JAPAN

A Historical Survey

5/10/73

JAPAN
A Historical Survey

MIKISO HANE
Knox College

CHARLES SCRIBNER'S SONS

Printed in the United States of America
Library of Congress Catalog Card Number 79–37178
SBN 684–12707–5 (Trade cloth)
SBN 684–12710–5 (College paper, SUL)

ACKNOWLEDGMENTS

Grateful acknowledgment is made to the following publishers for their permission to
reprint copyrighted material in this history:

GEORGE ALLEN & UNWIN LTD. for world rights outside the United States for
numerous quotations from Arthur Waley, trans., *The Tale of Genji*.

COLUMBIA UNIVERSITY PRESS for rights in the United States for extracts from the
Manyōshu: One Thousand Poems and for world rights for numerous quotations from
Ryusaku Tsunoda *et al.*, eds., *Sources of Japanese Tradition*.

DOUBLEDAY & COMPANY, INC., for world rights for three haiku and commentary
from Harold J. Henderson, *An Introduction to Haiku*, copyright © 1958 by Harold
J. Henderson.

GROVE PRESS, INC., for world rights for one haiku and its translation from Donald
Keene, ed., *Anthology of Japanese Literature from the Earliest Era to the Mid-Nine-
teenth Century*, copyright © 1955 by Grove Press, Inc., and for rights in the United
States and the Philippines for poetry, prose, and commentary from Donald Keene, ed.,
Japanese Literature: An Introduction for Western Readers, copyright © 1955 by
Donald Keene.

HOUGHTON MIFFLIN COMPANY for rights in the United States for numerous quotations from Arthur Waley, trans., *The Tale of Genji*.

JAPAN SOCIETY FOR THE PROMOTION OF SCIENCE for world rights outside the
United States for extracts from the *Manyōshu: One Thousand Poems*.

JOHN MURRAY LTD. for world rights outside the United States and the Philippines
for poetry, prose, and commentary from Donald Keene, ed., *Japanese Literature: An
Introduction for Western Readers*.

To Rose, Laurie, and Jennifer

Preface

I began work on this history several years ago because I felt that there was a need for a one-volume history of Japan that dealt fairly comprehensively with both the traditional and modern (post-Meiji) periods. There are several excellent histories of Japan available, but they tend to emphasize either the pre- or post-Meiji period, devoting relatively scant attention to the other. Although in terms of the time span involved I devoted proportionately more space to the modern period, I have tried to avoid slighting the essential aspects of pre-Meiji Japanese history.

My objective has been to present a general picture of Japanese history for the benefit of the non-specialist—the general reader as well as the college student—in the hope of furthering his understanding of present-day Japan. Even though Japan has undergone a period of "modernization" since the mid-nineteenth century, elements from the past have persisted in the society much more tenaciously than it may appear. The old maxim about the need to know the past in order to understand the present seems particularly true in the case of Japan.

The judgment as to what facts, events, and conditions are more important than others in understanding the nature of any history and culture is, of course, a subjective one. At times I may have pursued problems that intrigued me in greater detail than other historians might have done. I have also digressed from time to time by citing illustrative examples and graphic quotations, many translated from the Japanese, not only to enliven the account, but also to provide the reader with some sense of the atmosphere and mood of the times.

An ideal general history should provide facts as well as analyses of significant events, conditions, and developments. Given the limitation of space, the task of meeting both requirements becomes a difficult one, particularly because of the compelling necessity of presenting the basic facts. No interpretation is possible without the knowledge of the essential facts. I have attempted to supply adequate factual information for the reader to assimilate it and gain an analytical understanding of Japan.

So far as the overall structure of this history is concerned, I have attempted to present a balanced picture by incorporating all facets—political, social, economic, cultural, and intellectual. Naturally the emphases vary from period to period, but I sought to pay more attention to the social conditions of lower classes, that is, the peasants and the workers, than other general histories. I devoted considerable space to economic developments in the modern period because of the extraordinary growth of the Japanese economy since the Meiji Restoration. I also emphasized cultural and intellectual developments throughout because these are the areas where things of enduring values are produced, and what the people of any society have thought, perceived, and created speak meaningfully to peoples of all societies.

When I began writing this history I intended to play down the political aspects, but in the course of my work I was forced to conclude that the power struggle—and all that goes with it—is, after all, central to historical developments. It is one of the basic forces that move men and societies. Moreover the political story is the most convenient framework to link together all other elements and developments in a coherent account of a people's history.

In allotting space to the various eras, I ignored the time span of the eras and considered instead the relative importance that developments of a given period had in making Japan what she is today. The major events or developments of overriding importance in Japanese history that I have discussed are (1) the establishment of the imperial family as the ruling clan, (2) contact with China and the importation of Chinese civilization, including Buddhism and Confucianism, (3) the rise of the samurai class and the establishment of military rule, (4) the two-and-a-half centuries of Tokugawa rule, (5) contact with the West and the construction of the modern Meiji state, (6) the emergence of modern nationalism and militarism, (7) the Pacific War, and (8) postwar changes.

Topical chapter divisions of course do not mean that only those matters denoted in the chapter headings are discussed. The effects of the family system, the rise of the imperial court and the triumph of the feudal military class, and the influence of Chinese and Buddhist civilizations persisted throughout the centuries and their impact upon developments subsequent to their emergence have been noted repeatedly in later chapters.

In this work I have made extensive use of the works of other scholars and specialists, both Western and Japanese. I have relied particularly heavily upon the recent works of Japanese authorities and have endeavored to take into account their latest scholarly findings and interpretations. I have also translated from the original Japanese a considerable number of passages. These and quotations from Western sources are the only items that have been provided with source references in the footnotes. Sources for factual data and explanatory footnotes were kept to a minimum in order to avoid overloading the text with footnotes.

Japanese names have been given in the traditional style, that is, surname first and given name second. Traditionally the Japanese have identified historical figures by their given names. For the modern personalities, however, I have usually followed the practice of identifying them with their surnames except in cases where the artist or writer is known almost exclusively by a nom de plume that is used in place of his given name.

For the transliteration of Japanese names and terms I have used the Hepburn system. The vowels are pronounced as follows: *a* like the *a* in *father;* *i* like the *e* in *equal,* *u* like the *u* in *rule,* e like the *e* in *ebb,* o like the *o* in obey. A long mark over the vowels (-) means that the sound should be doubled in length. Diacritical marks were not used for such widely-known place names as Tokyo, Kyoto, Osaka, Kobe, Honshu, Kyushu, and Hokkaido. Singular and plural nouns are not distinguished in Japanese. Hence *samurai, daimyō, shōgun,* etc., could be singular or plural.

It would be impossible to thank all the people to whom I am directly and indirectly indebted for assistance in writing this history. I would, however, like to express my gratitude to my colleagues at Knox College for their valuable advice and assistance. I am also grateful to my many friends and mentors in Japan, especially Messrs. Minowa Shigeo, Tanabe Sadayoshi, and Kaji Ryuichi, for facilitating in countless ways my studies in Japanese history, and Professor Maruyama Masao, whose brilliant insights have helped me to gain a better understanding of Japanese history, particularly intellectual developments. I wish to thank Knox College and the Associated Colleges of the Midwest for the grants-in-aid that enabled me to spend the summer of 1968 in Japan and the academic year 1969–1970 on leave at the East Asian Library of Stanford University to work on this history. I am also indebted to the readers who went over the manuscript for Scribners, particularly Mrs. Barbara Wrubel, whose careful attention to details of style and consistency has improved the book immeasurably. The staff at Scribners has been extremely patient and generous in providing me with invaluable editorial assistance. I would like to acknowledge my great debt to Mr. Charles R. Boak, Mrs. Elsie Kearns, and, above all, to Mrs. Carol Cutler for going over the manuscript with such meticulous care.

Many people have helped me in typing the manuscript, but the person who performed the monumental feat of typing it over several times is my wife, Rose Michiko, who, in addition, has served as a most helpful critic and counselor.

MIKISO HANE

Contents

List of Maps

JAPAN

A Historical Survey

INTRODUCTION

Today Japan ranks seventh in the world in population size. More than one hundred million people are crowded into an area slightly smaller than the state of Montana. The islands that comprise the nation are mountainous, and only about 16 percent of the land is arable. Although the country is poor in natural resources, it is the world's third most productive industrial nation.

In the past Japan's place in the world was not as prominent as it is today. In fact, it was not until the nineteenth and twentieth centuries that her presence in world affairs began to be felt. In the first half of the twentieth century she emerged as a major military power in the Far East. After her defeat in World War II, Japan renounced militarism and has been concentrating since then on developing her economic strength.

Prior to the middle of the nineteenth century, Japan remained more or less isolated from the external world, with her contacts restricted primarily to her neighbors, Korea and China. In a sense Japan was a cultural satellite of China, under whose influence she remained for centuries following the introduction of Chinese culture into Japan during the fifth and sixth centuries. By adopting, adapting, and assimilating the products of Chinese civilization, Japan developed a culture and a way of life and established institutions and values that were distinctly her own, although traces of Chinese influence survived. In the nineteenth and twentieth centuries Japan was exposed to Western civilization and another period of importation and assimilation ensued. But the traditional attitudes, ways, and institutions have persisted; consequently, contemporary Japan cannot be adequately understood without examining her past.

It is interesting to speculate on the psychological effects that the introduction of Chinese civilization, especially the Confucian mode of thinking, has had upon the Japanese character and temperament. Confucianism emphasized the importance of order, harmony, self-control, composure, moderation, right conduct, proper decorum, and so on. In contrast to this, it has been asserted by the Tokugawa scholars of National Learning (see page 194) that before the advent of Chinese civilization the Japanese were unfettered by artificial rules and regulations about proper conduct. The spirit of the people was free and uninhibited; there was spontaneity of action and unrestrained expression of natural sentiments. If this was indeed the case, then the arrival of the Confucian value system meant the introduction of a diametrically opposed approach to life. In effect it entailed the insertion of an intellectual mode into the Japanese mental and spiritual life, which had heretofore been governed not by reasoned ideation, but by natural feelings that were motivated by immediately felt experiences.

The confrontation over the centuries between these opposing approaches to life must have caused deep inner conflicts and tensions within the Japanese psyche. This contention was surely aggravated further when the *samurai* (warrior), with his rugged, untamed activism, emerged as the dominant force in the eleventh and twelfth centuries. Conformity to an alien system of values that was designed to produce scholarly gentlemen was undoubtedly difficult for the spirited samurai, who lived by the sword. In the Tokugawa period (1600–1867) the rulers made a deliberate effort to inculcate Confucian concepts into the samurai class so as to make them capable of playing the role of scholar-official while still maintaining their function as warriors. Thus the dualism of intellect and spirit was perpetuated.

It is probably true that this conflict has never been fully resolved in the Japanese culture. The persistence of this inner tension may have given the Japanese society its dynamic quality, but at the same time it may have been responsible at least in part for the radical shifts in Japanese behavior —from extreme courtesy, decorum, and self-restraint to uninhibited activism and even violence—that have occurred periodically. Such drastic leaps from "civil" to "uncivil" behavior may be regarded as a reflection of the continuous struggle within the Japanese psyche between the alien Confucian notions (buttressed by Buddhism) and those elements that are indigenous to the culture.

Aside from seeking to understand the Japan of the present by investigating the Japan of the past, we can justify studying Japanese history— or, for that matter, the history of any people—because it is part of the common experience of humanity. Generally speaking, the problems confronting mankind are common problems, regardless of time or place. Man is faced with the task of working out his relationship with the cosmic or supernatural order, with the natural world or his physical environment, and with his fellowmen. He also faces the problem of understanding himself, achieving self-mastery, and thus gaining inner peace.

In the first instance, man seeks to define his place in the cosmic order of things as well as to comprehend and explain the mysteries of the universe. Religions, philosophies, and myths are created to enable him to cope with the unknown and the unknowable and to establish for himself a sense of direction, meaning, and identity. In Japan Shinto and Buddhism, among other religions, have served the needs of the people in this respect.

In terms of the second universal problem of man, that of adjusting to his physical environment, the salient fact about Japan is that it is an island nation, a circumstance that has significantly influenced the Japanese outlook and way of life. Although Japan was subjected to exernal influences, particularly from Korea and China in antiquity and from the West in the modern era, until the nineteenth century she was relatively free from the conflicts and struggles that beset the external world. The society functioned by and large as a cohesive, organic unit. The racial and cultural homogeneity that resulted from relative isolation fostered a strong sense of ethnocentrism, which was transformed in the modern era into a powerful current of nationalism.

The Japanese, nurtured in the natural beauty of the islands, developed an aesthetic sensitivity and a sense of identity with nature. Art and architecture have been molded by the Japanese attitude toward nature, just as a sense of unity with nature comprises an essential aspect of the indigenous religion, Shinto.

A more basic function of nature for man is to supply him with his material needs. Nature can be beneficent, but it can also be cruel and destructive. Japan has had her share of typhoons, floods, earthquakes, and droughts, which have made the people's struggle for survival arduous, but, in the main, nature has been relatively generous to the Japanese. The climate is mild, and the environment provides for the people's material needs. Despite the paucity of spacious open plains, the flatlands and hillsides have always produced sufficient food, except in years of crop failures, to enable the Japanese to survive. The seas surrounding the country supply the people with marine products, and the forests also provide for some of their basic needs.

Agriculture was the main source of Japanese livelihood for close to two millennia. This has profoundly affected the Japanese way of life and attitudes. The fact that the people had to work extremely hard to compel the limited land to produce an adequate amount of food has fostered in them the qualities of discipline and diligence. The need to work the land as a group resulted in the development and retention of strong family and communal ties. The availability of only a limited area of open lowland led to intense struggles by political leaders to gain and retain control of the more productive areas. Out of this struggle for land, and for the man-power to work the land, emerged the military class and the feudalistic political and social systems that prevailed from the late twelfth to the mid-nineteenth century. For the great part of Japanese history the soci-ety was divided roughly into two classes: the ruling class, which con-trolled the land, and the masses, who tilled the soil. The ruling class developed an aristocratic, militaristic outlook and life style, while the masses generally remained submissive to authority.

In the realm of interpersonal relationships, mankind has devised a variety of social and political institutions to govern and regulate human intercourse and has formulated diverse ideologies to buttress these insti-tutions. In Japan, as in most societies, the family emerged as the basic social institution. In addition to the family unit, wider kinship and clan groups developed.

The family system, which still remains the basic force in the Japanese way of life, has served as the prototype of many other social organizations. It determined one's status in the social order and molded one's outlook to a large extent. It was underpinned by Confucianism, which defined the cardinal human relationships in terms of the relationships among family members. The political system that prevailed throughout most of Japa-nese history was founded upon the concept of the family. The entire society was seen as one big family with the Emperor functioning as the "father," the head of the family. A familial structure also characterized the relationship between men involved in political, economic, social, and cultural activities.

The strong family system, with its hierarchy of age and sex and its em-phasis on obedience and submission to the head of the family, stifled indi-vidual initiative and spontaneity and reinforced the basically authori-tarian and hierarchical social and political order. The emphasis on the need to subordinate the individual's interest to the good of the whole and to maintain harmony in the group fostered the virtues of discipline, pa-tience, self-sacrifice, and the willingness to compromise. It also developed a sense of duty to the family and to the social circle to which one be-longed. The family system gave the Japanese a sense of continuity, a feel-ing of unity with the past and responsibility for the future. This is seen in the respect for ancestors and the desire to perpetuate the family line. But the emphasis on group solidarity also produced a parochialism that invariably placed the interests of one's own group above those of the outsiders and fostered a tendency to regard outsiders with suspicion.

An essential aspect of the story of man's relationship to his fellowmen is the continuous struggle for power in order to control manpower, land, and other resources. Power is necessary to maintain peace, order, and security in a society, but for the mc.t part it has been abused by those who wish to acquire the material, social, and psychological rewards it brings. Until the Industrial Revolution the quest for power was the most dynamic force in history and had the greatest effect upon people's lives. Although there have been occasional rulers who exercised power for the good of the people, by and large the quest for power has proved that the element that inflicts the greatest suffering and misery upon man is man himself. In a sense, history is the story of man's inhumanity toward his fellowmen. The history of Japan has been no exception.

Out of the struggle for power has emerged a variety of ideologies and institutions. In traditional Japan the principal ideologies were Shinto, the myths surrounding the emperor system, the code of the warriors, and Confucianism, the last an import from China. In the modern period the nationalistic myths about the uniqueness of the national character and spirit of Japan and, more recently, democratic and socialistic ideologies gained prominence. Among the political institutions that emerged and developed in traditional Japan were the *uji* (clan) system; the imperial institution, buttressed by the aristocracy; and the feudal-military system. In the modern age the clan oligarchy, bureaucracy, militarism, and democratic institutions have emerged as significant forces.

Japan's political history in the modern era has been shaped largely by her relationship with the outside world. When Japan encountered the Western powers in the mid-nineteenth century, her leaders set out to fortify and enrich the country in order to protect it against external encroachments and thus put the nation on the road to modernization and Westernization. As they achieved national security, they turned to the task of establishing Japan as a major world power, ultimately leading her down the path of imperialism to war and defeat.

The fourth problem confronting man has to do with himself. He seeks to understand himself and to govern his inner life in order to give his existence meaning and direction. To this end he attempts to comprehend the nature of "reality" and "truth" and to bring his life into harmony with what he perceives as real and true. He expresses his perception of the truth and the essence of things in terms of myths, religion, philosophy, art, and literature.

The Japanese did not create any grand philosophical system, but they did produce Shinto, and they embraced and modified Buddhism and

Confucianism. Zen Buddhism, the Japanese adaptation of the continental import, stands out as a notable example of man's effort to gain enlightenment (*satori*) by apprehending the essence of things through self-effort and then expressing in art the truth so perceived. Thus Zen reinforced the Japanese aesthetic sensitivity and made of Japanese art something more than a medium to please the senses. Suzuki Daisetsu, a Zen authority, remarked that the Japanese possessed a unique talent in turning abstract philosophical concepts into art and endowing commonplace things with aesthetic significance. They have even made arts of tea-drinking and gardening.

The aesthetic sensitivity of the Japanese had been highly developed before the advent of Chinese civilization and before Zen influenced their outlook. These cultural forces did contribute, however, to the creation of a uniquely Japanese aesthetic style. The Japanese appreciation of nature did not result in an art that merely imitated nature in exacting and precise detail. Instead, the aesthetic interpretations reveal attempts to improve upon nature by accentuating the available colors, textures, and forms. Thus in landscape gardening, for example, the artist imposes his design on nature by careful additions and reductions to formulate what he perceives as the essential patterns inherent in nature. This requires a keenly developed sense of composition—the ability to utilize form, line, space, and color in such a way as to create patterns and designs that have striking visual effects. The art of placement is a vitally important feature of every genre of Japanese art. This emphasis on arranging things in an aesthetically satisfying manner has so deeply penetrated the culture that it is manifested even in such commonplace matters as the placement of food on dishes. The Japanese artist has also displayed a scrupulous concern for details and this has contributed to the flowering of minor arts such as *bonsai* (dwarfed trees or shrubs grown in pots), *netsuke* (miniature carvings), ceramics, flower arrangement, and textile design.

In his cultural achievements man produces his most worthwhile and enduring creations. By exposing ourselves to what men of other ages and places have thought, felt, perceived, and done, we can deepen our understanding of ourselves and the human condition and enrich and give meaning to our own existence. Ultimately, this is the chief value of studying history.

CHAPTER 1

THE
EARLY
YEARS

GEOGRAPHIC SETTING

The Japanese archipelago, consisting of the four main islands of Hokkaido, Honshu, Shikoku and Kyushu, and over one thousand smaller islands, juts into the Pacific Ocean in a convex arc. The
total area of Japan proper is a little more than 142,000 square miles. To
the north the Russian-administered Kuriles, a large number of small volcanic islands, extend to Kamchatka Peninsula, while to the south the
Ryukyu Islands stretch out toward Formosa.

The Japanese islands are mountainous, with considerable volcanic activity. Offshore on the eastern side there are great submarine trenches, 5
or 6 miles below sea level. Along the coast on the same side the mountain tops reach 2 miles above sea level. This great range of elevation
from seabottom to mountain peak causes enormous strains and stresses,
resulting in constant shifts in the rock masses. Moreover, there are about
five hundred volcanoes in the archipelago, and earthquakes, a related phe-
nomenon, are commonplace occurrences, with an average of about fifteen
hundred tremors annually. Since 1596 there have been twenty-one major
earthquakes, each one resulting in the deaths of more than a thousand
persons.

Seventy-five percent of the country is hilly or mountainous, with an
average slope of more than 15 degrees. But nearly 65 percent of the land
with a slope of 15 degrees or less is tilled. The total area under cultivation, however, amounts to less than 16 percent of the land mass. The
highest elevations are located in the Gifu Node in central Honshu. A

dozen or more mountains measuring 10,000 feet are located in these high-lands known as the Japanese Alps. Mt. Fuji, 12,461 feet, is situated here.

There are no extensive lowlands in Japan. The typical plain is a small isolated area in a coastal indentation or in a mountain basin. The largest of the plains, the Kantō Plain, where Tokyo is located, has an area of only 5,000 square miles, or 3.2 million acres. Other major plains are the Nōbi Plain at the head of Ise Bay where Nagoya is situated (450,000 acres) and the Kinai Plain at the head of Osaka Bay where Kyoto, Osaka, and Kobe are located (310,000 acres). These are the most important plains, on which six of Japan's largest cities were built. Other fairly large plains are the Ishikari in southwestern Hokkaido, the Echigo in northwestern Honshu, the Sendai in northeastern Honshu, and the Tsukushi in northwestern Kyushu.

Rivers water most of these plains, but they are generally short, swift, and shallow and therefore not suitable for navigation. The two longest rivers are the Ishikari in Hokkaido (227 miles) and the Shinano in central Honshu (229 miles). The mountain rivers are important as sources of ir-rigation for the rice fields and hydroelectric power.

Japan proper has a remarkably long coastline, about 17,000 miles, or 1 linear mile of coast for each 8.5 square miles of area. The effect of this unusually long coastline is accentuated by the fact that most of the low-lands have sea frontage. This situation has fostered a strong maritime out-look in the Japanese. A large part of the coastline has indentations and irregularities that, together with the many tiny islands along the coastline, make the landscape strikingly beautiful and diverse.

Since the Japanese archipelago extends from 31° to 45° north lati-tude, there is a marked contrast in the climate between the northern and southern regions. Discrepancies in surface configurations, great differences in altitude, and diversity in the effects produced by the Pacific Ocean and the Japan Sea also account for notable differences in climate. A large part of Japan lies in subtropical latitudes. Consequently, in most areas climatic conditions are conducive to plant growth and are not too harsh for human comfort.

The monsoonal air masses affect the climate in a significant way. In the winter great waves of dry, cold polar air come from the Lake Baikal re-gion of Siberia. In the summer moist tropical and subtropical maritime air masses, originating over the warmer parts of the Pacific Ocean, move into eastern Asia. Thus while the winter winds are prevailingly from the northwest, the summer winds come from the southeast. The winters are colder and the summers hotter and more humid than normal for regions with Japan's latitude.

The two ocean currents washing the shores of Japan also influence her climate. A cold current from the north, the Okhotsk Current, and a warm

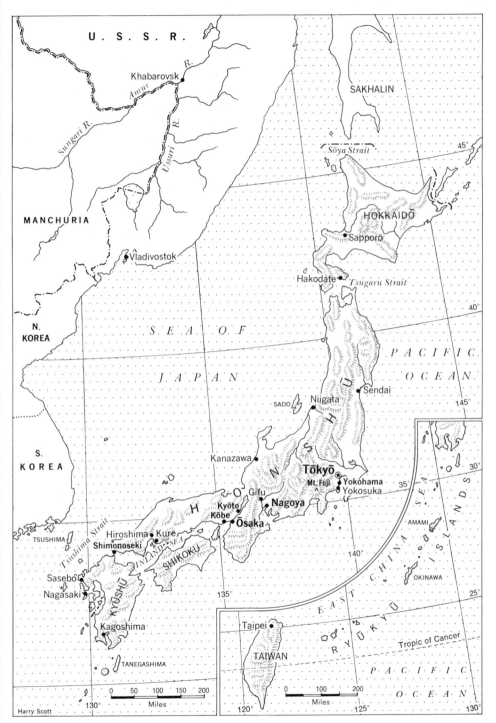

MODERN JAPAN.

stream from the south, the Japan Current, converge off northern Honshu. A smaller stream from the Japan Current swings into the Japan Sea from the Tsushima Strait and flows northward as far as Hokkaido.

During late spring and early summer a period of abundant rain, high humidity, and cloudiness sets in. This is the so-called *bai-u,* or plum rains. In the late summer and early fall violent storms and typhoons strike the islands, causing much damage to the rice fields as well as to the dwellings and the general landscape.

Japan's climate is much like that of the United States Atlantic seaboard or the Mississsippi Valley in similar latitudes. Temperatures in January range from about 10 degrees or 15 degrees in northern and central Hokkaido to 35 degrees or 40 degrees on the lowlands of central Honshu and 45 degrees in the extreme south of Kyushu. July temperatures in central and southern Japan range from 77 degrees to 80 degrees. August is slightly warmer than July in most areas. High temperatures combined with high humidity make the summers extremely sultry and oppressive.

Japan has a considerable amount of precipitation all year round; although it rains more in the warm months than in the winter, the difference in precipitation between summer and winter is not great. Even in the driest cool season there are 2 or 3 inches of precipitation each month and several times this amount in the warm months. Where precipitation is heaviest it may exceed 120 inches annually, while where it is lightest, in the Inland Sea region, it averages 40 inches per year.

Snow falls throughout the main islands, although it is light in the southern regions. It remains on the ground all winter in Hokkaido and in Honshu on the northern part of the Pacific side and all across the Japan Sea side. In the mountainous regions of western and northern Japan the snow reaches a depth of 6 or 7 feet in January.

The growing season varies from about 120 to 130 days in central and eastern Hokkaido to 250 days or more along the extreme southern and eastern littoral. The region around Tokyo has a growing season of 215 days.

Rice, grown in paddy fields, is the most important food crop produced. Today 55 percent of the cereal acreage consists of rice fields. Barley, wheat, oats, soybeans, potatoes, and a variety of vegetables are also grown. Tea and mulberry (for silkworms) constitute important supplementary income crops for farm families. Because only a little more than 15 million acres are arable, intensive cultivation is practiced, and terraced fields climb the hillsides of the Japanese landscape.

Since Japan is an island nation, the sea is an important source of food. Seafood is the chief source of protein in the Japanese diet. The warm Japan Current yields sardine, mackerel, tuna, bonito, skipjack, albacore, and seabream, while herring, salmon, cod, and crab are fished from the

Okhotsk Current. Many edible seaweeds are also extracted from the sea.

Japan is one of the most completely forested countries in the world. About 55 percent of the island is forested and another 8 to 9 percent is potential forest land. The forests are a source not only of timber but of charcoal, wood fuel, wood pulp, and a variety of foods. Broadleaf forests occupy about 50 percent of the forest land, while coniferous and mixed forests occupy 29 and 21 percent, respectively.

Japan does not have an adequate supply of mineral resources. Because coal, the most important of her minerals, is of poor quality, a supply of better quality must be imported for heavy industrial use. Petroleum resources are extremely limited; 98 percent of Japan's oil and petroleum products must be imported. Her iron mines supply only a small percentage of her industrial needs. The supply of copper, limestone, and sulfur is adequate, but lead, zinc, and phosphate and potassium materials for fertilizers must be imported.

THE MYTHOLOGICAL ORIGINS OF JAPAN

According to Japanese mythology—based upon the first historical accounts, the *Kojiki* (*Records of Ancient Matters;* completed in 712) and the *Nihongi* (*Chronicles of Japan;* completed in 720)—sky and heaven gradually separated from the primordial chaos in the universe, and five primal deities appeared. They were followed by a series of mated deities, ending with the creative pair, He-Who-Invites (Izanagi) and She-Who-Invites (Izanami). They stirred the sea with a spear and created an islet. Descending upon it, they created many other deities as well as the other islands of Japan.

Izanami died while giving birth to the Fire God and descended into the underworld of Yomi (darkness), where putrefaction and pollution prevailed. Longing to see his wife, Izanagi followed her into the land of darkness but was driven back by her because she was ashamed to be seen by him in her state of putrefaction. Returning from the land of darkness, Izanagi cleansed himself, and as he washed his left eye—left being the side of honor—the Sun Goddess, Amaterasu, was born, and from the right eye sprang the Moon God. As he washed his nose the Impetuous-Male-Deity (Susano-o), the Storm God, came into being.

The Sun Goddess and the Moon God ascended to the sky, the former to rule at Takamagahara (Plain of High Heaven) and the latter to serve as her consort. The Storm God was to rule over the earth. When Susano-o, who was an unruly character, visited his sister in the sky, he behaved obstreperously, damaging her rice fields and defiling her house with excrement. In anger Amaterasu shut herself up in a cave, darkening the world. To lure her out, the heavenly gods engaged in dancing and merrymaking. When Amaterasu opened the door of the cave to peek out to see what was taking place, the gods compelled her to leave the cavern, and the world was made radiant again. This story may be connected with ceremonies conducted during an eclipse of the sun or during the winter solstice to revive the waning power of the sun. It was also intended, some maintain, to signify the triumph of light over darkness, peace and order over savagery and destruction.

Susano-o was banished to the earth for his misconduct. He first traveled to Korea then to Izumo in western Honshu. From Izumo Susano-o's descendant, Ōkuni-nushi (Great-Land-Master) ruled the earth. The Sun Goddess, wishing to extend her authority to the earth, sent several messengers to persuade the Great-Land-Master to abdicate in her favor. After resisting several of Amaterasu's attempts to persuade him, the ruler of the earth finally agreed to submit to her authority. The Sun Goddess then sent her grandson, Ninigi (Ruddy-Plenty) to rule the earth.

Ninigi descended to the earth at Tsukushi in northern Kyushu and brought with him three items that became symbols of the imperial rule: a bronze mirror (a symbol of the Sun Goddess and of purity); a sword (courage), which was used by Susano-o to slay a huge serpent; and a curved-bead necklace (benevolence), which warded off evil spirits.

Ninigi's great-grandson, Waka-mike-nu (Young-Three-Hairs-Moor), left Kyushu to conquer the rest of Japan. Sailing through the Inland Sea, he entered the Kinki region (the area that encompasses Osaka, Kyoto, and Nara) and established his rule in Yamato in 660 B.C. He then became the first Emperor of Japan, Jimmu.[1]

Among other mythological figures two deserve mention, since they came to be popularly regarded as actual historical personages of heroic stature. One is Yamato-takeru (Mountain-Gate-Brave) who performed great military feats in conquering the rebellious people in the south (the Kumaso) and in the north (the Ezo). The other is the Empress Jingū, who is said to have led an expedition against Silla in Korea.

Mythological tales similar to those found in Japan are told in other parts of Asia, especially among the peoples of Southeast Asia and the nomads of northern Asia. The models for the stories concerning the origin of the universe, the age of the gods, superhuman kings, and heroic men may have been taken from Chinese myths by the ancient Japanese, but in the opinion of Joseph Campbell, an authority on mythology,

---

[1] The date 660 B.C. seems to have been arrived at by the compilers of the *Nihongi* in the following manner: The Chinese had a cyclical time system in which sixty years formed a small cycle, and 1,260 years a large one. An event of revolutionary significance was believed to occur every 1,260 years. The year 601 was such a year. The innovations introduced by Prince Shōtoku around that period could be interpreted as constituting a revolutionary event. Counting back 1,260 years from A.D. 601, 660 B.C. was arrived at as the year for the founding of the imperial government.

"the material that they dressed to this frame was of their own, comparatively childlike, folkloristic heritage, and the result was the most remarkable history of the world-as-fairytale" that the literature of mythology knows. This, according to Campbell, is particularly suitable to Japan, where "the extraordinary earnestness and profound gravity of the ideal of life is masked by the fashionable fiction that everything is only play." [2]

JAPANESE PREHISTORY

Archaeologists and historians fail to agree about the origins of the Japanese. There is a consensus, however, that the early inhabitants came from different areas in several separate waves of immigration. Some of the early inhabitants are believed to have been a Tungusic people who came from the northeastern region of the continent by way of Hokkaido or Korea. It is also thought that people of Malayan origin came from the south—from South China or perhaps from Southeast Asia—by way of Formosa and the Ryukyus, while others of Mongoloid origin came by way of Korea.

The Japanese language seems to have links with both the Polynesian and Altaic languages. Some authorities theorize that in the Jōmon period a language of southern origin was spoken, while in the Yayoi period a new language, Altaic in character, entered from the continent.

Until very recently there was no concrete evidence to substantiate the existence of paleolithic man in Japan, but archaeological discoveries since 1947 indicate that this may have been the case. Tools made of roughly flaked stone dating from perhaps two hundred thousand years ago have been discovered. Archaeological remains of microlithic artifacts, that is, tools of sharp-edged stone flakes, indicate that mesolithic man was present in Japan around 5000 B.C.

Among the early inhabitants of neolithic Japan were, it is believed, ancestors of the Ainus, a people of Caucasian origin who inhabit Hokkaido today. (There are at present only about fourteen thousand Ainus in existence.)

The early stages of the neolithic age in Japan, known as the Jōmon period, extended from about 4500 B.C. to 250 B.C. On the basis of carbon 14 tests made on archaeological finds, some authorities now contend that the Jōmon period started around 7000 or 8000 B.C. The term Jōmon (cord-marking) describes the type of decoration on pottery associated with this age. Most Jōmon earthenwares have designs of high relief

[3] Joseph Campbell, *The Masks of God: Oriental Mythology* (New York: Viking, 1962), pp. 465–66.

made with cord impressions. This era is divided into several periods based upon the changing style of pottery.[3] The patterns made by cord impressions became increasingly more complex in later stages.

Jōmon men lived primarily near the sea coast and gathered shellfish for food. A large number of shell mounds, principally in the Tokyo Bay area, have been found at archaeological sites that had been inhabited by Jōmon men. Those living in mountainous areas hunted game and lived on fruits, nuts, berries, and edible roots. Fish hooks made of animal bones and ground and chipped stone tools were used by men of the Jōmon period. These early people lived in pit dwellings covered over with thatched roofs. Evidently the houses were circular, had several supporting pillars for the slanting roofs, and a fireplace of earthenware or stone. Clay figurines have been found in the remains of these dwellings. These are believed to have been used to ensure fertility and guard against pernicious forces. It appears from the iconography of these idols that the sun and the spirits of stones were worshipped in this period.

The later years of the neolithic age are called the Yayoi period (ca. 250 B.C.–A.D. 250) because potteries belonging to this culture were first discovered at a place called Yayoi in Tokyo in 1884. The Yayoi pots, reddish in color, were wheel-made and are less elaborately decorated than Jōmon pieces. The designs are simple and neat, generally consisting of straight lines. Yayoi pottery, fired at a higher temperature, is technically superior to Jōmon pottery. A greater variety of earthenwares were produced in the Yayoi period. Basically there were three types: plain jars used for cooking, decorated urns for storing food, and more elaborately designed dishes on pedestals in which offerings to the gods were placed.

Yayoi culture is believed to have emerged around the third century B.C. in northern Kyushu. It would appear that it was influenced by two different cultural forces, one from the south and the other from the north. Rice cultivation, which was not yet practiced in northern China, came to Japan from the south. It may have been introduced from Southeast Asia or from South China by immigrants fleeing the Han conquerors, who were extending their control into South China. Perhaps it entered from South China by way of southern Korea. At any rate, the introduction of rice cultivation revolutionized the way of life of ancient Japan and established the basis for the economic life of the people until the industrial age.

While rice cultivation indicates a southern influence, the polished stone

---

[3] Recently anthropologists at the Smithsonian Institution have theorized that around 3000 B.C. a Japanese boat that had been blown off course landed in Ecuador, bringing with it Jōmon pots. These influenced the style of Valdivian pottery, which is nearly identical to Jōmon pottery. See the *New York Times*, January 3, 1966, p. 1.

implements of Yayoi culture show links with Korea, Manchuria, and northern China. As we have already noted, it is possible that during this period Japan came under the influence of people who belonged to the Altaic world. The Yayoi decorative designs resemble ornaments found in areas where the Altaic languages were spoken. Around the second century B.C. bronze and iron implements were introduced from China. Among the bronze artifacts were swords, halberds, and mirrors used for religious and ceremonial purposes.

The agricultural implements used in the Yayoi period were crude wooden and stone tools such as hoes, rakes, spades, semilunar knives, and adzes. In the later stages of the period, iron implements came to be used for household and agricultural purposes. For weapons, Yayoi men used bows and arrows and, after the introduction of iron, iron swords, spears, and halberds. Remnants of looms and fabrics indicate that weaving was also introduced from the continent in this period. Pits and caves were no longer utilized for dwellings. Huts were now constructed above the ground, and wooden posts and beams were used to hold up thatched roofs. The dead were buried in urns, dolmens, and stone cists; a variety of artifacts, many of Chinese origin, were buried with them.

In the Yayoi period there were two population centers, one near the present city of Nara in the Yamato plain and the other in northern Kyushu. Evidently they adhered to different religious cults. The people in Yamato used bronze bells for ceremonial purposes while those in Kyushu used gems and bronze spears, swords, halberds, and mirrors. While the bronze swords and halberds are believed to have come from the continent, the bronze bells used in the Yamato region are not found on the continent. These bells were fairly large, some as long as four feet, and were decorated with engravings of farming and hunting scenes.

The ritualistic use of these artifacts was evidently linked with political control. An ancient account states that shields and spears sent to the governors and chiefs were interred in the sacred hills to ensure the protection of the frontiers; thus the bronze spear became a symbol of divine presence as well as of power. That the possession of ritual symbols endowed the possessor with special authority is seen in the fact that the imperial family traditionally used three symbols—the sacred sword, mirror, and gem—to assert its special authority and legitimacy.

The first written accounts of Japan are found in the historical chronicles of China, specifically in the *History of the Kingdom of Wei* (a kingdom in North China, A.D. 220–265), written in A.D. 297, and in the *History of the Later Han Dynasty,* compiled around A.D. 445. These histories mention the existence of more than one hundred communities in Japan and note that a number of envoys were sent from Japan to the Han court

Two examples of prehistoric Japanese art: left, a terra-cotta Jōmon urn, ca. 200 B.C.; *right, a bronze bell of the late Yayoi period, ca.* A.D. *100–300. Both courtesy of the Cleveland Museum of Art: left, Purchase John L. Severance Fund; right, Gift of Mrs. Arthur St. Newberry.*

in what is the present-day city of Sian and to the Han governors in Korea. The first envoy is said to have arrived in the Han capital in A.D. 57. A golden seal presumably given to one of the rulers of northern Kyushu by an Emperor of Later Han China in the first century was found in 1784. Its authenticity has been questioned, but many authorities now consider it to be genuine.

According to the Chinese records Japan underwent a period of civil

17

strife in the second century A.D., but eventually the nation was unified under a queen referred to as Pimiku. Pimiku (or Himiko in Japanese, meaning daughter of the sun) was not a proper name but rather a term applied to female rulers in general. The Pimiku mentioned in the Chinese histories was a shaman, a priestess who served as an intermediary between supernatural forces and the people. The *History of Wei* states that Pimiku "occupied herself with magic and sorcery, bewitching the people. Though mature in age, she remained unmarried. She had a younger brother who assisted her in ruling the country. After she became the ruler, there were few who saw her. She had one thousand women as attendants, but only one man." [4]

Historians disagree about the location of the land ruled by Pimiku. The *History of Wei* states that Pimiku resided in Yamatai, located on an island southeast of Korea. This might indicate that Yamatai was in northern Kyushu, but if the distances given in the *History of Wei* were followed it would be located on the high seas. The similarity of the names might signify that Yamatai was actually Yamato in central Honshu, but Yamatai, which means gateway to the mountains, was not an uncommon place name.

All sorts of theories based upon mythological, linguistic, and archaeological evidence have been set forth to prove that Pimiku's kingdom was in either northern Kyushu or the Yamato plain, but neither side has been able to substantiate its contention. It would appear that northern Kyushu had much greater contact with the continent, but the *History of Wei* states that when Pimiku died in the middle of the third century a great mound was constructed as her tomb. This, the proponents of the Yamato thesis argue, proves that Pimiku ruled in the Yamato plain, because the practice of constructing large tombs did not prevail in northern Kyushu. This argument is fallacious, however, since evidently such practices did not prevail in Pimiku's time in the Yamato region either.

The hypothesis that Pimiku was the ancestor of the imperial family is also open to question. If she were it might not be unreasonable to assume that she was located in Kyushu, because it is likely that the ancestors of the imperial family did come from Kyushu and moved on to the Yamato region some time after Pimiku's reign. The theory that the imperial ancestors came from Kyushu is, again, a matter of debate, but with no conclusive evidence available one way or the other, there is no reason to reject the mythological account that the imperial ancestors left their homeland in Kyushu, moved along the Inland Sea, and entered the Yamato region, conquering hostile tribes on the way. The fact that the

[4] Ryusaku Tsunoda, trans., and L. Carrington Goodrich, ed., *Japan in the Chinese Dynastic Histories: Later Han Through Ming Dynasties* (South Pasadena, Calif.: Perkins, 1951), p. 13.

symbols of imperial authority—swords, mirrors, and gems—have been found in abundance in the burial sites of northern Kyushu would tend to uphold the Kyushu theory.

It is possible that the Kyushu people had imported new weapons (such as long swords and iron armor) and had learned new techniques of warfare (such as the use of warriors on horseback) from the continent and were thus able to overwhelm their rivals in central Honshu. Another group evidently traveled up the northern shores of Honshu along the Japan Sea and settled in Izumo, a place that figures prominently in Japanese mythology.

At any rate, by the middle of the fourth century the ruling family that had established its authority in the Yamato region had more or less unified Japan except for the outlying areas to the north, which were not pacified until the ninth century, and southern Kyushu. By A.D. 369 the rulers of Yamato had become strong enough to invade Korea and establish a foothold on the southern coast. The years roughly from the early fourth to the middle of the seventh century are conventionally referred to as the Yamato period.

JAPAN'S NEIGHBOR: KOREA

In A.D. 400 Korea was divided into three kingdoms, Koguryo in the northern half, Paekche in the southwest, and Silla in the southeast, a division that occurred during the second half of the first century B.C. and lasted till the second half of the seventh century A.D. In the central part of the southern tip there was a small area under Japanese control called Mimana or Kaya.

Koguryo quite naturally was under strong Chinese influence and had adopted Confucianism and Chinese institutions and practices. Paekche also had close Chinese ties, mainly with South China. It was frequently beset upon by its larger and more powerful neighbors and was willing to accept Japanese aid against both Koguryo and Silla. Silla was the least Sinified of the three kingdoms, although later it too began to adopt Chinese culture. Earlier the southeastern region had maintained close contacts with Japan, but with the establishment of the kingdom of Silla relationships became strained. By 562 Mimana, the Japanese foothold in the peninsula, had been annexed by Paekche and Silla.

In the middle of the seventh century Silla allied itself with T'ang China and put an end to the kingdoms of Paekche and Koguryo in 660 and 668, respectively. Then it succeeded in freeing itself from T'ang political domination and extended its authority over the entire peninsula, unifying Korea for the first time. Thereafter Korea remained unified except for brief periods. From the end of the eighth century Silla was plagued with internal disturbances. In 935 order was restored under the

Koryo dynasty, which remained in power until 1392. Korea, however, became tributary to the ruling powers of China. When the Mongols conquered China, they also made repeated military forays against Korea and in 1258 finally brought her to her knees. With the expulsion of the Mongols from China in 1368, Korea freed herself from the former's control but, under a new ruling family, the Yi, entered into tributary relationship with the new Chinese dynasty, the Ming. The Yi dynasty lasted from 1392 to 1910, when Japan annexed the peninsula.

EARLY YAMATO SOCIETY
(fourth and fifth centuries)

The period from the unification of Japan by the imperial family to the time when the country felt the massive impact of Chinese civilization is still a rather obscure era. The conditions that prevailed around the time of unification are matters of conjecture again. Pimiku, or Himiko, was a priestess who served as the medium conveying to the people the words and laws of the gods. Religious and political functions were regarded as being one and the same. Governmental functions were called *matsuri*— worship of or service to the gods. The act of being possessed by the gods when receiving their words was called *noru.* The noun of this word is *nori,* meaning law; laws, then, were divine decrees. Religion served as an instrument of political control. Ordinarily the shamans were females, so the rulers were usually women. The *History of Wei* states that after Pimiku's death a king was placed on the throne, but the people refused to obey him and civil strife ensued. To restore order, a girl of thirteen was placed on the throne.

As the imperial family extended its authority to outlying areas, it either appointed its own officials to manage the land brought under its direct control or allowed the conquered chieftains to continue as governors (*kuni-no-miyakko*). In areas not under the immediate control of the imperial family, the head of the *uji* of each area was allowed to manage his own land.

Th uji, customarily translated as clan, was a lineage group organized around the main family. Each uji had a patriarchal chief (*uji-no-kami*) and worshipped a guardian god (*uji-gami*). As a member of the ruling elite each uji controlled its own land and also had under its authority workers organized into associations or corporations (see below). The imperial family, before it gained ascendancy over the other uji, was one of the uji contending for land and power.

With the growth of imperial power, the number of kuni-no-miyakko increased. By the middle of the seventh century, just prior to the Taika Reforms, there were perhaps as many as 120 such officials. Around the fourth century the imperial government began to confer titles of nobility (*kabane*) upon the chiefs of the leading uji. Evidently these titles had been used prior to this, but the imperial family sought to assert its authority over the clan chieftains by assuming the right to confer them officially. With the titles went certain official functions and positions that were hereditary. Without a title one could not occupy a high government position. Among the patriarchal chieftains those claiming direct descent from the legendary first Emperor, Jimmu, or from the founding gods occupied the highest places in the political and social hierarchy. The former were given the title of *omi* and the latter *muraji*. The clans of the omi and muraji and the imperial family were the major landowners. Those chieftains who held the title "great omi" or "great muraji" were entitled to hold key government positions.

Another institution came into being about the same time as the kabane system, the hereditary associations or corporations called *be*. They were under the control of the imperial family and the leading uji. Members of these functional communities were required to perform fixed services for the uji to which they were attached or to supply them with certain commodities. They were not slaves, for they retained their personal freedom. The hereditary guilds of the later Roman Empire would be the closest Western analogy to these corporations.

As imperial power grew, the leading clans themselves were organized into functional corporations to serve the Emperor. For instance, the head of the Mononobe family, holding the title of muraji, was responsible for the maintenance of weapons for the imperial family. The head of the Ōtomobe family, also a muraji, was responsible for the safety of the Emperor. There were be for every category of occupation: those engaged in military and religious affairs, ricefield workers, fishermen, sake makers, weavers, grooms, smiths, potters, arrow makers, bow makers, mirror makers, lapidaries, cooks, scribes, and so forth. These classifications eventually came to denote family names, in the same way that words such as miller and smith came to be used as surnames in English. Immigrants from Korea and China, many of whom were skilled artisans, constituted important elements of the corporation system. For instance, toward the end of the third century A.D. a considerable number of weavers arrived in Japan from Paekche and were organized into a weavers' corporation. By the middle of the sixth century there were 7,053 households belonging to this community, numbering, it is estimated, over 30,000 members.

By subjugating the uji and making them serve as functional corporations, the imperial family was able to extend its control over the rest of the populace, because the be under the authority of the uji fell indirectly under imperial control. These institutions remained in existence until the Taika Reforms movement was initiated in the seventh century, although they had begun to deteriorate prior to that because of disputes over titles and positions among the leading uji.

RELIGION: SHINTO

As the imperial family extended its authority, its ancestral god, the Sun Goddess, became the chief deity of the entire land. She was enshrined at Ise, which is still today the sacred city of the native religion known as Shinto. Each uji had its own god, the uji-gami, who was usually the founder of the clan or a prominent ancestral figure. In addition it was believed that a whole host of gods or spirits were present in all things in nature. There were gods or spirits identified with the woods, streams, mountains, fields, rain, fire, water, stones, grass, trees, and so on. Some animals, such as snakes and foxes, were also believed to possess supernatural powers and were worshipped out of fear. Worship of the lingam, or phallus, was also practiced. All spirits and deities were referred to as *kami*, that is, superior beings.

In worshipping the kami, ritual purity was stressed, and purification rites constituted an important part of Shinto ceremonies. Even today the compounds of Shinto shrines are kept immaculate. Visitors to Shinto shrines usually wash their hands and rinse their mouths with water before entering the sacred grounds, and the Shinto priest waves his sacred wand over their heads to drive the evil spirits away and cleanse the worshippers spiritually.

The ancient imperial court employed an official whose function was to preserve the ceremonial purity of the entire community. It was his duty to observe the taboos and to conduct the rites of abstention. Another official was assigned the task of reciting the litany of purification twice a year to cleanse the people of pollution.

The ancient Japanese made no animal sacrifices to the gods because blood was considered to be defiling. Instead, grain, fruits, and vegetables were proffered to the kami in times of thanksgiving.

This preoccupation with cleanliness and purity was carried over into the moral outlook of the early Japanese. Instead of relying on abstract standards of good and evil, they judged everything in terms of purity and impurity: What was pure was good, what was soiled was bad. "To do good is to be pure; to commit evil is to be impure," states a thirteenth-century Shinto tract. Thus an "unclean" mind or heart was abhorred while a "clean" mind or heart was admired.

The early Japanese evidently did not possess a sense of guilt but were governed instead by a sense of shame. It was shameful to be polluted.

When Izanami was followed by Izanagi into the land of darkness and was seen in her state of pollution, she was humiliated and became angry at him for seeing her in that condition.

Another fundamental moral characteristic of the people of Yamato was their pragmatic, utilitarian nature. To the early Japanese what was agreeable was good, what was disagreeable was bad. The pleasant, the beautiful, the auspicious, and the valuable were all regarded as being good.

Since early Shinto was centered upon the uji, the concept of clan solidarity, with its stress on submission to the authority of the patriarchal chieftain, was emphasized. Defense of clan interests required military valor. This is reflected in Shinto by the worship of swords, spears, and bows and arrows as symbols of militaristic gods.

Shinto has been judged by a Western scholar to be "perhaps the most rudimentary religious cult of which we have an adequate written record. It has not advanced beyond crude polytheism; its personifications are vague and feeble; there is little grasp of the conception of spirit; it has scarcely anything in the shape of a moral code." [5]

Joseph Campbell tells a story concerning a Western sociologist who said to a Shinto priest, "You know, I've now been to a number of these Shinto shrines and I've seen quite a few rites, and I've read about it, thought about it; but you know, I don't get the ideology. I don't get your theology." The Shinto priest reflected for a moment and replied smilingly, "We do not have ideology. We do not have theology. We dance." This, according to Campbell, goes to the heart of the matter. "For Shinto, at root, is a religion not of sermons but of awe: which is a sentiment that may or may not produce words, but in either case goes beyond them. Not a 'grasp of the conception of spirit,' but a sense of its ubiquity, is the proper end of Shinto." [6]

Shinto rite is designed to evoke the sense of awe that inspires gratitude to the source and nature of being. "As such, it is addressed as art to the sensibilities—not to faculties of definition. So that living Shinto is not the following of some set-down moral code, but a living in gratitude and awe amid the mystery of things." [7]

Each community and each uji worshipped its own kami in sanctified grounds marked off by trees or fences. Later these primitive sanctuaries were replaced by shrines whose entrances were marked by wooden or stone portals known as *tori-i*, consisting of two quadrangular beams placed upon two round columns. Shinto ceremonies are simple and austere, consisting of thanksgiving offerings, the recitation of liturgies by the priest,

[5] W. G. Aston, quoted in *ibid.*, p. 475.
[6] *Ibid.*, p. 476.
[7] *Ibid.*, p. 477.

Terra-cotta Haniwa figures, 3rd–6th centuries. Left, courtesy of the Consulate General of Japan, New York; right, courtesy of the Cleveland Museum of Art, The Norweb Collection.

and dancing accompanied by singing and the playing of musical instruments.

SOCIAL PRACTICES AND CONDITIONS

The native religion of ancient Japan had no formalized theological or philosophical interpretation concerning the afterlife; apparently it was believed that after death one went to the land of darkness, where everything was polluted. Consequently, death was viewed as defiling. The *History of Wei* records that "mourning is observed for more than ten days, during which period they [the bereft] do not eat meat. The head mourners wail and lament, while friends sing, dance, and drink liquor.

When the funeral is over, all members of the family go into the water to cleanse themselves in a bath of purification." [8]

Upon the death of Emperors and great chieftains, huge sepulchral mounds were built to entomb them. This practice started around the end of the third century or the beginning of the fourth century. Some of the tombs were of immense dimensions; the keyhole-shaped barrow of Emperor Nintoku (early fifth century), encompasses 80 acres and is 90 feet high and 400 yards long. In terms of the area it occupies it is the largest tomb in the world. With the dead was buried a mélange of personal belongings and ornaments, such as bronze mirrors, swords, knives, curved beads, arrowheads, armor, and helmets.

Swords found in the tombs indicate that the long single-edged sword of Han China had replaced the short sword of early Yamato in popularity by the second half of the fifth century. Also by this time the paraphernalia of the mounted warrior had begun to replace the foot soldier's armor.

In addition to these objects, which were buried with the dead, a large number of clay images—known as *haniwa* (circle of clay)—were placed around the mound to strengthen the sides and prevent earth washouts. These terra-cotta figures, which represent human beings, horses, birds, armor, furnishings, utensils, houses, etc., have proven invaluable in enabling archaeologists to reconstruct the mode of life of that era. It is assumed that these artifacts were designed to replace human beings—perhaps slaves—who had formerly been buried alive with the dead Emperor or chieftain. "When Pimiku passed away," records the *History of Wei,* "a great mound was raised, more than a hundred paces in diameter. Over a hundred male and female attendants followed her to the grave." No archaeological evidence has been unearthed, however, to confirm that mass retainer burial was in fact practiced.

The *Nihongi* states that when the younger son of Emperor Suinin (who is thought to have ruled in the third century) died and his personal attendants were buried alive with him, "for several days they died not, but wept and wailed day and night. At last they died and rotted. Dogs and crows gathered and ate them." The emperor was grieved by all this, and five years later when the Empress died, he asked his ministers to devise a way to avoid burying her attendants with her. One of his advisers called together hundreds of clay workers and had them make figures of men, horses, and other objects and told the Emperor, "Henceforth let it be a law for future ages to substitute things of clay for living men, and to set them up at tumuli." The Emperor thereupon issued a decree stating, "Henceforth these clay figures must be set up at tumuli; let not men be

[8] Tsunoda and Goodrich, *Japan in the Chinese Dynastic Histories,* p. 11.

harmed." [9] This, it is generally agreed, is a purely legendary account of the origin of the haniwa. Cylinder-shaped haniwa were used at least a century before the time of this story. Sepulchral mounds ceased to be constructed after the introduction of Buddhism because Buddhists favored cremating the dead. By the beginning of the ninth century, cremation had become prevalent throughout the land.

In early Yamato society human sacrifice was practiced to propitiate the gods in order to ensure the successful construction of buildings, bridgeheads, and dikes. This practice survived as late as the seventeenth century, although it became increasingly uncommon.

Polygamy was common in this society, and marriages between close members of the family circle—such as half-brothers and sisters, aunts and nephews, and stepmothers and stepsons—took place. After marriage the wife continued to live with her parents; the husband either visited her periodically or came to reside with her family. This is an aspect of the matriarchal nature of early Japanese society. The prominent place held by female deities—after all, the chief deity of Japan is the Sun Goddess—and female rulers attests to this fact. Until the late eighth century the Japanese throne was frequently occupied by an Empress. Even during the Tokugawa period the imperial court was twice headed by women. Although Japan eventually became a decidedly patriarchal society, remnants of matriarchy persist to the present. For example, when there is no male heir, the family line is continued through the female issue.

As in other primitive societies, trial by ordeal was practiced in early Japan also. The *History of the Sui Dynasty*, written around A.D. 630, states, "Sometimes pebbles are put in boiling water and both parties to a dispute made to pick them out. The hand of the guilty one is said to become inflamed. Sometimes a snake is kept in a jar, and the accused ordered to catch it. If he is guilty, his hand will be bitten." [10]

The protection of the farmers' rice fields was one of the chief concerns of the society. Severe punishments were meted out to troublemakers who destroyed the banks of rice paddies, filled in irrigation ditches, removed water conduits, reseeded fields already seeded, and planted stakes in rice fields to cause harm to others.

Certain actions were considered to be unclean and polluting and were therefore condemned. Skinning an animal alive or skinning it hind-end first was such an offense. It was also believed that the gods viewed as unclean albinos and people with external tumors and warts.

The punishments meted out in ancient Japan were harsh. The *History*

---

[9] W. G. Aston, trans., *Nihongi* (New York: Paragon, 1956), part 1, pp. 178–81.
[10] Tsunoda and Goodrich, *Japan in the Chinese Dynastic Histories*, p. 30.

Part of the Shinto shrine in Ise, dedicated to Amaterasu, the Sun Goddess. Courtesy of the Japan National Tourist Organization.

of Sui reports that "it is customary to punish murder, arson, and adultery with death. . . . Other offenses are punished according to their nature— sometimes by banishment and sometimes by flogging. In the prosecution of offenses by the court, the knees of those who plead not guilty are pressed together by placing them between pieces of wood, or their heads are sawed with the stretched string of a strong bow." [11]

ARCHITECTURE

During the early Yamato period the simple but striking style of architecture that we see in Japanese shrines had come into existence. These shrines, with their raised platforms, boxlike structures, bargeboards extending above the roofs like the upper half of the letter X, heavy billets set crosswise across the ridges of the roofs, and unpainted, undecorated woodwork, were designed to blend into their natural surroundings. The early shrines still standing at Izumo and Ise are good examples of the style of architecture that prevailed during this protohistoric period.[12]

At Ise there are two shrines four miles apart, the Inner and the Outer shrines. The Inner Shrine was founded, according to the early chronicles, by Emperor Suinin and is dedicated to the Sun Goddess. The Outer Shrine is dedicated to the goddess of agriculture and sericulture. These shrines are surrounded by cedar trees in a beautiful setting. They are supposed to have been reconstructed every twenty years. The fifty-ninth rebuilding since the beginning of this practice in the seventh century took place in 1954. The buildings are constructed without nails or complicated joints, and the plain, unadorned style of the original shrines has been retained.

The early aristocracy lived in houses built on raised platforms, a style of dwelling that came perhaps from the southwest Pacific. Haniwa replicas of houses indicate that relatively substantial abodes were being built by the fourth and fifth centuries, perhaps with the aid of immigrant Korean workmen. The Koreans apparently introduced the practice of using planks in walls and roofs and taught the Japanese how to construct houses on an exactly regular plan using evenly spaced rectangular windows. Models have been found of two-storied buildings with fancy gabled roofs with overhanging bargeboards.

The haniwa figures with their simple but bold geometrical shapes are thought by art historians to be among the most interesting ancient sculptures. A characteristic that distinguished Japanese from Chinese art—

---

[11] *Ibid.*, p. 30.

[12] "One cannot but remark on the similarity of these buildings to those still used in Indonesia, notably by the Batak of Sumatra." Sherman E. Lee, *A History of Far Eastern Art* (Englewood Cliffs, N.J.: Prentice-Hall, and New York: Abrams, 1964), p. 74.

the fact that the Japanese artist let the material determine his technique rather than allow his designs to dominate the material—is seen in the use of clay by the haniwa makers. The Japanese artist's skill in using natural material effectively and his sensitivity to the natural environment have been distinctive features of Japanese art throughout history.

CHAPTER 2

THE ADVENT AND ASSIMILATION OF CHINESE CIVILIZATION

THE INTRODUCTION
OF CHINESE CIVILIZATION

The fifth and sixth centuries are truly significant from the point of view of Japanese cultural history because it was during those years that Japan was influenced by Chinese civilization on a massive scale, much in the manner in which she was subjected to the influence of Western civilization in the nineteenth century. With the introduction of the Chinese writing system and the infusion of Confucian and Buddhist thought and Chinese arts and crafts into the society, Japan became a "civilized" nation during this period. During the seventh and eighth centuries the continental culture and institutions were assimilated by the Japanese.

The recorded history of Japan starts with the fifth century, for writing was introduced from the continent around A.D. 400. The historical chronicles that are extant were not compiled, however, until the early part of the eighth century. Consequently not all of the Japanese accounts of events and conditions between A.D. 400 and the eighth century are reliable, but they augment other historical evidence to give us a fuller story of Japanese history than that which we have for the preceding period.

From the middle of the third century to the beginning of the fifth century there is no mention in the Chinese historical records of any contact with Japan (due, perhaps, to unstable conditions in China), but fifth century records mention a number of Japanese missions that arrived in China. The Japanese Emperors whose names are recorded in these chronicles can be identified as historical figures. The first Emperor who is regarded as a historical personage is Emperor Sujin, who ruled either around A.D. 240 or around 270–290. Some historians consider him the real founder of the imperial government in Yamato, not the legendary Emperor Jimmu mentioned in the mythologies. However, a number of historians regard Sujin, too, as mythical. There is general agreement, however, that the Emperors from Ōjin on are actual historical figures. Ōjin is believed to have reigned around A.D. 400.

Intercourse with the continent was carried on prior to the fifth century through Korea. Technical knowledge and material goods had previously entered Japan from the continent, but during the fourth and fifth centuries a large number of artisans and craftsmen immigrated to Japan. The Chinese who had fled their country after the fall of the Han government and had gone to Korea were again forced to escape the political turmoil there; they arrived in Japan in the early fifth century and were organized into functional communities (be) to serve the imperial family.

One of the most significant importations from the continent was the Chinese writing system. No doubt some knowledge of Chinese writing had filtered into Japan before its official introduction, but the story as stated in the chronicles is that during Emperor Ōjin's reign the King of Paekche in Korea sent an envoy, Wani, to Japan with a list of one thousand Chinese characters and a copy of the Confucian *Analects*. The introduction of the Chinese system of writing caused the Japanese vocabulary to be enlarged tremendously and new concepts to enter the Japanese intellectual world. A Japanese dictionary published in 1884 classified thirteen thousand words as of Chinese derivation, compared with twenty-two thousand words of purely Japanese origin. The introduction of the writing system was an epoch-making event that propelled Japan into a new stage in her history. Henceforth records were kept, chronicles were compiled, poetry was anthologized. Chinese literature and philosophy came to be studied, and Confucianism, one of the decisive forces in molding the Japanese character and mode of thought, started to establish its roots in Japanese soil.

Not long after the introduction of Chinese learning to Japan Confucian values and ideals started to be mirrored in the proclamations and decrees of the Japanese Emperors. Confucian virtues such as benevolence, righteousness, propriety, wisdom, and faithfulness were extolled, and the importance of maintaining proper relationships between ruler and subject and between father and son was emphasized. The idea that government should be founded upon the moral character of the ruler also entered Japanese political thought. Confucianism did not become deeply embedded in the Japanese way of life and thought until the Tokugawa era, when the ruling family adopted Neo-Confucianism as its official philosophy and actively inculcated Confucian moral ideals into the minds of the people. From around the fifth and sixth centuries, Chinese learning and Buddhism constituted the basic ingredients from which Japanese learning and culture emerged and developed.

In the sixth and seventh centuries the second impact from the continent was felt. Again, a large number of Koreans, escaping the political turmoil of their homeland, immigrated to Japan. With them they brought knowledge of medicine, the art of divination, and the calendar.

A far more momentous event was the introduction of Buddhism to Japan during this period. Again there are indications that some segments of the Japanese society, particularly the immigrants from the continent, were already familiar with Buddhism, but the official introduction and formal adoption of this religion did not occur until the latter half of the sixth century. In either 538 or 552, the King of Paekche presented Buddhist images and scriptures to the Japanese court with, it is said, the following message: "This doctrine is amongst all doctrines the most excellent. But it is hard to explain, and hard to comprehend. . . . This doctrine can create religious merit and retribution without measure and without bounds, and so lead on to a full appreciation of the highest wisdom. . . . Every prayer is fulfilled and naught is wanting." [1]

Whether or not to adopt the new religion became a matter of major political controversy at the imperial court. There were at that time two powerful factions competing for power. One group was led by the Mononobe family, in charge of arms, and the Nakatomi family, in charge of religious affairs. The other faction was headed by the newly risen Soga family, which was responsible for financial affairs. The former, representing the conservative faction, opposed the adoption of the new religion, while the latter, representing the new power bloc, favored it. Following a series of intrigues and open clashes, the Soga faction crushed the Mononobe family in 587, and the adoption of Buddhism was officially sanctioned. Thus, even the religion that was to play a vital role in molding the Japanese culture and character was initially a pawn in the struggle for power and influence.

BUDDHISM

Buddhism was founded in the sixth century B.C. in northern India by Gautama Buddha, who, distressed by the human suffering and misery that he saw around him, set out to discover a way to free his fellowmen from their suffering. After years of searching for the answer to his quest, he attained "enlightenment" and formulated what he believed to be the true principles of life, known as the Buddha's Four Noble Truths. Life, he

[1] W. G. Aston, trans., *Nihongi* (New York: Paragon, 1956), part 2, p. 66.

taught, is full of sorrow: birth, disease, old age, and death are misery. The second principle that Buddha taught was that the cause of all this misery is desire. The craving of the self to satisfy its ego results in the perpetuation of the cycle of birth-death-rebirth and, therefore, in endless misery. Thirdly, the only way to break this cycle and end suffering is to free oneself from this craving, that is, to extinguish the ego. Finally, the way to accomplish this is through an eight-fold path that entails adhering to right views, right intentions, right speech, right conduct, right livelihood, right effort, right mindfulness, and right concentration.

Right views consist of understanding the nature of reality, that is, the truth that life is in a constant state of change and flux; nothing is permanent or absolute. The phenomenal world is only an illusion; there is no absolute reality behind it. Neither the soul nor the self is an absolute entity. The self is actually an ever-changing composite of psychological states, part of a stream of universal consciousness. What persists after death is not the soul but *karma,* the result of our deeds. It is our ignorance that leads us to believe that we are individual entities and causes us to crave satisfaction of our selfish impulses. By following the eight-fold path and gaining self-mastery and self-knowledge, the sense of the self is extinguished and the state of *nirvana* is attained.

Because the Buddha never clearly explained what the state of nirvana is and because the exact nature of the eight-fold path is open to varying interpretations, many different Buddhist sects came into existence. But Buddhism can be divided into two major branches: Mahayana, or the Greater Vehicle, and Hinayana, or the Lesser Vehicle. The adherents of the latter group prefer to be called Theravada Buddhists or the followers of the Way of the Elders. Although Buddhism eventually declined in India, it spread to other parts of Asia and flourished as one of the major religions of the world. Theravada Buddhism spread into Southeast Asia, while Mahayana Buddhism extended into China, Korea, and Japan. The former stresses the attainment of the state of nirvana through self-knowledge and self-mastery, whereas the latter offers salvation with the help of bodhisattvas, merciful Buddhist deities who have attained enlightenment but have postponed entrance into the state of nirvana in order to help those who are incapable of gaining salvation by themselves.

As we noted, Buddhism was adopted officially in Japan because of the triumph of the Soga family over its political rivals. Buddhism's beneficence, the chronicles record, was judged in terms of its ability to outdo the Shinto gods in controlling the forces of nature, but no doubt the ruling class was most impressed by the learned scriptures and beautiful artifacts that accompanied the religion. In the early period of its adoption, Buddhism appealed only to a small elite, who either took a scholastic interest in its scriptures or were interested in its more esoteric and ritualistic aspects. The masses were at first largely unaffected by the new religion, but as Buddhist temples and monasteries began to be constructed, not only in the seat of the imperial government but also in the outlying provinces, the impact of Buddhism upon the lower classes began to grow.

PRINCE SHŌTOKU

After Buddhism was officially adopted in Japan, it found a powerful and enthusiastic supporter in the person of a very able leader, Prince Shōtoku (574–622), who exercised authority as regent to the Empress from 593 until his death. During his regency he sought to accomplish several things. One was the reorganization and consolidation of imperial authority. Another was the propagation of Buddhism. Third, he sought to restore Japan's influence in Korea, where her position had been declining since the loss of Mimana to the kingdom of Silla in 562. Finally, he endeavored to strengthen Japan's cultural ties with China.

There was an urgent need to reorganize the government and strengthen the position of the imperial court. The leading clans had ensconced themselves in the central government and had begun to overshadow the imperial authority. Moreover, the rivalry among the leading families was undermining the stability of the government. In the provincial areas, also, the clan chieftains and the provincial governors appointed by the imperial court were beginning to act independently of the central government, usurping the right of taxation and extending their power by seizing the lands of their weaker neighbors. There is some evidence to indicate that the general disorder of the period was caused in part by the rise in population and the consequent struggle over existing resources.

In order to deal with this situation, Prince Shōtoku initiated certain changes. Hoping to end the hereditary control of top government posts by the entrenched elite families and allow men of ability to rise to positions of importance, he established a table of ranks. There were to be twelve grades for government officials. Reflecting the Confucian influence, senior and junior ranks entitled "virtue," "benevolence," "propriety," "good faith," "righteousness," and "wisdom" were created. In theory, men of talent were to be appointed to these ranks and assigned appropriate government positions.

The Prince also promulgated in 604 what is known as the "Constitution of Seventeen Articles." [2] It is not a constitution as we ordinarily understand the term, that is, a document that defines the structure, functions, and powers of the government. Rather, it is a set of moral injunctions that were intended to serve as guiding principles for government officials.

---

[2] Prince Shōtoku's authorship of the "Constitution" has been questioned by some authorities, but further studies have convinced most historians that he did indeed compose the document, although some scholars remain skeptical.

These moral injunctions were meant to strengthen the authority of the imperial family. Article III states: "When you receive the imperial commands, fail not scrupulously to obey them. The lord is Heaven, the vassal is Earth. Heaven overspreads, and Earth upbears." Article XII decrees: "Let not the provincial authorities . . . levy exactions on the people. In a country there are not two lords; the people have not two masters. The sovereign is the master of the people of the whole country." [3]

Prince Shōtoku and the reformers who followed him not only adopted the Chinese view that the Emperor was the supreme ruler possessing the sanction of Heaven but went further and equated him with Heavenly power itself. Being the direct descendant of the Sun Goddess, the Emperor was not a mere mortal who received the Mandate of Heaven—a mandate that the Chinese Emperor received because of his superior moral character—but was a living god. Around this period or soon after the Emperor came to be referred to as *Aketsu-mikami* (manifestation of kami, or god) or *Arahito-gami* (kami appearing as man). Thus, although Confucian concepts were imported into Japan, the Japanese did not speak of the Mandate of Heaven, a basic principle in Confucian political philosophy. In a way, the military rulers (*shōgun*) who emerged later were the ones who received the Mandate of Heaven, that is, the imperial mandate to govern on behalf of the Emperor. Consequently, although they became the real wielders of power, they never eliminated the Emperor; they continued to pay lip service to him as if he were the true sovereign. The Emperor was necessary as the symbol of Heaven, and his outward approval, or even tacit consent, was indispensable to the shōgun.

It was also during Prince Shōtoku's time or slightly later that the term *tennō* (heavenly prince) came to be applied to the Emperor, rather than the terms *ō* (king) or *ōgimi* (great lord) used until then. The term tennō was also imported from China; the first use of the word is found in the *Shih Chi, Historical Records,* written by the great Chinese historian Ssu Ma-ch'ien in the first century B.C.

That Confucian concepts influenced the thinking of the Prince is discernible throughout the entire "Constitution." The Confucian ideals of propriety, good faith, harmony, etc. are upheld in different passages. The Legalist viewpoint is seen in this document in its emphasis on the necessity of properly meting out rewards and punishments.[4] As one might expect, Buddhist precepts are also embodied in the document. Article II, for example, reads, "Sincerely reverence the three treasures. The three

---

[3] For the Seventeen Articles see Aston, *Nihongi,* part 2, pp. 129–33.

[4] The Legalists, opponents of Confucianism, believed that moral precepts were useless in governing the people. Rigorous enforcement of the law was the method they favored.

treasures, *viz.* Buddha, the Law, and the Priesthood, are the final refuge of the four generated beings, and are the supreme objects of faith in all countries."

Throughout most of Japanese history an aversion to dictatorial rule prevailed. This is reflected in Article XVII of the "Constitution": "Decisions on important matters should not be made by one person alone. They should be discussed with many." This injunction did not immediately produce significant changes in the government, but it provided the basis for later attempts to centralize political power.

Prince Shōtoku failed to regain Japan's foothold in Korea, but he succeeded in broadening her contacts with China. He sent embassies to the court of Sui (581–618) and encouraged students and monks to travel to China to study her religion and culture. This policy was continued by his successors; during the T'ang period (618–907), sixteen missions were sent to China. Prince Shōtoku did not believe that Japan should play a subordinate role in her relationships with China. In the message he drafted for the Japanese Empress Suiko (554–628), he referred to her as the Emperor of the Land of the Rising Sun and to the ruler of China as the Emperor of the Land of the Setting Sun. At this early date we already see the highly sensitive national pride that was to characterize Japan's relationship with the outside world.

Prince Shōtoku, a devout Buddhist, studied the religion for years under the tutelage of a monk who had immigrated from Korea. He edited a series of Buddhist sutras and initiated the construction of several Buddhist temples. The most famous of these is Hōryūji, located outside of Nara.

THE TAIKA REFORMS

Prince Shōtoku's plan to strengthen the power of the central government failed to materialize during his regency, but it was attempted again by his successors in the middle of the seventh century. The Prince's hope of weakening the position of the entrenched elite families through the implementation of the new table of ranks was not fulfilled because it failed to replace the old kabane system as the basis for power and status in the government. In the provinces the leading clans continued to extend their landholdings at the expense of weaker clans and to poach upon public lands and forests. At the center, the Soga family, which steadily gained in power after their victory over the Mononobe and Nakatomi families, had fastened a firm grip on the government and began behaving in an arbitrary fashion, controlling the succession to the imperial throne. It appeared as if they might even usurp the sovereignty of the imperial family. Consequently, their opponents awaited an opportunity to oust them and to effect a general reform to strengthen the authority of the imperial court.

The situation in Korea also caused the political leaders in Japan to feel the acute need to strengthen the powers of the central government. Korea, it appeared, might fall under the control of T'ang China. If this were to happen Japan's security would be endangered. The Sui dynasty had invaded Korea three times during the second decade of the seventh century in an attempt to bring the kingdom of Koguryo under its control. These invasions had failed, but in 644 the founder of the T'ang dynasty led a huge army against Koguryo. Japan's old antagonist, Silla, cooperated with the T'ang authorities and attacked Koguryo and Paekche, hoping to establish its hegemony over all of Korea with the aid of the T'ang forces. The T'ang venture did not succeed this time either, but it alarmed the Japanese leaders and gave impetus to the reform movement. Both major movements to strengthen the imperial authority, the Taika and Meiji reforms, were initiated in part out of fear of foreign encroachments.

In 644 the foes of the Sogas rallied around Prince Naka-no-Ōe (626–671), who later became Emperor Tenchi, to liquidate the Soga family. A leading figure in this coup was Nakatomi-no-Kamatari (611–669), a descendant of the foes of the Soga family at the time of the Buddhist controversy. He founded the powerful Fujiwara family that was to dominate the imperial government for the succeeding four centuries or so.

With the removal of the Sogas the new ruling clique set about initiating political, social, and economic reforms. The object was to strengthen the imperial authority and weaken the influence of the powerful families entrenched in the outlying regions.

The series of reforms started by Prince Naka-no-Ōe and his supporters is referred to as the Taika Reforms, after the era name adopted by them. (The use of era names was one of the innovations introduced by the reformers.) An edict was issued in 646 calling for reforms, but not all changes were implemented immediately; they extended into the next century. In 702 the Taihō Code, a compendium of penal laws and administrative practices, was written. This was a codification of all the administrative and legal changes that had been implemented or had been under preparation since 646. The reformers looked to T'ang China for their models, though they did not, of course, introduce exact replicas of T'ang institutions and practices. For the sake of convenience we can consider the changes listed in the Taihō Code as the major aspects of the general reform movement labeled the Taika Reforms.

The initial step taken by Prince Naka-no-Ōe and the reformers was to reaffirm the supremacy of the imperial authority. "The imperial way," they asserted, "is but one. But in this last degenerate age, the order of

Lord and Vassal was destroyed. . . . Now, from this time forward . . . the Lord will eschew double methods of government, and the vassal will avoid duplicity in his service of the sovereign." [5]

The central government was reorganized. The offices of the great omi and the great muraji were abolished and replaced with the minister of the left, the minister of the right, and the minister of the center. The last of these served as the personal adviser to the Emperor and consequently was the most important government official. Initially Nakatomi-no-Kamatari held this post. Under the Taihō Code, the occupant of this post was made the highest administrative officer and was called the *dajō daijin* (chancellor). He presided over the *Dajōkan* (Grand Council of State), which included the minister of the left and the minister of the right. The former was in charge of all the adiminstrative departments and the latter served as his deputy. The office of dajō daijin was frequently left open, in which case the minister of the left usually served as the chief administrative officer.

Under the Dajōkan there were eight ministries or departments: Central Administration, Ceremonial, Civil Affairs, People's Affairs, War, Justice, Treasury, and Imperial Household. An Office of Deities (*Jingikan*), having precedence over the Dajōkan, was created to manage Shinto rituals at the court.

In local administration, the country was divided into 66 provinces, which were subdivided into 592 counties, which were in turn broken down into townships consisting of 50 households each. Provincial governors appointed by the central government were instructed to prepare registers of all the free and unfree subjects of the land and to investigate the titles of the clan chieftains claiming landownership and authority in their districts. Armories were to be built, and all weapons in the possession of private persons were to be stored in them.

These local reforms did not, however, spell the end of the authority of the clan chieftains; many were appointed governors of the provinces where they were entrenched. Generally speaking, the county heads were also chosen from among former landowners and clan leaders. Despite its desire to do so, the imperial government was not in a position to uproot all the vested interests in the outlying areas.

The provincial governors were given the power to levy taxes, but initially they did not have judicial authority. This remained in the hands of the county heads. The people, however, had the right to appeal the decisions of the county heads to the central government. The provincial governors' term of office was limited to about six years, but the county heads

[5] Aston, *op. cit.*, part 2, pp. 197–98.

held life-time tenures and their sons frequently succeeded them. Consequently they were able to develop and protect their interests in their respective counties.

The be, or functional communities, were abolished as part of the effort to undercut the strength of the major clans. This did not mean that the members of the corporations were made free and independent. Instead of being under the direct control of the clan chieftains they were now under the authority of the imperial government.

In the economic realm a significant attempt was made to change the nature of land tenure. Again following a practice of T'ang China, where a policy of maintaining equal landholding prevailed, the Taika reformers sought to equalize landholding in order to weaken the power that the clan chieftains exercised over the land and people under their control. For this purpose all land in the country was to be nationalized. To set an example, Naka-no-Ōe transferred his land and workers to the public domain in 646 and asked other property holders to follow suit. They did so without much resistance because they were usually appointed governors of the areas in which their interests lay. Thus, although in theory they derived their authority from the imperial government, in reality they managed to retain their former privileges and interests. Moreover, the plan to nationalize all land was not put fully into effect. Important clansmen were allowed to hold a certain amount of land, commensurate with their rank and position. By special fiat the Emperor also created tax-free estates for privileged members of the court or aristocracy.

The nationalized land was to be redistributed among the people. For this purpose a census was taken, and population registers were compiled. Everyone except slaves,[6] who were given smaller allotments, was to be given an equal share of land: 2 *tan* (1 tan was 30 paces long by 12 paces wide) for each male over the age of six and two-thirds that figure for each female. Members of the imperial family and nobility were entitled to larger allotments, from 16 to 160 acres, depending upon rank. Every six years a general redistribution was to be effected in order to ensure continued equality in holding.

An additional inducement to effect the land-reform program was the government's desire to increase its revenue by bringing private estates into the public domain. Consequently, at the same time the new land policy was introduced taxation was systematized, and a tax of 2 to 3 per-

---

[6] Estimates of the size of the population and number of slaves that existed during this time vary. Earlier estimates held that the overall population numbered between 3 and 3.5 million, with slaves constituting about 5 percent of this figure. More recently it has been estimated that the population was about 6 million, with the slave population running as high as 10 or 15 percent.

cent of the harvest was instituted. Estates held by monasteries and shrines, however, were exempt.

Although the land tax was fairly light, there were other forms of taxation that added to this burden. Each adult male was required to contribute to the government a fixed amount of such goods as silk and hemp fabrics. Corvée had to be performed for both the central government and the local authorities. The amount of labor exacted by the former was normally ten days a year but could be extended up to forty more days. When labor services were not needed the government asked for contributions of produce instead. The provincial governors could demand up to sixty days' service each year. In addition to the regular corvée, construction work on special projects such as the temples, shrines, and public buildings was required.

The Taihō Code also instituted military conscription. One-third of all males between the ages of twenty-one and sixty were required to serve from one to three years in the army. While the recruits were in the army they were obliged to provide their own weapons, food, and other necessities. Because of its ineffectiveness, however, the conscript army was abandoned in 792.

In theory the Taika Reforms opened government posts to men of ability and merit, but high government positions were still closed to men who did not rank high in the newly established system of court ranks. A person's standing in this system depended upon his family background or upon his success in examinations taken after attending the government college. The practice of choosing officials by means of examinations was also imported from T'ang China, but in Japan the college was open only to children of government officials, so government service was limited to those who were already members of the governing class. As a result, the new system did not in reality provide for "a career open to talent." The ruling class was determined to preserve the hereditary governing caste. In 682 the Emperor issued an edict stating, "Let the lineage and character of all candidates for office be always inquired into before a selection is made. None whose lineage is insufficient are eligible for appointments, even though their character, conduct and capacity may be unexceptionable." [7]

Another practice borrowed from China was the establishment of barriers (sekisho), check points in strategic places to restrict the movement of people. It proved particularly useful in controlling peasants fleeing from the tax collectors.

The establishment of a permanent capital was another practice adopted

[7] Aston, op. cit., part 2, p. 357.

from China. In 710 Nara was selected as the site for the new capital. Prior to this the seat of government varied with each Emperor because his residence became the center of government. Because death was regarded as defiling, no Emperor resided in the same house that the former Emperor had lived in. As a result, no permanent seat of government came into existence.

Now for the first time there was to be a capital city. This had a double significance because prior to this time hardly any Japanese community could have been called a city or even a town. Now an elaborate city and capital—modeled after the T'ang capital of Ch'ang-an, although only half its size—was constructed. It was laid out in checkerboard fashion with the imperial court placed at the center of the northern end of the city. A major thoroughfare, about 280 feet wide, ran through the center from north to south, dividing the city into two parts. One aspect of the layout of the Chinese capital that the builders of Nara did not adopt was the practice of building a wall around the city. At this time the Japanese were evidently less security-conscious than the Chinese. Perhaps they also abhorred the idea of cutting the city off from its natural environment. Public buildings, residences for the aristocracy, and many Buddhist structures were built in Nara, which became the center of political and cultural life in Japan from 710 to 784. The population of Nara at its peak is estimated to have reached 200,000. The years in which Nara was the capital are known as the Nara period.

The objectives of the Taika reformers were not fully attained and the changes introduced were not thoroughly implemented, but the imperial institution was strengthened and the authority of the central government was fortified. The Emperor was endowed with greater prestige and dignity. The central government's administrative organs were systematized, and its control over provincial and local areas was strengthened by eliminating the *be* and nationalizing the land. In theory, the people and the land were now in the public domain, not the private possessions of the clan chieftains. The systems of taxation and compulsory service and the penal code were all designed to strengthen the central government's control over the populace.

The power and prestige of the prominent clans, on the other hand, were not diminished. The uji leaders were now incorporated into the top rungs of the central government's new bureaucracy as high officials or as provincial and county governors. They retained the privilege of collecting the taxes from the areas to which they were assigned. Moreover, they were paid generous stipends, were exempt from taxation, and were given special considerations in the enforcement of penal laws against them. The status and privileges of the officials of the upper ranks were inherited by their children. Thus the leading families retained their special status. In addition they were acquiring a strong cultural tradition, which gave them a further advantage over the masses; they were becoming a cultural as well as a political aristocracy.

At the beginning of the eighth century the number of officials occupying the higher ranks of the bureaucracy is estimated to have been no more than 125 men. They held the highest offices in the central government and served as governors of the key provinces. In addition there were about ten court aristocrats who were involved in decision-making at the very top level. These two groups of men constituted the elite—politically, socially, economically, and culturally. The gap between the aristocracy and the masses was further widened by the fact that the aristocracy tended to remain in the capital and manifested a growing unwillingness to serve in the countryside.

CULTURE OF THE SEVENTH
AND EIGHTH CENTURIES

Chinese civilization had a more lasting impact on Japan in the cultural sphere than in the political and social realms. The art and architecture that came from China were primarily Buddhist in nature, and, as temples and monasteries were constructed throughout the land, the cultural level of the society was greatly enhanced. The shapely, well-balanced tile roofs, the many-storied pagodas, and the vermilion gateways of Buddhist precincts undoubtedly would have made a Chinese or a Korean visitor of this period feel very much at home.

The art of sculpture took root in Japan and flourished very rapidly, reaching a level of figural art "never surpassed in the Far East." [8] The Buddhist structures that were springing up throughout the countryside were embellished with expertly carved wooden images and glittering bronze figures of the Buddha, the Kannon (Bodhisattva Avalokitesvara), and other Buddhist deities. Paintings and frescoes with Buddhist motifs also added new dimensions to the culture of Japan.[9]

The most renowned of the Buddhist edifices was the Hōryūji. The original buildings, constructed in 607, were destroyed in a fire and were rebuilt at the end of the seventh century. Nonetheless, they are believed to be the oldest wooden buildings extant in the world today. The plan of the monastery was patterned after the style of building in the Chinese Six Dynasties (222–589), with a relatively asymmetrical arrangement of the buildings. The five-storied pagoda with its gently curving tile roof occu-

---

[8] Sherman E. Lee, *A History of Far Eastern Art* (Englewood Cliffs, N.J.: Prentice-Hall, and New York: Abrams, 1964), p. 146.

[9] In art history the period roughly from the middle of the sixth to the middle of the seventh century is known as the Asuka period, and the eighth century is called the Tempyō period.

Hōryūji, a Buddhist monastery in Nara. Founded in 607 by Prince Shōtoku, the principal buildings were constructed over a period of several centuries. Courtesy of the Consulate General of Japan, New York.

pies a prominent place in the compound, as does the Golden Hall. The structures convey a sense of order, balance, and cohesion; the pagoda in particular has a stately dignity and grace. The buildings use the Chinese bay system, a modified version of post-and-lintel construction employing intricate bracketing designed to transfer the weight of the heavy tile roof down through the wooden parts into the main columns that support the structure. The interior of the buildings is adorned with Buddhist frescoes and wooden and bronze statues. In 1949 the Golden Hall caught fire and the priceless frescoes were destroyed.

The construction of Buddhist monasteries was given further impetus by Emperor Shōmu (701–756), who ordered them to be built in all the sixty-six provinces. In Nara itself, the Tōdaiji, where a great bronze Buddha over 50-feet tall is housed, was constructed in the middle of the eighth century. The Great Buddha sits on a lotus petal with his right hand signifying "fear not" and his left hand making a boon-bestowing gesture. The Tōdaiji complex is much larger than Hōryūji, occupying about 20 acres. The columns, bracketing, and other architectural parts are also more elaborate and massive. The several halls house innumerable Buddhist images—made of dry lacquer, clay, wood, and gilded bronze—patterned after early and middle T'ang styles.

The Shōsōin, where more than six thousand objects from this era are housed, was also built in the Nara period. Among the treasures stored here are the oldest printed manuscript extant in the world, brocades, silk fabrics, screen panels, musical instruments, mirrors, bowls, ivory works, lacquerware, dance masks, and weapons. Many of these were imported from China. Some items show traces of Eastern Roman, Persian, and Indian influence. Evidently objects from distant areas had found their way to Japan. The articles stored in the Shōsōin are still in excellent condition because the log construction "breathes with the seasonal changes in humidity, keeping out the damp and allowing the dry air of late summer and fall to circulate freely." [10]

Buddhism was still restricted largely to the aristocracy during this period. The abstruse philosophy was beyond the comprehension of the masses. In fact, both upper and lower classes together were attracted more to the pomp and ceremony of the rituals, the glitter of the benevolent-and merciful-looking images and the special powers that they believed the Buddhist gods possessed than they were to Buddhist doctrine. In a way, Buddhism was regarded as a magical cult. The people prayed to the Buddhist deities to give them good fortune, good health, and prosperity and to ward off the evil spirits and help them escape the pains and miseries of life as well as the many hells whose existence popular Buddhism envisioned.

With the arrival of monks from the continent, however, a small circle of specialists began studying the religion seriously. Six Buddhist schools arose during the Nara period, but none became a major movement. Three became extinct, while three have survived to the present with only a small number of adherents. The largest of these, the Hossō school, aimed at discovering the ultimate reality of cosmic existence through the investigation of the specific nature of all existence and a mystical apprehension of the nature of the soul. The second, the Kegon sect, sought communion with Buddha, who embodies the cosmic soul, and, through him, communion with all beings. The third, the Ritsu school, emphasized monastic discipline and the mystical concepts embodied in the mysteries of the initiation ceremonies.

Some Buddhist priests were not content merely to engage in scholastic or mystical activities but sought to spread the word among the people and to do good works by building roads and bridges into previously inacces-

[10] Lee, *op. cit.*, p. 274.

sible areas. The most notable of these missionaries was a monk named Gyōki, who was first condemned as a rabble rouser and preacher of false doctrines but was later honored as a high priest.

The native religion, Shinto, retained the following of the masses but it began increasingly to pale next to Buddhism, because it had no priestly caste, no elaborate moral code, and no heaven or hell. Neither could it match the glitter and glamour of the Buddhist artifacts and rituals. Moreover, the wealth and profundity of Buddhist teachings greatly overshadowed Shinto. As a result, even at this early stage attempts were made by Shintoists to reconcile their traditional beliefs with Buddhists concepts so as to enhance Shinto's spiritual and intellectual standing. This kind of syncretism did not take concrete form until the following centuries, however. Like the Chinese, the Japanese did not demand exclusive loyalty to any one religion; a person could worship at both a Shinto shrine and a Buddhist temple. Thus Shinto and Buddhism coexisted peacefully.

Perhaps an even more significant cultural development of this period was the emergence of a native written literature. At the beginning of the eighth century, the mythologies and legends concerning the founding of Japan, which had been transmitted orally down through the ages, were transcribed in the *Kojiki* (*Records of Ancient Matters*) and *Nihongi* (*Chronicles of Japan*).[11] Both works were patterned after Chinese chronicles and contain a number of stories that are not part of the indigenous tradition.

The compilation of these histories was started in the 670s as a project to revise and expand two earlier accounts, one a genealogical record of the imperial family and the other a collection of old tales. These two histories, it is conjectured, were written in the sixth century, but neither has survived. Their existence is known only because they are mentioned in the *Kojiki*. It is believed that the *Kojiki* and the *Nihongi* were based on oral tradition, on the two earlier works, and on Chinese sources. Some parts may have been fabricated by the compilers, because one of the chief reasons for composing these chronicles was to justify and glorify the imperial rule. The *Kojiki* consists primarily of mythological and legendary tales, containing very little that might be regarded as historical. The *Nihongi*, however, focuses more upon history, extending its coverage to A.D. 697. Its reliability as a historical document for the earlier period is questionable, but its accounts from about the beginning of the sixth century are regarded as being fairly accurate, although still embellished with materials taken from Chinese sources.

Although they are not entirely reliable as historical documents, as records of myths and legends of early Japan the *Kojiki* and the *Nihongi* are

---

[11] The *Nihongi* is also known as *Nihon-shoki*.

significant. For one thing, they aided in establishing the tradition that claimed a divine origin for the imperial family. Partly because of the sanctity and authority conferred upon it by these accounts, the imperial family was able to maintain its special status above the rest of the society. These records became authoritative "scriptures" in the modern age when the ultranationalists turned to them to prove the uniqueness of the Japanese national polity.

The *Kojiki* and *Nihongi* symbolized the growing sense of ethnocentrism that is discernible in the seventh century. Japan is viewed in these accounts as a unique land. In fact, it was depicted as being at the center of the universe, and the ancestral god of Japan, the Sun Goddess, was seen as the ruler of the entire world. From around the middle of the seventh century the term Nihon, the place where the sun rises, came to be used to identify Japan. Much of the cultural activity of this era sprang from the Japanese desire to rise to the level of China.

Another significant literary accomplishment of this period was the compilation of the *Manyōshū,* a collection of over four thousand long and short poems from the earliest period—although the majority of the poems anthologized had been composed after the fifth century—to about 760. The collection is invaluable not only for its intrinsic literary merit, but because it reflects the moral and intellectual outlook of early Japan. It is noteworthy that it includes poems composed not just by Emperors and court nobles but also by nameless plebeians. Motoori Norinaga, an eighteenth-century authority on the subject, indicated that the outlook that prevails throughout the *Manyōshū* is one of spontaneous, unadorned expression of natural human sentiments—even excessive sentimentality. The Confucian ideals of order, control, and restraint had not yet begun to mold the attitudes of the Japanese. The anthology consists of poems about nature, the landscape, the four seasons, flowers, birds, moonlight, the sorrows and joys of life, and, above all, love.

The belief that a man must not lay bare his feelings regarding such "unmanly" sentiments as love for the opposite sex, particularly his spouse, had not yet become embedded in the Japanese mind, whereas by the Tokugawa period love of wife and children came to be condemned as self-indulgence. For example, the following poem probably would not have been composed later, after the military class had become dominant.

> My wife and I are one in heart:
>   However long we are side by side
> She is charming all the more;
> Though face to face we sit,
> She my cherished love,
> Is ever fresh as a new flower. . . .

What appear to be Buddhist and Confucian ideas are discernible here and there in the *Manyōshū*. For example, the following poems seem to reflect the Buddhist view of the ephemeral nature of life.

> Brief is this mortal life—
> Let me go and seek the Way,
> Contemplating the hills and streams undefiled.

> How brief is this lease of life,
> To think my days will end,
> Lost in those falling flowers of spring.

There are frequent expressions of loyalty to the Emperor, such as the following poem, which school children in prewar Japan knew by heart:

> At sea be my body water-soaked,
> On land be it with grass overgrown,
> Let me die by the side of my Sovereign!
> Never will I look back.

Faithful service to the Emperor was essential for the preservation of the honor of the family and clan.

> Our forefathers served the Imperial House
> With all their hearts faithful and true. . . .
> So cherished and clean is the name of our clan,
> Neglect it never, lest even a false word
> Should destroy this proud name of our father. . . .

The Spartan attitude of the warriors of later years had not come to the fore as yet. A warrior taking leave of his family at the command of his sovereign departs with a heavy heart:

> My wife and children gathering about here and there,
> Wailed like birds of spring,
> Their sleeves all wet with weeping. . . .
> Having left my dear ones far behind,
> My mind knew no rest
> While the pain of longing wrung my heart.[12]

---

[12] All of the poems quoted here are from the *Manyōshū*, edited by the Nippon Gakujutsu Shinkōkai (The Japan Society for the Promotion of Scientific Research) (Tokyo: Iwanami Shoten, 1940), pp. 139, 142, 151, 177, 179.

The poems of the *Manyōshū* reflect the Japanese outlook before it was strongly affected by Chinese culture. The influence of Chinese poetry and literature could not be kept out of the literary realm for long, however. In the newly established college and in the provincial schools the Chinese classics formed the core of the curriculum. The educated soon became well versed in Chinese poetry and literature, and they came to admire and emulate the works of such great T'ang poets as Li Po and Tu Fu.

In addition to utilizing Confucian concepts to buttress their political authority, the ruling authorities sought to instill in the people other aspects of Confucian thought. For instance, in 757 the Emperor advised every family to keep a copy of the *Hsiao Ching* (a Confucian discourse on filial piety) and learn its contents. The *Hsiao Ching* taught that filial piety forms the foundation of all virtues and that all other teachings must be based upon it.

In other cultural developments, musical instruments, including a variety of wind, percussion, and string instruments, as well as dances, including Indian-style dances, came from the continent.

SOCIAL AND ECONOMIC CONDITIONS

In the economic realm, too, the influence of the continent was felt. The use of better tools imported from the mainland, improved methods of irrigation, and the production of wheat in dry fields led to greater agricultural yields. From the middle of the seventh century, copper, gold, and silver mines came to be exploited more extensively. Prior to this most of the minerals used in Japan were imported from Korea. With the construction of better roads and the introduction of horse stations to facilitate travel for government officials, commerce expanded and markets began to spring up in the major cities. In 708 the government minted its own coins, but a money economy did not develop to any significant extent right away. Rice and fabrics remained the chief mediums of exchange during the Nara period.

Medical knowledge and drugs also came from China during this period, and the long tradition of Chinese medicine in Japan, which persisted into the twentieth century, was founded. This included the use of not only herbs but also acupuncture (treatment by needles) and moxacautery (cauterizing with moxa leaves).

The smallest administrative unit introduced under the Taika Reforms was the township or village, consisting of fifty households. The size of the households varied but usually they consisted of several small or nuclear families within an extended family. The census records show that one household in central Honshu had 96 members, 59 of whom were slaves. Another in northern Kyushu included 126 members, 37 of whom were slaves.

Although slaves had existed in earlier days, the Taihō Code made a clear legal distinction between slaves (*semmin,* or lowly people) and free men (*ryōmin,* or good people). Slaves could be bought and sold, but the masters did not have judicial authority over them; if a slave committed a crime he was tried by the magistrates. They were expected to work around the house and in the fields and also to perform corvée in place of their masters. It is believed that they were not treated too harshly, and their lot was more or less akin to that of household servants of later ages.

Although the Taika reformers adopted the patriarchal concepts of China, in reality it appears that women continued to enjoy a status equal to that of men. Family life still centered around the mother. In most instances husband and wife lived apart, and the latter kept and raised the children, but the practice of the father retaining the children was becoming more prevalent in the late seventh century.

Polygamy was still common among the upper class. The Emperor had a number of wives and concubines. The Taihō Code made provisions for the Emperor to have nine concubines. There were also over two hundred female attendants serving at the court. Empresses were usually chosen from the Emperor's immediate family circle, so close consanguineous marriages frequently took place. The first wife was usually chosen by the parents with political considerations in mind. Otherwise the young people were allowed to choose their own mates.

By the Nara period the aristocracy lived in houses with wooden floors and wooden or tile roofs. The common people, however, still lived in hovels with dirt floors, thatched roofs, and only primitive household furnishings. They usually went about barefoot, while members of the upper class wore wooden shoes or clogs, which were in use as early as the Yayoi period. Meals were taken only twice a day. Although Buddhism forbade the killing of living creatures and the eating of meat, the proscription was ignored by most of the people, and meat and fish were consumed.

INTERNAL AND EXTERNAL FOES

From the latter part of the seventh century Japan followed a defensive policy in her relations with Korea, in contrast to her earlier attempts to extend her political influence into the peninsula. Korea was now under the control of China and Silla, Japan's traditional foe, a potentially dangerous situation for Japan. Fearing a possible invasion from the peninsula, the Japanese rulers began to fortify northern Kyushu and southeastern Honshu. A military defense command was established at Dazaifu in Kyushu. The threat from Korea persisted even after Silla drove the T'ang forces out of the peninsula only a few years after they had joined forces to conquer Paekche and Koguryo. The Japanese kept their fortifications in good repair and kept a close watch on political developments in Korea.

Toward the latter part of the eighth and beginning of the ninth centuries the relationship between Japan and Silla became tense when the latter sent vessels to raid the Japanese coastal regions. In 894 Silla attempted to invade the island of Tsushima but failed. The potential threat of Silla contributed to the consolidation of the military tradition in Japan by compelling the Japanese to maintain military vigilance for nearly four centuries following Silla's conquest of Mimana in 562.

Internal forces—hostile domestic tribes—also kept the imperial government preoccupied with military preparedness. The tribes of Kumaso and Hayato in Kyushu and the Ezo in the north resisted the imperial forces for centuries. The racial origins of the Kumaso and Hayato are not known, but from the early years of the Yamato state the imperial government was compelled to send its warriors against them. The Kumaso tribe disappeared from historical accounts early, but it was not until the beginning of the eighth century that the Hayato were brought under control. By the middle of the seventh century the Ezo were driven out of the Kantō region and were pushed into northeastern Honshu.[13] They continued to defy the imperial government, however, which found it necessary to send expeditionary forces against them periodically. Advance outposts were established in the north, and constant vigilance was maintained. The general in charge of the expeditionary troops was given the title *seiitaishōgun,* generalissimo in charge of subduing the barbarians. (After the late twelfth century this office was used as a stepping stone to exercise military control over the entire land.) In the early eighth century the northern region was brought more or less under the imperial government's control, although a major campaign had to be launched against the Ezo again at the end of the century. Like Silla, these domestic opponents of imperial authority can be viewed as having contributed to the strengthening of military tradition early in Japanese history.

[13] Historians formerly believed that the Ezo were the ancestors of the Ainus, but considerable doubt has been cast upon this theory.

CHAPTER 3

THE
HEIAN
PERIOD
The Age of Court Aristocracy

In 784 Emperor Kammu (737–806) decided to move the capital in order to escape the influence of the powerful monasteries in Nara. He first moved to Nagaoka near Kyoto, but believing the new capital to be plagued with the spirit of the dead, he moved once again in 794 to Kyoto, which remained the seat of the imperial court until 1868.

The new capital was laid out in the same manner as Nara, that is, in a checkerboard pattern. It was built on a larger scale, however, extending about 3.5 miles from north to south and 2.5 miles from east to west. The imperial palace was located at the middle in the north and from it an avenue 300 feet in width ran south.

The city of Kyoto was then known as Heiankyō, so the period from 794 to the establishment of the military government in Kamakura in 1185 is labeled the Heian era. Several significant developments took place during this period, among them the deterioration of the institutions and practices established by the Taika Reforms, the decline of imperial authority, the ascendancy of the Fujiwara family, the rise of the court aristocracy and its culture, and, toward the end of the period, the emergence of tax-free manors and military supremacy in the provincial regions.

THE CENTRAL GOVERNMENT

The administrative system established by the Taika Reforms changed its character when two new governmental organs were created at the beginning of the ninth century. They were the *Kurōdo-dokoro* (Bureau of

Archivists) and the *Kebiishi* (police commissioners). The former served as the private secretariat of the Emperor, assisting in the drafting of imperial rescripts and decrees, the latter as the judicial and police agency. As personal advisors to the Emperor, officials in these offices came to wield more authority than the ministers in the Dajōkan. The Grand Council's authority was weakened further as regents to the Emperor emerged as powerful political figures in the latter part of the ninth century.

There were two types of regents, *sesshō* and *kampaku*. The sesshō served as regent during the minority of the Emperor or during the reign of an Empress. In 858 this post was occupied for the first time by a person not of royal blood, a member of the Fujiwara family who was a descendant of Nakatomi-no-Kamatari. The kampaku, whose post was first established in 884, governed on behalf of the Emperor regardless of the latter's age. By the end of the ninth century political power was concentrated in the hands of the Fujiwara family, which had come to monopolize the regency. During the tenth and eleventh centuries the office of the kampaku was made a regular organ of the government, and Fujiwara family members occupying the office ruled as virtual dictators. The Emperors during this period devoted their time mainly to ceremonial and cultural activities.

The rise of the Fujiwara family to the position of supremacy was a slow process, effected by gaining control of key government posts, acquiring large tax-free manors, and intermarrying with the imperial family. The apex of Fujiwara power, wealth, and glory was reached during the regency of Michinaga (966–1027), who dominated the court for thirty years. Two of his sisters were imperial consorts and two of their offspring became Emperors. Four of his daughters became imperial consorts, and two of his grandsons and one great grandson mounted the throne.

In most instances during this period the wife and children remained with her family, while the husband visited or came to live with them; as a result the maternal grandfather and uncles exerted great influence over the children. For this reason the Fujiwaras wedded their daughters to Emperors whenever possible. When a son was born out of such an arrangement, the Emperor was persuaded to abdicate and the young heir was placed on the throne, enabling the Fujiwaras to exercise political authority on his behalf. The new Emperor was apt to be provided with another Fujiwara girl as his consort, most likely his aunt or cousin. For example, the two emperors who were Michinaga's grandsons were both wedded to his daughters.

With all the power and wealth they desired at their disposal, the Fujiwaras in Michinaga's time wallowed in sumptuous luxury and extravagance while the common people lived in a state of abject poverty.

It is noteworthy, however, that although the Fujiwara family dominated and virtually overshadowed the imperial family, it made no attempt to liquidate it and establish a dynasty of its own. Respect for the Emperor was deeply embedded in the Japanese mind by this time, and the Fujiwaras could exercise power only by utilizing the prestige of the imperial family.

As regents, members of the Fujiwara family conducted the affairs of government through their own house organs staffed by majordomos and stewards who were also government officials. At first the Fujiwara family sought to uphold the Taika land reform program and endeavored to discourage the growth of tax-free estates (shōen, see p. 65). It kept its own holdings down to a minimum, also. As the acquisition of tax-free estates became prevalent, however, it, too, began to accept estates from donors as payment for the immunity from government control and taxation that it could grant. By the time of Michinaga's regency the Fujiwara family had accumulated huge holdings. Its power, however, was not based upon landholding but upon its marital ties with the occupants of the throne.

The domination of the imperial government by the Fujiwaras was finally broken during the middle of the eleventh century when the actual powers of government passed into the hands of the retired Emperor, who controlled political affairs from behind the throne.[1] This practice was initiated by Emperor Shirakawa (1053–1129). When he came to the throne there was no dominant figure among his Fujiwara relatives, so he was able to reassert the authority of the Emperor. After his retirement, in order to curb the Fujiwara family, he continued to exercise political power as the guardian of his successor, who was only eight years old. This practice was continued in the succeeding years and came to be known as the "cloister government," because after retirement the Emperors usually entered a monastery, forsaking the secular world. After Emperor Shirakawa's time the retired Emperors ran the government from the cloister. This situation did not end political intrigues at the court because the rivalry between the Fujiwara family and the imperial family was merely replaced by a power struggle between the Emperor on the throne and the retired Emperor in the cloister.

Emperor Shirakawa also brought the newly emerging regional military forces into the central political scene by using them as imperial guards as well as agents to subdue those who defied the imperial authority. This development not only evinced the declining power of the central government but also portended other changes.

The decline in the central government's authority was caused by its neglect of provincial administration and its inability to prevent the emer-

---

[1] The decline of the Fujiwara regency resulted partly from the fact that the paternal side of the family was growing in importance. Wives were beginning to leave their families to establish independent households with their husbands.

gence of tax-free estates as well as by the continuous power struggle and political intrigues. Moreover, political offices fell into the hands of incompetent, untrained, or immature officials. Important posts were treated as hereditary possessions of the privileged families and in some instances came to be occupied by youngsters barely in their teens.

In the eleventh-century novel *The Tale of Genji,* Prince Genji's son is given a court rank at the age of twelve but is chagrined at his father's insistence that he receive some education before occupying a high government post. "Did Genji think him so very stupid as to need, before he could work for the Government, a training with which everyone else seemed able to dispense?" he muses. Prince Genji recognized that training and education were being neglected by the children of the court aristocrats. "I have noticed," he says, "that children of good families, assured of such titles and emoluments as they desire . . . see no advantage in fatiguing themselves by arduous and exacting studies." [2]

CULTURE

The Heian culture was the culture of the court aristocracy, which manifested highly refined taste in art and literature and strongly developed customs and modes of behavior. This was an age when the court nobles placed heavy emphasis on form, appearance, and decorum. There were prescribed rules for all aspects of life. An art historian described the period thus: "Here was artifice rather than art. . . . What most occupied the thoughts of those courtiers were ceremonies, costumes, elegant pastimes like verse-making, and even love-making conducted according to rules." [3]

Composure was important at all times for a noble at the court, even if he were ill or inebriated. Laughing with one's mouth wide open or wailing out loud were considered to be in poor taste. It was a highly self-conscious age. How one appeared in the eyes of others was the never-ending concern of the members of the court circle. This extreme sensitivity to appearance and form became so deeply implanted in the Japanese mind that it seems to have become a prominent feature of the Japanese character.

Heian society was also a highly snobbish and status-conscious world, in which pedigree and birth determined everything. For instance, it fixed a person's place in the table of ranks, which in turn determined his position in the government, emoluments, power, and proximity to the Emperor. Common people were looked upon as insensible sub-human creatures and constantly referred to as "strange" and "grotesque." Even non-

---

[2] Murasaki Shikibu, *The Tale of Genji,* trans. Arthur Waley (New York: Random House, 1960), pp. 402, 405.

[3] Langdon Warner, *The Enduring Art of Japan* (New York: Grove, 1952), p. 32.

plebeians, if not of the same social status, were held in contempt. Prince Genji's son "winces" at having to mingle with his "shabby and uncouth" classmates. Sei Shōnagon, a renowned literary figure of this era, indicates her contempt for the common people in her masterpiece, *The Pillow Book*. Once when she was at a temple she found that "a throng of commoners had settled themselves directly in front of me. . . . They looked like so many basket-worms as they crowded together in their hideous clothes, leaving hardly an inch of space between themselves and me. I really felt like pushing them all over sideways." [4] The aristocrats in the capital were also very contemptuous of the country "rustics." Characters in *The Tale of Genji* constantly refer to the provincial regions as "uncivilized," "barbarous," "wretched" places.

The Japanese language is characterized by the many different levels of politeness that can be expressed by the proper use of polite and honorific terms. By the Heian period this practice too had become firmly established. Referring to things that were hateful to her Sei Shōnagon remarked, "It is particularly unpleasant to hear some foolish man or woman omit the proper marks of respect when addressing a person of quality; and, when servants fail to use honorific forms of speech in referring to their masters, it is very bad indeed." [5]

During the height of Fujiwara dominion, extravagant luxury, ostentatious display, and decadent sensuality prevailed at the court. Showy splendor characterized the costumes, buildings, furnishings, ceremonies, festivals, and processions. The comforts and pleasures of this world were pursued assiduously even in religious life.

The Heian court circle was also a society with highly polished aesthetic taste. Prince Genji shows a keen sensitivity to beauty in nature. "And when all these weighty matters are off my hands," he says at one point, "I hope I shall have a little time left for things which I really enjoy—flowers, autumn leaves, the sky, all those day-to-day changes and wonders that a single year brings forth; that is what I look forward to." [6]

When love notes were passed back and forth among the lovers in *The Tale of Genji*, the touchstones for worthiness were a beautiful handwriting and refinement of poetic expression. A girl composing a reply to a missive she received from Prince Genji

> knew that he would regard her cadences and handwriting
> very critically, expecting something hopelessly countrified
> and out-of-date. This made the framing of an answer all

[4] Ivan Morris, ed. and trans., *The Pillow Book of Sei Shōnagon*, 2 vols. (New York: Columbia University Press, 1967), vol. 1, p. 258.

[5] *Ibid.*, p. 28.

[6] Murasaki Shikibu, *op. cit.*, p. 380.

the more embarrassing. She chose a Chinese paper, very
heavily scented. "Some fault there must be in the stem
of this marshflower. Else it had not been left unheeded
amid the miry meadows by the sea." Such was her poem.
It was written in rather faint ink and Genji, as he eagerly
scanned it, thought the hand lacking in force and decision.
But there was breeding and distinction in it, more indeed
than he had dared to look for.[7]

The court aristocrats' aesthetic taste was also reflected in their acute
sensitivity to color and concern about combining proper colors in their
dress. They regarded slight errors in matching colors as an embarrassing
lapse in taste.

Heian society was also governed by what we may regard as superstitions. In a testament left by a tenth-century member of the Fujiwara
family, the daily routine for a young nobleman was prescribed. Upon
awakening he was to recite seven times in a low voice the name of the star
under whose sway he was. Then he was to cleanse his teeth with a toothpick, wash his hands, turn west and invoke the name of Buddha and also
pray to his Shinto god. After recording the events of the previous day in
his diary, he was to eat some gruel and comb his hair. Being a male it was
necessary to use the comb only once in three days. Then he was to trim his
fingernails on the day of the Ox and his toenails on the day of the Tiger.
Also choosing the proper day, he was to bathe once in five days. He was
to avoid bathing on the first of the month since this would lead to an
early death. If he were to bathe on the eighth day, he would live longer;
if he bathed on the eighteenth, he would be victimized by a thief; if he
did so on the day of the Horse, he would lose love and respect; and on the
day of the Boar, he would be dishonored.

These notions were based upon the Chinese concept of yin and yang
and the five elements. All things in the universe were believed to be governed by yang (male, or positive, force) and yin (female, or negative,
force) and by the five elements, namely, wood, fire, earth, metal, and
water. For purposes of divination a sexagenary cycle—consisting of the
twelve signs of the zodiac (rat, ox, tiger, hare, dragon, serpent, horse,
sheep, monkey, cock, dog, and boar) and the ten celestial stems (each of
the five elements was divided into two parts, the elder and the younger)—
was used. By consulting this, experts could comprehend the forces that
affected the lives of all men and discover which days would be auspicious
and inauspicious. These beliefs, intermixed with magical aspects of Buddhism and traditional beliefs in magic, sorcery, and evil spirits, gave the

[7] *Ibid.*, p. 457.

society a strong superstitious sense. Diviners played an important role. The court employed experts on the stars, the calendar, and the science of yin and yang. Fortunetellers, geomancers, and exorcists were relied upon heavily by the populace at large to help them select lucky days and avoid unlucky ones, observe the proper taboos, and exorcise the evil spirits. These beliefs and practices persisted into the modern era.

In the Heian period Japanese culture came into its own. To be sure, Chinese influence was still very pronounced in all areas of Heian culture. *The Tale of Genji,* which is hailed as the outstanding testimony to Japan's coming of age in the literary sphere, is honeycombed with allusions and references to Chinese poetry, literature, and history. But once we recognized the profound debt that Nara and Heian Japan owed to Chinese civilization, it would then not be a distortion of the situation to assert that in the Heian period, having assimilated and adapted what they had imported from China, the Japanese began to develop an art and literature uniquely their own.

Up to the ninth century the Japanese consciously imported the products of Chinese culture. Students and monks were sent to China to study, and Japan sought to emulate T'ang art, poetry, customs, patterns of behavior, and institutions. Toward the end of the ninth century, however, the long-standing practice of sending cultural missions to China was discontinued because of the internal difficulties confronting the T'ang government just prior to its downfall.

A conscious effort was made to free Japan from the excessive dependence on T'ang China, especially in literature, where the most significant developments had occurred. Although great emphasis was placed on the art of composing Chinese poetry during the early part of the Heian era, the composition of *waka,* a Japanese-style poem of thirty-one syllables, also gained in popularity at the Heian court. As early as the middle of the ninth century Fujiwara-no-Yoshifusa (804–872), the first member of his family to hold the position of regent, wrote, "the poems that we are dedicating [to the Emperor] are written in Japanese, and not a word of the land of T'ang is used. There is a sacred and ancient saying that Japan is a land blessed by the muses. It is the custom of this country to compose elegant poems in Japanese when the subject matters are the gods and the imperial family." [8] At the beginning of the tenth century Ki-no-Tsurayuki and three other poets compiled an anthology of waka called *Kokinshū* (*Collection of Ancient and Modern Poems*). It included eleven hundred poems from the time of the *Manyōshū.* In its preface Ki-no-Tsurayuki

[8] Quoted in Inoue Mitsusada, ed., *Kodai Shakai (Ancient Society),* vol. 2 of *Shin Nihonshi Taikei (A New Outline History of Japan),* 6 vols. (Tokyo: Asakura Shoten, 195?–1954), p. 294.

wrote: "The poetry of Japan has its roots in the human heart and flourishes in the countless leaves of words." [9]

The development of native literature was facilitated by the invention of two phonetic Japanese writing systems derived from the Chinese ideographs. It is not known exactly when the two systems were invented, but they were in use by the end of the ninth century. The phonetic alphabet known as *hiragana*, which is more cursive in form than the more formal *katakana*, became the vehicle for literary expression for the Heian court ladies. The ladies in attendance to the imperial consorts were usually selected for their intelligence. Consequently many displayed great interest in literature; in fact, they were largely responsible for the Golden Age of Japanese literature that flourished in the late tenth and early eleventh centuries. The literary masterpieces they produced not only became classics in Japanese literature, but at least one, *The Tale of Genji*, came to be included among the great works of world literature.

The Tale of Genji was the creation of Murasaki Shikibu (978–1016?), a lady-in-waiting to Empress Akiko, one of Fujiwara-no-Michinaga's daughters. At one point in the novel the author has Prince Genji explain why a novelist feels compelled to write.

> Again and again something in his own life or in that around
> him will seem to the writer so important that he cannot
> bear to let it pass into oblivion. There must never come
> a time, he feels, when men do not know about it. That is
> my view of how this art arose. Clearly then, it is no part
> of the storyteller's craft to describe only what is good and
> beautiful. . . . He is just as likely to have been struck
> by numerous examples of vice and folly in the world
> around him, and about them he has exactly the same
> feelings as about the pre-eminently good deeds which he
> encounters: they are important and must all be garnered
> in. . . . The novel is . . . not . . . a mixture of useful
> truth with idle invention, but something which at every
> stage and in every part has a definite and serious purpose.[10]

The story that Lady Murasaki recorded was set in the court life of her era and centered upon the love life of the central character, Prince Genji, and on other members of his family circle. The picture that Lady Murasaki paints has a decidedly feminine point of view. The novel focuses

[9] Quoted in Earl Miner, *An Introduction to Japanese Court Poetry* (Stanford, Calif.: Stanford University Press, 1968), p. 18.
[10] Murasaki Shikibu, *op. cit.*, pp. 501–502.

upon the thoughts and feelings of the various characters as they brood and fret about their relationships with members of the opposite sex. The author is not concerned about the physical relations between the various couples. What interests her is the emotional and psychological interplay.

Why, one may ask, has this work come to be ranked as a world masterpiece? It is certainly not intricacy of plot nor profoundness of theme that has sustained the interest of the Japanese readers for nearly a thousand years. What accounts for this is the author's graceful poetic style, her realistic description of scenes and events, her profound understanding of human nature, her sensitive treatment of subtle psychological moods, her ability to create delicate nuances and atmospheres. Above all, it is the overall aesthetic effect that the author successfully created that has drawn the Japanese reader to the novel down through the ages. Although it is one of the world's longest novels, the poetic effect is sustained throughout the work, and the Japanese approach it as a work of poetry rather than prose.

If one were to select the one mood that permeates the entire novel, it might be what Motoori Norinaga characterized as the sense of *mono-no-aware*, a sense of pathos. A melancholy sense of futility and despair occurs again and again, and a Buddhist awareness of the impermanence of all things permeates the entire work. "We must never forget," Genji says, "how uncertain everything in this world is." [11]

Lady Murasaki displays a wealth of knowledge about Chinese literature in her constant allusions to Chinese literary and historical figures and events. Women, Lady Murasaki realized, were viewed as inferior creatures in her age. For example, she has Genji remark, "But what was the good of trying to please women? If they were not fundamentally evil, they would not have been born as women at all." At another point Lady Murasaki writes, "women are not supposed to know anything about Chinese literature and I will not shock your sense of propriety by quoting any of the poems . . . ," [12] but her masterpiece reveals that she was herself one of the most learned and talented persons of the age.

In painting, also, a distinctive Japanese style, known as *Yamato-e*, emerged toward the end of the Heian era. Although initially Yamato-e dealt with Buddhist subjects, it began increasingly to depict secular scenes and tales based on the everyday lives of the Japanese. The objects depicted in this style are outlined with thin lines and filled in with bright colors. Sliding-door panels and screens were painted in the new style, but the most noteworthy medium where Yamato-e found expression was in the horizontal narrative-picture scrolls called *e-makimono*.

[11] *Ibid.*, p. 606.
[12] *Ibid.*, pp. 405, 666.

Among the most famous e-makimono is *The Tale of Genji*. It is not as strictly narrative as the scrolls that appeared in the next era, the Kamakura period. Each scene is followed by a text and can be regarded as a separate framed picture; their function is more decorative than narrative. Concerning the style of *The Tale of Genji*, one authority writes, "This is not a bold splashing about, but a carefully calculated art of placement, of juxtaposition of color and texture, but particularly of placement. Placement is almost everything, along with the interrelationships of elaborate patterns of angle and line, of triangle and square, and of the large over-all patterns found on the costumes worn by the participants." [13]

There were also notable paintings of Buddhist deities during the Heian period. Among them are a number of renowned paintings of the Fudō, a mainfestation of the cosmic Buddha Vairocana. He is depicted as a deity with fangs, fierce protruding eyes, thick eyebrows, and a powerful, muscular body. He holds a sword and a rope in his hands to combat the forces of evil and is framed by a raging fire. There were also representations of more serene Buddhist deities such as the *Fugen Bosatsu*, the Bodhisattva of wisdom and virtue, who is depicted as a graceful, elegant Heian beauty.

The art of calligraphy also flourished during this period, and a number of master calligraphers emerged. With the invention of the hiragana writing system, brush-writing in the cursive style became a highly polished and graceful art. The ability to write poetry in an elegant style was prized just as much as the content of the poem itself. A superior handwriting was a mark of learning and good breeding.

In the realm of architecture, too, a distinctly Japanese style began to appear in the construction of Buddhist temples in the early Heian era. The ground plans for the temples of this period were arranged in irregular, asymmetrical patterns to fit in with the lay of the land. One of the best-known structures of this era is the Phoenix Hall of the Byōdōin, which was built around the middle of the eleventh century in Uji near Kyoto. The Phoenix Hall is situated beside a pond, and its reflection in the water enhances the beauty of the total image. It is so named because its design suggests the mythical phoenix descending to the ground. It represents the Buddhist paradise on earth. In accordance with the developing Japanese style, the whole structure is fitted into the natural setting, but the building itself resembles the buildings depicted in ninth- and tenth-century Buddhist wall paintings in Chinese caves. The T'ang influence is also seen in the exact symmetry, lavish decoration, and bright red and

---

[13] Sherman E. Lee, *A History of Far Eastern Art* (Englewood Cliffs, N.J.: Prentice-Hall, and New York: Abrams, 1964), p. 307.

The Phoenix Hall of the Byōdōin, a temple in Uji, near Kyoto, was completed in 1053. The hall represents a phoenix about to land on earth: the central hall stands for the mythical bird's body; the lateral corridors are the wings; and the rear corridor, not visible in this photograph, is the tail. Courtesy of the Consulate General of Japan, New York.

white colors of the temple. The Phoenix Hall was used as an imperial villa as well as a Buddhist temple.

A style of architecture known as *shinden zukuri* characterized the dwellings built by the Heian aristocrats. It emphasized simplicity and lightness of construction. The wooden floors were raised, and the roof consisted of unpainted bark or reed. The pillars were also unpainted, and the walls were made of plain removable panels. Large rooms were partitioned by screens. These features foreshadowed the architectural style of the houses that emerged in later periods.

BUDDHISM

During the Nara period scholarship in Buddhist scriptures had been pursued by learned monks, but Buddhism did not extend its influence broadly among the masses. As we noted, there were monks such as Gyōki who went out among the people initiating a variety of projects for their benefit. Most of the powerful monasteries of Nara, however, concentrated on strengthening their political and economic position and made little effort to reach the masses.

Besides moving the capital away from Nara, partly to escape the political pressures of the monasteries, Emperor Kammu also encouraged the growth of new sects that might rival the older orders. These new Buddhist movements were led by two energetic leaders, Saichō (767–822) and Kūkai (774–835), who is also known as Kōbō Daishi. Saichō went to China in 804 and came under the influence of T'ien Tai (Tendai) and Ch'an (Zen) Buddhism. After his return he founded the Tendai sect in Japan. This sect based its teaching on the Lotus Sutra and contended that the Lotus Sutra was identical with the Living Buddha. The Nara sects had generally derived their doctrines from secondary sources instead of from the sutras. Saichō asserted the superiority of his position because he claimed that his doctrines were based on the actual words of Buddha. He upheld Mahayana Buddhism over Hinayana Buddhism and laid the foundation for its diffusion. He also broadened the basis of Buddhism in Japan by teaching that salvation was possible for all living creatures. All living things, he preached, are endowed with Buddha-nature. The way to salvation was moral perfection and contemplation.

Kūkai also went abroad to T'ang China and studied there for three years. He came under the influence of esoteric Buddhism, and returning to Japan, founded the Shingon (True Word) sect. The central deity in the Shingon sect is the Dainichi Nyorai. He was called Maha-Vairocana (the Great Illuminator) and was regarded as the primordial Buddha from whom all other Buddhas—which included deities and demons, saints and goblins from all religions—emanated. The Great Illuminator, Kūkai taught, is in all things in the universe. The body, speech, and thought of the Dainichi Nyorai constitute the life of the universe. The aim of the Shingon sect was to evoke the vitality of the "three mysteries" in the body, speech, and thought of everyone. In effect, each individual was to be divinely transubstantiated. To achieve this end special chants, spells, motions, and symbols were to be employed in the rituals; especially important were the mystic formulas, the "true word." When the mysterious powers of the Great Illuminator were evoked, salvation as well as mundane benefits could be realized.

The Tendai sect also employed certain esoteric practices. At the end of the Heian period the excessive reliance on magical formulae contributed to the outbreak of dissident groups that rejected esoteric Buddhism, offering a "purer" way to salvation.

Kūkai is also known for his artistic, literary, and linguistic achievements. He was one of the three outstanding calligraphers of his age and is credited with having invented the kana syllabary, although the authenticity of this attribution is questionable.

Both Saichō and Kūkai, like their predecessors, considered the protection of Japan as one of the chief functions of Buddhism. Saichō indicated that his incantations, prayers, and sermons were intended to serve the interests of the nation. Kūkai, too, professed his interest in serving the nation and offered this as the reason for his desire to establish his monastery on Mt. Kōya.

Another aspect of this growing strain of national conciousness in Buddhism is seen in the attempt to reconcile Buddhism with the native religion, Shinto. Some such attempts had been made earlier, but in the tenth century this movement, under the leadership of the Shingon sect, became more pronounced although it was not until later in the Heian period that it developed fully. This effort to syncretize Buddhism and Shinto is known as Dual Shinto. Its advocates explained that all deities on earth were merely manifestations or emanations of the primordial Buddha. Thus Shinto gods were not distinct and separate divinities but were merely emanations of the primordial Buddha under different names.

In spite of these new developments in Buddhism in the Heian era, it did not spread widely among the people until the end of this age, when the doctrine of the Pure Land with its worship of Amida Buddha came into existence. There were, however, some monks who went among the people to bring the blessings of Buddhism to them. Such a monk was Kūya (903–972), who traveled throughout the country constructing roads and bridges, repairing old temples, building wells, cremating corpses abandoned on the roadside, and reciting the name of Amida Buddha.

There is little doubt that Buddhism had begun to affect the thinking of the aristocracy in a very significant manner. Buddhist concepts run through all the major literary works of this period. References to Buddha and Buddhist doctrines and practices occur repeatedly in *The Tale of Genji,* and the concept of karma is ever present in the minds of the central characters.

Buddhism, however, like everything else, was becoming increasingly formalistic during the Heian period. Appearance rather than true piety, form rather than substance were stressed among the court aristocrats. The Buddhist temples and images were designed to appeal to the aesthetic taste of the observers rather than to their deep religious feelings. People often went to the temples for pleasure and entertainment rather than for devout religious worship. They were just as likely to pray for worldly success and ease as to pray for religious salvation.

Salvation was to be achieved through mechanical means, such as the

routine recitation of spells and magical formulae. The esoteric sects fortified this tendency. It was believed that quantity was more important than
quality. The more a person recited the formulae the better his chances of
salvation were. Thus, people kept track of the number of times they recited the incantations by setting aside one bean for each time an invocation was made. One person, it was said, accumulated 3,600,119,500 beans
in thirty years. It was also believed that the more images of Buddha
a person dedicated, the better his chances of entering the Buddhist paradise were. One retired Emperor had one thousand images of Kannon
made and housed them in a structure 384 feet long. Although this occurred in the thirteenth century it typifies the spirit of Heian Buddhism.

Despite all its defects the Heian period was a remarkable age. It was
one of the few periods in Japanese history when the accent was placed
heavily upon peaceful pursuits. Arts and letters were the primary preoccupation of the court aristocrats in Kyoto. Force and violence seemed
to have counted for little among them. Symbolic of this was the abolition,
at the beginning of the ninth century, of capital punishment for government officials. This policy remained in effect until the middle of the
twelfth century, when the military men came to the forefront. During the
Heian period political foes were sent into exile, not executed. The literature of this era seldom mentions bloodshed and violence. A man was admired for his literary and artistic talents, not for his military exploits.

But while the court aristocrats were pursuing aesthetic values and
amorous pleasures, a revolution was brewing in the countryside, and a
new age was about to emerge. The makers of the new era will be of an
entirely different breed and temperament—less concerned with propriety
and decorum, less sensitive to the refinements of arts and letters, less
squeamish about spilling blood. They will be more ruthless, more brutal,
more coldblooded. They will present the other face of Japan. The polite
Japan, the gentle Japan, the sentimental Japan will fade into the background for the time being. The age of "sweetness and light" will be replaced by an age of "blood and iron." The effeminate, placid age will be
superseded by a more masculine, dynamic one.

RISE OF THE SHŌEN

While political intrigues and a poorly staffed administrative system
were weakening the imperial government, significant changes were taking
place in the countryside: the land reforms and legal institutions introduced by the Taika Reforms were slowly deteriorating. One of the objectives of the reformers had been to eliminate the local forces that had
entrenched themselves between the central government and the people
in the countryside. The authority of the central government was to have

been extended throughout the nation, and taxation brought under its direct control. In actuality this plan was never fully realized, because some of the local magnates managed to maintain private control over their estates through special dispensations. Those local leaders who remained in power as governors of provinces and counties were also able to retain their prestige and influence in their traditional strongholds.

In areas where land reforms were put into effect, the plan to divide the land equitably among the people failed. The scheme to redistribute the land once every six years to prevent land concentration was not enforced vigorously. In 834 the cycle of periodic redistribution was extended to twelve years, but even then redistribution was not effected as scheduled.

As a result, land tended to become concentrated in the hands of the local magnates, Buddhist monasteries, court aristocrats, and high government officials. Another factor that contributed to the concentration of landholding was the reclamation of wastelands. In order to encourage this practice the government permitted all lands that were reclaimed to be held as private property with reduced rates of taxation. Originally the reclaimed land was to be retained as private property for one to three generations, depending upon the time and effort expended upon the project, but as the time for the reclaimed fields to be transferred to the public domain approached, the owners tended to neglect or abandon them. To cope with this situation, in 743 the government agreed to permit permanent ownership. This resulted in a significant increase in private estates. The monasteries were especially active in sponsoring reclamation projects. In addition, they purchased lands illegally from other landowners and also acquired additional plots as gifts. In many instances these were gifts in name only. Since the monastic lands were free from taxation, some landholders arranged to have the monasteries become the legal owners of their estates to escape taxation. Then by paying nominal rents to the monasteries they were able to retain their now tax-free lands. As a result, the larger monasteries, such as Tōdaiji and Hōryūji, became huge landholding institutions. The holdings of a monastery (*cum* "donors") might range from 1,000 to as many as 10,000 acres.

The court nobles, such as the Fujiwaras, eventually accumulated enormous landholdings because they could offer protection to the local landowners against the provincial governors, who had the authority to levy taxes. As a result, local landholders made the same kind of arrangement with the court nobles as they did with the monasteries. They would donate or offer the land in commendation to a powerful court noble and then be given back the land as a benefice and pay a nominal rent. Thus they gained freedom from taxation and from the legal control of the government and its agent, the provincial governor. The imperial court also granted thousands of acres of tax-free land to members of the imperial family and court favorites. Consequently, the number and size of tax-free estates began to grow. These estates, under civil proprietorship, were called shōen.[14]

The government granted two privileges to the shōen owners: freedom from taxation and the right to deny government officials or agents entrance to their estates. These privileges had to be granted officially by the government in each particular instance, and initially they were limited to monastic and shrine lands. Later, in some cases, the provincial governors took it upon themselves to grant these immunities. Eventually many owners of estates came to claim these privileges without any official sanction. For example, those landholders who had ties with powerful officials, court nobles, or monasteries could claim these privileges without official permission because their patrons could gain for them de facto exemptions from taxation and freedom from the authority of the magistrates. Free from official supervision, the shōen owners came to exercise complete police and judicial authority over their own estates. The government repeatedly issued decrees prohibiting the establishment of shōen without official approval. In 902, for example, a comprehensive ban on illegal possession of land, woods, and streams was decreed. Such prohibitions were futile, however, because the violators included members of the imperial court itself as well as high government officials and nobles upon whom the government had to rely for the enforcement of its decrees. The imperial family and the Fujiwara family, the two authorities that showed some interest in curbing the growth of the shōen, ended as major proprietors of tax-free estates themselves. By the beginning of the tenth century shōen existed throughout the country.

A local shōen holder might be free of all outside control or influence, or he might be under the nominal jurisdiction of powerful monasteries and court nobles in Kyoto, who would be his legal guardians. Some shōen were under the direct management of the monasteries and court aristocrats. These tended to be larger than the shōen held by local magnates, but some local chieftains also became owners of large shōen by extending their protection and control over lesser shōen owners.

Usually a certain portion of shōen land was reserved for the owner to cultivate, and the rest was rented out to tenant farmers who paid rent and provided labor services in return. In some instances there were small and medium-sized independent farmers who owned land in the shōen, but they were subjected to the political jurisdiction of the shōen owner. These independent farmers were known as *myōshu*, that is, owners of *myōden* (name fields) that had originally been acquired by reclaiming wasteland. The fields were named after the reclaimers of the land in

---

[14] *Shō* means village and *en* means farmland.

order to protect their property rights. Some tillers of the soil also acquired proprietary rights over the fields they worked and gained possession of them as myōden. In the twelfth century the myōden was made the basic unit of organization in the shōen. An effort was made to equalize the size of the myōden to about 1 acre in the provinces near the capital, but they varied greatly in size in the outlying regions.

The shōen owners employed agents or managers to handle the affairs of the estates. Those managers whose employers lived in Kyoto, far removed from the shōen, tended to acquire considerable authority. Some gained hereditary rights to their position as well as the right to collect a fixed amount of income from the shōen. In fact, everybody connected with the shōen—the tillers of the soil, the manager, the proprietor, and the patron—had specific rights in the shōen. This system of rights, which also included the right of officials such as county heads to maintain hereditary possession of their positions, was known as *shiki*.

With the increase in the number and size of the shōen, the area under the jurisdiction of the provincial governors decreased proportionately. Several attempts made in the eleventh century to ferret out shōen owners who had gained possession of their estates illegally failed to reduce the number of tax-free manors. By the twelfth century it was estimated that only about one-tenth of the land remained in the public domain under the authority of the provincial governors.

THE EMERGENCE OF THE WARRIOR CLASS (SAMURAI)

The rise of the shōen meant a steady decline in the authority of the central government. Taxes collected by the government decreased, and police and military power in the provinces fell increasingly into the hands of the local magnates. After the military conscription instituted under the Taihō Code was abandoned in 792, the local governors were required to maintain the necessary military forces. In order to fulfill their military tasks, the governors relied upon the local chieftains for assistance. As the authority of the central government declined, the shōen proprietors and managers had to rely upon their own resources to protect their property and preserve peace and order in the shōen. Thus they found it necessary to maintain their own private militias, which were manned initially by shōen workers as part of their corvée. The influence and power of the local chieftains increased as the inhabitants began to submit to their leadership in order to receive protection.

The size of the local armies grew as unemployed or displaced farmers, reduced to being vagrants or brigands, joined their ranks. The deterioration of the peasantry resulted in part from the fact that, as tax-free estates proliferated, the tax burden grew heavier upon those who worked the little-remaining taxable land. The exploitation of the peasantry by the local governors became more intense also. Many of the farmers fell into debt to the government or to moneylenders. Unable to pay their debts and unable to bear the burden of heavy taxes, they left the land and joined the ranks of the vagrants. The land they abandoned was taken over by the rising local landowning magnates.

As the local chieftains—usually shōen owners, managers of shōen whose owners resided in Kyoto, county heads, and, in some cases, provincial governors who had established their roots in the countryside—grew more powerful, they began to establish lord-and-vassal relationships with their followers. The hard core of their following consisted of vassals who had some sort of blood ties with them. This was, in a way, the clan or uji system of old—a tightly-knit unit based on kinship ties. In addition, among the followers of a local chieftain were those who had entered into a master-vassal relationship with him because of the circumstances discussed above. This relationship was formalized with the presentation of a name plate from the vassal to the lord. In return for the vassal's loyal services, the lord was expected to provide him with a piece of land or the right to collect taxes or rents from the land. Thus what was essentially a feudal relationship was established between the local lord and his followers. Unlike European feudalism, however, the peasants on the shōen were generally not serfs but either free tenants or independent, landowning farmers. The local lords and their followers constituted the ascending samurai class, which was to play a dominant role in Japanese political history from this time until the middle of the nineteenth century.

There was a hierarchy of lord-vassal relationships, since the lord himself might be a vassal of a more powerful chieftain, while the vassal might have followers of his own. Something like the system of sub-infeudation that existed in Europe in the Middle Ages began to emerge in Heian Japan.

Gradually larger and larger nuclei of power began to develop. The more powerful local military chieftains—those who were descendants of the imperial family or those who were related to powerful court aristocrats—tended to attract a larger following and succeeded in extending their control over an increasingly wider area. Thus, while the central government was neglecting to maintain its military strength, local lords were building formidable private armies to fight for economically productive and strategically important areas.

As the powers of the local military men grew, they began to defy openly the authority of the central government. Having allowed its military strength to decline, the central government was forced to call upon other local leaders to help curb the more recalcitrant military chieftains. In this way it inadvertently strengthened the position of certain local leaders over others and at the same time provided these military men with an excuse to interfere in its affairs.

As early as the tenth century, the government was confronted with two major uprisings that could not be suppressed without the aid of loyal local chieftains. One rebellion was led by Fujiwara-no-Sumitomo (?–941), who had been assigned by the government the task of subduing the pirates in the Inland Sea. After bringing the pirates under control he in turn defied the central government and plundered the western region between 936 and 941. Sumitomo was subdued, however, with the aid of a local military chieftain bearing the name Minamoto, a name that would have to be reckoned with later.

The other rebellion occurred in the east, in the Kantō region. In 939 Taira-no-Masakado (?–940), who had been extending his power in that area, declared himself the Emperor of Kantō and established his own government, modeling it after the Heian government. His rebellion was crushed in 940 when another member of the Taira clan turned on him. In quashing both of these uprisings, the central government had to rely upon the support of other provincial magnates, and it had to continue relying upon the help of the emerging military chieftains to maintain its authority in the countryside. This tended to strengthen those military families that cooperated with the imperial government, and power came to be concentrated in the hands of fewer and fewer families.

By the twelfth century the Taira and Minamoto families, two major military houses both claiming direct descent from Emperors of the Heian period, came to dominate the outlying regions. They both came to power first in the Kantō region where, because of the long history of conflict with the Ezo in the north, the military tradition was the strongest. The Minamotos distinguished themselves by subduing rebellious military chieftains in the Kantō region and in the north. They had also established close ties in Kyoto by catering to the interests of the Fujiwara family. Their power and prestige grew under Yoshiie (1041–1108), who attracted a large following not only because of his military exploits but also because of his generosity. When the imperial government refused to reward the troops under him for subduing the northern rebels, Yoshiie compensated them out of his own property. His popularity caused a large number of farmers and warriors to commend their lands to him. This alarmed the imperial government, and it felt compelled to prohibit further donations to him.

The Tairas first emerged in the Kantō region also but lost their base of power there as a result of Masakado's rebellion. A Western branch of this clan located in Ise emerged as the nucleus of Taira power. The Ise Tairas first gained prominence by helping the imperial government subdue rebels and pirates in the western regions. They strengthened their economic position by engaging in trade with Sung China and also by cultivating close ties with the cloister government.

In addition to these two major families, there was another power to the north, the Fujiwaras—unrelated to the Fujiwaras in Kyoto—who posed a potential threat to the other military families until the end of the twelfth century.

The struggle for power and land in the provinces resulted in the emergence of powerful military forces that eventually were in a position to dominate the central government.

CHAPTER 4

THE KAMAKURA PERIOD
The Triumph of the Samurai

We saw in the previous chapter how the authority of the central government steadily declined as the shōen dominated by local military chieftains grew in size and number throughout the land. It not only virtually lost control over the outlying areas, but its authority was undermined in Kyoto itself where there was a continuous power struggle between various imperial factions. In addition, the imperial government was challenged by the powerful monasteries in and around the capital, which had recruited inmates who were monks in name but warriors in reality. Most of these warrior-monks were farmers who wished to escape the heavy tax burdens and unemployed vagrants who sought a place of refuge. They were used by the monasteries to protect their shōen and also to coerce the government to grant special privileges and ecclesiastical posts to their members. In time the number of warrior-monks increased—some monasteries retained as many as several thousand men —and from time to time they poured into the streets of Kyoto to intimidate the government authorities. They contributed further to the political disorder by engaging in disputes among themselves. Particularly troublesome were the Kōfukuji of Nara, which was patronized by the Fujiwara family, and the Enryakuji of Mt. Hiei, an "order" founded by Saichō.

THE RIVALRY OF THE TAIRA
AND MINAMOTO CLANS

As noted earlier, two major military families rose to power in the countryside, the Taira (Heike) and the Minamoto (Genji). In 1156 a dispute at the court provided the Taira family with an opportunity to emerge as a significant force in Kyoto. A power struggle between the reigning Emperor and the retired Emperor broke out, and both factions appealed to the provincial military leaders for support. The Taira family, led by the able and ambitious Kiyomori (1118–1181), came to the aid of the reigning Emperor and defeated the rival faction, which was supported by Minamoto-no-Tameyoshi (1096–1156), the grandson of Yoshiie. This was not an outright confrontation between the Tairas and the Minamotos, however, because some members of the Taira clan fought on the side of the retired Emperor, while some Minamoto clansmen supported the Emperor. The most prominent of the latter was Tameyoshi's own son, Yoshitomo (1123–1160) who, after victory, was ordered by the Emperor to execute his own father. This power struggle is known as the Hogen Insurrection, Hogen being the era name for the years 1156–1158.

After the Hogen Insurrection both Kiyomori and Yoshitomo became influential at the court, but in 1159 Kiyomori managed to eliminate Yoshitomo when the latter, jealous of Kiyomori's growing popularity and power, supported dissident elements at the court and attempted to stage a coup, known as the Heiji Insurrection. Having failed, he was executed, together with those of his sons who had participated in the uprising. One son, Yoritomo (1147–1199), who was only twelve years old at that time, was saved from execution by the intercession of Kiyomori's stepmother. He was exiled to an island off Izu Peninsula instead. Yoshitomo's three younger sons by a concubine were also spared on the condition that their mother become Kiyomori's mistress. One of these boys, Yoshitsune, later emerged as the leading general of the Minamoto forces.

It now appeared that the Minamotos had been eliminated from the national scene and the paramountcy of the Taira family established. Kiyomori became virtually a dictator. He rose rapidly in court rank and in 1167 became dajō daijin (chancellor). His family members became high-ranking court officials. He married his daughter to the Emperor and his grandson thus became heir to the throne. His possessions were immense; in addition to controlling the governorships of thirty provinces, the Taira family owned over five hundred shōen. They gained such power and prestige that people came to say, "If one is not a Taira, one is not a human being."

Like all dictatorships, the Tairas tolerated no adverse criticism. The

Tale of the Heike, a historical romance written in the early Kamakura period, relates, "If there was anyone who spoke evil against the Taira and one of these [youths employed by the Tairas to patrol the streets of Kyoto] chanced to hear it, straightway summoning to him his fellows, they would violently enter that man's house, seize his treasures and household goods and bring him bound to Rokuhara [the Taira residence]. So that none were found to open their mouth about things they saw or knew." [1] But they could not control the secret feelings of the people. "The provinces are oppressed by the governors and the fiefs are abused by the commissioners; people are harried in all matters and there is no peace. . . . Outwardly all submit but inwardly there are none who do not dislike the Heike rule." [2]

Besides focusing upon the consolidation of his political position, Kiyomori endeavored to develop commerce with Sung China. He built the port of Hyōgo and excavated the Straits of Ondo near the city of Kure to facilitate this trade.

Unlike Yoritomo, his successor, Kiyomori did not seek to establish his own government. Instead he chose to rule through the imperial court in cooperation with the cloistered Emperor. As the balance of power shifted in favor of the Tairas, however, the imperial faction began to engage in intrigues to reduce the power of the clan. But the several conspiracies directed against the Tairas failed.

In 1180, however, anti-Taira uprisings broke out in the Kantō region and spread to the provinces near the capital. The leadership for this anti-Taira movement was provided, ironically enough, by Minamoto-no-Yoritomo who, while in exile, managed to build his military strength by joining forces with the Hōjō family, a local power in the Izu area. Yoritomo had, in fact, married a member of the Hōjō family, Masako. Heeding the imperial call to overthrow the Tairas, Yoritomo led his forces against them, and the two rival families confronted each other again. The struggle continued for five years. Tales of heroism and treachery, valor and cowardice, chivalry and cruelty fill the chronicles of this conflict.

The closing years of Taira supremacy were plagued by disastrous natural calamities, causing severe famines. A contemporary account describing the terrible famine of 1181–1182 describes conditions in Kyoto thus:

> Beggars swarmed by the roadsides, and our ears were filled
> with the sound of their lamentations. . . . Everybody

---

[1] A. L. Sadler, trans., *The Heike Monogatari,* in *Transactions of the Asiatic Society of Japan,* vol. 46, part 2, p. 10.
[2] *Ibid.,* p. 48.

was dying of hunger. . . . By garden walls or on the road-
sides countless persons died of famine, and as their
bodies were not removed, the world was filled with evil
odours. . . . The numbers of those who died in
central Kiōto during the fourth and fifth months alone
were 42,300. To this must be added many who died before
and after; while if we also reckon those who perished
in the various outlying quarters, the number has no limits.[3]

These conditions no doubt helped to undermine the position of the
Tairas. They had also incurred the opposition of the powerful monasteries and many local leaders. Eventually, the Minamoto faction emerged
victorious as Yoritomo consolidated his position in the east and broadened his base of support by welcoming all comers into the Minamoto
faction regardless of family or historical ties. Although the Tairas were
superior in number, the Minamotos had the advantage of superior leaders, among them Yoritomo's younger brother, Yoshitsune (1159–1189),
whose daring tactics led to many victories, and his cousin Yoshinaka
(1154–1184), who drove the Tairas out of the capital. Before the Tairas
were completely crushed, however, Yoritomo and Yoshinaka found their
ambitions to be incompatible. Yoshinaka was defeated and killed by
Yoritomo's men.

In the early stage of the conflict Kiyomori fell ill and died in the
spring of 1181, and the fortune of the Tairas, deprived of their able
leader, steadily declined. They were forced to retreat to the west and
were finally annihilated in 1185 by the Minamoto forces under the brilliant generalship of Yoshitsune, who was at that time only twenty-four
years old. Determined not to repeat the mistake that the Tairas had
made, Yoritomo had all the important members of the main Taira family executed. Even little children were not spared; all were drowned or
buried alive.

Yoritomo now set about consolidating his power. If Yoshitsune was
the military genius who made the Minamoto triumph possible, Yoritomo
was the political genius. It was said that the Tairas had failed to maintain their position because they had imitated the effeminate ways of the
court, neglecting to maintain a firm grip on the real source of their
power, their provincial strongholds. Yoritomo was determined not to
make the same mistake. Throughout the conflict with the Tairas, Minamoto military headquarters were at Kamakura. Even after his victory,
Yoritomo chose to remain in Kamakura, refusing to move to Kyoto.

[3] W. G. Aston, *A History of Japanese Literature* (New York: Appleton 1899), pp. 149–
51.

Thus the real seat of government was transferred to Kamakura, although the imperial government in Kyoto was still regarded as the legal government and was treated as such by Yoritomo.

Now we enter the period in Japanese history in which the military class dominated the country, a situation that prevailed for almost seven centuries. From 1200 on the imperial court and the Emperor were increasingly relegated to the background and played no role of real significance in the political life of the nation until the middle of the nineteenth century. Not only were the political, social, and economic patterns of the land set by the military, but the cultural, moral, and intellectual tone was also molded largely by the military outlook. Military domination would have a decisive and lasting effect in forming the Japanese mind, character, and temperament; in this sense the political triumph of Minamoto-no-Yoritomo was of paramount significance in Japanese history.

THE KAMAKURA SHOGUNATE (1185–1333)

After the defeat of the Tairas, Yoritomo, a jealous and ruthless man, set out to remove all potential rivals, including his brother Yoshitsune, who had gained renown because of his military exploits. Yoritomo suspected his brother of harboring political ambitions and sought to repress him. In anger Yoshitsune rebelled against his brother but failed to gain sufficient support. Yoritomo had him hunted down relentlessly and executed. When Yoshitsune's wife gave birth to a baby boy, Yoritomo had the child killed. Earlier he had had his son-in-law killed because he suspected him of disloyalty. He also did away with his half-brother Noriyori. Using the excuse that they had provided help to Yoshitsune, Yoritomo seized the opportunity to destroy the northern Fujiwara clan. By 1189 he had removed all potential military threats to his position.

Although there no longer remained anyone who might challenge his supremacy, Yoritomo did not attempt to bring the entire country under his direct control. He deferred to the imperial court as the legal government and obtained imperial sanctions for all his policies and decrees. At the same time he went about strengthening his political position. In 1185 he persuaded the imperial court to appoint him supreme constable and supreme land steward of all sixty-six provinces. The former office gave him military and police power over the entire country, and the latter the right to collect taxes from all public domains and the shōen. He also acquired the right to appoint provincial constables and land stewards at all levels—in provinces, counties, and townships. The right of Yoritomo and his successors to appoint and control these officials eventually eliminated the immunity from taxation and from official intervention that the shōen had heretofore enjoyed.

Yoritomo was also given proprietary rights over the lands he formerly held in the Kantō region, amounting to nine provinces. The governors of these provinces were appointed by Yoritomo from among his followers. Yoritomo also acquired the lands formerly held by the Tairas. This meant an additional five hundred shōen scattered throughout the country. Over these areas Yoritomo exercised direct control, just as the imperial court, the court nobles, the monasteries, and some of Yoritomo's own followers exercised proprietary rights over their shōen. To supervise his estates he appointed vassals whom he wished to reward as land stewards and managers of his holdings.

Yoritomo's authority was also felt in the public domains and in the shōen owned by the court aristocrats and the monasteries because the constables and land stewards appointed by him exercised authority over the lower officials in both sectors. His control over Kyushu and western Honshu was weaker than in eastern Honshu, where his direct holdings were located. He did not insist upon appointing land stewards to those areas where his influence was weak.

In effect a dual authority prevailed during the early Kamakura period. Yoritomo exercised direct control over the Kantō provinces and his own shōen scattered throughout the land. The governors of the eastern provinces were his appointees. He also held supreme military and police power over the entire country. On the other hand, the imperial faction still controlled a large number of shōen, and the provincial governors in the areas outside of eastern Japan were appointed from Kyoto. Nonetheless, these governors had to share their authority with the constables and land stewards appointed from Kamakura.

Although Yoritomo had to share the administration of the country with the imperial court, he was supreme in the military realm. In 1192 he was appointed seiitaishōgun, which made him officially the military commander-in-chief of the land. In order to exercise his military authority and manage the lands under his proprietorship, he established an administrative system in Kamakura known as the Bakufu (tent government). This was not intended to replace the imperial government in Kyoto but was designed to manage his "family" affairs. The system established by Yoritomo was a relatively simple one. There were three offices: the Office of the Samurai, the Administrative Office, and the Court of Appeals. The first organ dealt with promotions and demotions of the samurai and generally supervised their conduct. The second managed administrative, legislative, and legal affairs. The third functioned as a judicial board to settle civil disputes, particularly those involving land, among those samurai under Yoritomo's jurisdiction. To staff these offices Yoritomo employed members of the Kyoto aristocracy who, unlike many of his vassals, were well educated. The three offices were under the close supervision of Yoritomo, who made all the important decisions.

In local administration, as we have noted, Yoritomo appointed provincial constables and land stewards from among his followers. The constable had military and police authority. It was his duty to apprehend criminals, suppress rebellions, and, when summoned by the shōgun, to come to his aid with his warriors. He also served as the local liaison and administrative officer for the shōgun.

The land stewards were at first authorized to collect taxes from all the estates in the provinces to which they were assigned, whether public or private. This policy was opposed by the shōen owners in Kyoto, however, so the land stewards' tax-collecting power was limited to the public domains. The extent to which land stewards exercised their influence in the provinces varied from place to place, but they usually held considerable power. At the lower levels they exercised police power. Their authority was extended greatly after ex-Emperor Gotoba sought to overthrow the Kamakura forces in 1221. This attempt was crushed, and the estates of the nobles and monasteries who had supported the move were confiscated and placed under the jurisdiction of the land stewards. Throughout the Kamakura period the land stewards steadily increased their authority over the shōen not owned by the Bakufu. One of their duties was to collect the rent for the shōen owners, but in time they tended to ignore their responsibilities to the proprietors, concentrating instead on increasing their own incomes and control over the peasants on the land. By the end of the Kamakura period many stewards had acquired proprietary rights over the shōen and emerged as a new landholding class.

In discussing Kamakura society we should consider whether we can properly label it a "feudal" society. Although hitherto it has been customary to consider the Kamakura society feudal, recently a more cautious viewpoint has begun to emerge. Some authorities now feel that to call the Kamakura system of land administration feudalism would be an oversimplification, because the vassal was usually appointed to some office such as that of land steward or shōen manager and was not given a piece of land to control as his own fief. With the office went the right to extract some income from the land, but the actual proprietary rights were retained by the Bakufu or the shōen owner. Moreover, the feudal elements centering upon Yoritomo were still not the dominant forces in the political and social systems. Although the real power was in the hands of the shōgun, the administration operating out of Kyoto still controlled large parts of the country. Thus, we have something like a dual administration, with the Bakufu, or shogunate, operating—at least on the sur-

face—under the jurisdiction of the imperial government. For convenience, the term feudal can be used to designate the hegemony of the
military chieftains, but it should be clearly understood that this term
does not denote the same kind of system that prevailed in medieval
Europe.

During the Kamakura period, the earlier practice of submitting a name
plate at the ceremony of investiture was abolished, and the vassal merely
presented himself to his lord at the ceremony. As noted above, the benefice granted by the lord to the vassal was usually some office. In return the
vassal performed military duties in time of both war and peace and
helped defray the cost of his lord's expenses. For example, he had to
present gifts to the lord's household on such important occasions as births,
coming of age ceremonies, and weddings.

Although the tillers of the soil varied greatly in status, no peasants in
Kamakura society could be characterized as serfs. The most well-off were
the myōshu, who held title to land under the jurisdiction of the shōen
proprietors. The myōshu in outlying regions tended to have larger holdings and often used semi-slave workers to till the soil. Although the practice was illegal, impoverished peasants were often driven to selling their
wives and children as slaves to be used as household or farm workers. In
addition there were a variety of tenant farmers and hired workers.

THE HŌJŌ REGENCY

Yoritomo died in 1199 and was succeeded by his son Yoriie (1182–1204),
but the real power of the Bakufu passed into the hands of Hōjō Tokimasa (1138–1215), the father of Yoritomo's wife, Masako. When Yoriie
became ill in 1203, Tokimasa forced him to resign and made Yoriie's
younger brother, Sanetomo, the shōgun. He later had both Yoriie and his
eldest son assassinated. Since Sanetomo was a minor, Tokimasa made himself regent and exercised power as the actual head of the Kamakura government. We now have a situation in which the nominal government in
Kyoto was run by a regent, while the de facto government in Kamakura,
which was governing on behalf of the imperial court, was also controlled
by a regent.

In 1205 Tokimasa sought to eliminate Sanetomo also. Instead he was
ousted by his daughter Masako, Yoritomo's wife, and his son Yoshitoki,
who exiled him. Thereupon Yoshitoki became regent. In 1219 the figurehead shōgun, Sanetomo, was assassinated by Yoriie's other son. This
ended the brief era of the Minamoto shogunate. Following Sanetomo's
death the position of the shōgun was filled by court nobles from Kyoto.
The shōgun remained a mere figurehead, and the Hōjōs controlled the
Kamakura government as regents until its downfall in 1333. Thus, the
Minamoto rule was almost as brief as the Taira.

After Yoritomo's death the imperial court intensified its intrigues against the Bakufu. When the Minamoto shogunate ended with the death of Sanetomo, ex-Emperor Gotoba decided to take advantage of this situation and move against the Kamakura Bakufu. In May, 1221, he issued a call for all loyal military leaders to come to the support of the imperial family and overthrow the shogunate. The imperial court had gained the friendship of the military chieftains and constables in the Kyoto vicinity, and over ten thousand men responded to Gotoba's call. Faced with this threat and with the possibility that other military magnates might defect to the imperial faction, Masako rallied the Bakufu forces, reminding the vassals of the many favors that had been bestowed upon them by Yoritomo. She managed to marshal a huge force under the Kamakura flag and overwhelmed the imperial forces with ease.

This incident, known as the Jōkyū Insurrection, produced two significant results: (1) The supremacy of the Bakufu over the imperial court was clearly established; and (2) the Hōjō family gained absolute control of the Bakufu. The Kamakura government confiscated all the shōen of those who had taken part in the uprising—over three thousand estates—and established regional headquarters in Kyoto to maintain a check on the activities of the imperial court and to administer the western provinces.

Throughout the thirteenth century the Hōjō regents governed the land effectively without any major disturbances. The Bakufu's domains were scattered throughout the entire country, although there were some provinces in which it held no land. It held virtually all the land in the Kantō region, and in most of the other provinces its holdings were more extensive than estates owned by proprietors free from immediate Hōjō control.

One noteworthy innovation occurred in 1226, when the third regent, Yasutoki (1183–1242), established a council of state. The council consisted of eleven important military chieftains. They deliberated upon important questions and advised the regent, who was obliged to accept their decisions. Yasutoki also codified the customary practices that governed the relationships among the military elements.

In 1232 Yasutoki issued the Jōei Code, which was not strictly speaking a code of laws but rather a set of guidelines for jurists. Yasutoki explained that the object of the code was "to establish standards so that fair trials without regard to the disputants' social status can be held, and eliminate the unjust practice in which the disputants' power determines the outcome." Consisting of fifty-one articles, the code was based on customary law and dealt with property rights, land tenure, inheritance, duties and functions of officials, criminal punishments, and so on. It established a basis for the feudal laws and practices of subsequent periods. One noteworthy provision of the code was the right of women to inherit property and serve as vassals. This was not an innovation, however, but merely a codification of the practice in existence during the Kamakura period.

In other respects, too, women were accorded fairer treatment in this period than in the later Tokugawa era (1600–1867). Women who committed adultery were not punished very much more severely than adulterous men. (In the Tokugawa period such women were executed, while no stigma was attached to wanton behavior by men.) During the Kamakura period women played a much more active role than in subsequent eras. Some even led warriors into the field of battle; others proved their worth as able administrators. One of the ablest women of this era was Masako, who acted as one of the powers behind the shōgun after her husband Yoritomo's death and is sometimes referred to as the "nun-shōgun."

The Jōei Code classified people into three categories: samurai, commoners, and slaves. Unlike the Taihō Code, the Jōei Code did not give the upper classes privileged treatment. On the contrary, in some instances they were punished more severely than the common people for the same offense.

In the trials of this period documentary evidence and testimony by witnesses were weighed carefully by the magistrate in arriving at his verdict, but when such evidence or witnesses did not exist, the disputants were required to swear to the gods that their claims were true. The outcome was then determined by whether some ill omen or event befell a disputant in the following seven days. Among such signs were nosebleeding, sickness, choking while eating, the occurrence of misfortune among relatives, and being wet by a crow or a kite. Vestiges of the ancient trial by ordeal were still present.

THE MONGOL INVASIONS AND THE DECLINE OF THE KAMAKURA BAKUFU

During the early years of the Kamakura period, the friendly relations with Sung China that had been established during the Heian period were maintained. Sung influence was manifested in the Japanese economic realm in the form of imported copper coins, and, more significantly, in the cultural sphere in the form of Zen Buddhism and Sung-style painting and literature.

The most momentous political event in Sino-Japanese relations during the Kamakura period was the attempt of Kublai Khan (1216–1294) to bring Japan into the fold of the vast Mongol empire. The first Mongol invasion occurred in 1274 against northern Kyushu, but before the Mongols could successfully launch their attack, a typhoon struck and destroyed a large portion of their fleet. Expecting a second foray, the Japanese fortified northern Kyushu, and in 1281, when the Mongols did initiate a second attack with a force of about 140,000 men, they were turned back after seven weeks of fighting in northern Kyushu by the efforts of the Japanese warriors and yet another typhoon. These typhoons were interpreted as interventions by the gods and were later referred to as *kamikaze* (divine wind).

This grave threat to their independence aroused a greater sense of unity among the Japanese than the nation had ever before experienced, and a concerted effort to defend the country was made under the able leadership of Hōjō Tokimune (1251–1284), who had become regent at the age of eighteen and was only twenty-three when the Mongols launched their first attack.

Although the Mongol invasions were successfully repelled, the defensive efforts sapped the strength of the Kamakura Bakufu, especially its financial resources. Those who had taken part in the campaign expected to be rewarded for their services, but the Bakufu did not have any fruits of victory to distribute among the warriors. The samurai, disappointed and frustrated, began to grow increasingly disaffected from the Bakufu.

Changes in the economy were undermining the Kamakura society also. The military class was beginning to feel the pressures of the rising money economy. The samurai had fallen under the influence of the more elegant life of the court aristocracy, and were no longer satisfied with leading simple and frugal lives. While their expenses mounted, their income remained stationary because the amount of land they held remained more or less fixed or even decreased when divided among the children, a practice that prevailed during most of the Kamakura period.

Many of the landholding samurai were forced to sell or mortgage their estates in order to meet rising expenses. They also fell into debt to the emergent moneylenders. In order to cope with this situation, the Bakufu issued in 1297 an edict (*Tokusei,* or Act of Grace) canceling all debts and calling for the return to the samurai of all lands they had lost or sold. But this action only created quarrels and legal disputes and did little to alleviate the situation. At the same time land and power were being concentrated in the hands of the more powerful military leaders, especially the provincial constables, who were beginning to overwhelm the land stewards and the lesser samurai.

Thus political disorder began to increase in the provinces as the struggle for land and power continued among the Bakufu's vassals, constables, land stewards, and shōen owners. This also created disturbances and unrest among the peasantry, who were not only being oppressed more severely by the local authorities but were also beginning to be plagued by the growing number of brigands and thieves who raided and pillaged the countryside.

By the end of the Kamakura period there were many provincial military leaders who were powerful enough to challenge the Bakufu. The sense of loyalty that prevailed during the early years of the Bakufu had weakened with the passing of several generations. The original benefactors of the Kamakura samurai, the Minamotos, had long since passed from the scene. Meanwhile, the imperial court was constantly on the alert, waiting for an opportunity to recapture political power.

An imperial uprising against the Bakufu was attempted in 1324 but failed. Another insurrection was attempted in 1331; this one proved more successful. The military chieftains and constables around Kyoto and western Japan rallied to the support of the imperial court under the leadership of Emperor Godaigo (1288–1339). The most able and determined of these military chiefs was Kusunoki Masashige (?–1336), who carried on a struggle akin to guerrilla warfare against the Hōjō forces. For a while, however, it appeared as if this insurrection would fail, too, but the imperial faction was ultimately rescued by two powerful leaders, Nitta Yoshisada (1301–1338) and Ashikaga Takauji (1305–1358). Takauji was one of the generals whom the Hōjō family had counted on to crush the insurgents. With his defection the Hōjō family could no longer stem the tide and fell in 1333. This terminated the Kamakura era and ushered in a brief return to imperial rule, a period known as the Kemmu Restoration (1333–1336).

THE ETHOS OF THE SAMURAI

The cultural and intellectual outlook of the Kamakura period is identified closely with the military outlook and way of life. Although the term *Bushidō* (Way of the Warriors) was not yet used during this period, the ideals of the *bushi*, or warriors, that emerged with the rise of the military eventually developed into the concept of Bushido in the Tokugawa period. In the Kamakura period the samurai spoke of *"yumiya no narai,"* or "the way of the bow and arrow."

The ethos of the samurai demanded that the warrior live by the principles of duty, loyalty, integrity, honor, justice, and courage. Japanese history abounds with tales of warriors who acted nobly, chivalrously, and selflessly, but they were not always motivated by noble ideals. Underneath the high-sounding ideals lay an equally if not more powerful motivation: self interest. The world of the samurai, particularly in time of disorder when no strong controlling force existed, was a society in which the law of the jungle prevailed.

Expediency and opportunism guided the actions of many warriors who were ready to shift with the changing tide of fortune. "The past is the past, the present is the present," was the attitude that prevailed in the years when the fortunes of the Tairas and Minamotos were shifting rapidly. There are numerous examples of local chieftains switching sides when the prevailing political winds shifted. During periods of disorder and strife the inconstancy of the warriors became particularly noticeable. The years between 1337–1392, when the country was split into two factions, "might not inaptly be characterized as the Great Age of Turncoats." [4] The latter part of the sixteenth century is also noted for the absence of loyalty among warriors; then, too, they transferred their allegiance freely depending upon the rewards that were forthcoming.

For the sake of expediency, family loyalty and sentiments were sometimes sacrificed. Basically, however, family interests played an important part in the samurai's system of values. The family was the essential unit upon which the feudal relationship was constructed. The samurai built his power structure by extending his family ties to all his blood relations, enlarging it further by marital connections, and encompassing followers. Such a follower was virtually regarded as a family member and called "a man of the house" (*gokenin*) or "a child of the house" (*ie-no-ko*). The lord-vassal relationship was viewed as a father-son relationship. The individual warrior usually served his lord in the hope of extending the interests of his family. In general, individual interest and family interest coincided. When they clashed, however, personal interests often superseded family interests. Examples of a warrior spilling his brother's blood in disputes over land and inheritance occurred with distressing frequency.

Once a master-vassal relationship was entered into, ideally the vassal was expected to dedicate his entire life to the service of his master. In return for his loyalty and services, the master was expected to reward him. The entire samurai system was founded upon reciprocal relationships of services and rewards. The reward usually took the form of land or an office that entailed a certain income. The protection and security offered the vassal was also part of the benefit that he derived from his contract with his lord. The benefits that a vassal obtained from his master placed him under the latter's obligation, that is, *on*. Even a display of good will and benevolence by the master to his vassal would place the latter under the *on* of the former.

A close emotional and psychological bond between master and vassal could lead the vassal to serve his master selflessly without any anticipation of immediate rewards, but more often than not tangible rewards were expected. After serving in battle, vassals openly asked for compensations. When no rewards were forthcoming after the Mongol invasion, some warriors implied that unless they were properly remunerated, the Bakufu could not expect them to remain loyal. One of the reasons why the Kemmu Restoration failed was because the imperial faction could not properly compensate its supporters.

[4] James Murdoch, *A History of Japan,* 3 vols. (New York: Ungar, 1964 [1st edition 1902–1926]), vol. 1, p. 564.

On the other hand, when a strong sense of on did develop, the followers of the lord would join him in death. When the Hōjōs faced their downfall, thousands of loyal samurai committed suicide to share the fate of their masters. A samurai who enjoyed the special favor of his master was expected to accompany him to the next world, a tradition that continued even into modern times, dramatically demonstrated by General Nogi's suicide upon the death of Emperor Meiji in 1912. Even during the peaceful rule of the Tokugawa shōgun, the samurai were expected to join their dead lords by committing suicide. The Bakufu found it necessary to ban this practice in 1663.

The practice of committing suicide by disemboweling oneself with the sword (known as *seppuku* or *hara-kiri*) emerged around the end of the twelfth century and became a highly ritualized affair, particularly in the Tokugawa period. A warrior might be ordered to commit seppuku for violation of the samurai code of conduct, or he might voluntarily commit seppuku if he felt disgraced in any way. Warriors also committed suicide to expiate mistakes or transgressions, to protest against unjust actions, and to persuade superiors to refrain from following a certain course of action. Gruesome as this practice might seem it brings into focus one positive aspect of the code of the warrior, namely, the warrior's willingness to play the game strictly by the rules and assume total responsibility, paying the full price for whatever action he takes.

In order to be properly rewarded for heroic exploits in battle, witnesses were necessary. So it was said that "to cut into the enemy all alone, and die unseen by any witnesses is a futile action. This is called 'a dog's death.' Only when a warrior charges into the enemy and sacrifices his life while his friends are nearby would he gain fame, and his descendants be properly rewarded." [5] So honor and reputation were valued not only for idealistic reasons but for the tangible results that would accrue. The descendants who benefited from the heroic achievements of an ancestor were expected to be aware of the on owed him and to honor and revere him.

To gain fame and honor for himself and the family, the samurai, of course, had to excel in military exploits and be fortified with the Spartan virtues of courage, strength, discipline, and endurance. He was not to waste his time in aesthetic or cultural pursuits. "A person born into a military family," one warrior is purported to have said, "must pursue the way of the military. Of what use is it to allow the mind to concentrate on the moon and flowers, compose poems, and learn how to play musical instruments? What good would it do to play the *koto* [a Japanese harp] and flute in the battlefield? Members of my household, including women,

[5] Quoted in Ienaga Saburō, *Nihon Dōtokushisōshi (History of Japanese Moral Thought)* (Tokyo: Iwanami, 1951), p. 78.

must learn to ride wild horses, and shoot powerful bows and arrows." [6]

Above all the warrior had to be indifferent to considerations of life and death. Regardless of how one may romanticize the exploits of the samurai, his chief function was to kill his foe. Life had to be held cheaply, and a callousness necessarily characterized the samurai outlook. Thus not only were the warriors ruthless and cold-blooded about killing their enemies on the battlefield, they were also frequently as heartless in their treatment of the aged, women, and children, although the code of the warrior required the samurai to protect and aid the weak, the injured, and the defeated. For example, when Yoritomo was in exile in Izu he had a love affair with the daughter of the official who was assigned the task of keeping him under surveillance. A baby girl was born of this relationship. When the official, who had been away in Kyoto for several years, returned and found out about this affair, fearing the reaction of the Tairas, he threw the innocent little girl down a waterfall.

The Spartan virtues of the samurai were also demanded of women. Young girls were trained to repress their feelings, to harden their nerves, and even to use weapons. The samurai's treatment of women in the Kamakura period was quite different from the relationships of aristocratic couples during the Heian era. The samurai's wife was expected to go and reside with her husband. She was to aid him in advancing his family interests and to manage the affairs of the household. Upon his death she inherited his property and was expected to take charge of the family and perform the duties of a vassal. As the practice of equal inheritance was abandoned in favor of single inheritance, however, women's property rights declined as they were increasingly relegated to an inferior position.

The method of warfare during this period deserves some comment. The chief weapons used were the bow and arrow and the long sword. It is said that some Minamoto warriors used such powerful bows that it required three to five people to stretch the bow and shoot the arrow. The arrows for such bows were almost four feet long. Contending warriors usually faced each other on horseback. They wore suits of armor that did not provide full protection from the flying missiles, which might have a range of 45 to 110 yards. Each knight was armed with twenty to thirty arrows, which he usually shot while mounted. Once the arrows were depleted the warriors turned to single combat. Each warrior called out his name to identify himself and seek out a worthy opponent. As the two combatants approached each other on horseback, each warrior tried to cut down his opponent with his long sword. This was rather difficult to

---

[6] Quoted in Okada Akio, *et al., Nihon no Rekishi* (*A History of Japan*), 12 vols. (Tokyo: Yomiuri Shimbunsha, 1959–1960), vol. 4, p. 186.

accomplish, however, since the knights usually charged swiftly past each other. Hence each sought to knock his opponent off his horse, wrestle him to the ground, get on top of him, and use the dirk to slit his throat. The victor usually cut off his opponent's head to prove that he had finished him off or, if the victim happened to be an important foe, to be properly rewarded for it.

A certain code of combat was followed before the Minamoto-Taira conflict. For instance, both sides would agree on the site of combat and avoid using treacherous means to take unfair advantage of the enemy. But the Minamotos and Tairas were not playing a game; they were involved in a bitter struggle to the end. As a result, sneak attacks were frequently resorted to and came to be an accepted mode of combat. Also while at the beginning of the Kamakura era it was considered unfair to shoot the horse from under the opponent, later in the period warriors deliberately aimed at the underbelly of the opponents' horses. Warfare was becoming a much more ruthless and sanguinary affair.

BUDDHISM

During the Heian period Buddhism was a religion restricted primarily to the upper segment of the society, but in the Kamakura era it spread rapidly among the common people. There are several reasons why the Kamakura period became an era of religious ferment. For one thing it followed an age of disorder and chaos—the time of troubles at the end of the Heian and beginning of the Kamakura eras. Civil strife was widespread and continuous; great powers rose and fell. Moreover, man-made disasters were aggravated by natural calamities—earthquakes, floods, and droughts. Famines and epidemics followed. The Buddhist concept of the decline of the law and the end of the world (*mappō*) seemed to be becoming a reality. People turned to religion for consolation and security, but the older religious sects failed to satisfy their spiritual needs. The monks, who lived in worldly splendor and stressed the mechanical and ritualistic aspects of the religion, had removed themselves from the common people. Thus, to meet the spiritual needs of the people, several new sects came into existence.

The movement that won widespread adherence was Amida Buddhism, which had been introduced into Japan during the middle of the Heian period. It belonged to the Mahayana branch of Buddhism that—unlike Theravada Buddhism, which equated salvation primarily with the attainment of enlightenment through self-effort and the extinction of the erroneous sense of the self we possess—envisioned a rebirth into another world, a Buddhist paradise, a land of bliss. This was to be achieved through the aid of merciful Buddhas and Bodhisattvas who, after having attained enlightenment themselves, delayed their entrance into paradise in order to help those remaining behind gain salvation too. The Buddhist paradise is not the ultimate goal but rather a place where the individual incapable of attaining enlightenment by his own merit will be aided in doing so and will thus be able achieve the ultimate goal of nirvana, self-extinction. For the common people, however, entrance into the Buddhist paradise became a goal in itself.

Theravada Buddhism did not envision the existence of Buddhist deities, whereas Mahayana Buddhism conceived of a multitude of divine Buddhas and Bodhisattvas. The tendency to idolize and even worship the Buddha had developed early in history, however. By the first century A.D. he was represented in images that were venerated by the believers. Then Bodhisattvas—Enlightened Beings—came to be revered by some members of the Buddhist community. Next the doctrine of the Three Buddhas came into existence. The Buddha, it was taught, had three bodies—the Body of Essence, the Body of Bliss, and the Created Body. The Body of Essence was the primordial Buddha, permeating the universe. The historical Gautama Buddha was the Created Body. The Body of Bliss takes the form of many Buddhas, but for the development of Mahayana Buddhism in Japan the most significant of these was Amida Buddha, or Amitabha (Immeasurable Glory), who dwells in the Western Paradise where all the faithful can enter.

In the Heian period a monk called Genshin (942–1017) sought to propagate Amida Buddhism in Japan. He wrote the *Essentials of Salvation* and prepared the grounds for the emergence of the Pure Land Sect during the Kamakura period. Genshin was concerned with making salvation, that is, entry into the Western Paradise, possible for everyone, regardless of class status or sex. In his day, the path to salvation involved the understanding of difficult scriptures, metaphysical training, participation in complex rituals, adherence to rigorous spiritual discipline and purity of conduct, and the doing of good works, such as dedication of images and temples to Buddha. These things were not possible for everyone. How then could the common man gain salvation? It could be achieved through devotion to Amida Buddha and the recitation of his name, said Genshin.

Other monks preached this doctrine also, and the movement gained some following among the aristocracy.[7] But the powerful monasteries were still concerned primarily with the furtherance of their economic and political interests. As noted earlier, they even maintained their own armies to protect their interests. Initially, Amidaism had little effect on

[7] *The Tale of Genji* states: "It was at about this time that Genji put himself under the especial protection of Amida, Buddha of Boundless Light, beseeching the Blessed One that in due time his soul and that of the lady whom he had undone might spring from the same lotus in His Holy Paradise." Murasaki Shikibu, *The Tale of Genji*, trans. Arthur Waley (New York: Random House, 1960), p. 398.

the traditional religious practices of the major sects. It was still believed that the invocation of Amida's name had to involve an understanding of the profound meaning of that name and a mental visualization of the Land of Bliss to be truly effective. The blessings to be derived from the recitation of Amida Buddha's name by itself were slight. The troubles and disorder of the late Heian period, however, turned the people toward a religion that offered them a place in the Land of Bliss and an escape from the miseries of this world.

The monk who popularized Amidism and founded an independent sect was Hōnen (1133–1212). Hōnen offered those who could not save themselves by their own efforts an easy path to salvation. He taught that faith in the compassionate mercy of Amida Buddha and the sincere repetition of his name were sufficient for salvation and entrance into the Land of Bliss. Metaphysical training, spiritual discipline, and personal effort were not essential for salvation. It could be achieved by total reliance on the saving power of Amida Buddha.

In order to become independent of the older sects that emphasized traditional practices, Hōnen founded his own sect known as the Jōdo (Pure Land) Sect. His unorthodox views disturbed the existing sects, and he was subjected to constant persecution and was finally exiled from Kyoto late in his life. His sect flourished, however, and he won a wide following among the aristocracy as well as the common people. Yoritomo's wife, Masako, was one of his devoted followers.

Hōnen's disciple Shinran (1173–1262) simplified his master's teachings even further and made Pure Land Buddhism truly a religion of the masses. Hōnen and his other disciples believed that the more one recited the Amida Buddha's name, the better one's chances of salvation were. It was even asserted that Amida Buddha's name should be invoked 70,000 times a day. Shinran, however, taught that one sincere invocation of Amida's name was sufficient for a believer to gain salvation and entry into the Western Paradise. A person might, if he so desired, continue to repeat Amida's name in order to honor him, but it was not necessary for salvation. If repeated invocations of the name were necessary, Shinran reasoned, it would mean that salvation was still dependent upon individual effort. The believer would not be throwing himself completely upon the mercy and compassion of Amida Buddha. It would indicate a lack of faith in his saving power. Shinran even discontinued chanting the sutras, which until then was believed to contribute to the salvation of others. This too, Shinran held, would be contrary to the belief that only the invocation of Amida's name was necessary for salvation.

Shinran went further than his master in another aspect. He concluded that all external conduct was irrelevant to salvation. Whether one was moral or immoral made no difference in one's eligibility for entry into the Land of Bliss. Amida was not a stern judge but rather a compassionate savior. All men, good or bad, rich or poor, learned or ignorant, clerical or secular, would be saved by the merciful Amida. In fact, Shinran taught that a wicked person might have a better chance of being saved because he had to rely wholly on the mercy of Amida Buddha while a good man might be inclined to feel that he could rely on his own good conduct to gain salvation. What was necessary was complete reliance on "the other power." The *Tannishō*, a collection of Shinran's sayings, records that Shinran said, "If the good can gain salvation, there is all the more reason to believe that the wicked can win salvation."

Because external conduct was irrelevant to salvation, Shinran concluded that traditional injunctions against eating meat, drinking alcoholic beverages, and so on were unimportant. He also rejected all forms of ritualism and ascetic practices. Furthermore, he repudiated monasticism and clerical celibacy; there was no need for the clergy to maintain a different mode of life than the laity. He himself married and had a number of children. This does not mean, of course, that Shinran and his followers were unconcerned about moral conduct. Shinran believed that by giving oneself over completely to Amida Buddha one automatically became moral. As Shinran developed his own interpretation of Amida Buddhism, he and his disciples came to consider themselves the "True" adherents of the Pure Land Sect (Jōdo Shinshū).

The Pure Land Buddhists emphasized the significance of Amida Buddha over all other Buddhas and Bodhisattvas. The founder of Buddhism, Gautama Buddha, or Shakyamuni, was looked upon as only a teacher and transmitter of the faith, not a divinity to be worshipped. Amida Buddhist sects were truly egalitarian, in that they made salvation possible for the most humble and ignorant person. Shinran consciously sought to spread his teachings to the common people, and he gained a wide following, particularly among the peasants. It soon became the most popular of the Buddhist sects and even today has one of the largest body of followers.[8]

The second important Buddhist sect that arose during the Kamakura period was the Nichiren Sect (or the Lotus Sect) established by Nichiren (1222–1282). Nichiren was born into a lowly fisherman's family but founded a powerful Buddhist sect and became prominent enough even to defy the Bakufu. Some students of Buddhism question whether Nichiren can be classified as a Buddhist because of his narrow ethnocentric sentiments. It would be more appropriate to consider the Nichiren Sect as an offshoot of nationalistic Shintoism, asserts one authority on Buddhism. "Nichiren suffered from self-assertiveness and bad temper, and he

---

[8] The total number of followers of the Pure Land and True Pure Land sects was 20.4 million in 1968. Of these about 14 million belonged to the various branches of the True Pure Land Sect.

manifested a degree of personal and tribal egotism which disqualify him as a Buddhist teacher," he writes.[9]

Yet the source of Nichiren's religious faith was Buddhism. He preached that salvation was to be achieved by the repeated invocation of the Lotus Sutra, which contains the true teachings of Shakyamuni Buddha. The Lotus Sutra emphasizes the importance of the three bodies of Buddha, that is, the universal Buddha (*Dainichi Nyorai*, or the Body of Essence), Amida Buddha (the Body of Bliss), and the historical Buddha (the Created Body). Nichiren taught that all three should be regarded as a unity and equal in importance, unlike other sects that stressed only one of the three. Insofar as Nichiren taught that salvation can be gained by the simple recitation of the name of the Lotus Sutra, he paralleled the teachings of the Pure Land sects.

Unlike the other Buddhist masters, Nichiren was extremely dogmatic, intolerant, and aggressive. He violently condemned all other sects for what he considered to be their erroneous beliefs, and he looked upon himself as a reincarnation of the Bodhisattva of action mentioned in the Lotus Sutra. He embarked upon the task of eliminating the false teachings of the other sects and replacing them with his own "true" interpretation of the Buddhist scriptures. Unlike the other Buddhist sects, the Lotus Sect was militant, activist, and zealous, reflecting the personality of the founder.

In criticizing the other sects, Nichiren argued that the natural calamities, famines, and epidemics of his day were caused by the prevalence of false religions. He was particularly critical of Hōnen and the Pure Land Sect, but he did not spare the other sects either. In his criticisms of other religious leaders, he resorted to bitter invectives. He attacked all those who did not submit to his views and even turned his wrath upon Ninshō, a monk renowned for his charitable activities.

Nichiren emerges as one of Japan's earliest super-patriots. He did not limit himself to the task of saving the souls of individuals; he considered himself the savior of Japan. "I will be," he proclaimed, "the Pillar of Japan. I will be the Eyes of Japan. I will be the Great Vessel of Japan." [10] He predicted the invasion of Japan by the Mongols and insisted that the only way the country could be saved from this calamity was to adopt his religion. His aim was to make his the official state religion.

Nichiren emphasized the concept of requiting one's obligation (on) to the sovereign. This was to be achieved through faith and devotion to the Nichiren Sect. Service to the Lotus Sect was to be identified with service

---

[9] Edward Conze, *Buddhism: Its Essence and Development* (New York: Harper, 1959), p. 206.

[10] Quoted in Masaharu Anesaki, *History of Japanese Religion* (Tokyo and Rutland, Vt.: Tuttle, 1963), p. 198.

to the country. Conversely, he taught that Buddhism could not prevail without the country. Thus national security had to be the primary concern of all true Buddhists. The way to strengthen the country was through the propagation of the true faith. His teachings, he said, "are not designed to further my own interests, but the interests of the gods [kami], the ruler, the country, and all the people." He came to concern himself more with the salvation of the country than the individual. Japan to him was the land of the gods and was destined to become the center of the universal religion, that is, the Nichiren Sect.

Nichiren, like a good Shintoist, considered Japan to be a unique land. He compared India, where Buddhism was born, to the moon and Japan to the sun. The moon moves west to east, thus Buddhism moved from India to Japan. The sun moves from east to west, so, according to Nichiren's line of thinking, Japanese Buddhism would spread westward, back to India. He was happy, he said, to be born in a land that was protected by the Sun Goddess, Amaterasu.

His uncompromising, aggressive attacks on the other sects and his scathing criticisms of the Bakufu for supporting them repeatedly led Nichiren into difficulties, but he won a wide following among the samurai, who were attracted to his positive, dynamic point of view as well as to his emphasis on fulfilling one's obligations to the country through service.

The Nichiren Sect continued its growth and became one of the major Buddhist sects. It retained the unique character stamped upon it by its founder and continued to represent an unusual combination of Buddhism and militant ethnocentrism. In the modern era it contributed to the rise of ultranationalism and was used to support the imperialistic policies of the militarists. Today it is regaining its influence in the political sphere with activist programs spearheaded by its secular organ, the *Sōka Gakkai* (Value-creating Society), which in the late 1960s had a membership of more than eleven million.[11]

Zen Buddhism was the third significant Buddhist movement to emerge in the Kamakura period. Each of the three new Buddhist sects that arose during this era contributed something unique and significant to Japanese history and culture. Zen Buddhism had its greatest impact in the cultural sphere, in molding the aesthetic taste of the Japanese.

Zen, or Ch'an, Buddhism was, it was said, introduced to China by an Indian monk, Bodhidharma, about A.D. 520, although it is now believed that the doctrine of meditation had entered China much earlier. Some aspects of Ch'an Buddhism had entered Japan prior to the Kamakura period and were adopted by the older sects, but it was not until the Kama-

---

[11] The total number of people affiliated with the many branches of the Nichiren Sect came to over thirty-one million in 1968.

kura era that it emerged as an influential, independent movement. Zen Buddhism differed from the Pure Land and Nichiren sects in that it emphasized self-reliance, while they emphasized reliance upon external powers. The ultimate goal of the Zen Buddhists was not entrance into the Buddhist paradise but the attainment of "enlightenment" (satori), which involved the acquisition of insight into one's true or original nature and the comprehension of the nature of reality. Buddhists believe that beneath the surface manifestations that lead us to distinguish between the subject and the object, between this and that, there is an underlying unity or reality which, when the surface illusions are removed, can be perceived as a "great void," a reality that is infinite. The object of the Zen Buddhists is to enter this reality itself, not simply to come into contact with it as a Christian seeks to come into contact with God. When a person attains satori he becomes immersed in reality just as naturally as a fish finds itself in water.

Satori, according to the Zen Buddhists, is to be achieved through an intuitive grasp of the nature of reality by means of meditation and concentration, not by relying on the intellect or reasoned knowledge. Just as the hand that grasps cannot grasp itself, the reason that seeks to comprehend cannot comprehend itself. Satori occurs as a sudden and direct perception of reality. Study of the scriptures, metaphysical speculation, and performance of rituals are useless in this quest for enlightenment. All the embellishments and trimmings of the religion must be eliminated if man is to probe directly into his soul to grasp his Buddha-nature. When a person attains enlightenment and comprehends reality he cannot transmit it to others by use of words because it is a completely subjective process. The message that Bodhidharma brought to China was:

> A special transmission outside the scriptures;
> No dependence upon words and letters;
> Direct pointing at the soul of man;
> Seeing into one's nature and the attainment of Buddhahood.[12]

Zen Buddhism emerged in Kamakura Japan as a major force largely through the efforts of two monks, Eisai (1141–1215) and Dōgen (1200–1253). Both had traveled to China and studied under Ch'an masters. Returning to Japan they embarked upon the propagation of Zen Buddhism. Eisai founded the Rinzai Sect, and Dōgen the Sōtō Sect. No fundamental differences divided the two sects. The former, however, tended to empha-

---

[12] William Barrett, ed., *Zen Buddhism: Selected Writings of D. T. Suzuki* (Garden City, N.Y.: Doubleday, 1956), p. 61.

size the importance of *kōan,* enigmatic, paradoxical themes to be concentrated upon by the acolyte.

The kōan was designed to break the mind's customary habit of thinking in rational, logical terms and to force it to attain sudden, intuitive insights into reality. They simply serve as means of derailing the mind from the path of ratiocination.

One of the kōan given to an initiate to contemplate is "Listen to the sound of the Single Hand!" Another is "Thinking neither of good nor of evil, at this very moment what was the original aspect before your father and mother were born?" [13]

The kōan results in the liberation of the unconscious.

> Evoked by the enormous psychological strain of trying to
> force a solution of the insoluble kōan problem, enlighten-
> ment is experienced as the dawn of a new reality, in which
> the boundaries between the conscious and the unconscious
> disappear, and conscious and unconscious alike are openly
> revealed. The Zen disciple realizes the totality of human
> nature in its primal unity, prior to all discrimination and
> division.[14]

Although the Sōtō Sect did not reject the kōan, it emphasized *zazen,* or sitting in meditation, above all. While one is sitting in meditation the kōan is not employed, because the object of zazen is to free the mind from all mundane things. The kōan, the Sōtō adherents said, insofar as it is motivated by the desire to gain sudden insight into reality, is a manifestation of the self.

Zazen entails a prescribed posture, regulation of the breath, and special concentration to still the mind in order to control the emotions and strengthen the will. Then one looks into the "heart-mind" to discover the true nature of existence. The end of zazen was not only satori-awakening but also the spiritual and moral development of the practitioner, who, hopefully, will emerge a man of virtue and of all-embracing compassion and wisdom. In the process of sitting in meditation, Dōgen asserted, one's Buddha nature is being realized.

Although the practice of kōan might induce sudden enlightenment, zazen ordinarily does not result in sudden expansion of consciousness or the onset of a sudden sense of buoyancy and exhilaration. Even though a profound inner transformation takes place when satori is achieved, the

---

[13] I. Miura and R. F. Sasaki, *The Zen Koan* (New York: Harcourt, 1965), p. 44.
[14] Heinrich Dumoulin, *A History of Zen Buddhism* (New York: Random House, 1963), p. 132.

person himself, it is contended, may not even be aware of it initially. In some instances, however, a sense of elation and buoyancy evidently do occur. A Zen monk of the Meiji era (1868–1912) said of his experience of satori:

> I found myself, as it were, on the ground of the Great
> Death, and no awareness of the being of all things and of
> the ego remained. I felt only how in my body a spirit
> extended itself to ten thousand worlds, and an infinite
> splendor of light arose. . . . In a flash seeing and hearing,
> speech and motion, were different from every day. As I
> sought the supreme truth . . . my own self was clear and
> things appeared bright. In the excess of delight I forgot
> that my hands were moving in the air and that my feet were
> dancing.[15]

Because the Zen masters did not preach the easy way to salvation as did the masters of the Pure Land sects, Zen did not become a mass movement. Instead it tended to be a religion of the elite, those who had the strength of character and willpower to work out their own salvation. It gained a strong following among the samurai and the ruling class. It was said that "the Tendai is for the royal family, the Shingon for the nobility, the Zen for the warrior classes, and the Jōdō for the masses." [16]

Zen's emphasis on discipline, single-minded concentration, simplicity, and a direct and decisive approach to life and reality appealed to the samurai, who had to face the moment of truth constantly in the field of battle and act with singleness of purpose and firmness of will. Suzuki Daisetsu points out that Zen appealed to the samurai "because it teaches us not to look backward once the course is decided upon . . . because it treats life and death indifferently." [17] Thus Zen became the moral and philosophical mainstay of many military men in Japan from the Kamakura period to the modern age. Even in prewar Japan many military officers entered Zen monasteries to discipline themselves in order to face the enemy on the battlefield.

The Zen point of view played an important role in the formation of the Way of the Warriors, which required the samurai to conduct himself with honor, courage, and dignity in face of ever-present death. To live up to these ideals the samurai had to come to terms with the problem of death and conquer his fear of it. A seventeenth-century samurai wrote,

[15] *Ibid.*, p. 273.
[16] Daisetsu T. Suzuki, *Zen and Japanese Culture* (New York: Pantheon, 1959), p. 63.
[17] *Ibid.*, p. 61.

"The idea most vital and essential to the samurai is that of death, which he ought to have before his mind day and night." [18] Zen helped the samurai to cope with this problem. Takeda Shingen (1521–1573), a warlord of the sixteenth century and a student of Zen, advised his warriors, "devote yourselves to the study of Zen. Zen has no secrets other than seriously thinking about birth and death." [19]

Thus a close connection was established between Zen Buddhism and the warrior class. Zen certainly played a positive role in disciplining the samurai and training him to deal with the problem of death. But rising above considerations of one's own life and death could also entail a general indifference to the life and death of other people. In the words of an authority on Japanese thought, "to get accustomed to the idea of death is to treat death lightly." [20] Suzuki asserts that the Zen master does not use the sword to kill but that the sword itself performs its function automatically to eliminate the enemy that appears to injure the Zen swordsman. This explanation does not resolve the unpleasant paradox. To prepare the swordsman to kill efficiently is a far cry from the profound mercy and compassion that led Gautama Buddha to embark on his search for a way to relieve the suffering of his fellowmen.

This aspect of Zen Buddhism is, of course, only one phase of its varied contributions to Japanese life and culture. It contributed to the development and refinement of the tea ceremony, the art of gardening and flower arrangement, sword-making, the Nō drama, painting, ceramics, and haiku, as we shall see in later chapters.

Moreover, the Zen masters were certainly not indifferent to human suffering. There has been a long tradition of charitable activities on the part of Buddhist monks in Japan. There is a story that Eisai gave to the poor a piece of copper that was to be used to make a halo for an image of Buddha. When he was criticized for this, he replied, "You are right, but just consider the will of the Buddha. He sacrificed his very flesh and limbs for the sake of all mankind. If some men are about to die of starvation, would he not want us to give the whole Buddha figure to save them?" [21] Dōgen, too, sought to instill the spirit of charity among his disciples. A monk of the Tokugawa period, Ryōkan (1758–1831), who was known for his simple and humble way of life as well as his love of all living things, was a member of the Sōtō Sect. He extended his selfless love to his fellow men, aiding the poor, even showing compassion to thieves.

[18] Quoted in *ibid.*, p. 72.

[19] *Ibid.*, p. 78.

[20] Tsuda Sōkichi, *Bungaku ni Arawaretaru Kokuminshisō no Kenkyū* (*A Study of Japanese Thought as Manifested in Literature*), 4 vols. (Tokyo: Iwanami, 1951–1955), vol. 1, p. 617.

[21] Ryusaku Tsunoda, W. T. de Bary, and Donald Keene, eds., *Sources of Japanese Tradition* (New York: Columbia University Press, 1958), p. 248.

The two monks most renowned for their charitable social work during the Kamakura period, however, belonged to the Ritsu Sect, which emerged in the Nara period and enjoyed a revival during the Kamakura era. The two monks were Eison (1201–1290) and his disciple, Ninshō (1217–1303). Eison devoted his life to helping thousands of outcasts, beggars, the homeless, the sick, and lepers. Ninshō followed in his master's footsteps and built hospitals and homes for orphans, beggars, and outcasts and cared for the lepers. Every other day for several years he carried a young leper back and forth on his back 5 miles to the outskirts of Nara to enable him to beg in the streets.

During this period the practice of monks traveling throughout the countryside to extend the blessings of Amida Buddha became widespread. The most popular of these wandering saints was Ippen (1239–1289), whose followers eventually merged with the True Pure Land Sect. Ippen danced about while chanting the name of Amida Buddha and is credited by some with having originated the Bon dances performed to console the souls of the departed.

CULTURE

The pragmatic, realistic outlook of the samurai is reflected in the art of the Kamakura period. Portraits of actual personalities rather than idealistic images of Buddhist deities are a prominent feature of Kamakura art. The most famous such painting is one of Yoritomo. The artist presumably portrays him as he actually appeared, with relatively close-set eyes, a large curving nose, and a face wider at the bottom than at the top. The art of painting narrative scrolls (e-makimono) also continued to flourish. These picture scrolls were long, often more than 40 feet in length, and were unrolled from right to left. They depicted scenes from renowned battles or episodes from the lives of religious personalities such as Ippen. A scroll depicting the Heiji Insurrection is the most representative of the narrative picture scrolls. The paintings in this scroll are characterized by forcefulness, animation, and realistic details. The landscapes depicted in the scroll paintings of this era have also become more realistic, serving not simply as decorative settings but as representations of local scenes.

Another noteworthy feature of the scroll paintings of this period was the introduction of a satirical element into the medium. Comic-strip-like drawings of animals satirizing the human world—attributed formerly to a Buddhist monk, Toba Sōjō (1053–1140), but now believed to be works of the thirteenth century—are especially unique. Such animals as frogs, monkeys, and hares are used to make fun of the rituals of the Buddhist priests and the devotions of the pilgrims.

In sculpture, too, the spirit of the samurai is discernible. We have the vigorous, powerful, and somewhat grotesque—because of the exaggerated muscles and tendons—works of Unkei and Kaikei. They carved the 26 foot high Deva kings that guard the gateway of the Tōdaiji Temple in Nara, which was rebuilt at the end of the twelfth century after being destroyed by fire during the struggle between the Taira and Mina-moto families. These huge statues successfully convey a sense of tactile value, movement, and force.

In architecture the major effort was still expended in the construction of Buddhist temples. Reflecting the Zen influence, clarity of line and simplicity of decor were increasingly stressed. In domestic dwellings, also, the stress was on simplicity. In the middle of the thirteenth century the 42 foot tall Great Buddha of Kamakura was built. Representing the serene majesty of the Amida Buddha, the figure is in the yogi position, with legs crossed and hands in the gesture of meditation.

Being the age of the samurai, the art of sword making reached new heights of excellence, and many great master swordsmiths emerged, the greatest being Masamune (1264–1344), whose creations are valued today as rare treasures. It is said that no sword of any age or country can surpass the Kamakura swords. The samurai sword had to have a "blade keen enough to hack through armor but resilient enough not to snap on im-pact." In order to produce such a sword, the swordsmith forged a com-pound blade with carbon steel or white cast iron on the cutting edge, a mild metal in the center, and a fairly soft but unbrittle iron on the back. When steel alone was used, the process of welding and folding was re-peated until a blade consisting of more than four million layers of steel was forged. Armor making also became a fine art. The grand armor of this era was especially rich in decoration: gilt-bronze, patterned leather, and figured textile.

Monkeys worshipping a frog, a section of a handscroll attributed to Toba Sōjō (1053–1140). Courtesy of Kōzanji and the Benridō Company, Ltd.

The art of ceramics came into its own also, thanks to the influence of Sung China. The town of Seto, near Nagoya, became the center for pottery manufacture and has remained the leading ceramics center to the present. The term Setoware became a generic term for pottery in general. This art acquired greater significance in the next era (the Ashikaga period), when the tea ceremony became popular among the ruling class.

In literature the great romantic war stories, such as the *Tale of the Heike*, the *Rise and Fall of the Genji and Heike*, the *Tale of Hogen*, and the *Tale of Heiji*, were written during this period. They were not composed by the samurai themselves but by noblemen and priests, so the sentiments described in them do not directly represent those of the samurai. They do reflect the general outlook of the age, however, as well as the ethos of the samurai: martial valor, courage, loyalty, and integrity. The Buddhist outlook on life, with its emphasis on the ephemeral and transitory nature of all things and its belief in the inevitable fall of those who have risen, sets the tone of these works. Thus a sense of melancholy and sorrow pervades many of the tales, notably the *Tale of the Heike*, which depicts the heroic exploits of the samurai in the course of the rise and fall of the Taira clan. The tale starts with the lines:

> In the sound of the bell of the Gion Temple echoes the
> impermanence of all things. The pale hue of the flowers
> of the teak-tree shows the truth that they who prosper must
> fall. The proud ones do not last long, but vanish like a
> spring-night's dream. And the mighty ones too will perish
> in the end, like dust before the wind." [22]

This sense of the ephemeral nature of all things runs through the entire tale and is stated over and over. " 'Those who are born must die; those that meet must part,' is the way of the world. 'The last dew or the first drop,' one must go before the other, and whether one dies first or last, all must leave this world at last." [23] The only consolation in this life was to be found in a Buddhist renunciation of the mundane world and the hope of being reborn into the Western Paradise.

The *Hōjōki*, a collection of personal observations by Kamo-no-Chōmei (1151–1213) written in 1212, embodies the same sense of the ethereal nature of life. It starts with the statement:

> The current of a running stream flows on unceasingly, but
> the water is not the same: the foam floating on the pool

[22] Donald Keene, ed., *Japanese Literature: An Introduction for Western Readers* (New York: Grove, 1955), p. 78.

[23] Sadler, *op. cit.*, part 1, p. 207.

where it lingers, now vanishes and now forms again, but
is never lasting. Such are mankind and their habitations.
. . . In the morning some die, in the evening some are
born. Such is life. It may be compared to foam upon the
water. Whether they are born or whether they die, we
know not whence they come nor whither they go.[24]

During this period the composing of waka, a poem of thirty-one syllables—a pastime that flourished at the Heian court—continued to be pursued by the courtiers. At the beginning of the thirteenth century an anthology of waka was compiled under the auspices of a retired Emperor.
This was the *Shinkokinshū* (*New Collection of Ancient and Modern
Poems*), which, with the *Manyōshū* and the *Kokinshū*, constitutes one of
the three most prominent collections of early Japanese poems.

Several histories or chronicles were also written in this era. Of particular interest is the *Gukanshō* (*Jottings of a Fool*), written by a monk named
Jien (1155–1225). Its significance lies in the fact that Jien viewed the
course of Japanese history as a process governed by a general principle.
It was the first attempt at a philosophical interpretation of history in
Japan. Jien characterized Japanese history in terms of the Buddhist theory
of the periodic decline of the Law of Buddha. His age, he said, was an era
when the Law had already deteriorated. This view, as we noted earlier,
was common at the end of the twelfth and the beginning of the thirteenth
centuries. Jien divided Japanese history into seven stages and identified
the decline of the Law of Buddha with the decline in the authority of the
imperial family. Governed by this principle of decline and degeneration,
history moved forward inexorably in accordance with the Law. The rise
of the military, which had deprived the imperial house of all political
power, could not be challenged because this was brought about by the
general principle of history and was inevitable. One had to accept the
existing situation and await the return of the Law after the period of the
absence of the Law had spent itself.

[24] Aston, *op. cit.,* p. 146.

CHAPTER 5

THE ASHIKAGA PERIOD

The Emergence of the Daimyō

POLITICAL DEVELOPMENTS

When the imperial faction, aided by the discontented military chieftains and warriors, succeeded in overthrowing the Hōjō family, Emperor Godaigo took personal charge of the government, hoping to set a precedent for direct rule by the Emperor and to centralize power in the court. The Emperor was not powerful enough, however, to keep the military under control. What actually ensued was a government composed of both imperial and military elements.

The new government retained some features of the Bakufu. Samurai were appointed as high officials in the central government and as provincial governors and constables at the local level. The office of constable was a holdover from the Bakufu, but the imperial government was unable to abolish it and empower the governors with full authority in local affairs. In many instances powerful military chiefs held both the offices of governor and constable.

For various reasons the new government failed to win the support and confidence of the samurai. Emperor Godaigo first concentrated on making secure the holdings of the imperial court, the court nobles, and the monasteries. He also claimed most of the Hōjō holdings for the imperial court. The samurai who had aided the imperial cause expected to be rewarded generously and flocked to the capital to present their claims, but the imperial government failed to satisfy their demands. Furthermore, as the new government was being established disputes over boundaries and proprietary rights broke out frequently. The imperial government had to arbitrate these quarrels, but the settlements it made naturally failed to please all the disputants and added fuel to the fires of discontent with the Emperor. In addition, as soon as it gained power the imperial court began to renovate the imperial palace and taxed the samurai for this project. From the outset, then, there was considerable dissatisfaction with the new government.

The imperial family itself was weakened internally by a cleavage between the Emperor and his son, Prince Morinaga, who had led the imperial forces against the Hōjōs. The prince was accused of plotting to capture the throne and was assassinated while in custody of the Ashikaga family. At the same time local uprisings by forces antagonistic to the new government continued to break out in various areas.

Realizing that the new regime was on a weak footing, Ashikaga Takauji, who had played a decisive role in the victory of the imperial forces over the Hōjō family, decided to gain control of the government himself. The Ashikaga family had descended from Minamoto-no-Yoshiie and had held constabulary posts in two provinces, controlling a considerable amount of land in the Kantō region. When the Kamakura Bakufu fell, Takauji occupied Kamakura and became the leader of the Kantō warriors. Evidently Takauji was not completely trusted by the imperial faction and was not allowed to play any major role in the new government.

In 1335 Takauji led a military expedition to the Kantō region to crush a rebellion led by the remnants of the Hōjō clan. He then refused to return to Kyoto and remained in Kamakura. Thereupon the imperial government dispatched Nitta Yoshisada to subdue Takauji. Takauji, however, succeeded in defeating Yoshisada and moved on to Kyoto and occupied it temporarily. The imperial forces rallied to drive him out of the capital, however, and he was ultimately forced to flee westward. He then rebuilt his forces with the support of the Kyushu warriors and other military men who were discontented with the decline in their fortunes since the restoration of imperial rule. Takauji then marched back to the capital and defeated the imperial forces led by Kusunoki Masashige, who died in the course of the conflict.

Emperor Godaigo surrendered to Takauji and recognized the sovereignty of the new Emperor whom Takauji chose from a collateral line of the imperial family and had enthroned. However, when his supporters rallied the pro-imperial forces together, Emperor Godaigo fled south to Yoshino in the Kii Peninsula and established a rival government there in 1336. Until 1392 there were two imperial courts, both claiming to be the legitimate dynasty. The imperial court in Yoshino was known as the southern court, and the one in Kyoto the northern court.

Takauji became shōgun in 1338, but he was preoccupied with the task

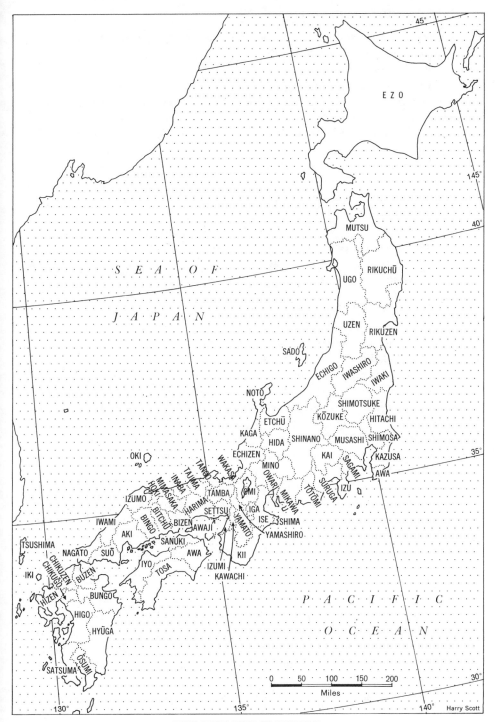

THE PRE-MEIJI PROVINCES.

of subduing his foes and therefore delegated his political functions to his younger brother, Tadayoshi. Even after Nitta Yoshisada, Godaigo's military chief, died in battle in 1338, the supporters of the southern court continued to resist the Ashikaga government. They were especially strong in the north and in Kyushu. In addition, the Ashikaga forces were weakened by armed conflict between Takauji and Tadayoshi. After the latter's death his adopted son continued the struggle against Takauji. Thus, in effect, the country was engaged in a triangular power struggle.

By the time of the third Ashikaga shōgun, Yoshimitsu (1358–1408), however, his clan had managed to extend its control over a large portion of the country. As a result, the southern court was persuaded in 1392 to return to Kyoto and to merge with the northern court, with the understanding that the imperial throne would be occupied alternately by the descendants of the two courts. This promise, however, was not kept by the northern court, and since that time only its descendants have occupied the throne.

ASHIKAGA RULE

Although Takauji did not make Kamakura his headquarters, he retained the governmental machinery of the Kamakura Bakufu when he established the shogunate in Kyoto.[1] He selected loyal vassals to serve as constables in provinces under his control. In 1367 the post of deputy to the shōgun was created, and the heads of three leading military families served alternately in this capacity. A governor-general was also appointed to oversee the administration of the Kantō region. The holder of this office resided in Kamakura and functioned as a semi-independent ruler of Kantō. Shōgun's agents were also appointed to oversee the northern provinces and Kyushu, but the Ashikaga government's control over these areas remained fairly precarious.

Because the Ashikaga rulers were challenged by rival forces throughout most of the fourteenth century, they were compelled to work closely with the leading military houses. Three major families (Shiba, Hosokawa, and Hatakeyama) alternately served as the shōgun's deputy. Yoshimitsu, the third Ashikaga shōgun, selected his department heads as well from leading military families. By gaining the cooperation of the major military houses, Yoshimitsu stabilized and strengthened his government. The foundations of the Ashikaga Bakufu were strengthened even further after rebellions by two major houses—the Yamana family, which held constabulary posts in eleven provinces, and the Ōuchi clan—were crushed in 1391 and 1399, respectively. It was under Yoshimitsu's shogunate that the southern

---

[1] The Ashikaga era is also known as the Muromachi period, after the Muromachi section of Kyoto, where all but the first three Ashikaga shōgun resided.

court finally agreed to end its struggle and merge with the northern court. Thus the Ashikaga Bakufu reached its apex of power and prestige during Yoshimitsu's rule. In 1394 Yoshimitsu transferred the title of shōgun to his son and became dajō daijin (chancellor), the first samurai to hold that position since Taira-no-Kiyomori. He soon resigned this post as well and became a monk, but he remained the real wielder of power.

Yoshimitsu not only enjoyed supremacy of power but indulged himself by expending huge sums of money on lavish architectural projects. The most famous of his undertakings was the construction of the Golden Pavilion, whose interior and exterior were covered with gold leaf, a dazzling symbol of the power and glory of the shōgun.

The demesne of the Ashikaga Bakufu was far less than what had been retained by the Kamakura Bakufu and its hold over the constables, particularly those in the outlying regions, was weak. It could not adequately finance its expenditures with income and taxes from the land and was consequently forced to rely heavily upon taxes imposed on the merchants in Kyoto, particularly the sake brewers and the moneylenders.[2] Emergency taxes on houses and rice fields were also frequently imposed.

After Yoshimitsu's death in 1408 the authority of the Bakufu began to decline, and the Ashikaga government experienced increasing difficulty controlling the major constabulary houses. The power of the constables in general had been growing steadily during the period of conflict between the southern and northern courts.

THE DECLINE OF THE SHŌEN

At the beginning of the Ashikaga period, the land throughout the country was held by a variety of proprietors. There were, of course, the direct holdings of the Bakufu. Then there were the shōen (estates) held by the imperial household, the court nobles, major monasteries and shrines. Important military houses, many holding constabulary posts, possssed shōen in their home provinces as well as in other provinces. Local military leaders, many of whom were land stewards, and local warriors who had ties of vassalage with the Bakufu or with a military chieftain also owned property. In addition there were independent farmers, the myōshu, who in some instances held a considerable amount of land and were influential leaders in their communities.

Because the central government was involved in a power struggle with rival elements during most of the fourteenth century, it was unable to extend its authority effectively to the outlying provinces. The power vacuum in those provinces was filled immediately by the leading military

[2] In 1425 there were 342 sake brewers in Kyoto, many of whom also engaged in moneylending.

chieftains, particularly those in constabulary posts. These provincial constables steadily extended their control over the shōen held by absentee proprietors and even over the estates held by the local military men. Initially the Ashikaga rulers transferred the constables from province to province, but this practice was soon discontinued and they became entrenched in the provinces to which they were assigned. By the middle of the fifteenth century a majority of the constables had acquired hereditary possession of their posts. Some constabulary houses held jurisdiction over more than a single province.

In order to enable them to defray the cost of maintaining military forces, Takauji granted the constables the right to collect one half of the rents collected in the shōen. This was intended to be merely an emergency measure, but the practice persisted. Moreover, many constables began to claim half the land of the shōen rather than simply to collect one half the rent. In some instances they persuaded the shōen owners to grant them the authority to collect the rents on the owners' behalf as well, thus gaining de facto control over the shōen. The constables also had the authority to impose corvée on the people in the shōen and to extract various dues and gifts as well.

In addition to these economic encroachments, the constables extended their political influence over the manors by converting many shōen officials and myōshu into their own "housemen" or vassals. In the fifteenth century many constables began to expropriate the shōen outright. For instance, in the beginning of the fifteenth century one court family reported that it had been divested of fourteen of its twenty-three shōen by the constables and their vassals. One monastery complained that four of its shōen had been seized by the constable. By the outbreak of the Ōnin War in 1467, the shōen owners had virtually lost control of their manors.

The local military men, such as the land stewards and the samurai, sought to remain independent of the constabulary families by maintaining direct ties with the Ashikaga family by becoming its retainers. As the power of the provincial constabulary houses grew, however, many local military men found it necessary or more advantageous to become vassals of the constable. If the local military leader was powerful, the constable appointed him as a deputy constable and secured his support in return. By the fifteenth century a considerable number of constabulary magnates controlled much of the country.

THE ONSET OF THE TIME OF TROUBLES

After Yoshimitsu died, the Ashikaga shogunate's authority began to decline. The constabulary chieftains began increasingly to assert their independence from the Bakufu. In 1416 a rebellion against the governor-general in Kantō broke out. Although this uprising was subdued, other political disturbances led by Kantō military chieftains followed. In addition, uprisings of local samurai began to occur with increasing frequency. In 1441 the sixth Ashikaga shōgun was assassinated by one of the leading constables. A young child was installed as the successor, but the real power came to be exercised by four major constabulary houses. Rivalry among these major families, as well as frequent power struggles within them, undermined the stability of the central government, however. The feuding culminated in a conflict, the Ōnin War, that split the entire nation into two contending military factions, one led by the Yamana family and the other by the Hosokawa.

The struggle was touched off by disputes over succession—both to the shogunate and to the family leadership of several major constabulary houses. (The two issues were intertwined because the Ashikaga shōgun had a voice in the selection of successors to the major constabulary families, while the major constabulary houses participated in choosing the successor to the shogunate whenever there was no obvious heir to the post.) The trouble started when a son was born to the eighth shōgun, Yoshimasa, after he had already named his brother as his heir. Yoshimasa's wife, supported by the Yamana family, sought to have her newly born son designated as the successor. The shōgun's brother, however, advanced his claim to the shogunate with the support of the Hosokawa family.

The quarrel over the succession to the shogunate, however, was not the basic cause of the outbreak of the conflict. It was merely a by-product of the power struggle among the leading constabulary houses. In the course of the civil war the dispute over the shogunate was lost sight of, and the rival claimants even switched sides: Yoshimasa's brother turned to the Yamana faction for help, and the Hosokawa family transferred its support to the shōgun's son.

The civil war, known as the Ōnin War, raged from 1467 to 1477. It ushered in the time of troubles known as the Age of the Warring States (*sengoku jidai*), which lasted for about a century. Initially some 250,000 men joined in the fighting in and around Kyoto. As the conflict became protracted, the struggle spread to other areas, and the entire country was devastated and desolated. Places were plundered, and many valuable treasures were destroyed; the people were subjected to atrocities, and the residents of the capital were compelled to flee to the countryside. During the war the authority of the Bakufu deteriorated rapidly. Even though the leaders of the rival factions in the Ōnin War finally settled their differences in 1477, the truce had little bearing upon the general political situation. By then the authority of the Bakufu was virtually nonexistent, and the struggle for land and power continued unabated not only in Kyoto, where contending factions sought to control the shogunate by supporting rival claimants to the post, but throughout the countryside as well.

THE RISE OF THE DAIMYŌ
AND THE WARRING STATES

The Ōnin War changed the entire political complexion of the country. With the Ashikaga Bakufu wholly incapable of asserting its authority over the land, a period of decentralized rule came into existence. Many of the constabulary houses that had dominated outlying provinces lost control over their home bases as they expended their energy and attention on the Ōnin War, which was fought mainly around Kyoto. New local leaders began to emerge. Many constabulary families were overthrown by their subordinates, adventurers, or local military chieftains. These new regional military leaders began establishing independent principalities in different sections of the country, using force and guile to enlarge their territories at the expense of their former masters and neighbors. This was an era when control of regional territory changed very rapidly. Rank and position counted for nothing. Lowly warriors challenged the authority of the mighty warlords, and peasants defied shōen officials and proprietors. Consequently this period came to be known as the era of *ge-koku-jō,* those below subjugating those above. The only thing that counted was power. The people of this period recognized that the old order was being overturned and that a new era free from the fetters of tradition was coming into existence. Yamana Sōzen, the leader of one of the contending forces in the Ōnin War, admonished a court noble, "I disapprove of the constant references you make to 'precedents.' In the future you must replace the word 'precedent' with the word 'the times.' " [3]

The new military leaders who emerged during these changing times are known as *daimyō.* The constabulary chieftains are also referred to as daimyō or *shugo* (constabulary) *daimyō,* but they were not quite like the freewheeling warlords who emerged after the Ōnin War. The daimyō of the period of the Warring States were in effect fully independent regional rulers. Although their backgrounds were diverse, they can be roughly classified into three types.

One group consisted of the constabulary families that survived the political upheavals and emerged even more powerful than before. An example would be the Shimazu family of Satsuma, which remained a formidable regional power until the Meiji Restoration. Another was the Takeda family of Kai; under Shingen, who drove out his father to take power, the Takedas became a major force in central Japan. Of the 142

---

[3] Quoted in Nagahara Keiji, *Gekokujō no Jidai (The Triumph of the Lowly Over the Mighty)* (Tokyo: Chūō Kōronsha, 1965), p. 2.

major daimyō in existence in 1563, however, only 32 families could claim to have been constabulary houses.

The second type of daimyō was the local military leader who prior to the Ōnin War had played a subordinate role as a deputy or vassal of a constabulary family. A notable example would be Asakura Toshikage, who replaced his master as constable of Echizen by taking advantage of the troubled times of the Ōnin War. His effectiveness in wielding power was recognized by the Hosokawa faction, which persuaded him to defect from the Yamana forces by offering him the constableship of Echizen. He was heartily detested by the court nobles for his ruthless expropriation of their shōen. Takeda Shingen's rival, Uesugi Kenshin, also came from a family that had served as deputy constable. Kenshin's father killed the constable to gain control of Echigo. Other examples of daimyō who rose to power from subordinate posts are the Mōri clan of western Honshu, the Oda family of Owari, and the Tokugawa family.

The third category of daimyō consisted of men who had been lowly samurai, frequently warrior-farmers, but had managed to rise rapidly to the top by taking advantage of the civil disorder and breakdown of authority. A striking example of this type of daimyō is Hōjō Sōun (1432–1519).[4]

Sōun was an unemployed warrior, but his younger sister was the concubine of Imagawa Yoshitada, a powerful constable in the region around present-day Shizuoka, so Sōun stayed with the Imagawa family as a guest. While he was there the samurai in the service of the Imagawa family rebelled and assassinated Yoshitada. With the Imagawa family confronted with an insurrection, other local chieftains, hoping to fish in troubled waters, intervened. At this point Sōun stepped in and succeeded in negotiating a settlement, placing the son of his sister and Yoshitada at the head of the Imagawa family. As a reward he was given a fief and was made the chief of a castle. With this as his base, Sōun used cunning and treachery to extend his power and territory. He made a surprise attack on the province of Izu while its leaders were engaged in a power struggle. After conquering the province of Izu, Sōun intervened in a family quarrel of the Uesugi family, a major power in the Kantō region, and gained control of the provinces of Musashi and Sagami. In order to extend his control over the entire Kantō region, he made another surprise attack on the fortress at Odawara, a strategic stronghold whose occupant controlled the main road that led into the Kantō region. Then by concluding alliances and by engaging in intrigues and acts of treachery, he managed to

---

[4] Sōun was not related to the Hōjō family of the Kamakura Bakùfu. The Hōjō family name was adopted by Sōun's son. This family is also known as Go-Hōjō (Later Hōjō) to distinguish it from the earlier one.

enlarge his base of power sufficiently so that his descendants were able to control the entire Kantō region. Some historians view Sōun's campaign to conquer the Kantō region as the beginning of the Age of the Warring States. The new Hōjō empire remained intact until 1590, when Toyotomi Hideyoshi sent 200,000 men to capture the stronghold at Odawara.

Despite his ruthlessness in his drive for power, Sōun was a benevolent ruler and concerned himself with the betterment of the lot of the common people. In fact his successful rise to power was based partly upon his policy of benevolent rule, which won him the support of the common people, the peasants, and the artisans. He told his retainers, "For the lord of the domain the people are his children. For the people, the lord of the domain is their father." [5] Whenever his warriors conquered new territory, he forbade them to touch a single item belonging to the people. He provided aid when necessary and reduced taxes from 50 percent of the crop to 40 percent.

Sōun's spectacular rise to power was not unique. The same story was repeated throughout the land. Lowly but ambitious and shrewd warriors connived and clawed their way to the top, replacing the established constabulary houses, perhaps to be overthrown by others even more resourceful and ruthlessly ambitious. The rapid turnover in regional political leadership is reflected in the fact that of the 142 major daimyō in existence in 1563, only 45 were still around thirty years later, when Toyotomi Hideyoshi established his hegemony over the entire country. In the era of the Warring States, then, the concept of loyalty that was supposed to govern the conduct of the samurai was hardly discernible. Self-interest and tough-minded realism seemed rather to guide the conduct of the ambitious warriors.

Unlike the constabulary lords, who had been responsible to the shōgun, the new military chieftains were responsible to no one. They were in effect independent warlords who had complete control over the land and the people on it. Their power depended upon the number of loyal vassals they retained. There were several categories of vassals: those who were blood relations of the daimyō, those whose family had served in the house for several generations or had become vassals early in the political ascendancy of the daimyō, and those who had been subjugated by force but still retained a degree of independence. The last category of vassals were regarded as potential foes and were treated as outsiders (*tozama*), in contrast to the others, who were regarded as hereditary (*fudai*) vassals. In addition to those vassals who were given fiefs to man-

---

[5] Quoted in Tsuji Zennosuke, *Nihon Bunkashi (Japanese Cultural History)* 7 vols., (Tokyo: Shunjūsha, 1955), vol. 4, p. 176.

age as their own, the daimyō maintained immediate retainers to serve as his attendants, personal guards, and managers of his demesne.

During the Kamakura and Ashikaga periods the vassal's authority over his "fief" had accrued from the post to which he was appointed, such as the office of land steward or shōen manager. With the office went certain rights and privileges (shiki, see p. 68), including the right to an income from the land, but the lord retained the right to collect rent from the peasants. The office rather than the land was central to the benefice. During the era of daimyō rule, on the other hand, the vassal was given full control over the land granted to him as his fief.

In order to prevent the fiefs from being subdivided into small, submarginal plots, the principle of primogeniture came to be enforced. This weakened the position of women, depriving them of the right of inheritance that they had heretofore traditionally held. In an age in which only naked power counted, women could no longer retain the rights they formerly possessed. They became mere pawns for military alliances and were forced to marry whoever their fathers or brothers believed would serve useful political ends.

In return for their fiefs the vassals not only owed personal military service to their lord but also had to provide him with a fixed number of men on horseback and foot soldiers. The number depended on the size of the fief the vassal was given. In the middle of the sixteenth century Uesugi Kenshin had 5,514 men at his disposal. They included 566 knights on horseback, 321 musketeers, and 3,609 peasants armed with pikes.

Muskets were introduced to Japan by the Portuguese in 1543. Japanese smiths quickly learned how to make them, and within a decade they were widely used by the contending daimyō.[6] As the size of the warring armies grew and the use of firearms became more widespread, an increasingly larger number of peasants were mobilized to fight for the warlords. In Uesugi Kenshin's army the ratio of peasants to samurai was three to one.

The daimyō usually maintained one castle that served as his home base and several auxiliary castles or fortresses in strategic spots. The auxiliary castles were guarded by his trusted vassals. The site of the main castle usually became a fairly lively and populous town, since merchants and artisans as well as the daimyō's retainers congregated there. Each daimyō encouraged merchants and skilled artisans to settle in his town to assist in the production and distribution of weapons,

---

[6] Firearms had been introduced from China in the fifteenth century and may have been used by some eastern daimyō before the Western muskets arrived. Since their use did not spread, the Chinese firearms were evidently not very effective.

food, and other necessities. In order to strengthen the economic foundations of their domains, many daimyō initiated public works projects, particularly in water control and irrigation.

For the purpose of governing their territories and guiding their retainers most daimyō issued "house laws." These laws were in effect moral injunctions and rules of conduct. The house laws of Sōun contained such articles as:

1. Rise early in the morning. If you rise late, the servants too will become lethargic and cease to be industrious, and private and public tasks will be neglected.

2. Do not seek to acquire swords and apparel as splendid as those owned by others. As long as they are not shoddy, do not fall into debt to obtain better ones.

3. Keep a book with you constantly and use every spare moment to read it when unseen by others.[7]

The daimyō kept a close check on his vassals, trusting very few men. He employed spies to make certain that his followers, particularly the latecomers to his camp, were not plotting against him. He also had a voice in determining his vassal's place of residence, choice of wife, and succession to the family headship.

To determine taxes and to maintain close surveillance over his domain, the lord took censuses and checked land titles, acreage, and yield. He exercised judicial control over all the people on his land, usually punishing both parties in a dispute. When a person committed a serious crime, the entire household—including servants and retainers—or community was also held responsible. Punishments were extremely cruel and inhuman. Impaling, crucifying, tearing apart, boiling, burning, and sawing the offender to death were common means of execution. The peasants had little protection against the samurai, who were permitted to cut them down with impunity.

THE PEASANTRY

During the period of civil strife following the establishment of the Ashikaga Bakufu, control over the peasants slackened, and they were able to assert themselves, acquiring more freedom by taking advantage of the rival claims of the constables and the proprietors of the shōen. The element among the peasantry that provided the leadership in their ascendancy were the independent farmers, the myōshu. Those peasants who were not myōshu either owned a small plot of land or worked for the myōshu or the proprietors of the manor. There were also warrior-

---

[7] Quoted in Tsuji Zennosuke, *op. cit.*, vol. 4, pp. 177–79.

farmers who stood socially between the myōshu and ordinary peasantry. They, unlike the peasants, were entitled to use surnames.

During the Ashikaga period the villagers were able to exercise a certain degree of autonomy in managing the irrigation system, utilizing the woodlands and meadows, and maintaining peace and order within the community. When the local authorities failed to offer them protection from plunderers they banded together to form their own defense forces. The residents of a shōen belonging to the Tōdaiji in Nara, in requesting that rental payments be suspended, complained about the difficulties inflicted upon them by the contending forces of the northern and southern courts as follows:

> The forces of the two factions came to the shōen day and
> night and expropriated our cattle, horses, resources,
> rice, soybean, etc. Realizing that we would starve to
> death unless some action were taken we, the shōen
> residents, met and decided to band together to defend
> the shōen with our own lives. As a result we were able
> to put an end to the pillaging. But our burden has
> remained heavy. After the constable and governor arrived
> we expected to enjoy peace and tranquillity but they
> continuously make demands upon us, first asking for
> recruits for their armies, and then demanding food,
> horses and equipments. If we refuse they threaten to
> arrest us as supporters of their enemies and to burn our
> houses down.[8]

Taxes under the Ashikaga Bakufu grew steadily more burdensome, until about 70 percent of the peasants' produce was being collected by tax and rent collectors. Under normal circumstances the lot of the peasants was a difficult one, but in times of famine they were reduced to starvation. Daughters were sold to brothels, and sons were sold to priests who indulged in pederasty. Many peasants left the villages to become beggars and vagrants. A particularly serious famine occurred in the middle of the fifteenth century. Between 1459 and 1461 the country was plagued by a series of meteorological catastrophes, including droughts, floods, and typhoons. In addition, a plague of locusts destroyed the rice crop. These successive calamities resulted in serious food shortages, and a great number of people began to starve. The consequences were disastrous for large cities like Kyoto. In two months during the winter of 1460–1461 it was estimated that 82,000 persons starved to death

[8] Quoted in Satō Shinichi, *Nambokuchō no Dōran* (*Conflicts Between the Southern and Northern Courts*) (Tokyo: Chūō Kōronsha, 1965), pp. 390–91.

in the capital. Yet there is no evidence that the Bakufu under Yoshi-masa—the eighth Ashikaga shōgun, who was interested primarily in the construction of attractive villas and gardens and in amusing himself with Nō plays and flower-viewing—took any measures to alleviate the suffering of the people except to have prayers intoned on behalf of the dead.

With the growing burden of taxation, mounting debts, periodic crop failures, and the ruling class's general indifference to the well-being of the peasantry, it is not surprising that the peasants began to riot in protest. In the fifteenth century peasant uprisings began to occur with increasing frequency. In 1428, when the entire nation suffered from crop failure and famine and mass starvation occurred, a major uprising broke out in the Kyoto region. The peasants in the province of Ōmi staged an insurrection demanding tokusei (acts of grace), that is, the cancellation of all debts. They were soon joined by peasants from adjoining regions as well as by the townspeople of Kyoto. They attacked temples and monasteries, sake merchants, pawnbrokers, moneylenders—destroying, looting, and tearing up certificates of loan. Similar uprisings followed in other areas, especially in the central and western provinces. Such disturbances continued to break out until the following year. They were directed not only against the Bakufu and shōen owners but against a new force in the countryside, the urban moneylenders who had become more active in the rural areas as commerce and a money economy grew in importance. The peasants in the Kantō region were kept under firmer control by the local authorities and were unable to register their complaints effectively, but isolated instances of peasant uprisings did occur there also.

In 1441, while the Bakufu was in a state of uncertainty following the assassination of the sixth shōgun, the peasants in the provinces around Kyoto staged an uprising, again demanding the cancellation of all debts. During the thirty-year rule of the eighth shōgun, Yoshimasa, eighteen peasant uprisings occurred. Yoshimasa issued thirteen decrees cancelling debts. That he issued these decrees so readily may have been related in part to the fact that the debtors were required to pay 10 percent of their debts to the Bakufu in return for having the other 90 percent cancelled.

The peasant uprisings contributed to the emergence of the local samurai as an important political force. The leaders of these uprisings were frequently shōen officials, lower-class samurai, or myōshu, who utilized peasant discontent to weaken the authority of the constabulary families and further their own political fortunes, a trend that was particularly strong following the Ōnin War. This meant that in the long run the interests of the samurai rather than those of the peasants were advanced. Eventually the lower-level samurai became retainers of some rising military chieftain and then, as members of the new ruling class, helped to keep the peasants under control. As the daimyō came to dominate the country they suppressed the autonomous tendencies that had been developing among the peasantry. They held the peasants collectively responsible for rents, taxes, and crimes. Generally speaking the samurai were more ruthless than the constables in collecting rents and taxes and in exacting corvée and military service from the peasantry.

Although the peasants' lot worsened as the daimyō became powerful, until a strong central authority was reestablished in the late sixteenth century there was always an opportunity for a peasant to take advantage of the unsettled conditions to climb up the social hierarchy. As we noted, they were brought into the daimyō's armies as foot soldiers in increasing numbers in the Age of the Warring States. If they served with distinction they were able to join the ranks of the samurai because no rigid caste system existed in this period. The most dramatic example of an individual's rise up the social and political ladder is the life of Toyotomi Hideyoshi, who rose from the peasantry to become the dictator of the entire country. Only rarely were groups of peasants able to acquire political power, however. The most notable exception was the peasants of Yamashiro Province, near Kyoto, who gained control of the province in 1485 and held it for eight years.

ECONOMIC GROWTH

During the Ashikaga period a significant change in the economic life of the country took place. Agricultural production increased, and commerce and industry began to expand. The reason for this change cannot be ascribed to any dramatic shift or innovation. Agricultural production had increased through the years as a result of gradual changes in the methods of farming. Increased production in agriculture stimulated commerce and then industry. There were also technical improvements in the industrial sphere—in salt making, mining, textile production, metalwork, pottery, sake brewing, and paper making. Furthermore, economic growth was stimulated by the peace and order that prevailed after the country was unified under the Kamakura Bakufu. Even when the central government was weakened during the latter part of Ashikaga rule, the damages done by military conflicts were evidently minor. Indeed, there is some reason to believe that the constant movement of warriors and the emergence of many population centers in the form of castle towns tended to quicken the pace of economic activities. At the same time, the renewal and intensification of contact with China, Korea, and the Ryukyus greatly stimulated economic growth.

In the densely populated area around Kyoto, Osaka, and Nara, known as the Kinki region, agricultural production was conducted on a small scale, but arable land was utilized intensively by terracing the hillsides. With the rise of the military families, new land was opened for farming in the Kantō and Kyushu regions. At the same time better tools and improved methods of farming came to be employed. Metal plows and hoes, which were not readily available for use by the common peasants before the Kamakura era, were now used by them. Draft animals also came to be utilized by a larger number of peasants. Better methods of irrigation through the extensive use of waterwheels were introduced. In the production of rice, the introduction of a new strain better suited to the climate and the use of the seedbed resulted in greater yields. In addition, two crops, rice and another grain or a vegetable, came to be grown in many areas during the latter part of the Kamakura period. With the increased use of draft animals, manure was used as fertilizer; human waste was also used for this purpose. The practice of burning trees and grass to enrich the soil had been followed since the end of the Heian period. In addition to rice and other grains, the production of fruits and vegetables for the newly established towns as well as the production of tea and silk increased during this period.

This increase in agricultural production inevitably stimulated commerce. Toward the end of the Kamakura era market towns came into existence. As early as the Nara period markets had been set up periodically under the auspices of local authorities, monasteries, and shrines. By the end of the Kamakura period they came to have fixed locations, although they were still open only several times a month. Not until the middle of the fifteenth century were they held as often as six times a month. Out of the markets grew new towns near, not surprisingly, monasteries, shrines, and seats of local political power and at crossroads and forks of rivers.

To sell one's product at such markets a merchant had to pay a fee to the local lord, monastery, or shrine that offered him protection. Initially the people who operated these markets were local peasants who came to sell their farm produce and handicrafts. Eventually, however, regular merchants came to dominate the marketplaces. As these markets grew in importance, merchant and craft guilds, designed to acquire and preserve monopolistic rights for the members, came into existence.

These guilds, or za, originated in the early twelfth century as associations designed to serve the needs of the court and the monasteries. With the rise in commerce the number of guilds increased, and during the Ashikaga period they existed throughout the country. Some guilds managed to acquire monopolistic rights that extended over the entire country. Most guilds, however, usually held a commercial monopoly in a single town or other limited area, with each guild specializing in a single commodity. The Kinki region had the greatest number of strong guilds.

There were guilds for practically every commodity in use at that time. For example, there were za for vegetable oil, rice, sake, salt, paper, straw mats, sliding doors, sedge hats, braziers, metal goods, candy, rice-cakes, noodles, fish, textiles, lumber, charcoal, and medicine. The za varied in size from as few as two members to more than fifty members; the average size, however, was about ten.

Although the primary object of the guilds was to establish and maintain a commercial monopoly, they also sought to acquire for their members such privileges as exemption from taxation and protection from outside competitors and lawless elements. In return a guild paid the protecting authority, either the local lord or monastery, a fixed fee. There were also artisans' and workers' guilds for blacksmiths, silversmiths, swordsmiths, carpenters, dyers, carriers, etc.

Another consequence of the rise in commerce was the emergence of a money economy. Although money existed during the Nara and early Heian periods, it was not widely used, and coins were not minted after the early part of the tenth century. In the eleventh century rice and silk were used as the chief media of exchange. In the twelfth century coins reappeared as a result of the revival of trade with China. By the fourteenth century Chinese copper coins were in wide use. The rise of a money economy made the control of copper, silver, and gold mines important, and they became the object of contention among the warring daimyō. In addition to coins, bills of exchange came to be employed by merchants engaged in long-distance commerce. They were also used to pay taxes. The earliest record of the use of bills of exchange comes from 1279.

The increased use and need of money resulted in the rise of moneylenders. Wealthy landowners, pawnbrokers, merchants—particularly sake merchants—and even monasteries and shrines engaged in moneylending. The borrowers, usually peasants, were charged high interest rates, starting at about 50 percent. The peasants, however, were not the only customers; the proprietors of the shōen also relied on the moneylenders. The Bakufu, too, borrowed money from the sake merchants and pawnbrokers. Many moneylenders later became government officials in charge of financial affairs and rose in the social hierarchy.

The expansion of commercial activities resulted as well in the emergence of wholesale merchants and in a growth of port cities. The ports around the Kinki region and the Inland Sea were the first to be built up, but cities were soon established on harbors in other parts of the country too. The city of Sakai near Osaka emerged as a flourishing port with considerable political power.

As an increasingly large volume of goods came to be transported on both land and sea, a large number of checkpoints and toll stations were established by local authorities to collect duty on goods in transit. It has been estimated that in 1462 there were 380 such toll stations between Kyoto and the mouth of the Yodo River in Osaka. Not only did the traveling merchants have to contend with these barriers to commerce, but they were frequently attacked by bandits and pirates.

A by-product of the increase in trade was the revival of the system of horse stations for official transportation and communication. This "pony express" system had been introduced as one of the Taika Reforms but was allowed to deteriorate. It was revived in many areas in the Kamakura period by the rising daimyō.

The merchants grew not only in number but also in importance in the market towns, ports, castle towns, and the towns that grew around monasteries and shrines. The dominant members among them were the wholesale merchants and the moneylenders. In some towns they collected taxes for the local lords and policed their communities. Sakai was an autonomous city run by thirty-six elders, primarily wealthy wholesale merchants. It had its own defense force and usually managed to defy the warlords in its vicinity. In 1568 it even refused to pay the levy demanded of it by Oda Nobunaga, although it was forced to submit the following year. Among other cities that retained a similar autonomy were Hakata in Kyushu and Ōminato and Uji Yamada, both in Ise. All this added up to a possibility that the towns of Japan would emerge as a significant political force, following the pattern of the medieval towns of Europe, but with the establishment in Japan of a strong central government in the late sixteenth century, the nascent urban forces were brought under control. In many instances the merchants cooperated with the daimyō who were working for the unification of the country, motivated no doubt by the desire to have peace and stability restored so that commerce could flourish.

A significant aspect of the expansion of commerce was the revival of trade with China. Following the decline of the T'ang dynasty the close relationship between China and Japan that had been maintained during the Nara and Heian periods abated, but with the unification of China under the Sung dynasty contact was reestablished. When the Sung court moved to the south (1127), Chinese commerce increased. Soon, however, as the Sung government became concerned with the excessive outflow of gold, silver, and copper, it began to restrict overseas trade. In 1245 it asked the Japanese authorities to limit the number of Japanese merchantmen sailing to China. Later, after the Mongol dynasty was established in China (1271), commercial contact between the two countries was again formally revived. Although the first official commercial exchange took place in 1325, informal trade had started earlier.

Around the fourteenth century Japanese pirates known as *wakō*, operating out of the islands of Iki and Tsushima off Kyushu, began to intensify their activities against the coastal cities of Korea. They also began to raid the coastal towns and villages of China. When the Ming government came into power in 1368 it sent an envoy asking the Japanese government to curb the pirates, but because the demand was presented in such a manner as to indicate that China considered Japan her subject state, it was rejected. The third Ashikaga shōgun, Yoshimitsu, was interested in expanding commercial relations with China, however, so he curtailed the wakō's activities to some extent. Nevertheless the pirates continued to make their attacks against Korea and China during the fourteenth and fifteenth centuries, frequently with the support of local lords in western Japan. The object of these raids was to steal food, such as rice and beans, and to kidnap villagers who could then be sold as slaves.

Legitimate trade between Ming China and Japan began to flourish under Yoshimitsu, who sought to ease the financial difficulties of his regime by such commerce. In 1404 a formal commercial treaty was concluded between the two governments, and the Bakufu periodically sent merchantmen to China. Formal commercial relations were ended under Yoshimitsu's successor but were revived by the fifth shōgun. In order to curb unauthorized trade with neighboring countries, the Ming government adopted a system of certification for those ships authorized to conduct commerce with China.

Trade with Korea was also reestablished around the same period and was conducted on an even larger scale than the commerce with China. Commercial relations with China and Korea enriched the daimyō and merchants of western Japan. The city of Hakata in Kyushu was the center of commerce with Korea, while official trade with China was carried on through the port of Hyōgo. After the Ōnin War, the Ōuchi and Hosokawa families tended to dominate the trade with China. Commerce was also conducted with the Ryukyu Islands, and Ryukyu merchants frequently served as middlemen between Japan, and Southeast Asia, and China.

Japan exported to China such things as swords, armor, copper, sulphur, lumber, fans, lacquerware, and pearls and, in return, imported raw silk, cotton thread, fine fabrics, dye, ironware, porcelain, paintings, books, medicine, and copper coins. From Korea Japan imported cotton goods, in exchange for copper, sulphur, and swords. Prior to this period

Japanese garments had been made largely of silk and hemp. With the increased production of cotton in Korea in the fifteenth century, the Japanese began increasingly to utilize cotton fabrics for clothing. In the sixteenth century Japan began growing her own cotton.

The contacts between China and Japan during the Kamakura and Ashikaga periods not only had economic significance but also resulted in the re-exertion of Chinese influence in the cultural realm. A large number of Japanese monks visited China, Chinese books were imported to Japan, and the advanced Chinese printing technique was introduced. Chinese painting, calligraphy, and ceramics influenced Japanese art, and Chu Hsi philosophy (see page 184) came to be known to Japanese scholars. The latest Chinese medical knowledge and drugs, as well as new food and culinary practices, entered the country.

During the Ashikaga period, commercial intercourse with Southeast Asia was established for the first time. Emissaries from Southeast Asian countries appeared in Japan occasionally during the fourteenth and fifteenth centuries, but trade was conducted largely through Ryukyu middlemen.

THE INFLUENCE OF ZEN BUDDHISM
UPON CULTURE

The influence of Zen on art reached its apex in the Ashikaga period. It molded the aesthetic taste of the Japanese and established standards of excellence for later generations to emulate. It fostered an appreciation of the simple and the austere, and a preference for imbalance and asymmetry.

The upsurge of creativity in the arts was given a significant boost by the eighth shōgun, Yoshimasa, who concerned himself more with cultural activities than with the art of government. Even during the Ōnin War he paid more attention to culture than to the power struggle that was fragmenting his land. He constructed the Silver Pavilion in Higashiyama in the northeastern section of Kyoto, creating a cultural style referred to as Higashiyama Culture. He not only initiated the construction of a complex of buildings in his villa but also personally patronized the masters of landscape gardening, Nō, flower arrangement, the tea ceremony, and painting. Yoshimasa's taste in all these areas reflected the growing influence of Zen.

Even before Zen came to Japan, the Japanese had developed a refined sense of beauty and appreciation of nature. The stark, simple, and unadorned designs of the early Shinto shrines attest to a love of simple, uncluttered beauty. A Japanese writer remarks "I find it difficult to accept . . . [the] view that the aesthetic sensibility of the samurai civilization should be attributed entirely to Zen, since I believe this civilization had its roots still deeper, in the traditional Japanese sensibility as expressed in the classical civilization." [9] Zen, however, extended the aesthetic sensitivity of the Japanese into many new areas of life and art. It is manifested in such militaristic pastimes as swordsmanship and archery as well as in the artistic activities of the poet, the calligrapher, and the painter. It also molded the arts of gardening, flower arrangement, and the tea ceremony.

Regarding the relationship between the last-mentioned art and Zen, Suzuki Daisetsu observes, "What is common to Zen and the art of tea is the constant attempt both make at simplification. The elimination of the unnecessary is achieved by Zen in its intuitive grasp of final reality; by the art of tea, in the way of living typified by serving tea in the tearoom." [10] Tea was imported to Japan from China before the Kamakura period, but Eisai is credited with making it a popular beverage. The ritual of the tea ceremony was also introduced from China by Zen monks in the late thirteenth century, and the art was adapted to Japanese tastes. Formally the ceremony is conducted in a small, simple room in a thatched hut in the quietude of nature. Its object is to foster the spirit of harmony, reverence, purity, and tranquillity.

The aesthetic tastes fostered in the tea ceremony are *wabi* and *sabi*. Sabi is an objective quality manifested in things and the environment. It is associated with "age, desiccation, numbness, chilliness, obscurity— all of which are negative feelings opposed to warmth, the spring, expansiveness, transparency, etc." [11] It is a quality of mellowness and depth that is acquired through use and aging. Wabi is a subjective feeling fostered by simple, almost rustic, and serene surroundings. It embodies the sense of solitude and melancholy but also of tranquillity that one experiences as one's Buddha nature comes to the surface in the simplicity and serenity of the teahouse and tea ceremony. An aesthetic taste related to these qualities is the preference for what is called *shibui,* that is, that which is austere, sober, and subdued. It is a quality that is in keeping with the Japanese taste for restraint and understatement.

The tea ceremony, then, is not merely a pleasant pastime. In its pristine form it has had profound aesthetic and spiritual significance, and the spirit fostered by it has deeply influenced Japanese art and life. In Suzuki's opinion such aesthetic and spiritual experiences take the place of spiritual constructs.

> If Japan did not produce any philosophical system of
> her own, she was original enough to embody in her

---

[9] Nyozekan Hasegawa, *The Japanese Character: A Cultural Profile,* trans. John Bester (Tokyo and Palo Alto, Calif.: Kodansha International Ltd., 1965), p. 48.

[10] Daisetsu T. Suzuki, *Zen and Japanese Culture* (New York: Pantheon, 1959), p. 271.

[11] *Ibid.,* p. 285.

practical life all that could profitably be extracted from
Confucianism, Taoism, and Buddhism and turn them into
the material for her spiritual enhancement and artistic
appreciation. . . . The Japanese are great in changing
philosophy into art, abstract reasoning into life,
transcendentalism into empirical immanentism.[12]

The art of the tea ceremony also contributed to the development of
ceramics, since the appreciation of the tea bowls used in the ceremony
was an essential part of the art of tea. In the latter part of the Ashikaga
era the influence of Korean pottery, which is characterized by crude
simplicity in contrast to the highly finished style of Chinese pottery,
came to be reflected in Japanese ceramics. The most significant developments in Japanese pottery, however, occurred in the latter half of the
sixteenth century.

The tea ceremony also fostered the art of flower arrangement since the
alcove in the tea room was decorated by a tray of flowers and twigs. Here,
as in other areas of Japanese art, placement is crucial. A flower arrangement is, in effect, a three-dimensional design, with forms and colors arranged in an aesthetically satisfying manner.

The influence of Zen during this period can also be seen in the art
of gardening. Gardens were laid out artistically earlier too, but during
the Ashikaga period, under the influence of Zen, a new style developed.
The master in this field was Musō Soseki (1275–1351), a Zen monk.
Musō was not interested in imitating nature but sought rather to reduce
things to the bare essentials. His work became highly symbolic. One of
the most famous of his creations is the Moss Garden at Saihōji in Kyoto,
a symbolic representation of the ideal "land of Zen." This style of landscape gardening culminated in the rock garden of Ryōanji, another temple in Kyoto. The rock garden was created at the end of the fifteenth
century either by Sōami (?–1525), who was a master in all fields of artistic
endeavor, or by his disciples. It consists of nothing but white sand and
fifteen natural stones arranged in five groups surrounded by a meager
growth of moss. The sand symbolizes the sea and the rocks signify islands.
Here natural forms are presented in their simplest terms, not unlike an
abstract painting.

In the residential buildings of this era, a style known as *shoin-zukuri*
came into existence. The simplicity and austerity manifested in Zen
teahouses were incorporated into the domestic architecture. The materials used were plain and simple. In the interiors straight lines created
neat geometric patterns in the corridors, ceilings, floor mats, and slid-

[12] *Ibid.*, p. 307

The rock garden of Ryōanji, a Buddhist temple in Kyoto. Sōami (?–1525) is thought to have designed the garden. Courtesy of the Consulate General of Japan, New York.

ing doors. The *shoin* was a room where Zen monks lived and studied, and its features were incorporated in private dwellings; for example, the recessed altar of the Zen monk's room became the alcove where artworks were displayed. These features have been retained to the present in Japanese houses.

Shōgun Yoshimitsu's Golden Pavilion, a three storied structure, was built in the shoin style. The building and its setting of trees, rocks, and a lake were carefully arranged to constitute a harmonious whole. Yoshimasa's Silver Pavilion was modeled after the Golden Pavilion but has

The Golden Pavilion in Kyoto was built in 1394 by the Ashikaga Shōgun Yo-shimitsu (1358–1408). The present edifice is a reconstruction of the original pavilion, which was destroyed by fire in 1950. The first two stories are lacquered black, the third is gilded. Courtesy of the Consulate General of Japan, New York.

only two stories. It, too, is surrounded by a beautiful garden, believed to have been designed by Sōami. Nearby is a building which contains a small tearoom that became the model for tearooms constructed subsequently.

Some authorities consider the influence of Zen to have been reflected most significantly in painting. About the middle of the thirteenth century the paintings of a Chinese Zen monk, Mu-ch'i, were brought to Japan, where they made a lasting impact upon Japanese *sumie* (ink drawing). Zen injected into painting and calligraphy an air of virility. Bold, forceful strokes characterize the works of the master sumie painters and calligraphers of this period. In sumie painting once the brush touches the paper the brushstroke cannot be changed, so the mental control of a person disciplined in Zen becomes essential. The artist

Landscape of Ama-No-Hashidate by Sesshū (1420–1506). From the collection of the National Museum in Tokyo; courtesy of the Consulate General of Japan, New York.

moves his brush delicately at first, then boldly across white paper, finally letting the imprint of the brush either fade out or end abruptly. The sumie painters of this period were not interested in a realistic imitation of nature but depicted the essence of things as they saw it. All unessential details are therefore left out of their paintings. The rhythm and movement of the brushwork, as well as its texture and overall design, are important in endowing these paintings with dynamism and vigor.

Josetsu (fl. 1400) is thought to have been the founder of the sumie school of painting in Japan, but only one of his works is extant. It depicts a man trying to catch a catfish with a gourd, a typical Zen proposition. It is generally agreed that the greatest artist to emerge out of this tradition was Sesshū (1420–1506). An authority on Japanese art commenting on the power of Sesshū's brush writes: "His strokes are sudden, strong, vehement, he seems careless of modulating them; and yet how magically all falls into place. It is this extraordinary mastery of forcible brush-stroke which gives Sesshū his supremacy with the Japanese: this, and the intensity and directness which he combines with unsurpassed greatness of spirit." [13] Ernest F. Fenollosa, a pioneer among Western students of Japanese art, asserts that Sesshū is the greatest master of the straight line and the angle in the history of world art. Sesshū used two styles: one utilizing sharp, angular, and relatively complex brushwork, and a soft, diffused, rather explosive yet highly simplified

[13] Lawrence Binyon, *Painting in the Far East* (New York: Dover, 1959), p. 180.

style. Although he was primarily a landscape painter, his paintings of the founder of Zen Buddhism, Bodhidharma, are known for their vigor and dramatic force. In the next era, another sumie artist, Miyamoto Musashi (1584–1645), who was also one of the greatest swordsmen of Japan, combined Zen aesthetics with the spirit of the samurai.

The influence of Zen can also be seen in the calligraphy of this period. In contrast to the gentle, cursive style that was popular during the Heian period, Ashikaga calligraphy was vigorous and masculine. As in sumie painting, the overall composition, the relationship between the brush-marks and the blank areas, and the movement and rhythm of the brush-strokes are important. But, in addition, the proper balancing of the component parts of each character, the relationship of adjacent charac-ters, and the variations in the size and density of the brushstrokes are of equal importance.

It was also during this era that the Nō drama reached new heights of artistic refinement. The Nō play grew out of the popular folk dances and plays that were performed at Shinto festivals to pray to the gods for abundant harvest and to give thanks after the harvest. They also served as entertainment for the common people. These dances were refined through the ages and in the Ashikaga period emerged as a serious dra-matic form. Nō was patronized increasingly by the upper classes and eventually came to be regarded as an aesthetic experience appreciated primarily by the culturally elite.

The Zen preference for simplicity and restraint is seen in the external aspects of the Nō plays. The stage, open on three sides, is simple and plain, having neither a curtain nor background scenery except for an old pine tree painted on the rear wall. The few stage properties that are used are symbolic and abstract. The movements and gestures of the all-male cast are highly stylized, formal, and carefully measured. Usually the principal actor wears a mask, but even without a mask the actor's face is frozen as if he were masked. Mime constitutes an important part of Nō dramas; feelings are expressed by symbolic gestures and move-ments. Weeping, for example, is signified by raising the hand to the eyes. The fan is manipulated to symbolize a variety of things, such as fall-ing leaves, rippling waves, and an ascending moon. The Nō performance is accompanied by a chorus that chants the story in a sing-song. The actors are dressed in brilliant costumes, luxuriously embroidered and brocaded.

The art of Nō was perfected by two men: Kan'ami Kiyotsugu (1333–1384) and his son, Seami Motokiyo (1363–1443), who enjoyed the patron-age of the third shōgun, Yoshimitsu. Seami's works are regarded as mas-terpieces and are still performed today. He was profoundly influenced by Zen and sought to convey in his works the sense of *yūgen*, or mystery, "what lies beneath the surface; the subtle as opposed to the statement."

OTHER CULTURAL DEVELOPMENTS

In the Ashikaga period learning began to spread downward into the society rather than being restricted to the elite, the court aristocrats and the priests. The warriors began to show an interest in education, and the local lords began to encourage learning among their followers. We have already caught a glimpse of this in the "house laws" of Hōjō Sōun. The process of cultural diffusion was facilitated during and after the Ōnin War when a large number of aristocrats and monks fled the turbulent capital, finding employment with the daimyō as educators and lecturers.

One manifestation of this growing interest in learning is the Kanazawa Library that was established in Kanazawa (near present-day Yokohama) in the middle of the Kamakura period. Even though it was allowed to deteriorate after the fall of the Kamakura Bakufu, twenty thousand volumes were recovered from this library. The Ashikaga Academy was also founded during the same period by the Ashikaga family in the Kantō region. Students from all over the country attended the academy. Although it was operated by Buddhist priests, Confucianism came to form the core of the curriculum, and students educated here returned to their home provinces to engage in educational work.

Another significant institution that emerged during this period was the temple school (*terakoya*). It became the practice of the samurai and wealthier peasants to send their children to Buddhist temples to learn how to read and write. Although this practice did not become widespread until the Tokugawa period, the origin of the temple schools can be traced back to the Ashikaga era.

The art of woodblock printing, which had entered Japan from China during the Kamakura period, flourished in the Ashikaga years as many Chinese printers sought asylum in Japan during the period of turmoil at the end of the Mongol and the beginning of the Ming rule. The Zen temples of Kyoto and Kamakura (known as the Temples of the Five Mountains) sponsored the printing of Buddhist texts.

Several significant works of history were produced during this era. One such history was written by a loyal supporter of the southern court, Kitabatake Chikafusa (1293–1354). This is the *Jinnō Shōtōki (The Records of the Legitimate Succession of the Divine Sovereigns)*, written in 1339. It records the history of Japan from its founding by the gods to the reign of Emperor Godaigo. Kitabatake emphasized that Japan was a unique land of the gods and that descendants of the Sun Goddess were destined to reign to eternity. Every subject of the Emperor, he insisted, must serve him with utmost loyalty.

The *Jinnō Shōtōki* is significant as an important Shinto document. Shinto was keeping its flame alive even during this era when Buddhism was winning widespread support. The tradition of seeking to reconcile Buddhism and Shinto, which had emerged during the Heian period as Dual Shinto, prevailed during this age, too, but there was also a move to subordinate Buddhism to Shinto. The proponents of this movement contended that the Japanese gods constituted the original divine substance, and the Buddhas and Bodhisattvas were manifestations of this, a reversal of the position taken by the earlier Dual Shintoists, who regarded the Japanese gods as manifestations of the universal Buddha.

Another important historical work—actually a historical romance—of this era was the *Taiheiki* (*Chronicle of Grand Pacification*). It is believed to have been the work of several writers and was completed around 1370. It describes the events from 1318, the beginning of the reign of Emperor Godaigo, to 1367, focusing on the Kemmu Restoration and the conflict between the imperial and Ashikaga factions. It is sympathetic to the imperial cause and depicts the heroic exploits of such men as Kusunoki Masashige and Nitta Yoshisada. It has remained the chief source of information for the early Ashikaga period. The saga was also in its day a source of popular entertainment; storytellers went about retelling its tales of military exploits, heroism, and virtue.

The people were entertained by other romantic and melodramatic tales of heroic warriors as well. One of the most popular subjects of the storytellers was Yoshitsune, Yoritomo's younger brother, who was idealized as a young man of valor, courage, and military genius. Fairy tales were popular in this era, too.

Another form of recreation enjoyed by the people at large were the Buddhist Bon dances that came to be performed in the early years of the Ashikaga period. The people also found emotional release in the annual festivals of the Shinto shrines and were occasionally entertained by farcical plays known as *Kyōgen*, which often satirized the members of the upper classes. The Kyōgen was eventually incorporated into the Nō theater.

In the religious life of the people, the custom came into existence of paying homage to stone images of various Bodhisattvas who, it was believed, bestowed diverse benefits upon the worshippers. The practice of going on pilgrimages to a number of widely scattered Buddhist temples also became popular among devout believers.

As for the Buddhist sects that emerged in the Kamakura period, both Nichiren and True Pure Land Buddhism were endowed with dynamic leadership that effected a kind of renaissance in the sects. The beliefs of the Nichiren Sect were propagated vigorously by its leaders, among whom was Nisshin (1407–1488), who, it was said, disciplined himself by such means of self-torture as pulling out his fingernails and piercing the open sores with a needle. When he aroused the wrath of the sixth shōgun, the shōgun had a red-hot iron pot placed on his head. Undaunted, Nisshin continued his work to gain converts. The zealous efforts of such preachers won the Nichiren Sect a large number of converts, particularly among the townspeople. It became especially popular in Kyoto and became something of a political force in the sixteenth century in that strife-ridden city.

Because Shinran, the founder of the True Pure Land Sect, did not believe in institutionalizing his movement, it was loosely structured. This situation was changed by Rennyo (1415–1499), who welded the movement into a well-structured religious sect and a political power as well. The sect became especially popular among the peasantry in the north central and western regions of Honshu. In the age of political disorder, the converts organized themselves into military bands and fought against hostile military chieftains. The True Pure Land Sect came to be known as the *Ikkō* (One Direction) Sect, and the military campaigns they launched against the warlords were called Ikkō Uprisings. In the last quarter of the fifteenth century, the Ikkō adherents staged six uprisings and eventually gained control of the province of Kaga. By the sixteenth century the Ikkō forces had become a major power in the Kyoto-Osaka area as well as in the north central and central provinces, constituting a formidable obstacle to the ambitious daimyō.

CHAPTER 6

THE RESTORATION
OF ORDER

During the Age of the Warring States, the Ashikaga shogunate not only lost its capacity to govern the outlying regions but found itself unable to maintain control over the provinces near Kyoto. Ultimately those provinces came under the control of new military leaders who emerged in that area. After the demise of the major constabulary houses, such as the Hosokawa family, the government fell under the domination of the Miyoshi family. It was then dominated by Matsunaga Hisahide, a vassal of the Miyoshi family, who rebelled against the Miyoshi clan and assassinated the thirteenth shōgun.

In the provinces a multitude of warring lords were contending for land and power. Their object was not to succeed merely as regional powers but to extend their authority over the entire country. The most critical power struggle occurred in the region between Kantō and Kyoto, where powerful warlords contended for supremacy. In the middle of the sixteenth century there were four major powers entrenched in this region: the Uesugis of Echigo, the Takedas of Kai, the Imagawas of Suruga, and the Hōjōs of Kantō. Among the lesser forces were the Oda family and the Matsudaira (Tokugawa) clan.

The clan that emerged triumphant was the Oda family, led by Nobunaga (1534–1582), who started the country on its path to reunification and order. The men who completed the task were Toyotomi Hideyoshi (1536–1598) and Tokugawa Ieyasu (1542–1616). These three men laid the foundation for the establishment of two-and-a-half centuries of stable military rule—the Tokugawa Bakufu. Their lives were closely interwoven. They were all born within one decade. Hideyoshi was Nobunaga's most able and trusted general. Ieyasu was at one time held captive by the Oda clan and later became Nobunaga's ally. Hideyoshi succeeded Nobunaga as the military chieftain of the entire land and in turn was succeeded by Ieyasu.

ODA NOBUNAGA

The Oda family had served as deputy constable of Owari and gained control of that province under the leadership of Nobunaga's father. Owari was located in a strategically critical spot, on the route from Kamakura to Kyoto. It was also a rich rice-producing and commercially active area with many market towns.

Nobunaga managed to extend his power by bold military tactics and politically beneficial alliances. For instance, he married his sister to a military leader of Ōmi, his adopted daughter to Takeda Shingen's son, and his daughter to Ieyasu's son. He was quick to take advantage of new tactics and weapons. He ended the traditional reliance on mounted knights by making effective use of foot soldiers armed with long pikes. When firearms became available he was among the first to arm his men with muskets. In a battle with the Takeda clan in 1575 he employed over three thousand musketeers, compared to the five hundred used by his foes, and won a decisive victory. He was also a daring tactician. In 1560 when the odds seemed to be overwhelmingly against him in his confrontation with the Imagawa clan, he launched a surprise attack against his rival's forces, which numbered ten times his army, and dealt them a crushing blow. This victory proved to be an important milestone in Nobunaga's rise to power. He proceeded to consolidate his position in central Japan and in 1568 moved into Kyoto where, after a struggle, Matsunaga Hisahide submitted to his superior force.

After he gained control of Kyoto, Nobunaga did not immediately claim suzerainty over the entire country but instead supported Ashikaga Yoshiaki as the shōgun of the land. He then turned to the conquest of the military chieftains controlling Ōmi and Echizen. In the process he encountered the opposition of the Ikkō (True Pure Land) forces and the monks of Mt. Hiei just outside of Kyoto. He turned his wrath against the latter, destroying the monasteries and seizing and executing not only the monks but the villagers, including women and children. About sixteen hundred people were killed in this blood bath.

Shōgun Yoshiaki became uneasy about Nobunaga's growing power and began conspiring with his foes. This finally induced Nobunaga to put an end to the Ashikaga shogunate. In 1573 Yoshiaki fled to the west and sought the aid of the Mōri family, the dominant power in western Honshu. In the east, the major clans of Hōjō, Takeda, and Uesugi were

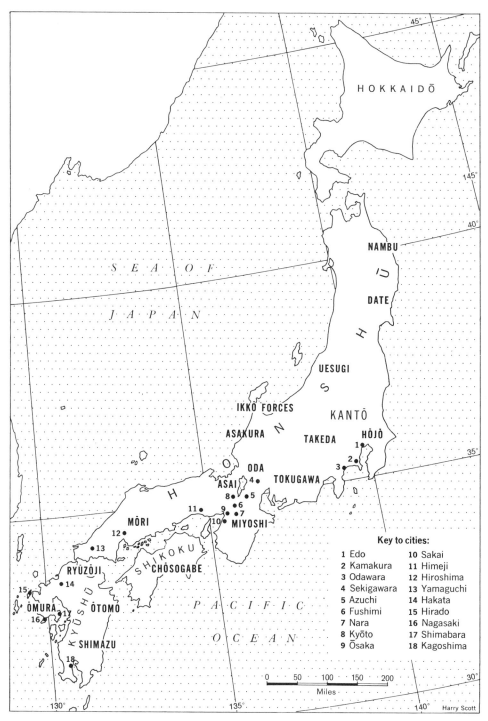

Key to cities:

1 Edo	10 Sakai
2 Kamakura	11 Himeji
3 Odawara	12 Hiroshima
4 Sekigawara	13 Yamaguchi
5 Azuchi	14 Hakata
6 Fushimi	15 Hirado
7 Nara	16 Nagasaki
8 Kyōto	17 Shimabara
9 Ōsaka	18 Kagoshima

Harry Scott

MAJOR DAIMYŌ, AROUND 1570.

132

engaged in a power struggle. Such rivalries among the daimyō played conveniently into Nobunaga's hands. By 1581 the Takeda forces were completely destroyed. The Uesugi clan remained a formidable power while it was led by Kenshin, who was an outstanding general and administrator, but its fortunes also began to decline after his death in 1578.

A situation that redounded to Nobunaga's benefit was the fact that, as it became evident that his power was ascendant, his foes' vassals began to defect to his side with increasing frequency.

The other political bloc that gave Nobunaga considerable trouble was the Ikkō forces, with their headquarters in Ishiyama Temple in Osaka. They were particularly powerful in the provinces of Kaga and Echizen. Kaga was under their complete control. In 1575 Nobunaga sent his men against the Ikkō forces in Echizen, capturing and massacring thirty thousand to forty thousand Ikkō adherents. In 1580 his men succeeded in driving the Ikkō forces out of Kaga. A peace settlement was finally effected between the Ikkō leaders and Nobunaga through the mediation of the imperial court.

Nobunaga then turned to the subjugation of the Mōri clan, which had been allied with the Ikkō forces. The general who was placed in charge of this campaign was Toyotomi Hideyoshi, who effectively used the siege, one of the favorite tactics of the contending warlords of this era, against his enemies. Hideyoshi turned two castles into veritable hells as he starved the defenders to death. He had placed still another Mōri fortress under siege when he received word of Akechi Mitsuhide's rebellion against Nobunaga.

Mitsuhide had joined Nobunaga's camp relatively late, after the latter captured Kyoto. Evidently he harbored a deep-seated resentment against the high-handed and sometimes abusive treatment accorded him by Nobunaga. In one battle Mitsuhide had sent his mother to the enemy as a hostage in order to persuade them to come out of their fortress to negotiate with Nobunaga. When the opponents did so Nobunaga, ignoring Mitsuhide's compact with them, apprehended and crucified them. Naturally the enemy forces executed Mitsuhide's mother.

When in June, 1582, Mitsuhide was ordered by Nobunaga to lead his men west to assist Hideyoshi against the Mōri forces, he decided to lead his army against Nobunaga instead. Caught wholly by surprise, Nobunaga was trapped in a Kyoto temple and committed suicide. Thus perished his dream of establishing his hegemony over the entire land. When he died he had possession of thirty-two of the sixty-six provinces.

Nobunaga was not only a masterful military leader, he was also an able administrator. He encouraged merchants to open markets in the areas under his control, offering them protection and immunity from taxation. He also curbed the monopoly of the guilds, opening the markets to all merchants. To facilitate the flow of goods he abolished toll stations and encouraged the building of ships and the construction of roads. He abolished corvée, sought to establish a uniform system of coinage, and initiated a cadastral survey. By Nobunaga's time contact with the West had already been established. He favored broadening ties with the outside world by encouraging foreign trade and welcoming the Christian missionaries.

Nobunaga was essentially a ruthless tyrant who was extremely self-willed. For example, he had a young serving maid executed because she had not cleaned the room thoroughly—she had left a stem of a fruit on the floor. He was also a vindictive man. A man once took a shot at him and was captured many years later. Nobunaga had the man buried in the ground with only his head exposed and had it sawed off. He was particularly merciless in his treatment of Buddhist monks. In addition to the massacre of the monks of Mt. Hiei, he at one time had one hundred and fifty monks who were attached to the Takeda clan's family temple burned to death merely because they had performed funeral services for the departed chief of the clan.

TOYOTOMI HIDEYOSHI

The man who succeeded Nobunaga as the foremost general of the land was born a son of a peasant in Owari. He left his stepfather's home when he was fifteen and became a servant of one of Imagawa's vassals. A few years later he entered Nobunaga's service as his sandal holder. He gained his master's recognition and eventually rose in rank, becoming one of Nobunaga's most successful generals. When he received word of Mitsuhide's mutiny, he quickly made peace with the Mōri forces, returned to Kyoto, and avenged his master's death. He then eliminated in battle those generals who were likely to challenge his claim to leadership as Nobunaga's successor, including the latter's son. He also managed to subdue the regional forces capable of threatening his aspirations for national leadership. He failed, however, to remove the man who was potentially his most dangerous foe, Tokugawa Ieyasu. With Ieyasu, Hideyoshi was compelled to conclude a negotiated peace. Otherwise he succeeded in gaining the allegiance or subduing all the major daimyō—the Hōjō clan in the Kantō region, the Date family in the north, the Shimazu forces in Kyushu, the Chōsogabe family in Shikoku, and the Mōri clan in western Honshu.

By 1590 Hideyoshi had accomplished what Nobunaga had failed to achieve: he had completed the task of national unification. All of his former rivals recognized his supreme authority as overlord and became his vassals, holding their domains as fiefs. They were no longer independent warlords beholden to no one. True, Ieyasu had not capitulated completely, but the two leaders had agreed to a truce. Hideyoshi sought to bind Ieyasu closely to him by adopting his son and by having Ieyasu marry his sister. Ieyasu supported Hideyoshi in the latter's campaign against the Hōjō clan and was given their Kantō holdings as a reward. In return, however, he was asked to relinquish his former holdings in the central region. This was no great sacrifice, since Ieyasu's new holdings —eight provinces—were immense. His domain constituted a little empire in itself, valued at 2.5 million koku.[1] Ieyasu built his castle in Edo (Tokyo) and consolidated his position in the Kantō region. His status was not that of a subservient vassal of Hideyoshi but virtually that of an ally.

Hideyoshi was made regent (kampaku) in 1585 and was appointed chancellor (dajō daijin) the following year. He also coveted the position of shōgun, but it had become customary to appoint only the descendants of the Minamoto family to that position. Hideyoshi contemplated having Ashikaga Yoshiaki adopt him as his son to qualify him for the post, but when he was appointed regent he pursued the shogunate no further.

Hideyoshi triumphed in the scramble for national supremacy by his superior generalship and his ability to make bold decisions and take resolute action. He could be ruthless but also magnanimous and is regarded as having been less cruel than Nobunaga had been. He was not as relentless in punishing his foes, permitting them to survive if they submitted. His vassals lived in fear of him nevertheless. A Jesuit missionary, Luis Frois, observed, "he is so feared and obeyed that with no less ease than a father of a family disposes of the persons of his household he rules the principal kings and lords of Japan." [2] Like all warlords of his era, he, too, had a vicious streak in him. He had adopted his nephew as his heir, but when his own son was born, he eliminated his adopted son by accusing him of disloyalty and forcing him to commit suicide. He then had the latter's wife, three young children, mistresses, and servants all put to the sword. Their bodies were thrown into a pit as if they were animals—hence their grave came to be known as "animal mound." When some unknown persons scribbled abusive remarks on his gate, Hideyoshi had eight townspeople of Kyoto arrested. On the first day he had their noses sliced off, the second day their ears, and on the third day they were strung upside down and impaled.

Hideyoshi was inordinately ambitious and, not satisfied with his conquests in Japan, harbored grandiose visions of building a great East

---

[1] The value of the fiefs was assessed in terms of the amount of rice they produced. In 1598 the official estimate of the rice yield of the entire land came to about 18.5 million koku. A koku equals 4.96 bushels.

[2] Quoted in James Murdoch, *A History of Japan*, 3 vols. (New York, Ungar, 1964), vol. 2, p. 209.

Asian empire. After subduing all of Japan he turned his attention abroad to Korea and China and launched an invasion of the continent.

Evidently Hideyoshi had only a vague notion about Korea and China and undertook the invasion without weighing carefully the implications of this move. He seemed to have regarded Korea as an extension of Japan, a land that he could conquer in the same manner in which he had subdued the daimyō. Perhaps there was some economic motivation involved such as the desire to control the trade with Korea. The merchants of Sakai were known to have favored expanding commercial contacts with Korea and China. Hideyoshi may have also wished to acquire more land to distribute among his followers and at the same time to use the expedition as a means of channeling the energies of the samurai—many of whom were unemployed—now that there was no outlet in Japan. Apparently there was also a general imperialistic spirit rising in Japan. The desire to expand abroad is reflected in the fact that a number of people emigrated to Southeast Asia during this period. Thus around the same time that England was emerging as a major sea power and expanding abroad, Japan, too, seemed to be on the verge of rising as a major colonial power, propelled by the people's desire to seek new havens and embark on new adventures.

It may also be that Hideyoshi's desire for personal glory, a megalomaniacal urge to leave his mark on history, was behind the Korean venture. In May, 1586, before he had subdued all his foes in Japan, he expressed to a Jesuit priest his wish to conquer Korea and China. He remarked that "his sole ambition was to leave a great name behind him after his death, for which reason he had resolved . . . to cross the sea at the head of a vast expeditionary force with the object of conquering Korea and China." [3] He asked the Jesuits to charter for him two large Portuguese galleons for this purpose. In return he offered to build churches throughout China and to force the populace to embrace Christianity en masse.

In 1593 Hideyoshi boasted to the Franciscan ambassador from the Philippines, "When I was born, a sunbeam fell on my chest and when the diviners were asked about this, they told me that I was to be the ruler of all that lies between east and west." The ambassador related that "he said that the people of Luzon should obey him; if they did not, he would send his men against them because they had nothing to do as there were no wars at the time in Japan." [4] He did send several messages to the Spanish governor of the Philippines demanding his submission.

[3] Charles R. Boxer, *The Christian Century in Japan, 1549–1650* (Berkeley, Calif.: University of California Press, 1951), pp. 140–41.

[4] Michael Cooper, S.J., ed., *They Came to Japan: An Anthology of European Reports on Japan, 1543–1640* (Berkeley, Calif.: University of California Press, 1965), p. 111.

Although his words regarding the Philippines remained idle threats, he did take action against Korea.

In the spring of 1592, Hideyoshi sent an expeditionary force of over 150,000 men into the peninsula. His armies—led by Konishi Yukinaga, a Christian general who came from a merchant family in Sakai, and by Katō Kiyomasa, who rose from the lower ranks with Hideyoshi—were able to move rapidly north and to capture Seoul in less than a month. Elated, Hideyoshi wrote his nephew, "I now intend to command the country of the Great Ming. And I shall appoint you Kwampaku [viceroy] of Han [China]." He also planned to send the Japanese Emperor to Peking and even began thinking of the possibility of conquering India.

But as the Japanese forces moved further north, they began to encounter greater difficulties. Japanese naval forces were not powerful enough to control the seas, and Korean warships equipped with guns and incendiary missiles were able to prevent Hideyoshi from sending his troops sufficient supplies and reinforcements. Moreover, as the Japanese approached the Chinese border, the Ming government became alarmed and sent its troops into Korea to stop Hideyoshi's armies. After several major but indecisive battles, an armistice was agreed upon. Negotiations on the final settlement of the war were entered into but the talks dragged on for two years without any conclusive agreement. Hideyoshi failed even to obtain the terms that the Ming officials had originally accepted. The Ming Emperor was misled by his officials into believing that Hideyoshi was prepared to become his vassal and sent an envoy to formalize the relationship. Hideyoshi, on the other hand, had been led to believe by his subordinates that the Chinese were ready to accept him as their Emperor. When he realized that the Ming government was not about to submit to his wishes, he exploded in anger and launched another invasion of Korea in 1597. A force of about 140,000 men was sent overseas again. The invading armies were once more initially successful, but before a decisive victory was won, Hideyoshi died in August, 1598, and the expeditionary forces were withdrawn. The fact that Hideyoshi's death resulted in the immediate termination of the plan to conquer Korea and China would seem to indicate that the scheme was primarily Hideyoshi's own creation and did not represent any underlying factors that engendered an inexorable drive for expansion into the continent.

For Korea these military attacks wrought devastation and desolation of the land and starvation and death for the populace. When the Chinese commander recaptured Seoul during the first invasion, he found that

> the country all about was lying fallow, and a great famine
> stared the Koreans in the face. . . . Famishing men fought

and killed each other, the victors eating the vanquished, sucking the marrow from the bones, and then dying themselves of surfeit. . . . This state of things naturally brought on an epidemic of the native fever . . . and the dead bodies of its victims lay all along the road.[5]

Not all Japanese were elated with Hideyoshi's Korean campaign. Hearing of the impending invasion of Korea, a monk in Nara wrote in his diary, "As I think of the suffering and vicissitudes that will befall all segments of that society, I feel nothing but sorrow for their plight. . . . It is indeed difficult to understand the reason for this unprecedented undertaking." [6]

HIDEYOSHI'S DOMESTIC POLICIES

Once Hideyoshi had subdued all of his foes and consolidated his position at home, he proceeded to stabilize the social order. During the period of strife, the peasants, suffering from the predatory actions of the warring factions, often banded together to protect themselves. As we saw earlier, peasant uprisings against the moneylenders occurred frequently. Many peasants also left the soil to seek refuge in the provinces of the more powerful or more benevolent lords. Thus there was considerable mobility and disorder in the countryside.

In order to restore order and stability, and in effect freeze the social order, Hideyoshi issued a decree in 1586 forbidding the peasants to move from the land. This sort of ban had been imposed by many daimyō at the local level prior to this, but under Hideyoshi it became a national policy. In 1591 he reiterated the ban against movement from the soil and decreed severe penalties not only against the peasants who left the land but also against those who aided or abetted a peasant's flight. At the same time, he prohibited the lower-class samurai from becoming farmers, merchants, or artisans and forbade all vassals from leaving the service of a lord without his consent.

In 1588 Hideyoshi issued a decree ordering the peasants to turn in all their weapons—swords and firearms—to the ruling authorities. During the period of disorder, many peasants fought as warriors; Hideyoshi himself had risen from the ranks of the peasantry. Many samurai, on the other hand, had tilled their own farms. This decree, which started the so-called sword hunt, was designed to make the class distinctions between the samurai and the peasants rigid and at the same time prevent the peasants from causing any trouble in the countryside. Hideyoshi's object

---

[5] Quoted in Murdoch, *op. cit.,* p. 346.

[6] Hayashiya Tatsusaburō, *Tenka Tōitsu* (*Unification of the Land*) (Tokyo: Chūō Kōronsha, 1966), p. 476.

was to bind the peasants to the soil and turn them into a class of serfs. The decree stated:

> The people of the various provinces are strictly forbidden to have in their possession any swords, short swords, bows, spears, firearms or other types of arms. The possession of unnecessary implements [of war] makes difficult the collection of taxes and dues and tends to foment uprisings. . . . Therefore the heads of provinces, official agents, and deputies are ordered to collect all the weapons mentioned above and turn them over to the government.[7]

Another measure taken by Hideyoshi to extend his control over the countryside was the nationwide cadastral survey that was conducted during 1582–1598. This survey enabled him to assess the value of the lands and check the legality of landholdings. The findings determined the amount of tax the peasants had to pay on each piece of land. Taxation rates differed according to locality, but generally the peasants were expected to turn over to the lord 50 percent of the crop. (Because the practice was not uniform, some lords demanded as much as 70 percent while others asked for less than 30 percent.) In time of crop failure, however, instead of gaining relief, they were expected to pay up to two-thirds of the harvest.

Hideyoshi called for a ruthless implementation of the land survey. He instructed one of the daimyō in charge of the survey:

> If any manorial lord objects to it, drive him and his vassals into the castle and annihilate them. Adopt the same policy towards the peasants. If they complain, kill all the peasants in the village. Even if the entire area or province is turned into a wasteland it would not matter. Go deep into the mountains and far across the seas in order to conduct a thoroughgoing survey.[8]

His order was followed faithfully by his officials. In other respects, too, Hideyoshi employed harsh measures against the peasants. He decreed that any peasant asking for tax exemptions (and any official who indulged the peasants in this matter as well) be punished. Peasants who neglected to work the land were also chastised.

---

[7] Ryusaku Tsunoda, W. T. de Bary, and Donald Keene, eds., *Sources of Japanese Tradition* (New York: Columbia University Press, 1958), p. 329.

[8] Okada Akio *et al., Nihon no Rekishi (A History of Japan),* 12 vols. (Tokyo: Yomiuri Shimbunsha, 1959–1960), vol. 7, p. 114.

When the cadastral survey was conducted, it was decided to use the koku as the standard of measurement for rice rather than the *kan* (8.27 lbs.), which had been used prior to this. The daimyō and warriors' land allotments were calculated in terms of the amount of rice they were entitled to receive as stipends. If a samurai's stipend was to be 100 koku of rice, he was given a fief that supposedly produced that amount. For his actual income he then levied rice rents on the peasants in his fief. If he imposed a 50 percent levy, his income amounted to 50 koku.

In order to minimize the threat from the daimyō, Hideyoshi sought to prevent them from joining forces against him. Daimyō families were prohibited from establishing marital ties without his permission and were forbidden to make military alliances or political agreements. Hideyoshi could and did move the daimyō around to different provinces to prevent them from becoming entrenched in one region. He stationed those whom he trusted in strategic areas and placed mutually hostile lords next to each other so they might check one another. He held about 2 million koku as his own demesne. These holdings were scattered throughout the country. In order to strengthen his financial position he controlled the gold and silver mines and exploited them intensively. He also maintained close control over the merchants of Kyoto and Sakai in order to exploit their financial resources.

MOMOYAMA CULTURE

The era covering roughly the years in which Nobunaga, Hideyoshi, and Ieyasu dominated the land is referred to as the Momoyama period in art history. The term Momoyama comes from the site near Kyoto where Hideyoshi built his Fushimi Castle.

The art of this period conveys a sense of vigor and vitality. The symbolic representation of the temper of the age is found in the castles built by the military leaders. These were massive fortresses designed for defense against armies equipped with firearms. They were usually patterned after Western fortifications, surrounded by a series of walls and moats. The castle itself consisted of a central tower flanked by a number of smaller ones. The main tower was usually six or seven stories high and was used as a final holdout. At the base of the superstructure were huge stone blocks. The entire edifice, with its white plastered walls and handsome tile roofs, usually dominated the surrounding landscape. Himeji Castle west of Osaka is the best preserved of the fortresses of this period.

Nobunaga built a huge castle in Azuchi near Kyoto, but it was destroyed in the conflict that was touched off by Mitsuhide's rebellion. Its main tower was seven stories high and the rooms were elaborately decorated, containing paintings by the leading artist of this age, Kanō

Himeji Castle in Hyōgo Prefecture took nine years to build; it was completed in 1609. Courtesy of the Consulate General of Japan, New York.

Eitoku. Hideyoshi constructed two massive fortresses, one in Osaka and the other in Fushimi. The former had forty-eight large towers; the main tower stood on a stone base 75 feet high, above which it rose 102 feet. Both of Hideyoshi's castles were destroyed in battle, but the Osaka castle was later rebuilt and is now equipped with an elevator. Many of the components of the Fushimi castle were removed to the Nishi-Honganji, headquarters of the True Pure Land Sect, and have been preserved to the present.

The construction of these castles and palaces fostered the other arts because the interiors of these edifices were elaborately decorated with painted walls, sliding doors, folding screens, and wood carvings. In tune with the military spirit of the age the predominant style of painting was vigorous and colorful. It was also grander in scale than that of the previous era, when elegance and gracefulness had been emphasized. Ink monochrome flourished in the preceding age but now opaque, bright color was used. The sliding doors and screens were painted in strong colors against backgrounds of gold leaf. The most renowned painter of this period was Kanō Eitoku (1543–1590), who painted for both Nobunaga and Hideyoshi. Unfortunately only a few of his innumerable works have survived, but those that remain are thought to typify his style: flat space, bold and simple designs, and bright colors. Some art historians consider Hasegawa Tōhaku (1539–1610) a greater artist than Eitoku. Tōhaku painted both in monochrome and color. He patterned his black-and-white paintings after the Chinese master, Mu Ch'i, using the soft-ink style in which everything is suggested rather than explicitly stated. In the use of color, also, he was a master, producing the finest works of this age. The paintings on sliding doors attributed to him display the brillance of color and boldness of design manifested by Eitoku but also show a delicacy of detail and a greater concern for perspective.

The warriors of this period displayed a great interest in the tea ceremony, resulting in the construction of a large number of teahouses and fostering of the craft of pottery. Hideyoshi was one of the most enthusiastic practioners of the ceremony, sponsoring elaborate tea parties. He enlisted the master of the tea ceremony, Sen-no-Rikyū, who also served Nobunaga, as one of his advisers. Sen-no-Rikyū, a Zen Buddhist, perfected the art of tea ceremony and gave it the simplicity, restraint, and austerity traditionally associated with it. He not only prescribed the form of the ceremony but the kind of utensils to be used, the design of the tearoom, and the setting in which the teahouse should be located. Unfortunately for Sen-no-Rikyū he got embroiled in political intrigues, lost Hideyoshi's favor, and was compelled to commit hara-kiri.

Stimulated by the demand for tea bowls, pottery making flourished, resulting in what is regarded as the golden age of ceramics. Glazed wares reflecting Korean influence as well as plain unglazed pottery were produced. The *Shino* wares, with their heavy translucent white glaze applied thickly and unevenly and then embellished with simple abstract designs; the *Oribe* wares, which took a great variety of shapes and ornaments; the *Raku* wares, usually black, with strong, simple shapes; and the *Karatsu* wares, with a brownish-gray crackled glaze and free flowing abstract designs, were some of the noteworthy products of this era.

CONTACT WITH THE WEST

In 1543 some Portuguese seamen whose vessel was blown off course landed on the island of Tanegashima off the shore of southern Kyushu. They were followed by Portuguese traders who arrived to establish commercial relations with Japan. The Portuguese were in turn followed by the Spanish, who first arrived in 1584. The city of Nagasaki became the main port of entry for traders.

The Western merchants brought to Japan silk fabrics, gold, sugar, perfume, medicinal herbs, and apparel from China, India, and other Asian countries. With the introduction of firearms in Japan, the demand for imported lead and nitrate also increased. In return Japan exported silver, copper, lacquerware, and pottery. Silver was one of Japan's main attractions for the Western traders. Some historians estimate that Japan was probably producing at that time one-third of the silver in the world.

The Dutch and the British soon followed the Portuguese and Spanish to Japan. The first Dutch ship arrived in 1600; the British came in 1613. Eventually the Dutch replaced the Portuguese as the chief Western traders in Japan.

The advent of the Western merchants stimulated Japanese interest in overseas trade, and they, too, began to send merchantmen to the south. Around the middle of the sixteenth century Japanese vessels sailed to Formosa, Luzon, Indochina, and Siam. Both Hideyoshi and Ieyasu issued official certificates stamped with red seals to Japanese ships (thus known as *goshuinsen,* or red-seal ships) engaging in overseas commerce. Only those vessels possessing these certificates were permitted to participate in foreign trade. The Japanese merchantmen of this period averaged 200 to 300 tons in size.

As commercial contacts with Southeast Asia increased, a number of Japanese—mostly merchants, masterless samurai, and Christians—began emigrating to such places as the Philippines, Annam, Cambodia, Java, and Siam, establishing Japanese settlements. It is estimated that in 1621 there were three thousand Japanese living near Manila. The Japanese population in Siam was about fourteen or fifteen thousand. The leader of the Siamese settlement, Yamada Nagamasa, became a prominent general at the court of Siam. When the Tokugawa Bakufu adopted a policy of national seclusion in the 1630s, these emigrants were isolated from their homeland and were eventually assimilated into the societies where they had settled.

CHRISTIANITY IN JAPAN

In 1542 St. Francis Xavier, who had helped to found the Jesuit Order, arrived in Goa in India to spread Christianity in Asia. He went to Kagoshima in 1549 and received permission from the daimyō of Satsuma to spread his religion there. From Satsuma he traveled to Hirado near Nagasaki and then to Yamaguchi and eventually to Kyoto for a brief stay. At the end of 1551 he left Japan to return to Goa, leaving behind about a thousand Christian converts. Other dedicated missionaries such as Luis Frois and Alexander Valignano arrived to take St. Francis's place.

The missionaries were generally favorably received by the Kyushu daimyō, who were motivated in part by the desire to engage in trade with the Western countries. By 1569 there were fifteen thousand converts in the Nagasaki area. The missionaries' task was facilitated by the fact that several daimyō became Christians and then compelled their followers to accept the religion. As a result, the Jesuits won many converts among the samurai class. Among the early daimyō converts were Ōtomo Sōrin of Bungo and Ōmura Sumitada of Hizen. In 1582 they sent four youths to Rome to see the Pope. Date Masamune, a daimyō of northern Japan, although not a Christian, sent an embassy of over sixty persons to Rome in 1613 primarily to facilitate trade with Spain. The embassy went to Rome by way of the Philippines, Mexico, and Spain, and returned in 1620 by the same route, after a two-year stopover in the Philippines.

The Christian missionaries were aided greatly by the fact that Nobunaga gave them his enthusiastic support. He did so in order to weaken and undermine his political foes, the Buddhists. A Jesuit missionary, Coehlo, observed, "This man seems to have been chosen by God to open and prepare the way for our holy faith. . . . In proportion to the intensity of his enmity to the bonzes [Buddhist monks] and their sects, is his good will towards our Fathers who preach the law of God." [9]

In 1560 the Jesuits had received permission to preach their religion in Kyoto, but in 1565, because of the complaints of the Nichiren Sect, the Emperor had prohibited the propagation of Christianity and compelled the missionaries to leave the capital. In 1568, when Nobunaga gained control of Kyoto, he lifted this ban. He also assisted in the construction of chapels in Kyoto and Azuchi. By 1576 there were over twenty thousand converts in the Kyoto-Osaka area alone. In 1582 it was estimated that there were about 150,000 Christians and 200 chapels throughout the country.

Although initially the missionaries were welcomed by the ruling class, who believed they could facilitate trade with the West and also inculcate such virtues as obedience and humility among the people, some men came to recognize the potential danger Christianity posed. A devout Christian might make an obedient vassal, but ultimately he was expected

---

[9] Quoted in Murdoch, *op. cit.*, p. 167.

to serve and obey a higher authority, God. If ever a Christian's duty to his master and his duty to God came into conflict, he was expected to choose God. When some samurai abandoned their masters for God and some children left their parents for their new faith, a sense of uneasiness began to beset some members of the ruling class. Nonetheless the future of Christianity in Japan appeared to be bright even after Nobunaga was eliminated by Mitsuhide. Then in 1587 Hideyoshi suddenly moved against the Christian missionaries, ordering them to leave the country within twenty days. He did not require the Japanese converts to renounce their faith, but he forbade Christian daimyō and samurai from forcing their religion upon the inhabitants in their fiefs. Upper-class samurai were prohibited from adopting Christianity without official permission.

Hideyoshi's motives for this action have remained elusive. When he succeeded Nobunaga as the overlord of Japan, he did not change his predecessor's policy toward Christianity. In fact, he seemed to be sympathetic to the missionaries, and granted them the same favors that Nobunaga had accorded them. He was certainly not sympathetic to the Buddhists whose power he sought to undermine. In the battle with the Shimazu forces of southern Kyushu, he had the support of the Christian daimyō of northern Kyushu. Apparently, Hideyoshi's physician was anti-Christian and filled his ears with the dangers and evils of Christianity. When Hideyoshi ordered one of his Christian vassals to renounce his religion and was disobeyed he suddenly issued the anti-Christian decree.

Just prior to issuing the ban Hideyoshi asked Coelho these questions: (1) Why do the missionaries seek to persuade his vassals to become Christians? (2) Why do they persecute Buddhist monks and destroy their temples? (3) Why do they eat beef when cattle are useful to mankind? (4) Why do the Portuguese buy the people of Japan and export them as slaves? These may have been some of the issues brought to his attention by his doctor and other anti-Christian advisers. It was true that the Portuguese traders did purchase a number of Japanese, particularly young boys and girls, to be sold abroad as slaves. They were sold not only to other Asian countries but some ended up in places as distant as Mexico and Argentina. The Jesuits were, of course, opposed to this practice and had the Portuguese king issue a decree against the slave trade in 1571, but there was no way to enforce the ban. Hideyoshi was concerned about this problem. He was also critical of the Westerners' custom of eating meat. When he issued the edict restricting Christian missionary activities, he also issued decrees against slavery and meat-eating.

Differences in other customs and moral standards caused some friction between the missionaries and the Japanese. One issue the missionaries were critical of was the loose sexual standards of the Japanese men, who in effect practiced polygamy. The upper-class men, in particular, had many concubines. Hideyoshi remarked, perhaps in jest, that if it were not for the Christian insistence on monogamy, he, too, might become a convert. The Jesuits were also critical of the practice of pederasty, which was common among the upper classes.

Initially, Hideyoshi did not rigorously enforce his decree against the Christians. The missionaries were not made to leave the country, as called for by the edict. As a result they looked upon Hideyoshi's anti-Christian outburst as an act of caprice. Although there was some reason to believe that the spread of Christianity might disturb the political order, Hideyoshi seemed unconcerned about the presence of the Christian daimyō. If any problems arose he was in a position to deal with them decisively. For instance, when the lord of the Nagasaki, Ōmura, turned the city over to the Christian Church and forbade the residence there of non-Christians, Hideyoshi appointed a deputy to govern the city and removed it from the Church's control.

Even after the ban, then, missionary work was conducted by the Jesuits, who were, however, very circumspect in their behavior so that Hideyoshi's wrath would not be again aroused, but new difficulties arose when another group of missionaries, the Franciscans, arrived from the Philippines in 1593. They, too, were received cordially by Hideyoshi. Being unfamiliar with the situation that prevailed in Japan, they were less discreet and more zealous in their work. Soon a rivalry between the Jesuits and the Franciscans developed. The Jesuits had hoped to retain a monopoly in spreading Christianity in Japan and had sought to keep the Franciscans out. The way in which the two orders went about their work was different: the Jesuits concentrated on converting the upper classes, while the Franciscans won more converts among the poorer classes. The Jesuits did not think highly of the "poxy lepers" and seedy ragamuffins who frequented the Franciscan hospices. While the "blind, halt, burned, deaf, dumb, lame—nearly all lepers" went to the Franciscan centers, the stately samurai attended the tea ceremonies held at the Jesuit establishments. The rivalry was evidently stimulated in part by the antagonism between Portugal and Spain—the Jesuits came from the former, the Franciscans from the latter.

For about ten years after the anti-Christian edict was issued the missionaries were permitted to carry on their work, but in 1597 they began to encounter more serious difficulties. In the fall of 1596 a Spanish galleon was shipwrecked off the coast of Shikoku. This offered Hideyoshi a chance to confiscate its rich cargo, and while he was deciding what to do with the vessel, the Spanish pilot-major, perhaps hoping to intimidate the Japanese officials, boasted that it was usual procedure for Christian missionaries to be followed by Spanish conquerors. This seemed to confirm what Hideyoshi's anti-Christian advisers had been telling him, so he decided to apprehend and execute the Franciscan missionaries who were working in the Osaka-Kyoto area. In late 1596 six Franciscan missionaries, fifteen Japanese Franciscan neophytes, and three Japanese Jesuit lay brothers, who were included by mistake, were arrested, paraded through the streets of Kyoto, Osaka, and Sakai, and then marched on to Nagasaki. In February, 1597, the twenty-four victims, plus two more neophytes who were apprehended along the way, were crucified, becoming the first Christian martyrs in Japan. Before he could start any large-scale persecution, however, Hideyoshi died, and the Christians enjoyed a short breathing spell under Ieyasu, who succeeded him as the overlord of Japan.

Ieyasu was also interested in expanding foreign commerce and opened all the ports to trade without any restrictions. As part of this policy he tolerated the Christian missionaries, although he did not retract the ban imposed against them by Hideyoshi. Consequently the missionary work continued. Before long, however, Ieyasu also concluded that Christianity was a potential political menace. There is some reason to believe that fear of the Catholic powers was instilled in the minds of the Japanese authorities by the Catholics' Protestant rivals, the Dutch. For instance, in 1610 the stadholder of the Netherlands sent a message to Ieyasu asserting that the object of the Catholics was to foment political dissension and civil strife. Moreover, unsavory behavior by some Japanese Christian officials undermined Ieyasu's complacency about the prevalence of Christian converts in Japan. With the way of distrust thus paved, the commissioner of Nagasaki had little trouble persuading Ieyasu to adopt an anti-Christian policy. Finally, on January 27, 1614, Ieyasu issued an edict banning the religion. Everyone was required to become a member of one of the major Buddhist sects, and records were kept on the people's religious affiliations. It is believed that there were about 300,000—some estimates run as high as 700,000—Christians in Japan when the edict was issued. Most of them were concentrated in northern Kyushu, with Nagasaki as the center, but some Christians could be found even in the northernmost areas of Honshu.

Persecution of Christians now began in earnest. The missionaries were ordered to leave the country. Many stayed behind, however, and went into hiding, but this time there were no powerful Christian daimyō to protect them and the converts. Daimyō who were suspected of harboring pro-Christian sentiments were compelled to prove their loyalty to the shogunate by purging their fiefs of Christians. Those who refused to renounce Christianity were burned to death. After Ieyasu's death in 1616, the attempt to root out Christians was carried out with even greater vigor. Hidetada, Ieyasu's successor, reiterated the decree ordering the missionaries to leave the country. Anyone helping them to hide was punished. To demonstrate its determination to root out Christianity, in September, 1622, the Bakufu publicly burned or decapitated fifty-five Christians in Nagasaki, including women and children.

The third Tokukawa shōgun, Iemitsu, who came to power in 1623, was an even more cold-blooded persecutor of the Christians than his father had been and often attended the torture sessions himself. A growing number of Christians were forced to become apostates through force and torture. The most common methods of torture were by water, fire, mutilation, and hanging into a pit headfirst. Ironically enough, the samurai tended to apostatize more readily than the common people —"the lame and the halt"—who had been converted by the Franciscans. Those who refused to renounce their faith were executed. Before their execution some were thrown into prisons so overcrowded that there was barely enough room to move. They were forced to endure terrible hunger, thirst, filth, stench, and disease. Often they were left there to rot. Frequently when a prisoner died, the corpse was left there for days. During the period from 1614 to 1640 between five and six thousand Christians were executed.

The climax of the anti-Christian campaign came with the Shimabara Rebellion of 1637–1638, involving Christians from Shimabara Peninsula and the nearby island of Amakusa, where Christianity had been firmly implanted. There were about ten thousand Christians in Amakusa Island, and when, at the beginning of the seventeenth century, the daimyō sought to eradicate the religion he failed because of popular resistance. When persecution became more severe, most of the Christians renounced their religion outwardly but remained Christians at heart. In 1633 a new daimyō was enfeoffed who mercilessly taxed the impoverished peasants. The people of Shimabara, too, were suffering at the hands of a brutal and rapacious daimyō, who tortured and abused those who were unable to pay their taxes. The peasants of Shimabara finally staged a general uprising against the daimyō in 1637.

Although the rebellion may have started out as a protest against the taxation policies of the lord, it soon took on a religious hue. The rebels openly proclaimed their adherence to Christianity and shouted the names of Jesus, Maria, and Santiago during their attacks. From Shimabara the rebellion spread to Amakusa, where the rebels chose a sixteen-year-old youth, Amakusa Shirō (1621–1638), as their leader. They also had the support of several resourceful masterless warriors who provided them with military leadership. After the Amakusa rebels were defeated on the island, they went to Shimabara and joined the insurgents there. About thirty-seven thousand people, including women and children, entrenched themselves in a strategically located castle and defied the Bakufu's forces that besieged them. They were finally reduced to near starvation and the stronghold was taken. Virtually all of the insurgents in the castle were massacred. The siege had lasted for three months, and the Bakufu had employed over 100,000 warriors against them, suffering a loss of 13,000 men.

The Shimabara Rebellion spelled the end of Japanese contact with the outside world. Indeed, the process of curbing Japanese relations with the external world had started earlier. In 1616 all foreign merchantmen, except those from China, were prohibited from entering ports other than Nagasaki and Hirado. Foreigners were permitted to reside only in Edo, Kyoto, and Sakai. In 1624 the Spanish were denied the right to trade with Japan, and the British voluntarily abandoned their attempts to develop commerce there. In 1633 Japanese ships without official authorization were prohibited from leaving the country. In 1636 all Japanese ships without exception were forbidden to leave Japan. Not only could the Japanese no longer go abroad, but those who had gone abroad were prevented from returning. In 1639, after the Shimabara Rebellion, the final edict, calling for a strict policy of seclusion, was issued. No foreign ships were allowed to enter Japanese ports, except the Dutch and the Chinese, who were allowed to trade at the small island of Deshima in Nagasaki Bay under restricted circumstances. The Dutch tradesmen were allowed to reside only on the island and could not travel elsewhere without special permission.

Initially there were no restrictions on trade with China. In 1685, however, the outflow of silver to China was limited to 6,000 kan (about 49,620 lbs.) and that to Holland to 3,000 kan. After 1715 only thirty Chinese ships were allowed to come to Japan each year, while Holland was permitted to send two vessels only. Export of copper was also restricted at this time. In 1813 the number of Chinese merchantmen allowed to call annually was reduced to ten.

All books from the West were banned in order to prevent Christian ideas from entering the country. From time to time Christians were uncovered and were either punished or executed. Between 1664 and 1667 two thousand Christians were arrested. The government remained vigilant, and it appeared as if Christianity had been successfully rooted out. But many hidden Christians survived, and when religious freedom was restored in the nineteenth century, a number of Christian families came out of hiding in the area around Nagasaki.

Japan was to remain closed to most of the world until Commodore Perry's arrival in 1853. This decision to sever external contacts was a momentous one for it meant that Japan was to be virtually cut off from the great scientific, technological, and industrial developments that unfolded in the West in the following two-and-a-half centuries.

THE INTRODUCTION OF WESTERN THINGS

As we noted earlier, the Portuguese introduction of muskets to Japan changed the mode of warfare. The construction of castles was also affected by the Western mode of building fortresses. Western navigation and ship-building techniques as well as Western mining techniques were adopted. Movable type was introduced to Japan by Valignano, and initially the Japanese used it to print a number of books. Woodblock printing was found to be easier to produce, however, so movable type ceased to be used. Western-style oil painting was also introduced at this time, and for a period the naturalistic style of the West was employed by some Japanese artists. Aside from Christian texts, the only literary work that was brought to Japan by the missionaries was *Aesop's Fables*.

The kind of commodities introduced from the outside was indicated by the new words, derived from Portuguese or Spanish, that came into use. These included birōdo (*velludo,* velvet), rasha (*raxa,* woolen cloth), sarasa (*sarsa,* printed cotton), jiban (*gibao,* underwear), kappa (*capa,* waterproof coat), shabon (*jabon,* soap), karuta (*carta,* cards), and tabako tobacco). Among the new words for foods were jagaimo (*jacatra,* pota-toes), kabocha (*camboja,* pumpkins), pan (*pan,* bread), and kasutera (*castella,* sponge cake). Even the popular Japanese dish tempura came from Portugal (*temporas,* meatless Friday). In addition, such articles as clocks, telescope lenses, and eyeglasses were introduced.

CHAPTER 7

THE EARLY TOKUGAWA PERIOD

With the death of Hideyoshi we enter a unique period in Japanese history: two-and-a-half centuries of military rule in which political peace and social stability were maintained. The Tokugawa rulers set about deliberately to freeze the political and social order and achieved their objectives remarkably well. Here, cut off from the rest of the world, was a small "world state." Arnold Toynbee characterizes the nature of this kind of world state in the following manner:

> The smallest human community constitutes the whole world for the people inside it if it is insulated from all other human communities on the face of the planet; and it will be insulated from them if its members feel that outsiders do not count. In this—and it is a very practical sense—even tiny Japan was a world state during her two centuries of insulation under the regime of the Tokugawa shoguns. . . . the world governments of the past have concentrated their energies on self-preservation; and they have tried to preserve themselves by a policy of freezing. They have tried to freeze not only their frontiers against the outer barbarians and not only the structure of public administration inside those frontiers; they have tried to freeze the private lives of their citizens as well. The most notorious recent instance of this policy is that of the Tokugawa regime in Japan.[1]

[1] Arnold Toynbee "How to Change the World without War," *Saturday Review,* May 12, 162, p. 17.

In this closed society the institutions, practices, values, attitudes, behavior, and mode of thinking of the Japanese were molded for two-and-a-half centuries. The present-day Japanese way of life and pattern of thinking cannot be clearly understood unless the nature of Tokugawa society is understood, for out of this setting the Japan and the Japanese of the nineteenth and twentieth centuries emerged.

THE TRIUMPH OF TOKUGAWA IEYASU

Of the three "unifiers" of sixteenth-century Japan, the man who finally triumphed and achieved the objective of establishing a new military dynasty was Ieyasu. He was the most patient, the shrewdest, and the luckiest of the three. Moreover, he had a broad vision—a historical perspective and political acumen—that the other two may have lacked. He was also willing to listen to criticisms about himself. "It is difficult," he said, "for anybody to recognize his own weaknesses. At the lower ranks friends and relatives can criticize each other. But those of higher standing do not have this advantage. They are approached by people who flatter them. . . . Thus, I appreciate all sorts of criticisms, even those dealing with minor faults." [2]

In order to survive in the ruthless world of the contending warlords, Ieyasu was willing to be just as pitiless as the next man. When Ieyasu and Nobunaga were allies, Nobunaga demanded that Ieyasu kill his wife and his son, who was married to Nobunaga's daughter, because he suspected them of intriguing against him. In order to avoid a conflict with the more powerful Nobunaga, Ieyasu complied by executing his wife and compelling his son to commit suicide. When Ieyasu set out to destroy the Toyotomi family he was merciless, sparing only two small children. Thousands of Toyotomi supporters were hunted down relentlessly, executed, and had their heads publicly exposed.

The experiences of his childhood taught Ieyasu to be patient and to endure hardships. His family, the Matsudaira clan, was a local power in Mikawa but was threatened by two powerful neighbors, the Oda and Imagawa clans. In order to avoid being crushed by them, Ieyasu's father allied himself with the more powerful Imagawa family and turned Ieyasu, who was then six, over to them as a hostage. Ieyasu was abducted by the Oda family, however, and remained their captive for two-and-a-half years. He was recaptured by the Imagawa forces and remained their hostage until the age of eighteen when, in 1560, Nobunaga defeated the Imagawa clan. After his liberation Ieyasu began building his family fortune in the Mikawa-Suruga region. As noted earlier, when Hideyoshi

---

[2] Watsuji Tetsurō, *Nihon Rinri Shisōshi* (*A History of Japanese Ethical Thought*), 2 vols. (Tokyo: Iwanami, 1952), vol. 2, pp. 372–73.

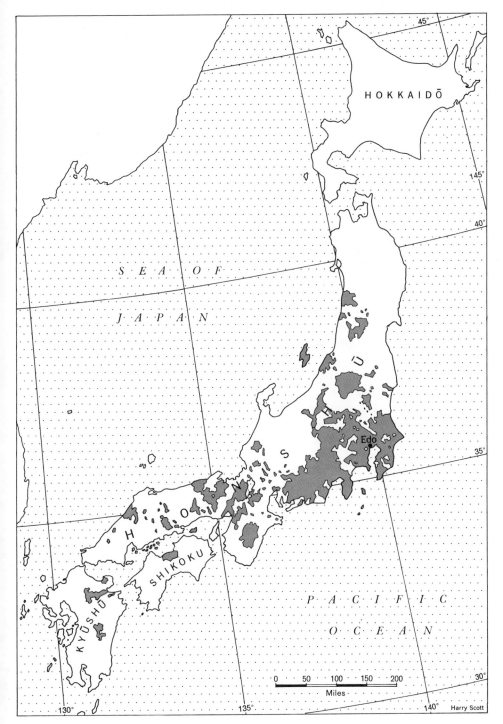

TOKUGAWA DOMAINS. 1664.

succeeded Nobunaga, Ieyasu had become such a formidable power that he could not be forcefully subjugated.

When Hideyoshi died his son and successor, Hideyori, was only five years old. Before his death Hideyoshi had established a council of five daimyō to assist Hideyori. The dominant figure in the group was Ieyasu, who soon made it clear that he had no intentions of being bound by the pledge to support Hideyori.

A development that played into Ieyasu's hand was the cleavage that occurred among Hideyoshi's generals between the "administrators" and the "combat officers." The former were led by Ishida Mitsunari (1560–1600); the latter included Katō Kiyomasa (1562–1611). The generals who made their reputation in the battlefields held in contempt those who had risen with the brush.

When it began to appear that Ieyasu was seeking to gather power in his own hands, Mitsunari called upon the Toyotomi family's loyal supporters to join forces with him to oust Ieyasu. This led to a great confrontation at Sekigahara in central Honshu in October, 1600. The two factions could be divided roughly into geographical regions: the western clans supported Mitsunari, while the eastern clans sided with Ieyasu. Hideyoshi's "combat officers," disliking Mitsunari, all joined Ieyasu's camp. A pitched battle was fought on the 20th of October, but Ieyasu managed to persuade one of Mitsunari's generals, a member of the Mōri clan, to become a turncoat and thus won the day. Mitsunari's faction suffered a crushing defeat, and Mitsunari himself was captured, paraded around Kyoto, Osaka, and Sakai, and executed. Ieyasu finally emerged as the successor to Hideyoshi.

Ieyasu proceeded immediately to confiscate the holdings of the daimyō who had supported Mitsunari. Some lost all their holdings, others had their fiefs reduced drastically. Toyotomi Hideyori was allowed to retain three provinces with 650,000 koku. His presence still posed a threat to the Tokugawa family because strong pro-Toyotomi sentiments prevailed in the land. Many generals loyal to the Toyotomi family had supported Ieyasu at Sekigahara merely because of their distrust and hatred of Mitsunari. Consequently Ieyasu was forced to exercise caution in dealing with the Toyotomi family. He succeeded in dividing the pro-Toyotomi faction by sowing seeds of mutual distrust among them. He had also bound many of Hideyoshi's former generals to him by rewarding them generously. Thus when he decided to move against the Toyotomi family, few generals came to their defense. A large number of masterless samurai, perhaps as many as 100,000, who were on the losing side in the Battle of Sekigahara did, however, come to their support. In the winter of 1614 Ieyasu sent his forces against the citadel of Osaka, but it proved to be impregnable. Thereupon Ieyasu offered to conclude an armistice if the Toyotomi faction would allow him to destroy some of the fortifications of Osaka Castle. The Toyotomi faction was under the impression that the agreement called for the destruction of the outer ramparts and the outer moat alone and agreed to the armistice. When the fighting ceased Ieyasu had his men fill in not only the outer moat but the two inner moats as well. This caused the Toyotomi faction to recommence fighting. This time, though, the Tokugawa forces were able to overrun the fortress and eliminate the Toyotomi family.

In 1603 Ieyasu was named shōgun. Unlike Hideyoshi he managed, by making appropriate changes in his family tree, to trace his ancestry back to the Minamoto clan. He retained Edo as his headquarters, and it became the de facto capital. In 1605 he resigned the post of shōgun in favor of his son, Hidetada (1579–1632), but until his death was the real wielder of power. He concentrated on organizing the political and social systems in such a way as to ensure the continuity of Tokugawa rule even after his death. In order to appreciate this continuity, however, one must first have an idea of the political events of the first half of the Tokugawa era.

In 1623 Hidetada was succeeded by Iemitsu (1604–1651), the able but ruthless shōgun who uprooted Christianity and closed the country. Iemitsu also tightened the Bakufu's control over the daimyō and instituted the system of *sankinkōtai* (see page 160), requiring the daimyō to spend every other year in Edo. In fact, the political system of the Tokugawa government acquired its basic form during Iemitsu's regime. In 1651 he was succeeded by Ietsuna (1641–1680). There was a minor disturbance during the latter's reign when some unemployed samurai, led by Yui Shōsetsu, plotted to overthrow the Bakufu, but the conspiracy was quashed before an uprising was ever staged. Ietsuna failed to play an active role in running the government and left the management of the affairs of state initially largely in the hands of his uncle, who acted as regent, and later to the councilors, who ruled the land as a committee. Since the personal leadership of the shōgun ceased to be important during Ietsuna's shogunate, when he died some of his councilors favored following the practice of the Kamakura Bakufu and proposed installing a member of the imperial family as the shōgun. The suggestion was rejected, however, and Ietsuna's younger brother, Tsunayoshi (1646–1709), was installed as shōgun in 1680.

During the first part of his regime Tsunayoshi was assisted by an able councilor, and he exercised strong leadership. During the latter half, however, his personal attendants and chamberlains gained considerable power, which they somewhat abused. Tsunayoshi became a protector of dogs because he was born in the year of the dog and was advised by a charlatan that he would have a male heir if he treated dogs in a kindly manner. Ultimately he became fanatical about this and severely punished anyone who harmed a dog. Engelbert Kaempfer, a German doctor who visited Japan during this period, observed: "Many a poor man hath been severely punished in this country, under the present Emperor's reign, purely for the sake of dogs." [3] Finally the shōgun forbade the killing of any living thing. One samurai was executed for killing a swallow. In Edo no fish, clams, or fowls could be sold. No one was to swat even a mosquito. Although Tsunayoshi's desire to protect living creatures was based partly on his Buddhist beliefs, he did not extend the principle of non-killing to human beings.

On the positive side, Tsunayoshi became interested in learning. He encouraged the study of Confucianism and established a Confucian academy. He also sponsored the compilation of histories.

Initially the Bakufu's finances were in good condition. But in succeeding generations the expenses mounted, while the revenues failed to keep pace. Many expensive projects were undertaken, such as the construction of the Tōshōgū Shrine in Nikkō honoring Ieyasu. The city of Edo experienced many devastating fires, and the silver and gold mines began producing less. Tsunayoshi not only led an extravagant life but also initiated a program of renovating many temples and shrines. Consequently the Bakufu's deficits continued to increase. In order to deal with the growing financial crisis, Tsunayoshi debased the coinage in 1695 and created an inflationary situation. Although the government's revenues were increased substantially by this means, deficits had again increased by the end of his reign. In 1708, in the last year of Tsunayoshi's rule, the Bakufu's revenues came to about 760,000 to 770,000 ryō, as opposed to expenditures of 1.4 million ryō.[4]

It was during Tsunayoshi's rule, however, that the culture of the townspeople flourished. This was the era of the Genroku culture that will be discussed in the next chapter. A famous incident involving forty-seven samurai who avenged the death of their lord also took place during Tsunayoshi's shogunate. It came to be cited as a shining example of faithful warriors who fulfilled their obligations to their lord.

The sixth shōgun, Ienobu (1663–1713), employed one of the most able of the Tokugawa scholars, Arai Hakuseki (1657–1725), to correct the abuses of the previous regime. One of the first things the new shōgun did was to withdraw the edict protecting all living creatures and release those who had been imprisoned for violating the edict. Hakuseki sought to revitalize society by re-emphasizing the Confucian code of conduct that

---

[3] Engelbert Kaempfer, *History of Japan*, 3 vols., trans. J. G. S. Schenchzer (Glasgow: MacLehose, 1906), vol. 3, p. 205.

[4] Although the value of both gold and rice fluctuated, one ryō is estimated to have been worth about 1.5 koku of rice around 1700 and about 1 koku around 1800.

called for proper decorum and etiquette. In an attempt to cope with the economic problems, Hakuseki issued new coins to replace the debased ones and sought to curtail the outflow of gold and silver by further restricting foreign trade at Nagasaki. It is estimated that in the hundred years or so following the establishment of the Tokugawa Bakufu one-fourth of the gold and three-fourths of the silver mined in Japan had left the country.

Hakuseki was a scholar with broad interests. He informed himself about the outside world through an Italian Christian missionary, Giovanni B. Sidotti, who had smuggled himself into Japan in 1708. Sidotti was captured and imprisoned until his death five years later. Hakuseki wrote a book about the West on the basis of what he had learned from Sidotti. He came to the conclusion that Western science and technology should be allowed to enter the country, but Christianity should continue to be banned. Concerning his discussions with Sidotti, Hakuseki observed:

> When he came to speak about his religion, it appeared to
> be not in the slightest respect like the true way. Wisdom
> and folly became suddenly interchanged in him; at first
> I had thought him very intelligent, but when he began to
> explain his doctrine, he became like a fool. . . . At this
> point, though, I knew that although Roman learning is
> well accustomed to deal only with matter and mechanics,
> and is acquainted with things derived from matter, yet it
> is not acquainted with things above matter.[5]

After he left his official post Hakuseki turned to the study of history. He adopted a rational, positivistic approach in his examination of ancient Japan, thus removing the veil of mysticism that had traditionally surrounded the "age of the gods."

The seventh shōgun, Ietsugu, under whom Hakuseki also served, was in office only for a short period as an infant. Yoshimune (1684–1751), who became the eighth shōgun in 1716, was one of the ablest of the Tokugawa shōgun. He reasserted the authority of the office, which had been left largely in the hands of the high officials since Iemitsu's rule. Like his predecessors, however, he failed to get at the root of the economic problems confronting the Bakufu and sought to cope with the difficulties by forcing the people to be frugal through moral exhortations and sumptuary laws. The government's difficulties could be traced, he was convinced, to the easy living and sagging moral life of the people. He thus

[5] "The Capture and Captivity of Pere Giovan Batista Sidotti in Japan from 1709 to 1715," a translation by W. B. Wright of Arai Hakuseki's *Seiyō Kibun*, in *Transactions of the Asiatic Society of Japan*, vol. 9, p. 166.

emphasized the military arts over literary efforts, and encouraged the samurai to engage in hawking and hunting.

Yoshimune also put into effect certain stop-gap measures, known as the Kyōhō Reforms (named for the Kyōhō period, 1716–1736), in order to increase government revenues. For example, he reduced the daimyō's stay in Edo (the sankinkōtai system; see page 160) to a half a year in return for rice contributions, a practice that was discontinued after a decade, however. In order to increase agricultural production he encouraged the reclamation of new land and the production of crops other than rice, such as sweet potatoes. To prevent the peasants from leaving the villages he attempted, with little success, to enforce the ban on the buying and selling of land. He also regularized tax collection by maintaining a fixed rate of collection over a number of years rather than relying on an annual assessment of the agricultural yield. He sought to disseminate practical knowledge. As part of this policy, in 1720 he eased the ban on the importation of foreign books, allowing them to enter the country as long as they did not contain Christian concepts.

The eighth shōgun also introduced legal reforms and in 1742 had the Code of One Hundred Articles—a compendium of the legal procedures and penal laws that were in effect up to his time—drawn up. He encouraged the populace to express their opinions through the use of suggestion boxes. In addition, he sought to utilize men of talent and was interested in aiding the sick and the poor.

Yoshimune was puritanical in his outlook and endeavored to uphold morality by censoring novels and other works of literature, insisting upon the expurgation of all lewd expressions. In order to discourage double suicides by lovers, he prohibited any mention of this practice. He also proscribed any discussion of the Tokugawa family in print. An effort was made to curb unlicensed prostitution and gambling.

Although Yoshimune succeeded in injecting a measure of energy into the Bakufu, the reforms that he instituted merely dealt with the external symptoms. The difficulties confronting the Bakufu arose from the basic nature of the society, and these attempts at reform were palliatives which merely delayed its deterioration.

THE POWER STRUCTURE

With the Battle of Sekigahara the supremacy of the Tokugawa family over the rest of the daimyō was established. Ieyasu did not seek to rule over the entire land directly, but the daimyō were no longer allowed to be the fully autonomous regional barons that they had been in the Age of the Warring States. They were in effect vassals of the shōgun and owed him loyalty and prescribed obligations. In the administration and control of the land, a division of power between the Bakufu and the daimyō, who retained authority in their han (domains), was effected. Thus the Tokugawa system of rule is referred to as the *baku-han* system.

The Tokugawa family retained a large portion of the country's land as its demesne. At the end of the Tokugawa rule the agricultural yield of the entire nation was estimated at about 30 million koku. The Tokugawa family retained about 7 million koku. Of this amount, between 2.6 million and 2.7 million koku was held as fiefs by the liege vassals or direct retainers of the Tokugawa family. The Bakufu's holdings were located not only in the Kantō region but in the central provinces and the Kinki area (the provinces around Kyoto) as well. The remaining 22 to 23 million koku were divided among the daimyō. The number of daimyō varied somewhat during the Tokugawa period but averaged about 270. Each daimyō held at least 10,000 koku, but the size of the daimyō's domain varied greatly. A large majority held less than 100,000 koku, and many held only the minimum 10,000 koku. Only sixteen han were officially valued as being worth more than 300,000 koku. The largest han was held by the Maeda family of Kaga, whose holdings were assessed at 1.02 million koku. Frequently the actual productive capacity was higher than the official estimate.

Initially the imperial court was granted an income of about 20,000 koku, but this was later increased to 30,000. The court aristocrats were restricted to meager stipends and led an existence of near privation.

There were three categories of daimyō: relatives of the Tokugawa family (*shimpan*), hereditary daimyō (fudai), and outside lords (tozama). There were only a few shimpan. The most important of these were the three main collateral houses established by Ieyasu's sons, the Owari, Kii, and Mito han. They, together with three houses established by the sons of the eighth and ninth shōgun, provided a successor to the shōgun if he did not have an heir. Other major shimpan included the Echizen and Aizu houses.

The fudai lords were by and large those daimyō who had been vassals of the Tokugawa family before the battle of Sekigahara. They not only functioned as rulers of their own han but served as high officials in the Bakufu. The tozama lords, of whom there were about a hundred, were those who had joined the Tokugawa faction later. Many had fought against it at Sekigahara, but some had remained neutral, and others had even fought on its side. The last group were regarded as friendly tozama lords and were rewarded after Ieyasu gained mastery over the land. Those who had fought against him at Sekigahara, with a few exceptions, found their holdings reduced substantially. The tozama holdings, however, tended to be larger than the fudai holdings. Of the sixteen largest han, eleven were held by tozama lords, four belonged to the shimpan, and only one was held by a fudai daimyō.

For a few decades the Bakufu pursued a policy of eliminating those lords it considered untrustworthy, even those who had supported it at Sekigahara. It also confiscated the holdings of those daimyō houses that experienced internal conflict over succession. In addition it exercised the right of escheat when a daimyō died without leaving an heir. Deathbed designations were not recognized. During the first half of the seventeenth century, 120 daimyō families lost their fiefs for diverse reasons, but the Bakufu discontinued exercising its right of escheat at about the middle of the seventeenth century.

The Bakufu kept strategic areas under its direct control or else allotted them to the shimpan or fudai daimyō. Those tozama lords who were not fully trusted by the Bakufu were generally located in the outlying regions or were placed in between two reliable houses.

The Bakufu took great care to prevent the daimyō, particularly the tozama daimyō, from endangering its supremacy. Daimyō families were prohibited from concluding marital ties without the Bakufu's approval. Castles could not be repaired without permission from the shogunate. An elaborate system of spies was developed to ferret out any budding conspiracies.

In order to maintain a close check on the daimyō, the Bakufu instituted the sankinkōtai (alternate attendance) system, requiring the daimyō to spend every other year in Edo. This compelled them to spend huge sums of money moving their households back and forth to the capital and maintaining expensive residences there. The resulting drain on their resources prevented them from accumulating funds that could be used against the Bakufu. In addition, the daimyō were required to leave their wives and children in Edo as hostages. Barriers or checkpoints were established at strategic points to control their movements.

The daimyō were also required to sign an oath of allegiance to the shōgun. As each new shōgun came to office, the daimyō had to renew their pledges and also to acknowledge the *Buke Shohatto* (Laws Governing the Military Households), which prescribed the mode of conduct for the samurai and daimyō.

The major obligation of the daimyō to the shōgun was to come to his aid in time of trouble with a fixed number of warriors, horses, and weapons. The number of warriors each daimyō was obliged to provide was determined by the amount of land he held and came to about two men per 100 koku. The daimyō was also required to provide material assistance and men for corvée when the Bakufu required them for special projects.

The daimyō was allowed a fairly free hand in the administration of his own han, but certain matters were placed outside his jurisdiction. The Bakufu retained the right to manage the country's foreign relations, and it also controlled such internal matters as coinage, weights and measures, and inter-han transportation.

The liege vassals of the shōgun were classified into two groups: the bannermen (*hatamoto*) and housemen (*gokenin*). They were in a way members of the "palace guard." The bannermen had the privilege of approaching the shōgun directly whereas the housemen did not. The latter also held smaller fiefs or stipends. These immediate servitors of the shōgun were at first given either fiefs or stipends, but the Bakufu eventually adopted the policy of removing the liege vassals from the land and having them reside in Edo, and thus by 1722 most of them were receiving stipends rather than holding fiefs. In the early eighteenth century there were over five thousand bannermen and seventeen thousand housemen. The daimyō also adopted the practice of paying their retainers stipends rather than alloting them fiefs. By 1690, 83 percent of the daimyō had their vassals on stipends.

ADMINISTRATIVE STRUCTURE

The administrative structure of the shogunate took its more or less final form during the third Tokugawa shōgun's regime. The shōgun, as the chief administrator, was assisted by several councilors. The highest ranking post was that of the *tairō* (great councilor). This position, however, was filled only under such special circumstances as the minority of a shōgun or in such extraordinary situations as the crisis caused by the arrival of Commodore Perry. During the early years of the Tokugawa Bakufu three tairō were appointed to function as a group, but eventually the number was reduced to one. They were chosen from among those fudai daimyō who were especially close to the Tokugawa family. The standing conciliar positions were those of the *rōjū* (senior councilors). Usually there were four or five rōjū who took turns each month managing the administrative affairs of the Bakufu. They were chosen from among the fudai daimyō with holdings of over 25,000 koku. Under their supervision were a number of important officials, such as the *ō-metsuke* (inspector general), whose function was to oversee the shogunate's relationship with the daimyō and keep a check on them. Various commissioners (*bugyō*) in charge of the major cities, financial affairs, and monasteries and shrines were under the direction of the rōjū. The city commissioners managed the administrative and judicial affairs of Edo and the other major cities under the Bakufu's jurisdiction.

There was also a group of three to five junior officials, the *wakadoshi-yori* (junior councilors), who were also chosen from among the fudai daimyō. Their task was to supervise the bannermen and housemen and to oversee the affairs within Edo Castle. Under their authority were the *metsuke* (inspectors), who also kept an eye on the bannermen and housemen. To manage its demesne the Bakufu appointed intendants. There were four intendants known as *gundai* and forty to fifty referred to as *daikan*. The former were in charge of Tokugawa domains with incomes of over 10,000 koku and the latter controlled areas with incomes between 5,000 and 10,000 koku. In order to maintain a close check on the imperial court, the Bakufu assigned a deputy in Kyoto. All of the court's activities were closely supervised, even its nominal ceremonial functions. The administrative machineries of the daimyō resembled those of the Bakufu, although there were local variations.

The manner in which the administrative system was established indicates that one of the chief concerns of the Bakufu was to maintain stringent controls over all elements in the society in order to ensure that its position would not be threatened from any direction. The other major preoccupation of the Bakufu was financial. It had to manage its affairs gent controls over all elements in the society in order to ensure that its vassals or the daimyō, although it could ask for contributions. Its primary source of income was the taxes levied on the peasants in its own demesne. It usually collected 40 percent of the harvest. In addition it imposed special levies to pay for public works, the horse stations, and extraordinary projects.

The Bakufu also derived some income from the mines, having kept the major ones under its direct control. It obtained loans, which were in effect forced donations, from the merchants. It retained the right to mint coins for the entire land, and it debased the currency from time to time when its financial situation became acute. The daimyō were permitted to mint their own coins and issue paper currency for use in their own han. These, however, had little value in other parts of the country.

THE ADMINISTRATION OF JUSTICE

The legal system that prevailed in Tokugawa Japan was not based upon the concept of rule-of-law as it evolved in the West. Rule-of-law upholds the supremacy of regular law as opposed to the exercise of arbitrary power; it means equality before the law with no immunities for the ruling or official class. In contrast, justice in Tokugawa Japan was administered according to "rule-by-status," in which discretionary powers were held by superiors within a multistatus social structure. The entire society was ruled by a concept of hierarchic relationship; distinctions between superior and inferior persons were constantly made. Not only could governing officials exercise arbitrary power over the common people, but the samurai class as a whole could exercise such power over them. There was little recourse for the commoner against the samurai, because bringing suits against superiors was proscribed and punishable.

Law to the common man meant submission to the will of those above. The ruling class justified its authority in terms of a moral order that stemmed from natural law, the basic principle of which was that men were unequal. Hence the decrees issued by the shōgun and the daimyō took the coloring of moral precepts and admonitions.[6] Laws, primarily sumptuary and proscriptive in nature, were issued in various forms from the beginning of the Tokugawa period, but little effort was made to systematize them. Some laws were applicable throughout the land, while others applied only to the Bakufu's demesne. Some laws were intended for the common people, some for the samurai, and some for the monasteries and shrines. Penalties for violating the laws were not clearly spelled out, although a common practice of a sort eventually emerged as magistrates followed precedents.

Under Shōgun Yoshimune an attempt was made to regularize the administration of justice with the compilation in 1742 of the Code of One Hundred Articles. Further additions and amendments were made, but by 1754 it had more or less assumed the form that was to prevail during the rest of the Tokugawa era. Altogether there were one hundred and three sections in the code.

A large number of crimes were punishable by death. Among such crimes was the failure to try to save one's parents trapped in a burning house. The code liberalized somewhat the penal practices that had prevailed prior to this, however. For instance, formerly a wide range of crimes resulted in the punishment not only of the culprit but also of his parents, brothers, wife, children, and in some cases even nephews and nieces. In 1691, for example, in the Bakufu's demesne in the north, a servant fell in love with his master's daughter, and they committed double suicide. Since he had evidently killed her first and then killed himself he was judged guilty of having murdered his master's daughter. Not only did the authorities crucify the corpse of the servant as an example, they also executed the servant's father and his older brother. The Code of One Hundred Articles limited the imposition of capital punishment for crimes committed by family members to the children of persons guilty of murdering their masters and parents. Capital punishment in such instances, however, was not inflicted upon samurai children. Instead they were banished to outlying regions.

Because of this practice of holding family members jointly responsible,

[6] Perhaps this tradition of moralistic decrees being issued by the wielders of power accounts in part for the fact that even in the modern era a tendency to equate morality with power prevailed. "We find a tendency . . . to estimate morality, not by the value of its content, but in terms of its power, that is, according to whether or not it had a power background." Masao Maruyama, *Thought and Behaviour in Modern Japanese Politics* (London: Oxford University Press, 1963), p. 10.

the custom of legally disowning members of one's family came into existence. Family members would then be protected from the misconduct of, say, a profligate son.

The hierarchical social structure and the concept of rule-by-status allowed a samurai to take the law into his own hands against the common people. The code permitted even the lowest of the samurai to execute on the spot petty townsmen or peasants if they addressed him in "coarse and improper language" or behaved insolently toward him. The code stipulated that "when one slays a rude fellow, it is to be deemed a [justifiable] cutting down, owing to the difference of high and low." [7]

As for the modes of execution, depending on the nature of the crime, a condemned man was crucified, beheaded with a sword, burned at the stake, or decapitated with a bamboo saw. In the last instance, the victim was pilloried for two days, and any passerby was permitted to saw away at his head with a bamboo saw that was placed beside him. Condemned men were frequently led through the streets, decapitated, and gibbeted. Other modes of punishment included banishment, house arrest, flogging, tattooing, handcuffing, and imposition of fines.

Under Tokugawa criminal procedures no one could be punished unless he confessed, so torture was used against those who, despite strong evidence of guilt, refused to confess to crimes involving murder, arson, robbery, breach of government barriers, or treasonable conspiracy. The modes of torture used included flogging, weighing down with stones, trussing up by binding the arms, legs, and body into a tight little bundle, and suspension on a beam with the arms pinioned and hands tied behind the back.

All the Bakufu officials, including the senior councilors, junior councilors, commissioners, and inspectors general, performed judicial duties by hearing disputes brought to the Bakufu by the daimyō, bannermen, housemen, townspeople, and peasants. Cases involving daimyō were heard by the higher officials. In special cases the high officials deliberated as a group and acted as the Bakufu's supreme judicial body. The peasants were denied the right to make direct appeals to the Bakufu so they remained at the mercy of their lords and the local officials. Those who made direct appeals did so with the full awareness that they would be executed regardless of the merit of their case.

The villagers had their own system of justice. There was a village code that dealt with such basic concerns of the village as taxation, agriculture, and community activities. Those who violated the code of conduct, written or unwritten, that regulated village affairs and the relationship between villagers were punished by the community. The punishments in-

[7] J. C. Hall, "The Tokugawa Legislation," in *Transactions of the Asiatic Society of Japan,* vol. 41, p. 776.

cluded, in ascending order of severity, apologies, fines, ostracism, and banishment. Ordinary disputes between villagers were mediated by the village headman or elders, and differences were usually resolved through compromises.

SOCIAL STRUCTURE

Prior to the Age of the Warring States it was common for the samurai to farm in time of peace and go off to the battlefield in time of war, but during the era of the Warring States, the samurai began to congregate in the castle towns. Thus a division of labor between the samurai and the farmers began to develop. Hideyoshi's sword hunt and freezing of occupation resulted in a four-class division of samurai, peasants, artisans, and merchants. The Tokugawa Bakufu adopted a policy of perpetuating this situation and maintained a rigid division of these four main classes. Birth determined every individual's social status. A samurai's son belonged to the samurai class, and the peasant's son remained a peasant. The establishment of the hierarchic social structure fixed the character of Tokugawa society and, to a large extent, of modern Japan. Class status and group relationship governed all social relations, and individualism was thoroughly repressed.

The ruling class justified this class structure in terms of Confucian concepts. Knowing one's proper place in society was one of the points emphasized by the Confucian scholars, particularly the Chu Hsi school, which became the official philosophy of the regime. The first official philosopher of this school, Hayashi Razan (1583–1657), wrote,

> Heaven is august, Earth is ignoble. Heaven is high, Earth
> is low. Just as there is a distinction of high and low between
> Heaven and Earth, in the society of men, a prince is noble
> while the subject is common. Proper decorum calls for a
> hierarchy between the noble and the common, the elder
> and the younger persons. . . . Unless the distinction
> between the prince who is noble and the subject who is
> common is maintained, the land cannot be governed. . . .
> If the Way that distinguishes the prince and the subject,
> and the father and the son is followed, and the principle
> of distinguishing the high and the low, the exalted and the
> vulgar is upheld, the Way of Heaven will prevail above,
> and human relationships will be clear below.[8]

The Bakufu's laws governing the military household stated that lord and vassal should observe what was proper to their stations in life.

[8] Ienaga Saburō, *Nihon Dōtokushisōshi (A History of Japanese Moral Thought)* (Tokyo: Iwanami, 1951), p. 106.

A person was expected to be totally submissive and obedient to his superiors and would never dare, of course, to criticize them.

The object of the Bakufu was to fix the social order and preserve the status quo. All innovations were rejected. An official decree stated, "Generally speaking in all things the ancient laws must be followed. New practices must be prohibited." An eighteenth-century Confucian scholar wrote, "It seems that in state affairs, if the laws and practices of those who founded the state are followed exactly and are not changed, the state will endure forever. If the descendants turn against the laws of their ancestors and devise new ones the state will fall into chaos and will surely perish." [9]

THE SAMURAI

In the hierarchic Tokugawa society the privileged class was the samurai, the governing class. It constituted about one-fifteenth to one-tenth of the total population. At the end of the Tokugawa era, there were fewer than two million members of the samurai class and about twenty-seven million commoners. Although the samurai was basically a military man, Ieyasu sought to identify him with the Confucian scholar-officials of China. Thus, he insisted that the samurai must not only be skilled in the military arts but must be well-educated, particularly in the Confucian classics.

Within the samurai class itself there was a hierarchy of rank and status. In general there was a broad division between the upper- and lower-class samurai. A nineteenth-century intellectual leader, Fukuzawa Yukichi, who came from a small han in northern Kyushu, reported that there were more than one hundred different degrees of rank in his han where there were only fifteen hundred samurai. Proper distinctions of status were maintained at all levels.

At the end of the Tokugawa regime there were 1,282,000 upper-class and 492,000 lower-class samurai and their family members. Between these two groups rigid social barriers existed. Ordinarily the lower-class samurai could not rise into the upper class regardless of how well they performed their duties or how faithfully they served their lords. There were considerable differences in the privileges enjoyed by the two classes. Upper-class samurai could ride horses and go hunting and fishing, but the lower-class samurai were denied these pleasures. Foot soldiers had to kneel on the ground when they encountered upper-class samurai. Intermarriage between the two classes was prohibited. There were, of course, great differences in the stipends they received. Toward the end of the Tokugawa era many lower-class samurai were unable to live on their stipends and were forced to engage in handicraft work at home to supplement their income —a truly humiliating thing for a samurai to have to do. There were com-

[9] Both quotations are from *ibid.*, p. 110.

plex rules and regulations to abide by in one's relations with other members of the samurai society, including intricate rules concerning the use of the proper style of language befitting the conversing parties' social status. There were also differences in apparel and the kind of fabrics that could be used.

At the beginning of the Tokugawa period, there was a considerable number of unattached samurai because a fairly large number of daimyō lost their domains in the early years of Tokugawa rule. The masterless warriors (known as *rōnin*) usually retained their samurai status and became teachers of swordsmanship or Confucianism. Some, however, were assimilated into the townspeople, while others became warrior-farmers known as *gōshi*. Among the gōshi were peasants who were given the privileges of samurai as a reward for some meritorious conduct or special service performed.

It was during the Tokugawa period that the code of the samurai came to be discussed in idealistic terms, largely by Confucian scholars such as Yamaga Sokō (see page 190). In time of strife the principle that guided the conduct of most of the samurai was self-interest, and the means to success was brute force and guile. The Tokugawa era, however, was a peaceful age. Hence the samurai was expected to be more than just a skilled swordsman; he was expected to be well-versed in the Confucian classics and to conduct himself in a manner befitting a gentleman-scholar. Whereas formerly his loyalty to his master was dependent upon the benefits his master could bestow upon him, now he was expected to remain loyal to his lord regardless of the latter's behavior. It was said, "Even if the prince does not behave like a prince, the subject must behave like a subject."

In the early eighteenth century a Saga Han warrior's thoughts concerning the ideal mode of samurai behavior were recorded by his disciple. The collection of his remarks, *Hagakure* (*Hidden Among Leaves*), came to be regarded as an embodiment of the essence of the samurai spirit. In emphasizing the importance of selfless service to one's master, the Saga warrior asserted, "As long as a person values his master, his parents will be happy and the Buddha and the gods will respond to his prayers. I have no other thought but to serve my master." Another point he emphasized was the need to come to terms with death. "I have discovered," he said, "that *bushidō* means to die."[10] By thinking continuously of death, he contended, a person will become free and be able to perform his duties more perfectly.

But the era of peace compelled the Bakufu to discourage the samurai from dying needlessly. In the early years of the Tokugawa period the

---

[10] Yamamoto Tsunetomo, *Hagakure*, 2 vols., ed. Shiroshima Masayoshi (Tokyo: Jimbutsu Ōraisha, 1968), vol. 1, pp. 27, 41.

practice of devoted vassals committing hara-kiri upon the death of their lords became widespread. When Shōgun Iemitsu died, thirteen men, including three high officials, committed hara-kiri. In order to put an end to the needless deaths, the fourth shōgun proscribed this practice in 1663. The Bakufu also sought to discourage vendettas, although it did not ban them. Those samurai who planned to avenge the death of their parents or masters were required, however, to obtain the permission of the Bakufu. From 1615 to the end of the century there were over a hundred instances in which vendettas were carried out. The most celebrated case was that of the forty-seven warriors who in 1702 avenged the wrong done to their daimyō. Although their action was regarded as a noble deed, they were ordered to commit hara-kiri by the Bakufu for having disturbed the public peace.

THE PEASANTS

The peasantry, constituting more than 80 percent of the population, theoretically ranked next to the samurai in the social hierarchy but in reality their status was lower than that of the townspeople. Like the townspeople, the peasants could not wear swords or use family names. They were bound to the soil and could not change their occupation.

In order to prevent the peasant landholdings from being reduced in size and to avert a rise in tenancy, in 1643 the Bakufu prohibited land from being bought and sold. In 1673 it proscribed the division of land among family members if it resulted in reducing the family holdings to below 10 koku or 1 chō (2.45 acres). This was designed to prevent family holdings from becoming so small as to make the payment of taxes difficult. This meant that younger sons could no longer become independent farmers. They had to remain in their parents' households as dependent members or become hired workers or indentured servants. The daimyō usually followed the Bakufu's policies in managing peasant affairs, but some did not adopt these proscriptive measures.

The peasant's life was regulated in minute detail by the ruling class. In the samurai's way of thinking, the peasant's *raison d'etre* was to serve the ruling class's economic needs. Everything was therefore directed to this end. The peasant was told to limit his crops to the five cereals (rice, wheat, beans, German millet, and millet) and to produce only rice in the wet fields. No arable land was to be left idle. In some han the officials determined when the peasants should get up and when they should start and stop their day's work. They were told not to waste their evening hours but to make straw ropes and sandals. Women were instructed to spin and weave.

In addition to advocating the virtue of industry, the ruling class sought to instill the concept of frugality among the peasants. They were instructed to consume as little food as possible. Millet rather than rice was to be their staple. Smoking, tea-drinking, and, above all, consumption of sake—for rice was used to produce it—were discouraged. They were also told to utilize barnyard grass and vegetable leaves as food. They were instructed to use only cotton for clothing and to bind their hair with straw instead of ribbons. Their dwellings were to be simple hovels. All forms of recreation and games were forbidden except on special occasions. Any peasant found amusing himself any other time was punished. Wives who idled their time away by such pastimes as flower-viewing and tea-drinking were to be divorced. Many of these admonitions were embodied in the Bakufu's edict issued in 1642. As the influence of the towns began to be felt in the villages, the officials began to concern themselves about ways to prevent the peasants from being contaminated by the extravagant ways of the townspeople.

The taxes usually amounted to about 40 to 50 percent of the crop, but the percentage tended to increase as the ruling class began to experience increasing financial difficulties. The general policy, it would appear, was to squeeze as much as possible out of the peasants, leaving them just enough to stay alive. "Sesame seed and peasants are much alike," an eighteenth-century senior councilor said. "The more you squeeze them, the more you can extract from them." [11] In a political guidebook written by Honda Masanobu, an influential adviser to Ieyasu, it is stated that all the rice except the amount needed by the peasants to stay alive during the year should be collected. In practice, however, not all daimyō and officials followed these maxims.

The amount of rice and other products each village was expected to pay was determined by land surveys. If the officials estimated that a particular village was capable of producing 500 koku of rice and rice equivalents in other crops, the village was classified as a 500-koku village. If the tax rate was 50 percent, under normal circumstances the officials counted on reaping 250 koku in rice and rice equivalents. The village as a whole was held responsible for the payment of the assessed tax. Each household's share of the tax burden was determined by the villagers themselves.

Because the actual yield in a given village differed from year to year, each year the officials came to examine the quality of the harvest and fix the exact amount to be paid. As noted earlier, in the Kyōhō era (1716–1736), Shōgun Yoshimune abandoned the annual crop survey and allowed a fixed rate to prevail for three to five years. The last previous nationwide cadastral survey had been made during the Kambun and Empō eras (1661–1681). This meant that in many instances newly re-

[11] Furushima Toshio, *Nihon Hōken Nōgyōshi (Japanese Feudal Agricultural History)* (Tokyo: Shikai Shobō, 1931), p. 83.

claimed plots were not included in the tax assessment, although some han did make surveys of just the newly reclaimed areas.

In addition to the land tax, as the years passed a large number of miscellaneous taxes came to be levied on the peasantry. By the late eighteenth century there were, according to a high Bakufu official, "a tax on the field, a tax on doors, a tax on windows, a tax on female children according to age, a tax on cloth, a tax on sake, a tax on hazel trees, a tax on beans, a tax on hemp . . . if the peasant added a room to his hut a tax was levied on it. . . ." [12]

Furthermore the peasants were called upon to provide labor to maintain roads and other public facilities. Villages along the main highways, such as those connecting Edo and other major cities, were required to provide men and horses to maintain the horse stations that were located at fixed intervals. For example, on the Tōkaidō connecting Edo and Kyoto, there were fifty-three such stations. Each station had a hundred men and a hundred horses ready for the use of travelers, especially the daimyō, on their way to and from Edo. Hamlets located within 10 to 20 miles of the main road had to provide three or four men and five or six horses for every 100 koku of rice produced.

In some han the officials were directed to confiscate the peasants' possessions, even their wives and children, if they failed to pay their taxes. Slavery was prohibited but temporary bondage was permitted. Thus, in order to pay their taxes and debts, the peasants frequently sold their family members into temporary servitude. In reality this resulted in permanent enslavement, because the contract could not be dissolved until the debt was repaid, and this the impoverished peasants could seldom do. The brothels of the big cities were filled with daughters of indigent peasants. In the villages themselves there were a considerable number of hereditary and indentured servants who were employed by the wealthier farmers. That the peasants' lot was a hard one was remarked upon frequently by contemporary observers. An eighteenth-century Bakufu official claimed that peasants were treated like beasts of burden.

Broadly speaking there were two classes of peasantry: those who possessed their own land and those who were tenants. The former came to be called hombyakushō (full-fledged farmers). They were recorded in the land registries and had to pay taxes. On the other hand, they had a voice in village affairs, belonged to the five-man group (see page 172), and had priority in the use of the woods, meadows, and irrigation water. The size of the landholding of the full-fledged farmers differed from place to place, but 1 chō (2.45 acres) was probably the average size, since they were forbidden to reduce their holdings below this figure.

Although records of peasant incomes and expenditures are rare, the

[12] Quoted in E. H. Norman, *Japan's Emergence as a Modern State* (New York: Institute of Pacific Relations, 1940), p. 23.

few that do exist show that the average peasant led a hand-to-mouth existence. A handbook written around the 1680s for officials of an unidentified region estimated that a peasant with a half a chō of rice field and a half a chō of upland could, by double cropping, produce 22.5 koku of rice and rice equivalents. His farming, living, and household costs came to 18 koku, leaving him 4.5 koku to pay his land taxes.

The farmlands were usually graded into three categories: superior, medium, and inferior. Although the expected yield differed somewhat depending on the location, 1 chō of superior rice field was expected to yield about 15 koku, medium grade field 13 koku, and poor field 11 koku. The expected yields for uplands were lower.

In the case of the above peasant, the handbook states that if his fields were rated medium, his taxable yield would be 12 koku. If they were rated superior, it would be 14 koku. The normal tax rate being 40 percent, he would have to pay 4.8 koku in the former instance and 5.6 koku in the latter. Thus he would have to go into debt to pay his tax. This tendency prevailed throughout the country, and the situation grew worse with the passing years.

Normally the peasants had their own plots of land to farm on a more or less permanent basis, but in some areas land was held in common by the entire village and periodic land distribution took place. This practice prevailed to some extent in twenty of the sixty-six provinces, and in some villages it survived until the end of the Tokugawa era.

In most villages there were a few fairly wealthy farmers who owned considerably more land that the average villager. They also retained a number of servants to work on the land. Some of these workers were hereditary servants who were in effect slaves. Others were indentured servants whose terms of service might run from ten years to a lifetime, depending upon the amount of money they or their families had borrowed. It is estimated that these servants accounted for as much as 10 percent of the population in the seventeenth century. In the later years of the Tokugawa era their number decreased as their masters found it more beneficial to allow them to work the land as tenants instead of indentured workers.

At the beginning of the Tokugawa rule, there was in certain regions a segment of the rural population who were in effect serfs of rural landlords. These workers were called *nago* (children of the landowners) and were attached hereditarily to their masters' household. Holding none of the rights and privileges of the independent peasants, the nago were completely dependent on their masters for the means of farming and were usually among the most impoverished members of the village. By the end of the Tokugawa era, the nago also were practically nonexistent; they, too, had become independent or tenant farmers.

The basic administrative unit in the Tokugawa era was the village (*mura*), which emerged after the shōen system collapsed. The shōgun and the daimyō's agents supervised village affairs and the collection of taxes, but each village enjoyed a degree of autonomy in the management of its affairs and in effect constituted a corporate body. It owned, bought, and sold property, borrowed and loaned money, and entered into agreements with other villages. Although all independent farmers had a voice in village affairs, an elite group of wealthy and prominent villagers dominated the community. Members of the elite families functioned as headmen and elders, serving as agents of the lord of the domain.

The headman was held responsible for keeping records, allocating each family's share of the land tax, collecting the taxes, adjudicating local disputes, maintaining public works, reporting infractions of the law, and so on. He was assisted in his work by the elders and other leading members of the village. When an important matter arose, a meeting of the hombyakushō was held to deal with it.

There was also a five-man group or neighborhood association consisting of five to ten householders. Members of this group were held jointly responsible for the payment of taxes and criminal acts committed by any of its members. In other words, the authorities used it as a self-policing body to maintain a close check on peasant life and enforce its many rules and regulations. The association also served as a mutual aid society, with members helping each other in time of need and sickness. This system first came into existence under Hideyoshi and was probably patterned after a similar institution that existed in China.

It was the Bakufu's policy to keep the peasants intimidated. When Ieyasu heard that the peasants were disturbed at the high-handed behavior of the falconers he is said to have remarked, "Let the falconers be as high handed as they please. This will make the peasants think 'if mere falconers act in such a manner how much more overbearing would high officials be?' and they will be afraid to harbor any disloyal thoughts. Willful farmers are the cause of peasant disturbances." [13]

The peasants' mental horizon was limited because each village tended to be isolated from the surrounding areas. Moreover, the ruling authorities deliberately kept the villages insulated from the towns. Their object was to keep the villagers ignorant. "A good peasant is one who does not know the price of grain," was a common saying among the ruling class. It was said that peasants and townspeople should be forbidden from studying. They were to be indoctrinated with the ideals and values convenient to the ruling class, that is, with such virtues as humility, obedience, and loyalty. By and large, the peasants endured their hardships with great patience, but toward the end of the Tokugawa era, as economic difficult-

[13] Rekishi Chiri Gakkai, ed., *Nihon Nōminshi (A History of Japanese Peasants)* (Tokyo: Rekishi Chiri Gakkai, 1924), p. 110.

ties increased, peasant uprisings began to break out with growing frequency.

THE TOWNSPEOPLE

The third and fourth classes in the social hierarchy were the artisans and the merchants. They were placed at a lower level than the peasantry because the economy was supported by the tillers of the land and, in theory, the samurai class respected and valued the peasants. In the official social hierarchy the merchants found themselves at the bottom of the order because the orthodox philosophy, Confucianism, held moneymaking in disdain. Confucius stated, "The superior man thinks of virtue; the inferior man things of possessions. . . . The superior man understands righteousness, the inferior man understands profit." [14]

A Confucian moralist of Tokugawa Japan, Kaibara Ekken (1630–1714), wrote that "the enlightened kings of the ancient period valued agriculture and curtailed industry and commerce. They respected the five grains and held money in disdain." Another Confucian remarked, "Merchants gain wealth without laboring, encourage luxurious living and undermine the people's minds. Farmers not only must be aided but they must also be respected while merchants must be suppressed and held in contempt." [15]

It was considered to be in bad taste for the samurai to concern himself with money, and ignorance about financial matters was seen as a sign of good breeding. This attitude prevailed to the end of the era and even into the Meiji era. Fukuzawa Yukichi reports that his father was outraged to hear that his children were being taught how to work with numbers. But the merchant class accepted its lot and function as dealers in money and made it its philosophy to accumulate as much money as possible. Chikamatsu Monzaemon (1653–1725), a Tokugawa playwright, had a merchant remark in one of his plays,

> A samurai's child is reared by samurai parents and
> becomes a samurai himself because they teach him the
> warrior's code. A merchant's child is reared by merchant
> parents and becomes a merchant because they teach him
> the ways of commerce. A samurai seeks a fair name in
> disregard of profit, but a merchant, with no thought to
> his reputation, gathers profit and amasses a fortune.
> This is the way of life proper for each. [16]

[14] These Confucian statements are quoted from Wing-Tsit Chan *Source Book in Chinese Philosophy* (Princeton, N.J.: Princeton University Press, 1963), pp. 27, 28.

[15] Both quotations are from Ienaga Saburō, *op. cit.*, p. 120.

[16] Chikamatsu Monzaemon, *The Major Plays of Chikamatsu*, trans. Donald Keene (New York: Columbia University Press, 1961), p. 332.

A writer who depicted the life of the townspeople, Ihara Saikaku (1642–1693), wrote, "Money is the townsman's pedigree, whatever his birth and lineage. No matter how splendid a man's ancestors, if he lacks money he is worse off than a monkey-showman." [17]

An early member of the famous business house of Mitsui, Mitsui Takafusa (1684–1748), compiled in the 1720s a history of merchant houses, focusing in particular upon houses that fell because of extravagance, neglect of business, and the practice of loaning money to the daimyō. The purpose of the work being didactic, Takafusa warned repeatedly against falling into these pitfalls. Merchants were admonished to never forget that their primary object was to make money. "For the townspeople," he wrote, "though there are many businesses, there is nothing that they can rely upon but the profits that accrue from gold and silver." A merchant must be frugal, prudent, and stick to his business. "Never waste your attention on matters which have nothing to do with your work," he advised. "Merchants who ape samurai or think that Shinto, Confucianism or Buddhism will preserve their inner heart will find that they will only ruin their houses if they become too deeply engrossed in them. How much more true is this of other arts and entertainments! Remember that it is the family business that must not be neglected for a moment." [18]

A significant spokesman for the merchant's point of view was Ishida Baigan (1685–1744), a philosopher who is regarded as the founder of the school of thought referred to as *Shingaku* (Teachings of the Heart). Baigan was born a farmer's son and found employment in a Kyoto merchant's shop at the age of twenty-three. He read everything he could get his hands on and later asserted that learning consists of reading books. He remarked, however, that "if one reads the books and does not know the heart of the books, it is not called learning. The books of the sages contain their own heart. Knowing their heart is called learning." [19] Hence the name for his school of thought.

Baigan upheld the opinion that the business of a merchant was to make money, and he sought to make the pursuit of profits a part of the Principle of Heaven. The merchant performed a useful function in society and in return received his "stipend" in the form of profits, just as the samurai received his stipend. He wrote, "If one calls receiving a stipend from one's lord 'greedy' and 'immoral,' then from Confucius

---

[17] Howard Hibbett, *The Floating World in Japanese Fiction* (New York: Grove, 1960), p. 37.

[18] Mitsui Takafusa, "Some Observations on Merchants," E. S. Crawcour, trans., in *Transactions of the Asiatic Society of Japan*, vol. 8, pp. 103, 115.

[19] Robert N. Bellah, *Tokugawa Religion: The Values of Pre-Industrial Japan* (Glencoe, Ill.: Free Press, 1957), p. 149.

and Mencius on down there is not a man who is moral. What sort of thing is it to say, leaving samurai, farmers and artisans aside, the merchants' receiving a stipend is 'greed' and that they cannot know the Way?" [20]

Baigan also emphasized the point that the common people, just as much as the samurai, were doing their duty as the shōgun's subjects. He rejected the distinction that the samurai made between themselves as subjects and the rest of the populace as common people. Peasants, merchants, and artisans were also subjects of the ruler; the only difference was in the work they performed. As proof of this common quality of the four classes, he cited a common principle that governed all classes. This was the principle of frugality. It was essential, he argued, not only for the merchants but also for the peasants and artisans as a principle that would cause them to "fear those above and realize their lowly status." It was also the basis of government. "The principle of loving the people," he asserted, "can be put into effect if in managing financial affairs frugality is practiced. Even if one wishes to love the people, it would not be possible if financial resources are lacking. Thus, it is clear that frugality is the basis for governing the land." [21] Frugality, then, was made the basis of the Confucian concept of benevolence (jen). It fitted in well with the ruling class's continuous interest in fostering frugality as a means to solve its economic difficulties.

Baigan and his followers gave public lectures to the townspeople to propagate their views. Their ideas even filtered into the countryside, as rural leaders invited them to speak in their villages. It would appear, then, that the virtues of frugality, diligence, and devotion to money-making were firmly embraced by a substantial segment of Tokugawa society. This fact no doubt contributed in part to the rapid rise of Japan as a commercial and industrial power after the Meiji Restoration.

Although the samurai held the merchants in contempt, in reality the townspeople's lot in general was much better than that of the peasants. It continued to improve as the merchants accumulated more and more wealth and eventually gained financial power over the ruling class. And, as we shall see below, they dominated the cultural world of the Tokugawa era.

As we noted earlier, commerce and a money economy were on the ascendancy during the Ashikaga period. Even during the period of the Warring States commerce was encouraged by the contending daimyō. Nobunaga sought to foster commerce as did Hideyoshi. With the advent of peace and stability under the Tokugawa Bakufu, conditions be-

---

[20] *Ibid.*, p. 158.
[21] Watsuji Tetsurō, *op. cit.*, vol. 2, p. 612.

came even more favorable for commercial expansion, even though this growth was limited to the internal market.

The area under cultivation increased considerably between 1600 and 1730, and it is estimated that the population grew from about eighteen million in the latter part of the sixteenth century to about twenty-six million by the early eighteenth century. These developments stimulated commercial expansion and, therefore, increased the number and size of cities, particularly castle towns. About one hundred and thirty cities emerged and flourished primarily as castle towns. Between thirty and forty of these had populations of over ten thousand.

As the Bakufu's seat of government and the secondary home of the daimyō, Edo grew into a major city almost overnight. Estimates of the size of its population in the early eighteenth century run from 800,000 to one million. As the chief port and commercial center of western Japan, Osaka had a population of about 400,000, and Kyoto, the traditional capital, remained the center of commerce and culture, with a population of about 350,000.

For purposes of transportation and travel the Bakufu improved old roads and built new ones extending out of Edo to key areas. Because the daimyō had to travel back and forth under the sankinkōtai system, there was a great deal of activity along the main roads. The most heavily traveled route was the Tōkaidō connecting Edo and Kyoto. Towns along the route flourished, with inns and shops serving the daimyō and their retinues.

The major cities had to be supplied with rice and other consumer and luxury goods by the wholesale and retail merchants. To transport rice and other commodities to these cities, coastal shipping was extensively used because of the difficulties involved in overland transportation. The most important sea route was that connecting Osaka and Edo, but the entire island of Honshu was ringed with sea routes linking the main cities.

Those among the merchant class who prospered most as purveyors of consumer goods to the major cities were the wholesale merchants and brokers. The daimyō of western Japan maintained warehouses in Osaka and those in eastern Japan kept similar ones in Edo. Rice was shipped from the home provinces to these cities and stored in warehouses for future dispersal. The daimyō employed merchants to manage these warehouses and brokers to convert their rice into money. These merchants enjoyed some of the privileges of the samurai and were paid retainers' stipends. Some merchants served as financial agents for several daimyō and received huge remunerations.

Osaka was the commercial center for sake, soy sauce, rape-seeds, dried sardines, cotton cloth, paper, and iron, in addition to rice. Kyoto was the center of textile and other handicraft trades. Later in the Tokugawa era, as regional specialties were developed, a large number of wholesale merchants and shippers dealing in inter-han trade grew in importance and wealth.

Among the townspeople there were two classes: those who owned their own houses and those who were tenants. The former were treated as citizens and were recorded in the official registries. In addition, of course, there was a great distinction between the wealthier merchants and the ordinary townspeople. The moneychangers and wholesale dealers grew enormously wealthy, particularly those dealing in rice, lumber, and textiles.

Some merchant houses lost their fortunes by incurring the wrath of the ruling authorities, but many wealthy merchant houses flourished and survived throughout the Tokugawa era. A few emerged in the Meiji period as major business and financial firms. Among them were the house of Mitsui, which started out in the moneylending and drapery businesses and flourished as brokers; the Kōnoike family, which got its start in sake brewing, moved on to shipping, and eventually became financial agents for many major han; and the Sumitomo family, which made its fortune mining copper.

The Bakufu appointed commissioners to administer the major cities. Edo, Kyoto, and Osaka each had two commissioners. The cities were generally allowed considerable autonomy, and mundane local affairs were managed by officials chosen from the townspeople. In Edo there were town elders and district headmen. The elders, who were chosen from three prominent families, acted as liaison officers between the townspeople and the city commissioners. The headmen coordinated the affairs of the local districts in the city. Like the villagers, the townsmen were also organized into five-man groups. Townspeople who owned real estate were required to pay taxes to defray the cost of maintaining public facilities. The taxes were paid in lieu of the corvée that they were originally required to perform.

The residents of Edo and the castle towns consisted primarily of the retainers of the Bakufu and the daimyō, and merchants, artisans, and workers. At the end of the Tokugawa era, 60 percent of the area of Edo was occupied by the samurai class, and 20 percent by temples and shrines. The townspeople, constituting about 50 percent of the populace, were crowded into the remaining 20 percent. They were usually located in fixed sections of the city on the basis of their trade. That is, the carpenters were located in one section, the masons in another, the smiths in still another, and so on. Likewise, the dealers in rice, fish, paper, dry goods, etc., were apt to be located in fixed sections of the town.

Merchant and craft guilds were organized by the townspeople to limit the number of merchants or artisans in a given trade. Among the artisans and craftsmen, a master-follower relationship developed, and personal ties similar to those that bound the samurai and his master came into existence. A similar relationship existed between the merchant and his helper, who was expected to serve the employer loyally in accordance with feudalistic ideals. In return the employer was expected to treat him as a member of his family and eventually provide him with his own shop.

One of the chief fears of the city dwellers was fire. In Edo alone there were eighty major fires during the Tokugawa period, adding seriously to the Bakufu's financial burden. The conflagration of 1657 destroyed 60 percent of the city and killed 102,000 people. In the early decades of the eighteenth century the Bakufu sought to compel the homeowners to use tile roofs in key sections of the city. The maintenance of effective fire-fighting units became a major concern of the officials and townspeople.

OTHER CLASSES

In addition to the four main classes, a fairly large segment of the society was treated as outcasts. The ruling class classified the common people into ryōmin (good people) and semmin (lowly people). The majority of the commoners belonged to the former category, but at the end of the Edo period there were about 380,000 people who fell into the latter group. Of this category there were two major classifications, *hinin* (non-people) and *eta*. Before the Tokugawa era the two were not clearly differentiated, but in the Edo period the eta were classed as people who were outcasts by birth, while the hinin were outcasts by occupation and social status, and could in rare instances rejoin the ranks of the ryōmin.

The origin of the eta class is not known, but it is believed that engaging in occupations considered to be defiling (such as slaughtering animals, butchering, and tanning hides), racial distinctions made in antiquity, descent from slavery, physical abnormalities, and diseases may have accounted for the beginnings of discriminatory treatment.

In the Tokugawa period the eta engaged in a variety of trades aside from tanning and butchering, such as the manufacturing of leather goods, baskets, straw sandals and mats, and tea whisks. Although they tended to be located in urban or semi-urban settings, there were also eta communities in rural areas, where they engaged in farming.

The hinin were itinerant entertainers, beggars, scavengers, prostitutes, and castoff commoners. As an example of how this category of people came into existence we find Shōgun Yoshimune punishing those who attempted double suicide by dropping them into the ranks of the hinin. The Bakufu used the hinin to take care of prisoners and to execute and bury criminals.

Usually the outcasts were ignored in official surveys, and in some maps their settlements were left out. Roads passing through these communities were not included in the calculation of distance. Although the hinin were not considered defiling, the eta were regarded as such and were severely discriminated against. They were required to live in fixed areas and were not allowed to marry outside of their caste. They were not permitted to socialize with or enter the houses of the "good people." They could not wear *geta* (wooden clogs) or anything but cotton clothing. In the late Tokugawa era, an Edo magistrate handed down a decision that held that the life of an eta was worth only one-seventh the life of a non-eta.

FAMILY HIERARCHY

In addition to the social class structure, there was a hierarchical order within the family. The father was at the top of the family hierarchy and held absolute authority. Filial piety was a virtue prized equally with loyalty to the lord. It was a moral ideal upheld by all thinkers and embraced by all segments of the society. There was, in addition, a hierarchy of age and sex. The younger brother had to defer to the elder brother and women to men.

The treatment of women, in particular, illustrates the authoritarian nature of the family system, especially in the samurai family. A samurai's wife was to be absolutely obedient to her husband and serve without any complaints, enduring all forms of hardship and abuse. Kaibara Ekken, who wrote a tract on the ideal conduct expected of women, said, "A woman has no prince to serve. She must consider her husband her master, and serve him with respect and deference." [22]

While a samurai's wife was expected to remain faithful to her husband and was punished by death for adultery, he was not restricted by similar moral strictures. She was taught that although a lower-class woman might display jealousy, it was unbecoming to a samurai's wife. While a man was permitted to have many wives, a woman was allowed only one husband in her lifetime. It was said that "even if the marriage had been arranged when the parties concerned were three or five years of age, if her mate dies, the girl must remain loyal to him all her life. This is the proper behavior for a member of a samurai family." [23]

A girl's marriage was arranged by her parents; she was given no voice in the matter. On the other hand, she could readily be divorced by her husband if he or his parents so desired. The ties between husband and wife were not to be sealed by love and affection. Their relationship was to be that of a superior and an inferior person. Thus proper decorum and etiquette had to be observed in their relationship. The son was re-

[22] Ienaga Saburō, *op. cit.*, p. 112.
[23] *Ibid.*, p. 113.

quired to place his parents' interests above those of his wife and children. It was said that "it is the normal way of the filial son to neglect his wife and children to serve his parents' interests." [24]

In one of Chikamatsu's plays a mother tells her daughter that "the most important test of a woman's training comes after she's married. You must treat your parents-in-law with the same devotion you have shown to your own parents, and your husband's brothers and sisters as if they were your own. When you are alone together with any other man you are not so much as to lift your head and look at him." [25]

This kind of total subservience to the husband was not demanded of the women of the lower classes, though the samurai's ideals did filter down somewhat. Writers representing the townspeople's ethos defended the natural expression of love between husband and wife, unlike the stoic samurai ideal that required the warrior to keep under complete control all his inner emotions. One writer, expressing the attitude of the townsmen, observed, "For the husband to love his wife, and the wife to be affectionate towards the husband and maintain a gentle and friendly relationship is the proper Way. If the affection of the husband and wife appears syrupy sweet to outsiders, an authentic relationship between husband and wife prevails." [26]

The notion that a woman should serve only one man was not adhered to rigidly by the townspeople. Ihara Saikaiu wrote, "We cannot label as immoral the longing of a married woman for another man, or her desire to have another man after her husband's death." Another writer observed, "Among the townspeople, for a woman to remarry after parting from her husband is not an unsavory matter. She is free to do so, and her relatives will help arrange the affair for her."

The ideal of filial piety, which superseded all other considerations—except, of course, loyalty to the lord—in the samurai family was not insisted upon quite so rigorously in the townsman's family. Love of one's wife and children was considered to be more powerful than love of one's parents by some men. "On being parted by death," one writer asserted, "it is sadder in the case of one's wife than one's parents and it is much more grievous in the case of one's child than one's wife." Some townsmen even made the relationship between husband and wife the basis of all ethical conduct. "The way of men originated with husband and wife. First there was man and woman, and then husband and wife. After that came the gods, Buddha and the sages. Thus, husband and wife consti-

[24] *Ibid.*, p. 115.
[25] Chikamatsu, *op. cit.*, p. 76.
[26] This and the rest of the quotations in this chapter are from Ienaga Saburō, *op. cit.*, pp. 143–46.

tute the source of all things." The complete subservience that was demanded of the samurai's wife to her mother-in-law was rejected by
some townspeople who advised the mothers-in-law not to harass their
sons' wives. These attitudes, however, ran counter to the mainstream of
Tokugawa thought, which was primarily Confucian in nature.

CHAPTER **8**

INTELLECTUAL AND CULTURAL DEVELOPMENTS IN TOKUGAWA JAPAN

CONFUCIANISM

In the Tokugawa period, Confucianism, which had entered Japan with the introduction of Chinese civilization, finally emerged as the dominant mode of thought. Specifically it was the Chu Hsi school of Confucianism that was adopted as the official philosophy of the Bakufu. At the core of the doctrine were the teachings of Confucius and Mencius along with interpretations made by later Confucian scholars, including Chu Hsi.

Confucianism was a practical moral philosophy concerned primarily with government and society. The restoration of order and stability during the troubled days of the late Chou period was Confucius' goal; thus he addressed himself mainly to the rulers—the princes and the officials. He looked back to the golden age of the Three Dynasties, that is, Hsia, Shang, and Chou. Confucius believed this was a time when wise, benevolent, and moral leaders governed over an orderly society. The rulers of this period had to follow the examples set by the ancient sage-kings, who governed in accordance with the Will of Heaven. Confucius said, "The superior man stands in awe of three things. He stands in awe of the Mandate of Heaven; he stands in awe of great men; and he stands in awe of the words of the sages." [1] The ruler, having this reverent attitude toward

[1] The quotations from Confucius and Mencius that appear in this chapter were selected primarily from Wing-Tsit Chan, *Source Book in Chinese Philosophy* (Princeton, N.J.: Princeton University Press, 1963), pp. 18 ff.

Heaven and the sages, was expected to acquire the virtues of benevolence (*jen*), righteousness (*i*), propriety (*li*), faithfulness (*hsin*), and wisdom (*chih*). Benevolence and righteousness were given special emphasis by Confucius and Mencius. Benevolence can be equated with love, humanity, or human-heartedness. Righteousness is justice, a categorical imperative demanding "what ought to be." Propriety, also translated as rituals, etiquette, or rites, has to do with human relationships and a scrupulous respect for distinctions of status. In other words, proper conduct meant conforming to what was regarded as the natural order of things. An individual must know the proper meaning of what he claims to be in order to behave properly. A prince cannot behave as a prince unless he knows the true meaning of the word "prince." The same is true of the subject, the father, and the son. Therefore, wisdom and the rectification of names are important. Confucius said: "Let the ruler *be* a ruler, the minister *be* a minister, the father *be* a father, and the son *be* a son."

The concept of loyalty was also stressed by Confucius and Mencius. *The Analects of Confucius* states, "Confucius taught four things: culture, conduct, loyalty, and faithfulness." Mencius said, "Humanity, righteousness, loyalty, faithfulness, and the love of the good . . . constitute the nobility of Heaven."

The ruler was to govern by moral example through the acquisition of these virtues. Mencius said, "Let the ruler be humane, and all his people will be humane. Let the ruler be righteous, and all his people will be righteous. Let the ruler be correct, and all his people will be correct. Once the ruler is rectified, the whole kingdom will be at peace." Accordingly, the role assigned to the ruler in the Confucian political system was highly paternalistic. The ruler was "the parent of the people" and he was "to dispense a benevolent government." If the ruler should fail to be virtuous, Heaven would reveal its displeasure and revoke the mandate to rule by bringing about natural calamities and social disorder. The people would then be justified in overthrowing the ruler. This aspect of Confucianism, however, was not stressed by the Tokugawa rulers and their Confucian supporters.

Confucius posited five cardinal relationships for man in social intercourse: lord—subject, father—son, husband—wife, elder brother—younger brother, friend—friend. In all of these relationships, an individual was to comport himself in accordance with the moral ideals propounded by the ancient sages. The most important of these relationships for the Confucians was that of father and son, or parent and child. Mencius rejected the ideal of universal brotherhood because he contended it was natural for a man to love his parents more than strangers.

Confucius also emphasized the importance of understanding and adhering to the rites (*li*) and music-dance (*yüeh*) compositions of antiquity.

These were the manifestations of the wisdom and virtue of the ancient sages. Rites were to regulate and refine human desires so that they would remain within proper bounds; music-dance compositions were to regulate human emotions so that they would be expressed in accordance with right principles.

In theory, Confucianism would seem to have the ingredients for creating an open society: the prince was admonished to employ men of talent, and the distinction between the superior and inferior man was based upon moral character, not birth or wealth. Basically, however, it was an elitist philosophy. Confucius said, "The common people may be made to follow it [the Way] but may not be made to understand it." Confucianism held the laboring man in low esteem while emphasizing the superiority of the learned class. Mencius wrote, "It is said 'some labor with their minds and some labor with their strength. Those who labor with their minds govern others; those who labor with their strength are governed by others.' Those who are governed by others support them; those who govern them are supported by them. This is a universal principle."

Confucianism was not a philosophy that encouraged independent or original thinking, since one was to follow the example of the ancient sages. Complete reliance on the words of the sages—not just the ancient sage-kings, but all the Confucian thinkers since Confucius—characterized the intellectual behavior of the later Confucians, including most of the Japanese Confucian scholars. Officially, in Tokugawa Japan, it was the Chu Hsi version of the philosophy, or Neo-Confucianism, that was adhered to faithfully.

THE CHU HSI SCHOOL IN JAPAN

The ascendancy of Confucianism in the Tokugawa period can be explained in part by the fact that the founder of the government, Ieyasu, favored it. There were also many objective circumstances that made its rise possible. For one thing, the social and political features of Tokugawa society were comparable to those of imperial China at the time of the emergence of Confucianism. Secondly, when the Tokugawa Bakufu was founded, Confucianism in Japan had changed in character compared to the earlier period.

Regarding the first point, the Tokugawa social structure resembled the feudal class structure of Chou China with its hierarchy of emperor, feudal lords, ministers, high officials, officials, and common people. Thus Confucianism, which was used to justify the social structure of Chou China, could also be used to justify the Tokugawa class structure.

Prior to the Tokugawa era, Confucianism was studied primarily at the imperial court as a philological discipline. It was also pursued by Buddhist monks for their personal intellectual interest and enjoyment. By the time the Tokugawa government was established, it had been transformed into a moral philosophy of broad interest and significance. This transformation was induced by the importation of Sung or Chu Hsi Confucianism. Sung philosophy was introduced into Japan during the Kamakura period by the Zen monks and was treated as an integral part of Buddhist learning. The scholars who liberated Sung Confucianism from this dependence on Buddhism were Fujiwara Seika (1561–1619) and his disciple, Hayashi Razan (1583–1657). The fact that they had the support of the single most influential man of the age, Ieyasu, greatly facilitated their task.

Ieyasu displayed an interest in Confucianism prior to the establishment of his government, and after meeting Seika in 1593, he frequently invited him to lecture him on Confucianism. Later, through Seika, Ieyasu met Razan and appointed him his political adviser in 1607. The Hayashi family then became the official philosophers for the Tokugawa regime.

Ieyasu decided that Confucianism could be utilized to strengthen the foundations of his government. Although he had gained power by the sword, he recognized the need to curb the militaristic sentiments of his vassals. The character of the samurai had to be changed from purely combative to a combination of military and "civilian" qualities. By encouraging them to study the Chinese classics, he sought to transform the samurai into Confucian scholar-officials.

It can be argued that the reason why Chu Hsi philosophy appealed to the Tokugawa authorities was simply that it was the school of Confucianism that was gaining currency at that time among Confucian scholars, particularly Seika and Razan. No doubt other Confucian schools could have been utilized just as effectively to uphold the authority of the ruling family. In Chu Hsi thought, however, certain characteristics can be discerned that might have had special appeal to the Tokugawa rulers.

Scholars of the Chu Hsi school held that all things in nature are governed by a universal principle, *li* (Principle), derived from the Supreme Ultimate, which may be equated with Heaven. The physical nature of all things is determined by *ch'i* (Ether). All men are endowed with the same Principle, but differences in their Ether are responsible for physical and moral variations. Some men have purer Ether than others, but everyone can strive to allow the Principle to emerge by clarifying the turbid Ether that obscures it. This can be achieved by "the extension of knowledge through the investigation of things" [2] As a person begins to understand the Principle he will be able to live in accordance with it and the Way of Heaven. The Japanese Chu Hsi scholars emphasized this linkage between Principle and Heaven: since all things are governed by Principle,

[2] On Chu Hsi's views see *ibid.*, pp. 588 ff., and Fung Yu-lan, *A History of Chinese Philosophy*, trans. Derk Bodde, 2 vols. (Princeton, N.J.: Princeton University Press, 1953), vol. 2, pp. 533 ff.

which is related to Heaven, the ruler, in performing his task, acts in accordance with the Way of Heaven. He is in effect an agent of Heaven who acts to enforce the principle of things. Accordingly, it becomes imperative for the people to obey the ruler.

The Japanese Chu Hsi scholars placed special emphasis on *taigi meibun* (doing one's duty to the lord in accordance with one's place in society). *Taigi* means supreme righteousness or supreme duty; *meibun* has to do with one's name and place, that is, knowing one's proper place. This concept was particularly convenient for the ruling authorities since the Principle required each man to observe what was proper to him. The ruler, thus, has certain duties to perform according to his "name" and "place" and in a similar manner, subjects have their duties to perform.

The Chu Hsi school, like earlier Confucians, emphasized the need to maintain proper human relationships in terms of the five basic relationships. This aspect of Confucianism was useful to the Tokugawa rulers who wished to establish a hierarchic society based upon the relationship between the lord and subject, between superior and inferior persons.

The Chu Hsi school of Japan adopted the Chinese Confucian scholars' point of view that the teachings of the ancient sages were unquestionable truths to be followed with absolute fidelity. One Confucian scholar remarked, "If I were to err because I had studied Chu Hsi, I would be erring in accordance with Chu Hsi's teachings so I would have nothing to regret." [3] As a result of this kind of thinking, there was a tendency on the part of the Tokugawa Chu Hsi scholars merely to repeat what their Chinese counterparts had written. A significant exception to this was Fujiwara Seika, the scholar who introduced Ieyasu to Chu Hsi philosophy. He was not as narrow in his outlook as later Chu Hsi scholars, and he did not reject outright the rival Wang Yang-ming school. He sought to interpret Shinto and Buddhist ideas with an eye toward reconciling them with Confucianism.

Seika's disciple, Hayashi Razan, was considerably more rigid, as evidenced by his highly critical attitude toward Buddhism and Christianity. On the other hand, he was interested in trying to reconcile Confucianism with Shinto. "Some people," he wrote, "ask what the difference between Shinto and Confucianism is. I would reply, the principles are the same. They only differ in deeds. . . . The Way of the Kings transforms into the Way of the Gods, and Shinto transforms into the Way. The Way is the Confucian Way." [4]

Razan also emphasized the importance of studying history because

---

[3] Watsuji Tetsurō, *Nihon Rinri Shisōshi* (*A History of Japanese Ethical Thought*), 2 vols. (Tokyo: Iwanami, 1952), vol. 2, p. 416.

[4] Maruyama Masao, *Nihon Seijishisōshi Kenkyū* (*Studies in the History of Japanese Political Thought*) (Tokyo: Tōkyō Daigaku Shuppankai, 1954), p. 155.

he believed it would reveal moral principles that were just. History could also be used to provide the ruling family with a legitimate claim to power. It is not surprising then that the Bakufu asked Razan to start compiling its family genealogy.

In his Confucian teachings Razan did little more than repeat the Chu Hsi doctrines. He emphasized the importance of combating human desires or selfishness and permitting one's "illustrious virtue" (the li endowed upon man by Heaven) to manifest itself. He also stressed the five human relationships and the five virtues. Particular emphasis was given to benevolence because he believed it encompassed the other four virtues. Righteousness, he said, was the basis of *giri,* man's moral duty and obligation. The principle of propriety was used by Razan to justify the hierarchical relationship between the noble and the base, the high and the low. Wisdom, he explained, consisted in understanding the principles of benevolence, righteousness, and propriety. Finally, faithfulness was equated with *makoto* or sincerity.

Another prominent Chu Hsi scholar was Yamazaki Ansai (1618–1682), the philosopher who said he would willingly err with Chu Hsi. He accepted Chu Hsi's words as unquestionable truth and did not permit his students to read any book that did not contribute to what he considered to be the essence of Chu Hsi philosophy: the principle of "devotion within, righteousness without." Like Seika and Razan, he sought to reconcile Confucianism with Shinto. This led him to what is known as *Suika Shinto,* a combination of the ethical ideals of Confucianism and the religious doctrines of Shinto. This was in tune with the growing tendency on the part of the Confucian scholars to syncretize Confucianism and Shinto. This trend persisted throughout the Tokugawa period.

Another Chu Hsi scholar worthy of attention is Kaibara Ekken (1630–1714), who played a significant role in molding the ethical ideals of Tokugawa society. He wrote moral tracts in a plain and straightforward style that were designed to disseminate Confucian ethical values among the common people. His work was easily understood and widely read. His didactic tract for women is an interesting example of his work and an illuminating statement of the concept of masculine superiority and feminine inferiority. In his *Great Learning for Women* he operates from the premise that the sole purpose of existence for a girl is to get married and serve her husband and his family faithfully, subserviently, and selflessly. A woman can accomplish this only by completely suppressing her individuality and natural emotions.

In the later years of his life Ekken began to disagree with the theoretical aspects of Chu Hsi philosophy, but he did not go so far as to reject them. He turned his attention, instead, to scientific research. He was trained as a physician, and his interest in natural science led him to do some significant work in botany.

Muro Kyūsō (1658–1734) was a scholar who remained an ardent defender of Chu Hsi philosophy, even as it came under increasing criticisms by the adherents of the Wang Yang-ming school and the school of Ancient Learning. "The Way of Heaven and Earth," he wrote, "is the Way of Yao and Shun. The Way of Yao and Shun is the Way of Confucius and Mencius. The Way of Confucius and Mencius is the Way of Ch'eng-Chu [Sung philosophers Ch'eng Hao, Ch'eng Yi, and Chu Hsi]." [5] He even went so far as to suggest that "useless" books of all other schools should be burned.

Kyūsō emphasized the Confucian notion that the ruler must govern for the good of the people, and he apparently favored the concept of equality among men. He wrote,

> The ruler is not inherently superior. He is superior
> in relationship to the people. . . . The people and the
> prince were in the beginning alike in being mere mortals.
> The people then came to the prince asking him to
> serve them. He agreed to do so. For this reason
> the people pay their respects to him and treat him
> as their prince. The fact that he has become prince
> and works for the people is merely the fulfillment
> of the agreement.

Here Kyūsō's political concepts resemble the theory of the social contract. The ruler, Kyūsō contended, derives his authority from the people. "The [feudal] domain is not given [to the feudal lord] by Heaven, nor is it given to him by the Prince. Needless to say he cannot seize it by force. It is given to him by the people." Thus it is the duty of the ruler to "work for the interest of the people." This theory, though unorthodox, was not intended to arouse the people. It was essentially an exhortation to the ruling class to live up to the Confucian ideal of benevolent rule.

THE WANG YANG-MING SCHOOL

One of the leading rivals of the Chu Hsi school in Japan was the philosophy of Wang Yang-ming of Ming China. Wang Yang-ming (1472–1528) began his philosophical career as a follower of Chu Hsi philosophy,

---

[5] The quotations from Muro Kyūsō are from Nagata Hiroshi, *Nihon Tetsugakushisō-shi* (*A History of Japanese Philosophical Thought*) (Tokyo: Mikasa Shobō, 1938), pp. 112–16.

but he departed from it and adopted the position that li (Principle) is a subjective or intuitive thing. "Mind is li. How can there be affairs and li outside the mind?" he asked. "The substance of the mind is the nature and the nature is li. Therefore, since there is the mind of filial love, hence there is the li of filial piety. . . . And since there is the mind of loyalty to the sovereign, hence there is the li of loyalty." [6]

Wang Yang-ming emphasized the importance of a person acting upon the truth as he individually perceives it. He spoke of the unity of knowledge and action: "There have never been people who know but do not act. Those who are supposed to know but do not act simply do not yet know." [7] This thesis that the truth can be apprehended subjectively and that the individual must act upon it, held special appeal for the samurai. The Wang Yang-ming school thus had a particularly strong following at the end of the Edo period in those han, such as Satsuma and Chōshū, where militant activists emerged who participated in the political movements leading to the downfall of the Bakufu.

The founder of the Wang Yang-ming school in Japan was Nakae Tōju (1608–1648). He was attracted to the philosophy by the thesis that truth is to be grasped intuitively, and that one had to act upon the truth so apprehended. In accordance with this tenet, Tōju believed that the way to clarify "the illustrious virtue" was to have "the mind read the mind." He focused upon the Confucian virtue of filial piety as an ideal of tremendous importance because of his belief that it constituted the very essence of man. This was the principle that distinguished man from the birds and the beasts. Tōju gave special emphasis to this quality because he was searching for a principle that would be common to all men and could thus serve as the basis for a moral outlook that would encompass all elements of the society.

Tōju's disciple, Kumazawa Banzan (1619–1691) denied that he belonged to any particular school of Confucianism and asserted that his source of ideas was the ancient sages. He claimed that he was willing to adopt the best aspects of both the Chu Hsi and Wang Yang-ming schools. He departed radically, however, from the Chu Hsi philosophy by embracing the concept that the principle of all things was located in the human mind. "Everyone knows," he contended, "that myriad principles and the mind are one. Myriad things in heaven and earth do not exist outside of the mind." [8]

---

[6] Fung Yu-lan, *A Short History of Chinese Philosophy* (New York: Macmillan, 1953), p. 309.

[7] W. T. de Bary *et al.*, eds., *Sources of Chinese Tradition* (New York: Columbia University Press, 1960), p. 579.

[8] Nagata, *op. cit.*, p. 81.

Banzan may have made a greater impact on the society than did his master, but his influence was similarly limited primarily to the samurai class. As a good Confucian he believed that the samurai had to follow the Way in order to qualify as the ruling class. It was for this reason that he focused upon ethical conduct and maintained that the samurai should strive to become like the scholar-officials of ancient China.

Banzan was a staunch supporter of the welfare of the peasants for he insisted that "the foundation of the nation is the people, and the foundation of the people is food." [9] His concern over the peasantry's economic difficulties led him to favor a return to the era of the warrior-farmers, that is, to the time before the class system was devised to separate the samurai and peasants into distinct classes. According to Banzan, taxes were low before the class division occurred. Afterwards, the tax burden on the peasants was increased in order to support the samurai and enable the warrior class to live in the castle towns. As an adviser to the lord of Bizen, he managed to have his plan tested but found that it was received unfavorably by both the samurai and the peasants.

Another reason for the difficulties of the peasantry, according to Banzan, was the rise of the merchant class and a money economy. To eliminate the consequent hardships imposed on the peasantry, he advocated a return to a rice economy. In this sense he may be labeled a reactionary. In order to relieve the lot of the people to some extent, he also urged a less stringent enforcement of "laws and etiquette." He believed that the rules of proper conduct and the laws of his day failed to reform bad men but caused hardships to honest men.

ANCIENT LEARNING

The other Confucian circle that challenged the orthodox scholars was the school of Ancient Learning. Actually, it is an oversimplification to classify these Confucians into a single school because they held divergent views and concerned themselves with different problems. The only justification for grouping them together is the fact that they all shared the belief that the essence of Confucianism was to be comprehended, not by studying what later scholars such as the Sung philosophers said, but by going directly to the texts of the ancient philosophers. The first of these philosophers of the school of Ancient Learning was Yamaga Sokō (1622–1685). He contended that the scholars of the Han, T'ang, Sung, and Ming dynasties had misled and confused the world by their interpretations of the ancient classics. Sokō claimed that since what the sages taught as recorded in the classics was self-evident, there was no

---

[9] Naramoto Tatsuya, ed., *Nihon no Shisōka* (*The Thinkers of Japan*) (Tokyo: Mainichi Shimbunsha, 1954), p. 117.

need for lengthy commentaries. His criticism of the official philosophy led him into serious difficulty with the authorities, and he was banished from Edo for a time.

Sokō felt that it was necessary to justify the existence of the samurai class, which in many ways had lost its function since peace prevailed under Tokugawa rule. Consequently, he set about defining the function of the samurai and the ideal way of life for them in his *Shidō* (*The Way of the Warrior*). In essence, he argued that the samurai were the custodians of the moral principles of the land, a role the warrior could claim only if he maintained his moral superiority. Sokō agreed with the Bakufu's contention that the samurai had to be well educated in the Confucian classics and history as well as skilled in the military arts. Above all, however, the samurai had to lead lives grounded upon just principles. It was essential that they comport themselves properly in all familial and social relationships. As guardians of the Way, the samurai had the responsibility of summarily punishing any member of the common classes who transgressed against the Way.

Unlike many Confucians, particularly the Neo-Confucians who insisted upon suppressing human desires, Sokō believed that the natural expression of human desires was good as long as it was done in conformity with the rules of proper conduct. If excesses were avoided, as they definitely must be, humanity and justice were sure to prevail.

Sokō was popular among the samurai as a teacher of military science. In his later years he became a royalist and a nationalist who looked upon the imperial family as the ultimate ruling authority. The shōgun was merely overseeing state affairs on behalf of the Emperor, as a good Confucian subject should. Sokō did not, however, seek to base the imperial authority on Shintoist notions of divine origin. He interpreted early Japanese history primarily in terms of Confucian concepts and explained that the Emperor was to be served in the manner that a loyal Confucian subject served his king. Sokō thus set the stage for the later Confucian scholars who became supporters of the imperial court.

Sokō was also an early nationalist who sought to assert the superiority of Japan over China. He referred to Japan as the Middle Kingdom, the center of the world. He thought she was superior to China, because, as he argued, only in Japan had proper relationships between lord and subject, father and son been truly observed and the moral ideals of the sages fully manifested.

Itō Jinsai (1627–1705) is another scholar who is identified with the school of Ancient Learning although there is no direct link between him and Sokō except for their common rejection of the Chu Hsi school and insistence upon going directly to the works of the early Confucians. Jinsai gave special emphasis to the Confucian *Analects* because he held that it alone could serve as "the standard and guide for the teaching of the Way in all times." Next to the *Analects* he stressed the importance of the *Book of Mencius,* which was the key to the understanding of Confucianism. Unlike Sokō, Jinsai did not link Confucianism primarily with the samurai class. He refused to accept any of the positions offered him by a number of daimyō and remained an independent scholar, living in poverty. Jinsai's influence, nevertheless, extended to a large number of people, for during his forty years of teaching, three thousand students attended his academy. After his death, his sons and disciples carried on his work.

Jinsai rejected the Neo-Confucian distinction between li and ch'i as well as the theory that li governs all things including human nature and moral principles. He restricted li to physical things and separated the Way of Man, which was his primary concern, from this. The Way of Man and the moral principles that constitute it are not, according to Jinsai, principles grounded upon the natural world, or human nature, which is part of the natural world. They are *ideas* and as such they exist independently.

Jinsai was not greatly interested in metaphysical theories; he was concerned primarily with practical morality. He placed special emphasis on benevolence, which he described as "a compassionate and loving heart reaching everywhere," and he considered this to be the ultimate goal of learning in Confucianism.[10]

Another Confucian scholar who defied the orthodox school and charted an independent course was Ogyū Sorai (1666–1728). He too emphasized the importance of studying the ancient Chinese texts and was known as a great Sinologist. He believed that in order to understand the Way of the sages, one had to understand ancient terms. Philological studies were extremely important, according to Sorai, because the meaning of words change in time and thus the true meaning of ancient terms could not be understood by applying later meanings of words to them. He also emphasized the six classics,[11] that is, works believed to have been produced during the era of the Three Dynasties. The fundamental principles of Confucianism were, he contended, to be found in these classics rather than in later interpretations.

Sorai was employed by Shōgun Tsunayoshi's personal adviser, and his opinion was often solicited by Shōgun Yoshimune's high officials. He did thus exert some influence on the Bakufu. A number of brilliant scholars

---

[10] Ryusaku Tsunoda, W. T. de Bary, and Donald Keene, eds., *Sources of Japanese Tradition* (New York: Columbia University Press, 1958), p. 421.

[11] The books of *Odes, History, Music, Changes,* the *Rites of Chou,* and the *Spring and Autumn Annals.*

emerged from his academy, and his school of thought dominated the intellectual scene during the mid-eighteenth century.

In many ways Sorai was one of the most radical Confucian thinkers of the Tokugawa era. Like Jinsai, he disagreed with the Neo-Confucian theory that li governs the nature of all things, including human nature and moral principles. He believed that the Way was not based on any principle of the universe, nature, or Heaven. It was in fact created by human personalities, the ancient sage kings of the Three Dynasties. All rules, regulations, and institutions were man-made, and so there could be no such things as a "natural" order of things or an order ordained by Heaven. The Way, according to Sorai, had absolute validity even though it was created by human beings, who became sages because of this rather than because they were morally perfect. The fact that he held the order of things to be man-made opened the way for later thinkers to entertain the idea that the existing feudal order, which had been created by man, was subject to change. The emergence of this line of thinking coincided with the entrance, in the nineteenth century, of Western political thought, which also held institutions to be man-made.

In discussing the Way, Sorai rejected the concept that the cultivation of personal morality necessarily leads to good government. He separated private morality and public affairs, and concluded that the Way, as formulated by the ancient sage kings, was primarily political in character. It was concerned with "how to govern the state and preserve peace in the land." [12] To achieve these ends, the ruler may, Sorai argued, use any means he deems necessary. This somewhat Machiavellian conclusion was tempered by his belief that benevolence and wisdom were virtues required of a ruler. Sorai said that benevolence meant "giving peace and security to the people," and that wisdom had to do with "recognizing good men and raising them to positions of responsibility."

Sorai claimed that the ruler had to emphasize "rites and music, and law enforcement and political administration" in order to govern effectively. He did not consider it worthwhile to argue, as the other Confucian scholars did, about the metaphysical basis and abstract meaning of morality. It is pointless, he held, to debate the question of whether human nature is basically good, as Mencius believed, or basically evil, as Hsün Tzu (ca. 300–237 B.C.) maintained. Man's nature is what it is and cannot be changed. Man can, however, pattern his behavior after certain moral standards and in this way learn to behave virtuously. Sorai opposed the constant moralizing of the other Confucian scholars and insisted that he was primarily interested in facts and substance, not

[12] The quotations from Sorai and analyses of his thinking are based on Maruyama Masao, op. cit.

idealistic concepts about morality. In this, he was unique among the Confucians. His emphasis on philological studies and his belief that Confucian concepts were man-made rather than based upon universal or natural principles influenced the thinking of the scholars in the school of National Learning.

NATIONAL LEARNING

The truly unorthodox school of thought of the Tokugawa period did not grow directly out of Confucianism but emerged as an independent intellectual movement. This school, referred to as National Learning, was influenced by Confucianism, Shinto, and even Buddhism. Essentially, however, it was an attempt to free Japanese learning from its excessive dependence on Chinese philosophy and literature. It failed to diminish significantly the influence of Confucianism during the Tokugawa period, but it did succeed in slowly extending its influence over the intellectual world until finally, in the Meiji era, it emerged as the central force of the nationalistic intellectual movement.

There was, as we observed, a movement to establish Japanese literature as an independent entity as early as the Heian period, but this attempt was not wholly successful. When the Tokugawa government made Neo-Confucianism the orthodox philosophy, Chinese learning enjoyed increasing domination over the Japanese intellectual scene. Partly as a reaction against this, and partly as a response to the Confucian emphasis on the past and historical studies, cultural nationalism emerged as an important force. Another contributing factor in the formation of National Learning was the interest in philological studies, which was stimulated by the scholars of Ancient Learning. Actually there were two schools of nationalistic learning: one developed in Mito Han and the other formed around Motoori Norinaga. It is the latter that is generally referred to as National Learning (*kokugaku*).

The Mito school grew out of the desire of Tokugawa Mitsukuni (1628–1700), the lord of Mito and grandson of Ieyasu, to compile a definitive national history. The project, *Dainihonshi* (*The Great History of Japan*), was started in 1657 but work on it was conducted sporadically, and it was not completed until early in the twentieth century. At the outset, Mitsukuni brought together more than one hundred scholars, including many Chu Hsi scholars, to work on the history. In compiling their work these men were guided by the concept of taigi meibun, the very principle that was stressed by Chu Hsi himself when he wrote his outline history of China. In Chou China the subjects owed supreme loyalty to the king; in a corresponding notion, Mito scholars concluded that in Japan supreme loyalty was due the Emperor. The shōgun, according to the scholars, was merely acting as the Emperor's loyal minister. By defining the relationship in this way, they saw no conflict between the two authorities. During the last stages of the Tokugawa era, the Mito scholars became more volatile in their expression of royalist sentiments, and eventually they came to favor direct imperial rule. Mito became one of the centers of opposition to the shogunate.

The origin of the National Learning school can be traced back to Keichū (1640–1701), a Buddhist monk who was interested in examining the *Manyōshū* from a literary viewpoint. He did not go beyond that to attempt to uncover the Way as it was embodied in ancient Japanese literature. A tenuous move was made in this direction by Kada-no-Azumamaro (1669–1736), who was interested primarily in conducting philological studies of ancient Japanese works such as the *Manyōshū, Kojiki,* and *Nihongi.* Kada-no-Azumamaro was also interested in establishing an academy where "imperial learning" would be pursued, but it was actually his disciple, Kamo-no-Mabuchi (1697–1769), who developed the concept of National Learning. Mabuchi wanted to study ancient Japanese literature with the hope of uncovering the Way of the sages by examining ancient words and making critical analyses of their meanings. In addition to studying ancient poetry and literature, Mabuchi included Shinto prayers among his objects of study.

His interest in ancient Japan and the imperial Way made him critical of Confucianism and the Chinese influence. He rejected the Neo-Confucian concept of li (Principle) and claimed that although the theories based upon this concept sounded reasonable, the fact that li was merely an abstract principle and not a practically applicable guide to experience was proven by the chaos and disorder that had characterized Chinese history. He advocated a rejection of this abstract philosophy and a return to the simple and pure ways of ancient Japan. He observed that the Way of the sages laid down all sorts of complex rules and regulations about proper conduct, which served to create a highly artificial society that prevented man from behaving naturally.

Mabuchi blamed all of Japan's evils on the introduction of Confucianism and artificial ways of China. He went so far as to claim that before Japan fell under Chinese influence, the nation was governed in accordance with the natural ways of the universe. "Confucianism made men crafty," he explained, "and led them to worship the ruler to such an excessive degree that the whole country acquired a servant's mentality. . . . the Confucian teachings had not only repeatedly thrown China into disorder, but they now had the same effect in Japan." He went on to declare the necessity of returning to the natural and simple ways of old Japan. "In ancient times," he wrote, "words and things were few. When things are few, the heart is sincere, and there is no need for difficult teachings. All will go satisfactorily even without teachings because men are honest." [13]

This condemnation of the influence of Confucianism and the emphasis on the simple, natural ways of ancient Japan were echoed and developed further by the most prominent figure among the scholars of National Learning, Motoori Norinaga (1730–1801). Norinaga, though born into a merchant family, was trained to become a doctor and studied medicine and Confucianism in Kyoto. His interest in Japanese literature and philology brought him under Mabuchi's influence. When the two men first met, Norinaga expressed his desire to study the *Kojiki* and Mabuchi advised him to begin instead with the *Manyōshū* because he felt it offered the best foundation for the understanding of ancient words. He claimed that without this knowledge the "true intentions of the ancients" could not be understood, and it would be impossible "to make a complete break with the Chinese mind." [14] Under the guidance of Mabuchi, Norinaga commenced work on the *Manyōshū* and then the *Kojiki,* which he ultimately devoted thirty years to studying.

Norinaga believed that the *Kojiki* embodied the Way of the gods, which was a political philosophy, not a religion. It was the "way in which the Emperor governs the land." Norinaga rejected the attempts to synthesize Confucianism and Shinto as well as the efforts to reconcile Shinto with Buddhism. These syncretic endeavors were intended to endow Shinto with theoretical doctrines, and he maintained that this was invalid because pristine Shinto did not really possess any abstract concepts at all. True Shinto, Norinaga claimed, was the Way of the gods that prevailed before the contaminating influence from the continent was felt. Consequently, he adopted a rigidly anti-Chinese, highly ethnocentric position, refusing to recognize the wisdom or superiority of the Chinese sages. He condemned them as imposters and asserted, "Sages surpass other people only in their cleverness."

In rejecting Chinese thought and all interpretations of the past by later scholars, Norinaga was even inclined, by virtue of his absolute faith in the Way of the gods, to reject rationalistic thought. "The acts of the gods," he said, "cannot be fathomed by ordinary human reasoning." He believed that man's intellect was limited and thus incapable of comprehending all things. This left open the possibility for "mysterious things," but, as he lamented, "disbelief in mysterious things has been brought about by the misguidance of the Chinese mode of thinking."

His belief in the mysteries of the universe and life enabled Norinaga

---

[13] Tsunoda *et al., Sources of Japanese Tradition,* pp. 517, 519.

[14] This and the following quotations from Norinaga are from *Motoori Norinaga Zenshū* (*The Complete Works of Motoori Norinaga*), 6 vols. (Tokyo: Yoshikawa Hanshichi, 1900–1903), vol. 4, pp. 49, 607, 393, 387, 853, 565, 556, and vol. 6, p. 219.

to accept the *Kojiki* as factual history. The Way of the gods was created by the ancestral gods of Japan, who were not abstract concepts like the Confucian "Heaven." They were divine beings that actually existed and were in fact the ancestors of the Emperors. Norinaga believed the Sun Goddess, who casts her light over the entire universe and is the founding Goddess of Japan, to be none other than the sun itself. Japan thus occupies a unique place in the world as the land favored by the gods.

An essential feature of the unique quality of Japan, according to Norinaga, was the imperial dynasty, which had survived unimpaired since it was established by the Sun Goddess. Consequently, the imperial family acquired special significance in his political thinking. The people did not belong to the shōgun or the daimyō but were subjects of the Emperor. This belief did not, however, lead him to reject the Bakufu because an integral part of his philosophy was to let nature take its course. As a result, he was willing to accept the status quo. "Things of this world," he held, "are beyond the scope of the human mind and designs. . . . Thus new laws must not be put into effect casually. If one were to rule in accordance with the trend of the times, and by following earlier precedents in all things, there may be slight defects but there will be no serious mistakes." He justified the rule of the shogunate by claiming, "Great shōgun have ruled the land ever since Azumaterunokami [Ieyasu] founded the government in accordance with the designs of the Sun Goddess Amaterasu, and by the authority vested in him by the imperial court. . . . The rules and laws of the founder and succeeding shōgun are all rules and laws of the Sun Goddess Amaterasu." Consequently, he could conclude that, "to obey the laws of the day is to follow the true Way of the gods."

Like Mabuchi, Norinaga believed in following the natural path, and he rejected the artificial rules and regulations about decorum and propriety that were stressed by the Confucians. "Man's feelings," he observed, "do not always follow the dictates of his mind. They arise in man in spite of himself and are difficult to control." [15] These spontaneous feelings, he insisted, should not be curbed unnaturally. As an example of this he noted that while alien philosophies teach man to transcend the sorrow and fear of death, these teachings are essentially invalid because they are contrary to the ways of human nature. To weep at the death of someone dear is an expression of true human nature and feelings.

Norinaga believed in the superiority of Japanese over Chinese poetry and ascribed its excellence to the fact that the former expressed human sentiments in an unrestrained fashion, whereas the latter sought to keep

[15] This and the following quotations from Norinaga are from Tsunoda *et al.*, *Sources of Japanese Tradition*, p. 534.

human emotions under control. In this sense we might say that Norinaga was a romantic. He observed that before the Chinese influence acquired roots in Japan there were many poems dealing with love. The reason for this was that the ancient poets gave free expression to natural human sentiments. Poetry, Norinaga insisted, should not be used for moral, didactic purposes. That is, the poet should not choose the good and reject the bad, instead, he should express in a natural and unadorned fashion both the good and the bad. In this Norinaga clearly ran against the dominant current of didacticism so prevalent in Tokugawa society.

AGRARIAN EGALITARIANISM

A thinker who stands virtually alone in that he cannot be included in any particular school of thought was Andō Shōeki (active during the first half of the eighteenth century), who rejected all the existing philosophies and religions. Shōeki was a physician who came from northern Japan, where the impoverishment of the peasantry was most severe. He was a forgotten figure until the twentieth century when his multivolume work was discovered.

Angered by the unjust system that exploited the peasantry, and motivated by his compassion for them, Shōeki became one of the harshest critics of the existing institutions and ideologies. He was not, however, an active revolutionary, and his views were known only to a small circle of friends. He traveled extensively and lived in Edo, Kyoto, Osaka, and Nagasaki, but he does not appear to have exerted a significant influence over the thinking of his age. He does, nevertheless, stand out as an example of one of the few independent-minded Tokugawa thinkers, and as a formulator of a uniquely utilitarian, egalitarian philosophy.

Shōeki regarded the existing order as an unjust system established by the usurpers of the people's land. "Rulers and sages," he charged, "have taken the country which was given by Heaven to the multitudes as their property, and turned it into their own domain from one end of the land to the other." [21] He believed that the agrarian class constituted the backbone of the society, and he was highly critical of the other classes. The samurai were corrupt and flattered their superiors while oppressing their inferiors; the artisans concerned themselves only with profits; the merchants relied on their clever tongues to make money and lead lives of comfort and ease. Only the peasants were engaged in "honest living by direct cultivation." Shōeki believed the country had fallen into a desperate plight, and the root of the problem, he said, could be found in

---

[21] The quotations from Andō Shōeki are from E. H. Norman, "Andō Shōeki and the Anatomy of Japanese Feudalism," in *Transactions of the Asiatic Society of Japan,* series 3, vol. 2, *passim.*

the existing class system. Simply stated, the consumers of rice had increased while the producers had not, and this plunged the country into terrible difficulties. "All this arises from the errors of the ancient sages," he wrote, "who created the four classes and discriminated between them, whereas originally all men were equal, one with the other."

Shōeki was severe in his criticism of the teachings of the sages, and like the Taoists and Rousseau, he believed that before "learning and civilization" arose man was free, happy, equal, and moral. The invention of writing and the emergence of many religions and philosophies gave rise to illusions and superstitions that served to replace the simplicity and purity of the "original world of Nature." He berated those who did nothing but talk while remaining idle and gluttonous, not producing "a single grain of rice." What the so-called saints and sages had said, he asserted, was less useful than "horse-dung."

Shōeki's touchstone was utility, not abstract moral concepts or theories. Ideologically his point of departure was the necessity of satisfying man's basic material needs. "Does the theory contribute to the economic well-being of man?" is the question he asked of all schools of thought. "Direct cultivation and happy eating, direct weaving and happy clothing—there is no Way but this. Talking of thousands of ways is false." Shōeki considered that the ideal society was one in which everybody performed economically productive work, following the course of nature and living in harmony. "In Nature there is neither order nor disorder. The people, all alike, cultivate as one man." In such a society there would be no need for anyone to rule over others. Man's natural activity, according to Shōeki, was to till the soil. Thus, if everyone engaged in "direct cultivation" complete freedom and equality would prevail because no one would have to take anything from or oppress his fellow man.

THE CULTURE OF THE TOWNSPEOPLE

In theory the townspeople were at the bottom of the social structure, but in fact they had acquired a great deal of economic power and had emerged as the most energetic and creative element in Tokugawa society. Tokugawa culture was, in reality, largely the creation of the townsmen. A high point in the economic well-being and cultural activities of the townspeople was reached in the Genroku period (this era name technically refers only to the years 1688–1703, but in practice this period actually encompasses a decade or more on both ends, thus covering at least the thirty years of Shōgun Tsunayoshi's rule, 1680–1709). This is not meant to suggest that the creative work of the townspeople promptly ceased with the end of the Genroku era. It was sustained to some extent throughout the remaining years of the Tokugawa period. The townsmen made lasting impressions on Japanese culture through their contributions to woodblock prints, haiku, novels, and drama—in both Kabuki and puppet plays.

This outburst of creative energy can be explained in part by the fact that the townspeople lacked outlets for their considerable wealth and energy in the political realm. Consequently, they applied themselves to the pursuit of physical and material pleasures that in turn stimulated the rise of town culture. The Kabuki and puppet plays emerged as popular forms of entertainment for the townsmen. The brothels where the wealthy merchants went to seek their pleasures provided material for the storytellers, the dramatists, and the woodblock artists. The various arts and crafts were able to flourish to the considerable extent that they did because the townspeople had the money to spend on expensive clothing, lacquerware, screens, tea bowls, books, prints, etc.

The Genroku era is known for the townsmen's exuberant, colorful, extravagant, and often ostentatious way of life. The mores, values, attitudes, and behavior of the rich merchants of Osaka, Kyoto, and Edo had a unique aura that fixed the tone of Genroku culture. It was Osaka that originally set the pace, for here the wealthy merchants dominated society. Kyoto was still under the cultural dominance of the court aristocracy, and Edo was under the control of the ruling samurai class. Engelbert Kaempfer, a German doctor who visited Japan in the late seventeenth century, said of Osaka,

> Even what tends to promote luxury, and to gratify all
> sensual pleasures, may be had at as easy a rate here as
> anywhere. For this reason the Japanese call Osacca the
> universal theatre of pleasures and diversions. . . . Hence
> it is no wonder, that numbers of strangers and travellers
> daily resort thither, chiefly rich people, as to a place, where
> they can spend their time and money with much greater
> satisfaction, than perhaps any where else in the Empire.[22]

In their pursuit of material happiness the wealthy townspeople were relatively free from the rigid code of ethics that regulated the conduct of the samurai. The literature of this era yields a vivid picture of their way of life, and it would be quite accurate to describe it as a blatantly hedonistic mode of existence. They lived in what was referred to as the *Ukiyo*, the floating world where the pleasures and joys of life were pursued without a thought for the future. This entailed "living for the moment, gazing at the moon, snow, blossoms, and autumn leaves, en-

---

[22] Engelbert Kaempfer, *History of Japan*, 3 vols., trans. J. G. S. Schenchzer (Glasgow: MacLehose, 1906), vol. 3, pp. 6–7.

joying wine, women, and song, and, in general, drifting with the current of life 'like a gourd floating downstream'." [23]

The wives of rich merchants vied with one another to gain recognition as the most elegantly attired lady of the land. Young men went about dressed as dandies, and homosexuality became widespread. Wealthy merchants replaced the samurai as patrons of the brothels where the hedonism of the pleasure-seeking townsmen was paid for by the heartbreak and degradation of the girls that had been sold into slavery.

PROSE FICTION

The hedonistic, erotic life enjoyed by the townspeople was reflected in their literature, that is, in the works described as *ukiyo-zōshi* (notes of the floating world). The originator and master of this form of prose fiction was Ihara Saikaku (1642–1693) of Osaka. Saikaku, a former merchant, began his literary career as a haiku poet and wrote primarily about the love lives of the men and women of his world. At one time he composed 23,500 haiku in twenty-four hours, a feat that attests to his prolific imagination and zestful energy. He wrote his first humorous, erotic novel, *The Man Who Spent His Life in Love*, in 1682 and produced more than two dozen volumes of this kind during the next decade. In his first book he described the love life of a rake whose amorous exploits began at the precocious age of eight and continued into lecherous old age. The hero has 3,742 women before he turns philosophical at the age of sixty. "I've been around every one of the pleasure quarters in this wide world, till I find," he says, "I'm quite emaciated by love; and now at last the floating world has lost all attraction for me." [24] His "emaciated" condition, however, does not stop him from sailing off in search of the fabulous Island of Women.

Saikaku did not moralize in his love stories; instead, he displayed an optimistic and sympathetic attitude toward man's foibles by depicting the exploits of his characters in a realistic but good-humored fashion. His novels demonstrate his keen awareness of the serious conflict between love and duty that confronted the lovers of the floating world. This was a theme that was also of particular interest to the playwright Chikamatsu (see pages 203–204).

In his later works Saikaku dealt with the economic life of the townspeople. He was an enthusiastic supporter of the system that enabled clever, resourceful, and diligent men to amass great wealth. This did not blind him, however, to the economic hardships besetting the townsmen

[23] Howard Hibbett, *The Floating World in Japanese Fiction* (New York: Grove, 1960), p. 11.
[24] *Ibid.*, pp. 42–43.

of the lower class who were constantly involved in a desperate struggle to make ends meet. Despite his awareness of the negative aspects of his society, he retained a fundamentally optimistic and positive outlook. The qualities needed for success in business, he held, were frugality, persistence, a pleasant manner, honesty, and imagination.

The popularity of the works of humorous and satirical writers like Saikaku attest to two significant facts: first, the printing of books had become common by the Genroku period and second, many Genroku townsmen, though not erudite, were at least literate. In numerous cities there existed something that was comparable to a lending library where books could be borrowed inexpensively.

Many didactic tales reflecting the moralism of the ruling class were written by Tokugawa writers. The master of this kind of prose fiction was Takizawa Bakin (1767–1848). He was born into the warrior class but married into a footwear merchant's family in order to be able to pursue his writing career. Bakin devoted twenty-eight years of his life to the completion of his major work, *Nansō Satomi Hakkenden,* which consists of ninety-eight parts. The novel is set in the period of the Warring States and has eight heroes, each having a noble dog for his ancestor. The dogs represent the Confucian virtues of benevolence, righteousness, propriety, wisdom, loyalty, sincerity, filial piety, and obedience. Bakin made clear distinctions between good and evil, for his primary goal was "to encourage the good and chastise the bad." This was a theme that had the approval of the ruling authorities.

Stories designed to entertain or morally uplift the townspeople continued to be written, and they were widely read during the remainder of the Edo period. The quality of the literature declined considerably as many writers sought merely to imitate the earlier masters.

THEATER

Another area that reflected the culture of the townspeople was the theater. The puppet theater (*Jōruri* or *Bunraku*) that originated in the Muromachi period as a ballad-drama and saw the addition of marionettes in the early seventeenth century, was perfected during the Genroku era. The Kabuki also gained a solid footing in this period.

Osaka was the center of the puppet plays. In these shows puppets perform actions that are described by a singer-narrator who is accompanied by *samisen* (a three-stringed instrument) players. The puppets are about one-third life-size, and each one requires three men to operate it. Official restrictions that were placed on Kabuki for moral reasons led to the domination of the theatrical world by the Jōruri by the middle of the eighteenth century. In order to compete with this form of theater, Kabuki borrowed heavily from it both in the style and in the actual plays performed. By the end of the eighteenth century Kabuki regained its popularity and has remained the leading dramatic form in Japan to the present.

The nature of Kabuki is described by a leading authority as follows:

> Kabuki fuses into a single form the arts of music, dance, acting, literature, as well as graphic and plastic arts. . . . Each of the arts within the combined art of Kabuki is responsible for certain effects. Music gives Kabuki its dynamics, its rhythm, and its continuous pace. Dance makes the actors concentrate on grace and determines a large part of Kabuki's special kind of movement and gesticulation. Acting adds the qualities of pantomime, speech, and declamation, and of course provides the important dramatic factor. . . . Graphic arts are utilized in the wide variety of scenery, properties, and costumes. . . . Plastic arts are rivalled in the frequent poses and studied groupings of the actors. [25]

Spectacle, providing the framework for all this, is specifically designed to please the eye, which is the primary objective of Kabuki. Color and motion are thus the two most important elements in this kind of drama, and they serve to make Kabuki a much more spectacular dramatic form than the Nō plays. Ingenious mechanical devices such as the revolving stage, trapdoors, and the passageway that runs directly through the audience enabled the Kabuki producers to solve many technical problems and thereby heighten the dramatic effects of the plays.

The Kabuki theater comprised one of the key elements of the Genroku world of pleasure. The colorful day-long performances attracted people from all ranks of society, "from shop-boys to samurai." Kabuki actors became the focus of popular attention, gaining as much fame as today's movie stars. Theatrical giants like Ichikawa Danjurō I and Onoe Kikugorō I founded acting dynasties that have survived to the present day and have sustained the essence of the Kabuki theater.

The playwright who made the greatest contribution toward increasing the repertory of the puppet and Kabuki plays was Chikamatsu Monzaemon (1653–1725), who wrote about one hundred and sixty plays. He was born into a minor samurai family but joined the ranks of the townspeople as an unemployed samurai. Chikamatsu wrote his first play when he was thirty and devoted the rest of his life to writing historical dramas and domestic plays about the ordinary people of his time. When he

---

[25] Faubion Bowers, *Japanese Theatre* (New York: Hill & Wang, 1959), pp. 177–78.

wrote about love affairs, the plot usually involved a hero who was either a samurai or a townsman, and a heroine who was a courtesan from the brothels. The play generally focused upon the conflict between love and duty or *ninjō* (human feelings) and *giri* (social and moral obligations). Frequently, the only way out of this conflict for the lovers was suicide.

The harsh demands of giri often necessitated heartless treatment of loved ones. Fortunately, however, ninjō tempered such actions. In one of his plays, a woman is almost forced to disown her son because of the dictates of giri, but ninjō leads her instead to steal money in order to help him. Ninjō, then, humanizes giri, which "denies the individual's right to be happy at the expense of society. In so doing it preserves society, as ninjō unchecked by giri must eventually destroy it." [26]

WOODBLOCK PRINTING AND PAINTING

Another art form that emerged from the world of the townspeople was woodblock printing, known as *ukiyo-e* (paintings of the floating world). The prints were made not only to be appreciated in themselves but also to illustrate the stories written by Saikaku and other novelists. Saikaku had done the illustrations for some of his works himself, but the artist who is usually given credit for making the woodblock print an important art form, Hishikawa Moronobu (1618–1694), also did some illustrations for him. Moronobu was followed by a galaxy of prominent woodblock artists: Harunobu, Utamaro, Sharaku, Hokusai, Hiroshige, to name a few. These artists created a sense of movement, form, and atmosphere by relying solely on line and color. They made no use at all of chiaroscuro or linear perspective because they did not want to give the prints a sense of the three dimensions; they were not to be realistic paintings. These artists did, nevertheless, succeed in conveying a feeling of gracefulness, sensuality, and warmth in their depiction of lovers, courtesans, and actors. In landscape paintings, artists such as Hokusai were able to capture the atmospheric tone of the scene and convey a sense of dynamic force and energy.

Among the more prominent of the woodblock artists was Suzuki Harunobu (1725–1770), who, it is believed, was the first artist to produce a full polychrome print. He did not restrict himself to conventional colors to brighten his prints but experimented with rosy-pink skies, kelly-green earth, jet-black skies, etc. As was the style with other woodblock artists, his subjects lacked individuality and consequently looked rather similar. His primary interest was not in depicting individual

[26] Monzaemon Chikamatsu, *The Major Plays of Chikamatsu*, trans. Donald Keene (New York: Columbia University Press, 1961), p. 35.

This and the following four illustrations are color woodblock prints by five Tokugawa masters of ukiyo-e *("pictures of the floating world"). This page, "Lovers Sharing an Umbrella" by Harunobu (1725–1770).*

personalities but in portraying the essence of femininity through the creation of doll-like creatures. Harunobu's trademark is his delicate and coquettish feminine figures. Feminine frailty is conveyed through the depiction of abnormally small hands and feet on his subjects. In order to accentuate their sensuous, erotic characteristics, Harunobu never has the

"Half Bust of a Beautiful Lady" by Utamaro (1753–1806). *Courtesy of the Cleveland Museum of Art, Edward L. Whittemore Fund.*

ladies stand erect but has their heads and bodies curved gracefully. The lines emphasize the richness of the fabrics adorning the figures and this adds considerably to their sensuousness.

Kitagawa Utamaro (1753–1806) is also known for his sensuous

Portrait of the Kabuki actor Otani Oniji III, by Sharaku (fl. 1794/5, d. 1801).
Courtesy of the Art Institute of Chicago, Clarence Buckingham Collection of
Japanese Prints.

"The Great Wave," a print from the series "Thirty-Six Views of Mt. Fuji" by Hokusai (1760–1849). Courtesy of the Museum of Fine Arts, Boston, from the series Fugaku Sanjurokkei.

feminine figures. His subjects, more voluptuous than Harunobu's, are generally tall and willowy with elongated faces. Many of them are semi-nudes, and the lines are ingeniously used to convey a sense of the smoothness and softness of the flesh. Utamaro was inclined to concentrate on the head and the upper part of the body, usually dispensing with the setting.

In contrast to Harunobu and Utamaro who focused upon delicate or sensuous women, Tōshūsai Sharaku (d. 1801) concentrated upon Kabuki actors. Departing from his activities as an obscure Nō actor, he produced about one hundred and forty-five prints in ten months during 1794/1795. He realistically depicted the intense facial expressions and exaggerated poses employed by Kabuki actors at climactic moments in the plays. His prints lack the gentleness and charm of the other artists' works, but because the lines are stronger, they convey a powerful sense of vigor, vitality, and movement. His unconventional realism did not endear him to his contemporaries, who were accustomed to stylized portraits of handsome actors, and he disappeared from the public scene after his very brief career as a woodblock artist.

Katsushika Hokusai (1760–1849) and Andō Hiroshige (1797–1858), known for their scenic color prints, are perhaps better known in the West than the other woodblock artists. Hokusai, who led a flamboyant and turbulent life, is regarded as a giant among the Tokugawa print-makers. He first called attention to himself by painting an enormous portrait of the Bodhidharma, which was 60 feet high. He then drew two sparrows that were so tiny they could be seen only with a magnifying glass. He perfected his art late in life and produced his masterpieces after he was sixty. Among the better known of his prints are the series on *The Thirty-Six Views of Fuji, Waterfalls, Bridges,* and *Imagery of the Poets.* The last series shows great poets placed in a variety of natural settings, such as Li Po admiring a tremendous waterfall. He also produced thousands of sketches of human beings in every conceivable posture and situation.

His prints project an aura of majesty, as manifested in some of his views of Mt. Fuji, and a tremendous sense of force and energy, as seen in his prints of waterfalls and towering waves. Hokusai was also a master of dramatic composition who was able to use color in such a way as to capture the unique atmosphere of a particular moment. A striking example of this is the *Red Fuji,* one of his masterpieces. "Light effects as a device in art reached a high watermark in this picture, and it is no wonder that it served as a source of strong inspiration to painters of the impressionist school in France." [27] Like the other woodblock artists, Hokusai produced erotic prints. His "spring pictures" are considered to be the most profound, constituting "one of the major accomplishments of ukiyo-e."

Hokusai was a dedicated craftsman who devoted his entire life to his art. At the age of seventy-five he wrote,

> Since the age of six I have had the habit of drawing
> forms of objects. Although from about fifty I have often
> published my pictorial works, before the seventieth year
> none is of much value. At the age of seventy-three I was
> able to fathom slightly the structure of birds, animals,
> insects, and fish, the growth of grasses and trees. Thus
> perhaps at eighty my art may improve greatly; at ninety it
> may reach real depth, and at one hundred it may become
> divinely inspired. At one hundred and ten every dot and
> every stroke may be as if living.[28]

He signed this essay, "The old man crazy about drawing."

Hiroshige's series, *Fifty-Three Stations of the Tōkaidō,* is probably the

---

[27] Tokuzo Sagara, *Japanese Fine Arts* (Tokyo: Japan Travel Bureau, 1955), p. 198.
[28] Robert T. Paine and Alexander C. Soper, *The Art and Architecture of Japan* (Baltimore, Md.: Penguin, 1955), p. 153.

"Rain Shower on Ōhashi Bridge" by Hiroshige (1797–1858). *Courtesy of the Cleveland Museum of Art, gift of J. H. Wade.*

best known work of the Tokugawa woodblock artists. Hiroshige was interested in the relationship between light and natural phenomena and sought to capture the moods of nature and the atmospheric conditions— the mist, the moonlight, the raindrops, and the falling snow—of the different seasons. He was particularly successful with his snow scenes, as he made effective use of blank space while taking full advantage of the beauty of Japanese paper. His rain scenes were rendered in a unique and refreshing fashion by his use of bold parallel lines to indicate rain. "No one," writes an art historian, "had revealed to us so freshly the beauty of the rain; rain showering like light javelins that shine in the returning sun, or mingling with the mist and with the wind that bends and tosses a long ridge of blotted pines, or descending in straight rods that hiss on ground or water, or trailing delicate threads that caress the trembling willows." [29]

Japanese woodblock artists profoundly influenced the French impressionists of the nineteenth century. In particular it was the manner in which light and atmosphere were treated in the scenic color prints by Hokusai and Hiroshige that impressed the French artists.

Traditional decorative art—screen paintings and paintings on lacquer and pottery—also flourished during this era. One of the most prominent of the decorative style painters, and certainly the greatest lacquer artist of the age, Ogata Kōrin (1658–1716), emerged from among the townspeople. His works are known for their simplicity and elegance of form and color as well as the forcefulness of the brushstrokes. His most famous work is a pair of screens representing a row of irises with their dark-and-light blue blossoms and soft-green leaves arranged in an overall design that is set against a gold background.

An artist who painted in a more naturalistic style than the men who preceded him was Maruyama Ōkyo (1733–1795). A folding screen depicting pine trees in the snow reveals his preoccupation with modeling as a technique for evincing the roundness of forms. His paintings also possess more realistic details than the works of other decorative style painters.

A school of painting that evidently emerged as a reaction against the naturalistic school of Ōkyo was the *Nanga* (Southern painting), which sought to follow the Southern School of China. Nanga painters relied upon inspiration rather than a studied technique, and they regarded painting as an activity that educated men pursued for enjoyment. The best artist to emerge from this school, Ike-no-Taiga (1723–1776), showed an impressive mastery of calligraphic lines and subtle tone variations. His paintings are characterized by a brush-dotted texture and a rolling

[29] Lawrence Binyon, *Painting in the Far East* (New York: Dover, 1959), pp. 266–67.

"Fishing in Springtime," a hanging scroll by *Ike-no-Taiga* (1723–1776). *Courtesy of the Cleveland Museum of Art, Edward L. Whittemore Fund.*

rhythm. A master haiku poet, Buson (1716–1783), was also a Nanga painter.

In pottery, porcelainware came to be produced in the Edo period. Such products as *Imari* wares with their elaborate decorations and rich colors, and *Kakiemon* wares with their elegant decorations on a pure white body gained renown even in the West. The Kakiemon wares in particular were imitated by the porcelain makers of Holland, Germany, and England.

HAIKU

Another significant cultural development of the Tokugawa era was the emergence of haiku—a seventeen syllable poetry—as a major literary form. It is usually identified with the culture of the townspeople even though the greatest haiku poet, Matsuo Bashō (1644–1694), was born into a samurai family and traveled around the countryside as a Buddhist priest in order to avoid the bustling towns. Haiku was popular among the townspeople—for that matter, it was greatly favored by men of every walk of life.

Haiku is linked intimately with Zen Buddhism. Suzuki Daisetsu points out that haiku "ought to be an expression of one's inner feeling altogether devoid of the sense of ego. The haiku poet in this sense must also be a Zen-man." In explaining the brevity of the haiku poem, he remarks, "At the supreme moment of life and death we just utter a cry or take to action, we never argue, we never give ourselves up to a lengthy talk. Feelings refuse to be conceptually dealt with, and a haiku is not the product of intellection. Hence its brevity and significance." Therefore, "a haiku does not express ideas but . . . it puts forward images reflecting intuition." [30]

Its extreme brevity occasionally makes haiku sound flat, pointless, and even nonsensical when it is translated into another language. Donald Keene explains that the effectiveness of haiku depends upon the realization of the basic principle that the poem have these two elements: a general condition and the momentary perception. "The nature of the two elements varies but there should be the two electric poles between which the spark will leap for the haiku to be effective; otherwise it is no more than a brief statement." [31] As an example, here is one of the most frequently cited haiku by Bashō:

[30] Daisetsu T. Suzuki, *Zen and Japanese Culture* (New York: Pantheon, 1959), pp. 225–27, 240.

[31] Donald Keene, *Japanese Literature: An Introduction for Western Readers* (New York: Grove, 1955), pp. 40–41.

> The ancient pond
> A frog leaps in
> The sound of the water.

In this haiku Bashō was seeking to express two principles, change and permanence. The first line evokes the eternal component: the timeless, motionless water of the pond. The second line gives the momentary element in the form of the frog's movement. The point where the momentary intersects the eternal is the splash of the water.[32]

In his book *Narrow Road of Oku*, Bashō discusses the circumstances that induced him to compose some of his poems. He mentions the time, for example, when he came upon Minamoto-no-Yoshitsune's last battle scene and, as he sat there weeping, he recalled this poem by the T'ang poet, Tu Fu:

> Countries may fall,
> But their rivers and mountains remain.
> When spring comes to the ruined castle,
> The grass is green again.

The result of this experience was his writing of the following haiku:

> The summer grasses—
> Of brave soldiers' dreams
> The aftermath.[33]

The keen sense of finesse possessed by a great haiku poet distinguishes him from an ordinary poet, as this story about Bashō will illustrate. When he was just starting out as a haiku teacher, he was out walking one day with a student who, upon seeing the darting dragonflies in the field, composed this haiku:

> Red dragonflies!
> Take off their wings,
> And they are pepper pods!

Bashō is said to have exclaimed, "No! That is not haiku. If you wish to make a haiku on the subject, you must say:

[32] *Ibid.*, p. 39.
[33] Donald Keene, ed., *Anthology of Japanese Literature from the Earliest Era to the Mid-Nineteenth Century* (New York: Grove, 1955), p. 369.

> Red pepper pods!
> Add wings to them
> and they are dragonflies! [34]

Haiku has come to be composed by people from all segments of the society since Bashō's days, and in this sense it can be said to have contributed to the growth of cultural democracy in Japan. In the Tokugawa era even the peasantry produced a great haiku poet, Issa (1763–1827). He wrote of insects, birds, and animals, manifesting a strong compassion for all living things. For instance, seeing a fly about to be swatted, Issa felt that it was praying for mercy and cried out:

> Oh, don't swat
> the fly! He wrings his hands!
> He wrings his feet! [35]

EDUCATION

One further noteworthy aspect of Tokugawa culture is the fairly widespread diffusion of learning that took place. Education of the common people was carried on in the *terakoya* (temple schools) by Buddhist and Shinto priests in the rural areas and frequently by masterless warriors in the towns. Children were taught the rudiments of reading and writing and the use of the abacus. Girls also attended these schools and learned the skills and modes of behavior deemed at the time to be suitable to their sex.

A considerable number of children successfully learned how to read and write in the towns. In the villages, however, education was largely restricted to the children of prominent farmers. The number of terakoya increased greatly toward the latter part of the Tokugawa period, and, although no accurate figures are available, it is estimated that perhaps there were from ten to fifteen thousand temple schools in existence. Twenty or thirty pupils attended an average-sized terakoya.

The children of the samurai were especially well-educated. They attended private schools or han academies where they were taught calligraphy, the Chinese classics, some arithmetic, etiquette, and the military arts. In the later years of the Edo period, the han academies began to admit some students from the common classes. It is believed that literacy among the samurai men was almost 100 percent. This is a

---

[34] Harold G. Henderson, *An Introduction to Haiku* (Garden City, N.Y.: Doubleday, 1958), pp. 17–18.

[35] *Ibid.*, p. 133. (The author has substituted "swat" for "mistreat" in Henderson's translation.)

rather astonishing achievement. Over all, slightly more than 40 percent of all boys and about 10 percent of all girls were receiving some kind of formal education outside of their homes by the end of the Tokugawa era. In 1870 the literacy rate in Japan was considerably higher than that which exists in most underdeveloped nations today. It is likely that Japan compared favorably in this respect with some of the European countries of the nineteenth century. In light of this, it is not at all surprising that Japan was able to launch so successful a program of modernization and industrialization after she opened her doors to the outside world again.

THE STATE OF BUDDHISM

In addition to performing funeral services, Buddhist priests did contribute to the education of the common people, but little creative work was actually done by them in the way of furthering the spiritual well-being of the masses. They had captive clienteles because everyone was required to affiliate with a Buddhist temple, and their work with the laymen tended, as a result, to fall into a regular routine.

Buddhism as a religious and philosophical movement remained relatively stagnant during the Tokugawa period. The main intellectual activities of the various sects consisted in the formulation of doctrinal systems and orthodox dogmas. None of the sects challenged the orthodox philosophy, Neo-Confucianism, and they all seemed content to cooperate willingly with the ruling authorities. The Bakufu had some difficulty with a small segment of the Nichiren Sect who refused to participate in officially sponsored ecumenical religious functions. This was the only group that caused any trouble and eventually those who did not cooperate were suppressed. Some of the dissenters managed to survive by going underground, much like the Christians did.

A renaissance of a sort took place in the Zen Rinzai Sect under the leadership of Hakuin (1685–1768). He systematized the existing kōan and created a number of new ones, formulated a method of achieving satori, and trained a large number of disciples. The kōan system and method of training that Hakuin established have remained in effect to the present. He insisted upon continuous zazen practices and kōan study. The discipline of a Zen disciple, Hakuin taught, did not cease with the attainment of satori, because the training that followed was of equal or greater importance. He emphasized the importance of moral behavior, without which satori was not possible, and the value of good health, which was necessary for the rigorous training. Hakuin was also a talented painter and calligrapher.

The age of creativity that characterized the Genroku period and the few decades that followed it also coincided with the period in which the Bakufu began to feel, with increasing intensity, the pressures of the growing economic crisis. We shall now turn to an investigation of this and other related problems that plagued the Bakufu for the last remaining century of its rule.

CHAPTER 9

THE LATE TOKUGAWA PERIOD

POLITICAL DEVELOPMENTS

In 1745 Shōgun Yoshimune turned over the shogunate to his son, Ieshige, but he remained the de facto ruler until his death in 1751. It is not surprising that Ieshige proved to be a rather ineffective shōgun—he was an invalid with a rather serious speech defect. During the reign of the next shōgun, Ieharu, chamberlain Tanuma Okitsugu and his son became influential figures wielding great power. In fact, during the last fourteen years of Ieharu's reign, Okitsugu, acting as senior councilor, held near dictatorial power. As a result, Ieharu's regime (1760–1786) is referred to as the Tanuma era.

Unlike Yoshimune, who sought to solve the Bakufu's economic difficulties by reducing expenses, encouraging frugality, and increasing agricultural production, Okitsugu hoped to resolve the difficulties by debasing coinage, granting monopolistic rights to wholesale dealers in return for payment of fees, and taxing the merchant guilds. In order to reverse the unfavorable balance of trade and curb the outflow of bullion, he sought to increase exports. He also initiated various reclamation projects. There is little question that Okitsugu sought to serve the public good; but there is also no doubt about the fact that he was more than casually interested in advancing his own private interests in the hopes of accumulating a vast fortune. Consequently, standards of rectitude began to decline throughout the official hierarchy, while graft and bribery, though surely engaged in to some extent under previous administrations, became widespread practices. One observer noted, "Villagers rush about in agitation crying out that officials are coming to assess the tribute; for days on end shrines and temples are piled high with all kinds of rare presents for them." [1]

In spite of Okitsugu's efforts to solve the Bakufu's financial difficulties, natural calamities aggravated the situation, and conditions failed to improve. A great famine broke out between 1783–1787, the prices of goods soared, and rice riots occurred frequently. Okitsugu was blamed for most of the difficulties and, with the death of Ieharu, he was summarily removed from office.

Under Shōgun Ienari (1773–1841), Yoshimune's grandson, Matsudaira Sadanobu (1758–1829), emerged as the chief Bakufu official. Sadanobu had gained a reputation as an able and enlightened administrator while he was the head of a small han in northern Honshu. During the great famine of 1783, while hundreds of thousands of people starved in the neighboring han, he took measures to ensure that not a single person in his han would perish from lack of food.

The treasury was nearly depleted when Sadanobu became the Bakufu's chief councilor in 1787, a year of great floods, inflation, food shortages, and rioting. In order to cope with the crisis, Sadanobu started what has been called the Kansei Reforms (the Kansei period, for which the reforms are named, was 1789 to 1801). The policies that he adopted were conservative in nature and patterned after those of his grandfather, Yoshimune. He concentrated, for instance, on reducing expenditures and encouraging frugality. He also imposed price controls, but they proved to be ineffective. In order to be prepared to cope with future famines, he increased the Bakufu's rice reserves and required the daimyō to set aside 50 koku for every 10,000 koku of rice they collected. After reducing the expenditures of the city of Edo, he had 70 percent of the savings set aside as relief for the needy and as low interest loans for the poor. He also established a vocational training program for the unemployed and the vagrants in Edo. In 1789, in order to relieve the Bakufu's liege vassals who had fallen in debt to the rice brokers, he canceled all the debts that they had incurred before 1784 and reduced the interest rates on those incurred after 1784.

In the hope of increasing agricultural production, Sadanobu encouraged the peasants in the cities to return to the countryside. He issued sumptuary laws prohibiting them from indulging in any wasteful or extravagant activities. This was intended to foster frugality among the peasantry. He also attempted to impose standards of austerity on the townspeople; he even went so far as to attempt to tighten their moral values by curbing unlicensed prostitution, censoring books that he

---

[1] E. H. Norman, "Andō Shōeki and the Anatomy of Japanese Feudalism," in *Transactions of the Asiatic Society of Japan*, series 3, vol. 2, pp. 57–58.

deemed prurient, and banning mixed bathing of persons over the age of six.

In order to cope with the rising tide of unorthodox philosophies, Sadanobu issued the Kansei ban on heterodoxy and prohibited the teaching of any philosophy other than the Chu Hsi version of Confucianism in the Bakufu's schools. He also adopted a policy of denying employment in the Bakufu to anyone who had been trained in unorthodox philosophies.

It was during this period that Russia began probing Japan's northern islands. Sadanobu was not at first concerned about this, and in fact he arrested an advocate of national defense, Hayashi Shihei, for criticizing the Bakufu for neglecting its defenses against external threats. Later he did come to recognize the need to fortify the northern coastal regions.

In spite of his strenuous efforts, Sadanobu failed to solve the basic problems of the Bakufu. He remained in office for only six years, but his puritanical asceticism did manage to cramp the life style of influential people in the shōgun's entourage, including the ladies in the inner palace.

Sadanobu's departure was followed by an era of laxity under the leadership of the hedonistic Ienari, who was shōgun for the more than fifty years from 1786 to 1837. Even after his resignation, Ienari dominated the Bakufu until his death in 1841. Moral standards declined and graft and bribery became rampant once again. Government expenditures rose along with the considerable personal expenses of the self-indulgent shōgun (he had forty wives and concubines to support). The price of rice remained low, but the cost of other commodities rose sharply. The only steps taken by the Bakufu to deal with its financial difficulties were to repeatedly debase the coinage and make requests of wealthy merchants for financial contributions. Between 1806 and 1813 the Bakufu called upon the merchants and villagers to contribute money three times, and over 1.4 million ryō was collected. The Bakufu's difficulties, however, continued to multiply as famines broke out frequently and, as we will see later, peasant uprisings increased in size and number. In addition to the internal difficulties, pressures from the outside world were becoming more serious.

After Ienari's death another attempt at reforms was made, this time by the chief councilor, Mizuno Tadakuni (1793–1851), in what is called the Tempō Reforms. Like Sadanobu, Tadakuni also endeavored to tighten moral standards, reduce expenses, encourage frugality by issuing many sumptuary laws, and curtail extravagance in food and clothing. In addition, he restricted what he considered to be frivolous and wasteful activities, such as festivals, Kabuki, Nō, and other forms of entertainment. He even sought to curtail the operation of pawnshops, public bathhouses, hairdressers, and the like.

Like Sadanobu, Tadakuni encouraged the initiation of reclamation projects and hoped to increase agricultural production by compelling the peasants who had migrated to the cities to return to the villages. In addition, he sought to curtail secondary work such as weaving because he believed that it reduced the time the peasants could spend tilling the soil.

Tadakuni also sought to curb inflation by the fixing of wages and prices. Convinced that a free flow of goods would reduce high prices, he ended the monopolistic privileges that had been granted to the wholesalers and merchant guilds by the Tanuma administration. This of course resulted in the loss of the fees they had been paying the Bakufu, and to offset this reduction in revenues Tadakuni found it necessary to compel the wealthy Osaka merchants to donate money to the Bakufu. As another means of increasing the Bakufu's income, he sought to bring under its direct control the land held by the bannermen and daimyō in the vicinity of Edo and Osaka. This measure, however, was so vigorously opposed by the parties concerned that he was forced to abandon it. This episode served to unite the opposition against him while providing the catalyst that eventually brought about his dismissal. As was the case with Sadanobu, Tadakuni's austerity program displeased a great many people, including the shōgun's consort. As a result, he was removed from office in 1843, only two years after he had initiated the Tempō Reforms. He made a brief comeback in 1844 but was dismissed again after a short term in office. Many of his reforms were rapidly undone soon after he fell from power.

All the while he was in office Tadakuni encouraged the daimyō to follow his example by urging them to institute similar reforms in their han. Many failed to respond, but some han, such as Chōshū, did in fact initiate their own reform programs. None of these attempts were very effective, but some han did manage to reduce their expenses and tighten official control over the marketing of cash crops. During his tenure in office Tadakuni was also very much aware of the trouble China was having with the British, and he sought to strengthen his nation's military defenses by training the warriors in Western gunnery.

All the reforms initiated by the various Bakufu officials were basically ineffective because, though they were honestly intended to solve the Bakufu's economic difficulties, they were aimed at achieving this by actually preventing changes, that is, by curbing the rising merchant class and money economy. Essentially, the reform programs pointed to a return to the predominantly agrarian, natural economy of early Tokugawa. It was with the best of intentions that the reformers persisted in adopting reactionary measures. But sumptuary laws to enforce simple living and uplift the people's moral standards could not solve the Bakufu's financial problems, nor could these legal maneuvers prevent the disintegration of the closed society. The Bakufu thus approached the middle of the nineteenth century having failed to solve its basic economic difficulties. At this juncture it was confronted with a major external crisis that ultimately brought about its downfall—the arrival of Commodore Perry. Before we turn to this event, however, let us examine more closely the economic difficulties of Tokugawa society.

ECONOMIC PROBLEMS

The basic cause of Tokugawa society's problems lay in the fact that the economy was supported by an agrarian base that, though expanded, was not sufficiently broad to meet either the increasing needs of the ruling class, whose size and standard of living did not remain static, or the rising expectations of the common classes. From the end of the seventeenth century, in particular, commerce began to grow, thus creating an economy evermore incompatible with agrarianism.

Large urban centers emerged and the demand not only for basic necessities but also for what the ruling authorities regarded as luxury goods steadily increased. In order to meet these needs of the cities, the production of nonessential agricultural and industrial goods had to increase and consequently, the number and size of local business entrepreneurs, wholesale dealers, and shippers grew. The sankinkōtai system also served to stimulate economic growth by increasing commercial and industrial activities along the routes that the daimyō crossed in their travels to and from Edo. There were, necessarily, growing expenditures, which the daimyō sought to meet by fostering the production of cash crops and industrial goods that could be marketed to other han. Now that a greater variety and better quality of fabrics, utensils, household goods, and art objects was available, the taste and standard of living of the samurai as well as the wealthier elements in the towns and villages rose substantially. Such improvements, however, also tended to raise the level of expectation of the other segments of the society. An increased imbalance between income and expenditures resulted. Despite the fact that over the years rice production grew at a rate greater than the increase in population, the people, instead of enjoying an augmented sense of ease and satisfaction, became increasingly restless about an economic and financial situation they found uncomfortable and dissatisfying.

We have already discussed some of the economic problems plaguing the Bakufu, and we shall now turn to an examination of those confronting the daimyō and the samurai. Ogyū Sorai observed in the 1720s that whereas thirty or forty years earlier lower-class samurai never wore formal ceremonial suits and were unable to furnish their houses with *tatami* (reed mats), they now not only had better household furnishings and fancy formal suits, but their hair smelled of perfume, and their sword guards were decorated with gold and silver inlays.

To be sure, the daimyō were certainly enjoying much greater luxury if the samurai were living in better houses and wearing finer clothing. According to Sorai,

> In the way in which they comport themselves throughout
> the day, in their garments, food and drink, household
> furnishings, dwellings, employment of servants, the
> conduct of their wives, the retinues that accompany them,
> the manner in which they travel, the ceremonies of
> coming of age, marriage and burial—in all these matters
> they naturally tend to be extravagant in accordance with
> the trend of the times.[2]

The samurai and the daimyō needed more money to maintain their more elaborate style of living, and their financial needs were made ever the more acute by the recurrent periods of inflation that beset the land. The monetary problems of the daimyō were further intensified by the need to defray the cost of traveling back and forth to Edo and maintaining two residences, one in the home province and one in Edo. The extent to which this cut into the daimyō's budget is illustrated by the example of Saga Han. In the mid-seventeenth century 20 percent of its expenditures were applied to travel costs for the sankinkōtai, and 28 percent was used for its residence in Edo.

The Bakufu added to the financial burdens of the daimyō by requiring them, whenever it felt the need to do so, to participate in public works and other expensive tasks. Saga Han, for example, devoted 4 percent of its expenditures to guarding Nagasaki. In 1754 Satsuma, already in debt for 800,000 ryō, was asked to assist in the construction of a water-control project along the Kiso River in central Honshu. Participation in this project made it necessary for Satsuma to raise more than 200,000 ryō. To obtain the money, the already over-taxed peasants had to be taxed even further. After the completion of the project, the Satsuma official in charge committed hara-kiri to atone for the hardships inflicted upon the people.

In addition to these expenses, the daimyō's financial difficulties were aggravated by such calamitous events as floods, droughts, famines, and

[2] Maruyama Masao, *Nihon Seijishisōshi Kenkyū* (*Studies in the History of Japanese Political Thought*), (Tokyo: Tōkyō Daigaku Shuppankai, 1954), p. 120.

fires. Consequently, many han were continuously plagued with budgetary deficits.

There were only a limited number of ways in which the daimyō could cope with the rising costs of their personal and public needs. One way was to borrow from the wealthy merchants, and there were, in fact, some merchant houses that specialized in loaning money to the daimyō and samurai. An interesting example of this was Yodoya Tatsugorō, whose wealth was legendary. So many daimyō had fallen deeply in debt to him that the Bakufu finally confiscated his fortune in 1705. The ostensible reason given for this action was that he was living in an outrageously extravagant fashion, far beyond the limits suitable to a person of his social status.

The Kōnoike family records showed that in 1706 its loans to the daimyō totaled over 278,000 ryō, and by 1795 this amount had risen to more than 416,000 ryō. After the Tokugawa era, the descendants of one merchant family found three cases full of certificates of loans to daimyō amounting to ten million ryō.

In order to extricate the daimyō and the samurai from their indebtedness, the Bakufu sought to compel the merchants to settle for less than full payment of outstanding loans. In some instances it called for the total cancellation of long-standing debts, inflicting great losses upon the merchants. For instance, when Senior Councilor Sadanobu canceled debts in 1789, ninety-six financial agents lost a total of about 1.2 million ryō. Some daimyō, in arranging the terms of a loan, demanded that they be given anywhere from one hundred and fifty to two hundred years to repay the debt. These measures naturally caused many merchant houses to become bankrupt, and induced others to become extremely wary about loaning money to military men. This in turn forced the daimyō and the samurai to abandon their traditional attitude of superiority and appeal to the wealthy merchants for money with lowered heads. In order to cultivate the good will of the merchants, they gave them seasonal gifts, extended special commercial privileges, and accorded them the rights of the samurai, such as the rights to bear swords and receive stipends.

The subservience of the warrior class to the wealthy merchants led one contemporary observer to remark, "When the great merchants of Osaka get angry, the feudal barons of the land quake with fear." [3] Another commentator wrote, "Both large and small daimyō . . . are constantly plagued by their creditors to pay their debts and have no peace of mind worrying about how to make excuses. They fear the sight of

[3] Sakata Yoshio, Meiji Ishinshi (A History of the Meiji Restoration), (Tokyo: Miraisha, 1960), p. 19.

moneylenders as if they were demons. Forgetting that they are samurai, they bow and scrape to the townspeople." [4]

Another way in which the daimyō sought to increase their revenues was by taxing the peasants more heavily. There was a limit, however, to this approach. Some han made occasional tax reassessments to take into account the increase in rice production, but there is some evidence to indicate that in many han this was not actually done because of the laborious tasks involved in making thoroughgoing surveys. Many daimyō followed the example of the Bakufu reformers and periodically attempted to reduce their expenses by implementing austerity programs, but these measures repeatedly failed to solve their financial problems. Some daimyō sought to cope with their difficulties by reducing the samurai's stipends, but naturally this only worsened the already serious plight of the samurai. Some other measures that were resorted to were the extraction of forced loans from the merchants and the issuance of currencies valid only in the han.

The daimyō did adopt some measures that yielded very positive results. Many han attempted to increase their revenues by expanding agricultural production. They reclaimed wastelands, initiated water-control projects, built irrigation systems, and introduced improved methods of farming and better strains of seed. As noted below, the acreage under cultivation was substantially increased, and greater yield per unit of land was achieved. It appears, however, that even this increased agricultural yield failed to meet the growing expenditures of the Bakufu and the han.

Another positive measure that was adopted by the Bakufu and the han was the fostering of the production of crops and handicraft goods that could be marketed to other han. As a result, many han came to be known for special products. Some han even concentrated on the production of high quality rice with the intention of competing more effectively for the urban rice market. Many han were known for their textiles, pottery, timber, and fish, while other han managed to produce commodities not readily available elsewhere, such as salt, sugar, indigo, wax, tea, and paper. Villages near major cities like Edo concentrated on producing vegetables for the urban consumers. Some han exploited the mineral resources that had not been claimed by the Bakufu. A few han in the south and the west managed to increase their revenues by engaging in trade with Korea and the Ryukyu Islands; for instance, Tsushima Han, which was officially valued at 20,000 koku, managed to raise its revenues to about 200,000 koku by trading with Korea.

In marketing the commercial and industrial crops many han either

[4] Maruyama Masao, *op. cit.*, p. 125.

established han monopolies or granted monopolistic rights to selected entrepreneurs. In order to compete effectively with other han while increasing their own revenues, han authorities paid the producers of the cash crops minimum prices. This frequently became a source of conflict between the peasants and the authorities.

The Bakufu and the daimyō were feeling the pressures of rising expenditures, but the samurai felt the imbalance between income and outlay even more acutely. As we noted earlier, the samurai had also become accustomed to a more elegant way of life. Their expenses were growing, and their economic woes were further intensified by the fact that they had a fixed income in rice even though the price of rice tended to drop in time of abundant harvest. The price of other commodities, however, not only did not drop, but in some instances rose.

Another economic development that hurt the samurai was the policy adopted by the Bakufu and some daimyō to withhold a certain amount of rice stipends from time to time. In Chōshū as early as 1646 the retainers were asked to "loan" one-fifth of their stipends to the han. Later the amount was raised to one-third and then to one-half of their stipends. These were meant to be only temporary measures, but such reductions often lasted for years. During the time between 1742 and 1762, for example, the Chōshū retainers were asked to take reductions annually, and for seven years in a row they were required to accept reductions of 50 percent. This practice, which was also followed by other han, forced the samurai to fall deeper and deeper into debt, and had the effect of weakening the samurai's sense of loyalty to their lords who, they felt, were failing in their duty to provide them with adequate means of living. A critic at the end of the eighteenth century observed, "Some daimyō have now ceased to pay their retainers their basic stipends. These men have had half their property confiscated by the daimyō as well, and hate them so much that they find it impossible to contain their ever-accumulating resentment." [5]

Occasionally the samurai would be aided when the Bakufu and the daimyō ordered a cancellation of debts, but before long they were heavily in debt again because the basic situation remained unchanged. Consequently, the poorer samurai were reduced to selling their military equipment and there are instances of a few who even sold their daughters. Some turned to banditry, but the most common solution open to the lower-class samurai was to engage in some sort of handicraft work such as repairing umbrellas, lanterns, wooden clogs, or household utensils. This kind of menial work was considered beneath their dignity, but

[5] Donald Keene, *The Japanese Discovery of Europe, 1720–1830* (Stanford, Calif.: Stanford University Press, 1969), pp. 168–69.

they were compelled to do it in order to survive. It was not uncommon for some samurai to establish family ties with merchant houses as a means of escape from financial problems. A samurai might adopt a young man from a merchant family or permit his son to marry a merchant's daughter.

In addition, peacetime conditions had brought about a deterioration in the warriors' moral standards. Many samurai began to frequent places of entertainment—the brothels and the theaters—which existed primarily for the pleasure of the townspeople. It was estimated that in the middle of the eighteenth century 70 percent of the patrons of Edo's brothels were samurai. One observer, bemoaning the moral decay of the samurai, surmised that seven or eight samurai out of ten were effete weaklings.

To some extent, the economic distresses and consequent changes in moral standards of the ruling class tended to blur the social distinctions between the samurai and the merchant classes. At the same time, the bonds between the lord and his followers were weakened. These changes, together with the penetration of commercial interests into the rural areas and the growing unrest of the peasantry, were beginning to strain the existing social and political order.

THE LOT OF THE PEASANTS

The peasantry was the segment of the society that supported the national economy and endured hardships and miseries in silence. The expanding money economy was affecting them most adversely and, after the Genroku era, as the Bakufu and the daimyō faced growing financial difficulties, the plight of the peasants appeared to worsen as they were taxed even more heavily.

The infiltration of money and commercial economy into the villages also meant the penetration of Genroku culture. This was true despite the attempts of the Bakufu to keep the villages insulated from the more extravagant ways of the cities. As might be expected, the desire for better living conditions grew among the peasants, and they began to purchase items that the authorities regarded as luxury goods. They also needed money to buy fertilizers and agricultural implements. Their expenses were rising at the same time that the authorities in many han were increasing the rate of taxation in order to meet their growing expenses. This situation became even more serious when, in some instances, the peasants were compelled to pay taxes several years in advance. As we noted previously, there were also numerous additional taxes besides those levied on the rice crop. The peasants were also subject to corvée, the most burdensome being the obligation to provide men and horses for the courier or horse station system.

There is some indication that the ruling class was not uniformly ruth-less in its financial demands, but this is not to say that the taxation was not burdensome. Some daimyō, in fact, raised the tax rate to exceed 50 percent, and in a few extreme cases, the peasants were forced to pay 70 percent of the harvest. It should be noted that while many daimyō revised the method of assessment in order to increase the tax yields, the han in the poorer sections of the north and in the mountainous areas were espe-cially stringent in exacting taxes. On the other hand, the Bakufu retained its taxation rate of 40 percent. During the latter half of its rule it usually managed to collect about 1.6 million koku from its assessed holdings of something over 4 million koku. In 1744, by revising the method of assess-ment, it managed to raise its intake to 1.8 million koku. After 1766, how-ever, its tax revenues gradually declined.

Abuses occurred in all the han when some ambitious officials sought to impress their lords by increasing the tax yields. At the same time, how-ever, there were officials who sought to further and protect the interests of the people and gained renown as practitioners of "benevolent rule."

An important point to consider in assessing the tax burden on the peas-ants is the fact that no nationwide land survey was made after the Kam-bun and Empō eras (1661–1681). The area under cultivation, however, had been steadily expanded through reclamation, and the productivity per acre of land was increased substantially through the years by better plant varieties, greater use of fertilizers, and improved methods of farming. The area under cultivation in 1598 was 1.5 million chō, whereas by the Kyōhō era (1716–1736) it had risen to 2.97 million chō. Agricultural production in 1598 was estimated at 18.5 million koku, whereas by the Genroku era (1688–1703) it had risen to 25.78 million, and by 1834 it had reached 30.43 million. In light of the fact that no nationwide land survey had been made since the latter half of the seventeenth century, it is possible that the amount of rice and other crops left in the hands of the villagers may not have decreased even though the tax rates rose. Moreover, in or-der to encourage the reclamation of wastelands the officials were usually willing to overlook the fact that taxes were not paid on reclaimed plots, or else they imposed only a nominal levy. One study of eleven widely scattered villages indicates that from around 1700 to 1850 the official as-sessment of productivity varied very little, that is, there was no substantial movement upward. The same was true of the tax rate; no significant changes had occurred in these villages. This of course was a period during which productivity was still increasing.

It would appear then that in spite of the financial pressures facing them, the Bakufu and many daimyō did not tax the peasants as severely as they might have. The growing determination of the peasants to resist additional levies and arbitrary measures may have been partially responsible for this. Furthermore, the changing attitude of the villagers perhaps accounts for the increase in uprisings at a time when the standard of living of the peasants may have been higher than that of their ancestors who lived during the early stages of Tokugawa rule.

There are also strong indications that the larger amount of rice and other products that remained in the villages after taxation did not benefit all the villagers equally, but was in fact primarily directed to the advantage of the wealthier members. The villagers who were likely to increase the yield per acre and to enlarge their holdings through land reclamation were the wealthier farmers. This was the case because of the additional expenses and labor needed for such undertakings. These wealthy and thus prominent villagers were the ones to hold the key village posts, and this enabled them to determine each producer's share of taxation. It appears that in many villages the increased yields and greater holdings were not taken into account in allocating each producer's share of the tax burden.

The fact that the wealthier villagers were benefiting from the taxation system is reflected in the many complaints lodged by the poorer peasants that they were being taxed more heavily than the rich. The clash of interests can also be seen in the growing number of peasant disturbances that were directed against the headmen and other prominent villagers. This is in sharp contrast to the many earlier disturbances, which were led by the village leaders to protest the policies of the Bakufu or han officials.

The rising rate of tenancy also indicates that the gap between the rich and poor peasants was widening. It was illegal to buy or sell land, but this law was frequently circumvented, and even some merchants purchased land in the villages. Most of the land belonging to the poorer peasants, however, passed into the hands of the wealthy villagers who held mortgages on the fields of impoverished farmers. The percentage of tenancy varied greatly from place to place, but it is estimated that in areas where the commercial economy had penetrated deeply, that is, near the major cities and the main roads, it had risen to 50 percent by the nineteenth century. Accompanying this increase in tenant farmers was an increase in the number of hired workers on the larger farms and in the village handicraft industries. A further indication of the growing disparity of wealth in the villages can be seen in the changing pattern of landholding: the number of large and very small holdings increased while medium-sized holdings decreased.

The wealthier villagers, in addition to enhancing their wealth through greater productivity per acre and acquisition of more land, began investing their money in the commercial and industrial enterprises that were developing in the rural areas. Many were already involved in traditional commercial activities such as the lending of money and the selling of daily necessities (e.g., sake, salt, soy-sauce, oil) to the villagers. Now some began to participate in such "manufacturing" enterprises as spinning, weaving, pottery making, and other handicraft industries. Others ventured into the business of marketing the cash and industrial crops that were produced in their villages. At the same time, urban merchants came to the villages to market these crops and became members of the rural communities. The consequence of this was the development of a group of rural dwellers, known as gōnōshō (rich farmer/businessman), who came into existence in villages that were affected strongly by the commercial economy.

An early nineteenth-century observer made the following remarks concerning the growing disparity between the rich and the poor villagers: "the wealthy farmers have forgotten their rank, have been given the right to have surnames, wear swords or even have yearly allowances. They are addicted to wearing beautiful clothes, practice military arts, study Chinese books and poetry, and even call courtesans from the prosperous centres to their homes." [6] Essentially, then, they were living like members of the samurai class. In sharp contrast to this, the poorer farmers, he noted, were falling deeper into debt and losing their land. In the less productive sections of the country, the poorer peasants found it difficult to raise a family and resorted to infanticide and abortion. A social critic writing in the later stages of the Tokugawa era claimed that in the northern provinces the number of children killed annually exceeded sixty or seventy thousand.

The fact that the population remained stable and even decreased from time to time after the eighteenth century indicates that a large percentage of the peasantry was leading a marginal existence. In 1721 the population of the common classes was officially noted to be twenty-six million. It fluctuated between twenty-five and twenty-seven million from that date until the end of the Tokugawa era.[7] Figures prior to 1721 are not available, but if we accept an estimated figure of eighteen million for the period 1573–1591, it is conceivable that the population increased by ten million from the end of the sixteenth century to the beginning of the eighteenth.

The population during the latter half of the Tokugawa era was held down by periodic famines and epidemics, and by abortion and infanticide. Mass starvation resulted whenever there were serious crop failures, which were caused by droughts, excessive rainfall, floods, typhoons, cold weather, or locusts. There were in all thirty-five famines in the Edo pe-

---

[6] Hugh Borton, "Peasant Uprisings in Japan of the Tokugawa Period," in *Transactions of the Asiatic Society of Japan*, series 2, vol. 16., p. 10.

[7] For the total population, two to three million must be added to account for the daimyō and samurai, and their servants, as well as the outcasts, who were excluded from the census. It should be noted that in some instances children were not included in the count either.

riod. In 1732, for example, swarms of locusts descended upon western Japan, practically ruining the entire rice crop of that region. This is known as the Kyōhō famine, and contemporary estimates held that while it lasted 969,900 people died of starvation. No doubt this figure is highly exaggerated, but it does, nevertheless, indicate the strong impression that large-scale starvation made upon observers. In 1755 cold weather destroyed the crops in the north, and as a result, in one han alone it was reported that one out of five persons died of starvation. In 1773 droughts preceded a plague that claimed the lives of two hundred thousand people. This death toll rose as the plague spread through the northern provinces, with Sendai Han reporting the loss of three hundred thousand people. This was followed by the great Temmei famine that began in 1783 and lasted until 1787. It was caused by continuous bad weather: excessive rainfall, unseasonably cold weather, and drought. The year the famine started Mt. Asama in central Japan erupted causing much death and destruction. The bad weather and persistent crop failures continued year after year and the northern provinces, which were again affected most seriously, experienced such mass starvation that the people were finally reduced to practicing cannibalism. No accurate figure is available on the number of people who starved to death in the Temmei famine, but one contemporary observer wrote, "during the three years of bad crops and famine which occurred since 1783, over two million people in Ōu Province alone starved to death." [8] This is an overestimation, but it is believed that several hundred thousand persons did perish, and much of the northern region remained uninhabited and untilled for years.

In the Tempō era another major famine occurred that lasted from 1833 to 1836. Once again the northern provinces were most severely affected. Tsugaru Han, which was said to have lost eighty thousand persons in a single year during the Temmei famine, lost another forty-five thousand.

The effects of these famines and catastrophes are reflected in the decreases in the population that followed each major outbreak. As a result of the Kyōhō famine of 1732–1733, the population of the common people dropped from 26.92 million in 1732 to 26.15 million in 1744, when the next census was taken. Just prior to the Temmei famine, the population was 26.01 million, but it declined to 25.08 million in 1786, and then dropped even further to 24.89 million in 1792.

PEASANT UPRISINGS

The peasants did not remain completely passive when confronted with the rigid control and exploitation of the ruling class, growing economic

---

[8] Keene, *op. cit.*, p. 182.

hardships, and periodic disasters. There was little they could do about natural calamities, but they could and did protest against abuses on the part of the officials and demand relief in times of famine and disaster.

Recent studies show that between 1590 and 1867 there were 2,809 peasant disturbances. During the early years of Tokugawa rule these disturbances tended to occur more frequently in the poorer regions. Later on, however, they began to break out increasingly often in the more advanced areas, thus indicating that the penetration of commercial economy was causing difficulties in the villages. The number of peasant uprisings rose significantly in the latter half of the Edo period. This was also true of the Bakufu's own domain: from 1590 to 1750 the Bakufu was faced with 146 peasant disturbances in its demesne, while between 1751 and 1867 it was confronted with 401 incidents.

The protest movements took various forms. The peasants could, of course, submit petitions through regular channels, but such actions were not effective since they could so readily be blocked at the lower levels. Illegal actions took the form of mass flights into another lord's domain, forceful demonstrations, violent uprisings, and submission of petitions that bypassed the lower authorities and went directly to the daimyō or Bakufu. With the passage of time, the protest movements tended to grow increasingly violent, and from about 1710 forceful demonstrations and violent uprisings constituted between 40 and 50 percent of all protests. The houses and warehouses of the rich farmers, merchants, and moneylenders were frequently the objects of attack.

In a study that was made of 2,755 peasant outbursts, it was determined that taxation, having been named in 628 of the incidents, was the most prevalent cause of violent action. The other incidents involved the following immediate causes: 355 were directed against some aspect of the administrative system; 214 involved demands for relief and assistance; 158 were rice riots; 146 were directed against abusive Bakufu or han officials; and 134 were protests against arbitrary measures taken by the authorities. In the later stages of the Edo period there was an increase in protests against the village leaders and merchants who had monopolistic rights.[9]

During the latter half of the Tokugawa era, the number of participants and the areas covered by the disturbances tended to grow in scope. In 1738, eighty-four thousand peasants in Iwaki Province in the north participated in a demonstration against excessive taxation. In 1754, one hundred and sixty-eight thousand peasants were involved in an outburst against unfair taxation in Kurume Han in Kyushu. In 1764, two hundred thousand peasants in the Kantō region rioted to protest the burdens of

[9] The source for these figures on peasant disturbances is Aoki Kōji, *Hyakushō Ikki no Nenjiteki Kenkyū* (*A Chronological Study of Peasant Uprisings*) (Tokyo: Shinseisha, 1966), p. 13.

corvée in the horse stations. Following the Temmei famine, violent uprisings involving thousands of peasants broke out with increasing frequency. One of the major riots in the nineteenth century was the 1831
uprising in Chōshū, where one hundred thousand peasants rioted, demanding a reduction in taxes and protesting the han's monopolistic policy in marketing industrial crops.

It is interesting to speculate as to why peasant unrest grew in the latter
half of the Tokugawa period when, compared to the first half, more food
and other commodities were available. The population remained more or
less stable after the eighteenth century while rice production increased
somewhat, so there must have been more food to go around.[10] A partial
answer is found in the fact that this was the time when the three major
famines of the Edo period occurred: the Kyōhō famine of 1732–1733, the
Temmei famine of 1783–1787, and the Tempō famine of 1833–1836. In
the decade or so during and following these major famines, the number
of peasant disturbances increased significantly.

This period of increasing unrest also coincided with the growing financial difficulties of the Bakufu and the han. The various measures they
adopted to cope with the situation, such as the Kyōhō, Kansei, and
Tempō reforms, caused the people inconvenience and hardship. The
growth of commercial economy and its consequent effects in the villages
also gave rise to unrest by causing dislocations in the countryside. The
economic difficulties caused by opening the country to the West touched
off a large number of peasant disturbances in the 1860s. We have already
made note of the growing conflict between the wealthier villagers and
poorer peasants, which also contributed to the increase in agrarian
troubles.

Another possible contributing factor that should not be overlooked is
that the peasants were getting bolder in challenging the ruling class because the latter had lost some of its militaristic qualities. The samurai
were no longer hardy warriors, they were more like gentleman-scholars
who had been softened by urban living. Very few samurai lived in the villages where the peasants dwelled, and when these outsiders did appear it
was only to collect taxes. Finally, the greater productivity and the improved standard of living being enjoyed by the village leaders and the
townspeople must have had the double effect of raising the expectations
of the peasants while making them more militant.

In some instances the protestors did succeed in gaining concessions and
in having their grievances redressed; but, in all cases of violent or illegal

---

[10] During the seventeenth century the rice production increased by about 40 percent
while the population may have grown by about 50 percent. From the early eighteenth
century, however, the population remained fairly stable until the end of the Tokugawa
era while the rice production grew about 18 percent by 1834.

action, the leaders were arrested and punished because any sort of conspiracy or group action was strictly prohibited. In order to ferret out the instigators, the suspected leaders were tortured cruelly and forced to confess. They were then beheaded or crucified. Some were buried alive.

The peasant uprisings were not motivated by any desire to change the social or political order. They were simply protest actions calling for redress of specific grievances. The peasants remained politically unsophisticated partly because of the Bakufu's success in keeping them isolated and politically ignorant. The rulers followed the adage that "the peasants should not be informed but should be made to depend upon the ruling class." Peasant riots did break out, particularly in the Kantō and northern regions, when the Bakufu was being overthrown by the imperial forces. These were called *yonaoshi ikki,* uprisings to reform the society, but they were isolated actions directed primarily against the wealthy villagers.

It was not only the peasants who were forced to resort to violence because of economic difficulties; the urban poor also began to stage violent demonstrations. Inflationary prices and food shortages were the primary causes for these urban riots, which were usually directed against the rice and sake merchants and the pawnbrokers.

Prior to the Kyōhō (1716–1736) era, only eight urban disturbances had occurred, and only one of these involved any violence. After 1717, however, 332 instances of urban conflict were recorded, and most of them entailed rioting and violence. One of the most widespread urban rice riots occurred late in the spring of 1787 in the wake of the Temmei crop failures and famine when fifty separate violent incidents broke out in cities throughout the country.

The Tempō famine also touched off rice riots in the cities, where shortages and inflated prices caused rampant hunger and starvation. This series of disturbances culminated in a major uprising in 1837 in Osaka, which was led by a former police officer and a Wang Yang-ming scholar, Ōshio Heihachirō (1792–1837). Ōshio was outraged at the indifference of the Osaka city commissioners and the rich merchants, such as Mitsui and Kōnoike, to whom he had unsuccessfully appealed for help. Instead of taking any positive action to alleviate the unfair conditions, one of the city commissioners accused Ōshio of violating the ban on making direct appeals to higher officials. Ōshio, as a result, decided that the only course left to him was to lead the people in an uprising against the rich and the established authorities. He had only about three hundred followers, largely impoverished townspeople and peasants from nearby villages, but they managed to set fire to one-fifth of the city. The uprising was quickly crushed, and he was forced to take his own life.

Urban disturbances continued to break out. The crisis facing the Bakufu and established authorities became acute after the advent of

Perry, and the number of urban riots increased. Seventy such outbursts were recorded between 1854 and the fall of the Bakufu.

AGRICULTURAL IMPROVEMENTS

Agricultural production, as noted above, did not remain static during the Tokugawa period. A variety of factors contributed to the increased yields in rice and other crops. There was a far greater and more extensive use of fertilizers—in addition to night soil, manure, grass, leaves, and ashes, dried fish and lees of vegetable oil came into use. The variety of plants also increased considerably, and it is estimated that the number of rice varieties swelled from about one hundred and seventy-five in the early seventeenth century to over two thousand by the mid-nineteenth century. Irrigation systems were improved with wider use being made of water wheels and treadmills. In the northern and Kantō regions, sericulture became important as a supplementary source of rural income.

The production of commercial and industrial crops began to increase throughout the country. Cotton, indigo, sugar cane, tobacco, silk worms, tea, wax tree, etc. were produced by the peasants to supplement their income or at the behest of their lords. Despite the increasing production of cash crops and growing commercial activities, Tokugawa Japan was still predominantly an agricultural country, not a commercial one. It is estimated that in the 1860s only about 20 percent of the agricultural products reached the commercial market, whereas a century later the figure grew to 60 percent.

The fishing industry remained an important part of the Tokugawa economy, as did mining, forestry, and the various handicraft industries. Somewhat larger production facilities, especially in textiles, were emerging at the end of the era. Commercial capital began to enter the process of production to some extent, and the more advanced areas of the economy were showing signs of industrial growth. In view of the overall picture, however, all these changes were not really significant enough to affect the fundamentally agrarian character of the economy.

Not many Tokugawa thinkers concerned themselves with the practical aspects of farming, but there were a few who did. Among the more notable of these were Ōhara Yūgaku (1797–1858) and Ninomiya Sontoku (1787–1856). Yūgaku, although born into a samurai family, was disowned for having killed a man in a duel and spent years wandering around the country. He finally settled in a village in the Kantō region, just as the Tempō famine broke out. Deeply distressed at the suffering of the peasantry, he sought to devise ways in which to assist them. In 1838 he organized a cooperative credit union encompassing four villages. Each member was required to transfer to the cooperative a plot of land worth five ryō, and the profits from this land were then put into a fund that was to be used to assist the members in time of need. Yūgaku also introduced better methods of farming and initiated a land improvement program. In addition, he sought to instill a wholesome outlook into the peasantry and taught that the nature of things and the Way were fixed by the unity of Heaven and Earth. The common people too were created by this unity, so they were obliged to follow the Way. This consisted in practicing filial piety, adhering to one's station in life, and respecting the samurai.

In spite of his positive contributions to agrarian life, and his essentially pro-establishment philosophy, Yūgaku was accused by the authorities of disturbing the existing order in the village and of exceeding his proper station in life by daring to propagate his own philosophy. He was forced to dissolve the cooperative before being incarcerated. After his release he committed hara-kiri.

The other agrarian reformer, Ninomiya Sontoku, referred to as the "peasant sage of Japan," was born into a peasant family and remained a tiller of the soil and a spokesman for the peasantry all his life. His family was plunged into the depth of poverty by the Temmei famine and a destructive typhoon. Through hard work, Sontoku more than restored the family fortune and became a minor landlord of 4 chō. Like Yūgaku he also sought to help his fellow peasants improve their lot. He taught them the importance of making long-range plans, and advised them to make an annual budget in which they were always to plan on spending less than they expected to make. He also proposed the establishment of voluntary credit unions, a suggestion that was adopted by a fairly large number of villages in Sagami, where Sontoku came from, as well as in the neighboring provinces. He was active in relief work during the Tempō famine, and as he gained renown as an agrarian expert, he was sought out by many han to assist in revitalizing villages that had fallen into decay.

Sontoku believed that the peasants must be instilled with a philosophy of life that would be fitting to them while enhancing their well-being. Each person, he taught, owes his existence and well-being to his ancestors and society and, therefore, has as his duty the following of the doctrine of Repayment of Virtue, which calls for hard work, thrift, and sharing what one can with others. Sontoku's interpretations of the Way of Heaven and the Way of Man were pragmatic and utilitarian: the Way of Heaven is the way of nature as seen in the physical world; the Way of Man is fixed by man's necessity to survive in nature. Thus, the Way of Man tells us "rice is good and weeds are bad; to build a house is good, to destroy it is bad. . . . All that is convenient for man is good and all that is inconvenient is bad." [11]

[11] Nagata Hiroshi, *Nihon Tetsugakushisōshi* (*A History of Japanese Philosophical Thought*) (Tokyo: Mikasa Shobō, 1938), p. 237.

Unlike other Tokugawa thinkers, Yūgaku and Sontoku concerned themselves with practical problems and not with theoretical or idealistic moral concepts. This propensity to direct one's attention to practical matters came to be manifested increasingly in the intellectual world of the late Edo period.

INTELLECTUAL CURRENTS: REFORMERS AND CRITICS

During the latter half of the Tokugawa regime, heterodox views came to be embraced by a growing number of thinkers and Chu Hsi philosophy, the official ideology, no longer dominated the intellectual scene. The Kansei edict prohibiting heterodox studies was issued in 1790 by Matsudaira Sadanobu, and it was intended to combat the rising tide of unorthodox points of view. It could, however, neither curb opinions critical of official policies nor restrict the diffusion of non-Chu Hsi, or for that matter, non-Confucian philosophies.

There were several schools of thought among the heterodox thinkers. Of course these cannot all be neatly classified into fixed categories, but for the sake of convenience we can list the following: the school of thought that was influenced by Dutch or Western learning; the pragmatic, rationalistic critics of the existing order; the nationalists of the Mito school; and the nationalists of the school of National Learning.

The school of Dutch learning (*rangaku*) came into existence after 1720, when the Bakufu relaxed its ban against Western books and permitted works not containing Christian ideas to enter the country. This led a small circle of interested scholars to begin studying Dutch in order to become acquainted with Western science. Japanese-Dutch dictionaries were compiled, and these men started to pursue such subjects as astronomy, physics, electricity, plant studies, cartography, geography, and medicine. The pioneer students of this school included Aoki Konyō (1698–1769), who compiled a dictionary of the Dutch language, which he completed in 1758, and Hiraga Gennai (1729–1779), a versatile man who was not only interested in Western science but also in playwriting and Western painting. In his scientific work he engaged in botanical studies, conducted experiments in electricity, produced asbestos, and made a thermometer. He also taught Western painting, and among his students was Shiba Kōkan (1738–1818), who became the foremost exponent of the Western style of painting.

The Bakufu was interested in encouraging the study of astronomy and built an observatory in Edo in 1744. Surveying and cartography were also studied at this center, and it was through mastery of these fields that Inō Tadataka (1745–1818) managed to survey the entire Japanese coastline and produce an accurate map of the country. Among the early advocates of the Copernican theory were Miura Baien (1723–1789) and Shiba Kōkan. Baien, though a Confucian scholar, developed a naturalistic philosophy that departed from the traditional theoretical explanation of the nature of things. He believed that the principles underlying the natural world could be understood only by studying things in the physical world, and not by projecting assumptions about human nature onto the natural world. He emphasized the importance of developing a thoroughgoing spirit of inquiry and scepticism but the comprehensive system of logic that he formulated was too complex to be easily understood by his contemporaries. It was not until very recently that his position in the history of Japanese thought as a unique and original thinker came to be appreciated.

The science that had the greatest influence on the fostering of Dutch studies was medicine. Among the pioneers in this field were Maeno Ryōtaku (1723–1803) and Sugita Gempaku (1733–1817). In 1771 they had an opportunity to watch a dissection being performed, and they were thus able, through direct observation, to compare the human anatomy with the illustrations and descriptions in a Dutch book on anatomy. They were profoundly impressed by the accuracy of the Dutch work and so appalled at the erroneous notions they had formerly held that they set about doing a translation of the Dutch text, which they had published in 1774. This was the first openly circulated Dutch book that was translated into Japanese, and it did much to arouse the interest of fellow scholars.

Dutch studies were advanced significantly when Philipp Franz von Siebold, a young German doctor, arrived in 1823 to serve as a medical officer at the Dutch factory in Nagasaki. He was allowed to open a clinic and a medical school outside the city, and it was here that he taught fifty-seven Japanese medical students. In 1828 Siebold got in trouble with the authorities when it was discovered that he was planning to take a map of Japan with him on his projected trip back to Europe. He was expelled from the country as a suspected spy, but he was able to return in 1859 after Japan opened her doors to the West.

The Confucians began to attack Dutch studies as interest in them mounted. Ōtsuki Gentaku (1757–1827), an advocate of Dutch learning, responded as follows to the critics: "Dutch learning is not perfect, but if we choose the good points and follow them, what harm could come of that? What is more ridiculous than to refuse to discuss its merits and cling to one's forte without changing." [12] The scholars of Dutch studies grew increasingly critical of the Bakufu's anachronistic policy of seclusion and began as a result to experience growing official hostility. These men were bringing about an expanded awareness of the outside world and had become a force that could not be ignored.

[12] Keene, *op. cit.*, p. 25.

Russian movements in the north along with stories about European activities in the rest of Asia induced some Japanese thinkers to turn their attention to the problems of national defense. They also considered, though usually in private, the policies that they thought Japan should adopt in coping with the foreign powers. Hayashi Shihei (1738–1793) was one of the first of these thinkers to call for the adoption of appropriate defense measures to meet the impending threat from abroad. He urged the use of Western military science and arms, especially cannons, to repel the foreign naval vessels. The Bakufu, then under the direction of Matsudaira Sadanobu, arrested him for publishing a book dealing with the affairs of state, but he had already set a precedent for such discussions, which others were to follow. In the nineteenth century Takano Chōei (1804–1850), who had studied under Siebold, and Watanabe Kazan (1793–1841), who was a student of the Dutch language, an accomplished painter, and an experienced administrator, expressed their disagreement with the Bakufu's policy of driving away all foreign ships approaching Japanese shores. For this they were both persecuted and driven to suicide.

The practical and rational critics and analysts of Tokugawa society had acquired, in addition to what was noted above about Dutch learning, some knowledge about the West. One of these men, Honda Toshiaki (1744–1821), favored development of foreign trade and colonization in order to strengthen Japan's economy. He believed that the government was responsible for the economic miseries of the people, and he was convinced that the ruling class had to provide vigorous leadership to change Japan into a wealthy, industrial nation like some of the European countries.

Toshiaki believed that in order to strengthen the economy, centralized control had to be established. He felt it was particularly important to bring shipping and trade under state control. "As long as there are no government-owned ships and the merchants have complete control over transport and trade," he wrote, "the economic conditions of the samurai and farmers grow steadily worse." [13] In foreign policy he favored an expansionist course of action and bemoaned the fact that Hokkaido, Sakhalin, and Kamchatka were not being colonized. "Since," he wrote, "it is a national obligation to attempt to increase the size of the country, even if this involves invading other countries, it makes me speechless with despair when I realize that we have permitted all of our possessions to be snatched away by another country." [14] His desire was to make Japan "the greatest nation in the world." Toshiaki was highly critical of the Bakufu and favored drastic changes, but because he did not publicize his ideas, he

[13] *Ibid.*, p. 176.
[14] *Ibid.*, p. 221.

did not encounter any difficulties from the authorities. Consequently, he also failed to exert much influence on the thinking of his age.

It is interesting to note that men like Toshiaki and Satō Nobuhiro (1769–1850) already recognized key concepts about the necessity of adopting Western science and technology and the importance of developing the nation's economy for military purposes—an idea that was to have full sway in the early Meiji period. Nobuhiro had studied Dutch and was interested in a variety of practical subjects. He was also seriously concerned about the external threat and was deeply disturbed by China's defeat in the Opium War. Like Toshiaki, he believed in strengthening the economy in order to strengthen the nation; that is, he believed in what came to be known as a policy of *fukoku kyōhei* (enrich and strengthen the nation). Nobuhiro served as an adviser to Senior Councilor Mizuno Tadakuni and to several daimyō, so his ideas received the attention of the ruling authorities. His proposal for drastic economic reorganization was not adopted but when the Bakufu sought to regulate the economy more stringently after 1855, it is believed that Nobuhiro's ideas had something to do with it.

In order to revitalize Japan's economy, he advocated the establishment of a highly centralized totalitarian government that would have the authority to control the entire economic life of the society while fully utilizing and completely regulating all natural and human resources. He suggested that the country's industries be divided into eight divisions with every person being assigned to a given occupation and strictly forbidden from engaging in any other work. The existing political order and the class system were to be abolished, of course, and the ruler given autocratic powers that would allow him to "manage freely the entire nation of Japan as if it were his hands and feet." [15]

Nobuhiro, under the influence of the Shinto nationalism of Hirata Atsutane, whose views are discussed later in this chapter, envisioned Japan extending her divine rule over the rest of the world. "In terms of world geography," he argued, "our Imperial Land would appear to be the axis of the other countries of the world, as indeed it is. Natural circumstances favor the launching of an expedition from our country to conquer others, whereas they are adverse to the conquest of our country by an expedition from abroad." [16] It appears that an awareness of the outside world quickly led to the rise of expansionistic nationalism.

There were a number of other rationalist critics of the existing order who contemplated various ways of strengthening the society. Kaiho Seiryō (1755–1817), for example, advocated that since commerce consti-

[15] Maruyama Masao, *op. cit.*, p. 346.

[16] Ryusaku Tsunoda, W. T., de Bary, and Donald Keene, eds., *Sources of Japanese Tradition* (New York: Columbia University Press, 1958), p. 577.

tuted the basis of the social order industrial activities should be extended to all segments of the society. Shiba Kōkan recognized the superiority of Western science and favored establishing trade with Russia. He also expressed egalitarian ideas: "from the emperor, and shōgun above, to the samurai, peasants, merchants, artisans, pariahs, and beggars below all are human beings." [17] Yamagata Bantō (1748–1821), a scholar who had emerged from the merchant class, also recognized the superiority of Western science and adopted a materialistic, atheistic point of view. He noted the prevalance of conflict between the ruler and the people in Japanese history and, like Shiba Kōkan, asserted that all men were equal.

The nationalists, both the Mito school and the school of National Learning, though not yet in favor of overthrowing the Bakufu, were beginning to put increasing emphasis on the importance of the imperial family. They believed in "revering the emperor and respecting the Bakufu," and they tended to be outspokenly anti-Western. The Bakufu officials were willing to tolerate expressions of respect for the imperial family as long as these were accompanied by similar declamations about the Bakufu, but they were not willing to condone pro-imperialist expressions that at the same time implied a criticism of the Bakufu. In the eighteenth century two followers of Yamazaki Ansai's school of thought were punished by the Bakufu as exponents of pro-imperial, anti-Bakufu sentiments. They were Takenouchi Shikibu (1712–1767), who was exiled, and Yamagata Daini (1725–1767), who was executed. Proroyalists in the early nineteenth century were careful not to step into the danger zone.

This was true of Aizawa Seishisai (1782–1863) of Mito, one of the earliest advocates of the policy of sonnō jōi (revere the Emperor and repel the barbarians). He argued in traditional fashion that obedience to one's lord and adherence to the Bakufu's laws signified loyalty to the Emperor. In 1825 he wrote a book called New Proposals in which he set forth his nationalistic, pro-royalist opinions. This book appeared at a time when Japan's peace was being threatened by the attempts of foreign vessels to enter her ports. In fact, it was in 1825 that the Bakufu issued an order to fire upon all foreign ships approaching Japanese shores. Seishisai's New Proposals had a significant impact on the thinking of his contemporaries, and the volume came to be regarded as something of a Bible for the nationalistic patriots of the period.

Seishisai embraced the Shinto concepts of the divine origin of Japan and the uniqueness of the imperial family, who were descendants of the Sun Goddess. He held Japan to be "at the vertex of the earth" and the nation that sets the standard for others to follow. He elaborated upon

[17] Nagata, op. cit., pp. 250–51.

the concept of Japan's *kokutai* (national polity), a theory that combined elements from Shinto mythology, Confucian ethics, and Bushidō. It was this theory that emerged in the twentieth century as a key element in the ideology of the ultranationalists. Japan's kokutai was unique, Seishisai asserted, because the nation was founded by the Sun Goddess and because the imperial line, which stems directly from her, has survived inviolate through the ages. Concepts of loyalty to the sovereign and filial piety were thus handed down to the Japanese people by the Sun Goddess herself.

Seishisai possessed a narrow, xenophobic point of view, as the following statement of his vividly illustrates.

> Today the alien barbarians of the West, lowly organs of
> the legs and feet of the world, are dashing about across
> the sea, trampling other countries underfoot, and daring,
> with their squinting eyes and limping feet, to override
> the noble nations. What manner of arrogance is this! . . .
> everything exists in its natural bodily form, and our
> Divine Land is situated at the top of the earth. . . .
> It [America] occupies the hindmost region of the
> earth; thus, its people are stupid and simple, and are
> incapable of doing things.[18]

As might be expected, he was highly critical of the scholars of Dutch learning. He accused them of being taken in by Western theories and of seeking to transform the civilized Japanese way of life into that of the barbarians. He was also rabidly anti-Christian, contending that Christianity's aim was to devour the countries that it entered.

The nationalists of the Mito school, although they were sympathetic to certain Shinto concepts, were basically Confucians, and as such they sought to reconcile the concept of taigi meibun with loyalty both to the shōgun and to the Emperor. Consequently, they did not agree fully with the scholars of National Learning who were critical of Confucianism.

The central figure among the scholars of National Learning during this period was Hirata Atsutane (1776–1843), a zealous Shinto nationalist. In seeking to place National Learning above all other schools of thought, he contended that all learnings, including Confucianism and Buddhism, were encompassed in Japanese learning, "just as the many rivers flow into the sea, where their waters are joined." [19] Atsutane hoped to establish Shinto's supremacy over all other doctrines, and he was al-

---

[18] Tsunoda *et al., Sources of Japanese Tradition,* p. 596.
[19] *Ibid.,* p. 543.

most irrational in his criticisms of Confucianism and Buddhism. He had been exposed to Western knowledge and was influenced to some extent by Christian concepts, which were entering the country through Chinese publications. For example, he equated the early Shinto gods Izanagi and Izanami with Adam and Eve, and in one of his works he quoted the New Testament as if it were a Shinto text.

Atsutane sought to provide Shinto with a clearly defined theology by presenting a monotheistic interpretation of the religion, and by emphasizing life after death. He may have borrowed these two concepts from Christianity. In contrast to Motoori Norinaga, who envisioned two creator gods—Takami-musubi and Kami-musubi—Atsutane contended that Takami-musubi was the sole Creator God who made heaven and earth. He was, Atsutane said, omnipotent, the holiest among the many gods, and ruler over the world from his abode in heaven. In his concept about life after death, Atsutane again departs from the earlier Shintoists, who held that after death, the soul went to the polluted land of *Yomi*. According to Atsutane, the soul enters the land of spirits, where it joins the gods. This earthly life, then, is only a temporary abode for man. It is "the place where we are tested for good and evil. It is a temporary world where we are allowed to live for a short while. The invisible land is our real world." [20]

Atsutane's ethnocentric nationalism was manifested in his belief that Japan, because she was begotten by the gods and thus especially favored by them, ranks far above other countries. People all over the world, he claimed, refer to Japan as the land of the gods, and call the Japanese people descendants of the gods. Even the humblest of the Japanese, being descendants of the gods, are superior to others. He held the Chinese in contempt as being unclean, and although he compared the Dutch to dogs, he did recognize their devotion to intellectual pursuits and their superiority in the sciences. Atsutane was not one of the furious anti-foreigners who insisted on "repelling the barbarians." He sympathized with the seclusionist policy of the Bakufu but favored adopting those elements of Western science and technology that would benefit the country. He did not advocate overthrowing the Bakufu even though he was a Shintoist, and he believed that there was no conflict between revering the Emperor and upholding the Bakufu.

Atsutane, however, was fanatical in his opposition to Buddhism. He criticized its ascetic rejection of the mundane world, and he attacked the major Buddhist sects as "enemies of the gods." He renounced the Buddhist concept of satori (enlightenment) and contended that true en-

[20] The source for this and the quotations that follow is Nagata Hiroshi, *op. cit.*, pp. 254 ff.

lightenment was to be attained by following one's natural inclinations. True enlightenment, he said, "is understood as soon as it is explained to a person. It can be performed at once; it is not a difficult matter at all. It is what a person is born with; it is his nature." According to Atsutane, an enlightened person feels affection for his parents, loves his wife and children, and allows his innate sentiments to have free and natural expression. "Shakyamuni Buddha and Bodhidharma," he argued, "behaved contrary to this way so they were neither enlightened nor followers of the true Way." Consequently, he advocated the abandonment of "all things that smell of Buddhism" and the cultivation of "the Yamato spirit."

Atsutane's influence was widespread. His anti-Buddhist sentiments found considerable support and took concrete form in the anti-Buddhist outbursts that followed the Meiji Restoration. His Shinto nationalist concepts have had a great impact upon the nationalistic thinking of modern Japan.

CHAPTER 10

THE FALL OF THE TOKUGAWA BAKUFU

ARRIVAL OF COMMODORE PERRY

The coming of Perry in 1853 turned out to be an epoch-making event in Japanese history, but even before his arrival the Bakufu's seclusionist policy was already being challenged by the arrival of other foreign vessels. Russia was the first nation to start probing the shores of Japan. In 1771 a Russian adventurer, Baron von Benyowsky, who had been exiled to Kamchatka, seized control of a small vessel with the aid of some other convicts and sailed to Awa in Shikoku. Benyowsky pretended to be a Dutchman and told the Japanese that Russia was planning to attack Hokkaido the following year. This caused consternation among the Japanese officials and stirred the advocates of national defense, such as Hayashi Shihei, into action. In 1778 a Russian merchant ship came to Kunajiri Island off western Hokkaido and asked the local daimyō to enter into commercial relations. This offer to engage in trade was repeated in the fall of 1792 when a Russian ship, the *Ekaterina,* arrived at Nemuro in Hokkaido to return some castaway Japanese seamen. The authorities rejected the offer but told the Russians to sail to Nagasaki and present their request there. Adam Laxman, the commander of the ship, decided, however, to return to Russia without bothering to go on to Nagasaki. In 1804 the head of the Russian-American Company, Rezanov, arrived in Nagasaki and requested the establishment of commercial relations. He too failed to persuade the Bakufu to abandon its seclusionist position.

In the face of increasing Russian activities in the north, especially in

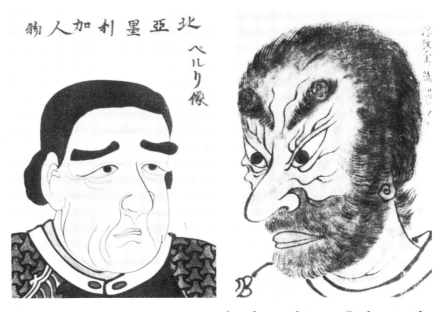

北亞墨利加人物

ペルリ像

Two contemporary Japanese views of Admiral Perry: left, an official portrait by an unknown artist; right, a print of Perry labeled "true portrait," from the Black Ship Scroll. Left, courtesy of the Library of Congress; right, courtesy of the Honolulu Academy of Arts.

Sakhalin and the Kuriles, the Bakufu began to concern itself with the defense of the northern regions, and in 1808 sent a survey team out there and across into eastern Siberia. Under the leadership of Mamiya Rinzō, the group verified the fact that Sakhalin was in fact an island and not a peninsula attached to Siberia. Russian interest in the Far East abated during the Napoleonic Wars, and it was not until 1847, when Nicholas Muraviev was appointed governor-general of eastern Siberia, that she began to press upon Japanese shores again.

England and America were also beginning to display some interest in opening Japan's ports. In 1818 the British sent a vessel to Uraga, near Edo, and asked for the commencement of commercial relations, but they too were summarily turned away. Also arriving on Japanese shores were whaling ships looking for food and water. As a result, in 1825 the Bakufu issued an edict ordering forcible ejection of all foreign ships from Japanese coastal regions. Upon receiving word of the Chinese defeat in the Opium War, the Bakufu began to strengthen its military forces by manufacturing cannons and training men in gunnery. In 1842 the edict of 1825 was relaxed by Senior Councilor Mizuno Tadakuni, and it was ordered that ships drifting accidentally to Japanese shores were to be provided with food, water, and fuel. Fundamentally, however, the basic

246

seclusionist policy remained unchanged. For example, in 1844 when William II of Holland sent a message to the Bakufu courteously explaining the world situation and urging that Japan open her doors, his advice went completely unheeded.

The nation that finally succeeded in persuading Japan to open her ports was the United States. She was becoming a significant Pacific power and consequently sought to develop commercial relations with Asian nations. In addition, the United States had whaling ships roaming the north Pacific that needed supply bases and shelter. Moreover it was felt that arrangements had to be negotiated for the protection and care of American seamen shipwrecked on Japanese shores, who were heretofore treated as unlawful intruders by the authorities.

In 1837 an American merchant ship, the *Morrison,* arrived with the aim of establishing contact with Japan, but she was promptly driven off. The leader of this mission then recommended to the United States government that a naval expedition be sent to open Japanese ports. In 1846 Commodore James Biddle was dispatched with two American warships, but he too failed to achieve his objective. Finally, Commodore Matthew Calbraith Perry was given the assignment and on July 8, 1853, he arrived off the coast of Uraga with four warships. Edo was plunged into a state of crisis when the "blackships" sailed into Edo Bay, ignoring the protesting Japanese on little boats. Perry was determined to accomplish his mission, so he refused to be shunted aside and gave the Bakufu three days to accept President Fillmore's letter to the shōgun asking for humane treatment of shipwrecked seamen, permission for American ships to enter Japanese ports for coal and supplies, and, if possible, trade between the two nations. The Bakufu had no choice but to accede to Perry's demands and allowed him to land in Uraga. He delivered the letter and then departed stating that he would return early the following year for an official reply.

Perry's arrival placed the Bakufu in its most difficult predicament since its founding. It had virtually ignored the outside world for more than two hundred years and now found that it could no longer continue to do so. The Bakufu officials knew that Japan was incapable of withstanding any military assault by the Western powers, but the ruling class was severely divided on how to deal with the difficulties posed by Perry. The blind fanatics favored "repelling the barbarians," but men who were better informed realized that such action was pure folly. The gravity of the situation and the Bakufu's inability to deal with it resolutely made it necessary to include radically new elements in the deliberative and policy-making processes. The Bakufu's officials turned for advice to the imperial court and all the daimyō, including the tozama (outside) lords, as well as to the shōgun's liege vassals. This, of course, gave potential opponents of the Bakufu and the politically ambitious elements an opportunity to move into the center of the political arena. The Bakufu was forced, reluctantly, to abandon its seclusionist policy, and the opposition then used the issue of jōi (repelling the barbarians) as a means to badger and embarrass it. At the same time, the inclusion of the imperial court in the decision-making process made it a rallying point for critics of the Bakufu. Thus sonnō (revering or honoring the Emperor) was tied in with jōi as a political weapon with which to assail the Bakufu.

In response to the Bakufu's call for advice concerning the American request, seven hundred memorials were submitted. No one, however, managed to formulate a brilliant solution. Some men suggested that the Bakufu accede to Perry's demands, but a majority of the replies advanced the desirable though unrealistic position that the policy of seclusion be retained while war be avoided at all costs. A few of the respondents, on the other hand, did advocate going to war against the intruders. The most eminent proponent of this policy was the lord of Mito, Tokugawa Nariaki (1800–1860), who contended that "if we put our trust in war the whole country's morale will be increased and even if we sustain an initial defeat we will in the end expel the foreigner." He bemoaned the fact that "In these feeble days men tend to cling to peace; they are not fond of defending their country by war." [1]

There were many men who agreed that the only practical solution would be to stall the Americans as long as possible. This, however, was not a feasible plan simply because Perry did return early in 1854, just as he had promised, and this time he had eight "blackships" with him. The Bakufu's officials were overwhelmed by this show of force and, fearing an attack if Perry's requests were not met, agreed to open two ports —Hakodate in Hokkaido and Shimoda on the tip of Izu Peninsula—to American ships, to treat shipwrecked sailors properly, and to permit a consul to reside in Shimoda. The most-favored-nation clause was also included in the treaty even though the Bakufu did not actually agree to establish commercial relations. This agreement, the Treaty of Kanagawa, was signed on March 31, 1854. England, France, Russia, and the Netherlands soon concluded similar agreements and thus brought to a close Japan's long period of seclusion. In effect this signaled the beginning of the end for the Tokugawa Bakufu, for its opponents and critics could now begin to intensify their attacks against it, criticizing its inability to stand up against the Western powers.

In August, 1856 the American government sent Townsend Harris to Shimoda to press for a commercial treaty. Some Bakufu officials, realiz-

---

[1] W. G. Beasley, trans. and ed., *Select Documents on Japanese Foreign Policy, 1853–1868* (London: Oxford University Press, 1955), pp. 103, 107.

ing that the Western powers were far in advance of Japan in military, economic, and technological affairs, concluded that Japan could no longer refuse to establish full diplomatic and commercial relations with foreign powers. Iwase Tadanari, the official who was given the task of negotiating with Harris, was convinced that Japan had to open her doors and persuaded the Bakufu's high officials to accept this fact. Several leading daimyō also became convinced of the wisdom of opening the country, but one of the most influential of them, Tokugawa Nariaki, remained adamant in his opposition and sought to win the support of the imperial court. Emperor Kōmei (1831–1866) was surrounded by advisers who were grossly ignorant of the world situation, and so it was not exceedingly difficult to persuade him that opening the country would be disastrous. He decided, therefore, to support the anti-foreign faction.

In the meanwhile, Harris and the Bakufu's officials concluded their negotiations on a commercial treaty and the senior councilor, Hotta Masayoshi (1810–1864), seeking to allay the very strong opposition led by Nariaki, asked for imperial approval of the treaty. Masayoshi expected immediate imperial consent, but the Emperor remained firmly committed to the policy of jōi. It was at this point that Ii Naosuke (1815–1860), who had just been appointed tairō (great councilor), decided that the treaty would have to be signed without imperial sanction. The Bakufu's officials, intimidated by Harris' information that the British and French fleets, fresh from their triumph over the Chinese, were on their way to extract greater concessions from Japan, finally signed the commercial treaty on July 29, 1858. It provided for the immediate opening of three ports to trade and the addition of two more a few years later. Duties of a varied scale on imports and 5 percent on exports were agreed upon. Edo and Osaka were to be opened for foreign residents by 1862 and 1863. American citizens were granted extraterritorial rights and freedom of worship in Japan. Similar treaties were concluded with England, France, Russia, and the Netherlands.

THE IMMEDIATE CONSEQUENCES

The impact of these contacts with the West was felt immediately in the political realm, even though involvement with foreign nations remained essentially limited until the Meiji government came into existence. The effects of the new relationships also became discernible in the cultural and economic areas, and the treaty ports such as Yokohama with their Western residents began to grow into important centers of Western culture.

In 1860 a Japanese embassy was sent to the United States to exchange ratifications of the treaty, and in 1861 another mission was dispatched to Europe. These trips exposed a considerable number of influential

Japanese to the Western world, and some of them, like Fukuzawa Yukichi, a leading Meiji educator, returned convinced of the need to adopt Western practices and institutions. The general mood of the country nevertheless remained strongly anti-Western, so these men were compelled to remain silent until the advent of the Meiji era. The Bakufu, however, did recognize the need to train some officials in Western languages, and in 1857 it opened the "Institute for the Investigation of Barbarian Books." Initially only Dutch was taught, but by 1860 other Western languages were added to the curriculum, and in 1863 the institute was officially turned into a government college for Western studies.

Various educational programs served to increase the exposure of many Japanese to Western culture. In 1862 the Bakufu sent a group of eight students to study in Holland, and this example was soon followed by several han. In 1863 Chōshū dispatched five students to England and in 1864 Satsuma sent sixteen more there. A number of students also went abroad on their own initiative, and many young men in Japan began to study Western languages with Western missionaries and Japanese instructors who were qualified in this field.

Commerce with the West, although still limited, began to increase in the sixties. Exports exceeded imports until 1866 when the trend was reversed, and the total combined figure, not including arms and ships, exceeded thirty-two million dollars. The chief trading partner was England, with whom 80 percent of Japanese trade from 1859 to the downfall of the Bakufu was conducted. Raw silk was the main item of export; tea, copperware, marine products, and lacquerware were among the other major export commodities. Imported goods included cotton yarn, cotton cloth, woollen fabrics, ironware, and sugar.

The tremendous demand for such items as silk and tea resulted in increased production, but it was quite insufficient to meet the enormous requests for these commodities. The demand for raw silk in particular created serious domestic shortages and inflationary prices. On the other hand, the importation of cotton yarn and cotton cloth had most adverse effects on the domestic producers. Foreign trade did, nevertheless, have the vitally important consequence of stimulating the growth of some factories in which many workers were brought together under one roof to work using reeling machines or processing tea. These factories were, of course, still limited in number and size, and the dominant mode remained domestic handicraft production.

A feature of foreign trade that particularly disturbed the Bakufu was the inordinate outflow of gold. Gold coins were exchanged with silver at a ratio of about one to five in Japan while the world rate was about one to fifteen. This meant that foreigners could make an enormous profit by first exchanging silver for gold in Japan and then taking the gold to China, where it commanded its full value in the world market. Before the Bakufu corrected the situation by debasing its gold coins in 1860, about 500,000 ryō in gold coins had flowed out of the country.

From a political point of view, the agreement to enter into commercial and diplomatic relations with the Western nations proved to be disastrous for the Bakufu. The anti-foreign faction began to grow increasingly disenchanted with the Bakufu, and it commenced openly to espouse the cause of the imperial court. Thus, the movement "to revere the Emperor and repel the barbarians" began to congeal into a formidable force as it gained the support of a growing number of activist warriors known as *shishi* (men of high purpose). Ii Naosuke came under severe criticism for having signed the treaty with the United States without imperial approval, and the opposition to him soon became intermeshed with the struggle over succession to the shogunate.

The struggle to pick his successor unfolded even before the weak and feeble-minded Shōgun Iesada (1824–1858) passed away. One faction, which included the daimyō of Echizen and Satsuma as well as some reform-minded Bakufu officials, favored Nariaki's son, Yoshinobu (1837–1913), also known as Keiki, who had a reputation as an individual of considerable ability and intelligence. The support of the anti-foreign faction was guaranteed him simply by virtue of the fact that he was the son of an avowed anti-Westerner. Keiki was also favored by some proponents of the open-door policy who believed that the old guard among the top Bakufu officials had to be removed.

Ii Naosuke, representing the fudai daimyō who traditionally controlled the top Bakufu posts, led the faction opposed to Keiki. They feared that his succession to the shogunate would mean the control of the Bakufu by Nariaki, who was not only anti-Western but sympathetic to the imperial court as well. In order to block Keiki, Ii supported the candidacy of Iemochi, the shōgun's cousin and eight-year-old head of Kii Han. Ii succeeded in making Iemochi shōgun and then began persecuting those who had opposed his policies or had supported Keiki. He placed Nariaki under house arrest, forced Keiki to retire, contrived the dismissal of anti-Bakufu court advisers, and executed the active samurai opponents and critics of the Bakufu.

Among Ii's victims was Yoshida Shōin (1830–1859), a zealous patriot and the leader of the young extremist warriors of Chōshū (see page 253). Another victim was Hashimoto Sanai, a warrior of Echizen, who was condemned for having worked for the candidacy of Keiki. Unlike the other critics of Ii, Sanai had favored opening the country. Ten warriors, including two who died in prison, were condemned to death, and many others were exiled to offshore islands. From Ii's point of view, he was merely upholding the authority of the Bakufu, for lower level warriors were forbidden from interfering in state affairs. The zealots, however, were no longer bound by such considerations as "knowing their place." In order to avenge the death of their fellow warriors, a group of activists from Mito waylaid Ii in March, 1860, as he was entering Edo castle and assassinated him. This deprived the Bakufu of its strong man, and forced its officials to try to cope with the opposition by winning over the cooperation of the imperial court. Consequently, the center of political action began shifting to Kyoto.

THE MENTALITY OF SONNŌ JŌI

Many proponents of sonnō jōi, the movement "to revere the Emperor and repel the barbarians," were young warriors who came primarily from the lower rungs of the samurai hierarchy, although there were a few from the middle segment of that class. Some well-to-do farmers' sons as well as priests and scholars could also be found among their ranks. Mito, Chōshū, Satsuma, and Tosa produced the largest number of these men, but they were to be found in other han also.

These samurai, usually referred to as shishi, were inclined to be fiery extremists as well as fanatical political activists. They were usually expert swordsmen who rigorously upheld such traditional samurai values as duty, courage, and honor. Some of the shishi outgrew their earlier limitations and managed to emerge as perspicacious statesmen; by and large, however, they were men who lacked the vision to discern a meaningful role and place for Japan in the context of the changing world scene. They were not inclined to be reasonable and tended instead to be ruled by their passions. Self-righteous, intolerant, and dogmatic to the extreme, they envisioned themselves as the saviors of Japan, men with a sacred mission. They were convinced that they were on the side of truth, justice, and right, and that they were the only true patriots while those who failed to agree with them were self-serving traitors. The shishi were, in effect, the forerunners of the ultranationalist extremists of prewar Japan.

The shishi constituted only a minority in their han, but the influence they wielded was very strongly felt because of the readiness with which they would use force against those who disagreed with them. There were frequent outbursts of violence as the shishi repeatedly tried to seize power. In Chōshū and Satsuma they eventually did capture the han leadership. Their uprising against the established leadership in Mito, however, was crushed. In Tosa, even though they assassinated a moderate han official they failed to intimidate the han leaders and were finally driven out.

Later, however, as the daimyō moved closer to the sonnō position, some of the shishi were restored to their good graces. Their terrorist tactics made the extremists a force to contend with not only in their own han but in Kyoto and Edo as well.

The shishi were as a rule rabidly anti-Western, but they disagreed about the tactics to be used in achieving their ends. Some men favored driving the Westerners out and closing the country; others favored opening the country in order to enable Japan to adopt Western military methods and thus become powerful enough to cope with the Western threat.[2] Some of the Bakufu officials who went along with the open-door policy did so because they felt it was an ineluctable necessity, but at heart they favored the seclusionist policy and the preservation of the old feudal order.

Sonnō jōi sentiments are generally believed to have originated in Mito, with men such as Aizawa Seishisai and the Fujitas (father Yūkoku and son Tōko) among the early advocates. Initially, the proponents of sonnō jōi did not advocate an anti-Bakufu policy, believing that loyalty to both the imperial court and the Bakufu was possible. After the arrival of Perry, however, and the conclusion of the commercial treaties, the sonnō jōi movement took a sharp anti-Bakufu turn.

The man who emerged as the leading spokesman of this movement was Yoshida Shōin, a brilliant shishi from Chōshū, who was the son of a low-ranking samurai. He studied Chu Hsi Confucianism and Yamaga Sokō's military science, read treatises on Wang Yang-ming philosophy, and was exposed to Western technology in Nagasaki. In 1851 he went to Edo and became a disciple of Sakuma Zōzan, a leading student of the Dutch language and Western science. He also traveled to Mito to see Aizawa Seishisai, whose works he had studied earlier. The arrival of Perry had a decisive effect on him and, believing that he should get to know his enemy, he sought to board an American ship to go abroad to study. He was arrested for violating the law of the land, and was turned over to his han to be placed under house arrest. After his release, Shōin started a private school to indoctrinate the young men of his han with his loyalist, nationalistic point of view. Among his students were the future

---

[2] This latter group would correspond to what Arnold Toynbee calls the "Herodians": "The 'Herodian' is the man who acts on the principle that the most effective way to guard against the danger of the unknown is to master its secret; and, when he finds himself in the predicament of being confronted by a more highly skilled and better armed opponent, he responds by discarding his traditional art of war and learning to fight his enemy with the enemy's own tactics and own weapons." In contrast, the 'Zealot' reverts to 'archaism evoked by foreign pressure.' (Arnold Toynbee, *Civilization on Trial and the World and the West*, New York: World Publishing, 1958, pp. 167–73.) Perry's arrival brought forth these two types in Japan, and it was the Herodians who ultimately won out.

leaders of Meiji Japan, Itō Hirobumi and Yamagata Aritomo, as well as one of the three architects of the Meiji Restoration, Kido Kōin, and the would-be leaders of the extremists in Chōshū, Takasugi Shinsaku and Kusaka Genzui—a truly impressive galaxy of disciples. Shōin believed that the old leaders were completely incapable of solving the national crisis, and so he envisioned the establishment of a new order under the leadership of people like himself and his followers, the "grass-roots heroes." His followers in Chōshū did indeed play a major role in overthrowing the old order.

Shōin was intensely anti-foreign and a loyal adherent to the Shintoistic notion of the divine nature of Japan. "One must," he wrote, "worship and revere the gods. The country of Yamato is . . . the honorable country which was founded by the lordly Gods." [3] His anti-Western sentiments burst forth with the coming of Perry, and he exhorted the Japanese people to unite and drive away the "wily barbarians." He was convinced that new leadership and new ideas had to be injected into the government in order to cope with the national emergency. He did not advocate the Bakufu's overthrow until it signed the commercial treaty with Harris without first receiving imperial sanction. When it finally did so, he turned against it in wrathful indignation that epitomized the feelings of the advocates of sonnō jōi:

> It is clear that the Americans' intentions are harmful to
> the Land of the Gods. It has been proven that the words of
> the American envoy have caused the land of the Gods to
> be dishonored. In view of this, the Emperor, in extreme
> anger, decreed that relations be severed with the American
> envoy. This command the Bakufu was obliged to obey
> without delay but it failed to do so. It behaved with
> arrogance and independence, and made flattery of the
> Americans the highest policy of the land. It gave no thought
> to the national danger, did not reflect upon the national
> disgrace, and disobeyed the imperial decree. This is the
> Shōgun's crime. Heaven and earth will not tolerate it. The
> anger of the Gods and men have been aroused. Now it
> would be proper to destroy and kill in accordance with the
> fundamental principle of righteousness. No mercy should
> be shown. [4]

[3] David M. Earl, *Emperor and Nation in Japan* (Seattle, Wash.: University of Washington Press, 1964), p. 183.

[4] Maruyama Masao, *Nihon Seijishisōshi Kenkyū (Studies in the History of Japanese Political Thought)* (Tokyo: Tōkyō Daigaku Shuppankai, 1954), pp. 355–56.

Shōin used all his resources in opposing the Bakufu and frequently plotted to take direct action against its officials. Six months before his death, he wrote, "As long as the Tokugawa government exists, American, Russian, English, and French control over Japan will continue. The situation is indeed critical. How can any red-blooded person bear to see our great nation which has remained independent and unconquered for three thousand years become enslaved by other nations?" [5] When the commercial treaty was signed with the United States, Shōin was so outraged that he conspired with his followers to assassinate one of the Bakufu councilors. He was arrested, turned over to the Bakufu, and later executed.

Sakuma Zōzan (1811–1864), Shōin's master, was also highly nationalistic, but he responded differently to the advent of the West. Zōzan was a Chu Hsi Confucian, but he was also interested in Western learning and had studied the Dutch language. He was particularly fascinated by Western science and technology, and in recognition of Japan's need to adopt Western military and naval techniques, he became an expert on Western gunnery. He had a wide following as a teacher and influenced many young men. Zōzan, unlike Shōin, favored opening Japan's doors in order to adopt Western science and technology. His attitude toward Western knowledge is reflected in the following statement:

> In teachings concerning morality, benevolence, and
> righteousness, filial piety and brotherly love, loyalty and
> faithfulness, we must follow the examples and precepts of
> the Chinese sages. In astronomy, geography, navigation,
> surveying, the investigation of the principle of all things,
> the art of gunnery, commerce, medicine, machinery and
> construction, we must rely mainly on the West. We must
> gather the strong points of the five worlds and construct
> the great learning of our imperial nation.[6]

Essentially, then, he favored the morality of the East and the scientific expertise of the West. He became identified with the policy of opening the country and was assassinated by fanatical sonnō jōi advocates. His faith in Eastern morals and Western science was the very attitude that was to be embraced by many of the leaders of Meiji Japan. Basically, the Japanese were interested in the external aspects of Western civilization while they sought to retain in their inner life those elements that they regarded as being intrinsically Japanese.

[5] *Ibid.*, pp. 356–57.
[6] Naramoto Tatsuya, ed., *Nihon no Shisōka (The Thinkers of Japan)* Tokyo: Mainichi Shimbunsha, 1954), p. 237.

THE RISE OF THE ANTI-BAKUFU FORCES

The assassination of Ii Naosuke brought about some readily observable changes in the political picture. As we have already noted, the imperial court loomed larger in the national political scene. At the same time the tozama han, particularly Satsuma, Chōshū, and Tosa, as well as the han related to the Bakufu, Aizu, and Echizen, began to exert their influence on the national political arena. Furthermore, with Ii gone the Bakufu's leadership fell to more moderate officials who sought to neutralize their zealous opponents while effecting an alliance between the imperial court and the Bakufu. Emperor Kōmei agreed to this strategy of cooperation in the belief that the Bakufu would in return adopt the policy of driving out the Westerners. The alliance, known as *kōbu-gattai* (union of the court and military), was cemented by the marriage of Shōgun Iemochi to the Emperor's younger sister Princess Kazunomiya, in early 1862. This policy was supported by the daimyō of Satsuma, Echizen, and Aizu.

The shishi angrily opposed this policy and launched a campaign of terror, assassinating those who had cooperated with Ii in suppressing the shishi as well as those who had supported the marriage of Iemochi and Princess Kazunomiya. Another target of the anti-Western fanatics was naturally enough the foreign officials. Starting with the killing of two Russian sailors in the summer of 1859, a number of Westerners were murdered, among whom was Henry Heuskin, Harris' Dutch language interpreter, who was killed in January, 1861.

The most active elements among the shishi emerged from Chōshū. The lord of Satsuma was able to keep the extremists in his han under control, but the shishi in Chōshū were able to operate in a rather free-wheeling manner. The lord of Chōshū was willing to leave the management of political affairs to his chief officials. Around 1860, when the Chōshū leaders adopted a policy of playing an active role in the national scene, the han leadership was in the hands of Nagai Uta, an official who favored a policy of moderation. He sought to play the role of a mediator between the court and the Bakufu when Ii's departure offered Chōshū an opportunity to move into the national political arena. Nagai also favored the policy of opening the country to the West. His ideas were vehemently opposed by the shishi, and his failure to effect a reconciliation between the court and Bakufu offered his opponents, led by Kusaka, a perfect opportunity to discredit him. He was ultimately ordered to commit hara-kiri, and the Chōshū leadership passed into the hands of the proponents of sonnō jōi.

Contrary to the expectations of the advocates of kōbu-gattai, the terrorists managed to swing the court back to a rigidly anti-Western position. Emperor Kōmei dispatched a messenger to Edo calling for the im-

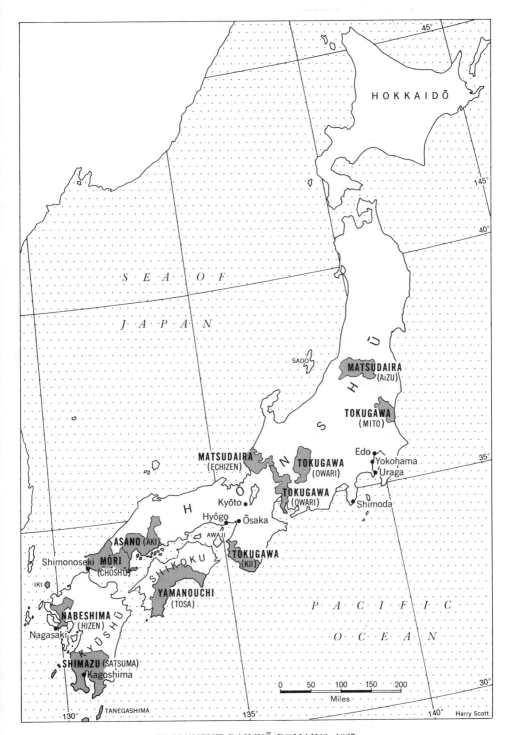

PROMINENT DAIMYŌ DOMAINS, 1867.

mediate expulsion of the foreigners. In early 1863 the shōgun and Keiki, who had been appointed his guardian, traveled to Kyoto to confer with the imperial court regarding the command. Seeing that the imperial court was dominated by the jōi faction, the daimyō who were opposed to such a policy, including the lord of Satsuma, departed for their home provinces. As a result, the Bakufu officials were forced to agree to implement the policy of jōi and May 10, 1863, was set as the date the policy was to go into effect.

The deadline arrived with the extremists of Chōshū firing upon Western ships passing through Shimonoseki straits. As might be expected, the Western powers were swift to retaliate and three American and French men-of-war attacked the Shimonoseki shore batteries, before landing and completely destroying the gun emplacements. The attacks, however, against the Western vessels passing through Shimonoseki straits nevertheless continued. During the following summer, England, France, the United States, and Holland sent seventeen warships against Chōshū, destroyed its forts, and routed its forces on land. This caused Chōshū to abandon its blind anti-Western stance and begin Westernizing its military forces. In a similar way, Satsuma also underwent a kind of baptism by fire in the summer of 1863, when British warships attacked Kagoshima in retaliation for the killing of an Englishman the previous fall. This encounter resulted in bringing the British and Satsuma officials closer together.

In the fall of 1863, the political faction favoring a union between the imperial court and Bakufu finally succeeded, with the support of Satsuma and Aizu, in driving the Chōshū warriors out of the imperial court. The anti-Bakufu court advisers were also expelled from Kyoto. Swordsmen organized to support the Bakufu retaliated against the violence-prone anti-Bakufu shishi, and the lord of Aizu, the constable of Kyoto, kept the city under tight control.

Once the Chōshū radicals and the anti-Bakufu court officials were out of the way, the relationship between the Bakufu and the court improved. In order to fulfill its promise to expel the foreigners, the Bakufu agreed to close the port of Yokohama. The court accepted this pledge as adequate proof of the Bakufu's willingness to reimpose the policy of seclusion.

Chōshū now became the base for all the anti-Western, anti-Bakufu extremists. They succeeded in persuading the han leaders to re-enter Kyoto by force, and in the summer of 1864, the men of Chōshū marched against the imperial seat. They were driven back by the Satsuma-Aizu forces, and in the course of the conflict some of the extremist leaders, including Kusaka Genzui, lost their lives. In the fall, the Bakufu sent a punitive expedition against Chōshū. Having just been rather severely chastised by the Western powers, Chōshū was in no condition to engage the expeditionary army in combat. Consequently, it acceded to the Bakufu's demands that those responsible for the attack against Kyoto be executed. Leadership in Chōshū was then taken over by the conservatives.

The extremists who called themselves the "righteous faction," under the leadership of Takasugi Shinsaku (1839–1867), rebelled against the conservative officials in 1865 and succeeded in re-establishing their political influence. Takasugi had the support of those auxiliary militia units who were trained in Western military techniques and equipped with Western arms. These units had been organized in 1863 by Takasugi, who was authorized to do so in order to defend the han against the Western powers. A fairly large percentage of each unit consisted of peasants because of the fact that non-samurai men were now allowed to join. The samurai, who composed 25 to 30 percent of the personnel, provided the leadership. Masterless samurai and townsmen were also among the militiamen. The establishment of militia units that were open to non-samurai became necessary because upper-class samurai disdained the use of rifles, convinced that it was a dishonor to abandon their swords. Membership in the auxiliary militia opened the way to political success for many lower-class samurai. Future leaders such as Kido Kōin (1833–1877), Itō Hirobumi (1841–1909), Yamagata Aritomo (1838–1922), and Inoue Kaoru (1835–1915) were active in these units.

Even before the crushing defeat by the Western powers, some sonnō jōi leaders in Chōshū were beginning to realize the necessity of adopting Western military techniques and arms. The naval assaults by the Western powers naturally enhanced this already growing awareness. In addition, Itō Hirobumi and Inoue Kaoru had traveled abroad and returned thoroughly convinced that Japan could not return to her former seclusionist position. They began to urge their fellow shishi to accept the policy of broadening contacts with the outside world for the purpose of strengthening the nation. Kido Kōin and Takasugi shared their views. These men ceased concerning themselves solely with the interests of their own han and began thinking of the well-being of the entire nation. They concluded that the establishment of a strong centralized authority was essential if Japan were to withstand the foreign menace.

In order to strengthen Japan, they believed that it was necessary to attend to Chōshū first. Consequently, after Takasugi's rebellion, the han leadership adopted the policy of fortifying Chōshū's military power. Ōmura Masujirō (1824–1869) was given the assignment of building the Chōshū army into a modern military force. Western vessels as well as thousands of Western rifles were purchased through an English arms merchant, Thomas Glover. The money to purchase these ships and weapons was taken out of a special reserve fund that Chōshū had established in 1762 and preserved even when the han budget was running a yearly deficit.

Chōshū was busy strengthening its military forces as a momentous turn of events was occurring on the national scene. The policy of uniting the court and Bakufu was beginning to disintegrate; at the same time, behind-the-scene machinations aimed at bringing together the two rival han, Satsuma and Chōshū, were beginning to meet with some success. A group of daimyō, including those of Satsuma, Tosa, and Aizu, and Bakufu officials headed by Keiki, worked together to maintain harmony between the court and Bakufu after the departure of Chōshū from Kyoto. Soon, however, dissension began to break out because, while the leaders of Satsuma wanted a government controlled by the major han, a faction in the Bakufu was seeking to revive their autocratic powers. The leader of this group was Finance Commissioner Oguri Tadamasa (1827–1868), who was a member of the embassy that had visited the United States in 1860. Oguri hoped to modernize the Bakufu's military forces, reduce the influence of Chōshū and Satsuma, and establish a strong national government under the Bakufu. In order to accomplish this, Oguri favored obtaining the support of a Western power and turned to Leon Roches, the French minister, for advice and assistance.

Shimazu Hisamitsu (1817–1887), who was regent to the daimyō of Satsuma, disapproved of the new trend in the Bakufu and began to entertain the thought of joining hands with his former foe, Chōshū. Prior to this, the radicals in Satsuma, headed by Saigō Takamori (1827–1877) and Ōkubo Toshimichi (1830–1878), had begun agitating for the adoption of an anti-Bakufu position but Hisamitsu had restrained them. Now that he was changing his attitude toward the Bakufu, they came to the fore as key leaders of the anti-Bakufu faction.

The man who served as a mediator between Satsuma and Chōshū was Sakamoto Ryōma (1835–1867), a shishi from Tosa who had outgrown the narrowly anti-Western position he had originally embraced. He now favored opening the country and introducing reforms at the national level. He brought Saigō of Satsuma and Kido of Chōshū together, and in early 1866 the two men agreed upon an alliance.

In June of that year the Bakufu, now led by the centralists, decided to eliminate Chōshū as an obstructive element once and for all and sent a second expeditionary force against it. This time, however, many major daimyō refused to support the move. Satsuma, naturally, declined to go against its recently acquired ally. Chōshū instituted a policy of total mobilization to stop the Bakufu's forces. Its troops were better trained, better armed, and their morale was higher so it is no surprise that they managed to rout the expeditionary army. This failure revealed the

Bakufu's weakness and served to strengthen the determination of the opposition to overthrow it.

Satsuma was also taking steps to modernize its armed forces by purchasing Western arms. Like the Bakufu and other han, Satsuma also had financial difficulties, but the measures it had put into effect during the Tempō era placed it in a far stronger financial position. It repudiated its debts to the merchants, reduced the samurai's stipends, encouraged the production of cash crops, and fostered trade with the Ryukus. In particular, it successfully exploited the sugar cane production on its offshore islands by allowing no other crops to be produced and by keeping stringent controls over the peasants. Those, for example, who produced poor quality sugar were severely punished. The han authorities established a rigid monopoly on sugar, using Draconian methods to ensure its control; for instance, anyone who engaged in the private sale of sugar was put to death. The use of such ruthless measures enabled Satsuma to increase its sugar production to the point where it came to supply more than one half of all the sugar sold in Osaka. Principally because of its sugar monopoly, it managed to accumulate reserve funds, which it was able to draw upon when it began to modernize its armed forces.

Satsuma was a particularly dangerous foe of the Bakufu for numerous reasons. First, it was the second largest han, with an official yield of 770,000 koku. Second, it was located in the most distant part of the country, and this made it difficult for the Bakufu to exert its authority. Third, Satsuma had a far larger percentage of samurai in its population than any of the other han. Here the ratio of samurai to commoners was one to three, whereas the national average was one to seventeen. Fourth, the civilizing influence of the urban centers was much diminished in Satsuma, and the warriors tended as a result to retain a hardier and more militaristic outlook than the samurai of other han.

In evaluating the potential threat against the Bakufu, it should be noted that Chōshū also had a larger ratio of samurai to commoners— one to ten—than the national average. The Bakufu, in sharp contrast to Chōshū and Satsuma, retained fewer samurai than even its own scale called for, based on the official assessment of agricultural productivity. This was also true of Owari and Aizu, both collateral houses of the shogunate. Traditional feudal values along with a deep sense of loyalty and dedication to the han were strongly embedded in the Chōshū samurai. In its productive capacity, moreover, Chōshū was among the top ten han with more than 700,000 koku, well over the official estimate. In view of all these factors, the combination of Satsuma and Chōshū can be seen as posing a very serious threat to the Bakufu.

The opposition han were aided by the fact that the Bakufu lacked strong and resolute leadership. The shōgun died during the course of the second expedition against Chōshū, and although everyone's choice for successor was Keiki, he lacked confidence in his own ability to cope with the situation and hesitated for several months before accepting the offer. He then moved to strengthen the Bakufu by following Oguri's line of thinking. He also turned to the French minister Roches for advice and initiated steps to modernize the army and navy as well as the administrative system.

These moves disturbed the opposition leaders because they feared that if the Bakufu succeeded in introducing reforms and in strengthening its military forces, it could possibly regain its former status as the paramount authority. Consequently, the opponents, led by Saigō Takamori, Ōkubo Toshimichi, and Kido Kōin, moved swiftly to effect the overthrow of the Bakufu. They joined hands with the anti-Bakufu court nobles led by Iwakura Tomomi (1825–1883), the most able of the court aristocrats, and began to make plans for the restoration of power to the imperial court.

THE MEIJI RESTORATION

Sakamoto Ryōma managed to persuade his fellow clansman, Gotō Shōjirō (1838–1897), to work for a peaceful solution to the power struggle at the same time that the Satsuma-Chōshū faction was plotting to overthrow the Bakufu. Under the prompting direction of Sakamoto and Gotō, Yamanouchi Yōdō (1827–1872) urged Shōgun Keiki to restore the powers of government voluntarily to the young Emperor Meiji, who had just ascended the throne. Keiki agreed to the proposal and in November of 1867 he formally petitioned the Emperor to accept the restoration of power.

In describing his reasons for making this momentous decision, Keiki later explained that he had concluded that the restoration of power to the court was absolutely essential to the resolution of the crisis facing the country. Several loci of power had developed and he was searching for a political system that would incorporate the various factions in such a way as to allow the new government to function effectively. At this point, he wrote,

> Matsudaira Yōdō (Lord of Tosa), submitted his memorial
> calling for the establishment of upper and lower houses.
> I decided that this was indeed a good proposal. The
> upper house would consist of court aristocrats and the
> daimyō and the lower house would consist of selected han
> warriors. In this way all matters would be decided by public

opinion, and the actual task of restoring imperial rule
would be accomplished. As a result I acquired the courage
and the confidence to bring about the restoration of
imperial rule.[7]

The daimyō of Tosa as well as Gotō Shōjirō wanted to avoid a civil
war that might offer the Western powers a chance to intervene and thus
compromise Japan's independence. They also envisioned the establishment of a government that would be run along parliamentary lines,
with the shōgun serving as the Prime Minister. Evidently Keiki also expected to become the chief executive of this new government. He may
have relinquished his authority as shōgun, but as the head of the Tokugawa domains he was still a major feudal lord. The Tokugawa clan was
bound to be a significant force in the new order as long as this situation
remained unchanged. The anti-Tokugawa faction, however, had no
intention of permitting the Tokugawa family to dominate the new government. They were prepared to destroy the Tokugawa clan by force if
necessary, and they had even obtained a secret imperial mandate to do
so. In a conference of court aristocrats, and leading daimyō and their retainers, Iwakura, with Ōkubo and Saigō's support, demanded that the
Tokugawa family relinquish its entire holdings and that Keiki renounce
all his authority.

Yamanouchi Yōdō fought strenuously to preserve a place in the new
order for Keiki and the Tokugawa clan, but his efforts were completely
undermined by Saigō's machinations. Convinced that an armed conflict
was necessary if the Tokugawa clan was to be completely liquidated,
Saigō decided to incite the Tokugawa forces into attacking by hiring a
large number of ruffians and hoodlums in Edo to provoke their retainers.
The latter fell into the trap set by Saigō and raided the Satsuma residence in Edo. News of the conflict soon reached Keiki and he and his
advisers felt that they could no longer endure the humiliations being
inflicted upon them by the Satsuma-Chōshū faction. They decided to
take up arms against them even though this meant defying the imperial
court, which was now in the grip of the Satsuma-Chōshū clique. Consequently, the Tokugawa forces were branded as rebels. Even Yōdō of
Tosa was forced to join the Satsuma-Chōshū faction against Keiki.

In the ensuing battle, the Tokugawa forces were easily routed at Toba-
Fushimi outside of Kyoto. Keiki fled to Edo and permitted his commander, Katsu Kaishū—who was convinced of the necessity of establishing a new order—to surrender Edo without a fight in April, 1868. Keiki
was placed under house arrest, and he subsequently retired to Shizuoka.

[7] Sakata Yoshio, *Meiji Ishinshi* (*A History of the Meiji Restoration*) (Tokyo: Miraisha,
1960), p. 202.

Some loyal Bakufu warriors continued to resist the imperial forces in the vicinity of Edo, but they were soon subjugated. The overthrow of the Tokugawa Bakufu was thus achieved without the country undergoing a major civil war.

The end of more than two hundred and sixty years of Tokugawa rule and the subsequent restoration of imperial rule was primarily a political event, although it has been interpreted by many Japanese historians as the product of the new social and economic forces that developed during the latter part of the Tokugawa era. It is unquestionably true that social and economic problems had begun to trouble the Bakufu, but these had not become serious enough to undermine its political authority. Elements of the ascending social and economic forces—the townsmen and the peasantry—were not the ones that challenged the existing order of things. The opposition faction emerged from the same political, social, and economic background as the Bakufu. Basically the struggle that resulted in the downfall of the Bakufu was an old-fashioned power struggle between traditional feudal power blocs. Specifically, it was a struggle between the Bakufu and, primarily, Chōshū and Satsuma. The failure of the former and the success of the latter was not directly related to the rise of the peasantry, the emergence of the merchant class, and the growth of commercial capitalism. The Meiji Restoration was certainly not a bourgeois revolution. Furthermore, peasant uprisings were not politically motivated or even directly involved in the actual overthrow of the Tokugawa government.

The outcome of the power struggle was the result of a variety of factors. For one thing, the Satsuma-Chōshū forces were militarily better prepared and possessed more able leaders. They did not gain their advantage over the Bakufu through a more significant growth in commercial capitalism or by virtue of a stronger consciousness among the merchants and the peasantry in their domains. Neither did these forces in the Bakufu's domains align themselves with the Satsuma-Chōshū faction to assist them against the Tokugawa clan. The two han were better prepared militarily because they were financially capable of purchasing modern weapons from the West. This was not the result of their having moved from an agrarian to a commercial economy. As we noted, Chōshū had a special reserve fund that was utilized to purchase weapons, and Satsuma maintained strict control over its economy and had a profitable sugar monopoly.

The crucial factor that made the difference in the rivalry between the Bakufu and the opposition han was leadership. A large number of zealous, highly capable shishi who were willing to take drastic actions to achieve their objectives were present in Satsuma and Chōshū. Many new leaders had also emerged from the lower rungs of the samurai class in these han. The Bakufu, on the other hand, lacked strong leadership, and control remained largely in the hands of the more conservative, high-ranking members of the feudal hierarchy.

In the smaller political communities of the han it was easier for able men from the lower ranks of the samurai to gain recognition and be utilized in time of crisis. In the larger political world of the Bakufu, on the other hand, the upper levels of the hierarchy were crowded with unimaginative, conservative men, and the chances of a low-ranking samurai attracting the attention of the higher officials were extremely limited. After he became shōgun, Keiki claimed that he sought to utilize "men of talent," but by that time it was too late. Furthermore, it is entirely possible that if Keiki himself had been rigorously determined to retain political power at all costs, the outcome may have turned out differently. He was severely lacking in determination and will power, so he hesitated and procrastinated. The inevitable consequence of this was that power slipped away from the Bakufu almost by default.

Probably the single most important factor, however, that contributed to the downfall of the Bakufu was the arrival of the Western powers. The Bakufu, as the authority directly responsible for foreign relations, was confronted with an impossible dilemma. Perry's arrival forced the Bakufu into opening a Pandora's box that brought the imperial court as well as the daimyō and its retainers into the decision-making process. This was followed by a series of crises that were set off by the signing of the commercial treaty with the United States without first securing imperial sanction. The Western powers were demanding still broader contacts and the Bakufu's opponents were thus given additional opportunities to play upon anti-foreign sentiments and to forge an emotionally charged movement—the sonnō jōi movement—that cut across han barriers.

The Bakufu was unable to adopt a definitive policy that they could pursue with firmness. It wavered between opening the country and succumbing to the pressures exerted by the exclusionists. The Bakufu staggered along without resolute leadership after Ii Naosuke, who was willing to use strong measures to curb the advocates of sonnō jōi, was eliminated. The lower-ranking samurai, who would not have been permitted to meddle in the affairs of state under normal circumstances, were able to use terrorist means to intimidate and sometimes eliminate their political foes.

The opposition leaders used every opportunity to harass the Bakufu in its management of foreign affairs. The Chōshū proponents of sonnō jōi fired upon Western vessels, and when they were directly confronted by the foreign powers they sought to shift the blame to the Bakufu by claiming that they were following its orders to expel the intruders. In

1867, as the deadline for the opening of the port of Hyōgo approached, the leaders of Satsuma insisted that the Bakufu renege on its agreement to open the port because, as they claimed, it was too close to Kyoto and would be offensive to the imperial court. At the same time, the leaders of Satsuma were in fact themselves dealing with the Western powers by purchasing ships and arms from them. In order to embarrass the Bakufu, the British, in collusion with the Satsuma-Chōshū faction, were pressing for the opening of the port, fully expecting the Bakufu's opponents to block it. In the ensuing crisis the opposition forces were expected to overthrow the Bakufu. Ernest Satow, the British minister's interpreter, recalled "I hinted to Saigō that the chance of a revolution was not to be lost. If Hiogo was once opened, then good-bye to chances of the daimios." [8]

Clearly, the situation that most seriously contributed to the undermining of the Bakufu's authority and self-confidence was the arrival of the Western powers. Without the crisis engendered by this situation, the Bakufu would not have collapsed as soon as it did. The end of Tokugawa rule, needless to say, did not bring about a completely new age and a new society overnight. In the course of the Meiji era significant transformations took place, but the new was built upon the foundations of the old. The attitudes, values, practices, and institutions that molded the Japanese mode of thinking and behavior prior to and during the Tokugawa era continued to govern the thought and actions of the people during the Meiji era and for a long time afterwards. Added to the old, however, were many new elements. These involved not only science and technology, but new political, social, and cultural ideas were also imported. All of these were to contribute to the very difficult period of transition that ensued. Our next task is to survey this aspect of Japanese history.

[8] Ernest M. Satow, *A Diplomat in Japan* (London: Seeley, 1921), p. 200.

CHAPTER 11

THE MEIJI RESTORATION
The New Order

In the fall of 1868 the era name Meiji was proclaimed. Edo, renamed Tokyo, was designated as the new capital. In the following spring the Emperor moved into the former Edo Castle. Thus commenced the Meiji era, which was to last until 1912.

What was the situation confronting the new leaders of Japan as they took over the reins of government from the Tokugawa Bakufu? First of all, who were the new leaders? The Emperor was a callow youth, no more than a figurehead, and although he is believed to have been an intelligent, able person he would remain by and large a symbol of authority for the forty-five years of his reign. The powers of government at the beginning of the Meiji period were in the hands of a small clique of court aristocrats, the most prominent of whom were Iwakura Tomomi and Sanjō Sanetomi (1837–1891), and members of those han that had played decisive roles in the overthrow of the Bakufu: from Satsuma, Saigō Takamori, Ōkubo Toshimichi; from Chōshū, Kido Kōin, Itō Hirobumi, Inoue Kaoru, and Yamagata Aritomo; from Hizen, Ōkuma Shigenobu; and from Tosa, Itagaki Taisuke and Gotō Shōjirō. There were also han chieftains who still regarded themselves as members of the power elite, the most influential being Satsuma's Shimazu Hisamitsu. In the beginning, however, power was concentrated in the hands of Iwakura, Sanjō, Ōkubo, Kido, and Saigō. Japan, it would seem, was endowed with a rather considerable number of very capable and far-sighted men who, despite their many faults, could certainly be labeled as statesmen. These men may have had to fight for their power, but essentially, they were patriotic individuals possessed of a strong sense of public responsibility, dedication, energy, and vision. Their leadership was collective, that is, no single person emerged as a strong man, and they ruled in accordance with the time-honored tradition of collective leadership and consensus politics.

The task confronting the new Meiji leaders was stupendous. The immediate and overriding necessity was to strengthen and enrich the nation (fukoku kyōhei). Japan was still in a precarious position even though there seemed to be no concrete evidence to indicate that the Western powers were interested in colonizing Japan as they had done with other Asian nations. There was, however, real fear in the minds of the Bakufu and the Satsuma-Chōshū factions that England or France might intervene if a serious civil war erupted. Both nations had already demonstrated in China their willingness to resort to force. Japan had been baptized by the gunfire of the British men-of-war at Satsuma and by the combined forces of the Western warships at Chōshū in the early 1860s. In the treaties she had concluded with the Western powers she had been compelled to accept unequal terms. She was deprived of the right to regulate her own tariffs, and the Western residents in the treaty ports were granted the privilege of extraterritoriality. Japan had to grant the Western nations most-favored-nation treatment, but she was not given the same right in return.

Clearly, Japan was viewed as a backward nation by the Western powers. The Meiji leaders did in fact recognize that in terms of military strength and economic development, Japan was indeed far behind the Western Nations. They even suspected that this was true in political, social, and cultural affairs. Consequently, they set as their primary task the development of military and economic power so as to protect Japan from becoming a victim to any external menace. They wanted to join the community of nations as an equal member and thus be eligible to participate in the game of international power politics.

To achieve the goal of increasing the national wealth and power it was necessary first of all to strengthen the foundations of the new government, which were still quite fragile. There were remnants of pro-Bakufu forces that were continuing their resistance against the Meiji government. These were mainly in the northern sections, the most prominent being Aizu Han. An expeditionary force had to be sent to subdue them as well as the bands of samurai who were conducting guerrilla-type warfare against the imperial government. The most famous band of warriors who resisted the Meiji government was the Shōgitai, whose members numbered two to three thousand. They continued to harass the imperial forces in Edo even after the Bakufu had officially surrendered the city.

It took the military skill of Ōmura Masujirō, who was well-versed in Western military techniques, to subdue them. Resistance was also sustained in Hokkaido by the Bakufu's naval commissioner, Enomoto Takeaki, who fled there with the Bakufu's warships and established a so-called republican government. By the early summer of 1869, he too was subjugated.

The most serious threat to the new government, however, was posed, not by the overt opponents of the new ruling authorities, but by the daimyō who were still entrenched in the local domains. The Bakufu's overthrow did not automatically end the daimyō's control over their han. Only the Tokugawa family and the northern han that forcefully resisted the new government were eliminated or had their holdings reduced. There were still about 270 large and small han that retained their status as autonomous authorities.

One of the major tasks confronting the new government was the subordination of these local authorities to the central government and the construction of a new administrative machinery for the entire nation. It also had to eliminate the castlike organization of the society if it wished to modernize successfully the political system, the armed forces, and the economy. In the financial realm the Meiji government, faced with an almost completely empty treasury, had to regulate its sources of revenue, systematize the currency, and pay its debts. In order to enrich the nation, as fukoku kyōhei demanded, the economy had to be revolutionized; that is, Western-style industries had to be introduced, agriculture techniques improved, and foreign trade fostered. This meant not only the importation of the products of Western technology such as railroads, telegraphs, and steamships, and the establishment of Western-style factories, but also the training and education of the people so that they could be employed in the new enterprises.

In other words, in order to achieve the goal of fukoku kyōhei Japan had to be modernized, Westernized. The men who succeeded in overthrowing the Bakufu did so by riding the crest of the wave of anti-Westernism, but once they gained power, it became imperative that they abandon their anti-Western position and embrace in its stead a policy of establishing full cultural and commercial relations with the West. This, of course, angered the true believers of jōi, who assassinated men like Ōmura Masujirō and Yokoi Shōnan[1] because they were regarded as the chief exponents of Westernism.

The fact that Japan was to open its doors completely to the outside

---

[1] Yokoi, a former adviser to the daimyō of Echizen, was an exponent of fukoku kyōhei. He was accused by the jōi advocates of favoring republicanism and Christianity.

world even in the face of some internal opposition, was signified by the proclamation in April, 1868, of the *Charter Oath of Five Articles,* stating:

1. Deliberative assemblies shall be widely established and all state affairs decided by public opinion.
2. All classes, high and low, shall unite in actively carrying out the administration of affairs of state.
3. The common people, no less than the civil and military officials, shall be allowed to pursue whatever calling they choose so that public apathy may not beset the land.
4. The evil customs of the past shall be abandoned and everything based on the just laws of Heaven and Earth.
5. Knowledge shall be sought throughout the world so as to invigorate the foundations of imperial rule.

The Five Articles, originally drafted by two men who were sympathetic to constitutional, parliamentary government, were revised by Kido Kōin in order to make the references to the common people and parliamentary government somewhat less explicit.

The business at hand for the new leaders, then, was the establishment of a new order and the modernization of Japan. The Meiji leaders were at the same time faced with the problem of consolidating their grip on the machinery of power. They had to dislodge those who formerly held power while fending off the efforts of new opponents who were seeking to expel them in the name of "freedom and popular rights." By the middle of the 1880s the Meiji leaders had not only launched Japan on its path to modernization, but they had also gained a firmer grip on the reins of power as they emerged in the form of a small group of tightly knit timocrats who came to be known as the *genrō* (elder statesmen). They were Itō Hirobumi, Yamagata Aritomo, and Inoue Kaoru from Chōshū, and Kuroda Kiyotaka, Matsukata Masayoshi, Saigō Tsugumichi, and Ōyama Iwao from Satsuma. These government leaders were providing official direction in creating a new order of things. Non-government leaders from the intellectual and cultural realms, by fostering the cultural movement known as *bunmei kaika* (civilization and enlightenment) and the political movement known as *jiyū minken* (freedom and popular rights) were also working toward the modernization of the society.

POLITICAL CHANGES

Early in 1868, after the Tokugawa forces were routed at Toba-Fushimi, the imperial faction established a provisional government. In June, this was replaced by a new political machinery, and what is sometimes referred to as the Constitution of 1868 was proclaimed, establishing a Council of State (*Dajōkan*) with supreme political authority. The Council of State had a threefold division, legislative, executive, and judicial, and in theory the principle of separation of powers was to prevail. In reality, however, the men who held key positions did not operate under the restraints of this kind of government and a few men exercised power that cut across administrative divisions.

Further changes in governmental structure were made in the summer of 1869, but the form of government that the Meiji leaders finally settled upon and retained (until the cabinet system was introduced in 1885) was the one adopted in the summer of 1871. On this occasion the Council of State was divided into three parts: the Central Board, the Right Board, and the Left Board. The Central Board was the supreme organ of the government and made final decisions on all questions of policy. It was headed by the *dajō daijin* (chancellor), and included the *dainagon* (deputies), who were later replaced by ministers of the left and right, and a number of councilors. The Left Board, although it was originally designed to perform legislative functions, acted merely as an advisory body. The Right Board consisted of heads of departments and their deputies. The departments of foreign affairs, finance, war, public works, imperial household, education, Shinto, and justice were created at this time. The department of home affairs was added in 1873. In theory the Right Board was separated from the Central Board, but because influential councilors also served as heads of departments, policy-making and administrative duties tended to merge.

Power was being drawn increasingly into the hands of the Satsuma-Chōshū leaders, while the court nobles and former daimyō gradually faded into the background. The post of dajō daijin was occupied by Sanjō and that of minister of the right by Iwakura, but the real authority actually rested with the councilors, who were primarily men from Satsuma and Chōshū.

Tampering with the administrative system of the central government did little to strengthen its authority because of the continued existence of the anachronistic feudal domains. From the outset of the Meiji era, men like Kido were convinced that it was imperative to compel the daimyō to return their domains to the Emperor just as the shōgun had done. Fortunately for the Meiji government, the leaders from Satsuma, Chōshū, Tosa, and Hizen managed to persuade their lords to take the initiative in adopting this policy, and in March, 1869, the daimyō of the four han appealed to the Emperor to accept the restoration of their domains. Apparently, they regarded this action as a mere formality in which the Emperor would agree to their offer but then would reinvest them with authority over their former han, and perhaps even add more land as a reward for their loyal gesture. Other daimyō quickly followed suit fearing that otherwise they might be considered less loyal to the new imperial government than the four daimyō that initiated the policy. The government formally accepted the restoration of the han lands in July, and ordered the remaining daimyō who had not voluntarily returned their domains to the court to do so. The former daimyō were reappointed as hereditary han chieftains and paid one-tenth of the han income as salary. The samurai retainers of the ex-daimyō were given a fraction of their former stipends as income.

The process of returning han lands to the Emperor was completed by early 1870. Some han chieftains, like Shimazu Hisamitsu, were disillusioned with the outcome of the transaction because they had been led to believe that they would have autonomous power in the han and be allowed to retain their own armies. Now that all the daimyō had relinquished their authority to the imperial government, however, the Meiji leaders proceeded to eliminate han government entirely by replacing the han with prefectures.

The smaller han were facing bankruptcy and some han officials petitioned the government to abolish them by the end of 1869. The government complied with these requests and brought several small han under the authority of the prefectural governors. Some han leaders were vigorously introducing reforms, but others did nothing to meet the challenges of the new era. Internal unrest among the peasantry and the samurai was also a problem in many han, and in order to suppress the malcontents the central government had to acquire immediate jurisdiction over the han. The government, moreover, needed the revenues that could be collected from the han: the agricultural production of the entire country at this time was estimated at thirty million koku, but the central government had only eight million koku under its control.

In order to replace the han with prefectural governments under the direct control of the central government, the Meiji leaders needed the cooperation of the most troublesome han, Satsuma. An effort was made to persuade Hisamitsu to enter the government, and although he personally refused, he did agree to allow Saigō, who had returned to Satsuma soon after the Meiji government was established, to join the central government. In the summer of 1871 Saigō began to serve as one of the first councilors of the government. Evidently, he did so expecting to build a strong government around the shizoku (former samurai).

The final decision to abolish the han was made with Saigō's entry into the government. In order to cope with any resistance that it might encounter, the central government organized an imperial army consisting of warriors provided by Satsuma, Chōshū, and Tosa. In August, 1871, a decree was issued formally abolishing the han and replacing them with prefectural units headed by governors sent from the center. A number of han welcomed this decision because of their severe internal weaknesses and financial troubles. Even those who were not wholeheartedly in favor of this policy nevertheless accepted the change without opposition because the settlement was very favorable to the former ruling caste. These daimyō were allowed to retain an income that was equivalent to one-tenth the income of their former han, and of course now they had none of the expenses involved in managing the han. The central government assumed the debts that had been incurred by the han, and undertook the responsibility for the paper currencies that had been issued by them. In effect, the central government had bailed the han out of their financial difficulties and thus provided the former daimyō with very little to complain about. The people who were placed in a difficult situation were the former retainers of the daimyō. Their plight will be discussed later.

The reorganization of the government in accord with the system adopted in 1871 was effected with the successful abolishment of the han and their replacement by the prefectures. A centralized bureaucratic government was beginning to emerge, and the key leaders, aside from Sanjō and Iwakura, were coming primarily from the four han of Satsuma, Chōshū, Tosa, and Hizen, with men from Satsuma and Chōshū predominating. These leaders, however, were not in complete agreement about the kind of government that should be established. The faction led by Ōkubo and Kido tended to prefer a strong centralized bureaucracy, while the faction represented by Saigō favored making the shizoku the core of the government.

The government, now that the decision to replace the han with prefectures was made, decided to move forward by sending a special mission abroad to lay the groundwork for revising the treaties that the Tokugawa Bakufu had concluded with the Western nations. The Meiji leaders wanted to remove the unequal provisions of the treaties, which were renewable in 1872. It was believed that the mission would also prove to be an important educational experience for the new leaders since they would be given an opportunity to observe directly Western societies in action. They were to study with particular care those legal and political institutions and practices that might be necessary to adopt if the Western nations were to be persuaded to revise the unequal treaties. The mission, which was led by Iwakura and included among its members such top government officials as Ōkubo, Kido, Itō, and Inoue, departed for the United States and Europe toward the end of 1871.

A caretaker government was established while members of the Iwakura Mission were abroad with the following men holding key positions: Saigō, Itagaki Taisuke, Etō Shimpei, Soejima Taneomi, and Ōkuma

Shigenobu. It was agreed that no major changes were to be introduced, but this was a rather unrealistic restriction in light of the fact that the Iwakura Mission was to remain abroad for a year and a half or more at a time when there were many pressing problems, such as growing agrarian discontent, threatening the country. As it turned out, many significant reforms and innovations were in fact made in the courts, the schools, the land tax, the military, the postal system, and the calendar.

So far as the mission itself was concerned, it failed to achieve its primary goal of persuading the Western powers to revise the treaties on the basis of equality. The members of the group, however, did return impressed with what they saw of Western industries, technology, and certain aspects of political life, particularly in Bismarckian Germany.

LOCAL GOVERNMENT

In 1871 the government reorganized the registration systems that had existed in the Tokugawa period (in which separate registers were kept for each class) and established a uniform system of family registration. The task of maintaining the records was turned over to the local administrative districts that were established by bringing together several villages under the authority of a "minor district." Several of these were then joined together to form a "major district." The administrative heads of these units were appointed from above, and in effect they became members of the new bureaucratic class.

In 1878 the artificial division of the country into districts was abolished, and the towns and villages were made the basic administrative units. In 1880 town and village assemblies were established, the members of which were elected, to deal with matters prescribed by national law.

The administrative authority immediately below the central government was the prefectural government. Initially the former han, regardless of size, were transformed into prefectures so that there were three *fu* (metropolitan prefectures) and 306 *ken* (prefectures). During the following years the smaller ones were consolidated and the larger ones broken up until 1888 when the final redistricting occurred dividing the nation into three fu and forty-three ken, including Okinawa. The prefectural governors were appointed by the central government, and they became its administrative arms.

SOCIAL REFORMS

The class system perpetuated by the Tokugawa government was one of the feudal vestiges of the society that had to be eliminated. The removal of feudal class distinctions began in 1869 when the daimyō began relinquishing their control over the han. They and the court aristocrats were classified as *kazoku* (peers), the upper-class samurai as *shizoku,* and

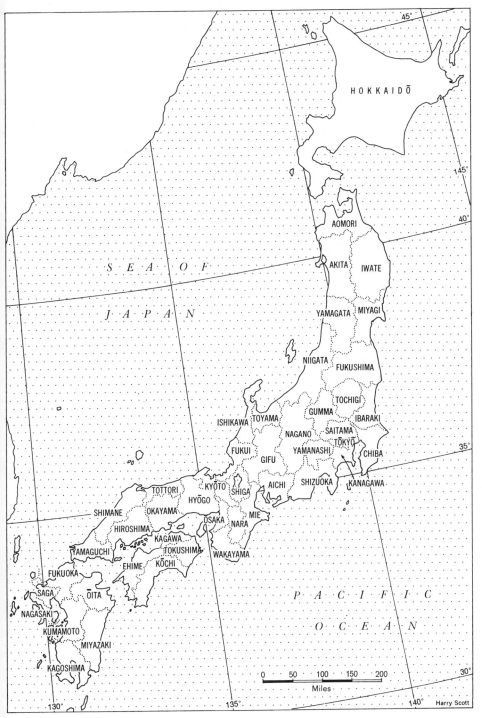

JAPANESE PREFECTURES.

the lower-class samurai as *sotsu*. In 1870 the common people, classified as *heimin*, were permitted to adopt family names, and 1871 intermarriages between the upper and lower classes were allowed. The common people were now given the right to wear formal apparel and travel on horseback, previously the exclusive privileges of the samurai. Also in 1871 wearing of the distinctive hair style and the characteristic sword bearing (which was ultimately banned in 1876) were made optional for the kazoku and shizoku. The samurai's right to cut down disrespectful commoners with impunity was also abolished. Aside from government officials, kazoku and shizoku were now permitted to become farmers, merchants, or artisans.

In 1872 the government reclassified the populace into three categories: kazoku, shizoku, and heimin. The lower-class samurai, the sotsu, were now reclassified as heimin. The purpose for retaining these distinctions, the government held, was for genealogical identification.

Another class of people who in theory were uplifted from their place at the bottom of the society were the outcasts, who had heretofore been treated as unclean members of the society. This group totalled about 400,000 people, or slightly over 1 percent of the population. The Meiji government abolished legal bias, but in reality social and economic discrimination against the outcasts did not cease, and,in fact, it continues to the present.

Equality was to prevail among all classes, theoretically, but in practice, the kazoku and shizoku were still accorded privileged treatment by law. In the code of 1873, for instance, both these groups were allowed to pay fines rather than face imprisonment for minor crimes. For offenses that resulted in incarceration with hard labor for commoners, kazoku and shizoku were imprisoned without hard labor. Commoners who became government officials, however, were accorded the same treatment as members of the shizoku. The government officials in effect constituted the new privileged class.

In the fall of 1872, as a by-product of the *Maria Luz* affair, slavery and human traffic were made illegal. The Peruvian ship *Maria Luz*, which was engaged in coolie traffic, arrived in Yokohama for repairs in the summer of 1872. Some coolies escaped and asked for aid. The Japanese, in extending assistance to them, were then confronted by the Peruvian authorities with the embarrassing fact that slavery was commonly practiced in Japan. This led the government to ban slavery, although "voluntary" servitude in houses of prostitution was permitted.

PENSIONS FOR THE KAZOKU AND SHIZOKU

As noted above, the central government adopted the policy of paying the former daimyō and samurai a portion of their feudal incomes and stipends. This naturally created a considerable drain on the government's revenues. Approximately one-third of the tax revenues collected in the period from the abolishment of the han to Saigō's rebellion in 1877 (see page 303) had to be allocated for these payments. The government had assumed in addition to this all the debts of the han. Consequently, about half of the government's total income was expended to meet these old feudal obligations.

In order to ease its financial burdens the government decided to commute the pensions in 1876. The pensioners were paid off in government bonds that were issued with interest rates varying in accordance with the former stipends. The recipients of smaller stipends may have been granted higher interest rates, but the original stipends of the upper class were so much larger that the 476 kazoku received one-third of the sum allocated for the commutation bonds, thus forcing the 320,000 shizoku to share the remaining two-thirds. The income of the kazoku dropped to about 45 percent of what they formerly received, but compared to the shizoku they were still well off. Many invested their money in land, business, and banks. The upper and middle-class shizoku saw their income decline by as much as 47 to 74 percent. The lower-class samurai, however, were the ones who were affected most adversely, for they experienced an 88 to 98 percent drop in income. Their average annual income came to about twenty-nine yen, which was comparable to the pay of an ordinary soldier who, however, also received free room, board, and clothing.

The abolition of the class system and the adoption of the pension plan meant that the former samurai were actually dispossessed. As a result, they were bitterly disappointed in the new order and fell into a dangerously rebellious mood. This in part accounts for the growing number of samurai uprisings that broke out in the seventies. Only 10 percent of the former samurai managed to obtain government positions. Some went into teaching, the army, and the police force, but the vast majority found it necessary to enter occupations totally alien to their background and aptitude, such as agriculture, commerce, and handicraft work. Some became so impoverished that they were reduced to selling their daughters to the houses of prostitution.

REVISION OF THE LAND TAX
AND THE PLIGHT OF THE FARMERS

In accordance with its policy of removing feudal restrictions, the Meiji government lifted the ban on the export of rice in the summer of 1871. In the fall of that year it also removed the restrictions on land utilization and gave the farmers the freedom to grow whatever they chose. Private ownership of land, established by the issuance of title deeds, was recognized, and in the spring of 1872 the right to buy and sell land was finally granted.

The levy on rice was collected in the traditional manner and in accordance with the rates that had been fixed by the former daimyō until 1873, when a tax reform was instituted. This required the holders of title deeds to pay taxes in money at 3 percent of the assessed value of the land, while at the same time local taxes were limited to one-third of the national tax. This new system of taxation, however, did not lessen the burden of the farmers because the amount due remained close to what was collected under the old order; that is to say, the 3 percent tax on the land came to about 33 percent of the total yield. This was two to seven times the rates prevailing in Europe at this time. In some instances in fact, the farmers had to pay even heavier taxes than they did in the Tokugawa era because collection under the Meiji government was much more stringently implemented.

During the Tokugawa period peasants were allowed to utilize the woods and meadows belonging to the lord of the han for firewood and fodder, but now these were no longer open to them. They were now, along with the woods and meadows belonging to the community, classified as state property. The farmers agitated for a reduction in the land tax, and they did manage in 1876 to have the rate lowered to 2.5 percent. The fact still remained, however, that the agrarian sector was paying for the cost of modernizing and industrializing the nation. During the period from 1875 to 1879, 80.5 percent of the government's tax revenues were derived from the land tax. The farmers were not allowed to deduct the equivalent of their wages from the taxable land value even though the wages of the townsmen were not taxed. The only favorable aspect of the land tax revisions as far as the peasants were concerned was the elimination of community responsibility for taxes.

The government did little to discourage the diffusion of tenancy because its primary interest was in the collection of the land tax. The question of land ownership mattered little to the officials, and at this time about one-third of the arable land was held in tenancy. The average tenant paid in excess of 60 percent of his crop to the landowner, who used about half of this to pay the land tax while retaining the other half as his revenue. The tenant's share, after payment of miscellaneous dues, came to about 32 percent of the crop. In the Tokugawa period the tenants kept on the average 39 percent of the yield. Many of the landowning farmers actually possessed very little land—about 40 percent of the farm families owned 1.1 acre or less.

Agrarian poverty was intensified by a variety of factors in addition to the heavy burden of taxation. Fluctuations in the price of rice affected the farmers adversely, and the penetration of the money economy into the countryside greatly increased their expenses. Those farmers who supplemented their income by raising silkworms were at the mercy of the fluctuating price of silk. The rural household industries were very badly hurt by the importation of cheap foreign manufactured goods, and the growth of Western-type factory production in Japan threatened their continued existence altogether.

New measures introduced by the Meiji government, such as universal military conscription and compulsory education, also added to the burden of the agrarian families. The pressures that were brought to bear by the implementation of these programs led to an increasingly large number of farmers being dispossessed of their lands. As a result, peasant disturbances began to increase and many village leaders, hoping to improve rural conditions by gaining a voice in the political arena, became active in the popular rights movement.

LEGAL REFORMS

It was noted earlier in discussing Tokugawa justice that the legal system prevailing then was based on the notion of rule-by-status rather than on the concept, prevalent in the west, of rule-of-law. From the Western point of view then, the legal practices in mid-nineteenth century Japan certainly seemed arbitrary, offering no protection for individuals unfamiliar with Japanese ways. The attacks against the Westerners who unknowingly violated the customs of the land hardened their distrust of Japanese justice. Consequently, there was little likelihood that the unequal treaties would be revised unless Japan adopted Western legal institutions and practices.

The Meiji authorities were eager to develop a legal system that would be acceptable to the West and they turned to the French model because, unlike the unwieldy Anglo-American common law, it had the advantage of having been codified. French laws were also especially appealing because they were administered by a corps of professional judges. This was in sharp contrast to the Anglo-American practice of dividing the functions between judge and jury, in which the former determined matters of law and the latter matters of fact, a distinction unknown to the Japanese.[2]

The legal system that emerged in the Meiji period is defined by some legal scholars as rule-*by*-law rather than rule-*of*-law because although there was a formal commitment to the concept of administration under law, there were no legal limitations set on policy formation or legislation. Rule-of-law in which these limitations are fixed by the law in deference

---

[2] An option making it possible to receive jury trials in criminal cases was provided for in 1923, but it was little used before being suspended in 1943.

to a consideration of fundamental human rights and the electoral process did not come into existence until the post-war era.[3]

The court system that emerged under the Meiji Constitution consisted, from the lowest to the highest, of summary police courts, district courts, local courts, courts of appeal, and the Court of Cassation, which heard appeals on points of law from inferior courts. A separate court system (Court of Administrative Litigation) was set up to deal with cases involving administrative authorities. This of course meant that administrative abuses could not be brought under the scrutiny of the courts of law.

A penal code and a code of criminal procedure were prepared and adopted in 1880 and 1890 with the assistance of a French adviser, Gustave Boissonade. A commercial code was designed with the aid of a German legal authority, Hermann Roesler, but it was not put into effect until 1899. The drafting and adoption of the civil code, the final version of which was patterned largely after the German model, was delayed until 1898.

THE POLICE SYSTEM

Under Tokugawa rule a police system whose primary function was the protection of the people did not exist. The law enforcement officials during this period functioned primarily as instruments charged with the responsibility of keeping the people under control. Some Japanese observers who went abroad were impressed by the courteous and helpful behavior of Western policemen, and they brought back with them the concept that the primary functions of the police should be to maintain law and order and to protect the people. The repressive, authoritarian tendency of the law enforcement officers, however, could not easily be altered. Initially the police were placed under the jurisdiction of the local governments, but in 1874 they were brought under the control of the Ministry of Home Affairs in accordance with the recommendation of Kawaji Toshiyoshi, who is regarded as the founder of the modern Japanese police system. He envisioned the police as an instrument for strengthening the nation, and he outspokenly favored the establishment of a "police state" in which the police would play a key role in maintaining "the good health" of the nation by aggressively ferreting out undesirable elements.

The Meiji government gradually centralized police power. Under the cabinet system that was introduced in 1885, the Minister of Home Affairs retained supervisory authority over the prefectural police. Prefectural

---

[3] Dan F. Henderson, "Law and Political Modernization in Japan," in Robert E. Ward, ed., *Political Development in Modern Japan* (Princeton, N.J.: Princeton University Press, 1968), p. 415.

police commissioners were appointed by the central government and were made responsible to the police commissioner in the Ministry of Home Affairs. The authority of the police was extended: it was given the power to censor the press and control political activities; it was granted the authority to regulate aspects of personal behavior by curtailing such things as nudity, heterosexual bathing, etc. It became an institution to be feared rather than an organization to which the people could turn for help and protection.

THE ARMY AND THE NAVY

In order to establish a strong central government and also cope with external problems, the Meiji government found it necessary to raise its own army instead of relying upon those maintained by the han. The need for a national army was generally agreed upon, but there was dispute over the question of the kind of army that should be established. Kido and Ōmura Masujirō favored one based upon universal conscription whereas Ōkubo advocated establishing a national army made up of the former samurai of the major han, Satsuma, Chōshū, and Tosa. Kido feared the power of the shizoku and objected to this scheme; Ōkubo, on the other hand, distrusted the commoners who might gain power if universal conscription were introduced. In Satsuma, where Ōkubo came from, about 20 percent of the population belonged to the shizoku class and thus constituted a force that had to be reckoned with. In 1871, with Iwakura in support of Ōkubo's position, the government established an army consisting of six to eight thousand warriors of Satsuma, Chōshū, and Tosa.

Ōmura became the object of hatred by the shizoku because his military plan would have deprived them of their traditional function. He was assassinated by reactionary samurai but the plan for universal conscription did not die with him, despite continued opposition by conservative officials. Eventually, Yamagata Aritomo succeeded in creating a new army that was based on universal conscription and in January, 1873, the military conscription law was promulgated. All male subjects, with certain exceptions, became liable for military conscription at the age of twenty.

Not only was universal conscription unpopular with the shizoku, who resented being deprived of their traditional function, but the common people also objected to being drafted. The use of the term "blood tax" for the obligation to serve in the military led to the belief that blood would be taken from the conscripts. It was even rumored that they would be killed and then turned over to foreigners who would extract oil from their corpses to be used for food. As a result, uprisings protesting military conscription broke out in different parts of the country. The new army, however, despite these difficulties, became an established institution, and by 1883 all the men in the army were conscript soldiers. The shizoku eventually came to accept the new system and in fact played a significant role as officers in the new army, which was designed after the Prussian model. The generals were primarily men from Chōshū and Satsuma, with the men from the former predominating.

The government was also faced with the task of building a modern navy, but plans for this did not materialize rapidly and it was not until 1875 that the government ordered three ironclad warships from England. As late as 1889, Japan had only three ironclad vessels and three composite (iron and wood) ships. The navy, modeled after the British prototype, was dominated by Satsuma men.

The soldiers had no *esprit de corps,* no sense of identity with the national interest or concept of public service, and so the government sought to foster such attitudes by issuing an imperial rescript to the soldiers and sailors in 1882. It emphasized such virtues as loyalty, duty, service, obedience, and valor, while urging the men to abstain from political activities. The rescript stressed in particular the special role they were to play as servants of the Emperor.

ECONOMIC DEVELOPMENTS

It was necessary to revolutionize the basically agrarian economy and transform the nation into an industrial society if the policy to "enrich and strengthen the nation" was to be realized. Meiji Japan had to enter the stage of modern economic growth and this necessitated: (1) the application of modern scientific thought and technology to industry, transportation, and agriculture; (2) continuous and rapid rise in real product per capita together with high rates of population growth; (3) rapid and efficient transformation of the industrial structure (*e.g.,* shift from agriculture to manufacturing); (4) international contacts.

The years 1868–1885 are seen by economists Ohkawa and Rosovsky as a transition period during which the groundwork was laid for the initial phase of Japan's modern economic growth, which begins in 1886 and extends to 1905. The second phase runs from 1906 to 1952. This is followed by a period of postwar growth that commences in 1953.[4]

Tokugawa Japan was essentially an agrarian society characterized by the small peasant cultivator who lived just above the subsistence level. "Isolated islands of modernity existed and exist in most backward countries, and these should not be confused with the genuine beginnings of an industrial revolution. A few spinning mills and iron foundries cannot

---

[4] Kazushi Ohkawa and Henry Rosovsky, "A Century of Japanese Economic Growth," in William W. Lockwood, ed., *The State and Economic Enterprise in Japan* (Princeton, N.J.: Princeton University Press, 1965), pp. 52–53.

be said to change the industrial structure of a country with a population of some thirty million people." [5] Government figures of 1874 indicate that at that time, in a way that was typical of pre-modern manufacturing patterns, textiles and food accounted for over 70 percent of the value of all manufacturing output. The amount of foreign trade after the arrival of Perry continued to remain very small, although of the four criteria of modern economic growth this was the one most clearly in evidence. At best, the following can be said:

> The Japanese economy of the 1860s was reasonably, but not outstandingly productive for a traditional economy. It had a high potential for saving and was already showing signs of quickening economic growth. At the same time a number of other features made it more responsive than most traditional economies to economic stimuli. It was basically commercial with a well-developed system of national markets. The population was comparatively well educated and economically motivated. Because of efficient and productive taxation systems and its tradition of economic activity and control, government was well placed to play an important role in the process of economic modernization.[6]

Under these circumstances the government had to play an active role in removing many of the feudal barriers and in creating and stimulating the conditions necessary for modern economic growth. As noted earlier, it abolished the Tokugawa class system along with the privileges customarily accorded to the samurai. Internal checkpoints that obstructed travel and trade were removed, and freedom of occupation was granted. The government fostered better agricultural techniques, instituted a uniform system of land tax, and established a new financial base by creating a public budget system and a modern currency and banking system. It also actively propagated Western knowledge and introduced compulsory public education. More directly, it encouraged the development of new industries by, among other things, building and operating key enterprises, constructing model plants, and granting government subsidies to private entrepreneurs.

The government took the initiative in constructing modern transportation and communication systems, which were essential for the modernization of the economy. The first railroad line, the Tokyo-Yokohama Rail-

---

[5] *Ibid.*, p. 58.
[6] E. Sydney Crawcour, "The Tokugawa Heritage," in *ibid.*, p. 44.

way, was opened in 1872, and this was followed by the Tōkaidō line linking Tokyo and Kobe, which was completed in 1889. In 1869 the telegraph line between Tokyo and Yokohama was completed, and in 1871 a postal system linking Tokyo and Osaka was introduced. In shipping, the government gave its support to the Mitsubishi Company so as to enable it to compete with foreign companies. By 1893 Japan had 2,000 miles of railroad, 100,000 tons of steam vessels, and 4,000 miles of telegraph lines. Shipyards, arsenals, foundries, machine shops, and technical schools were established and operated with foreign technical advisors.

In the realm of industrial development, the government established the first modern silk filature in 1870. Cotton spinning mills were built or re-equipped with modern imported machinery. Experimental factories were built for the production of cement, tile, sugar, beer, glass, chemicals, woolen fabrics, and so on. Using foreign technicians, the government also played a role in developing the mining industry, particularly copper, coal, and precious metals. In order to foster and stimulate interest in industrial development, it also staged an industrial exposition in 1877, in the midst of Saigō's rebellion. Needless to say it placed great stress on agricultural improvement, and also sought to encourage animal husbandry by establishing experimental stations.

In this transitional period neither agricultural nor industrial growth was spectacular.[7] Modern-style factories were still limited in number and rather small in scale. In 1886, for example, the steam power used for industrial purposes totaled 4,094 horsepower distributed through 217 plants.

The government did play a very significant role in the industrialization of Meiji Japan, but it was not the only force that was to contribute to a transformation of the economy. Private entrepreneurs took advantage of the fresh opportunities and initiated new enterprises, and despite the low standard of living, private savings did accumulate. Rural leaders also played an active role by introducing new agricultural knowledge into the villages. The one area, however, in which the government's role was critical was in the fiscal realm. The Meiji government was in a precarious financial situation when it came to power in 1868. During the period from September, 1868, to December, 1872, total public expenditures amounted to 148.3 million yen while revenue came to only 50.4 million yen. The government sought to offset this imbalance by issuing

[7] The estimate of percentage increase in paddy rice yield in a given area from 1873–1877 to 1883–1887 is believed to have been between 2.5 and 6.6 percent. One economist estimates that the annual growth rate of agriculture over the period 1873–1877 to 1918–1922 was 1 percent while others estimate it at 2.9 percent. Harry Oshima, "Meiji Fiscal Policy and Economic Growth," in *ibid.*, p. 355. Cf., James Nakamura, "Growth of Japanese Agriculture, 1880–1935," in *ibid.*, p. 305; Kazushi Ohkawa and Henry Rosovsky, "A Century of Japanese Economic Growth," in *ibid.*, pp. 69–70 note.

nonconvertible paper notes and by borrowing from big merchant houses and foreign nations. In 1872 it authorized the establishment of national banks and retired nonconvertible notes; in 1873 it instituted the land tax. Its financial position, even with the implementation of these measures, was still strained because so much of its revenue had to be used to fulfill the feudal obligations that it had assumed.

In 1877 the government was involved in the fiscally damaging enterprise of crushing the major uprising led by Saigō, and this necessitated the issuance of an additional twenty-seven million yen in notes. The government was also compelled to allow banks to issue notes, up to 80 percent of their capital, against bonds deposited with the treasury. This encouraged the kazoku and shizoku, who were paid off in bonds in the commutation of stipends, to invest in the national banks, which then issued additional bank notes. The total amount of notes in circulation rose from 106.9 million yen in 1876 to 164.4 million yen in 1879. This created a serious inflationary situation that saw the price of rice nearly double. The government's real income dropped drastically and it was compelled to introduce new taxes on sake and tobacco, and reduce its expenditures in developing new industries.

Confronted with this critical situation, Matsukata Masayoshi (1835–1924), who became finance minister in 1881 and remained in charge of fiscal affairs for the next sixteen years, adopted a policy of reintroducing convertible currency, severe austerity, and deflation. He ended public operation of costly factories and mines, introduced new indirect taxes, and started redeeming public debts. Under his financial management the government saved an average of 28 percent of its current revenues. Half of these savings were used for capital formation and the other half was retained as surplus. The quantity of money was reduced by about 20 percent and commodity prices fell sharply. In 1884 the general price level dropped to 75 percent of what it had been in 1881, interest rates declined, and foreign payments shifted in Japan's favor. In 1885 Matsukata reformed the banking system by establishing the Bank of Japan, which replaced the national banks as the bank of issue. Matsukata thus restored the financial health of the government and gave the country a modern currency system and an effective budget structure. Japan was finally ready to enter the stage of modern economic growth.

Matsukata undoubtedly deserves great credit for his achievements, but it should be noted at the same time that his taxation and deflationary policies had serious adverse effects on the farmers and created severe hardships that ultimately led to agrarian riots. Increased taxes on sake and tobacco, and indirect taxes burdened the common man more than the rich. Deflation was especially painful for the farming population because, although money was dearer, the land tax rate remained the same. The price of rice in Tokyo dropped 50 percent in the years between 1881 and 1884, and this meant that the peasants had to allot twice as much rice for tax payments. In 1881 the peasants utilized 16 percent of the total rice production in tax, whereas in 1884 they had to allocate 32.8 percent. Local taxes also increased as a result of the central government making the local authorities responsible for some of the services that it had formerly provided.

A noteworthy characteristic of the developing economic policy was the close cooperation that was established between the government and certain favored business interests, a policy that culminated with the emergence of gigantic business houses, the *zaibatsu*. Cooperation between the big merchant families and the new government began when houses such as Mitsui, Shimada, Ono, and Kōnoike supplied the imperial forces with funds, through donations or loans, during their conflict with the Bakufu. On the other hand, the big merchant houses also maintained close ties with the Bakufu, and thus made certain they would be on the winning side regardless of the outcome of the struggle.

Special consideration was given to these houses when the imperial faction triumphed. For instance, the merchant houses were used as tax collectors by the government. This proved to be a particularly lucrative enterprise since the farmers were required to pay their taxes in money and thus had to convert their rice into currency. Functioning as rice dealers and tax collectors, merchant houses such as Mitsui made huge profits by buying and selling the rice turned in for tax payments when the market price was the most advantageous to them.

The government facilitated the entry of these houses into the banking business when a system of national banks was established in 1872, and encouraged their expansion into the industrial realm by transferring many state-owned enterprises to them at very low prices. In 1880 a law enabling the government to transfer factories to private hands was enacted and factories in nonstrategic industries such as cotton spinning, glass making, and cement were turned over to private firms.

Initially the government maintained control of mining, with the exception of the Sumitomo Company, which was allowed to keep the Besshi copper mine, the largest in the country. As time went on, private firms increasingly moved into this industry. The Miike coal mine was obtained by the Mitsui Company, a few gold mines were acquired by the Furukawa Company, and a number of gold and silver mines went into the hands of the Mitsubishi Company in 1896.

The government supported and subsidized the Mitsubishi Company in the area of shipping. It gave thirteen ships that had been used as military transports during the Formosan expedition of 1874 to the founder of the company, Iwasaki Yatarō, and from 1875 the government subsidized his shipping business by granting it an annual subsidy of 250,000 yen for fifteen years. Later, as the shipping company amalgamated with another firm and formed the *Nippon Yūsen Kaisha* (Japanese Mail Line), the government granted it a yearly subsidy of 880;000 yen. The Mitsubishi Company was provided even further assistance when, in 1887, the government sold it the Nagasaki Shipyards. State support of sea transport was extended because, for strategic and economic reasons, it was deemed necessary to have a strong merchant fleet that was capable of competing on equal terms with foreign shipping firms.

There were frequently close personal bonds between key members of the government and the major business houses. Inoue Kaoru, for example, had close ties with the House of Mitsui, and the main reason the company was able to acquire the Miike coal mine was that it had obtained information about its competitors' bids from the Minister of Finance, Matsukata. Ōkuma was Iwasaki Yatarō's close friend.

EDUCATION

At the time of the Meiji Restoration some traditional scholars hoped to make Confucianism or Shinto the basis of learning. This was the case because what had presumably taken place was the "restoration" of imperial authority and traditional values. In 1869 a traditionalist scholar who believed that the object of education should be the elucidation of the "imperial way," was made the head of the Bureau of Educational Studies. It was intended that Shinto be made the national religion and the foundation of education. The goal of education, as stated in an official proclamation issued in 1870, must be the inculcation of "respect for the enlightened way of the kami [gods], and the clarification of human relations. The multitudes must rectify their minds, perform their work diligently, and serve the imperial court." The Bakufu's Confucian academy, the Shōheikō, was reactivated as the center of learning for Confucianism and Shinto.

This essentially reactionary trend in educational thought was soon challenged, however, by those who represented the movement to "enlighten and civilize" the country. They maintained that in order to modernize Japan, Western educational ideas and practices had to be adopted. The movement was led by private educators such as Fukuzawa Yukichi (1835–1901), but the need to adopt and adapt Western educational concepts and institutions was also recognized by the more progressive of the government leaders.

The importation of Western knowledge necessarily required that a high level of literacy be achieved. The literacy rate of Tokugawa Japan was indeed relatively high, as we noted earlier, but the Meiji leaders set out to eliminate illiteracy completely. They issued the Education Ordinance of 1872, which stated that there shall be "no community with an illiterate family, nor a family with an illiterate person." [8] Universal education was instituted by this act and every child was, in theory, required to attend school for eight years. The philosophy underlying this system was utilitarian and pragmatic, as the preamble to the Education Ordinance demonstrates:

> In order for each person to make his way in life, husband
> his wealth wisely, enjoy prosperity in his business, and
> attain the goal of his life he must develop his character,
> broaden his knowledge, and cultivate his talents. . . .
> [All this, however,] cannot be achieved without education.
> For this reason schools are established. . . . Learning is
> like an investment for success in life. How can anyone
> afford to neglect it?

The practical aspect of learning was emphasized by the observation that:

> Language, writing, and arithmetic used in daily affairs as
> well as the affairs of the shizoku, officials, farmers,
> merchants, and practitioners of all kinds of arts and crafts,
> and matters pertaining to law, politics, astronomy,
> medicine, etc., that is, all things that man concerns himself
> with belong to the domain of learning.

The new approach to learning was contrasted with the old approach in which:

> Learning was regarded as the business of the samurai and his
> superiors while the peasants, artisans, merchants, women
> and children paid no heed to it, having no notion of
> what it meant. Even the samurai and his superiors who
> pursued learning tended to claim that it was done for the
> good of the state and were unaware of the fact that it was
> the foundation for success in life.

This emphasis on the practical nature of learning reflected the thinking of Fukuzawa Yukichi, who had a significant influence on early Meiji education. He rejected the study of classical literature and poetry and

---

[8] This and the following passages are the author's translation from the original text.

argued that learning should be practical because it must be applied to real life and used to improved the livelihood of the people and enrich the nation.

The structure of the educational system of 1872 was patterned after that of the French. The country was divided into eight university districts, each containing thirty-two middle school districts. Each of these was to include two hundred and ten elementary school districts. All of this, however, merely remained a plan on paper and very few universities or middle schools were actually established in the early Meiji era. Not many elementary schools were built either, and much of the instruction that did in fact go on took place in private homes and Buddhist temples.

Normal schools were established, with the assistance of an American educator, Marion M. Scott, in order to train teachers for the new schools. Scott was a follower of Pestalozzi, the Swiss educational philosopher who emphasized the use of actual objects, models, and specimens in instruction.

The cost of education was borne by the taxpayers, that is, primarily by the farmers. A tuition of between 12.5 sen and 50 sen per student per month was also charged.[9] This tuition, if paid in full, would have been prohibitive for most families since the average income per month for the common people was 1 yen 75 sen in 1878. Only a small percentage of the tuition was collected, however, and it covered only 10 percent of the educational costs.

The curriculum of the elementary schools was influenced mainly by the American educational system. The textbooks, containing lessons about Western societies and civilization, were written by men like Fukuzawa or else they were translations of Western schoolbooks, especially American readers. Particular emphasis was placed on the introduction of scientific knowledge.

Traditionalists steeped in the Confucian classics scoffed at the effort to teach children about "peaches, chestnuts, and persimmons," while pupils failed to be stirred by accounts of Napoleon and other Western heroes. School attendance began to rise despite the financial burden on the masses and the seeming irrelevance of much of what was being taught. There was only 28 percent attendance in 1872, but this figure rose to 40 percent by 1878. The number of girls in school, however, remained small, and even as late as 1887 the ratio of boys to girls in school was three to one. The traditional notion that girls were inferior and had no need for an education was partly responsible for this lag.

In order to accelerate the pace of student enrollment and gain greater public support for the schools, the Minister of Education Tanaka

[9] There are one hundred sen to the yen.

Fujimaro (1845–1909), with the assistance of David Murray, a professor from Rutgers University, revised the educational system in 1879. Tanaka, following the example of the American school system, decentralized the Japanese schools, and a locally elected school board was introduced in each community to establish and maintain the schools. The period of compulsory education was fixed at four years, with each school year consisting of four months. All of these reforms, however, failed to strengthen the educational system, which may in fact have become even weaker because in some instances the local communities chose to close the schools or amalgamate them in order to reduce expenses.

In 1880 Tanaka was replaced and a new ordinance was issued that served to centralize the system again while giving the prefectural governors greater authority over the schools. The length of compulsory education was changed to three years, but because the school year was extended to thirty-two weeks, the period of school attendance was in reality made longer. In 1900 the period of attendance was extended to four years and the system of charging tuition was abolished.

During the 1880s a more conservative philosophy began to permeate the educational system. A conscious effort was made to replace the more libertarian, individualistic values that were taught in the schools with traditional virtues such as loyalty to the Emperor, filial piety, and benevolence and righteousness. The teaching of "morals" was made compulsory and many of the textbooks then in use, like Fukuzawa's works and the translations of Western texts on moral science, were replaced by books that were Confucian or Shinto in orientation. Japanese history came to be emphasized in an effort to acquaint students with the virtues of their own country.

All this was part of the rising tide of cultural nationalism (see page 322) that was becoming increasingly discernible around this time. There was a marked shift away from the concept that education was intended to serve the interests of the individual and toward the philosophy that it was primarily aimed at serving the ends of the state. The movement dictating tighter control over educational content continued, and in 1883 a policy of state textbook certification was adopted with more stringent curbs being added in 1886. At first, textbooks had to be compiled in accordance with guidelines delineated by the Ministry of Education, but finally in 1903 the government took direct charge of the actual compilation and publication of primary school textbooks.

Significant steps in the direction of tighter control of the schools, and indoctrination and training of the young to serve the interests of the state were taken in 1886 under the leadership of the Minister of Education, Mori Arinori (1847–1889). He issued a series of educational ordinances directed at introducing greater uniformity in the educational system while patterning it somewhat after the military. He introduced military drills in the schools, selected an army officer as the head of the first president of the higher normal school, and organized the students in the normal school dormitories as if they were soldiers in barracks. Textbooks were also brought under closer government scrutiny. The University of Tokyo, which was established as a successor to the Bakufu's colleges, was renamed the Imperial University of Tokyo and brought under the close supervision of the Ministry of Education. In fact, it was turned into an actual component of the state in which professors and students were expected to pursue learning that would further the interests of the state. Its chief function was to produce properly indoctrinated and trained future bureaucrats and leaders of the state.

Mori paid special attention to the education of the teachers, the molders of the young. The object of their training and indoctrination, he contended, was the creation of decent human beings who possessed the virtues of "obedience, friendship, and dignity." The last virtue was to be manifested in issuing and obeying commands.

By the 1880s, in line with the rise of conservatism, the American influence in educational thinking began to give way, and Japanese educators began to look to the Germans for guidance. The educational philosopher to whom they turned was Johann Friedrich Herbart. He focused his attention on the development of a student's moral character and held that the object of education should be the development of an enlightened will that is capable of making distinctions between right and wrong. These were particularly appealing notions at this time because of the growing tide of reaction against the superficial imitation of Western ways, and the desire on the part of the traditionalists to restore Confucian moralism to the educational sphere. This revival of moralism in education culminated in the issuance of the Imperial Rescript on Education in 1890, a document that will be discussed later.

CIVILIZATION AND ENLIGHTENMENT

In the cultural and intellectual realms, the first decade or so of the Meiji era was characterized by frantic efforts to adopt Western concepts, practices, and products in order to become "civilized." Initially, both the government and private leaders agreed upon the necessity of "civilizing and enlightening" the nation, which meant in essence, the adoption of the utilitarian, rational, scientific, and technological aspects of Western civilization.

Students were sent abroad, Western scholars and specialists in all fields were invited to Japan to assist in the modernization of the country, and a massive educational effort was launched to "enlighten" the populace. A large number of books, pamphlets, and journals were published to spread knowledge about the West. Many of these were translations of Western works, while others were written by Japanese.

As we noted earlier, after Perry's arrival the leaders of the Bakufu as well as many han realized the need to study Western languages and obtain information about the West. Consequently, some students were sent abroad to study while a growing number of young men began to study Western languages, particularly English, from Western missionaries and Japanese instructors. There was, however, strong opposition to Western learning by the exponents of the sonnō jōi movement until the Meiji government came into existence. With its establishment, the policy of seeking "knowledge throughout the world" was officially adopted, thus ushering in the era of "civilization and enlightenment." The government encouraged the movement to "civilize" and Westernize the people because it realized that this was essential if Japan was to become as rich and powerful as the Western nations.

Fukuzawa Yukichi was one of the leading private proponents of "civilization and enlightenment." Through his enormous publications he contributed more than any other individual toward the education of the people about the West. It is estimated that between 1860 and 1893, 3.5 million copies—if the several volumes of some of the titles were counted separately, this figure would climb to nearly 7.5 million copies —of his published works circulated among the reading public. Fukuzawa began publishing his *Conditions in the West* just prior to the fall of the Tokugawa Bakufu, and it became the most widely read and most influential book of that era. It provided the Japanese public with some inkling of the Western way of life and institutions.

With the advent of the Meiji era, when it became permissible to criticize the traditional way of life and values, Fukuzawa became a vociferous advocate of Western liberalism, thus ceasing to be merely a purveyor of information about the West. The values he extolled were freedom, independence, self-respect, rationalism, the scientific spirit, pragmatism, and what might be called "bourgeois materialism."

The best known of Fukuzawa's works that were designed to transform the mode of thinking of the people were *Encouragement of Learning* published between 1872 and 1876, and *Outline of Civilization* published in 1875. In the earlier work he emphasized the importance of education, arguing that all men are equal at birth but distinctions develop because of differences in education. He believed that what must be pursued was practical, scientific learning that was based upon the spirit of inquiry and skepticism. He also emphasized the necessity of strengthening the spirit of freedom and independence in the people in order to guarantee the independence of Japan. He rejected the paternalistic, hierarchic, repressive values of the past and called for the fostering of individualism. In his *Outline of Civilization,* Fukuzawa continued to emphasize the importance of freedom in strengthening the spirit of the people, upon whom the advancement of civilization depended.

Fukuzawa's significance as the chief exponent of "civilization and enlightenment" is enormous, but there were also other scholars and writers who contributed to the diffusion of Western knowledge and sought to "enlighten" the people. Many Western books, such as Samuel Smiles' *Self-Help* and John Stuart Mill's *On Liberty,* were translated and widely read. Educational societies such as the *Meirokusha* (Meiji Six Society), organized by Fukuzawa and his friends, spread Western ideas and knowledge through their journals. The following were among the founding members: Nakamura Masanao, who translated Mill's *On Liberty*; Nishi Amane, who introduced utilitarianism and positivism to Japan; Mori Arinori, who became Minister of Education in 1885; and Katō Hiroyuki, who later turned to Social Darwinism and German statism. Newspapers also came into existence and began to flourish, but they tended to focus on political issues. They became primarily instruments for the government or the opposition forces, and did not concentrate on the diffusion of knowledge about Western civilization.

The number of students going abroad to study increased substantially with the advent of the Meiji era. In 1873 there were 373 students studying in the West. Approximately three hundred students came to the United States between 1865 and 1885. England was also a popular destination and in the early seventies there were more than one hundred students in London alone. Western language schools, particularly those for English, mushroomed and flourished. In 1874 there were 91 foreign language schools with a total enrollment of 12,815 students.

The Meiji government also invited a large number of Western scholars and specialists to assist in the task of modernization. They were particularly prominent in the field of education: in 1874 there were 211 Western professors in the higher schools; in 1877, 27 of the 39 professors at Tokyo University were from the West. The number of Western educators, technicians, and advisers in Japan hit a peak of 524 in 1874 and then began to decrease gradually.

The Christian missionaries were another important source of information about the West and its values. They translated the Bible into Japanese, established mission schools and charitable institutions and, as noted below, had as their students many prominent Meiji leaders. Guido Verbeck was among the more influential missionaries, and he served in various capacities in Japan from 1859 to 1898. In 1871, while he was a college professor, more than a thousand students attended his lectures on the American Constitution and the New Testament.

There was a movement to adopt Western artifacts and customs at the same time that the government was adopting the policy of Westernization in order to strengthen and enrich the nation, and Fukuzawa and his cohorts were instilling and fostering the "spirit of civilization" in the people. This extended from such things as interest in Western languages and Christianity, to Western art, apparels, hair style, and even the eating of beef. The technological products of the West, of course, were regarded with awe by the people. In a popular children's song, the following ten most desirable objects were enumerated: gas lamps, steam engines, horse-drawn carriages, cameras, telegrams, lightning conductors, newspapers, schools, postal mail, and steamboats. Baseball was introduced as early as 1872, and by the late 1880s it had become a part of the sports programs in the higher schools.

The admiration for Western things and the concurrent contempt for things Japanese led some men to suggest that the Roman alphabet be substituted for the traditional writing system, and that the English language replace Japanese. It was also suggested that intermarriage with Occidentals be fostered in order to improve the Japanese racial stock. This low regard for things native resulted in precious art objects being abused or allowed to leave the country freely for Western museums. Woodblock prints by prominent artists were used to wrap fish and vegetables; many Buddhist temples and treasures were destroyed; and precious wooden structures were used as fuel. The attacks against Buddhist artifacts were, to be sure, primarily the result of anti-Buddhist sentiments, but the lack of respect for traditional things is also reflected in these actions.

The segment of the society that found it most difficult to adjust to the new ways was the peasantry. Consequently, government leaders encouraged the publication of popular, easy to read works on "enlightenment and civilization" and endeavored to persuade the masses by rational arguments to adapt themselves to "civilized" ways.

At the upper levels of the society the desire to emulate Western ways culminated in the efforts of the government leaders to imitate the social life of the West by holding fancy costume balls at the *Rokumeikan,* a social hall built for the aristocracy. This style of living flourished for half a decade during the 1880s, but the growing sense of discrimination against Western ways coupled with a revival of cultural nationalism resulted in strong criticisms of the undignified behavior of some of the government leaders. The decline in this lavish social life occurred just about the time when the era of indiscriminate imitation of the West was coming to a close.

RELIGION

At the outset of the Meiji era, an effort was made to establish Shinto as the state religion in order to fortify the foundation of imperial rule. Initially the government established the *Jingikan* (Department of Shinto) and placed it above the Dajōkan. Steps were taken to end the syncretic tendencies that had prevailed between Shinto and Buddhism in the past. The Shintoists initiated a frenzied move to suppress Buddhism, and consequently many Buddhist buildings and artifacts were damaged or destroyed. The anti-Buddhist trend at the center was followed by many local authorities with the result that a large number of Buddhist temples were eliminated. For example, in Toyama Han in north central Honshu, 1630 temples were abolished leaving only seven remaining ones to serve the entire han. The government, however, soon abandoned its policy of actively suppressing Buddhism, partly to check the activities of the extreme anti-Buddhists, but also because it realized that popular support of Buddhism could not be eradicated. It was also feared that the vacuum created by the weakening of Buddhism might be filled by Christianity.

Having lost the patronage and protection of the ruling class, and being confronted with challenges from Shinto and Christianity, some Buddhist leaders began to bestir themselves from centuries of relative inaction. They endeavored to revivify the religion that had lost its vitality during the halcyon days of Tokugawa rule, when every person was required to register with a Buddhist temple.

The government insisted on functioning as a religious and moral agent even after it had abandoned its plan to impose Shinto upon the people as the official religion. It established the Board of Religious Instruction in 1872 to propagate the Great Teaching, whose principles were based upon Shinto nationalism. Efforts at Shinto revival abated with the onrush of Westernism, but the religion did manage to stage a comeback by the late 1880s. Shinto and Confucian moralism gained a powerful outlet in the Imperial Rescript on Education of 1890.

The Meiji leaders, out of an ardent desire to be accepted by the West, adopted the principle of religious freedom in 1873, thus putting an end to the long proscription against Christanity. The Meiji government had, prior to this, retained the Bakufu's ban against Christianity and continued the persecution of the Japanese Christians, particularly the many thousands who had surfaced around Nagasaki after the centuries of hiding that followed the religious persecution of the seventeenth century.

Missionaries had been permitted to work in the treaty ports to serve the Western residents who lived there. Through their educational and medical work they also managed to establish contacts with the Japanese. Some missionaries, like J. C. Hepburn, made enormous contributions to Japanese culture. A Japanese-English dictionary was compiled by Hepburn and published in 1867. He also devised a system of Romanizing Japanese words. Many future leaders of Meiji Japan came under the influence of the missionaries. For example, toward the end of the Tokugawa era Guido Verbeck had among his students in Nagasaki, Saigō Takamori, Gotō Shōjirō, Ōkuma Shigenobu, Soejima Taneomi, and Etō Shimpei; L. L. Janes in Kumamoto influenced a number of young men including Tokutomi Sohō, who became a leading exponent of liberalism and nationalism; W. S. Clark in Sapporo, Hokkaido, was the teacher of such men as Nitobe Inazō, a prominent educator, and Uchimura Kanzō, who became a leading Christian.

The percentage of Christian converts before the Second World War remained fairly low—there were 300,000 Christians in the 1930s out of a total population of about 80 million—but many of them came from the upper rungs of the society and were rather well-educated. They had developed a strong political and social consciousness and as a result they exerted a much greater influence upon the society than the relatively small number might otherwise indicate.

CHAPTER 12

THE CONTINUING
MEIJI REVOLUTION (I)
Political Developments

The revolutionary changes that were introduced by the Meiji leaders and the large-scale exposure to a totally new civilization profoundly affected all segments of the society. The reactions to this were varied: some sought to resist or challenge the alterations, others reacted positively by adjusting to the new situation and contributing to the process of modernization. The government leaders continued to introduce changes in a persistent attempt to adapt Western institutions and practices to make them suitable for Japan. In the middle decades of the Meiji era they managed to reinforce and consolidate the changes they had introduced while moving toward the goal of "enriching and strengthening" the nation. In the next two chapters we shall first examine the reactions, responses, and consequences that followed the initial phase of the Meiji revolution, and then have a look at the continuing process of that revolution.

The group that was most adversely affected by the initial changes was the former privileged class, the samurai. Now, with the loss of their hereditary stipends and rights, they had to shift for themselves in a strange new world that was apparently bent on destroying the values and institutions that were familiar to them. Some managed to join the emergent establishment by becoming government officials, military officers, policemen, and teachers. Others entered the business world and became successful participants in the emerging commercial economy; but many more were reduced to penury through unproductive attempts at what they considered to be degrading activities such as farming, shop-keeping, handicraft, or common labor. Those who resented being denied a share of political power turned to antigovernment activities and occasionally staged armed uprisings, but more often these individuals turned to political agitation for democracy and parliamentary government by participating in the freedom and popular rights movement, jiyū minken. These disgruntled men also constituted the core of anti-establishment intellectuals who often turned to journalism as a vehicle for launching their attacks against the government.

The peasantry was another, and rather considerable, segment of the society that experienced serious alterations in their customary way of life. They were, to be sure, enjoying greater freedom, but at the same time they had to defray the cost of modernizing the country and shoulder new compulsory duties such as military service and the education of their children. The peasantry frequently resorted to violence as a means of resisting the exacting arms of the efficient new government.

Discontent was not limited to the samurai and the peasantry. In the intellectual and cultural realms too there were those who regarded with distaste the vogue for Westernism and the many superficial changes that were being imposed at the expense of traditional values. The old ways, it was felt, deserved protection against the mindless pursuit of the new. It is probably true that some of the men who believed this were pure reactionaries of Shinto and Confucian proclivities, but many were individuals of discriminating taste who had undergone the exposure to Western civilization and still maintained that there were many things worthy of preservation in the traditional culture and way of life. Thus a growing tide of cultural nationalism began to rise around the middle of the 1880s.

This movement, however, should not be seen as a wholly new force in Meiji Japan; from the outset the architects of the new order were motivated by the desire to defend Japan against the potential menace from the outside and to build a strong and rich nation. The driving force behind the Meiji leaders was nationalism, and they never lost sight of their ultimate objectives in spite of the turbulence that buffeted them from all sides.

The most fervid advocates of Westernism were also motivated by considerations of national interest. For example, Fukuzawa Yukichi wrote in his *Outline of Civilization*, "There is no other way to preserve our independence except through the adoption of [Western] civilization. We must advance toward civilization solely for the purpose of maintaining our national independence." [1] Nonetheless, the tone of the country became more obviously nationalistic in the 1880s, reflecting an ascend-

---

[1] *Fukuzawa Zenshū (The Collected Works of Fukuzawa)*, 10 vols. (Tokyo: Jiji Shimpōsha, 1925–1926), vol. 4, p. 256.

ancy of cultural nationalism as well as a growing militancy in Japan's relations with her Asian neighbors.

The Meiji government managed by the 1890s to establish the new order on a firm footing in spite of the resistance and unfavorable reactions that its revolutionary measures produced. This does not mean, of course, that the Meiji leaders had resolved all the difficulties facing the nation or that the entire populace was satisfied with or benefiting from the new order. Modernization did not really improve the economic or physical condition of the masses very much. The uncertainties and the turbulence that faced the Japanese at the outset of the Meiji era, however, were more or less resolved, or at least muted, by the 1890s. The people had been given a sense of identity with the nation and the living god-figure, the Emperor, along with a sense of mission in the expansionist struggles that were unfolding on the Asian continent. By and large the people retained this sense of identity and purposefulness until the fateful day when the city of Hiroshima vanished in the devastation of atomic holocaust.

POLITICAL REACTIONS

In order to evaluate the events that occurred in the political realm before the new order was stabilized, we must return to nearly the beginning of the era, to the time when the Iwakura Mission went abroad. A caretaker government was left in charge at home with the understanding that no significant innovations were to be initiated by them. This, of course, was impossible, and they did in fact introduce many new measures, such as the freedom to buy and sell land, the educational ordinance, military conscription, land tax revision, and judicial reforms.

Nothing upset the absent government leaders more, however, than the ill-conceived plan to provoke Korea into committing hostile actions against Japan in order to establish a pretext for launching an invasion of that country. This scheme became the pet project of the chauvinistic Saigō Takamori. He was motivated not only by zealous patriotism, but also by the hope that the conquest of Korea would serve as a means of restoring the former samurai to a place in the sun.

Saigō was certainly one of the most enigmatic figures of the Restoration. In many ways he was a selfless participant in and supporter of causes in which he believed. He was also a cunning Machiavellian who arranged, for example, to provoke the Bakufu forces in Edo when it appeared as if a compromise solution might effectively resolve the differences between the imperial and Bakufu factions. Yet he was not personally ambitious for political power; in fact, he left the seat of the new government that he had helped to establish and returned to Satsuma to concentrate on han reforms. In this respect he was, perhaps, an anachronism in the new age for he acted out of a stubborn adherence to an old fashioned notion that it would have been improper to place himself above the lord of Satsuma as a high government official. Saigō also seemed to be wedded to the interests of the lower-class samurai, and he was most unsympathetic to both the feudal aristocracy and the peasantry. The garnering of special privileges by the new Meiji leaders disturbed him a great deal, as did the intrusion of mercantile interests into the government and the growing trend toward utilitarian materialism. What he seemed to favor was the establishment of a military dictatorship based upon the lower-class samurai. He may have believed that a successful invasion of Korea would strengthen his faction and thus facilitate the establishment of military rule.

The ostensible excuse offered by the chauvinists for launching an attack against Korea was the allegedly insulting public pronouncement made by the Korean government about Japanese merchants illegally engaging in trade in their country. Saigō's proposal to stage an invasion of Korea was supported by the other officials of the caretaker government, with the exception of a few men, including Ōkuma Shigenobu (1838–1922). Among those concurring were Itagaki Taisuke (1836–1919), Foreign Minister Soejima Taneomi (1828–1905), Minister of Justice Etō Shimpei (1834–1874), and Gotō Shōjirō. Itagaki did not share Saigō's proclivity for military rule but he was very much in sympathy with the idea of giving the shizoku a greater role to play in the new society. It was this sentiment in fact that led him some time later to agitate for popular rights, an effort aimed essentially at securing a share of political power for the shizoku. Itagaki also seemed to have envisioned the invasion of Korea as a means of strengthening the central government against the remnants of the old order. Etō emerged from the ranks of the poorer samurai and seemingly favored liberal measures, but once he gained power as a high government official, he inclined toward a policy of authoritarianism.

The Iwakura Mission had not completed its itinerary when word reached them about the decision to move against Korea. Kido and Ōkubo were sent back to Japan in the middle of 1873 for the specific purpose of seeing to it that Saigō's plan be blocked. They argued that internal reforms had to be effected before any foreign ventures could be undertaken. Nevertheless, the nominal head of the government, the dajō daijin, Sanjō, had decided to dispatch Saigō to Korea as a special envoy to gain redress for the alleged insults to Japan. A concerted effort was made when Iwakura returned from abroad to force Sanjō to reverse his decision. Tremendous pressures by the opposing factions finally caused him to resign, whereupon Iwakura became acting dajō daijin and cancelled the Saigō mission to Korea.

Outraged at this decision, Saigō and the other advocates of the Korean war, Itagaki, Gotō, Etō, and Soejima, resigned from the government. Kido also left at this time, but he did so for reasons of poor health. Ōkubo then took charge of the government, relying upon Itō and Ōkuma as his key assistants. Thus, from October, 1873, until his assassination in May, 1878, Ōkubo was the de facto head of the government.[2] He created the Ministry of Home Affairs and assumed the chief post himself. This gave him jurisdiction over the police system, which he used to keep political dissidents under control. His basic objectives were to establish a strong central government while seeing to the rapid development of Japanese industries. The entrenchment of Ōkubo in power was a victory for the faction that advocated modernization; it was also the triumph of the new bureaucrats over the feudalistic elements of the government.

The Ōkubo government did little to mollify the discontented shizoku, but it did launch what proved to be an unsuccessful invasion of Formosa in 1874 partly as a means of providing an outlet for the chauvinism of the advocates of the Korean war. The official justification for the invasion had to do with fifty-four shipwrecked sailors from Okinawa who were massacred by head-hunting Formosan aborigines. The Chinese government's refusal to assume responsibility for the incident provided Ōkubo with an excuse for dispatching an expeditionary force to the island. The move was opposed by the British, and the military campaign floundered miserably. The question was finally resolved through negotiations with the Chinese government.

The hope of the dispossessed samurai that they might regain their special status had by now completely vanished. Saigō had departed from the central government and the only recourse left to them, it appeared to many, was armed opposition to the Ōkubo regime. There had been active samurai opposition to the new order prior to this time. Early in 1870, for instance, the samurai of Chōshū, who were demobilized with very little compensation, were led by anti-Westerners to stage an uprising in cooperation with peasants and townspeople who were infuriated over rising prices. Similar antigovernment disturbances led by reactionary samurai broke out in various parts of the country at around the same time. The Meiji government continued to diminish the privileges of the shizoku, and its rejection of the proposal to invade Korea coupled with Saigō's departure from the government gave these frustrated and increasingly bitter ex-samurai a cause to rally around.

The first major uprising to be staged by the advocates of the Korean war was the rebellion led by Etō in Saga Prefecture in February, 1874.

---

[2] Sanjō resumed the post of dajō daijin, and Iwakura became Minister of the Right. Nominally they held positions superior to Ōkubo's but the de facto head was Ōkubo.

Etō, with the support of reactionary, anti-Western elements who wanted to restore the former lord to power and reinstitute the samurai's stipends, led about twenty-five hundred men against the prefectural government. Ōkubo viewed this as a major threat that, if not crushed swiftly, could touch off an uprising enveloping all of Kyushu. Assuming supreme military and judicial power, he moved troops from three garrisons against the rebels. Etō had expected other discontented men, including Saigō, to come to his support, but when no one rallied to his flag, he was defeated and later hanged.

The suppression of the Saga Rebellion, however, failed to put an end to antigovernment uprisings. In October, 1876, a band of two hundred warriors in Kumamoto rose in rebellion. This incident was touched off by the government's ban on sword-bearing, but among the complaints mentioned by the rebels were the issue of Westernization, the diffusion of Christianity, and the termination of their stipends. The rebellion was easily suppressed. It was soon followed, however, by a similar uprising of four hundred warriors in Fukuoka Prefecture and an insurgency in the city of Hagi in Chōshū led by Maebara Issei (1834–1876), a former councilor in the Meiji government, who was a proponent of the Korean war. Maebara opposed military conscription and had also shown himself to be a friend of the common man when, as governor of Echigo, he cut taxes in order to aid the people suffering from floods. He was reprimanded for this and subsequently became disillusioned with the new government. He considered their harsh treatment of the former samurai to be particularly outrageous. Maebara's rebellion was crushed and he was executed.

All these unsuccessful efforts by the discontented samurai were preludes to the ultimate showdown, the confrontation with Saigō, the man toward whom all disgruntled shizoku looked with great hope. Many newspapers and journals advocating popular rights were sympathetic to Saigō, and the more extreme of these incessantly called for the overthrow of the "oppressive and despotic" government. Copies of inflammatory articles were widely distributed in Kagoshima, and this served to fan the already smoldering antigovernment sentiments.

Upon his return to Kagoshima, Saigō started a private school with branches throughout the prefecture, and he concentrated on the military training and indoctrination of youths. The prefecture was controlled by Saigō's followers and was in reality an autonomous region, a state within a state. Not a penny of the taxes that were collected was handed over to the central government. Here, none of the Meiji reforms such as the termination of samurai stipends, land tax revision, adoption of the new calendar, or the ban on sword-bearing were enforced.

In order to bring Kagoshima under the control of the central government, Ōkubo sent police agents into the prefecture to examine the situation, and at the same time he ordered the removal of some arms from the arsenal in Kagoshima. The outraged Kagoshima men captured the police agents and forced them, under torture, to say that they were assigned the task of assassinating Saigō.

Saigō's followers then urged him to rise up against the government and, even though he realized that the Kagoshima forces could not hope to defeat the government's troops, he agreed to challenge them. Thus, in February, 1877, Saigō announced that he had some questions to ask the government and that he planned to proceed to the capital with his followers. He began his move toward Kumamoto with fifteen thousand warriors, and as he continued on his way he was joined by thousands of additional men. At the peak of his campaign Saigō's supporters numbered about forty-two thousand men.

The central government appointed a royal prince as supreme commander and moved its new conscript army against the challengers. Saigō's men first attacked Kumamoto castle, fully anticipating to take it with ease because of the fact that it was being defended by "dirt farmers." Contrary to expectation the fortress withstood a fifty day siege until it was relieved. The imperial forces that arrived in Kumamoto engaged Saigō's men in a fierce battle lasting twenty days; finally, however, the insurgents were forced to retreat to the south. The conflict dragged on until September, but the imperial forces had clearly gained the upper hand and Saigō, realizing that there was no hope left, committed hara-kiri. Thus ended the career of one of the chief architects of the Meiji Restoration and a heroic figure in the eyes of many Japanese, even those who opposed him.

This rebellion, known as the *Seinan War,* was unlike the other uprisings in that it constituted a major civil conflict. The government utilized more than 60,000 men, of whom 6,278 died in battle and 9,523 were wounded. Saigō's forces consisted of more than 40,000 men, 20,000 of whom were killed or wounded. At the end of the conflict, 2,764 men were executed.

The government's victory was a triumph for the conscript army of "dirt farmers," and served to destroy the myth that only the shizoku were capable of fighting with discipline and valor. The conflict also brought to an end, once and for all, armed resistance to the new government by the shizoku. They now turned to the other alternative method of challenging the new oligarchy, that is, the popular rights movement that was emerging as a significant force under Itagaki's leadership.

Before we turn to this movement we shall examine the other segment of the society that reacted against the government policies, the peasantry.

AGRARIAN UNREST

The Meiji restoration did not materially improve the lot of the peasantry in spite of the belief that the victory of the imperial faction would result in a better way of life for them. The peasants in many regions staged what is referred to as *yonaoshi ikki* (uprisings to reform the society) when the imperial and Bakufu forces were struggling with each other. Their attacks were often directed against the rich and the leading members of the villages, but in the Kantō region where the Bakufu lands existed, peasant uprisings took on a distinctly anti-Bakufu coloring. Pro-imperial forces deliberately sought to stir up the peasants against the Bakufu by promising them a 50 percent reduction in taxes. Initially Saigō sanctioned this move. The most prominent of the warriors who incited anti-Bakufu peasant uprisings was Sagara Sōzō (1839–1868), the organizer of the *Sekihōtai*, "the band committed to the repayment of the imperial debt with blood." The movement began to spread, but as it did the anarchistic, antitaxation tendencies grew increasingly strong, with the result that the leaders of the imperial forces became disenchanted with these uprisings and began to condemn the men who had stirred up the peasants. The leaders, including Sagara, were arrested and executed. Consequently, as far as many peasants were concerned, the new government had come into power by deceiving them.

Peasant distrust of the new government persisted and agrarian disturbances continued to erupt throughout 1869. The peasants demanded cancellation of debts, termination of feudal dues, reduction in rent, and land reforms. In 1870 there was a large-scale uprising in Matsushiro Han (in present Nagano Prefecture) involving seventy thousand people. The central government sent its troops into Matsushiro and then executed or imprisoned more than three hundred of the leaders.

The peasant disturbances of the first few years of the Meiji era were directed against traditional grievances, but as the government began to introduce new actions or procedures that disturbed the way of life to which the peasants were accustomed, these measures became the objects of protest activities. In 1873 thirty-seven peasant disturbances broke out and among the grievances mentioned were military conscription, compulsory education, high taxes, and the removal of the restrictions against the eta. Major riots broke out in Okayama and Fukuoka prefectures. In the latter three hundred thousand people were involved in the destruction of 4,590 buildings and 181 telegraph poles.

At the end of 1876, large peasant uprisings occurred in central Japan, touched off by what the peasants regarded as unfair tax assessments. The government, deeply concerned at this time about a possible confrontation with Saigō, decided to appease the peasants and reduced the land tax from 3 percent to 2.5 percent of the land value. During the years between 1876 and 1880 the government increased its overtures toward the peasants and sought to foster in the people a closer sense of identity with the new order by having the Emperor tour about the country.

The village leaders turned increasingly to the popular rights movement as a way of gaining concessions from the government that would alleviate agrarian poverty. With the deflationary policy adopted by Matsukata, the economic plight of the peasantry worsened drastically. The price of farm products dropped and agrarian revenues were cut in half, but at the same time there were increased excise and local taxes. As a result, a growing number of peasants fell into debt to usurious moneylenders, and by 1884 the debts incurred by agarian families reached the astronomical figure of two hundred million yen. Many peasants, unable to repay their debts, lost their homes and land to the moneylenders and the banks. The severity of their problem is illustrated by the following example. At a time when 1 koku of rice was worth about 5 yen, the debt per family in one county in Kanagawa Prefecture came to 108 yen. This figure becomes rather staggering in view of these statistics: 1.6 koku of rice was produced per tan (0.245 acres) of rice paddy[3] and the average holding was about 1 chō (10 tan), thus the average rice harvest per family came to about 10.6 koku, or about 53 yen. In 1885 more than one hundred thousand families went bankrupt.

Matsukata's policy also severely hurt the peasants who depended on the silk industry for supplementary income. The price of raw silk dropped 50 percent and the villagers in Kanagawa, Shizuoka, Saitama, Yamanashi, and Nagano prefectures, where the raising of silkworms was prevalent, felt the effects of this most acutely. The farmers organized protest groups known as the Debtors party and the Hardship party to fight for the reduction of debts.

Peasant uprisings continued throughout 1883 and 1884 with troubles finally culminating in the Chichibu Uprising of November, 1884. Like other rural areas, Chichibu county residents (in the Kantō region) suffered from the 50 percent drop in the price of raw silk and fell heavily into debt. A Hardship party was organized, calling for a ten-year moratorium on debts, extension of payments over a forty-year period, reduction in local expenses, and cancellation of schools for three years as a measure to reduce expenditures. These demands were not met and the leaders decided to resort to force. Under the direction of a prominent village leader, Tashiro Eisuke, more than one thousand people attacked the homes of moneylenders and local government offices, destroying certifi-

[3] James I. Nakamura, "Growth of Japanese Agriculture, 1875–1920," in William W. Lockwood, ed., *The State and Economic Enterprise in Japan* (Princeton, N.J.: Princeton University Press, 1965), p. 299.

cates of debt. Then, joined by additional supporters, a group of five thousand men marched toward what is now the city of Chichibu. The government, under the leadership of Minister of Home Affairs Yamagata Aritomo, became alarmed and moved the military police as well as the regular troops against the undisciplined rebels. They were scattered within ten days, and the government then executed the main leaders and imprisoned others.

Uprisings on a smaller scale were staged by the Hardship party in other areas, but they too were readily suppressed. What followed in the villages was extreme scarcity of food, starvation, and infanticide. A prominent Japanese social historian recalled hearing, in the late 1880s, a story of a father who, unable to bear the agonies of his starving children, decapitated them to release them from their miseries. This same historian also observed that peasant families in Ibaraki Prefecture during this period had only one boy and one girl; the others were killed at birth.[4] The suicide rate was extremely high around 1885–1886. A majority of the poor did not "break the law" and resort to violence—they starved to death in silence.

The number of tenants, as might be expected, increased sharply, with close to 370,000 farmers suffering forced sales for arrears in the payment of the land tax between 1883 and 1890. In the early years of the Meiji era 20 percent of the cultivated land was farmed by tenants; this figure rose to 40 percent in 1887 and then to 45 percent in 1910, a year in which 39 percent of the tillers of the soil owned no land at all. The rent the tenants had to pay ranged from 45 to 60 percent of the crop on rice fields, while in some extreme cases, 80 percent of the crop was collected as rent. Another indication of the growing impoverishment was the diminishing number of men who qualified to vote by paying five yen or more in tax. Taking the year 1881 as index 100, for 1886 it was 84, for 1891 it was 64, and for 1894 it was 59.

In the difficult years that followed the Chichibu Uprising, the government did nothing to assist the peasants and only advised them to work harder. The Liberal party, organized by Itagaki, and the urban intellectual journalists whose political agitations had helped to arouse antigovernment sentiments in the countryside, did nothing to assist the agrarian insurgents. They denounced the Chichibu rebels as arsonists, gangsters, and hoodlums. The leaders of the Hardship party movement, if they were able to avoid being jailed, joined the ranks of the dispossessed or went into hiding. One leader of the Chichibu Uprising remained in hiding for thirty-five years in the backwashes of Hokkaido.

[4] Irokawa Daikichi, *Kindai Kokka no Shuppatsu* (*The Beginning of the Modern State*) (Tokyo: Chūō Kōronsha, 1966), pp. 320–23.

THE MOVEMENT FOR POPULAR RIGHTS

The movement for popular rights (minken), although related to some extent to the discontent and despair of the peasantry, was more a product of the dissatisfaction of the shizoku, who wanted a share of the power that had been gathered in the hands of the Satsuma-Chōshū oligarchy. Furthermore, most of the advocates of popular rights were influenced by Western political philosophies and thus were motivated by a certain degree of idealism.

The rural segment of the movement was represented by the gōnō, well-to-do farmers and prominent members of the villages, who were not only wealthier but also better educated than the ordinary peasant. Their ancestors had served as village leaders during the Tokugawa era. What the gōnō wanted was to persuade the wielders of power to recognize the problems facing the agrarian communities. They hoped to compel them to introduce reforms or offer concrete assistance. Many of the organizers of the Debtors party and the Hardship party were from the gōnō, and they also took part in the popular rights movement at the local level.

Initially it was the Tosa faction led by Itagaki that constituted the core of the minken movement. This was probably the case because of the "liberal, democratic" tradition that had been implanted in Tosa by such leaders as Sakamoto Ryōma. Itagaki and Gotō Shōjirō, who was attracted to the idea of parliamentary government even before the Tokugawa Bakufu fell, both came from Tosa. Itagaki became the chief spokesman for the movement after he split with the government over the Korean question. He returned to Tosa and organized a small political party.

In January, 1874, Itagaki, Gotō, Etō, and Soejima together with four other men submitted a memorial to the government calling for the establishment of a national assembly. The petitioners based their arguments on the tenets of Western liberalism, frequently quoting John Stuart Mill. They complained of official despotism and contended that for the good of the country free public discussion had to be permitted. The establishment of a national assembly, they argued, would be the best way to achieve this. The presentation of the memorial, which marked the beginning of the minken movement, aroused public interest and touched off animated discussions among journalists and intellectuals concerning the question of whether or not the Japanese people were ready for parliamentary government.

The Meiji Restoration had a revolutionary impact on the entire society insofar as it loosened the bonds of traditional institutions and unleashed the heretofore restrained energies and ambitions of people throughout the social hierarchy. The enthusiasm for new ideas and institutions was not restricted to the upper classes and the urban dwellers; educated leaders of the rural communities played very significant roles in the political and educational realms by establishing political societies, opening village schools, and propagandizing for popular rights and "civilization and enlightenment."

Many young men who had been educated in Tokyo or at least exposed to its politically stimulating atmosphere, returned to the countryside to practice law or to set up newspapers, thus establishing centers of political action. Fiery lecturers were brought to the countryside to educate and arouse the rural residents. The popular rights movement consequently changed from being primarily a movement of the discontented shizoku to one that included well-to-do farmers and merchants. For example, Kōno Hironaka (1849–1923), who was born into a prominent village family, became one of the key leaders in organizing political societies among leading rural farmers and merchants.

An important driving force in the popular rights movement was the group of intellectuals and journalists in Tokyo who published newspapers, journals, and tracts. These influential men went on lecture tours to stir up support for the movement and arouse opposition to the government. Among these were the followers of Fukuzawa Yukichi, who himself began to adopt an increasingly moderate position as the minken movement became more and more radical.

In order to cope with the intensifying attacks against the government, the officials introduced press control laws to curb the activities of the journalists. In 1875 a press law was enacted that severely restricted political criticisms and called for preliminary censorship by the Ministry of Home Affairs. Heavy fines, imprisonments, and suspensions confronted violators of the law. The code was made even more stringent in 1876, and by the end of that year forty-nine editors and reporters were fined or imprisoned. More than two hundred writers were punished during the five year period following enactment of the press law. These measures, however, did not prevent the newspapers from proliferating. The major ones were concentrated in Tokyo, but regional papers also began to increase in number. In 1883 there were 199 newspapers throughout the country, and in 1890 there were 716. The influence that the press exercised in molding public opinion was considerable, even though in the early years the circulation of even the major papers was no more than several thousand copies daily.

Faced with the growing criticisms by the press, the activities of Itagaki and the political societies, and the ominous presence of Saigō's state within the state in Kagoshima, Ōkubo and his cohorts decided that the government must be strengthened by bringing Kido back into the fold. Before he would accept the invitation to return to the government, Kido insisted upon the inclusion of Itagaki in order to check the power of the Satsuma faction. In January, 1875, a conference was held in Osaka and both men, after provisions to broaden the base of power were agreed upon, consented to enter the government as councilors. No meaningful political reforms were made, however, and consequently, Itagaki left the government in October, once again turning to the popular rights movement. Kido also resigned when he realized that the Osaka agreement was not being implemented. He died soon after in May, 1877. During the Saigō rebellion some members of Itagaki's political society contemplated staging an uprising in support of Saigō, but the movement failed to materialize and the plotters were arrested.

The failure of Saigō's rebellion served to intensify the agitation for the establishment of a national assembly, and its advocates organized political societies throughout the country. Itagaki and his faction formed a political party, the *Aikokusha* (Patriotic Society); it became the rallying point of the popular rights movement, and local chapters were organized throughout the nation. In March, 1880, the minken leaders organized the *Kokkai Kisei Dōmeikai* (Association for the Establishment of a National Assembly) and then submitted a formal petition asking for a national assembly, but the government refused to accept it. During 1880 more than 240,000 persons signed similar petitions calling for a national assembly.

Political agitation grew more intense and the government responded by striking back at the agitators with the issuance in April, 1880, of the Law of Public Meetings, severely restricting political gatherings and associations. This did not, however, dampen the ardor of the political activists. On the contrary, they sought to develop even greater strength for the movement by establishing a national political party, the *Jiyūtō* (Liberal party). They declared their political objectives to be: the extension of civil rights, national progress and prosperity, equality of rights, and constitutional government.

The motives of the leaders of the popular rights movement varied from an idealistic desire for reforms to, among other things, a tremendous thirst for power. In most of the men there was, to be sure, a fairly strong strain of nationalism. The frequent use of the term *aikoku* (patriotism) in their organizations is indicative of this characteristic. In their pronouncements they make constant reference to the need to establish a national assembly in order to strengthen the nation. For instance, the Memorial of 1874 stated: "We fear . . . that if a reform is not effected the state will be ruined. Unable to resist the promptings of our patriotic feelings, we have sought to devise a means of rescuing it from this danger, and we find it to consist in developing public discussions in the empire." [5]

The popular rights leaders did not concentrate solely upon the establishment of a national assembly in the central government. They also focused their attention on the prefectures, where they sought to build strongholds in the councils. The central government, however, repeatedly intervened to prevent any nationwide organization of the prefectural councilmen from being set up.

From the beginning there were elements in the government who favored the establishment of a constitutional government with some form of parliamentary body. Kido returned from his visit abroad with the Iwakura Mission convinced that a constitutional government was essential if Japan was to emerge from isolation as a strong nation. He did not, however, favor granting the people a real voice in the government; he preferred the establishment of a constitutional monarchy with much of the power being retained by the ruler. Nevertheless, he was not in sympathy with the trend in which power was being gathered into the hands of a small clique.

Ōkubo Toshimichi also believed that eventually a constitution would have to be adopted, and as early as 1873 he requested Itō Hirobumi to look into the possibility of drafting a constitution. Gotō Shōjirō, who was in and out of the government, was a supporter of constitutional government, as was Ōkuma. Itō and Inoue Kaoru were also sympathetic to the idea although they did not have specific ideas about the form it might take.

The popular rights movement received an unexpected boost from the government when a cleavage devloped between Itō and Ōkuma, the two men who emerged as leaders after Ōkubo's assassination in May, 1878, at the hands of a Saigō sympathizer. As the pressure for the establishment of a national assembly increased, Iwakura advised the Emperor in December, 1879, to ask the councilors to submit written opinions on the advisibility of drafting a constitution. With the notable exception of Ōkuma, all the councilors submitted their memorials without undue delay, and they generally favored the establishment of some sort of constitutional government while insisting upon a gradual approach. The only person who took a radical position was Ōkuma. He delayed for some time before presenting his recommendations in March, 1881. He counselled that a parliamentary government modeled after that of England be established immediately.

[5] W. W. McLaren, ed., "Japanese Government Documents," in *Transactions of the Asiatic Society of Japan,* vol. 42, part 1, p. 428.

Itō exploded in anger when Iwakura showed him Ōkuma's proposal three months later because he believed that Ōkuma had not been frank with him and Inoue when they had discussed the question earlier. Ōkuma had violated one of the cardinal principles of Japanese politics, that is, the need for each individual to work with the group to which he belongs without departing radically from the consensus. Any attempt by a man to outdo or rise markedly above the others could not be tolerated for it threatened to disrupt collective leadership, which was the very principle that governed the Meiji oligarchy.

Moreover, Itō could not agree with Ōkuma's proposal to establish a parliament immediately; nor could he accept the plan to model the Japanese government after the British example. It seemed to Itō that Ōkuma was taking a more radical position than other councilors in order to curry favor with the minken advocates and thus consolidate his own political position. In anger Itō threatened to resign, saying he could not serve in the government with Ōkuma. Iwakura managed to arrange a temporary truce between the two men by postponing further discussion concerning the national assembly.

The truce was broken, however, over another issue. In the summer of 1881 the government decided to sell its holdings in the Hokkaido Colonization Commission for 380,000 yen. This was a project into which it had invested fourteen million yen. The recipient of this largess was a Satsuma entrepreneur who was a friend of Kuroda, the official in charge the Hokkaido project. News of this transaction became known, and the government's critics launched a vigorous major campaign against what they considered to be a scandalous giveaway plan. The attack was spearheaded by the followers of Fukuzawa, who used the press and public opinion to full advantage.

Itō and his fellow officials looked upon this fresh assault on the government as a conspiracy on the part of Ōkuma, Fukuzawa, and the Mitsubishi interests to use this issue as a lever to overthrow the government. The move to expel Ōkuma from the government was thereupon initiated. His dismissal on October 12, 1881, was accompanied by a purge of his followers and those of Fukuzawa. At the same time, in order to placate public opinion, the government publicly announced its intention to draft a constitution and establish a national assembly by 1890.

Ōkuma and Fukuzawa vehemently denied the existence of any conspiracy, but what they said at this point mattered little. The Satsuma-Chōshū faction had its way. The by-product of the Itō-Ōkuma rivalry was of major importance: the government was forced to make a decision to frame a constitution and to establish a national assembly earlier than it had expected.

This announcement by the government took the wind out of the frenzied attacks that were being launched against the oligarchy and compelled the advocates of popular rights and national assembly to start getting ready for the election and the convocation of the assembly. The followers of Itagaki had been preparing for the formation of a national political organization, so they were able to establish the Liberal party immediately after the government made its announcement on the constitution. Itagaki was chosen as the party's president. Among the other leaders were the early fighters for minken and parliamentary government such as Gotō Shōjirō, Kōno Hironaka, and Baba Tatsui. That the party ideologists, Ueki Emori and Nakae Chōmin, were deeply influenced by Rousseau's *Social Contract* is clearly evidenced by their statement of principles, which starts with the sentence: "Liberty is the natural state of man and the preservation of liberty is man's great duty." It goes on to declare: "we will spread the heavenly bestowed liberty and control man-made authorities; at the upper level, we will correct and improve politics, and at the lower level we will foster the spirit of self-government." [6] The Liberal party leaders advocated popular sovereignty, but they also felt compelled to pay homage to the authority of the Emperor. The problem of reconciling these two conflicting principles continued to plague many minken advocates.

The second party that emerged was the Constitutional Reform party (*Rikken Kaishintō*), which was organized by the followers of Ōkuma and Fukuzawa.[7] This party was inclined to be more conservative than the Liberal party, and looked upon English parliamentary government as a suitable model. The two intellectual assistants to Ōkuma, Yano Fumio and Ono Azusa, were both influenced by English liberalism. The latter in particular was attracted to Bentham's Utilitarianism.

Reform party members believed that by following the English model the imperial institution and popular rights could be reconciled. The party eschewed violence and tended to appeal to the propertied, "respectable" members of the society, as these remarks from Ozaki Yukio, a lifelong fighter for parliamentary government reveal: "We of the Reform party decided to follow a moderate course in contrast to the Liberal party, which was organized mainly by hot-blooded members of the shizoku who tended to rely on radical actions. Hence we looked for members among those who were well educated, owned property, and were respecta-

    [6] Robert A. Scalapino, *Democracy and the Party Movement in Prewar Japan* (Berkeley, Calif.: University of California Press, 1953), p. 69.
    [7] The *Kaishintō* has sometimes been called the Progressive party, but we shall label it the Reform party here in order to distinguish it from its successor party, the *Shimpotō*, which has also been referred to as the Progressive party.

ble." [8] The party also had close ties with capitalistic interests, such as Mitsubishi, and continued to strengthen its association with business leaders. Unlike some segments of the Liberal party, the Reform party members did not get involved in the agrarian protest movements. Its essentially conservative character led Itagaki to scoff at it as a party designed "to please the old and the rich."

The two opposition parties expended more energy fighting each other than they did combating the government. Numerous factors account for the inability of the Liberal party and the Reform party to cooperate. The differences in ideology may not have been basic, but they certainly were provocative; in addition, there were dissimilarities in the bases of support, in the temperament and personality of the leaders, and in the regional, social, and economic ties. Another factor contributed to serious fission within the parties themselves. From their very inception, there was present in the political parties the same characteristic that governs the behavior of today's Japanese political parties; that is, the existence of numerous factions built around the party leaders. In a sense it might be regarded as "bossism," but it would not be wholly accurate to depict the situation in this manner because a great deal more than personal ties were involved; regional loyalties also played a part in keeping the factions together. This led not only to the formation of different parties, with the Tosa faction generally gathering around Itagaki and the Hizen faction around Ōkuma, but also to the operation of numerous cliques within each party at any given time. For example, when the first Diet was convened the Liberal party was split into four main factions.

The personal ties were patterned after the traditional master-follower or father-son relationship, so that the paternalistic, authoritarian, and hierarchical mode of behavior present in the family prevailed in the political parties as well. Each member had fixed rights and duties, and he behaved in the manner that was expected of him. This situation resulted in the absence of any strong sense of personal responsibility. Those men who possessed power thought of their actions as being dictated by their position and hence beyond the realm of personal responsibility, whereas the followers, having no right to make independent decisions or take independent actions, possessed no sense of individual responsibility. Consequently, irresponsible, erratic actions were taken from time to time by the leaders and rank-and-file members, thus seriously undermining the party movement at critical moments.

A third group, the Constitutional Imperial party (*Rikken Teiseitō*), was organized as a progovernment party, but it failed to develop into a

---

[8] Ozaki Yukio, *Gakudō Kaikoroku (The Memoirs of Gakudō)*, 2 vols. (Tokyo: Yūkeisha, 1952), vol. 1, p. 77.

major force because the government leaders were unsympathetic to political parties in general, and did not actively support it. This party was opposed to the popular rights movement and parliamentary government.

In order to build their bases of support the two opposition parties sent speakers on tours to rally the public to their cause. The Liberal party was particularly successful in developing a fairly broad base of support in the countryside by attracting the provincial landowners and businessmen as well as the peasantry. The well-to-do rural leaders were especially active, and they frequently sponsored public lectures and workshops.

The government leaders became concerned about this extension of party influence into the countryside. Consequently in June, 1882, they issued a law on public assembly that gave the prefectural governors the authority to curb public lectures and other political activities. The law also prohibited any party from establishing local organizations or developing ties with other organizations for the purpose of sponsoring public political talks. As a result, many local political organizations were forced to disband, and this in turn caused the more radical party members, particularly from the Liberal party, to support those who turned to direct action. Some became involved in the local agrarian uprisings, such as the Chichibu affair.

In April, 1882, while Itagaki was on a lecture tour, he was attacked by an assassin in Gifu. Fortunately, he was not seriously hurt, but this incident shocked and aroused the indignation of the party members. In order to remove the symbolic head of the party movement from the political scene and in this way attempt to cool down the heated political atmosphere, the Meiji leaders suggested that Itagaki take a trip abroad with funds provided by Mitsui. To the chagrin of his less flexible political allies, Itagaki accepted the offer and went abroad together with Gotō Shōjirō. This produced a serious split in the Liberal party that resulted in the more radically inclined Baba Tatsui (1850–1888) and others quitting it. Itagaki's behavior not only divided his own party, but it also exacerbated the rivalry between the two opposition parties. The Reform party leaders heaped scorn on Itagaki for accepting the financial backing of Mitsui, while the loyal followers of Itagaki struck back criticizing Ōkuma's ties with Mitsubishi.

At the local level the confrontation between the officials representing the central government and the opposition forces grew increasingly acrimonious. In 1883 an authoritarian official, Mishima Michitsune (1835–1888), was appointed governor of Fukushima Prefecture. Mishima boasted that he would not allow a single arsonist, burglar, or member of the Liberal party to exist in the area under his jurisdiction, and he repeatedly closed down public lectures that were sponsored by the Liberal party chapter in Fukushima. Popular opposition against him intensified as he launched a road-building project that was to be implemented by forced labor and higher taxes. The peasantry, encouraged by the advocates of popular rights, began organizing to resist Mishima's policies. At this point the well-to-do agrarian leaders began to dissociate themselves from the peasantry, realizing that there was an inherent conflict of interests between the two groups. Mishima started to arrest the peasants and party leaders and thus touched off a peasant protest movement that had to be dispersed by sword-wielding policemen. This was followed by a mass arrest of Liberal party members, including Kōno Hironaka. Officials of the central government, such as Iwakura and Yamagata, hoped to use this incident as an excuse to launch a general attack on the popular rights movement. They weakened the prefectural councils, curbed the right to make petitions, placed even greater restrictions on the press, and permitted the police to carry swords with a cutting edge.

Rural uprisings continued to break out in spite of these repressive actions by the government, and while many Liberal party members, particularly those at the top level, began condemning the reliance on violence, others were driven to more extreme measures. For instance, in May, 1884, some Liberal party members led three thousand peasants in Gumma Prefecture against a local moneylender and the police. The leaders of the incident were arrested and punished; some died while being tortured. This, however, did not deter other radicals of the Liberal party. In September, 1884, in Kabayama in Tochigi Prefecture, Kōno's nephew led an uprising with fifteen other men. They raised the flag of revolution and called for freedom and the overthrow of despotism. The rebels were easily suppressed and seven of the insurgents were executed while others received life or long-term prison sentences. The authorities, led by Mishima, who was now governor of Tochigi, used this occasion to arrest the Tochigi Liberal party members indiscriminately.

The Kabayama insurgents were condemned by political party members, journalists, and even the Liberal party leaders. This incident had the effect of hastening the dissolution of a party that was already badly divided. Less than a year and half before the uprising, Itagaki, already quite disturbed by growing radicalism, had proposed dissolving the party. He contended that radical political movements were out of step with the times, but he was persuaded to withdraw his proposal by Hoshi Tōru (1850–1901), a leader of the moderates who was emerging as a key figure in the party. The Kabayama incident, however, induced Itagaki to revive his proposal to dissolve the party. This time his suggestion was adopted and the Liberal party was disbanded in October, 1884, despite the opposition of Hoshi, who was then incarcerated in Niigata.

The Reform party did not fare much better than the Liberal party in its efforts to build a viable political organization before the first Diet elections were held. Ōkuma began to favor the idea of dissolving the party, but he was opposed by a faction led by Numa Moriichi (1843–1890), one of the founders of the party. As a result, Ōkuma left the party in December, 1884, with many of his followers. A remnant of the members, however, managed to keep the party alive even after a majority had resigned. It would appear that it was impossible to sustain interest in the party movement before the constitution came into existence. This was primarily due to the fact that until then the parties could not play a truly meaningful role in the power struggle.

The opponents of the government, however, remained ready at all times to grasp any opportunity to rally public opinion against it. In 1887 Hoshi and Gotō Shōjirō united the advocates of popular rights in an attack against the government for considering treaty revisions that they contended were a national disgrace. According to the provisions of the treaty being negotiated, the entire country was to be open to Western residents. Furthermore, legal cases involving Europeans were to be tried by Western judges. Perhaps most offensive of all was the provision that Western nations were to review the legal codes that were to be adopted by Japan. The French legal adviser, Boissonade, opposed the proposed revisions because he felt they infringed upon the sovereignty of Japan, but the government leaders nevertheless decided to proceed with the changes. Appealing to the nationalistic sentiments of the people, Gotō and other minken leaders organized the Union of Like Thinkers to protest the government's policy. They also added other issues, such as the abolition of the system of peers and the reduction of arms and taxes, to the protest movement. The government had to postpone its plan to revise the treaties, but it retaliated by issuing the Peace Preservation Ordinance and ejected from Tokyo 570 men whom it regarded as troublemakers.

FORTIFICATION
OF THE CENTRAL GOVERNMENT

Itō went abroad to study European constitutions in order to prepare for the drafting of the Japanese document, and he remained there for more than a year and a half during 1882–1883. Ostensibly he went to Europe with an open mind, but it is generally agreed that he had already decided to use the Prussian constitution as a model. Inoue Kowashi, one of Itō's key assistants in drafting the constitution, had translated it into Japanese in 1875. Hermann Roesler, a German professor of jurisprudence, arrived in 1878 to serve as legal adviser to the government, and he lent support to the idea of adopting the basic features of the Prussian constitution.

In light of the fact that the Meiji leaders had already decided on the kind of constitution that should be adopted, Itō's prolonged study abroad may have been unnecessary, but he did gain the prestige and understanding of theoretical ideas necessary to refute the critics who would have preferred the English model. He wrote in a letter to Iwakura:

> Thanks to the famous German scholars Gneist and Stein,
> I have come to understand the essential features of the
> structure and operations of states. . . . The situation in
> our country is characterized by the erroneous belief
> that the words of English, American, and French liberals
> and radicals are eternal verities. . . . I have acquired
> arguments and principles to retrieve the situation.[9]

Itō established the Office for the Study of the Constitution immediately upon his return from abroad. Before he could turn his attention to the tasks of drafting the constitution, however, he found it necessary to introduce certain governmental changes as a way of preparing for the day when power would have to be shared to some extent with the political parties. Consequently, he did not begin serious work on the constitution until 1886. A number of significant measures were adopted to fortify the emperor system and the power of the oligarchy. First, in July, 1884, Itō created a new system of peers who were to serve in the upper house of the projected parliament as a check on the popularly elected lower house. The new peerage was modeled after the German system with five ranks: prince, marquis, count, viscount, and baron. Approximately five hundred persons were selected from the existing kazoku, high government officials, military and naval officers, and other prominent men to serve as peers. Itō himself became a count as did Yamagata and Inoue. In 1888 the Privy Council, consisting of key members of the oligarchy, was created for the specific purpose of examining the proposed constitution. Even after this task was completed, it remained in existence as a special advisory body to the Emperor. As an organ functioning outside the purview of the constitution, it served as a stronghold of the oligarchy.

Two posts, independent of the cabinet, were created as additional means to prevent the imperial institution from falling under the influence of the political parties in the event that they gained control of the government. The Ministry of Imperial Household and the office of the Lord Keeper of the Privy Seal were filled by members of the oligarchy, giving them direct access to the Emperor. Another measure designed to strengthen the imperial family was the enlargement of its material holdings. Real property increased by nearly 6,000 times between 1881 and 1890 (from 634 chō to 3,654,000 chō). Its holdings in stocks and bonds

---

[9] George Akita, *Foundations of Constitutional Government in Modern Japan, 1868-1900* (Cambridge, Mass.: Harvard University Press, 1967), p. 61.

were also increased substantially, and by 1887 they were worth nearly eight million yen.

In the area of administrative changes, the Dajōkan was replaced by a cabinet system in December, 1885. There were ten ministers, including the Prime Minister who was responsible to the Emperor. Itō became the first Prime Minister, and the cabinet included all the top leaders of the oligarchy except Kuroda. A neat balance was maintained between Chōshū and Satsuma with four ministers each, and it transpired that until Ōkuma became Prime Minister in 1898 the office was rotated between Chōshū and Satsuma men. A civil service system was introduced and government officials below the highest level were, with some exceptions, to be chosen by examination. This measure was designed to prevent a takeover of the bureaucracy by the political parties in case they gained control of the government. The bureaucracy quickly developed into a formidable bulwark of the oligarchy. This was a society in which respect for and fear of the government officials had a long tradition, and the people continued to be overawed by these men. The attitude referred to as "respect for officialdom, contempt for the people" became deeply embedded in modern Japan.

The Imperial University of Tokyo became the most prestigious of the institutions of higher learning. The path to success in life was the route that led through government run middle and higher schools, the Imperial University of Tokyo, and up the ranks of the bureaucratic hierarchy. Government operated schools and the bureaucracy were thus linked closely together in this status conscious society to produce the new elitist "Mandarin" class.

In 1888 local administrative reforms were made in order to establish a system of local self-rule that was designed to preserve the influence of the well-to-do. The cities, towns, and villages were granted the right to manage their own affairs through local assemblies and mayors who were chosen by the assemblymen. These assemblymen, however, were elected by voters with property qualifications, but in 1890 only 103 persons out of 1,000 held the franchise. An additional provision aimed at ensuring that the wealthy would possess greater power was the procedure giving these first-class voters the right to choose one-third of the assemblymen. A further measure was the rule that mayors were to serve without pay. The poor were thus rather effectively prevented from holding office.

Above the towns and villages in the hierarchy were the counties, with no real administrative function. Next came the prefectural governments, whose governors were appointed by the central government. The prefectural assemblymen were chosen from the ranks of the county, city, town, and village assemblymen who paid more than ten yen in national taxes.

This arrangement for choosing local assemblymen remained in effect until 1899.

THE CONSTITUTION

In the fall of 1886 serious work on drafting the constitution was started by Itō. In this task, he was assisted by Inoue Kowashi, Kaneko Kentarō, and Itō Miyoji, all bright, able men who occupied the second rung of the power structure in Meiji Japan. Inoue Kowashi (1843–1895) was the real architect of many of the conservative policies of the Meiji government. In addition to working on the constitution, he helped to draft the Imperial Rescript on Education, served as Minister of Education, and was a member of the Privy Council. Kaneko Kentarō (1853–1942) attended Harvard Law School during 1876–1878, served in two of the cabinets headed by Itō, and later joined the Privy Council. Itō Miyoji (1857–1934) served in Itō's cabinet as secretary and minister and also became a member of the Privy Council. He continued to exert his influence from behind the scenes until as late as the 1930s.

In the summer of 1887 Itō and his three assistants prepared the final draft of the constitution, which was then checked by Roesler. Next it was examined by the Privy Council headed by Itō, who had resigned the premiership in order to chair the council. In the course of the discussions two contradictory positions were simultaneously upheld by Itō. First, when it was suggested that the Diet should be given the right to appeal to the Throne regarding illegal actions by government officials, Itō objected saying, "This constitution was drafted to strengthen the authority of the ruler and make it weightier." Second, when Mori Arinori suggested replacing the term "rights of the subject" with "status of the subject," Itō held that "the spirit behind the constitution is to limit the authority of the ruler and protect the subject's rights." [10] In view of this, it can be said that "The Meiji Constitution was essentially an attempt to unite two concepts which . . . were irreconcilable: Imperial absolutism and popular government." [11] Consequently, if the constitution was to function effectively compromises had to be made, but the side that was destined to make the major concessions was the one representing the popular elements.

After more than six months of deliberations in the Privy Council, the constitution was promulgated on February 11, 1889, as a gift from the Emperor to the people. It was, as Itō stated, designed to shore up imperial authority. Sovereignty was lodged in the Emperor, who held supreme com-

---

[10] Irokawa Daikichi, *op. cit.*, pp. 440–41.
[11] Scalapino, *op. cit.*, p. 150.

mand over the armed forces and possessed broad executive authority. He had the power to declare war, make peace, and conclude treaties. He was to control the administrative system and appoint the officials. He also held supreme authority over the legislative body for he "convokes the Imperial Diet, opens, closes, and prorogues it, and dissolves the House of Representatives." Legislation had to pass the two houses of the Diet, but the Emperor held a veto power and possessed the authority to issue imperial ordinances. Government officials, including cabinet ministers, were responsible to the Emperor, not the Diet.

The Diet consisted of two houses, the House of Peers and the House of Representatives. Seats in the upper house were to be filled by members of the imperial family, peers, and individuals appointed by the Emperor. The three hundred members of the House of Representatives were to be elected by the people on the basis of a limited franchise.

The lower house, which represented the popular elements, had limited power since, in addition to the Emperor, the House of Peers could veto its legislation. It had no authority over the government officials, and its control over the budget was restricted. Certain items in the budget could not be changed and if the Diet failed to pass it the government was authorized to operate on the basis of the previous year's budget. The Diet, however, did have to approve tax bills. This is where the opposition was able to exercise a certain degree of control over the executive branch because, as the need for military and naval expenditures grew, the government was often compelled to ask for new taxes.

The popular elements were curbed not only by the written provisions of the document, but also by virtue of the fact that they were hindered by institutions and practices not provided for in the constitution. We have already noted, for example, the special status of the Privy Council. The Satsuma-Chōshū oligarchs also constituted an informal group of genrō, or elder statesmen, that met whenever the need arose to decide upon policies of major importance. The fact that the constitution was subordinated to the throne gave the real power to this clique of genrō because they in fact controlled the Emperor.

Another institution that lay outside the purview of the popular elements was the armed forces, which were controlled by the oligarchs. The mantle of army leadership, after Ōmura Masujirō's assassination in 1869 and Saigō's departure from the government, fell to Yamagata, who had the army virtually become his private dominion. The military was designed to serve as the stronghold of the emperor system—that is, the oligarchy—and as noted above, the concepts of loyalty and service to the Emperor were rigorously instilled in members of the army and navy.

Yamagata, at the advice of his protégé Katsura Tarō, who had just returned from serving as military attaché in Germany, established the general staff office in 1879 in order to keep the military independent of civilian control. The supreme command was then placed completely beyond the control of the popular forces and even the cabinet under an ordinance issued in 1889 and revised in 1907. On matters concerning military command and military secrets, the chief of the general staff was given the right to report directly to the Emperor, thus by-passing the cabinet. The military, already freed from interference by civilian leaders, acquired the power to intervene in political matters when an imperial ordinance was issued in 1900 that stipulated that only active officers of the two top ranks in the army and navy could hold the posts of war and naval ministers. This in effect gave the army and navy the power to veto cabinets of which they disapproved.

In theory the people were guaranteed certain rights and liberties in the constitution, but these were restricted "within the limits" of the law. Official abuses, for example, could not be challenged in the regular courts because they had to be brought to the Court of Administrative Litigation, whose authority could not extend into areas left to official discretion, which was indeed extensive. Hence in reality the Japanese subjects were only given very limited rights and freedom.

CHAPTER 13

THE CONTINUING
MEIJI REVOLUTION (II)
Cultural, Economic, and
Social Developments

CULTURAL NATIONALISM

Early Meiji, as we noted above, was a period in which the vogue for Western things was widespread and the tide of "civilization and enlightenment" swept through all facets of Japanese life. From about the middle of the 1880s, however, the frantic pursuit of Western things began to abate and a more critical, discriminating look at Western culture and institutions came to be taken. This kind of swing of the pendulum was to be expected for after fairly extensive exposure to Western civilization, the people were beginning to develop more discriminating tastes and faculties.

Excesses in imitating Western ways, such as the behavior of the high officials at the *Rokumeikan* parties, contributed to the fortification of reactionary sentiments among those who wanted to revive Shinto or Confucian concepts and values. The critics of the blind emulation of Western ways were not, however, simply reactionaries. Most of these "cultural nationalists" were rational men who wanted to adopt the best from the West without having the people lose either their appreciation of things Japanese or their sense of cultural or national identity.

The influence of Confucian traditionalists was evident in the realm of moral education. The Confucian moralists were unhappy about the wave of individualism and utilitarianism that swept into Japan in the early Meiji years. The leading foe of this trend and the key spokesman for Confucian virtues was Motoda Eifu (1818–1891), who, as tutor to the Emperor, had a great deal of influence at the court. He regarded with distaste the pragmatic attitudes held by men like Itō and Inoue Kaoru, who were willing to condone the pursuit of self-interest and the spread of materialism for what they claimed was the sake of developing the nation's economy. Motoda, who was imbued with Confucian values, believed there was a basic and irreconcilable conflict between self-interest and the public good. He believed that the decline of morals brought about by Western ways had to be corrected by the inculcation of the virtues of benevolence, righteousness, loyalty, and filial piety. Motoda's position was akin to that of Sakuma Zōzan, who believed in Eastern morals and Western science. Eastern morals were based on a hierarchical social order in which benevolence from above was to be reciprocated by obedience from below.

Motoda had an ally in Nishimura Shigeki (1828–1902), who was familiar with Western concepts and was active as an "Enlightenment" thinker when he was a member of the Meirokusha (see page 293). Nishimura was convinced, however, that moral education had to be conducted by the government, and he wanted the imperial family to exert its influence in this area. Mori Arinori became Minister of Education in 1885, and he favored stressing moral education in the schools but he did not believe that the Confucian moral philosophy should be the basis for this.

Criticism concerning the absence of guidance on the question of moral education became more vocal, with the result that a plan to issue an imperial rescript on this matter gained favor, and by the time Yamagata became Prime Minister, such a plan was finally implemented. Inoue Kowashi and Motoda Eifu collaborated in drafting the rescript, which was issued on October 30, 1890. The document was based on the Confucian five human relationships, and called for loyal service to the state and the throne; filial piety; modesty; observance of the law; and furtherance of the public good. According to the rescript, the moral precepts were "the teaching bequeathed by Our Imperial Ancestors . . . infallible for all ages and true in all places." The rescript appealed to nationalistic sentiments by making the foundation of morality uniquely Japanese and by binding the throne and the people together in a common moral purpose. It served as a valuable instrument in making the young people loyal subjects of the Emperor, since it was recited by every school child every morning much in the manner in which American school children pledge allegiance to the flag.

The dilemma that some Christian leaders subsequently found themselves faced with demonstrates how closely the credo verged on being a state religion. In January, 1891, for example, the rescript was received in the school where Uchimura Kanzō, a conscientious Christian, was teaching. He refused to bow reverently toward it because he believed that to do so would be tantamount to recognizing the Emperor as a divinity. He was denounced as a traitor and summarily dismissed from the school. In 1893 a renowned philosopher at the Imperial University of Tokyo contended that Christianity was incompatible not only with the spirit of the rescript but also with the Japanese national polity (kokutai). Buddhism, which earlier had suffered at the hands of intolerant Shintoists, had by now recovered, and many of its leaders joined the nationalistic attacks against Christianity.

Besides these kinds of purely reactionary elements in cultural nationalism, we also find a group espousing what might be called "enlightened nationalism." This movement was led by men like Shiga Shigetaka (1863–1927), Miyake Setsurei (1860–1945), and Kuga Katsunan (1857–1907), who were not fundamentally anti-Western. Essentially, they wanted to establish a firm cultural or national identity that would enable them to adopt the best from the West while preserving the best, or the "essence," of Japan. They feared that if the blind imitation and worship of things Western continued the Japanese would lose their identity. One member of this circle lamented, "Our people are no longer Japanese. The country is no longer Japan."

In 1888 the leaders of the enlightened nationalist movement organized the Society for Political Education and issued a fortnightly journal entitled *Nihonjin* (*Japanese*). Their objective, Shiga wrote, was to preserve the national essence (*kokusui*). Many people tended to equate the concept of kokusui with reactionary traditionalism. Consequently, the society issued a manifesto stating,

> We seek to overcome the current evils by admonishing the
> so-called Westernizers who see the superb beauty of another
> country and forget the excellence of their own. We differ
> from those who rashly believe that preservation of
> *kokusui* means merely preservation of old things inherited
> from our ancestors and who mistakenly believe that we
> want to resist Western things and close the road to
> innovation and progress.[1]

Miyake had studied under Fenollosa (see page 326), and perhaps he was influenced by his teacher's concern for the preservation of Japanese culture. The best from the West in the realms of "truth, virtue, and beauty" must be adopted, according to Miyake, in order to augment aspects of these qualities already possessed by the Japanese. He took a position similar to Mazzini's in propounding a philosophy of nationalism that held that "to work for the good of one's country is to work for the good of the

---

[1] Kenneth B. Pyle, *The New Generation in Meiji Japan: Problems of Cultural Identity, 1885–1895* (Stanford, Calif.: Stanford University Press, 1969), p. 70.

world. The elevation of the special characteristics of one race contributes to the general advancement of the human race." [2] He was a liberal nationalist who was very much opposed to militarism. It was a great disappointment to him that the nationalism he had helped to foster turned to anti-foreignism and to a form of conservatism that stubbornly resisted social and political reforms.

Kuga believed that national independence was not possible without national pride. This, however, was not to be confused with self-aggrandizement or with blind anti-Westernism. Kuga claimed that his concept of nationalism was in harmony with universal love. In 1889 he started a newspaper, Nihon (Japan), to uphold the principle of "Japanism."

Some of the early advocates of Westernism and internationalism also began to have second thoughts. Most of the exponents of Westernism, such as Fukuzawa, were motivated by nationalistic impulses and believed that the best way to strengthen Japan and thus ensure her independence was through Westernization. These men, however, became increasingly critical of the indiscriminate worship of Western things that was unfolding in the early Meiji period. In his Encouragement of Learning, Fukuzawa stated that the spirit of scepticism must also be applied to the examination of Western civilization. A few years after this volume appeared, he remarked that progress in Japan depended upon a proper balance between Japanese and Western concepts. He criticized the Westernizers for imitating Western ways without possessing any knowledge about Japan.

Fukuzawa, however, did not abandon his faith in Western liberalism and individualism, and he consistently opposed the growing xenophobic, anti-Western sentiments. Some early Meiji Westernizers, however, did begin to stress the importance of traditional moral values and the Chinese classics while turning to German statism as a philosophy more compatible to Japan. At the same time, German idealism was replacing English utilitarianism as the dominant Western philosophy in the academic realm.

The most dramatic shift from liberal internationalism to militant nationalism was made by Tokutomi Sohō (1863–1957), who was influenced by Christian humanism and English liberalism. In 1886 he wrote a book entitled The Future Japan, in which he called for peace and attacked militarism and expansionism. The following year he started a journal, The Nation's Friend, with the avowed aim of leading the "new Japan" along the path of peace and democracy. The outbreak of the Sino-Japanese War saw Tokutomi, in a radical change of position, become an active supporter of the war effort. He completely abandoned his earlier idealistic beliefs when the Triple Intervention occurred (see page 355),

[2] Murakami Shunryō and Sakata Yoshio, Meiji Bunka-shi: Kyōiku Dōtoku-hen (Meiji Cultural History: Education and Morality) (Tokyo: Yōyōdō, 1955), pp. 555–56.

forcing Japan to return the Liaotung Peninsula to China. He concluded that force alone counted in this world, and he became a vociferous advocate of imperialism and militarism. Tokutomi remained an influential spokesman for expansionism to the end of the Second World War.

The arts was another area in which a significant revival of interest in things Japanese took hold. Ironically enough this movement was started by a Westerner, Ernest F. Fenollosa, an American who had arrived in Japan in 1878 to teach philosophy at the Imperial University of Tokyo. He soon became interested in Japanese paintings and woodblock prints and developed into a serious student of Japanese art. His studies led him to the conclusion that "the Japanese were denying an artistic heritage which they should honor and which the West could no longer overlook." He urged the Japanese to "return to their nature and its old racial traditions, and then take, if there were any, the good points of Western painting." [3] He advised them to establish an art school, assist and subsidize artists, and educate the public about art as a means of reviving their traditional art. He uncovered many long neglected works and prepared a list of national art treasures for the government. He succeeded in restoring the use of the brush in primary school art classes where, during the mania for Western things, it had been replaced by the pen. With a missionary zeal he launched a virtual one-man campaign to revive Japanese art—and he succeeded.

Among Fenollosa's students at the University of Tokyo was Okakura Kakuzō (1862–1913), who became his devoted disciple and a central figure in the revival of Japanese art. Fenollosa and Okakura were instrumental in founding the Tokyo School of Art, which concentrated on the teaching of traditional art. Artists such as Kanō Hōgai and Hashimoto Gahō were rescued from obscurity and poverty to participate in the renaissance of Japanese art.

Okakura, like his teacher, emphasized the importance of securing the foundations of the traditional culture before adopting from the West. He wrote, "We shall be ready more than ever to learn and assimilate what the West has to offer, but we must remember that our claim to respect lies in remaining faithful to our own ideals." He was not impressed by the West's pursuit of progress on the basis of mechanical civilization, and he questioned: "When material efficiency is complete, what end will have been accomplished?" He believed that for Japan, Asia served as "the true source of our inspiration," even though in some areas she had already risen above her Asian mentors. "The expenditure of thought involved in synthesizing the different elements of Asiatic culture has given to Japa-

[3] Lawrence W. Chisolm, *Fenollosa: The Far East and American Culture* (New Haven, Conn.: Yale University Press, 1963), p. 51.

nese philosophy and art a freedom and virility unknown to India and China." [4]

In literature, expressions of cultural nationalism did not appear as distinctly as they did in the visual arts. During the early years of Meiji translations of Western novels were read, and political novels with Western themes were written. An example of the latter is Yano Fumio's *Keikoku Bidan (A Noble Tale of Statesmanship)*, a historical romance based upon Plutarch's depiction of the life of Epaminondas.

The first real step toward the modernization of Japanese literature occurred when Tsubouchi Shōyō (1859–1935), a student of English literature, wrote *The Essence of the Novel* in 1885. Tsubouchi rejected the traditional view that novels were essentially instruments of moralism in which virtue must be rewarded and evil punished. He condemned the writers of his era for modeling their stories after the didactic novels of such Tokugawa writers as Takizawa Bakin. The primary task of the novelist, Tsubouchi argued, was the realistic depiction of life. The aspect of experience that must be of primary concern to the novelist is human emotions, which must be described in a psychologically accurate manner. Tsubouchi's own attempt, however, to put his theories into practice was not very successful.

The novelist who did succeed in writing the first important realistic Japanese novel was Futabatei Shimei (1864–1909). He was strongly influenced by Russian writers, such as Turgenev and Goncharov, and he was responsible for the translation of many Russian novels into Japanese. His first novel, *The Drifting Cloud,* was written between 1886 and 1889, and it was done in a realistic and colloquial style, rather unlike the formal literary mode used by the novelists before him. It depicts dispassionately and somewhat humorously the behavior and thoughts of an ineffectual young man who, lacking will power and decisiveness, mopes about the girl he loves but with whom he fails to take any positive action. *The Drifting Cloud,* influenced strongly by Western realism, can be said to have inaugurated the era of modern Japanese literature.

Even in the early stages of the development of modern Japanese literature, some writers manifested a desire to cling to traditional ways. Two very prominent authors, for example, turned back to the Tokugawa writers of the Genroku era for their inspiration. Ozaki Kōyō (1867–1903), a popular writer of the second half of the Meiji era, studied the works of Saikaku and modeled his style of writing after him. Kōda Rohan (1867–1947) was also strongly influenced by Saikaku, and his major works, dealing with the pre-Meiji era, show clear signs of Buddhist thought. Kōda

[4] Kakuzo Okakura, *The Awakening of Japan* (New York: Appleton, 1905), pp. 6, 97, 186, 188, 220.

held Bakin in high regard as a writer who did more than simply reflect the conditions and mores of his society by making acute and perceptive observations. He saw the virtue of sincerity (*makoto*) being manifested in the great literary works of the Tokugawa era, while in the other arts he noted the virtue of tenacious perseverance being depicted.

The interaction of Western and Japanese literary traditions produced an era of great creativity that culminated in the period spanning 1905–1915, when scores of talented writers produced an abundance of significant works. Mori Ōgai (1862–1922) was among the prominent writers of this era. He had studied medicine in Germany, and while serving as a medical doctor in the army he translated the works of Goethe, Schiller, Ibsen, and Hans Christian Andersen, and wrote a few novels of his own. He rejected utilitarian values and condemned the imitation of Western naturalism that was practiced by his fellow writers. Mori himself wrote romantic novels that focused on the fulfillment of the self. He turned increasingly to traditional subject matters for his stories and displayed a growing admiration for the samurai, who lived only for the sake of honor. Forms and conventions, he also believed, were very important. He wrote, "If tea ceremonies were empty forms, the august ceremonials of the state together with ancestor-worship rituals would be empty forms also." [5] Concerning the past he said, "Civilization rests on history. To realize a well thought out ideal is an impossibility. One should never forget that ethics and customs which have been verified over many centuries must have a good core; otherwise they would not have endured so long." [6]

The naturalist writers sought to emancipate the individual from the conventions of the society and dealt honestly and openly with matters that were traditionally shunned or glossed over. For instance, Tayama Katai (1871–1930), who is regarded as a leading naturalist writer, dealt with the lustful passions that bewitched his heroes. Another writer who is regarded as a pioneer among naturalists is Shimazaki Tōson (1872–1943), who won renown for his novel *Hakai* (*The Broken Commandment*), which depicts the inner torments of an eta who conceals his social background. Shimazaki produced semi-autobiographical works that also embodied criticisms of traditional as well as contemporary attitudes and ways. He culminated his literary achievements with *Yoakemae* (*Before the Dawn*) in which he depicts the effects of the Meiji Restoration on a rural community.

The influence of the various Western literary trends and authors became more pronounced, and many writers were beset by the problem of resolving the conflict between traditional and Western impulses. There

---

[5] Mitsuo Nakamura, *Modern Japanese Fiction, 1868–1926* (Tokyo: Kokusai Bunka Shinkōkai, 1968), part 2, p. 19.

[6] Tatsuo Arima, *The Failure of Freedom, A Portrait of Modern Japanese Intellectuals* (Cambridge, Mass.: Harvard University Press, 1969), p. 79.

was an outburst of "Japanism" in the literary realm following the Sino-Japanese War. Takayama Chogyū (1871–1902), the chief spokesman of this movement, formulated the credo for "Japanism," which called for "reverence of the national ancestors, the embodiment of the will of the nation's founders, vigilance in military preparedness even in time of peace, and the attainment of greater unity among the people."[7] Once he fell under the influence of Nietzsche, however, he readily abandoned the belief that the individual should be subordinated to the state and concluded that the unique individual, the superman, must be emancipated from all restraints. He resolved his inner conflict between the principles of statism and the notion of the superman by turning finally to Nichiren Buddhism. He saw in Nichiren a superman who "pursued the truth through the state."

A writer who straddled the Meiji and Taishō (1912–1926) periods and who is still widely read is Natsume Sōseki (1867–1916). He studied in England and began his career as a teacher of English literature. Natsume disliked the intensity of the naturalists and sought to maintain a certain aloofness from life. He wrote in a detached, dispassionate fashion, taking his subject matter from the quiet routine of daily life. He was particularly interested in delving into human relations at the family level, examining the contradictions, frictions, egoism, loneliness, foolishness, and dullness that were disclosed there.

Initially his works revealed a sense of humor in his clever satirizing of human foibles, but as he probed deeper into the inner workings of the mind and dealt with life more philosophically, his tone grew increasingly somber. He was also deeply disturbed by the problems created by the influence of Western civilization, and he had little hope that Japan would succeed in resolving these. He believed that the nation had failed to cope with, or digest, Western civilization, and those who were not content with merely dealing with it in a superficial manner would surely end up suffering from nervous exhaustion. A character in one of his novels asks, "But wouldn't Japan develop more and more in the future?" and another answers, "It will perish."

In poetry, works of long stanzas, exceeding the traditional limit of thirty-one syllables, became an accepted form of expression. Further innovations were introduced when poems came to be written in the colloquial style, and subjects dealing with everyday life and familiar social problems came to be treated. One of the most prominent of the late Meiji poets who represented this new approach was Ishikawa Takuboku (1885–1912). He wrote,

[7] Toki Yoshimaro, *Meiji Taishō-shi: Geijutsu-hen (Meiji-Taishō History: The Arts)* (Tokyo: Asahi Shimbunsha, 1931), p. 199.

Our ideal can no longer be fantasies about goodness and beauty. We must rigorously reject all fantasies and concern ourselves with the only truth that remains—necessity! This indeed is all that we should demand of the future. We must now examine the present with the utmost precision, courage, and freedom, and there we must discover the necessity of tomorrow. Necessity is the most reliable ideal.[8]

A renaissance was effected in the realm of haiku by a poet who more properly belongs to the cultural nationalism of the *Nihonjin* school. This was Masaoka Shiki (1867–1902), who worked briefly for the magazine *Nihon* and started a school of haiku known as the "Nihon School." Shiki,[9] out of a tremendous love for Japan, wanted to preserve the best in the traditional culture and vigorously opposed the Westernizers. In seeking to revivify haiku, he instructed his disciples to "be natural," "keep the words tight," eliminate adverbs, verbs, and particles as far as possible, and use real rather than imaginary pictures. He believed that since haiku was not logical, no process of reasoning should appear on the surface. Furthermore, he contended that because haiku is so concise, delicacy cannot be applied to human affairs, whereas it can be put to use with natural objects. Here are two examples of Shiki's haiku:

> Cold moon:
> shadow of a tombstone
> shadow of a pine.

> Night,
> I wait for you:
> Again the cold wind turns to rain.

Western drama was introduced into the theater as European plays were translated and then staged. At the same time an effort was made to revitalize Kabuki. Modern drama, or at least a theatrical form closer to real life, which dealt with Meiji problems also came into existence. One of the things that the supporters of the theater managed to accomplish was the uplifting of the status of playwrights and actors, who were traditionally held in low regard by learned men. High government officials and scholars were invited to attend new and traditional plays. This effort had the active support of men like Inoue Kaoru, and as a result, the prestige of

[8] *Ibid.*, p .315.

[9] Shiki, like many other Japanese writers and artists, signs his works with his given name and is therefore better known by that name than by his surname.

the theater world was gradually enhanced. In 1887 Inoue invited the Emperor to his home for a Kabuki performance, and this was the first time that a Kabuki play had ever been performed in the presence of an Emperor.

INITIAL MODERN ECONOMIC GROWTH

The period between 1886 and 1905, as we observed earlier, is defined by Ohkawa and Rosovsky as the period of "initial modern economic growth." In this phase, the machinery, factories, corporations, etc., that came to characterize the modern Japanese economy began to develop significantly. Nevertheless, the economy was, for the most part, still dependent upon agriculture for its growth. In 1898, 82 percent of the people still lived in towns and villages of populations under ten thousand. This period then was characterized by the coexistence of the traditional and the modern forms of the economy, plus a composite sector that combined aspects of both. This hybrid element took the the form of small shops using modern techniques and non-wage family labor.

There was a considerable growth in the traditional phase of the economy after 1885. This was necessary for the eventual realization of a modern economy because it provided the capital, labor force, food for the workers, and exports (such as tea and silk) that would be required to offset the imports needed for industrialization. Furthermore, this development created a domestic market for the industrial goods that were produced. The traditional sector's potential to expand reached its limit around 1905 and its growth rate began to decline, thus bringing an end to the initial phase of the modern economic growth. In the next phase the modern segment was no longer as dependent upon the traditional component and relied more upon its own strength and exports to develop rapidly.

There has been some disagreement about the rate of growth in the traditional phase because of the unreliability of statistical data and the tendency to underestimate the yields during the early Meiji period. Recognizing the tenuous nature of the statistics of this period, we can nonetheless make use of them as helpful indicators. Taking 1910–1914 as index 100, from 1885–1889 to 1905–1909 the index of food production rose from an estimated 57 to 85 and the production of raw material from 22 to 78. In the twenty-five years before World War I, the total production of food and industrial materials doubled. Rice production increased by 40 percent between 1885–1889 and 1910–1914. This was achieved by means of a 25 percent increase in yield per acre along with an increase in cultivated land. A 7 percent increase in cultivated area in rice was achieved between 1878–1882 and 1888–1892, and about 25 percent in the fifty years after 1885–1889. This greater yield per acre was accomplished through the use of more and better fertilizers, better seeds, double cropping, and improved methods of farming.[10] The well-to-do villagers played an important role in the diffusion of new agricultural knowledge by publishing farm journals and by taking the initiative in adopting new techniques.

There may be some disagreement about the extent to which Japanese agricultural production increased, but there is no question about the fact that industrial growth was largely sustained by the traditional segment during this period. In the early 1870s the land tax constituted 90 percent of the state revenue, in 1882 more than 80 percent, and in 1893, 45 percent. In subsequent years the tax burden on the farmers continued to be higher in comparison to what the merchants and industrialists shouldered. In 1908, for example, 28 percent of a farmer's income was paid in taxes while a merchant or industrialist paid only 14 percent. The labor force for the growing textile industries was supplied largely by young girls from the farming communities. Raw silk and tea provided the chief export commodities; in fact, during the period from 1868 to 1893 raw silk accounted for 42 percent of Japan's total exports.

The rapid growth in the modern or industrial phase occurred after the Russo-Japanese War (1904–1905), but there was considerable expansion during the second half of the Meiji era. Imports and exports doubled from 1889–1893 to 1899–1903, and doubled again during the next decade. Coal consumption in industry and transportation rose from two million tons in 1893 to fifteen million tons in 1913. Railroad mileage more than tripled and freight ton-mileage increased seventeen times. During this period a number of large-scale industries came into existence, and this trend was fostered and supported by the government for military and political reasons. Government initiative, subsidy, and protection were readily extended to those industries that were deemed essential to national interests. One area in which this was particularly apparent was in railroad construction. Nevertheless, serious financial difficulties kept the pace of construction rather slow.

As early as 1873 the government decided to rely primarily on private enterprise for railroad construction, but because of their strategic and economic significance, it kept close watch over the work and provided assistance whenever it was needed. In the 1880s private firms began building the trunk lines linking the major cities.

Railroad construction enjoyed a minor boom in the 1880s as a result of substantial government backing. Private companies owned 671 miles

---

[10] There is disagreement about whether or not these factors actually had as much impact as is generally assumed. See James I. Nakamura, "Growth of Japanese Agriculture," in William W. Lockwood, ed., *The State and Economic Enterprise in Japan* (Princeton, N.J.: Princeton University Press, 1965), pp. 291–95.

of railroad by 1889 compared to the 551 miles of tracks owned by the state. The number of private railroad companies increased from twelve in 1889 to twenty-four by 1895. Following the Sino-Japanese War the railroad business expanded even further and seventeen new companies came into existence.

The recession that followed the war brought considerable financial difficulties to the railroad companies, and as a result, the government decided to nationalize the industry. It began taking over the railroads in 1906, at which point there were 37,283 miles of private tracks and 1,499 miles of railway owned by the state.

Railroad travel in its early stages was a luxury that only the very rich could afford. For example, the third-class fare between Shinagawa in Tokyo and Yokohama was 31.25 sen in 1872, but at this time the highest paid girl worker in a textile plant was receiving only 7.8 sen a day. The most common means of transportation was the ricksha, which was invented in Japan in 1870, and by 1877 there were 136,761 registered rickshas.

The government also played an active role in the development of marine transportation. As noted earlier, the government turned over to Mitsubishi the transport ships it had purchased for the Formosan expedition as well as some additional vessels, and granted it subsidies so as to enable it to compete effectively with foreign shipping companies. Government assistance was extended to other shipping firms as well, and by the Sino-Japanese War merchant ships numbered 528 with a tonnage of 331,000. By 1906 the shipping tonnage came close to 700,000, and in 1913 half of the overseas trade was carried in Japanese bottoms, this as compared to less than 10 percent before the Sino-Japanese War.

The government paid similar attention to the development of heavy industry and mining. Initially the state operated a number of enterprises in strategically important fields, such as metallurgy, machinery manufacture, and shipbuilding. Fairly early in the Meiji period the policy of turning plants operated by the state over to private businessmen was adopted, but the government did retain the major arsenals, dockyards, machine shops, and wool and clothing plants for the use of the armed forces, and tobacco factories. Overall, however, state-run enterprises occupied a relatively small portion of the economy. In 1914 government plants employed only 12 percent of the total number of factory workers.

The state initially sought to operate the major mines; after 1885, however, it began to turn these over to private enterprise. Improvements in equipment and technique were introduced, but by and large the method of extraction remained primitive and the miners had to work under hazardously difficult conditions. Nonetheless, there was a steady increase in mineral production. In 1877, 3.4 million yen worth of minerals was produced; by 1887 the figure had climbed to 8.2 million yen. The building of the railroads facilitated coal mining; while in 1874, 220,000 tons of coal were mined, in 1897, 5 million tons were produced.

In the iron industry no significant growth occurred until the state-operated Yawata Iron Works began production in 1901. In that year the output of pig iron jumped to 56,000 tons and steel to 7,500 tons as compared to 26,800 tons and 1,000 tons respectively in 1897. The number of private steel companies increased after the Russo-Japanese War, and there was a significant rise in iron and steel production. In 1913 pig iron production came to 243,000 tons and steel output advanced to 255,000 tons.

The shipbuilding industry, in which Japan leads the world today, made very little headway in the Meiji period. The production of machinery also showed only modest advancement, and most of the equipment used in the various industries had to be imported. For example, almost all the machines used for cotton spinning came from England.

The industry that expanded most rapidly and remained the most important component of the economy until the Second World War was textile manufacturing. In 1900, 70.7 percent of the factories in Japan were involved in textile production. They consumed 46 percent of the motor power used in all industries and employed 67 percent of the factory workers.

Japan attained a dominant position in the silk industry by the First World War. Mechanization in silk filature occurred slowly at first, but the pace was accelerated after the Sino-Japanese War. Prior to the war, in 1892, 50 percent of the raw silk was produced by hand-reeling; by 1910, 70 percent was produced by machine-reeling filature. The size of the filature plants began to grow also. In 1909, of the 3,720 plants, 471 with more than 100 workers employed over 49 percent of the total number of workers in this field. The number of hand-reeling establishments in the countryside remained high, however, and in 1913 there were still about 285,000 shops of this kind.

The output of raw silk increased from 7.5 million pounds annually in the period 1889–1893 to 27.9 million pounds during 1909–1913. In 1897, 24 percent of the world's raw silk came from Japan, 39 from China and 27 from Italy. By 1904 these figures had changed to 31 percent from Japan, 24 from China and 26 from Italy.

It was in cotton textile production that the industrial revolution first occurred, with the extensive use of machinery in large plants. The man primarily responsible for the rapid mechanization in this field was the industrial entrepreneur, Shibusawa Eiichi (1840–1931). A few cotton spinning plants were established in the first decade of the Meiji period, but they failed to increase production sufficiently and a large sum of money had to be devoted to the importation of cotton yarn and cloth. During this time 36 percent of the money spent on imports was expended on cotton textile goods. In 1878 the government sought to correct this situation by establishing model plants and importing spinning machines that were turned over to private entrepreneurs with very favorable terms of payment. These measures were effective, but the really big step forward in this field was taken by Shibusawa. He received financial support from businessmen and aristocrats and established a huge plant in Osaka that began operating in 1883. Shibusawa used steam power, and he was able to run his 10,500 spindles day and night by bringing electric lights into his plant. The year after he began operation, Shibusawa was able to pay a dividend of 18 percent to the investors. By 1888, eleven hundred workers were employed in his Osaka Spinning Mill plants. Other industrialists followed the methods employed by Shibusawa and, between 1886 and 1894, thirty-three new plants were established in the vicinity of Osaka. In 1896 the Spinners' Association led by Shibusawa managed to have the import duties on raw cotton and the export duties on cotton yarn abolished.

The tremendous expansion in productive capacity led to rapidly increased output in this field. In 1896, with the domestic demand now being met, producers began to turn to foreign markets, particularly China. Exports to that country rose until 1903 when they began to decline because of competition from foreign cotton textile producers as well as from the growing Chinese textile industry.[11] As a result cotton textile producers began to turn to the manufacture of cotton fabrics. In general, however, weaving remained essentially a cottage industry during this period of initial modern economic growth.

Weaving machines were employed in the manufacture of glossy silk for export, but in the production of brocades for domestic consumption traditional hand weaving was retained. The export of silk fabrics, particularly to the United States, steadily increased from about 1.5 million yen in 1889 to 21 million yen in 1899. The figure continued to rise in the next two decades, reaching a peak of 160 million yen in 1919. Cotton and silk textile products constituted the most significant part of Japan's exports. In 1913 they amounted to nearly three-fifths of her total exports.

The large-scale use of machines in the textile industry was followed by similar developments in other areas. The first modern pulp factory was established in 1889 and by 1896 paper was being exported to China. Sugar refining plants were founded in 1895 and sugar manufacturing

---

[11] Japanese investors began establishing plants in China and by 1913, Japanese capitalists owned one-fourth of the spindles in the Chinese cotton industry.

took a great leap forward after the acquisition of Formosa. Substantial gains were made throughout the 1890s in the production of cement, chemical fertilizers, drugs, beer, matches, and glass.

The most significant growth in industrial production occurred in the next phase (1906–1930), but by the time of the Russo-Japanese War we could say that Japan was well on her way to becoming an industrial nation, even though most of the work was still carried on in small establishments or workshops. This condition prevailed through the pre-World War II period and even in the postwar era. In 1930 there were over one million tiny shops, each employing on the average of three persons, in many cases family members.

In terms of the percentage of people employed in factories, Japan was not yet an industrial society. Around 1913 only one-seventh of the country's total labor force was employed in manufacturing industries. The nation was still predominantly agrarian. At the turn of the century three out of five families were still engaged in farming; that is, in 1903 out of a total of 8.4 million families, 5.4 million of them were on the farm.[12]

THE PLIGHT OF THE WORKERS

Industrialization created new jobs for the people but it also imposed new hardships upon the working class. In traditional Japan the relationship between the employer and the employee was assumed to be one of benevolence and kindness from above and loyalty and obedience from below. The ideal may not have always been followed in practice, but the employer was nevertheless expected to take a lifelong interest in the well-being of his employees. His interest was not to be limited to the employees' activities in the shop; but much as if he were their father, he was to take their personal affairs, such as health, marriage, and family problems, as his direct concern.

The new industrialism that came into existence in Meiji Japan changed this relationship into an impersonal contract, a strictly business transaction. Some wily employers might have rationalized their exploitation of the workers in terms of the traditional values of benevolence and loyalty, but as the factories grew in size, it became clear that personal contacts between the employer and employee could not possibly be maintained. In the joint stock companies naturally there was no way

[12] In 1880, 81 percent of the workers were in agriculture, fishing, and mining. In 1900, this figure dropped to 69 percent and by 1920 it had fallen even lower to 55.4 percent. In the fields of manufacturing and construction the percentages for the same years were: 6.4, 13, and 19.4, and in commerce and transportation they were 6.4, 10.1, and 15.5. (William W. Lockwood, *The Economic Development of Japan* [Princeton, N.J.: Princeton University Press, 154], p. 462.)

to establish the traditional father-son, master-follower (oyabun-kobun) relationship between employer and employee. As a result, what frequently came to prevail was unrestrained exploitation; there were no laws regulating age, hours, wages, or working conditions.

In the textile factories and the mines conditions were particularly bad, and there was extensive exploitation of female labor. Nine out of ten workers in weaving sheds and silk filatures were women, and in the cotton spinning mills around the turn of the century 80 percent of the operatives were women. In 1897, 49 percent of the workers in these mills were girls less than twenty years of age; 13 percent were younger than fourteen, and some were even less than eleven. These girls were recruited from the countryside and were under contract to work in the factories for a fixed length of time in exchange for a sum of money that was advanced to them. They were then housed in company dormitories ostensibly to protect them, but in reality the purpose of the facilities was to prevent them from running away.

In 1893 a reporter visited what was then regarded as a model cotton spinning plant where working conditions were reputedly excellent, and he discovered that most of the operatives were girls between the ages of thirteen and twenty-four. They worked in twelve-hour shifts in order to keep the factory running day and night and they were given only one rest period of thirty to forty minutes in which to eat. The workers were kept at their task for as long as nineteen hours if the plant was busy. Their food was poor and the bedding inadequate. Only two girls out of sixteen hundred workers received twenty-two sen a day in wages; two hundred or so earned eleven sen or more; most of them were paid eight to ten sen; some received as little as four sen. They were charged for their food, having to pay two sen a meal, or one yen eighty sen for the month.

Working conditions were worse than this in the small weaving shops. One employer kept his workers locked in the plant and dormitory, forced them to work until they produced a fixed quota, fined them, punished them by reducing their food, and on occasion even stripped and beat them. Similar conditions prevailed in the silk filature plants, many in fact being small sweat shops. Even in the larger factories the wages were lower than in the cotton spinning mills. The death rate of the girl workers in textile mills was high, with many contracting tuberculosis and beriberi.

The overall pay in the textile industry remained low, even lower than was the case in India. In 1891 the labor cost to produce 100 pounds of cotton yarn was 135.5 sen for Japan and 151.9 sen for India. Men received better pay than women, and workers in heavy industry received better wages than those in textile plants. For example, in 1898 the average pay for men, including the salaries of executive officials, in ten cotton spinning plants was 24.5 sen a day compared to 13.9 sen for women; in 1901 workers at the Nagasaki shipyard received an average pay of 54.4 sen a day.

Low wages were justified by the employers, who claimed that it was necessary so as to enable them to compete effectively with the industrially advanced Western nations. Fukuzawa, a vocal spokesman for the businessmen's cause, admitted in 1893 that the Japanese textile workers were paid one-tenth the wages of their British counterparts, but he agreed with the employers that the cheap labor was necessary. The profits that were extracted by the owners and stockholders, however, were not at all modest. For example, five years after it went into production, Shibusawa's spinning company was paying dividends of 30 percent.

Another area in which harsh abuses occurred was in mining. One of the reasons for this was the fact that prisoners were used in the mines. This practice, although common in many of the state enterprises in the early Meiji era, was being discontinued in most of the privately owned mines. The Miike coal mines, however, which were the main source of coal that was extracted for export, utilized forced labor from 1873 to 1931. To be sure, the percentage of prisoners that were used there steadily declined. In 1889 it was 13.3 percent, while in 1907 it was down to 5.5 percent. The low cost of labor accruing from this practice enabled Miike to compete on more favorable terms than other mining firms. This led the Mitsubishi-owned Takashima Coal Mining Company to agitate for the sale of the Miike coal mines to private business.

At the same time, in order to compete with the cheap labor of the Miike mines, Takashima exploited its workers even more stringently, housing them in barracks as virtual prisoners, and working them for twelve hours for thirty sen a day. Any suspected slackers were punished severely. In 1888 a reporter for the magazine *Nihonjin* noted that the temperature in the mines got as high as 120 to 130 degrees. Oxygen was scarce so it was difficult to breathe, but the miners were not allowed to pause and rest. Guards went around clubbing those who slackened their pace of work, while troublesome workers were trussed up and whipped. Those who attempted to escape were beaten savagely. In 1884, when a cholera epidemic broke out, one half of the three thousand miners died of the disease. The victims were taken out and burned one day after they contracted cholera, whether they were dead or not. These conditions frequently led the Takashima miners to riot out of sheer desperation.

Faced with the cry of unfair competition, the government decided to sell the Miike coal mines. Mitsui purchased them in 1888 and, with the government's consent, continued to use prison labor. Under ordinary circumstances mining was a hazardous occupation. Not only was it backbreaking work, but the foul air shortened the miner's life, and frequent cave-ins and explosions took a high toll.

The workers were not the only ones affected adversely by the mining industry. Serious problems of pollution began to develop. The first celebrated case involved the damages caused by the poisonous elements that flowed into rivers of the Kantō region from the Ashio copper mines. The noxious ingredients killed the fish, ruining the fishing industries along the river routes. Moreover, the mining industry had stripped the adjacent areas of timber, thus creating serious erosion problems. This then brought about floods that spread the poisonous elements into the farm lands, causing a great deal of damage. In 1891 the matter was called to the attention of the government by a Diet member, Tanaka Shōzō (1841–1913), but to no avail. The desolation of the countryside became more critical and finally a major protest demonstration was staged in 1900, but it was readily quelled by the police. The leader, Tanaka Shōzō, in desperation submitted a direct petition to the Emperor as he was leaving the Diet. The government, however, was readily able to dispose of the matter by claiming that Tanaka was insane.

The pay for workers in the heavy industries was better in comparison to the situation in the textile industries. Here too, however, private entrepreneurs sought to cut costs by reducing wages and by decreasing the number of workers while requiring the remaining laborers to make up for cutbacks by putting in more hours per day.

Christian leaders and men who were influenced by Western social reform movements began to criticize these conditions in the factories and the mines. The businessmen and their spokesmen adamantly opposed any government intervention in the way of giving protection to the workers, claiming that they were adhering to the tradition of "benevolence and kindness." Moreover, they argued that any deviation from the principles of laissez-faire, which fostered the growth of Western industries, would surely hamper Japanese industrial development.

The government was slow to act on behalf of the workers, partly because many high officials had close business ties, but primarily because they were mainly interested in industrial growth. Thus, the state supported the business interests at the expense of the workers. The Civil Code of 1890 upheld the concept of "freedom of contract," and state authority was used to prevent the workers from staging strikes. The Police Regulation of 1900 made it virtually a crime to organize and lead workers out on strikes.

Faced with the opposition of the industrialists, who were backed by the state, the advocates of reform were severely restricted in their efforts to organize the workers, and by the turn of the century labor movements were still in their infancy. Workers did stage strikes out of desperation, but they were usually sporadic, unorganized affairs. The strikes that occurred before the Sino-Japanese War were especially ineffective. The first strike on record was staged in 1886 by a hundred female workers in a cotton mill in Yamanashi Perfecture. The number of strikes began to increase after the Sino-Japanese War, with the government recording thirty incidents of labor disputes within one four-month period in 1897. This increase in labor unrest was caused by inflation, which was not accompanied by any increase in wages.

In 1897 the first serious move was made to organize the workers when the Society for the Protection of Trade Unions was established under the leadership of Takano Fusataro (1868–1904) who had spent some time in the United States and was an admirer of Samuel Gompers, the American labor leader, and of Katayama Sen (1859–1933), who had studied at Grinnell College and Yale Divinity School and was also influenced by the doctrines of Christian socialism. Out of this movement spearheaded by these men, three labor societies emerged: the Association of Ironworkers, the Society to Reform the Railroads, and the Printers' Association. The objectives of these groups were still limited, and they all emphasized mutual assistance by the workers, played down strikes, and made it clear that they were for reforms, not revolutions. The members of the association for railroad workers were the most aggressive, and they staged a strike in the spring of 1898 in northern Japan, protesting the firing of "agitators" and demanding better treatment.

The government's efforts to curb the movement forced the labor leaders to try to organize more effectively and thus attempt to carry the struggle into the political arena. In 1901 Katayama Sen and five other men organized the Social Democratic party (*Shakai Minshutō*). The party was immediately disbanded by the government, but the leaders intensified their activities and propaganda work on behalf of socialism.

After the turn of the century the government did enact some legislation aimed at regulating conditions in the mines and the factories. In 1905 a mine act and in 1911 a factory act were put into law but, because of opposition from the industrialists, they were not enforced until 1916. The provisions were very modest. All mines and factories employing more than fifteen workers were required to limit the workday for women, and children under fifteen, to twelve hours, including one hour of rest. The minimum age of employment was set at twelve, except for light work, in which case the limit was ten years of age. No action was taken on night work.

SOCIAL CONDITIONS

The impact of industrialism, of course, was not all negative, although the positive effects were not felt by the masses until the twentieth century. As late as 1913 one scholar concluded "the mode of living—housing, food, clothing, and other factors of living—has not made noteworthy improvement. The mass of the people live in just the same way as they did during the feudal regime." [13]

In many small ways, however, changes for the better did occur even before the turn of the century. To what extent economic changes in the Meiji era improved the quantity and quality of the food would be difficult to assess. Agricultural production did increase but so did the population; specifically, the population increased from 35.9 million (index 71) in 1875–1879 to 50.6 million (index 100) in 1910–1914, while food production rose from somewhere below index 57 and increased to index 100. Economists, who have made a conservative estimate of the extent to which agricultural production increased in the Meiji period, contend that the caloric consumption per capita per day may have been over 2,100 during 1878–1882 and did not change significantly through 1915–1925, rising perhaps to about 2,300.

There does not seem to have been much improvement in the quality of the food. Rice and other cereals constituted the bulk of what was consumed. In 1889–1893, 0.9 pound per capita per year of meat was consumed and in 1900, 29 pounds of fish. The taste of some of the food was improved by greater use of sugar, although again the per capita consumption was not high—10.4 pounds per capita annually in 1896–1898. Nevertheless, this was enough to make the diet more interesting for peasants who in the past were condemned to a diet of rice, barley, sweet potatoes, vegetables, and occasionally, fish.

Housing remained poor and clothing did not improve much for the masses, but even in the countryside machine-made cotton fabrics replaced hand-woven cloth, and some Western-style clothing began to appear. Matches, soap, and kerosene lamps made life more convenient. In the cities there were gaslights and rickshas. Later, of course, there would be electricity and bicycles.

The effects of the new age were felt most forcefully in the towns and villages located near railroads or near new factories. The technological and industrial changes together with the other new institutions—schools, newspapers, and military conscription—brought the outside world into the villages, and a broader perspective and a new way of life began to

[13] Quoted in *ibid.*, p. 34.

develop. In recalling the changes brought about by the establishment of a cotton spinning mill in his village in 1890, one observer noted that the easygoing tranquillity of the town vanished forever as

> three times a day the factory whistle echoed throughout the village shaking violently the stagnant air of the community. The impact the factory had upon the village was greater than the arrival of Perry's warships off the coast of Uraga. Consequently, traditional attitudes about social status and family standing disappeared quickly and were replaced by standards of wealth and poverty.[14]

For the peasants who lived within commuting distance of the factories, a way to supplement their income now became available. Fathers and sons often found work in the factories, leaving mothers and younger children to till the soil. This alleviated the traditional problem of under-employment in the farm villages. The more ambitious young men, drawn by the job opportunities and the more exciting life of the cities, left their villages, causing the agrarian leaders to bemoan the fact that the seductive cities were draining the villages of energetic young men.

Insofar as the effect of modernization in the area of health and sanitation was concerned, there is little evidence that much improvement took place in the first half of the Meiji era. In fact, with factories operating under the hazardous, unhealthy conditions described above, the mortality rate remained high among women of child-bearing age and young men. Medical care remained inadequate, although in 1900 there were 0.75 doctors for every one thousand persons. This figure does not compare too unfavorably with 1.1 in 1966 when you consider the fact that modern medicine had to start from the very beginning in early Meiji. Life expectancy around 1891–1898 was 42.8 years for men and 44.3 for women. It remained approximately the same in the pre-World War II years. In the 1920s and the 1930s the infant mortality rate was well over 100 for every 1,000 live births as compared to 14.8 for every 1,000 in 1967. The overall death rate in 1920 was 25 persons out of 1,000 as compared to 6.7 out of 1,000 in 1967.

Crowded conditions and inadequate sanitation resulted in frequent outbreaks of epidemics. Cholera epidemics began to occur in the late Tokugawa years; the bubonic plague first broke out in 1899. The diseases tended to get out of control almost immediately after striking, and then they spread very rapidly. In 1879 there was a cholera epidemic

---

[14] Sumiya Mikio, *Dai-Nipponteikoku no Shiren* (*The Crucible of Imperial Japan*) (Tokyo: Chūō Kōronsha, 1966), p. 63.

in which more than 105,700 persons died. In 1886, a similar epidemic took the lives of 108,400 victims, and in the same year more than 20,000 persons died of typhus and dysentery, and 18,000 of smallpox. In 1886, then, more than 146,000 persons died as a result of epidemics. These epidemics continued to break out; in the second and third decades of Meiji more than 800,000 people died of one kind or another of these rapidly spreading diseases. The manner in which the victims were cared for was inadequate, to say the least. In 1892 Erwin Baelz, a German doctor who was teaching at the University of Tokyo, visited a smallpox hospital and observed,

> A scandalous state of affairs. There are four hundred
> patients, often fifty new cases every day, eight doctors
> some of whom have had very little experience, and
> twenty nurses. Wooden sheds with torn paper windows
> in wintertime. That's the way Tokyo treats the sick.
> Cholera—typhoid—smallpox! Not one hospital for
> such epidemic cases where the poor wretches are as well
> cared for as a horse in a good stable! [15]

Another area in which the new age failed to eliminate a traditional hazard was the frequent incidence of large-scale fires. These monstrously destructive fires continued to plague the cities just as they had in the Tokugawa period. Between 1876 and 1892, over sixty thousand houses went up in flames in the city of Tokyo. This amounted to about one out of four dwellings in that city.

Another unfortunate legacy of the Tokugawa era that modernization failed to have an ameliorating effect on was the houses of prostitution. As noted earlier, slavery was banned but "voluntary servitude" was permitted. There were six sections in Tokyo where these establishments were located, and between 1883–1888 there were anywhere from three to five thousand prostitutes kept in bondage in these brothels. A Swiss official in Japan observed that the girls were "publicly exposed like animals on display, to be freely scrutinized by all comers. After first examining the goods, they are purchased and used by the first man who sets the price. The impression I got of these unfortunate creatures was one of utmost misery." [16] Similar establishments existed in all the cities throughout the country. Many of the girls were sold into bondage by impover-

---

[15] Erwin O. E. Von Baelz, *Awakening Japan: The Diary of a German Doctor*, trans. Eden and Cedar Paul (New York: Viking, 1932), p. 98.

[16] Irokawa Daikichi, *Kindai Kokka no Suppatsu (The Beginning of the Modern State)* (Tokyo: Chūō Kōronsha, 1966), p. 107.

ished peasant families, victims of economic necessity and a feudalistic sense of loyalty to the family.

Efforts to end this practice and free the girls were spearheaded by Christians as early as 1882, but to no avail. In 1899–1900, however, a movement led by a missionary, U. G. Murphy, forced the courts to recognize the right of the prostitutes to leave the brothels. The girls were still obliged, however, to repay the money that had been advanced to their families for their services. The movement to free the prostitutes was joined by the Salvation Army and Christian journalists and for a short period their efforts were rewarded. Some houses of prostitution went out of business, but this was only a temporary victory. The system survived until the end of the Second World War.

CHAPTER 14

POLITICAL
DEVELOPMENTS
IN LATER MEIJI

The decade or two following the promulgation of the constitution and the convocation of the Diet was a period of trial and error in Japanese politics. Both sides, the oligarchy and the opposition parties, endeavored to learn how to fit the Diet into the political framework of the country. The idea of government functioning under a written constitution with the participation of a Diet that was composed of elected representatives was certainly a revolutionary concept. Despite all the theoretical discussions that had taken place before these institutions were adopted, the actual incorporation of these elements into the political life of the society required patience, willingness to compromise, and common sense—qualities that seemed scarce enough on both sides of the political battleline.

The internal power struggle was closely related to Japan's foreign relations. The opposition parties frequently used national interest as an issue to arouse popular opinion and support against the government, while the ruling clique, on the other hand, used external crises to deflect assaults launched by the opposition. The fact that the opposition parties were just as chauvinistic, perhaps even more so, than some government officials, did not augur well for the future of parliamentary government. Their willingness to support militarism and expansionism necessitated their subordination of internal political goals to these ends. In the 1880s, as Japan became increasingly involved in Korean affairs, Fukuzawa was speaking for many of the advocates of popular rights when he said, "The question of control of political power at home is insignificant compared to the question of national interests. Even if the government in form and name is autocratic, as long as it is capable of extending our national interests, I am satisfied." [1] In effect, Fukuzawa was nudging the movement toward its eventual demise a half a century later.

Another trait that weakened the political parties was their lack of unity of purpose and cohesiveness, which was no doubt the result of the persistence of traditional behavior and values. As we noted earlier, not only were there intense conflicts between the parties, there were also various incompatible factions within each party that based their loyalties upon sectional and personal ties. The existence of these cliques led to numerous intra-party squabbles.

Factionalism and personal rivalries could have been expected to divide the oligarchs too, but the Meiji leaders, faced with the threat that the political parties might usurp their power, managed to subordinate their personal and factional interests. By and large they acted as a cohesive group until the turn of the century when Itō organized a political party. The Satsuma and Chōshū factions shared the powers of government, alternating the post of the Prime Minister and more or less dividing the armed forces, with Satsuma dominating the navy and Chōshū the army. Eventually a rivalry of a sort did develop between Itō and Yamagata, but in the main they managed to work together as parts of a group in which power was shared collectively by the members. No one individual stood out above the others, that is until Itō and Yamagata began to emerge as the two most prominent leaders. The concept of the genrō was developing and with it came the expectation that each member be loyal to the group and behave in a manner appropriate to a genrō. This, in effect, meant that individuals were to refrain from establishing ties with a political party.

The collective exercise of power and the emergence of the Privy Council and the council made up of the genrō, which operated outside the confines of the constitution, as political bodies of primary importance tended to obscure the real locus of power. In addition, since all governmental actions were taken in the name of the Emperor, the system itself tended to draw a veil over those who actually exercised power. The Emperor could not personally be held responsible for any particular action because he was "sacred and inviolable." As a result, the notion of *kuromaku* (the man who pulls the strings from behind the black curtain) came to play an important part in Japanese political thinking. The decision-making process tended to obfuscate the location of responsibility because "go-betweens, informal meetings, and group discussions were con-

---

[1] *Fukuzawa Zenshū* (*The Collected Works of Fukuzawa*), 10 vols. (Tokyo: Jiji Shimpōsha, 1925–1926), vol. 8, pp. 23–24.

sistently used to reach decisions for which no individual or group was ordinarily responsible." [2]

To be sure, the desire to maintain power strongly motivated the oligarchs, but it is also true that they were sincere men who honestly wished to serve the state and the public good. They were convinced that they were better qualified to do this than the opposition party members. In order to retain their grip on political power, they took advantage of institutions and forces not available to the opposition, such as the emperor system, the bureaucracy, the army and navy, the police, and the general public's willingness to follow those in power. In addition, of course, they were able to play upon the weaknesses of the opposition by aggravating their internally divisive conflicts through support of one faction against another. Frequently, they were able to induce key leaders to leave the opposition altogether and join their camp by offering them government posts.

PARTISAN POLITICS: 1887-1894

As we noted in an earlier chapter, the opposition forces led by Gotō Shōjirō launched an offensive against the Itō cabinet in 1887 by opposing the negotiations for treaty revisions. Itō was forced to discontinue the negotiations, but he tried to split the opposition by bringing Ōkuma into the cabinet as Foreign Minister. This not only failed to weaken the Union of Like Thinkers, but it also served to annoy his fellow clansman, Yamagata, who disapproved of Ōkuma's entry into the government.

In the spring of 1888 Itō resigned his post in order to devote full attention to the drafting of the constitution and Kuroda (1840–1900) became the new Prime Minister. His cabinet also encountered difficulties in connection with treaty revisions with the result that the task was turned over entirely to Ōkuma, who had remained on as Foreign Minister in the new cabinet. The opposition party leaders persisted in their objections because Ōkuma, like Itō before him, was also willing to open the entire nation to Western residents and to allow Western judges to sit in trials involving Westerners. The other members of the oligarchy also disapproved of these concessions, and when Ōkuma was injured in an assassination attempt, they used this occasion to remove him from his post. As a result of these difficulties, Kuroda resigned in October, 1889, and was succeeded by Yamagata.

At the time the announcement was made that elections for the Diet were to be held on July 1, 1890, the opposition forces were in a state of disarray. Gotō had abruptly deserted his cohorts in the Union of Like

---

[2] Robert A. Scalapino, *Democracy and the Party Movement in Prewar Japan* (Berkeley, Calif.: University of California Press, 1953, p. 150.

Thinkers to join the Kuroda cabinet, and this splintered the opposition into many factions. Itagaki sought to revive the old Liberal party but failed. Separate factions led by Itagaki, Ōi Kentarō, and Kōno Hironaka agreed to cooperate during the election, after which these three groups, joined by a faction from Kyushu, merged to form the Liberal party once again.

The first Diet elections were held in July, 1890, as scheduled. The franchise was limited to male subjects over twenty-five years of age who paid a national land or income tax of fifteen yen or more. Priests, teachers of religion, active servicemen, and the insane were denied the right to vote. Those who did qualify numbered 450,365 out of the total population of 39,383,300 (i.e. 1.14 percent of the population). The country was divided into 257 electoral districts with each one having one representative, except for those with more than 180,000 residents, in which case two seats were given. There were 214 districts with one representative and 43 with two. The voter was required to sign his name and place his seal on the ballot. In the first national elections, 93.9 percent of those eligible to vote cast their ballots.

There were 130 Liberal party and 41 Reform party members in the lower house when the first Diet convened. A progovernment party won 67 seats and merged with other similar groups to form the *Taiseikai* (The Great Achievement Society) with 79 members. As for the social composition of the first Diet, 109 members were shizoku, 191 members were commoners, and 88 members fell into the category of absentee landowners by virtue of the fact that they paid more than 90 yen in land tax.

The government's avowed position was "to stand above parties," a policy that was proclaimed by Prime Minister Kuroda immediately after the constitution was promulgated. Itō, the man who framed the constitution, took a similar position holding that the bringing of political parties into the government would be extremely undesirable since the government had to maintain its independence. Yamagata was even less willing than Kuroda and Itō to cooperate with political parties, and he persisted in his rigid opposition to granting these organizations a role in government.

The Diet convened on November 25, 1890, and immediately there was a clash with the government as the opposition factions attempted to cut the budget. Part of these cuts though involved those items excluded, under Article 67 of the constitution, from the Diet's jurisdiction and consequently, Yamagata was inclined toward standing firm and, if necessary, even going so far as to dissolve the Diet. However, the desire not to mar the inauguration of constitutional government by such a drastic step prevailed, and a compromise was reached. Factionalism in the parties also played a significant role in this affair since the Tosa faction of the

Liberal party was persuaded (the critics said bribed) by the cabinet to split with the opposition and vote to uphold Yamagata's position.

In order to split the opposition, the Meiji leaders did not restrict themselves to such tactics as bribery. They frequently resorted to more persuasive techniques, such as the employment of thugs to exert physical force against Diet members. A cleavage developed within the Liberal party between those who were in the Diet and those who were not. The latter, led by Ōi Kentaro (1843–1922), sought to intimidate the weak-kneed Diet members, with the result that a group of Tosa men finally split with the party and formed a separate organization.

Just as the political parties could not maintain unity, there were signs that a cleavage was developing among the government leaders. Itō was dissatisfied with the way in which Yamagata dealt with the Diet; when this became known to the latter, he resigned his post. This was the beginning of the growing fission between the so-called "civil" faction of the genrō, represented by Itō and Inoue, and the "military" faction, which was headed by Yamagata and included the remaining genrō, namely, Kuroda, Matsukata, Saigō Tsugumichi (1843–1902), and Ōyama (1842–1916).

Upon Yamagata's resignation, Itō was again asked to form a cabinet but he refused, passing the task on to Matsukata, who organized a new government in May, 1891. Matsukata adopted an uncompromising stance toward the opposition at the encouragement of his Minister of Home Affairs, Shinagawa Yajirō (1843–1900) who was a follower of Yamagata and an inveterate foe of parliamentary government and political parties.

The opposition parties had by this time somewhat fortified their positions. The Liberal party leaders had expelled the more radical faction led by Ōi and curtailed the power of the non-Diet members. In addition, cooperation between the Liberal party and the Reform party was agreed upon in a meeting between Itagaki and Ōkuma. Ōkuma was thereupon "purged" by the government again, losing his membership in the Privy Council.

The second Diet convened in November, 1891, and the opposition parties, bent upon a confrontation with the government, began to slash the budget submitted by Matsukata. His response was swift and decisive —dissolution of the Diet. Matsukata, now fully determined to increase the number of progovernment representatives, decided to intervene in the election. Shinagawa implemented the plan by instructing prefectural and local government officials to employ whatever means were necessary to obstruct the opposition candidates. Not only did government agents intimidate the voters by conducting house to house visits telling them that a vote for opposition candidates was an act of disloyalty toward the Emperor, but they also bribed the voters and even employed thugs, hoodlums, police, and military troops to attack the opposition forces physically. Violence was particularly severe in Kōchi and Saga prefectures, the home bases of Itagaki and Ōkuma. Elections had to be postponed in Saga because of the extensive government intervention. Nationally, 25 deaths and 388 injuries were officially reported.

Despite the measures taken by the government, the opposition parties nevertheless managed to win the election by securing 163 seats; the progovernment faction got only 137. As soon as the third Diet was convened, the opposition parties sought to impeach the government by introducing a resolution memorializing the Emperor to dismiss the cabinet. The motion failed by three votes because some members did not favor involving the Emperor in the struggle. Thereupon a motion of no-confidence was passed by a vote of 154 to 111. The House of Peers also passed a resolution reprimanding the government for its actions in the election, but it supported Matsukata against the lower house's efforts to reduce the budget.

Matsukata was forced to resign in July, 1892, when the Minister of War and the Minister of the Navy resigned as a protest action against the inclusion of Ōkuma's friend in the cabinet. Itō was also disturbed by the way in which Matsukata had managed the election, and he consequently forced Shinagawa's removal from the cabinet. He had already begun to weigh the possibility of establishing a government party to deal with the difficulties posed by the opposition in the Diet.

Upon Matsukata's resignation, Itō took over the premiership again with the understanding that the other genrō would join the cabinet to give it the strength necessary to cope with the opposition forces. As a result, Yamagata, Inoue, Ōyama, and Kuroda entered what was to be labeled the Cabinet of Elder Statesmen.

The fourth Diet convened and once again the opposition trimmed the budget by disallowing monies needed for naval expansion and the bureaucracy. The government refused to accept the cuts since they fell under Article 67 of the constitution, which excluded these items from the Diet's jurisdiction. Itō, finding that the impasse could not be resolved, asked the Emperor to issue a rescript forcing the Diet to accept his budget. The Emperor pointed to the importance of national defense and pledged a certain sum of his own money, asked the civil and military officials to contribute part of their salaries, and requested the Diet to appropriate the remainder of the funds. The opposition parties had no choice but to acquiesce in the face of imperial intervention.

The fact that their opposition could be quashed so readily by imperial intervention had a demoralizing effect upon the party men. This caused many to become cynical, leading them to yield to compromises and accept bribes. To make matters worse, the cleavage between the opposition parties began to widen again at about this time. The behind-the-scene efforts to bring Itō and the Liberal party together was in part responsible for this situation. Moreover, a growing divergence of opinion on foreign policy between the Liberal and the Reform parties began to develop, with the latter taking a harder line.

The fifth Diet met in November, 1893, only to find the political parties in serious disarray with the de facto leader of the Liberal party, Hoshi Tōru, under severe criticism by his own party members for maintaining covert ties with the government. He was also accused of accepting bribes, and his foes ultimately succeeded in having him expelled from the Diet. The split in the opposition forces was offset, however, by the fact that conservative, anti-party Diet members joined in the attack on the Itō cabinet for its vacillating and irresolute foreign policy, and in particular for its weak stand in regard to treaty revisions. Among the leading critics of Itō's foreign policy was Shinagawa, behind whom, it was believed, stood Yamagata.

Itō finally dissolved the Diet after repeatedly proroguing it. The next Diet, also consisting of a majority hostile to Itō, passed a motion of non-confidence, severely attacking his foreign policy. In June, 1894, Itō again dissolved the Diet, this time after it had been in session for only half a month. Clearly, a serious internal crisis was in the making. Precisely at this point, however, the domestic exigency was suddenly resolved by the eruption of a crisis abroad. The Korean government had asked the Chinese government to send troops to help quash a rebellion that was led by a religious cult, the Tong Hak (Eastern Learning) Society. Overnight the opposition parties and the press diverted their attention away from the internal conflict to focus on the Korean situation, and they collectively rallied behind the government's policy of intervention. The seventh Diet as well as the eighth, both of which were convened during the Sino-Japanese War, gave enthusiastic support to the government's foreign policy and war efforts.

THE KOREAN QUESTION
AND THE SINO-JAPANESE WAR

Japan had from the outset of the Meiji era harbored imperialistic designs toward Korea. Saigō's plan to contrive an incident to enable Japan to go to war against her was noted in an earlier chapter. In August, 1875, Japanese men-of-war ventured into Korean waters at Kanghwa Bay where they were fired upon by coastal defense forces. Japan used this incident as an excuse to persuade Korea, under the threat of force, to agree to establish diplomatic and commercial relations. Six months later, in February, 1876, Korea agreed to open three ports and accepted an unequal treaty, not unlike the ones that the West had imposed on China and Japan. The treaty may have held Korea to be an independent nation, but China still regarded her as a tributary state.

In Korea, conflicts were taking place between the conservatives and the progressives who, looking to Japan as a model, wanted to reform and modernize the nation. In 1882, an uprising broke out that was directed against the ruling family, which was dominated by the queen's relatives, the Min family. The movement took an anti-Japanese turn because of the government's practice of employing Japanese officers to reform the army. Furthermore, the shortage of rice and the inflation were blamed on Japanese merchants who, it was charged, had hoarded Korean rice. The rebels forced the king to flee and attacked the Japanese legation. The movement widened its antagonism toward outsiders and became decidedly anti-foreign when the conservative regent, Taewongun (the Grand Prince), who had been out of power since 1873, took over the leadership. The Chinese government, at the request of Queen Min, thereupon intervened.

In Japan the war faction, led by Yamagata, favored intervening for the purpose of gaining territorial concessions. A force of fifteen hundred troops was landed at Inchon, but the rebellion was subdued by the Chinese forces, and Japan had to be content with receiving indemnities. This incident spurred on the Japanese militarists to expand the armed forces in anticipation of further difficulties in Korea and of a potential confrontation with China over that nation. In 1882 a ten-year plan to expand the army was formulated, and in 1885 it was put into effect. The navy also launched a program of expansion and its budget continuously increased from 1883.

The conservative nationalists, the progressives, and even the radicals were united by a determination to protect Japanese interests in Korea. They also favored supporting the Korean reformers led by Kim Ok-kyun and Pak Yong-hyo. The opposition party members, however, were behaving in an irresponsible fashion because, although they were generally jingoistic when it came to the question of Korea and China, they continuously sought to reduce the government's military and naval budget.

China's position in Korea, after the troubles of 1882, was much strengthened by the presence there of her own military force, headed by Yüan Shih-k'ai. The Korean reformers, with the encouragement of some leading Japanese, such as Fukuzawa and Gotō Shōjirō, staged a coup against the Min faction in December, 1884. Kim and Pak had the support of the Japanese legation in Seoul, but the coup was crushed by the Chinese forces and the Japanese minister had to flee with the rebel leaders. Thereupon the Japanese government, ignoring the fact that their own officials were at fault, dispatched Foreign Minister Inoue

Kaoru and two battalions to Seoul, demanding an apology as well as indemnities. Public opinion in Japan, led by the liberals, called for a tough stand against Korea and China. Itagaki even organized and trained a volunteer army in Kōchi, while Ōi Kentaro actually made plans to go to Korea and assassinate the leaders of the Min faction. The plot was uncovered and Ōi was arrested by the Japanese authorities.

Realizing that Japan was not yet ready for war, the government leaders led by Itō took a more responsible position and sought a peaceful settlement. Itō went to Tientsin to negotiate with the Chinese leader, Li Hung-chang, and concluded the Li-Itō Convention, which provided for the withdrawal of Chinese and Japanese forces and military advisers from Korea. Both nations also agreed to notify each other if and when they planned to send troops into Korea in the future.

In Korea, Chinese influence was exerted on behalf of modernization by the Chinese resident, Yüan Shih-k'ai. Meanwhile Japanese commercial activities continued to increase in Korea, and this, in the opinion of the Koreans, only added to their economic woes. Japanese merchants cornered the Korean rice supply and imported manufactured goods, such as cotton fabrics and sundry items for household use. Unrest among the people continued and a series of popular disturbances broke out in the decade following the 1884 incident.

The discontent among the Korean people enabled a conservative religious cult, the Tong Hak Society, to gain popular support. It was basically anti-foreign and anti-Japanese in character. The founder of the organization incorporated religious ideas from native shamanism, Taoism, Buddhism, Confucianism, and even Catholicism to start a movement that, he claimed, would save Korea from Western encroachments while enriching and benefiting the poor and the lowly. In 1894, the Tong Hak Society staged uprisings in the southern provinces with the support of impoverished peasants. This movement provided the poor with a way of venting their anger against the officials who had been exacting heavy taxes from them. Unable to suppress the insurgents, the Korean government was forced to ask Yüan Shih-k'ai for assistance.

The Japanese government immediately decided to dispatch a brigade of troops when it received a wire from its Korean legation on June 2, claiming that the Korean government was planning to ask for Chinese military assistance to quell the rebellion. Three days later a decision was made to establish a supreme military command under the Emperor and begin mobilization. It appears, then, that the Japanese government was actually ready to go to war even before there was any real cause to do so.

The main architects of the policy that led to war were vice-chief of staff of the army, General Kawakami Sōroku, and Foreign Minister Mutsu Munemitsu (1844–1897). By the time the Chinese government notified the Japanese government on June 7 of its decision to send troops into Korea, the Japanese soldiers were already on their way to Korea. They landed at Inchon despite the report by the Japanese minister in Korea that everything was under control. In order to find an excuse to justify the continued presence of these forces in Korea, Mutsu conceived of a proposal that called for Sino-Japanese intervention in Korea for the purpose of bringing about reforms there. China rejected this proposal, whereupon the Japanese government went ahead and submitted their demands to the Korean government while at the same time ordering their own minister in Korea to find a pretext that would enable them to take direct action before some foreign power, namely Russia or England, had an opportunity to intervene.[3] In line with this policy, Japanese troops moved into the palace, placed Taewongun in power, and then compelled him to request the withdrawal of Chinese troops from Korean soil. On July 25, a naval clash occurred off the coast of Inchon between Japanese warships and Chinese vessels transporting reinforcements to Korea. The Japanese authorities then dispatched their troops against the Chinese forces on July 29 before finally declaring war on China three days later.

So far as the fighting itself was concerned, the Japanese army, better trained and better equipped, managed to drive the Chinese forces out of Korea without too much difficulty. The First Army, under General Yamagata, moved against Pyongyang and captured it in two days. The Chinese forces were then pursued to the north, and by the end of October Yamagata crossed the Yalu into Chinese territory. In addition, the Japanese navy gained supremacy of the seas by defeating the Chinese navy on the Yellow Sea on September 17. By controlling the seas, the Japanese were able to send the Second Army, under Ōyama, to the Liaotung Peninsula. On November 22, Ōyama's men captured Port Arthur, which had been built as an impregnable fortress. The Second Army was then sent to Shantung Peninsula to attack the port of Weihaiwei from the land while the Japanese navy attacked, and by February ultimately destroyed, the Chinese fleet that was anchored there. The First Army marked time during the winter months and subsequently launched its offensive against the southern Manchurian cities in February of 1895. It was then poised to strike against Peking.

At home the Japanese public was intoxicated by the repeated victories, and under the leadership of such liberals as Fukuzawa Yukichi and Tokutomi Sohō, the people were calling for the continued prosecution of

---

[3] England had offered to mediate between China and Japan, but China flatly refused. In July, England and Japan concluded a new treaty by which, among other things, England agreed to renounce extraterritorial rights for British subjects in Japan. Soon after this other Western nations agreed to revise their treaties and Japan finally resolved the problem of unequal treaties.

the war until Peking fell. The entire nation was united behind the war effort, and the Diet swiftly approved the military appropriations requested by the government. Even Christian leaders, like Uchimura Kanzō (1861–1930), regarded the military effort abroad as a just war that was being fought to assist Korea against Chinese oppression.

The government officials were, to be sure, pleased with the moralistic sentiments that united the people behind it, but they were also realistic enough to understand what Japan's limitations were and they were thus keenly aware of the danger that might result from a crushing defeat of China. Itō concluded that "if Peking is captured, the Ch'ing government will collapse and riots will break out throughout the land. Then the major powers will move in their troops, using as a pretext the need to protect their nationals in China. Also Japan would have no one to negotiate with and would be faced with an impossible situation." [4] As a result, the government moved with caution in spite of the fact that the press was clamoring for the annexation of Formosa, Manchuria, and other Chinese provinces. The two major political parties were vying to outdo each other in their imperialistic greed.

By the end of 1894, China showed its willingness to negotiate a settlement, and in March, 1895, Li Hung-chang arrived in Shimonoseki to work out a peace treaty. After a slight delay caused by a Japanese fanatic's attempt to assassinate Li, the two parties agreed to the Treaty of Shimonoseki. The terms provided for China to do the following: recognize the independence of Korea; cede the Liaotung Peninsula, Formosa, and the Pescadores to Japan; pay an indemnity of 200 million taels (360 million yen); conclude a commercial treaty with Japan similar to those China had contracted with the Western powers; open four additional ports; permit Japanese vessels to navigate the Yangtze River; allow Japanese subjects to engage in manufacturing in China. The human toll that Japan paid in the Sino-Japanese War came to more than 17,000 dead, a majority of whom had succumbed to the frigid Manchurian weather.

The Sino-Japanese War successfully launched Japan's career as an imperialistic power by giving her increased influence in Korea, an outpost to the south in Formosa, and a substantial toehold on the continent in the Liaotung Peninsula. The war also gave her an opportunity to display to the other powers that she was a serious rival and a threat to their own imperialistic designs. The country that was most upset by this development was Russia. She had her own designs on Korea and Manchuria and consequently persuaded France and Germany to join her in

[4] Hiratsuka Atsushi, *Itō Hirobumi Hiroku* (*The Confidential Papers of Itō Hirobumi*), 2 vols. (Tokyo: Shunjūsha, 1930), vol. 2, p. 105.

protesting the Japanese acquisition of the Liaotung Peninsula. France supported Russia because she was her ally; Germany backed Russia because she wanted that nation to turn East rather than get involved in European affairs. Furthermore Germany, as seen in her acquisition of concessions in Shantung in 1898, also had ambitions in China. France also gained certain privileges in southern China, while Russia, as noted below, extended her influence in Manchuria.

This liaison of Russia, France, and Germany provided a turn of events that was not wholly unexpected so far as Itō and Mutsu were concerned. Faced with the Triple Intervention they saw no alternative but to accede to the demand to return the Liaotung Peninsula to China. In exchange, Japan received an additional thirty million taels in indemnity from China.

This was a shocking blow to the Japanese public, and the public opinion makers exhorted the people not to forget the galling experience. The government reacted by immediately launching a program of vast military expansion. The number of army divisions, which totalled seven at the beginning of the Sino-Japanese War, was increased to thirteen by 1903. The naval tonnage, which had stood at 63,100 tons was increased to 153,000 tons by 1902. The defense allocations increased annually from constituting 29.5 percent of the total budget in 1890, to 55.6 percent in 1897.

China had ceded Formosa to Japan but this did not mean that she could simply move in and take over. Neither the Chinese residents of the island nor the indigenous inhabitants were willing to accept Japanese rule, and in May, 1895, Formosa declared its independence. Japan landed her troops and managed to disperse the Chinese forces on the island. The native inhabitants, however, persistently refused to accept Japanese rule and continued to carry on guerrilla warfare. The military campaign of subjugation was continued until 1896, but the guerrillas were not fully vanquished. The Japanese losses as a direct result of combat was small and only amounted to 164; but 4600 men died of malaria and other tropical diseases, and more than 20,000 had to be sent home because of illness.

Pacification by force was clearly not succeeding. In 1898, General Kodama Gentarō was appointed governor-general. He was convinced that the repressive measures adopted by his predecessors only served to fortify native resistance. His plan was to follow a policy of promoting the welfare of the populace as a means of winning their good will. He appointed Gotō Shimpei (1857–1929), who had proven himself an able administrator, as head of civil administration. He introduced such measures as land tenure reforms, health and sanitation programs, railroads, postal system, telegraph, and other public services. The production of rice and sugar was increased through the adoption of scientific and improved methods in farming and land utilization. The implementation of these measures led to the restoration of peace and order, and subsequently, to a flourishing economy. The colonization of Formosa thus proved to be a fairly successful venture.

The other legacy of the Sino-Japanese War, the Korean situation, continued to plague the Japanese government. During the Sino-Japanese War it had tried to introduce reforms there but failed to accomplish very much. Instead it got caught in the rivalry among Queen Min, Taewongun, and pro-Japanese reformist factions. In 1895, Inoue Kaoru was sent to Korea as the Japanese minister and he managed to place the pro-Japanese Pak Yong-hyo in charge of the government. Pak, however, was soon driven out by Queen Min's faction, which had Russian support. The queen began to cooperate more and more with Russia and this forced the new Japanese minister in Korea, Miura Gorō, to bring Taewongun out of retirement again. In October, 1895, they staged a coup against the queen, killing her and many of her lady attendants. These atrocities placed Japan in a most unfavorable light in the eyes of the Western powers; the Japanese government recalled Miura and his supporters and had them arrested. Anti-Japanese sentiments in Korea, however, did not abate. The king fled to the Russian legation and condemned the pro-Japanese faction, whose leaders were thereupon killed. Hence, it appeared as if Japan's influence was waning while that of Russia was ascending. The rivalry developing between Japan and Russia in Korea contributed to the eventual outbreak of hostilities between the two nations.

POSTWAR DOMESTIC POLITICAL DEVELOPMENTS

The domestic political scene after the Sino-Japanese War saw Itō and the Liberal party coming to terms and agreeing to cooperate. The leaders of the Liberal party wanted a share of the political power and they were also anxious to beat the rival Reform party to the seat of that power. They realized that the methods used in the Diet before the war were clearly not enabling them to achieve their objectives. Now that the government had the support of the Liberal party, it had little trouble passing its bills, including a record budget. In April, 1896, Itagaki entered the cabinet as Minister of Home Affairs. Despite Itō's growing flexibility toward political parties, he insisted that Itagaki sever his ties with the Liberal party before joining the government.

Japan's foreign relations, particularly with Russia, were growing precarious, so when Foreign Minister Mutsu resigned because of ill health, Itō planned to bring Matsukata and Ōkuma into the government in order to form a cabinet that would foster national unity. Itagaki, however, strenuously opposed letting Ōkuma join the government and Matsukata, on the other hand, refused to join the cabinet without Ōkuma. Itō thereupon decided to resign, turning the government over to Matsukata.

One of the reasons why the Meiji cabinet heads gave up the premiership so readily was that as members of the oligarchy they really did not remove themselves from the seat of power. They were genrō, and thus they remained a permanent part of the power elite as long as the oligarchy retained its power. There were, of course, disagreements and some personality clashes, but no genrō ever sought to remove a fellow oligarch from the inner circle. Hence Itō, who had been burdened with the office of Prime Minister for four years, gave up his post over an issue that was not really insurmountable.

Matsukata, in forming his cabinet, appointed Ōkuma as Foreign Minister. Prior to this the Reform party was reorganized and it merged with other minor parties to form the Progressive party (*Shimpotō*). This group gave their support to Matsukata, who was thus able to get his program through the Diet. As a reward, members of the Progressive party obtained many high posts in the bureaucracy. This alliance of convenience soon dissolved, however, because Matsukata became disturbed by the party's many ambitious members who wanted still more cabinet posts and a voice in formulating general policies. The Progressive party members decided that Matsukata would not meet their demands and they broke with him, joining the Liberal party in a call for a vote of no-confidence against him. Thereupon Matsukata dissolved the Diet and resigned. Once again Itō was asked to form a cabinet, which he did in January, 1898.

Itō intended to try once more to establish a coalition government that would include the leaders of the two major parties. He approached Ōkuma and Itagaki but was unable to meet their demands for key cabinet posts. Consequently, he formed another "transcendental" cabinet, that is, a cabinet above the parties.

The election held in March saw the Liberal party win 98 seats, thus again emerging as the largest party, this time, however, the Progressive party was close behind with 91. Itō sought to bring Itagaki into the cabinet, but his friend and Minister of Finance, Inoue Kaoru, objected. Itō was forced to face the Diet without the support of the Liberal party and in consequence of this, his proposal to increase the land tax suffered a crushing defeat. Thereupon he dissolved the Diet.

By now it was clear that the Satsuma-Chōshū faction could no longer govern effectively without the support of one or the other of the major parties. The only reason the political parties failed to gain greater power was their inability to work together. The oligarchy had consistently managed to take advantage of the feuds between the parties to split and thus effectively weaken the opposition. Now, however, after numerous efforts to achieve a coalition with the oligarchs had failed, the two parties finally decided to give interparty cooperation a try. On June 21, 1898, the Liberal and Progressive parties voted to dissolve themselves, and on the following day they joined together to form a new organization, the Constitutional party (*Kenseitō*).

Itō now faced a difficult situation because this union of the two parties meant that he could no longer play one group against the other. The way to meet the challenge, he believed, was to form his own political party. He conferred with his ally, Inoue Kaoru, and asked him to obtain the support of the business leaders. Inoue contacted the business tycoons and was able to win over men like Shibusawa Eiichi. Nonetheless, Itō failed to gain as much backing as he had hoped to receive. Iwasaki Yanosuke of Mitsubishi refused to support the movement because of his ties with Ōkuma and the Progressive party, and as a result of this, other business leaders began to hesitate also. The most adamant opposition to Itō's new political plans, however, was provided by his erstwhile political partner, Yamagata.

There had been no open break between the two men prior to this, but their relationship had become somewhat strained ever since constitutional government was initiated. Itō and Yamagata were certainly the outstanding statesmen among the Meiji leaders and both were equally dedicated to serving the national interests. Neither can be faulted when it comes to public service, patriotism, and unselfish devotion to the state; but there were differences between their temperaments and beliefs.

Compared to Yamagata, Itō was not only more flexible and more "civilian" in his outlook, he was also far more humanistic. He was most distressed about the killings that wars inevitably entailed and, in commenting on the Russo-Japanese War, he once lamented to Baelz, "The fight goes on. Massacre without end." He had a warm, open personality, and tended to be rather fun-loving. Baelz, who knew him well, called him "a devotee of Bacchus and Venus." Itō was apparently a fair and just man; he was not at all vindictive, nor did he tenaciously seek to control people or power. Baelz made this observation after Itō's death:

> He was neither choleric nor swashbucklerish, being
> tranquil in manner and almost always with a friendly
> smile . . . lighting up his face. He was disinclined to use
> strong measures. . . . In personal relationships Prince
> Itō was the unassuming and persistently cheerful little man

that he had been thirty years earlier when I became
acquainted with him as plain Mr. Itō.[5]

Even his critics credit him with having a broad perspective, an ability
to get able men to work with him, and a talent for harmonizing conflicting forces. He was a moderate—conservative in some respects, progressive in others. It is said that of all the Meiji leaders, Emperor Meiji
trusted and liked Itō the most. His major weakness was his tendency to
be indecisive, and this became a particularly serious flaw toward the end
of his career.

If Itō can be equated with yang (the positive personality), Yamagata
represents yin (the negative). The impression that history records of
Yamagata is of a severe, formidable, and inflexible figure. He was more
austere, more disciplined, and more rigid than Itō, whose warmth and
openness he lacked. Yamagata was cautious and calculating, and as his
follower Katsura remarked, he was also vengeful and unforgiving.

Politically, Yamagata was much more conservative and authoritarian
than Itō. He was the personification of the stern militarist, something of
a Machiavellian who was willing to use any means to keep the oligarchy
in control of power. His critics say that he contributed to the decay of
the political parties by using bribery as a means to undermine and
weaken them. Some even regarded him as a petty schemer. He gathered
around him able men who shared his conservative philosophy and, like
Shinagawa, they were inclined to rely on ruthless tactics to suppress the
opposition. He managed to establish a tremendous power base in the
army and the bureaucracy, but he seemed not to have won the affection
of many men.

Yamagata objected vigorously when Itō concluded that the political
dilemma facing the government could only be resolved by the formation
of a progovernment party.[6] In a meeting of the genrō, Yamagata contended that if Itō organized a political party, he would essentially be
paving the way to party government. "This would clash with our national polity, run counter to the spirit of the constitution granted by
the Emperor, and would degenerate into a democracy. I fail to understand why you seek to join the mice who form factions and take such an
irresponsible action."[7] Yamagata went on to admonish that it was unbecoming for a genrō to engage in such activities. As a result of these

---

[5] Erwin O. E. Von Baelz, *Awakening Japan: The Diary of a German Doctor,* trans.
Eden and Cedar Paul (New York: Viking, 1932), p. 392.

[6] It has also been suggested that Itō actually favored the idea of forming a political
party in order to curb the influence of the militarists led by Yamagata.

[7] Masumi Junnosuke, *Nihon Seitōshiron (Discourses on the History of Japanese Political Parties),* 4 vols. (Tokyo: Tōkyō Daigaku Shuppankai, 1965–1968), vol. 2, p. 295.

rebukes, Itō threatened to renounce all official ranks and ties and carry on as a plain citizen. Arguing that he could not maintain his cabinet without a political party, he proposed to resign and turn the government over to the Constitutional party. The other genrō were shocked at this proposal but, when Itō asked who among them would volunteer to form a new cabinet, none would come forward. Thereupon Itō resigned his post and recommended to the Emperor that Ōkuma and Itagaki be asked to establish a new cabinet.

The first party cabinet was formed on June 30, 1898, and for the advocates of popular rights the long struggle seemed to have ended in final victory. Yamagata wrote to one of his friends, "The Meiji government has finally fallen. . . . There is no need for a defeated old general to speak of wars any longer. There is nothing left to do but retire." [8] Itō was more sanguine: "Both Ōkuma and Itagaki are Japanese like us. There is no danger at all that they will let quarrels among Japanese affect relations with the outside world and lead the state astray." [9]

It was premature of the parliamentary leaders to rejoice in their victory for they were still unable to overcome the most formidable obstacle, their inability to work together. Moreover, despite what he might have said, Yamagata had no intention of retiring. Regardless of who headed the cabinet he could still exert considerable influence through the Minister of War, Katsura. The generals and admirals refused to cooperate with the new cabinet without Yamagata's consent, and this state of affairs ultimately forced Ōkuma and Itagaki to ask the Emperor to intervene. As a result, the war and naval ministers in the Itō cabinet were asked by the Emperor to continue to serve in the new cabinet. Katsura, who was Yamagata's loyal follower, remained as Minister of War and Saigō Tsugumichi continued as Minister of the Navy. Hence, it was from the very outset that Ōkuma and Itagaki had to contend with Yamagata's agents in the cabinet. Even before the cabinet was formed, Katsura pressed Ōkuma about armaments and made him agree not to reduce arms in spite of the fact that this had been the policy publicly declared by the Progressive party.

Theoretically there was one united party, but in fact, the old party divisions remained, and from the beginning partisan rivalry prevailed. To begin with, there was the thorny problem of dividing the cabinet posts between the two factions. The Progressive party seemed to have gotten the lion's share in that Ōkuma held the posts of Prime Minister and Foreign Minister, while three other posts were filled by Progressive party members. The Liberal party on the other hand, held only three

[8] *Ibid.*, p. 297.
[9] *Ibid.*

posts, with Itagaki serving as Minister of Home Affairs. The fierce contest for other high government posts further aggravated the hostilities between the two factions, and when a general election was held in August, they vigorously competed with each other despite the fact that nominally they belonged to the same party.

The breakup of the Ōkuma-Itagaki cabinet came about quickly through a quarrel over a cabinet post. In criticizing the influence of big business in politics, the Minister of Education, Ozaki Yukio, had said that Mitsui and Mitsubishi would be presidential candidates if Japan were a republic. Ozaki made it quite clear that he was speaking of a hypothetical situation and strictly for the purpose of illustration, but the members of the oligarchy and the Liberal party pounced on this speech to force his resignation. Ōkuma replaced him with another Progressive party member, Inukai Tsuyoshi (1855–1932), despite Itagaki's demand that a member of the Liberal party be given that post. Thereupon Hoshi, who had been rebuffed in his attempt to become Foreign Minister, proposed that the Constitutional party be dissolved and that the Liberal party members leave the cabinet. This was accomplished on October 29. The Liberal party reestablished the Constitutional party without the men from the Progressive party, who thereupon set about forming the *Kenseihontō* (Main Constitutional party).

Despite Ōkuma's willingness to carry on without the support of the old Liberal party men, he was compelled to resign. The Ōkuma-Itagaki cabinet had survived only four months. The political parties proved incapable of working together; rather than see their rivals succeed, they were willing to betray them and sell out to the genrō clique.

Hoshi had promised Yamagata the support of the Constitutional party in return for cooperation in overthrowing the Ōkuma cabinet. As a result, Yamagata returned to office in November, 1898, at which time Katsura advised him to take a tough stand against the political parties. If necessary, he said, "the Diet must be dissolved repeatedly, and even if the constitution has to be suspended the irresponsible activities of the political parties must be stopped." [10] Yamagata, however, felt he needed the support of the Constitutional party, and he managed to gain its backing without having to allocate any cabinet posts to it. The man who was instrumental in keeping the Constitutional party linked to Yamagata was Hoshi, who used a considerable sum of money to keep the party members in line. In addition, during this period Yamagata had obtained 980,000 yen from the secret funds of the imperial household to buy votes in the Diet. By resorting to bribery, Yamagata persuaded enough Diet members to support his tax bill, which substantially in-

[10] *Ibid.*, 302–3.

creased land and residential taxes, so that he was able to pay for military expansion.

The change in the land tax, which was scheduled to remain in effect for five years, entailed an increase from 2.5 percent of land value to 3.3 percent. Among other bills passed by the Yamagata cabinet was the revision of the voting regulations pertaining to the Diet as well as the composition of that body. The qualification for suffrage was dropped from 15 to 10 yen, and the representation for the cities was increased, with the result that the total number of representatives rose from 300 to 369. Moreover, the secret ballot was adopted at this time. This bill was passed in 1900 and put into effect for the elections of 1902.

Yamagata was genuinely concerned that the spoils system would corrode the bureaucracy completely if the political parties had their way. Consequently he revised the civil service regulations by removing from the appointment list all the bureaucratic posts, with the exception of a few top positions, and bringing them under the examination system. In so doing, Yamagata made certain that the spoils system would not undermine the bureaucracy, while at the same time he ensured its semi-autonomous existence as a bulwark of conservatism. The bureaucrats defied not only the political parties and the Diet, but at times they even challenged Itō. Yamagata revised the army and navy regulations to stipulate that only active army and navy officers of the two top ranks would be eligible to serve as ministers of the war and navy. He also enacted the Police Regulation of 1900, which was designed to curb the organizers of labor unions.

The members of the Constitutional party decided to terminate their collaboration with Yamagata when they realized that he was freezing the party politicians out of the bureaucracy as well as the cabinet. The Yamagata cabinet did stay in office for several months after the break with the party, however, because of the international crisis caused by the outbreak in China of the Boxer Rebellion of 1900–1901. The ever-ambitious Constitutional party leaders, such as Hoshi, then turned to Itō in an attempt to gain access to the government.

Itō had been planning to organize his own political party, and he was touring the country calling for an organization that would not make party interests its chief concern but would make the weal of the state its primary objective. The Constitutional party leaders invited him to join their group as its head, but he refused, insisting upon the necessity of a new party that would correct the defects inherent in the existing parties. Thereupon the Kenseitō leaders decided to dissolve their own party and join Itō's emerging organization.

As chief advisers in forming his party, Itō relied upon Hoshi and a newcomer to the political scene, Hara Kei (1856–1921), a former foreign office official who was then president of a major newspaper, the *Ōsaka Mainichi*. Itō's plan was to form a national party that would include representatives from all segments of the society, not only existing political party members but businessmen and bureaucrats as well. He was, however, opposed to the entry of "propertyless scoundrels." As it turned out, the core of his organization came from the Constitutional party; that is, they were old Liberal party members who had abandoned Itagaki and rushed to Itō's side because he offered them a much better chance of gaining power. The party was formally established in August, 1900, as the *Rikken Seiyūkai* (Association of Friends of Constitutional Government), and it included at its inception 152 Diet members, 111 of whom were from the Constitutional party. The Emperor supported Itō's venture into party politics by contributing 100,000 yen.

Yamagata had indicated his desire to resign in August in favor of Itō, but the task of organizing his party was not yet completed and Itō refused. Yamagata resigned anyway in the following month fully expecting, his critics said, that the Seiyūkai would be hopelessly disrupted if it had to come to power before the various factions within the party had managed to accommodate each other.

Itō was thereby forced to form his fourth cabinet in October, 1900, well before he and his party were ready to assume power. He filled all the cabinet posts with Seiyūkai men, with the exception of the ministers of foreign affairs, war, and navy. The Seiyūkai held a majority in the Diet, so Itō did not encounter much opposition in the lower house, but he ran into serious difficulties in the House of Peers. Yamagata had managed over the years to turn the upper house into his power base by appointing his followers to it. Moreover, the upper house had been purposely designed by Itō himself to curb the popular elements, and the peers thus resented his alliance with party men because they felt such an affiliation could result in a substantial strengthening of the lower house. In order to embarrass the Itō government, anti-Itō peers criticized him for not pursuing a more aggressive policy in China, where it was clear the Western powers were extending their spheres of interest. They also launched an attack against Itō's Minister of Communications, Hoshi, who was implicated in a graft scandal. Hoshi was forced to resign, and Hara was appointed to replace him. The peers then proceeded to reject Itō's tax bill, which had already passed the lower house. They repeatedly refused to heed his pleas and remained intransigent, whereupon Itō again turned to the Emperor and succeeded in having him issue a rescript asking the peers to coöperate. They reversed themselves immediately and passed the tax bill intact.

The House of Peers nevertheless remained hostile toward Itō, resenting the fact that he had once again turned to the Emperor to extricate himself from his difficulties. In the lower house the opposition party, the Kenseihontō, tried to have him censured, but the motion failed to carry. Many high-ranking bureaucrats also objected to Itō's political party ties; some officials of the Ministry of Justice even threatened to go on strike because the Diet had not approved an increase in their salaries. Internal divisions beset the cabinet when the Minister of Finance clashed with Seiyūkai cabinet members over the question of government spending on public enterprises. Itō procrastinated in resolving the internal conflict and, in May, 1901, he resigned his post after remaining in office for only seven months.

Thus, Itō's experiment with party government, which had aroused the hopes of many, failed miserably. Itō weakened rather than strengthened his position by seeking to be a member of the genrō clique and at the same time head of a political party. He could no longer count on the wholehearted backing of the genrō and the other components of the oligarchy, such as the House of Peers and the bureaucracy; yet his support in the Diet was not substantial enough to enable him to function without those establishment forces.

It turned out that the fourth Itō cabinet was the last one to be headed by a genrō. These men tried to perpetuate their tradition of leadership when Itō resigned, and they gave Inoue Kaoru the task of heading the next government. He failed in his effort to form a cabinet, however, and the genrō were then compelled to turn to Katsura Tarō (1847–1913) and Saionji Kimmochi (1849–1940), who were at that time in the second rung of the power structure. For the next twelve years the cabinet was to be headed alternately by these two men, although the genrō did continue to exercise power from behind the scenes. The man who turned out to be the most influential figure was Yamagata, not Itō, who went into semi-retirement.

Katsura had risen to the top in the army as Yamagata's follower, and he became Minister of War in January, 1898, in the third Itō cabinet. He served in that capacity in the Ōkuma, the second Yamagata, and the fourth Itō cabinets. The cabinet that he formed in June, 1901, contained several Yamagata men. He lacked support in the lower house but managed to get through the Diet session by appealing to Itō, who directed the Seiyūkai to support Katsura's budget. In 1902, Katsura enhanced his prestige by concluding the Anglo-Japanese alliance.

During the same year, the first general election for the Diet since the franchise had been enlarged took place. The Seiyūkai still maintained a slim majority, with 189 seats out of 376, while the Kenseihontō won 104 seats. This election resulted in a decline in the number of representatives from the agrarian, landowning class and an increase in those from the legal profession. The business class was not heavily represented in the

Diet, but their influence was fairly strong because of the fact that many agrarian representatives had invested their money in business and were consequently very sympathetic to those interests. The businessmen's influence in politics continued to grow as they broadened their ties with the major parties. The enhanced status of the merchant class, which was formerly scorned by the shizoku, was reflected in the growing numbers of businessmen who were accorded the status of peers.

Katsura had to deal with the combined opposition of the Seiyūkai and Kenseihontō when he faced the newly enlarged Diet. In order to expand the armed forces Katsura sought to renew the land tax of 1898, but this was opposed by the party members. Failing to get Itō to intervene, Katsura was forced to dissolve the Diet. The new Diet, however, turned out to be equally hostile, but this time Katsura managed to work out a compromise.

Exasperated with Itō's dual role as genrō and party head, Katsura, in consultation with Yamagata, asked the Emperor to request Itō to sever his ties with the Seiyūkai and become the head of the Privy Council. Itō, in effect, retired from active politics in July, 1903, because he was unable to defy the imperial command.

Itō's place as head of the Seiyūkai was taken by Saionji, a court noble who in his youth was interested in Rousseau's political philosophy. The political parties continued to bicker with Katsura, but he was now faced with a far more serious problem than domestic political infighting. This was the growing crisis in Russo-Japanese relations.

CHAPTER 15

THE
CONCLUSION
OF THE MEIJI ERA

THE RUSSO-JAPANESE WAR

After the Sino-Japanese War a rivalry between Russia and Japan developed in Korea, where the Russians seemingly had gained the upper hand by emerging as the king's protector. In the middle of 1896, Japan and Russia signed an agreement providing for mutual financial assistance to Korea and limitations on troops that could be stationed there. Russia, however, tended to be more active in Korea than was warranted by the agreement, and another convention, the Nishi-Rosen Agreement, was signed in April, 1898, reaffirming the provisions of the prior arrangement. Russia also agreed not to "hinder the development of commercial and industrial relations between Japan and Korea." Russia was more interested in extending her interests in Manchuria than in Korea, so a number of Japanese officials favored a policy of persuading Russia to recognize Japan's special interests in Korea in return for Japanese recognition of Russian interests in Manchuria. Russia, however, was unwilling to relinquish her influence in Korea.

Japan continued to expand her economic activities in Korea and by the turn of the century, she accounted for more than three-quarters of that country's foreign trade. Japan exported cotton products to Korea and imported rice. She also constructed railroads in south Korea, from Inchon to Seoul and from Pusan to Seoul, and she then began to move into the Yalu River Valley to develop the timber industry in a move to counteract the Russians, who had also gained timber concessions there.

Russia, in search of an ice-free port in the East, was entrenching herself in Manchuria. She had already put China in her debt by intervening to force Japan to relinquish the Liaotung Peninsula and by, at the same time, loaning her the money necessary to pay Japan additional indemnities. In May, 1896, when Li Hung-chang went to Moscow to attend the coronation of Nicholas II, China and Russia signed an alliance, the Li-Lobanov Treaty. Russia agreed to defend China against any Japanese attacks, and in the event that Japan attacked Russia, China was to open all her ports to Russian warships. The two nations also agreed to build a railroad across northern Manchuria, which was to be financed by a new Russo-Chinese bank. This line was to be called the Chinese Eastern Railroad, and it was to link the Russian Trans-Siberian Railroad with Vladivostok. The immediate territory through which the railroad passed was to be under the authority of the Russian Ministry of Finance.

The next Russian advances in Manchuria occurred after Germany acquired concessions in the Shantung Peninsula in 1898. Russia persuaded China to lease the Liaotung Peninsula and Port Arthur for a period of twenty-five years. She also obtained the right to build the South Manchurian Railroad, linking Harbin with Port Arthur. Thus Russia acquired from China what she had forced Japan to relinquish three years before. Port Arthur, though an ice-free port, was cut off from Vladivostok by Korea. Consequently, the Russian expansionists believed that they could not allow Japan to control Korea. Russia moved her troops into Manchuria when the Chinese Boxer Rebellion broke out in 1900 and then asked for further concessions from China as a condition for withdrawal. China, with Japanese diplomatic support, resisted these demands and compelled Russia, in April, 1902, to agree to a three-stage withdrawal of her troops from Manchuria.

These Russian activities in Manchuria and her continued interest in Korea caused some Japanese officials, led by Katō Kōmei (1860–1926), who was Foreign Minister in the fourth Itō cabinet, to begin to advocate an alliance with Britain as a way to strengthen Japan's position in case war should break out. Katsura soon became Prime Minister and he asked the Japanese ambassador to England to sound out the British on the idea of an Anglo-Japanese alliance; he received a favorable response.

England was now prepared to abandon her policy of splendid isolation because she had felt the adverse effects of this policy during the Boer War of 1899–1902. Also, because of the growing international tension in Europe, she felt she could not safely extend her forces to the Far East for the purpose of checking Russian ambitions there. An alliance with Japan, however, would ensure the protection of British interests in that part of the world.

In Japan there was disagreement between the faction led by Yamagata,

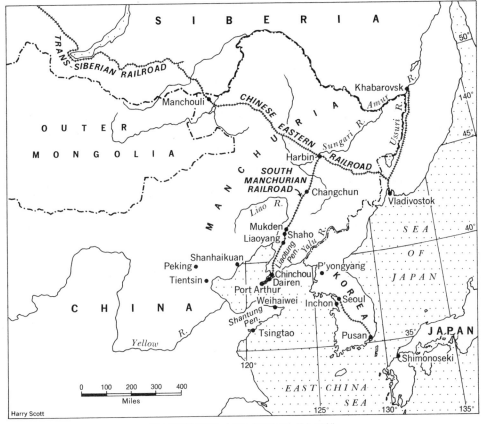

MANCHURIA AND KOREA. CA.1905.

which favored an alliance with Britain and the faction led by Itō, which felt that war could best be averted by arriving at some sort of understanding with Russia. Prime Minister Katsura and Foreign Minister Komura favored an alliance with Britain, whereas Inoue supported Itō's position. Talks with England were started when the British foreign secretary, Lansdowne, asked that serious consideration be given to the proposed alliance. As Anglo-Japanese talks were proceeding, Itō took advantage of an opportunity to go abroad (to receive an honorary degree at Yale University), and then proceeded to Russia to investigate the possibility of resolving the differences between the two nations. Itō's efforts not only produced negative reactions in Russia, they actually spurred on the negotiations with the British and, in January, 1902, the Anglo-Japanese Alliance was concluded.

The two nations agreed to maintain the status quo and general peace in East Asia, and to respect the independence and territorial integrity of China and Korea. They also recognized their respective spheres of interest in China as well as Japan's special interests in Korea. The alliance also provided that in the event one of the parties got involved in a war with another nation, the other party was to remain neutral unless the first party was attacked by more than one power.

The alliance, which was to run for five years, did not deter Russia from continuing to pursue her interests in Manchuria and Korea. Many high Russian officials wanted to avoid creating a situation that might lead to a war in the Far East, but one of the Tsar's advisers, A. M. Bezobrazov, persuaded him to take a more aggressive stance. As a result, the exploitation of the Yalu River Valley timber concessions was continued, and a viceroyalty in the Far East was established at Port Arthur, which was being turned into a major naval base.

Russia completed the first stage of her withdrawal of troops from Manchuria by October, 1902, as scheduled, but instead of making further moves when the second stage was supposed to start in February, 1903, she made additional demands on China. The Japanese leaders held a special meeting and agreed to pursue negotiations with Russia on the basis of the following: guaranteeing the independence and territorial integrity of China and Korea; recognizing Japanese and Russian rights and interests in Korea and Manchuria; and acknowledging Japan's special relationship with Korea. In an effort to resolve the differences between the two nations, four formal discussions between the two countries were conducted. Russia nevertheless continued her efforts to extend her privileges in Manchuria and in Korea, where she leased the port of Yongampo and began fortifying it.

Negotiations between Russia and Japan were proving unfruitful, and disagreement about how to cope with this situation began to develop among the Japanese leaders. The older leaders were anxious to avoid an armed conflict with Russia; Itō in particular was convinced that Japan could not possibly emerge victorious in such a war. On the other hand, the middle-ranking officers and officials took a chauvinistic position, while at the same time public opinion was also becoming increasingly jingoistic. Katsura later recalled to Baelz, "He himself had for a long time been reviled [by the press] day after day as a traitor and a coward, simply because he had wanted to avoid war if at all possible." [1]

Japan submitted her final proposals to Russia on January 13, 1904, and they were taken by the Russians to constitute an ultimatum because in urging quick action the Japanese insisted that "further delay in the

[1] Erwin O. E. Von Baelz, *Awakening Japan: The Diary of a German Doctor*, trans. Eden and Cedar Paul (New York: Viking, 1932), p. 312.

solution of the question will be extremely disadvantageous to the two countries." An agreement could not be reached, however, because Russia was unwilling to give Japan a completely free hand in Korea and Japan was unwilling to grant Russia a free hand in Manchuria. Neither side, of course, asked the Koreans or the Chinese how they felt about the situation.

The Japanese government, having failed to effect an agreement, decided on war on February 4. It notified the Russian government of its decision to break off negotiations and of its intention to take such independent action as it deemed necessary for the defense of its interests. On February 6, Japanese ships moved into Korean waters and headed toward Port Arthur for the purpose of destroying the Russian Pacific fleet. There was a naval skirmish off the coast of Inchon on February 8, and each side blamed the other for firing first. The main fleet, under Admiral Tōgō, proceeded to Port Arthur and attacked the Russians there on February 9, severely damaging several Russian warships. On February 10, Japan declared war. The initial Japanese moves in the Russo-Japanese War are often compared to her attack on Pearl Harbor, but in this case the Russians had ample warning of what was coming.

Despite Itō's pessimism about the chances for victory, Japan was in far better condition than Russia to fight the war. It was, first of all, much to her advantage that the fighting was to take place close to her home base. She had a trained manpower of about 850,000 men, with 180,000 in the active forces, and a male population of about 4 million who were capable of bearing arms. Her navy consisted of seven battleships, thirty-one cruisers, and additional smaller craft.

Russia, of course, had a much larger population from which to draw her fighting men, but she had the considerable problem of transporting them more than five thousand miles from Moscow to Port Arthur. The Trans-Siberian Railroad at Lake Baikal was not yet completed, so the troops had to be ferried across or marched over the ice in the winter. She had 135,000 troops east of Lake Baikal when the war started. Under the most favorable of conditions before the war she was able to transport about seven thousand men a month from Russia to Manchuria. At the outset of the war, however, the rate was lower because of numerous technical difficulties. Her fleet in the Far East consisted of seven battleships, eleven cruisers, and some smaller craft.

In the first few weeks of the war the Japanese fleet crippled the Russian vessels at Port Arthur and immediately gained supremacy of the seas. This enabled Japan to send her troops to Korea and Manchuria without any threat whatsoever from the Russian fleet. The First Army defeated the Russian forces that were defending the border between Korea and Manchuria and then crossed the Yalu River into Manchuria on May 1.

The Second Army landed on the Laiotung Peninsula and closed in on Port Arthur. The Third Army and the Fourth Army were added to these forces, and Field Marshal Ōyama, one of the genrō, was made commander in chief and had as his chief of staff General Kodama, who was regarded as the most able strategist among the Japanese generals.

On May 26, the Second Army clashed with the Russian forces around Chinchow and for the first time encountered assault from machine guns, a weapon that the Japanese would not have until the closing months of the war. In this encounter the Japanese suffered thirty-five hundred casualties but managed to capture the port of Dalny (Dairen), thus enabling General Nogi, commander of the Third Army, to concentrate on the seizure of Port Arthur.

The Russian commander, General Kuropatkin, planned to fight a defensive war until the Russian forces could be sufficiently strengthened by reinforcements. The Japanese, hoping to deliver a crushing blow before the arrival of those fresh troops, moved the First, Second, and Fourth armies toward Liaoyang where one hundred and forty thousand Russian troops were concentrated. The Japanese were outnumbered, but Ōyama nevertheless launched an offensive, and after twelve days of fighting the Russians commenced an orderly withdrawal to the north. The Japanese forces managed to drive Kuropatkin out of Liaoyang, but they suffered severe losses of fifty-five hundred dead and eighteen thousand wounded. The total Russian dead and wounded came to sixteen thousand.

In October, Kuropatkin launched an attack against the Japanese forces at Shaho but the results were indecisive. At this point it appeared that the Russians had superior fire power to the Japanese, who were, however, better led. There was relatively little action on the Manchurian plains until the battle of Mukden took place in the following spring.

From May to the end of the year, the Japanese launched a series of attacks against the Russian troops that were besieged in the fortress of Port Arthur. Every major attack resulted in heavy casualties for the Japanese soldiers led by General Nogi, who came under growing criticism for the futile and reckless expenditure of human lives. The port had to be taken before the Baltic fleet, making its slow and tortuous trip to the Far East, arrived. Finally on December 5, after bloody losses, they captured the 203 Metre Hill, from which the Japanese managed to shell the fortress and the Russian warships that were in the harbor. In January, after 240 days of fighting, including 156 days of direct siege, General Stessel decided to surrender the fortress. The Japanese toll of dead and wounded reached 57,780 in this conflict, while the Russians suffered 28,200 dead and wounded. General Stessel was severely berated for his action because when the fortress was surrendered there were 24,369 officers and men and 2.5 million rounds of small arms ammunition still left. However, more than half of the Russian soldiers were incapacitated.

The fall of Port Arthur gave a tremendous boost in morale to the Japanese, while in Russia criticism against the Tsar and the bureaucracy mounted. The revolutionaries were delighted. Lenin hailed the defeat saying, "the capitulation of Port Arthur is the prologue to the capitulation of Tsarism." [2]

The biggest land battle of the war was fought in March, 1905, at Mukden where three hundred thousand Japanese forces faced three hundred and ten thousand Russian troops. After a fierce ten-day battle the Japanese forces occupied the city as the Russian army retreated further north. The fall of Mukden was hailed as a major triumph although it did not constitute a decisive victory for the Japanese. The Russian army was still entrenched in the north awaiting further reinforcements and the arrival of the Baltic fleet, with which they hoped to wrest the command of the seas from the Japanese navy. The Japanese casualties at Mukden were estimated at seventy thousand and the Russian losses at ninety thousand.

The Baltic fleet, led by Admiral Rozhdestvensky, started its eighteen thousand mile trek in October, 1904. After a long and arduous journey fraught with difficulties, the weary Baltic fleet finally arrived at the Tsushima Straits on May 27, 1905, where Admiral Tōgō was waiting for it. He had accurately concluded that the Baltic fleet would try to make its way to Vladivostok by sailing between Korea and Japan rather than taking the longer route to the north of Japan. The naval battle, lasting twenty-four hours, resulted in a smashing victory for the Japanese fleet, which outdid the Russian ships in tactics and in the accuracy of its guns. Twenty Russian ships were destroyed, five were captured, six were interned in neutral ports, and only four managed to reach Vladivostok.

The Japanese victory had a decisive effect on the peace moves that had been in the offing since the fall of Port Arthur. The initiative for peace had been taken by President Theodore Roosevelt, who feared that the balance of power in the Far East would be upset if Russia were driven completely out of that area. Despite the victories, the Japanese leaders were aware of Japan's limitations in manpower and material resources. Her national debt, for example, had risen during the war from 600 million to 2.4 billion yen. There are indications that even as early as July, 1904, Japanese officials were seeking ways to settle the war, but the Russians were not ready to participate in peace talks until the Baltic fleet had a chance to engage the Japanese navy in combat.

[2] Quoted in Bertram D. Wolfe, *Three Who Made A Revolution* (Boston: Beacon, 1955), p. 279.

After the Battle of Tsushima, however, both combatants were willing to accept President Roosevelt's invitation to negotiate. Russia still had sufficient manpower and resources to carry on the war, but there was a growing restlessness among her people, and the country was rife with troublesome revolutionary activities.

During the war the Japanese public was overwhelmed by a tide of patriotism and national pride, and they supported the war effort with enthusiasm and selfless dedication. Not all thinking Japanese, however, succumbed to the impetuous call of nationalism. Some men, admittedly only a small number and primarily from among the Christians and the newly emerging socialist group, continued to express anti-war sentiments even after the actual outbreak of hostilities. This time the Christian leader, Uchimura Kanzō, did not support the war effort. He had been disillusioned with the results of the Sino-Japanese War, which not only failed to ensure the independence of Korea but, he believed, also brought about moral decay in Japan. He did not, however, take any overt action to oppose the war with Russia.

The leaders of the embryonic socialist movement, such as Kōtoku Shūsui (1871–1911) and Sakai Toshihiko (1870–1933), were aggressive in their opposition to the war. In November, 1903, they started a newspaper called the *Heimin Shimbun* (*The Commoner Newspaper*) and proclaimed egalitarianism, socialism, and pacifism as their guiding principles. As socialists, they viewed the war as a conflict not between the people, but instead between the aristocrats, militarists, and capitalists of the two countries. They sent an open letter to the Russian Social Democrats when the war broke out pledging their friendship because "for socialists, there are no distinctions of race, region, or nationality. You and we are comrades, brothers and sisters. We have no reason to fight each other. Your enemy is not the Japanese people, but it is the so-called patriotism and militarism of today." [3] The letter was printed in the Social Democrats' newspaper, *Iskra,* with the editors expressing complete agreement with the Japanese socialists. Kōtoku and Sakai's continued opposition to the war resulted in their imprisonment and the suspension of the *Heimin Shimbun.* Antiwar sentiments were also expressed by some writers. Yosano Akiko, for example, wrote a poem calling upon her brother not to sacrifice his life or kill the Russians. She asks, "Whether the fortress of Port Arthur falls/or does not fall,/is it any concern of yours?" [4]

In early August the Japanese and Russian delegations met in Portsmouth, Maine, to participate in peace talks. The Japanese delegation

[3] Sumiya Mikio, *Dainipponteikoku no Shiren* (*The Crucible of Imperial Japan*) (Tokyo: Chūō Kōronsha, 1966), p. 290.
[4] Fukao Sumako, *Yosano Akiko* (Tokyo: Jimbutsu Ōraisha, 1968), pp. 85–86.

was headed by Foreign Minister Komura Jutarō (1855–1911), and the Russian party was led by the veteran statesman Count Witte. Komura was instructed by his government to: (1) gain a free hand for Japan in Korea; (2) obtain the Russian concessions in the Liaotung Peninsula and also the South Manchurian Railroad between Harbin and Port Arthur; and (3) if possible, persuade the Russians to pay an indemnity and cede Sakhalin Island to Japan.[5] Russia's position at Portsmouth was that she had not been defeated and if necessary she could and would continue to carry on the war. The Tsar was determined not to pay any indemnity and not to cede any Russian territory.

The plenipotentiaries of the two countries met for about a month, from August 10 to September 5, but they were unable to agree on the Japanese demands for an indemnity and the cession of Sakhalin Island. A settlement was finally reached, with Japan withdrawing her demand for an indemnity and Russia agreeing to relinquish the southern half of Sakhalin Island. The terms of the Portsmouth Treaty provided for Russia to transfer to Japan, with the consent of China, the Liaotung Leasehold, the southern section of the Chinese Eastern Railroad, and the coal mines that had been worked by the Russians. The two nations agreed to withdraw their forces from Manchuria, except for guards to protect their respective railroads. Russia recognized Japan's "paramount political, military, and economic interests" in Korea, and ceded the southern half of Sakhalin Island.

The Japanese public, which had been so thoroughly intoxicated by the succession of military victories that they were completely unaware of the nation's inability to continue waging war any further, received the news of the peace treaty with incredulity, and they reacted with violent opposition to it. They had been led to expect far greater territorial gains, perhaps the cession of all the land east of Lake Baikal. Expansionist newspapers and opportunistic political leaders stirred up public anger with the government, focusing their wrathful expressions on Katsura and Komura, who were accused of betraying the country by accepting a humiliating treaty. Public meetings were held condemning the government and calling for the renunciation of the treaty and the continuation of the war. The movement was led by such ultranationalists as Tōyama Mitsuru (1855–1944), a leader of an ultra-right-wing group, the *Genyō-sha*,[6] and by leaders of the opposition party, such as Kōno Hironaka.

---

[5] The way had already been laid for the acquisition of Sakhalin by the Japanese seizure of the island in July, 1905. During early Meiji both Russia and Japan had claimed the territory, but in 1875 the two countries signed a treaty by virtue of which Japan agreed to recognize Russia's claim to Sakhalin Island in return for Russian recognition of Japanese rights to the Kurile Islands.

[6] The organization was named after *Genkainada*, the straits between Kyushu and Korea.

On September 5, protesters who had gathered to denounce the treaty soon turned into a violent mob that attacked public buildings, police stations, Christian churches, and a progovernment newspaper. The rioting continued the following day, throwing Tokyo into a state of anarchy, with the result that the government was compelled to impose martial law. It suppressed those newspapers that were publishing incendiary editorials and arrested two thousand rioters.

The public might have been dissatisfied with the peace settlement, but there is no question that the Russo-Japanese War established Japan as a major military and political power. The goal set by the Meiji leaders in the middle of the nineteenth century of "enriching and strengthening" the nation was seemingly achieved at last. Japan's victory had a great psychological impact upon the other Asian nations who were suffering from Western imperialism in that it proved conclusively than an Asian nation could successfully challenge Western powers in the battlefield. Furthermore, the Japanese triumph gave great impetus to nationalistic movements throughout Asia—in China, Vietnam, Indonesia, Burma, and India. Japan's success also brought about a shift in the attitude of Western nations toward her. This was especially true of England and America, who had been sympathetic to her during the Russo-Japanese War. Now, however, that the Russian advances into Manchuria had been stopped, Japan was seen as a potential threat to the balance of power in the Far East and to the open-door policy in China. Henceforth, Japan and the United States would find themselves frequently at odds on international controversies.

Victory in the war was achieved at a heavy cost: two hundred and twenty thousand men dead and wounded. The people had been willing to endure the suffering and sacrifice because they were convinced that a better life would follow the war. The amelioration of conditions did not, however, come about as anticipated, and the struggle for social and economic justice became more intense. The war, in fact, had strengthened both the emperor system and nationalism to a considerable extent, so the advocates of reforms were faced with even more formidable obstacles.

AFTERMATH OF THE RUSSO-JAPANESE WAR: FOREIGN AFFAIRS

In November, 1905, Komura proceeded to Peking and obtained China's consent regarding the Portsmouth Treaty provisions on the Liaotung Leasehold and Manchuria. In addition, he gained additional railway and economic concessions in Manchuria. The Japanese government then established the South Manchurian Railway Company to manage its railroad and other interests in south Manchuria. In order to prevent the other powers from extending their influence into Manchuria, Japan signed a secret agreement with Russia in 1907, which in effect divided Manchuria into Japanese (south) and Russian (north) spheres of interest. This move was initiated partly in response to the activities of the American railroad magnate, E. H. Harriman, who was seeking to gain railroad rights in Manchuria.

Korea was another area into which Japan moved swiftly. She wanted to consolidate the advantages acquired by Russia's recognition of her paramount interests there. Japan, in extending her influence, received the sanction of the United States by means of the Taft-Katsura memorandum of July, 1905. In this agreement the United States in effect consented to Japanese control of Korea in return for Japan's assurance that she would not extend her influence into the Philippines. In the following month, when the Anglo-Japanese Alliance was renewed, England also recognized Japan's paramount interests in Korea.

Having received the green light from the major powers, Japan then proceeded to turn Korea into a protectorate and, finally, a colony. In November, 1905, Itō Hirobumi, who was sent to Korea as the Japanese envoy, established a Residency General, whose primary task was the management of Korea's foreign affairs. This arrangement was put into effect in February, 1906, and Itō became the first Resident General. His primary intention was to introduce enlightened policies in Korea that would capture the loyalty of the Korean people. The Koreans, not unreasonably, bitterly resented the violation of their sovereignty and made no distinction between "good" and "bad" imperialists.

Itō did not restrict himself to controlling Korea's foreign affairs, he boldly interfered in her internal affairs as well. In July, 1907, he forced the Emperor to abdicate in favor of his son, who then agreed to give the Resident General the right to introduce administrative and legal reforms along with the right to appoint high-ranking officials. The Korean army was soon dissolved, whereupon patriots withdrew to the hills to organize opposition to the Japanese. Itō responded by moving twenty thousand Japanese troops against the rebels and burning down the villages where Korean nationalists were active. The resistance was not a minor affair— it is estimated that in 1907 fifty thousand men were involved in combating the Japanese and that by 1908 the number had risen to seventy thousand. Between July, 1907, and July, 1908, some 11,962 Korean "rioters" were killed.

On October 26, 1909, as Itō arrived in the Harbin railroad station to confer with Kokovtsov, the Russian finance minister, he was assassinated by a Korean patriot, An Joong-gun, who had vowed with his comrades to murder Itō and the Korean collaborators. Thus, the most significant architect of Meiji Japan died at the age of sixty-eight in a railroad car in northern Manchuria.

Yamagata and Katsura had both favored the annexation of Korea, but Itō had hoped to delay this action as long as possible. With his death, the annexationists moved swiftly and, in August, 1910, Korea was absorbed by Japan, and "the hardest and most relentless form of Imperial administration" [7] was imposed upon Korea.

AFTERMATH OF THE RUSSO-JAPANESE WAR: INTERNAL AFFAIRS

After the loose ends remaining from the peace settlement, such as the negotiation with China, were disposed of, Katsura decided to resign. He took it upon himself to recommend to the Emperor that the head of the Seiyūkai, Saionji, be his successor. In so doing, Katsura broke with precedent because usually the genrō conferred only among themselves to choose the Prime Minister. During the Russo-Japanese War, Katsura had promised to turn the government over to Saionji in return for the cooperation of the Seiyūkai. One of the conditions of that agreement was that Saionji was not to form a party government, and as a result, the government that came into existence on January 7, 1906, had only two Seiyūkai men in the cabinet, one of whom was Hara, who became Minister of Home Affairs.

The Saionji government, having come into existence under Katsura's auspices, continued its predecessor's policies in regard to the budget, retention of the emergency taxes, and nationalization of the railroads. This last measure encountered some difficulty since the Foreign Minister, Katō Kōmei, who was representing Mitsubishi's interests, opposed nationalization. He resigned, however, and the measure was approved by the Diet.

Now that the Ministry of Home Affairs was under the direction of Hara, Yamagata became concerned that the power base that he had built in the bureaucracy would be eroded. Consequently, he set out to undermine the Saionji government, beginning his attack by criticizing its laxness in controlling the socialists. Saionji had taken the position that "socialism too is one of the great movements of the world and should not be suppressed recklessly by police power. The more moderate socialists should be guided properly so that they too may contribute to the nation's progress." [8] Hence, when the socialists applied for official approval in early 1906 for a political party they had organized, the government readily granted it. Katayama Sen and men from the *Heimin Shimbun* were among the leaders of this new Socialist party. The membership

---

[7] Francis Hilary Conroy, *The Japanese Seizure of Korea: 1886–1910* (Philadelphia: University of Pennsylvania Press, 1960), p. 381.

[8] Shinobu Seizaburō, *Taishō Demokurashiishi* (*A History of Taishō Democracy*), 3 vols. (Tokyo: Nihon Hyōron Shinsha, 1954–1959), vol. 1, p. 89.

was split between those led by Katayama, who favored employing legitimate means and working through the Diet, and those led by Kōtoku Shūsui, who favored direct action. The activists tended to gain the upper hand when it came to organizing public protests.

In March, 1906, a public meeting to protest a projected increase in streetcar fare resulted in mob action and violence, and the subsequent arrest of many socialist agitators. The publication of the *Heimin Shimbun* was revived, but because of the provocative articles that filled its pages, it constantly came into conflict with the authorities. In February, 1907, the radicals, led by Kōtoku, managed to persuade the Socialist party to modify its policy from one of working for socialism "within the limits of the nation's laws" to one favoring a more aggressive position. This led the government to order its dissolution. In June, 1908, at a meeting of the socialists, two red flags with the words "Anarchism" and "Anarchic Communism" were hoisted. This resulted in the mass arrest of the participants.

Yamagata had advised the Emperor of the need for stricter control of the socialists just prior to the Incident of the Red Flag, and when this event took place he urged the Minister of War, Terauchi, to quit the cabinet. Saionji was informed of this, whereupon he immediately resigned without offering a plausible explanation, befuddling and disappointing those who had high hopes for the cabinet as the opening wedge for party government. Those who worked with Saionji during this period agree that he lacked political ambition; he was described as being "intelligent, indolent, and indifferent."

In July, 1908, the second Katsura cabinet came into existence. Katsura still retained the collaboration of the Seiyūkai through an understanding with Hara that he would pass the reins of government back to Saionji again. Despite some restiveness on the part of the more aggressive Seiyūkai members, Hara was able to keep the party in line. The Kenseihontō, on the other hand, was still unable to break out of its doldrums, strictly adhering to its negative position of inflexible opposition. During the second Katsura cabinet, the party merged with some minor parties and organized the *Rikken Kokumintō* (Constitutional Nationalist party).

Katsura dealt with two important problems during his second tenure. The first of these was an external issue having to do with the annexation of Korea. The second was a domestic issue involving a conspiracy to assassinate the Emperor. The plot was hatched by those on the extremist fringe of the socialist movement, the leader of which was Miyashita Takichi (1875–1911), a factory worker whose social conscience was aroused by the *Heimin Shimbun*. He conceived the idea of assassinating the Emperor after reading a book on anarchism. He tried, unsuccessfully, to gain the support of Katayama Sen, who at this time was convinced that reforms could be achieved through legitimate means and was working for universal suffrage. Miyashita then contacted Kōtoku Shūsui. After being released from jail for his anti-war activities during the Russo-Japanese War, Kōtoku had come to the United States and spent some time in San Francisco and Berkeley becoming acquainted with refugee anarchists from Russia. Upon his return to Japan he became the leader of the extremist socialists. By the time he was approached by Miyashita, however, Kōtoku had become a syndicalist and was convinced that the way to bring about a socialist society was through general strikes rather than individual acts of terrorism.

Miyashita managed to obtain the support of three other socialists, all close followers of Kōtoku. In May, 1910, before the conspirators could put their plan to assassinate the Emperor into effect, they were arrested together with a large number of other socialists, including Kōtoku. Twenty-four persons were charged with treason; twelve, including Miyashita and Kōtoku, were executed, and the rest were sentenced to life imprisonment. Some of those who were executed, were, like Kōtoku, innocent of the crime with which they were charged.

Out of a deep sense of anger and despair, one writer, Tokutomi Roka (Tokutomi Sohō's brother), had the following to say in an address to students at the First Higher School:

> Looking at it from the long-range interests of the nation, we have executed twelve anarchists now but planted the seeds which will produce innumerable anarchists in the future. The government officials who killed the twelve conspirators in the name of loyalty to the Throne are in fact the ones who are truly disloyal and unrighteous subjects. My friends, Kōtoku was killed as a rebel who conspired against the existing government. But we must not fear rebellions. We must not be afraid to become rebels ourselves. What is new is always revolutionary.[9]

The Katsura government was very much frightened by the conspiracy to assassinate the Emperor, and it therefore set out to repress all socialists. Its aversion and consequent vindictiveness reached such extremes that a school principal who had ordered some magazines on socialism just to find out what it was all about was fired from his post and prevented from ever gaining other employment. A book entitled *Society of Insects* was banned because of the word "society." The government then rallied the conservatives in the House of Peers to block a bill providing for uni-

---

[9] Sumiya Mikio, *op. cit.*, p. 444.

versal male suffrage that had already passed the lower house in March, 1911. One opponent in the upper house said, "This [universal suffrage] is based upon the theory of natural rights . . . and is founded on extremely dangerous thinking." The government disbanded the Association for Universal Suffrage, which had been in existence for ten years, and arrested anyone advocating universal suffrage. The political parties were so intimidated by these measures that they prohibited their members from introducing any bill calling for universal suffrage.

THE DEATH OF EMPEROR MEIJI

In August, 1911, Katsura again transferred the reins of government to Saionji. The major event during Saionji's second cabinet was the death of Emperor Meiji in July, 1912. The death of an Emperor need not necessarily mark the end of an era, but in this case it certainly did. The generation of leaders who had ruled in his behalf had also passed from the scene or were in virtual retirement; only four genrō, all in their seventies, were still living—Yamagata, Matsukata, Inoue, and Ōyama. The only one, however, who was powerful and ambitious enough to keep meddling in public affairs was Yamagata. The mode of control that the genrō had utilized for years was becoming ineffective, and the transition from their domination to party government took the form of Katsura and Saionji alternating in the office of Prime Minister. This game à deux was to come to an end also, and soon no cabinet could survive without the cooperation of one of the major parties. This change in the style of government was foreshadowed in the last Katsura cabinet (December, 1912–February, 1913), which was to last only two months because of the combined opposition of the major parties. Clearly, the days in which the oligarchy could pretty much have its own way were over.

On the international front, Japan's victory in the Russo-Japanese War brought the realization of the nation's initial objective of gaining recognition as a major power in the Far East. It also pulled Korea, an area that had been tantalizing the expansionists from the outset of the Meiji era, under her direct rule, thus bringing to a close phase one of her imperialistic dream. Japan had joined the ranks of modern nations.

The economy, as noted earlier, progressed to the second phase of modern economic growth around 1906. The working class was getting more restless and the socialists, though suppressed temporarily, were emerging as a force with whom the ruling class would very soon have to reckon. In 1906 more than a thousand miners at the Ashio copper mines rioted in protest against low wages and abuses by company officials. This was followed by troubles first in the Besshi copper mines and then in a coal mine in Hokkaido. During 1905–1906 workers in several major shipyards and arsenals rioted for higher wages. The year in which the

Emperor died was beset with major strikes throughout the land. The strike by the Tokyo streetcar workers that occurred in January is regarded as the first well-planned strike in Japan.

Emperor Meiji appears to have been manipulated by the genrō, but there is no question that he was very well-informed. To be sure, Itō and Yamagata were able to exercise what power they did only by virtue of the fact that the Emperor agreed with the policies they pursued. In the words of Tokutomi Sohō, "the general order in the nation was tied to the person of the Emperor." [10] He carried on his ceremonial functions with majesty and dignity. His presence is what gave Meiji Japan its special flavor.

The Emperor symbolizes the form of political authority and this makes his ceremonial functions so important, particularly in a country like Japan. Western observers have noted that,

> The familiar Western contrast of form and content is almost without meaning in the Orient. In this contrast, as well as in the word "form" itself, disparaging connotations are implicit. We say disapprovingly that a man observes the forms rather than the promptings of his inner nature; that he thinks in superficial analogies, regarding certain purely external features as the essential characteristics. In Japan and China, however, the formal is possessed of a constitutive meaning.[11]

Baelz, who had served the imperial court as a physician, made the following observations about the Emperor's personality and character. He had a retiring, "one might almost say a shy, disposition," And in fact he left the palace only when he had to perform public functions for he preferred to stay in a small suite of private rooms most of the time. "He had no taste for sumptuous festivals or decorative posturings before the world's eyes." [12] He was known to be frugal and displayed a concern for the well-being of the people as well as for particular individuals. For example, when Yamagata wanted to replace General Nogi for failing to capture Port Arthur swiftly, the Emperor rejected the proposal because, as he said, "if he were relieved, Nogi would probably not remain alive."

The institution of the emperor constituted the main pillar of the Meiji political system. It was the single most effective instrument em-

[10] Tokutomi Iichirō, *Taishōseikyokushi-ron* (*Discourses on the History of the Taishō Political Situation*) (Tokyo: Minyūsha, 1916), p. 46.

[11] Emil Lederer and Emy Lederer-Seidler, *Japan in Transition* (New Haven, Conn.: Yale University Press, 1938), pp. 100–101.

[12] Baelz, *op. cit.*, p. 395.

ployed by the ruling elite to retain their authority. The transformation of the imperial court from an empty institution, virtually unknown to the masses during the Tokugawa era, into an institution that claimed unquestioned, absolute sovereignty was one of the key achievements of the Meiji leaders.[13]

The Emperor was given a religious, a political, and a military function to perform in the society. He retained his historical function as the god-king, who acted in a religious capacity as the intermediary between the gods and the people. The ancient concept of the unity of religion and government still prevailed, and the Emperor was thus considered to be the spiritual and moral leader of the people. Politically, he derived his authority from his ancestors as well as from the Meiji constitution, which legally invested in him the sovereign power of the nation. The military function he had was that of supreme commander of the army and navy; all members of the armed forces were to remain loyal to him above all, while serving him "as limbs serve the head."

The moral textbooks, the Imperial Rescript on Education, and the constitution all contributed to the development in the people of a sense of loyalty and attachment to the Emperor. For example, the moral textbooks depicted the Emperor as the father of the entire nation, and loyalty to him was equated with the virtue of filial piety. The Sino-Japanese War also had an important effect in strengthening the emperor system. Baelz observed that the victory was

> explained as the outcome of the wonderful peculiarities of the Japanese and, in this self-adulation, talk of the "immemorial dynasty" of the imperial house played a great part. The upshot was that the position of the imperial family was strengthened by the crisis. . . .
> His portrait hung on the walls of every office, every school, and on ceremonial occasions all those present solemnly bowed their heads before it. An edict was issued describing the Emperor as the father of his people, and this edict was made the foundation of moral education in Japan. Thus was there revived a quasi-religious worship of the Emperor as the symbolical representative of the nation.[14]

This kind of reverence for the imperial symbol brought tragic results also. One popular novelist recalled that his father, who was a principal

[13] As late as 1880, Baelz lamented on the Emperor's birthday, "It distresses me to see how little interest the populace take in their ruler. Only when the police insist on it are houses decorated with flags." (*Ibid.*, p. 62.)

[14] *Ibid.*, pp. 115–16.

of a primary school, was compelled to take the blame and commit hara-kiri when the Emperor's photograph, which was "enshrined" at the school, accidentally burned in a fire.

Emperor Meiji had, by the latter period of his life, won the affection and loyalty of most of his subjects and when news of his illness appeared, thousands of people gathered before the imperial palace to pray for his recovery. Concerning his death, the central figure in one of Natsume Sōseki's novels says, "at the height of the summer, Emperor Meiji passed away. I felt as though the spirit of the Meiji era had begun with the Emperor and had ended with him. I was overcome with the feeling that I and the others, who had been brought up in that era, were now left behind to live as anachronisms." [15] On the day of the Emperor's funeral, General Nogi and his wife committed suicide so as to join him in death.

MEIJI JAPAN: AN ASSESSMENT

Despite all the difficulties and problems that beset the people, the Meiji era can nevertheless be considered to have been a magnificent half-century for Japan, perhaps the most remarkable such period in all her history. She emerged, with a modern army and navy, from a secluded feudal nation into one of the world's major powers. Japan had industrialized sufficiently during this period to lay the groundwork for the next phase of her growth, in which she was to rank economically among the major industrial nations. She had adopted Western political and legal institutions and was consequently accorded equal treatment by the Western powers, who relinquished the special privileges they had acquired from her in the mid-nineteenth century. Party government had not yet come into its own, but it was very definitely on the horizon. Constitutional government, though imperfect, had unquestionably become an established institution; and if rule-*of*-law had not yet become a reality, at least rule-*by*-law had come about.

Some critics have labeled the Meiji government "totalitarian," but there was certainly nothing like the kind of authoritarianism that had prevailed half a century earlier. There was still, of course, aristocrats and commoners, and the gap between the rich and the poor did continue to grow. However, there was legal equality and, theoretically, an open society with some degree of social mobility had come into existence.[16] Universal education had been introduced; in 1900 tuition fees were eliminated, and in 1907 compulsory education was extended to six years.

---

[15] Natsume Sōseki, *Kokoro*, trans. Edwin McClellan (Chicago: Regnery, 1967), p. 245.

[16] An indication, though minor, of developing social mobility can be seen in the increase in the percentage of commoners in government posts, both civil and military, from 1891 to 1899. In 1891 the percentage was 29; it rose to 35 by 1895 and to 42 by 1899.

Despite the two-year extension, school attendance was over 98 percent in 1908.

The extent to which Japan was modernized by the end of the Meiji era is a matter of controversy. Okakura Kakuzō remarked at the turn of the century, "Accustomed to accept the new without sacrificing the old, our adoption of Western methods has not so greatly affected the national life as is generally supposed. One who looks beneath the surface of things can see, in spite of her modern garb, that the heart of Old Japan is still beating strongly." [17] A Western observer saw strong imprints of old Japan in "the ideal of feudal loyalty, the patriarchal system, the attitude toward women, the exaltation of the martial virtues." [18]

Vestiges of traditional Japan were still strongly embedded in the social practices and the attitudes of the people. In the rural areas, in particular, the traditional ways and values still governed all phases of the people's lives. Western individualism certainly had not permeated the society, and it would appear that even later, in the Taishō era, when "democracy" was in ascendancy, the rugged individualism so characteristic of Western societies never really triumphed. This was also true in the highly competitive business world where the contending parties typically organized themselves around groups. Family-centered business empires like the Mitsui, Mitsubishi (Iwasaki), Sumitomo, and Yasuda constituted cliques of financial and business interests. Lafcadio Hearn, writing at the turn of the century, observed that the Japanese continued "to think and to act by groups, even by groups of industrial companies." Hearn goes on to point out that,

> In theory the individual is free; in practice he is scarcely
> more free than were his forefathers. Old penalites for
> breach of custom have been abrogated; yet communal
> opinion is able to compel the ancient obedience. . . .
> No man is yet complete master of his activities, his time,
> or his means. . . . The individual of every class above
> the lowest must continue to be at once coercer and co-
> erced. Like an atom within a solid body, he can vibrate;
> but the orbit of his vibration is fixed.[19]

The ruling class deliberately fostered and strengthened the familial characteristics of Japanese life in the new institutions that were emerg-

---

[17] Kakuzo Okakura, *The Awakening of Japan* (New York: Appleton, 1905), pp. 189–92.
[18] E. H. Norman, *Japan's Emergence as a Modern State* (New York: Institute of Pacific Relations, 1940), p. 8.
[19] Lafcadio Hearn, *Japan, An Attempt at Interpretation* (New York: Macmillan, 1913), pp. 420–27, 496.

ing. We have already noted this in the concept of the state and the Emperor.[20] In the industrial realm, factory owners were depicted as being fathers of the workers, and as such they were expected to manifest a paternalistic interest in their welfare by, for example, sponsoring mutual aid societies and training the girl workers in the domestic arts of sewing and flower arrangement. In return the workers, as children, were expected to be obedient and loyal to their employers, their fathers. Even the large business combines, the zaibatsu, were basically family-centered organizations. In the army also an effort was made, after the Russo-Japanese War, to equate the relationship between the company commander and the soldier with that of father and son. Paternalistic "benevolence" and "humaneness" failed, however, to humanize the army, which on the contrary became one of the most mercilessly disciplinarian and inhumane institutions in the world.

Bearing these qualifications in mind, we can still say that Japan at the end of the Meiji era was well on the way to becoming a modern, industrial power. The question is frequently raised about why Japan managed to modernize in fifty years or so while China, which was exposed to the West much earlier, fell so far behind. No doubt, a complex webbing of intertwining reasons accounts for this, but first some of the obvious differences in the situations facing the two countries should be noted. For one thing, Japan was a much smaller, more compact nation in which there was a stable, fairly centralized political system in existence even during the Tokugawa period. In China the pull toward regionalism got stronger as the central government weakened, whereas in Japan, even though the regional forces managed to overthrow the central government, they replaced the Bakufu with a much stronger central government instead of establishing divers regional ones. Throughout the country, as a result, it could effectively enforce its policy of "enriching and strengthening" the nation.

Another obvious difference in the situations facing the two countries is that the Western powers interfered much less in the internal affairs of Japan than they did in China, which was ultimately reduced to the status of a semicolonial nation. Still another noteworthy difference has

---

[20] The prewar Japanese family usually consisted of the stem family, that is, a man, his wife, his unmarried siblings and children, and his eldest son and his family. The family register that was kept at the local government office was based upon the stem family. The head of the household held legal ownership of the family property, had the right to determine the occupation of family members, determined the place of residence, and approved or disapproved of marriages and divorces. A son under thirty years of age and a daughter under twenty-five had to obtain the approval of their father and the household head in order to marry. In return for his rights, the family head was responsible for the well-being of the family members. The principle of primogeniture governed the succession to the position of family head.

to do with the fact that Japan was ruled by a military class that by its very nature was much more practical than the Confucian scholar-officials of China. The challenge posed to Japan, and to China for that matter, was primarily military in essence. The Japanese warriors immediately recognized the need to adopt Western arms and military techniques if they were to modernize and thus cope effectively with the foreign threat. They further realized that any program of modernization would depend heavily upon the adoption of Western science, technology, and industrialization. They were even willing to adopt Western political and social systems if these were deemed necessary for national survival.

In striking contrast to this rather pragmatic approach on the part of the Japanese military class, the Chinese ruling class was immersed in a sense of cultural superiority and enthnocentrism. This, of course, is quite understandable when you consider that China had been the center of the Asian world—which to the Chinese was the entire world—for thousands of years. China had a civilization that could be traced back three thousand years or more, and her institutions, values, and ways had served the needs of the society for more than two thousand years. As far as the Chinese were concerned, the golden age was in the past and if disorder or troubles came about, they occurred because the people had departed from the traditional values and ways. As a result, whenever the country was faced with difficulties, and this includes the crisis in the nineteenth century, the ruling class endeavored to reform the institutions and tighten the moral standards to approximate as nearly as possible those of the golden age of the past. It did not seek to resolve the problems by introducing innovations or by adopting alien institutions and values.

Japan, on the other hand, had been historically receptive to outside influences. As we observed earlier, for several hundred years after the fifth century she readily adopted and adapted Chinese civilization on a large scale. Subsequently from time to time she continued to subject herself willingly to influences from Korea and China. In the sixteenth century she even welcomed the advent of Christian missionaries. The ultimate rejection of Christianity, as we saw, was not due to cultural intolerance, it was strictly the result of political considerations. This long inbred tendency to learn and borrow from other cultures led the Japanese, when they were exposed to Western civilization in the nineteenth century, to reject the counsel of the seclusionists and turn enthusiastically to the importation of things Western. There was no psychological barrier to hinder seriously an all-out effort at modernization.

Another key factor that contributed to the relatively rapid modernization of Japan was the attitude or character of the people. The masses had been trained to be obedient and work hard during the centuries of feudal rule. Lafcadio Hearn made this observation about their tradition of obedience: "The probable truth is that the strength of the government up to the present time has been chiefly due to the conservation of ancient methods, and to the survival of the ancient spirit of reverential submission." Hearn goes on to comment about the great sacrifices willingly made by the people and their unswerving obedience "as regards the imperial order to acquire Western knowledge, to learn Western languages, to imitate Western ways."[21]

Undeniably the Japanese have always been a well-disciplined, industrious, and energetic people; and unlike people living in extremely impoverished countries, hard work enabled them to survive. These qualities should not, however, be considered as having given the Japanese an edge over the Chinese because the latter were also extremely diligent and industrious. Nevertheless, it is true that the Chinese were probably less regimented than the Japanese because they were not ruled by a sword-bearing military class that was ready to cut down any commoner who stepped out of line. The virtues of hard work, thrift, self-discipline, obedience, and selfless service had been instilled in the Japanese people by the edge of the sword.

It is also possible that the Japanese in the nineteenth century possessed a much more dynamic outlook than their contemporaries in China. Like the Chinese, the Japanese were influenced by Confucianism but, in addition, they were molded by Shinto and the outlook of the warrior. Also, Zen Buddhism flourished to a greater extent in Japan than in China. Shinto had the effect of accentuating national pride, the sense of being unique, and the desire to excel. The samurai outlook fostered activism, stressing spiritual discipline, physical superiority, and military excellence. Zen Buddhism, which influenced the samurai more than the other classes, made the ruling class vigorous, decisive, and highly disciplined.

Another noteworthy factor is that Japan was endowed with a large number of exceptionally able leaders during the critical years of Meiji. These men had the foresight and will power to chart the course of Japan and channel the energy of the people into enterprises that contributed to "enriching and strengthening" the nation. The Meiji Restoration was brought about by four outstanding leaders, Saigō, Ōkubo, Kido, and the court noble, Iwakura. They were succeeded as architects of the new Japan by statesmen like Itō, Yamagata, Inoue, Matsukata, and Ōkuma. At the center was an enlightened monarch who knew precisely who could be trusted and relied upon. At the nongovernmental level there were outstanding educators and *philosophes,* like Fukuzawa, who helped

[21] Hearn, *op. cit.,* pp. 454–55.

to create the necessary climate of opinion for the advancement toward "civilization and enlightenment."

In the business realm a significant number of enterprising leaders emerged from the samurai class to build the new industrial society. Iwasaki Yatarō would be an especially prominent example, and as one economist notes, "the role of the samurai families in founding Japan's business class can hardly be exaggerated." [22] There were even some business leaders who emerged from an agrarian background, like Shibusawa, although his would be an exceptional case. The traditional merchant houses, of course, provided their share of leaders even though they tended to adhere more closely to merchandizing and banking. They did not actually turn to industrial activities until new blood was injected into them from the former samurai class. In this respect, also, Fukuzawa played an extraordinary role in that his academy produced a large number of exceptionally able businessmen who became key executives in the major companies and thus played crucial roles in the industrialization of Japan.

Another factor to be noted is the relatively high rate of literacy that prevailed in Tokugawa Japan. This meant that not only was the samurai class literate but also the leaders among the villagers and some common peasants were able to read and thus could be exposed to ideas from the West through books, tracts, and journals dealing with "civilization and enlightenment," as well as scientific and technological matters. The Meiji leaders were consequently able to count upon a fairly large body of informed and intellectually sophisticated leaders at the middle and even lower levels of the society to assist in the task of propelling the nation toward modernization.

As we noted earlier, economic developments in the later stages of the Tokugawa era were sufficiently favorable for a fairly rapid transformation to take place from a feudal economy to a modern economic system.

At the end of the Meiji era it would have been difficult to assess whether or not modernization would be beneficial to the nation and the people as a whole. In fact the answer is still not available today, but Japan like other modern, industrial nations is now faced with the task of reevaluating the entire process of modernization and the consequent changes that science, technology, rationalism, and individualism have brought about. For the Japanese of the Meiji era, modernization was already a mixed blessing. The cost was borne primarily by the masses in terms of the following: the greater burdens imposed upon the peas-

---

[22] Yasuzō Horie, "Modern Entrepreneurship in Meiji Japan," in William W. Lockwood, ed., *The State and Economic Enterprise in Japan* (Princeton, N.J.: Princeton University Press, 1965), p. 195.

antry; the dehumanizing practices that accompanied industrialism in the exploitation of factory and mine workers; and the brutalizing effects of modern militarism.

The Meiji leaders envisioned as the object of modernization, not so much the well-being of the people, as fukoku kyōhei, the enrichment and strengthening of the nation. In terms of the goals they had established, they were well on the way to achieving their objectives. In the process, however, the masses were treated merely as means to an end, as laborers and cannon fodder. Voices were, nevertheless, beginning to be heard speaking up for the rights and welfare of the masses. The reign of Emperor Taishō was to be characterized by the ascendancy of democratic forces.

CHAPTER 16

ERA OF PARLIAMENTARY ASCENDANCY (I)

The Emperor Taishō (1879–1926), who succeeded Emperor Meiji, was in poor health and did not take as active an interest in the affairs of the state as his father did. His physical difficulties, moreover, made it necessary for his son to assume his duties in 1921 and act as regent. Hence, Emperor Taishō did not leave a strong personal imprint upon his reign in the way that Emperor Meiji did. The most serious consequence of the Emperor's weakness was that it created a situation in which the imperial institution could be more easily manipulated by the genrō clique, who were trying at the time to shore up their diminishing authority against the ascendant political parties. Nonetheless, the genrō, for all their desperate and scheming tactics, were incapable of preserving the tradition of nonparty government. They were unable to turn or hold back the tide of history because each man that came to head the government was compelled at one time or another to find some link and base of support in the existing political parties. In September, 1918, the first true party government came to power under Hara. This form of rule, except for a brief hiatus, was to hold sway in Japan until the assassination of Prime Minister Inukai on May 15, 1932.

The period covered in this and the following chapter is the era during which democratic forces reached their high point in prewar Japan. It coincides roughly with the first part of the second phase of modern economic development when the so-called modern sector of the economy grew significantly. This development intensified the reformist activities of the labor and socialist leaders. In the meanwhile Japan, regardless of who was in charge of the government—bureaucrats or party leaders—continued its policy of continental involvement, which kept the military forces actively involved in politics even in the halcyon days of party government.

INTERNAL POLITICAL AFFAIRS: 1912–1918

The chief political problem confronting the second Saionji government was the army's desire to increase its size. In 1906, a decision had been made to expand the army from seventeen to twenty-five divisions. In the first phase of the expansion program four divisions were to be added, but only two of these had been added by 1911. Since it was Saionji's policy to reduce expenditures, he favored delaying the army's project further. At the same time, however, he agreed to increase naval expenditures. The Minister of War, General Uehara, tendered his resignation to the Emperor when he discovered that the Saionji cabinet did not favor creating the two additional divisions immediately. Lacking the positive support of either Yamagata or Katsura, Saionji again resigned.

The leaders of the government, after failing to find a suitable successor to Saionji, finally turned once again to Katsura, who had been placed in semiretirement as the Lord Keeper of the Privy Seal. He formed a cabinet consisting largely of bureaucrats because, having been disappointed in his past associations with the Seiyūkai, he was not about to make any efforts to reestablish ties with Hara and his followers.

Katsura was confronted with strong opposition from the very outset. The journalists and party politicians aroused public opinion against the army's demands for more divisions, while the business leaders, who favored reducing government expenditures, vehemently opposed increasing the defense budget. The party leaders with the support of business leaders, especially Mitsui, proceeded to organize the Association to Protect Constitutional Government (*Kensei Yōgokai*) in order to eradicate the "han oligarchs." The supporters of the association held rallies directed against the ruling clique.

Katsura concluded that he needed to establish his own power base in the Diet and, following the path taken by Itō in 1900, he set out to organize a new political party under his control. He turned to the faction in the Nationalist party (the former Kenseihontō) that had previously indicated a desire to collaborate with him, and in so doing he produced a serious split in that group. Katsura also expected a fairly large number of Seiyūkai men to break with their party and join him, but his organizational campaign failed to draw even a single one of them. His new party, the *Rikken Dōshikai* (Constitutional Association of Friends), consequently attracted only eighty-three Diet members.

The Seiyūkai leaders now threw their support behind the Association to Protect Constitutional Government and then joined forces with the remnant of the Nationalist party to push for a vote of no-confidence against Katsura. Thereupon Katsura prorogued the Diet and got the Emperor to issue a rescript to Saionji asking him to resolve the political crisis. Saionji felt obliged to comply with the Emperor's wishes, but he explained to the party leaders that he understood that they were representatives of the people and as such they would naturally have to persist in representing their views. Saionji severed his ties with the Seiyūkai and as chief retainer of the nation joined the ranks of the genrō. The Seiyūkai, however, refused to withdraw the no-confidence bill and, in effect, defied the imperial command. Katsura had decided to dissolve the Diet but, faced with growing support for the opposition, he unexpectedly resigned instead. Thus, public opinion and the opponents in the Diet succeeded in overthrowing the Katsura cabinet. This event is referred to as the Taishō Political Crisis.

The genrō, Yamagata and Matsukata, now joined by Saionji, selected Admiral Yamamoto Gonnohyōe (1852–1933) of Satsuma as Katsura's successor. Yamamoto agreed to form the new cabinet with the understanding that the Seiyūkai would support him. As a result, three Seiyūkai men, including Hara, joined the cabinet organized in February, 1913. Once again the Seiyūkai leaders failed to adhere to their pledge to break the power of the ruling clique and abandoned the Association to Protect Constitutional Government.

The Yamamoto cabinet introduced several popular reforms. For one thing it succeeded, even in the face of strong opposition from the army, in revising the regulation, which was originally proposed by Yamagata in 1900, requiring the ministers of war and navy to be active generals or admirals of the two top ranks. The regulation was revised to make those who had already retired from these two top ranks eligible for these posts. Under the prodding of Hara, Yamamoto revised the civil service regulation that proscribed political appointments of high ranking bureaucrats, making the post of vice-minister an appointive position. Yamagata tried to block this change in the Privy Council, but Yamamoto threatened to purge that organ of the government and pushed through the revision. He also reduced the size of the Privy Council from twenty-eight to twenty-four and cut the number of bureaucrats by more than sixty-eight hundred. Together with other government personnel, a cut of ten thousand employees was effected, reducing the budget for the year 1913 by 11 percent. Yamamoto, however, was not bent on economy for the sake of economy; the savings were to be used for naval expansion.

Just when it appeared as if Yamamoto had devised a very strong and stable cabinet, a wholly unforeseen event wrecked it all. In January, 1914, the news broke that Japanese naval officers had been bribed by the Siemens Munitions Firm of Germany to obtain contracts for munitions and wireless materials. In the course of the investigation other instances of bribery involving naval officers came to light, whereupon the opposition parties seized this opportunity to strike at Yamamoto and rouse public opinion against him. At a protest rally held in Tokyo, clashes between the police and the protesters occurred, intensifying public hostility toward the government. The Yamagata faction then decided to take advantage of the situation and overthrow the Yamamoto cabinet by vetoing the budget in the House of Peers and then refusing to reconsider its position.

Yamamoto was consequently forced to resign, and as he did so, he recommended that Hara be appointed his successor. However Yamagata, who was not about to accept a party government, sought instead to have his follower Kiyoura Keigo selected to form the next cabinet. This posed a difficult situation because the navy refused to cooperate when Kiyoura failed to agree to call a special session of the Diet for the purpose of restoring the navy's budget, which had been cut (with Kiyoura's support) by the House of Peers. Inoue then pushed Ōkuma's candidacy, and got Yamagata's reluctant agreement.

Ōkuma, who had been out of politics for fifteen years since his retirement as head of the Kenseihontō, had been devoting his attention to social work and to Waseda University, which he had founded earlier. He accepted the premiership and immediately set about gaining the cooperation of Katō Kōmei, who was then the head of the Dōshikai. Next Ōkuma turned to Inukai and Ozaki, his erstwhile supporters. Ozaki, who was with a splinter group of a minor party, decided to enter the cabinet. Inukai, who was with a truncated Nationalist party, refused, however, because he would not work with the Dōshikai, which had been created by splintering the Nationalist party. The bureaucratic, pro-Yamagata faction was heavily represented in the Ōkuma government, which was formed in April, 1914. In effect, the old champion of party government had become something like an agent for the oligarchic clique.

One of the very serious problems that faced the Ōkuma government soon after its accession to power was the outbreak of the First World War. Foreign Minister Katō Kōmei wanted to seize the opportunity to take over the German concessions in China and also enhance Japan's status in the international arena by participating on the side of the Allied powers. The excuse for joining the war was provided by a British request for Japan's participation in accordance with the Anglo-Japanese Alliance. Soon thereafter, Britain had second thoughts about Japan's entry, but Katō had already pushed through the war plans without even conferring with the genrō—a step that certainly did not endear him to the latter. He was determined, however, to end genrō and military intervention in the realm of the formation of foreign policy.

The Japanese forces captured the German fortress at Tsingtao on the Shantung Peninsula and the German island possessions in the Pacific. Other than this, Japan's active role in the battle was limited to the use of her warships to patrol the Mediterranean toward the latter part of the war.

The other major foreign-policy matter that faced the Ōkuma government was the presentation of the Twenty-one Demands to the Chinese government in January, 1915 (see page 399). This was another decision that Katō made without first consulting the genrō, and the unfavorable international repercussions that ensued further hardened the genrō's opposition to him.

On the domestic front, Ōkuma pursued a policy of naval and military expansion. He sought to add the two army divisions that had been on the army's agenda since 1906, but the Seiyūkai and the Nationalist party so adamantly opposed this measure that Ōkuma found it necessary to dissolve the Diet. In the general election that followed in March, 1915, Ōkuma launched a major campaign to aid the Dōshikai. This was the first time that a Prime Minister campaigned personally in Diet elections. Not only did Ōkuma make whistle-stop campaign speeches throughout the country, but his Minister of Home Affairs, Ōura, a follower of Yamagata and a member of the bureaucratic clique, made major changes in the prefectural governorships and then had the new appointees campaign for progovernment candidates. Considerable money was spent on buying votes. As a result of this all-out effort, the Dōshikai increased its Diet seats from 99 to 150 and the Seiyūkai representation fell from 185 to 104. With additional backing provided by the minor parties, Ōkuma now had majority support in the Diet, and this enabled him to pass the measure to add two army divisions.

The economy was flourishing because of the First World War and so it appeared that Ōkuma would remain in power for some time. However, now that the Seiyūkai had been weakened and the army enlarged, the genrō and the bureaucratic clique felt that Ōkuma had served his purpose. He was no longer needed, so their agents in the House of Peers began to set the stage for his elimination by criticizing his inept handling of foreign affairs and by attacking his fiscal policies.

Obstruction by the House of Peers finally forced Ōkuma to give up the premiership in the fall of 1917. He sought to install Katō as his successor but Yamagata, who was still opposed to a party man heading the government, found him to be particularly objectionable because as Foreign Minister, Katō had by-passed him in formulating foreign policy. Yamagata managed to have his own choice, General Terauchi Masatake

(1852–1919), the Resident General of Korea, appointed as Prime Minister.

Terauchi formed a cabinet that was supposedly "above parties," but he did seek and receive the cooperation of Hara and the Seiyūkai. The *Kenseikai* (Constitutional Association), which had been formed by the Dōshikai and two minor parties, called for a vote of no-confidence against Terauchi, and he had to dissolve the Diet. In the ensuing election of April, 1918, the Seiyūkai managed to increase its representatives by about fifty, while reducing Kenseikai seats by eighty.

In the realm of foreign affairs, Terauchi had to cope with the unstable China situation as well as with the problems arising out of the fall of the tsarist government in Russia. The issue, however, that ultimately brought the Terauchi cabinet down was inflation.

The Japanese economy was undergoing a recession when the First World War broke out, and the situation worsened because the war initially reduced foreign trade. The price of rice and other grains continued to drop until mid-1916, when the trend was finally reversed. Japanese exports began to rise from the middle of 1915, as the belligerent nations were unable to supply goods to foreign markets. Japan sold war supplies as well as other necessities to the Allied nations while at the same time increasing her exports to Southeast Asia and North and South America. In 1915, her exports reached an unprecedented 708 million yen, and they continued to increase, reaching 1.96 billion yen in 1918. Her balance of payments, which was unfavorable just prior to the war, shifted, so that by the end of the war she had accumulated a favorable balance of 2.8 billion yen. This resulted in tremendous economic expansion, increased circulation of currency, greater demand for goods, and inflationary prices. Taking the year 1914 as index 100, in 1916 the price index rose to 144, and by 1918 it was up to 230. As is usally the case, the rapid increase in prices was not followed by higher wages. Consequently, real wages declined from index 100 in 1914 to 68 by 1918. Strikes, even though they were illegal, steadily increased in number as a result of the tremendous economic pressures.

The most pressing problem that confronted the government was the increase in the price of rice, which doubled between January, 1917, and July, 1918. This situation produced virulent riots throughout the country in the summer of 1918. In July, the housewives of a small fishing village in northcentral Honshu demonstrated against the high price of rice, and when news of this action spread, riots erupted in other areas of the country. The price of rice nevertheless continued to rise. By the middle of August, massive rice riots hit all the major cities, with the protesters attacking retail stores and warehouses of rice merchants as well as other shops and homes belonging to the rich. These riots, which lasted for fifty days until the middle of September, involved hundreds of cities, towns, and villages. A total of 700,000 people took part in the disturbances and more than 1,000 of them were killed or injured. The government called out army troops and arrested 25,000 persons when the police failed to quell the rioters; more than 700 were prosecuted and 71 were sentenced to prison for 10 years or more. The government officials, believing that the situation was being aggravated by the sensationalist and sympathetic approach taken by the newspapers, sought to impose severe curbs on the press. This, of course, only increased public hostility against the Terauchi government.

These riots, the largest and most widespread in Japanese history, had several significant effects. They not only forced out the Terauchi cabinet, but fear of the violent mobs they assembled brought rival political leaders of the establishment, such as Hara and Yamagata, closer together. They also created a sense of urgency about the need for immediate social reforms and extension of the franchise. Thus, the riots actually gave a boost to democracy and to the labor and socialist movements.

The political parties, however, were somewhat cautious about joining the critics of the government, for clearly the riots of the masses were also a threat to the party members. Yamagata wanted Saionji to head the government again after Terauchi resigned, but this new member of the genrō responded to the invitation by urging that a party government under Hara be permitted to try its hand instead.[1] Yamagata, who had fought and resisted party government throughout his political career, finally accepted the inevitable and agreed to Saionji's proposal. Unlike Katō, Hara had neither circumvented established practices nor neglected to pay proper deference to the elder statesmen.

In September, 1918, the first real party government in Japan came into existence. Hara was not a member of the House of Peers so he was hailed as "the commoner Prime Minister." The long struggle for party government led by the advocates of popular rights had finally achieved its desired goal, which, ironically enough, was realized by cooperating closely with genrō officialdom. Hara's accession to power was a landmark for parliamentary government, even though nonparty cabinets would follow for a few years.

FOREIGN AFFAIRS

The second decade of the twentieth century saw a growing Japanese concern over developments in China, where revolutionary forces under the leadership of Sun Yat-sen together with traditional military chieftains like Yüan Shih-k'ai had succeeded in bringing an end to the Manchu

[1] The only surviving original genrō at this time were Yamagata and Matsukata; Inoue had died in 1915, and Ōyama in 1916. Saionji was the sole new addition to the clique of genrō.

dynasty. A republic was established under Yüan Shih-k'ai, but political stability did not follow. Instead, internal divisions persisted as Yüan sought to establish a new dynasty. The republicans continued to carry on their struggle at home and abroad, but when Yüan died in June, 1916, China found herself lacking a strong central government and an era of "warlordism" was ushered into existence. Sun Yat-sen nevertheless continued his campaign to unify the country under a program calling for nationality, democracy, and people's livelihood. As a result of this fragmentation of authority in China, Japan was confronted with tempting opportunities to extend her influence and interests in that country.

During the first decade of the twentieth century, a considerable number of Chinese students came to Japan to study because they were convinced that her approach to modernizing society provided a model that their own country should follow. One source estimates that, whereas there were fewer than one hundred Chinese students in Japan in 1900, by 1906 there were thirteen thousand.[2] Sun Yat-sen used Japan from 1897 to 1903 as a base from which to carry on his revolutionary activities. He then spent a great deal of time in Europe and America before returning to Japan in 1905 in order to organize the *T'ung-Meng-Hui* (United League), by which he hoped to give the revolutionary movement a cohesive structure.

Many of the visiting students established close friendships with Japanese political leaders who were interested in assisting the Chinese in reforming their country. The following list of sympathetic Japanese suggests the nature of the support that Sun and the Chinese revolutionaries attracted: Tōyama Mitsuru (ultranationalist), Inukai Tsuyoshi (champion of parliamentary government), Kita Ikki (radical nationalist), and Kōtoku Shūsui (radical socialist).

There was also a fairly large number of Japanese who went to China as what were called rōnin (masterless warriors) to play a hand at political intrigue and revolution. Some went out of a sense of altruism, some were motivated by the spirit of adventure, and some, of course, wanted to advance the cause of Japanese imperialism. Tōyama and Inukai supported these continental rōnin, one of the more prominent of whom was Miyazaki Torazō, who became Sun Yat-sen's close friend and supporter. There were also those men who were primarily interested in establishing business enterprises in China for the purpose of engaging in a kind of economic imperialism. Among them was Mori Kaku, who was not only a businessman interested in the economic exploitation of China

[2] In 1924, 50 percent of the executive-committee members of China's Nationalist party had been educated in Japan. Between 1903 and 1921, 42.5 percent of all Chinese students studying abroad were in Japan.

but also a political intriguer who envisioned his role in China as comparable to that of Britain's Clive in India.

Attention had been focused upon Manchuria and Mongolia before the Russo-Japanese War, and many adventurers moved into that region to prevent Russian expansion in the Far East. The *Kokuryūkai* (The Amur River, or Black Dragon, Society) was formed in 1901 by Uchida Ryōhei (1874–1937), who was interested in furthering Japanese interests in Manchuria and Mongolia. This organization sent intelligence agents into these areas and Siberia, with the ultimate aim of making the Amur River into one of Japan's boundaries. The desire to achieve this goal was fortified with the victory in the Russo-Japanese War. The man who emerged as the real leader of the Genyōsha as well as the Kokuryūkai was Tōyama Mitsuru, who was to remain the patriarch and the gray eminence of the ultranationalistic expansionists until the Second World War. All right-wing politicians looked to him for guidance and advice, and his charismatic personality further enhanced his enormous following by attracting young "patriots" who were willing to kill and die for him.

Growing Japanese interest in China was reflected in the increasing number of Japanese residents in Manchuria, the Yangtze River Valley, and other parts of China. In 1900, there were only about 3,800 Japanese in China, but this figure rose to well over 26,600 by 1910, and to 133,930 by 1920. Most of these inhabitants were concentrated in the big cities of Manchuria. During the First World War political intrigues in these areas were supported by the general staff of the army as well as many other high-ranking officials.

One of the most controversial actions taken by the Japanese government toward China during the Taishō era was the submission of the Twenty-one Demands to the Yüan Shih-k'ai government in January, 1915. Ōkuma and his Foreign Minister, Katō, engineered this scheme and had the demands grouped under five headings. The first had to do with the transference of German rights in Shantung Province to Japan as well as granting her the right to construct a railway line there. The second called for the recognition of Japan's special position in south Manchuria and eastern Inner Mongolia. The third group dealt with the establishment of a Sino-Japanese company that would be given a mining monopoly in certain areas of the Yangtze River Valley. Group four asked that no harbor, bay, or island along the coast of China be ceded or leased to any other power. Group five involved the most controversial set of demands. Among other things it asked the Chinese government: to employ Japanese political, financial, and military advisers; to establish joint Chinese and Japanese police forces wherever necessary; to purchase 50 percent or more of China's arms from Japan, or else establish joint Sino-Japanese arsenals that would employ Japanese engineers and use Japanese materials; and to grant to Japan the right to construct railroads in south China.

These demands were presented at a time when the major powers were preoccupied with the World War and were thus unable to intervene. The only country that Yüan Shih-k'ai's government could count on for support was the United States, but she was not willing to exert much pressure on Japan. Secretary of State Bryan claimed that the United States frankly recognized that the territorial contiguity existing between Japan and Shantung, south Manchuria, and eastern Mongolia necessarily created special relations between the two countries involved. Bryan did, however, go on to say that his government objected to those demands that came under groups four and five.

Negotiations between the Chinese and Japanese governments continued for several months. Japan made threatening gestures by increasing the forces she had stationed in Manchuria, Shantung, and Hankow. Yüan stalled, unable to defy Chinese public opinion, which was enraged at the Japanese action, while at the same time hoping for third-power support.

In early May, the Japanese government deleted most of the demands in group five and presented Yüan with an ultimatum. He had no choice but to accede, and on May 25, the two nations signed an agreement that in effect conceded to Japan all the demands in the first four groups. The agreement, however, brought few actual benefits to Japan, while it stirred up tremendous Chinese hostility. The governments that succeeded the Yüan regime never recognized the legitimacy of the concessions gained by the Japanese.

Japanese-American relations tended to become strained because Japanese activities in Manchuria and China conflicted with the American concept of the open door in China. At the same time, the issue of Japanese immigration into Hawaii and the United States was causing tremendous ill feelings. Japanese immigration into Hawaii began to increase in the last decade of the nineteenth century, and by 1900 there were 61,000 Japanese immigrants in Hawaii, constituting 40 percent of the island's population. There were also 24,000 Japanese immigrants in California. Agitation against this immigration intensified in the West Coast states, and the Japanese government consequently sought to curb the flow of its people out of the country. There was, however, nothing it could do to prevent the Japanese in Hawaii from moving to the mainland of the United States. From 1902 to 1907, 39,531 Japanese immigrants came directly to the mainland from Japan, and 32,855 arrived from Hawaii.

President Roosevelt vetoed a piece of clearly discriminatory legislation that had been passed by Congress, but he could do nothing about prejudicial activities that were going on at the local level. In San Francisco, for example, the local press, with rousing headlines about the Yellow Peril, and the Asiatic Exclusion League managed to foment considerable animosity toward Japanese immigration. In 1906, the San Francisco school board issued a "separate school order" providing for the segregation of Oriental children in the public schools in order "to save White children from being affected by association with pupils of the Mongolian race." The order was clearly directed at Japanese pupils (Chinese children were already segregated), who were called vicious and immoral. It was further charged that these pupils were overcrowding the school system, although at that time there were only ninety-three Japanese youngsters enrolled in the twenty-three San Francisco schools.

Roosevelt succeeded in blocking the entry of Japanese immigrants from Hawaii, Canada, and Mexico, while persuading the Japanese government to conclude a "Gentlemen's Agreement" in 1908 to restrict the flow of its people to the United States. The agreement severely limited the inflow of Japanese immigrants, but it did nothing to reduce the agitation against these people that continued to mount in California. Anti-Japanese riots broke out in San Francisco in May, 1907, and there was even considerable talk of war between the United States and Japan. In 1913, an Alien Land Act was passed prohibiting aliens from owning land or leasing land for more than three years. In 1920, the right of Japanese to lease lands was denied completely, and in 1922, the Supreme Court of the United States held that the Japanese were ineligible for citizenship. In 1924, Congress passed an immigration act that annulled the Gentlemen's Agreement of 1908, and prohibited persons who were not eligible for citizenship from entering the country at all.

These measures aggravated Japanese-American relations, which were at this time already coming into conflict in the political arena of the Far East. Here, however, conflicting interests were resolved, if only temporarily, by political agreements. For instance, in 1908, when there was talk of a Chinese–German–American alliance, the Root-Takahira notes were exchanged wherein the United States and Japan pledged: to respect each other's territorial possessions in East Asia and the Pacific; to uphold the status quo in these regions and maintain the open-door policy; to respect China's independence and integrity. The statement, however, was couched in such vague rhetoric that both sides later disagreed about what was specifically intended. Japan interpreted the agreement to mean that she was not to attack the Philippines in return for a free hand in Manchuria.

As we observed earlier, an American railroad magnate, E. H. Harriman, was interested in acquiring railroad rights in Manchuria. The effort to extend American interests in that part of the world was carried on after Harriman's death by Secretary of State Knox, who wanted to neutralize foreign-owned railroads in Manchuria. Moves along this line only succeeded in driving Japan and Russia toward a virtual alliance to defend their common interests there.

The entry of the United States into the First World War raised hopes that American support could be garnered for Japan's claims to the German concessions in both Shantung and the Pacific islands north of the equator. Japan also wanted the United States to recognize her "paramount interests" in China, but such a commitment was refused. The only product that was to emerge from the Japanese overtures was the Lansing-Ishii notes, which recognized Japan's special interests in China while reaffirming the principle of China's territorial integrity and the open-door policy.

The next issue that exacerbated her relations with the United States was Japan's desire to send troops into Siberia following the fall of the Russian Provisional Government. The subsequent emergence of the Bolshevik government in the fall of 1917 brought an extension of Soviet control eastward into Siberia. The Japanese government under Terauchi then considered the possibility of countering this movement by establishing an independent anti-Soviet state in eastern Siberia. Without American consent, the Japanese leaders, including Terauchi and Yamagata, were unwilling to take aggressive action in the Far East, however, and at this point the United States was not willing to see Japan move into Siberia, even if it was to combat communism. The army leaders, headed by the vice-chief of staff, General Tanaka Giichi, continued to agitate for the dispatching of an expeditionary force into Siberia, and when the Cossack leader Semenov started his anti-Bolshevik movement in northern Manchuria, the Japanese army supplied him with weapons. Soon thereafter, when some Japanese were killed as a result of a clash between Bolshevik and anti-Bolshevik forces, the Japanese navy landed its marines in Vladivostok.

The American position on the question of intervention shifted when Czechoslovakian troops, which were moving across Siberia to return to the Western front, clashed with Soviet forces. The United States finally responded to the English and French appeal for intervention in order to extricate the Czech forces. In July, 1918, America and Japan agreed to send military units under Japanese command into Siberia to assist the Czech troops. The United States limited its expeditionary force to 7,000 men, while Japan, on the other hand, eventually dispatched 72,000 soldiers into Siberia.

The original intention was to confine military operations largely around Vladivostok, but the Japanese forces were sent as far as Irkutsk. This seriously disturbed the United States, who then withdrew her troops just as soon as arrangements were made to repatriate the Czech soldiers. All American soldiers were withdrawn by April, 1920, whereas the Japanese, hoping to control at least the Chinese Eastern Railroad in northern Manchuria, if not the entire region east of Lake Baikal, remained in Siberia until the latter part of 1922. Japan, headed now by Katō Kōmei, ultimately withdrew her troops for two primary reasons: first, considerable international pressure, particularly from the United States, was being brought to bear upon her, and secondly, the Soviet government was finally succeeding in consolidating control over Russia. Nevertheless, Japan did keep her troops in northern Sakhalin until 1925. In January of that year, under the leadership of Foreign Minister Shidehara, diplomatic relations were officially established between Japan and Soviet Russia. Essentially, Japan's intervention in Siberia accomplished nothing positive, while it served both to reinforce the distrust of Soviet leaders toward foreign powers and to impair even further Japanese relations with the United States.

The world powers met in Versailles in January, 1919, to work out a peace settlement after the First World War, and Japan participated as one of the major powers even though her role in the war had been limited. The Japanese delegation, headed by Saionji, had as one of its key objectives the legalization of Japanese control over the former German holdings in both Shantung and the Pacific islands north of the equator. Despite vigorous Chinese opposition and reluctance on the part of the United States, Japan got what she wanted. She did, however, fail to achieve something very significant, and that was the inclusion of a clause on racial equality in the Covenant of the League of Nations. Unfortunately, this effort was blocked by the Western powers.

The decade following the conference at Versailles was a period of international cooperation for Japan, which, in part at least, was brought about by the relative decline in the influence of the militarists and the emergence of party government. The formulation of foreign policy fell into the hands of men such as Shidehara who believed in cooperating with other nations.

In order to settle the differences that remained unresolved by the Versailles Treaty and also to end the naval armament race that was breaking out among England, the United States, and Japan, an international conference was convened under the auspices of the United States. In August, 1921, President Harding invited Great Britain, France, Italy, and Japan to Washington for the purpose of discussing the limitation of arms and related questions concerning the Pacific and the Far East. To the meetings devoted to these last problems, China, Belgium, the Netherlands, and Portugal were also invited.

The economic boom enjoyed by Japan came to a close with the end of the First World War. Her imports began to exceed her exports, and the need for economic retrenchment was acutely felt. Even the most ardent advocates of naval arms expansion came to recognize the urgent necessity to reduce expenditures. Consequently, the Japanese government, under the leadership of Hara, readily accepted the invitation to the Washington Conference. A number of agreements resulted from this gathering. Among the more important ones were the Four Power Pacific Treaty involving the United States, Great Britain, France, and Japan; the Five Power Naval Treaty agreed to by the United States, Great Britain, France, Italy, and Japan; and the Nine Power Treaty, which all the participants at the conference signed, dealing with the principles and policies to be followed concerning China.

The signatories to the Four Power Pacific Treaty agreed to respect each other's "rights in relation to their insular possessions and insular dominions in the region of the Pacific Ocean." All controversies were to be settled by a conference of the four powers. The earlier Anglo-Japanese Alliance was to be terminated upon ratification of this new treaty.

American Secretary of State Hughes took the initiative regarding the limitation of naval armament by making concrete proposals on the opening day of the conference. He suggested that the naval tonnage ratio of 5–5–3 be set for the capital ships of the United States, Great Britain, and Japan, respectively. Japan preferred a ratio of 10–10–7, but her delegation, headed by Admiral Katō Tomosaburō, accepted the American proposal with the proviso that the status quo would be maintained in the fortifications and naval bases in the Pacific. The United States had ports that could serve as naval bases, but none had been adequately fortified in 1921. Not included in this agreement were those American naval bases and fortifications located adjacent to the coasts of the United States, Alaska, and the Panama Canal Zone. France and Italy accepted a ratio of 1.75 each to the 5–5–3 ratio for the other nations. The naval agreement did not cover auxiliary crafts or submarines. The signatories also agreed to abstain from using "asphyxiating, poisonous, or other gases and all analogous liquids . . . in war."

In the Nine Power Treaty the parties concerned pledged to respect "the sovereignty, the independence, and the territorial and administrative integrity of China." Furthermore, they affirmed the open door by agreeing to maintain equal commercial opportunities in China for all nations, with no country seeking special rights and privileges. The sentiments were noble, but no nation was actually willing to renounce the unequal treaties imposed on China during the nineteenth century. Moreover, no effective sanctions were instituted to enforce the Nine Power Treaty.

Japan and China settled their differences on Shantung at the Washington Conference. Japan agreed to return the province to China but retained control of the Tsinan-Tsingtao Railway and its properties for fifteen years. Even though the problem of Shantung was solved, Sino-Japanese relations remained severely strained. The Versailles settlement unleashed an outburst of nationalism in China that was led by students and intellectuals. They staged what is known as the May Fourth movement, a patriotic demonstration directed against Japanese imperialism, and they also initiated boycotts of Japanese goods in all the major cities.

The tense situation between the two countries was no doubt seriously aggravated by the Japanese militarists who continued their intrigues in Manchuria and North China, backing warlords who might serve their ends and intensifying the exploitation of iron and coal mines.

The following episode involving Chang Tso-lin provides a good example of Japanese intervention in China's political affairs and the deteriorating effects of that interference. In July, 1920, Chang, in cooperation with other warlords, drove Tuan Ch'i-jui, a warlord backed by Japan, out of Peking and succeeded in holding the capital until 1922. At that time he was removed by a coalition of warlords headed by Wu P'ei-fu who, the Japanese believed, was supported by England and the United States. In 1925, the Christian General Feng Yü-hsiang rebelled against Wu and gained temporary control of Peking, but he in turn was driven out by the combined forces of Tuan Ch'i-jui and Chang Tso-lin. Late in 1926, when one of Chang's more progressive generals rebelled against him, Japanese militarists in Manchuria intervened on Chang's behalf and thus enabled him to gain supremacy in Manchuria and North China. As a result of Japan's participation in this struggle, there was a further intensification of antagonistic sentiments toward her in China.

Earlier in 1925, anti-Japanese feelings were aroused when a textile workers' strike against Japanese plants in Shanghai had led to bloodshed as the British police sought to suppress the demonstrators. Thus, despite Foreign Minister Shidehara's efforts to establish friendly relations by restricting Japanese interference, Chinese public opinion continued to grow inflamed by Japanese actions.

Nationalistic opposition also confronted Japan in Korea, where after annexing the nation in 1910, Japan imposed military rule. All the governors-general were either admirals or generals; the military police controlled the police force; and civilian officials, even teachers, carried sabers with them. The Koreans were granted no political rights and were denied freedom of speech and assembly.

The Japanese rulers confiscated large areas of farmlands from the Korean peasants, using as an excuse their failure to register their land

and establish legal ownership in a given period of time. The Korean peasants, most of whom were illiterate, had no understanding of what the legal technicalities were all about. The unregistered land was nationalized and then sold cheaply to Japanese land development companies and immigrants. By the end of 1918, one firm had acquired about 122,000 acres of rice paddy and 49,000 acres of dry land. A large number of Korean peasants were consequently reduced to tenancy or vagrancy. The Korean market was dominated by Japanese goods because measures had been introduced restricting the development of indigenous Korean industry. This massive importation of Japanese manufactured goods also undermined the traditional Korean handicraft industries. The Japanese landowners, merchants, and moneylenders prospered under this program of domination and exploitation, while the Koreans became increasingly impoverished.

At this time the Wilsonian concept of self-determination was gaining wide publicity, and those Koreans who were in exile intensified their efforts to gain freedom. Students and Christian leaders within the country also began agitating for independence.[3] On March 1, 1919, the day set for the funeral of the Korean king, the people staged a nationwide peaceful demonstration, calling for independence. The Japanese authorities labeled the participants as rioters and used the army to suppress the demonstrators ruthlessly. The Koreans used whatever means they had to strike back, but after two months the resistance was brought under control. Japanese officials reported 1,962 Korean casualties and close to 20,000 arrests. This, however, did not put an end to the movement for independence, which was continued by Korean nationalists abroad. Among them was Syngman Rhee, who used Hawaii as his base. Disillusioned by the lack of concern for their fate by the Western powers, many Korean nationalists turned to the Russians for support.

Admiral Saitō Makoto was appointed governor-general by the Hara government after these disturbances. He proclaimed a policy of "cultural rule," but the changes that Saitō introduced were at best superficial, such as the replacement of the military police with regular police, and the termination of the practice of having officials and teachers wear uniforms and bear sabers. As a matter of fact, the number of police actually increased tremendously, from about 1,400 to 16,900. Cooperative Koreans were given seats in advisory regional councils, but these administrative bodies had absolutely no authority. The economic exploitation of Korea continued, and as half of her rice crop was shipped to Japan, her own per capita consumption of rice dropped by 47 per-

---

[3] There were about two hundred thousand Christians in Korea out of a total population of twenty million.

cent between 1912 and 1933; that is, the per capita consumption of rice by Koreans was 78 *shō* (one shō equals 3.81 pints) in 1912, and this figure dropped to 60 shō in 1918, and then down to 41 shō in 1933. Japanese rice consumption, on the other hand, came to 115 shō. The Koreans were compelled to augment their diet by millet imported from Manchuria.

ECONOMIC DEVELOPMENTS: 1906–1930

After the Russo-Japanese War the Japanese economy entered the second phase of modern economic growth, which extends roughly from 1906 to 1952. This phase has been broken down into two periods by Ohkawa and Rosovsky: 1906–1930 and 1931–1952. In the first period, the growth in the modern sector of the economy was accelerated while the traditional sector failed to grow as rapidly. As a result the gap between the two segments slowly widened. The output per worker in the modern sector increased by about 6 percent as compared to 2–3 percent in the traditional sector. In the second period of this phase, the growth of the economy was stimulated by the political and military policies of the government, and was affected by abnormal circumstances, that is, war, defeat, and occupation.

The rapid growth in the modern sector during the first period, 1906–1930, was stimulated by the Russo-Japanese War. There were greater government expenditures in armaments and in transportation resulting from the nationalization of the railroads; new markets were developing in the freshly acquired colonies; a stronger home market was coming into being as a result of increased per capita income.

The decline in the traditional sector during this same period was caused in part by competition from both the modern sector of the economy and the colonies. The growth of this sector was also stunted as a consequence of these key factors: by 1905, the limits to which new arable land could be opened had been reached, and the maximum increase in yield per unit of land had been achieved.

The gap between the modern and traditional sectors created a noticeable difference in living standards, and the impoverished rural dwellers became increasingly dissatisfied. Greater efficiency in productivity in the modern segment resulted in a reduced demand for labor. This placed at the disposal of the industries a ready supply of cheap labor. At the same time low incomes, particularly in the traditional sector, limited the growth of the domestic market. By the end of the 1920s, the Japanese economy was confronted with a serious crisis.

A general idea of the extent to which the economy in the modern sector developed during this period can be obtained by the following statistics. Taking the years 1910–1914 as index 100, by 1925–1929 manufacturing production had risen to 313, the volume of imports to 242, and exports to 217. As for specific industries, manufacturing production in the textile industry increased from index 100 in 1910–1914, to 270 in 1925–1929; metals and machinery increased to 355 in the same period; chemicals and ceramics to 453; electricity and gas to 653. The number of factories that were equipped with power machinery increased from 9,155 in 1909, to 48,555 in 1929. The number of factory workers increased from 1,012,000 in 1909, to 2,384,000 in 1929. At the same time, however, the number of small factories remained high. In 1934 there were a million workshops employing less than five workers. In 1909, the percentage of private factories employing between five and nine workers was 52.1, and in 1934 it was 56.5.

Compared to the increased production in the industrial realm, production in the traditional sector showed relatively modest advances. For instance, taking the year 1910–1914 as index 100, agricultural production rose to 129 by 1925–1929, fisheries to 299, and mining to 157. Food production rose to 135 while the population rose to 125 (that is, from 50.6 million to 61 million). In other words, food production managed to stay only slightly ahead of the population growth.

In spite of the rather significant growth in the modern segment, Japan was still not a predominantly industrial nation. The percentage of workers engaged in the primary industries of agriculture, fishing, and mining declined from 81 in 1880, to 69 in 1900, and then to 55.4 in 1920, but it was still as high as 51.1 in 1930. Also, the standard of living did not improve significantly, although conditions for people in the modern, urban areas were somewhat better than in the traditional, rural sections. Taking the increase in food production and imports together there was a 20 percent rise in per capita food supply from 1910–1912 to 1925–1927. There was, however, a 40 percent increase in the use of all clothing fibers per person. During the decade after 1926, there was little change in the per capita intake of food, which remained at about 2,300 calories per day. So far as the life expectancy figures were concerned, there was no improvement over the previous decades. In fact, during 1921–1925, male life expectancy dropped somewhat to 42.06 years as compared to 43.97 years in 1899–1903 and 44.25 years in 1909–1913. Japan's mortality rate during this period was much lower than other Asian countries and comparable to France, Spain, and Eastern European countries.

The physical comfort and convenience of the people, however, continued to improve with the greater use of electricity in homes, the development of bus and railway transportation, and the widespread use of bicycles. By the end of the 1930s, nine out of ten homes were wired for electric lighting, and all of the 11,500 towns and villages (with the exception of about 200 small and very remote hamlets) had electricity.

The wages of the industrial workers did increase during this period. Taking the year 1914 as index 100, wages rose to 317 by 1925–1929. This apparently dramatic increase was offset by the cost of living, which rose from 100 to 204. Thus, the increase in real wages came to 55 percent. This nevertheless still meant a very austere existence of minimal subsistence for the working man.[4] This relatively slow rise in the standard of living at a time when the modern sector of the economy was growing at such a substantial pace is the result of numerous factors, such as considerable growth in population; a high rate of savings and investment; unfavorable price ratio in imports and exports; high expenditures in armaments and strategic industries; and tremendous costs in the colonies.

Another very important factor that contributed to holding down the standard of living, even in the face of remarkable growth in the modern sector of the economy, was the vastly unequal distribution of wealth. A great body of the peasant and urban working families still had annual incomes of less than 800 yen by 1930. They constituted 10.6 million out of 12.6 million families, but they were the recipients of only half of the country's household income. At the top, about 24,000 families (a scant 0.0019 percent of the nation's total households), with incomes exceeding 10,000 yen, possessed over 10 percent of the aggregate family income. Above this group at the uppermost level, 19 households had incomes over 1 million yen and, at the very bottom, 2,232,000 families (18 percent of the nation's total households) received 200 yen or less, constituting a mere 3.8 percent of the national household income.

The concentration of wealth at the top reflects the concentration of industrial and commercial enterprises in the hands of a few large business combines, the *zaibatsu*. Depending on the scope of the definition, there were from ten to twenty big business houses classified as zaibatsu in prewar Japan, and there were four indisputably gigantic ones: Mitsui, Mitsubishi, Sumitomo, and Yasuda. These huge business houses owned powerful banks and extended their activities into all areas of industry and commerce. As immense as these businesses were, they all remained essentially family owned and run. Sumitomo enterprises were almost all

---

[4] The average urban worker earned an income of three yen (about seventy-five cents) a day in 1935–1936, and he had to spend at least a third of it to maintain even the simplest diet. His rural counterpart subsisted on a still smaller income. A comparison of real consumption per capita in Japan and the United States (in terms of 1955 dollars) reveals that in 1910 it was $156 for Japan and $723 for the United States; in 1925 it was $248 and $955; and in 1940 it was $196 and $1,084. (Alan H. Gleason, "Economic Growth and Consumption in Japan," in William W. Lockwood, ed., *The State and Economic Enterprise in Japan*, Princeton, N.J.: Princeton University Press, 1965, pp. 439–40.)

controlled by one family, while the Mitsubishi combine was held and run by two Iwasaki families. The Mitsui interests were controlled by eleven branches of the Mitsui family that acted as a unit in accordance with formal household rules—policy was decided by a family council and 90 percent of the wealth was held collectively.

The machinery used to manage the vast holdings of these gigantic enterprises involved the domination of each combine by a holding company where the bulk of the house fortune was usually concentrated. From this point, company control was extended through "a network of subsidiaries and affiliates by intercorporate stockholdings, interlocking directorates, management agreements, and loans from the combine bank." [5]

The House of Mitsui was the largest and most powerful of these combines. In early Meiji it was active in commerce and banking before moving into mining and lumbering. Subsequently it branched out into textiles, shipping, warehousing, sugar, metals and machinery, and many other industries. By 1937, it owned properties valued at 1.635 billion yen, while its control extended over a business empire that was worth a great deal more.

Yasuda remained by and large a banking combine, and in 1944 it controlled assets in excess of 40 billion yen in banking and 2 billion yen in other enterprises. Sumitomo was engaged in mining, but in 1945 it also had investments in 123 companies spread over 30 industries. The Mitsubishi combine in 1944 controlled 25 percent of the nation's shipping and shipbuilding, 15 percent of coal and metals, 16 percent of warehousing, 16 percent of the bank loans, 21 to 35 percent of electrical equipment, 50 percent of flour milling, 59 percent of sheet glass, 35 percent of sugar, and 15 percent of cotton textiles.

Curiously enough, despite the fact that giant combines dominated the economy, no single one of them had an outright monopoly in any industry, though there are a few isolated examples of companies that came very near to this. For instance, the Ōji Paper Company controlled 75 percent of the output of Western-style paper; and in the steel industry, Nippon Seitetsu (Japan Ironworks), which was formed by a merger of the government-operated Yawata Ironworks and six private companies, produced nearly all of the pig iron and 52 percent of the raw steel in Japan and Korea in 1934. In the main, however, several major firms collectively dominated most critical industrial areas.

The growth of the major combines was fostered by the government since it believed that large concerns were vital to the development of the nation's heavy industries, foreign trade, and colonial enterprise. There

[5] William W. Lockwood, *The Economic Development of Japan: Growth and Structural Change, 1863–1938* (Princeton, N.J.: Princeton University Press, 1954), p. 215.

were also close links between government officials and the families of these huge businesses. An increasing number of top executives from the zaibatsu circle began occupying high government posts. The zaibatsu also developed close associations with the major political parties by providing them with considerable financial support. Consequently, neither the government nor the political parties showed any inclination to curb the growth of large business combines through legislation. In 1927, the Japanese government reported that "Japan has no particular legislation forbidding or establishing control over trusts and cartels. The judicature has not concerned itself with this question." [6]

The lack of government restraints made it quite simple for the bigger firms to eliminate or absorb smaller competitors. Not only were the zaibatsu able to increase efficiency, cut costs, and hire more able men, but because they dominated the field of bank credit, they were able to maintain control over customers, suppliers, and even those competitors that they did not actually take over.

Unquestionably, the zaibatsu played a significant role in the rapid development of the Japanese economy by investing their profits in new enterprises, developing export markets, building strategic industries, innovating, and taking considerable risks. There is a negative side to this picture, however, and that is that they also contributed to the growing disparity between the rich few and the poor masses. Through the concentration of economic power at the top, they stifled the growth of a strong middle class while curbing the rise of a vigorous trade-union movement.

The agricultural realm of the economy was also characterized by a concentration of wealth in the hands of a few. After World War I, there was a slight tendency toward dispersion of landownership, but in 1935, 3,415 big landowners owned 4.7 percent of the nation's cultivated land, while 4,765,000 farm families, each with holdings of less than 7.35 acres, owned only 56 percent.

SOCIAL REFORM MOVEMENTS: LABOR

The labor problems created by industrialism also grew in magnitude as the modern sector of the economy expanded. The number of factory workers continued to increase, but their rights and welfare remained inadequately protected. The demand for export goods intensified during World War I, and even the minimal factory law of 1911 was violated. For instance, match factories used children under eight years of age to meet the demand created by the inability of the Swedish producers to export matches to Southeast Asia.

The workers were essentially at the mercy of a fluctuating economy that

[6] *Ibid.*, p. 220.

went into a state of boom and inflation during World War I. This, as we observed, brought about the violent rice riots of 1918. The boom was followed in 1920 by a depression in which exports dropped 25 percent and the price of manufactured goods and textiles dropped 50 to 60 percent. This resulted in a serious decline in production and the elimination of many companies that had emerged during the wartime boom. This depression also hit the countryside as the price of cocoons and rice dropped by 50 percent or more. The economy managed to pull out of the tailspin somewhat by 1922, but in 1927 it underwent an even more severe crisis. In between, extreme hardship befell the people as a consequence of the Great Earthquake of 1923.

Socialist leaders had remained somewhat inactive in the labor movement since the trial and execution of Kōtoku and his followers. Consequently, labor leadership had to come from a different direction. In 1912, Suzuki Bunji (1885–1946), a Christian social worker, organized the *Yūaikai* (Fraternal Association) and emphasized the need for harmony between labor and capital. This focus on cooperation secured for the organization the support of prominent business leaders such as Shibusawa. By 1916, the membership had swelled to ten thousand. After observing the labor movement in the United States in 1915, Suzuki changed his focus to some extent and began supporting the right of workers to organize and strike. Thus, the Yūaikai started to develop into a labor union, whereupon the political authorities and the employers began to harass its members. On the other hand, this change in the organization gained it additional supporters from the ranks of college graduates. Among them was Nozaka Sanzō, who became a prominent leader of the Communist party in the post-World War II period.

The socialists, led by Sakai Toshihiko, and anarchists like Ōsugi Sakae and Arahata Kanson began to move cautiously into the labor field again. Initially, the socialist movement was led by intellectuals and theorists who had little connection with the working class, so they failed to establish rapport with the workers.

An increasingly large number of strikes began to be staged, even though they were illegal. In 1914, there were 50 strikes involving only about 7,900 workers, but in 1919, there were 497 strikes in which more than 63,000 workers participated. There was a slight decline in strike activities during the early twenties, but they began to increase again in the mid-twenties, with a growing number of workers joining unions. In 1921, there were 103,400 union members, while in 1926, there were about 385,000. This, however, constituted only 6 to 7 percent of the industrial workers.

In 1919, the Yūaikai began to broaden its base as a labor organization and changed its name to *Dainihon Rōdō Sōdōmei Yūaikai* (The Yūaikai of the All Japan Federation of Labor). Its declaration of principles proclaimed, "Man is by nature free. The working man is a human being. He is not to be bought and sold in the wage market." Among its objectives were the freedom to organize labor unions, the elimination of child labor, and the establishment of minimum wages. It also called for universal suffrage, revision of the Police Regulation Law, and democratization of the educational system.

A major triumph for the labor movement was achieved in 1919, by the workers of the Kawasaki shipyards in Kobe. They won an agreement for an eight-hour workday by engaging in "sabotage," which involved slowing down the pace of work. Following this, the eight-hour workday was obtained by workers in other heavy industrial plants. Female workers in textile plants, however, still labored for eleven or twelve hours a day.

In 1920, the first May Day demonstration was staged in Tokyo and the participants called for a minimum wage law, an eight-hour workday, a solution to the unemployment problem, and repeal of the Police Regulation Law. The Yūaikai held its national meeting in the same year, and the tone of the organization showed a significant change, with the more radical leaders speaking in terms of overthrowing the capitalists and capturing the means of production for the workers. There were still some who believed in working within the existing system, such as Kagawa Toyohiko, a Christian social worker (see page 422), and they became increasingly disenchanted by the growing militancy of the advocates of direct action.

In the twenties, the struggle for leadership between the radicals and moderates continued. The syndicalists led by Arahata resorted to direct militant action whenever the opportunity presented itself, while the moderates, on the other hand, continued through peaceful means to struggle for collective bargaining, protection against unemployment, and retirement payments. In 1921, a major labor dispute broke out at the Kawasaki and Mitsubishi shipyards in Kobe. The companies used the lockout, and then the governor of Hyōgo Prefecture moved army troops against the strikers, arresting more than three hundred leaders and thus effectively breaking the strike. This diminished the influence of the moderates such as Kagawa, and greatly enhanced the following of the syndicalists and the Marxists in the unions.

After the Great Earthquake of 1923, strikes again began to increase along with a swelling in the membership of unions. However, leadership struggles and cleavages continued to undermine and weaken the movement. In 1925, the Communist-led unions broke from the All Japan

Federation of Labor and organized the Labor Council (*Rōdō Hyōgikai*). In the meanwhile, the political authorities were becoming somewhat more flexible. In 1925, for example, the Police Regulation Law was revised to eliminate the restrictions imposed on labor activities. At the same time, however, laws were adopted providing for compulsory arbitration in public enterprises and defense industries, and control of violence in labor disputes.

A depression preceding the worldwide Great Depression struck Japan early in 1927, and dealt the labor movement a severe setback. Labor, in fact, never recovered from this as Japan then moved on to militarism, and the government tightened its control over all aspects of the society, including labor movements.

AGRARIAN REFORM MOVEMENTS

The efforts in the cities to organize factory workers were mirrored in the rural areas by like attempts to organize tenant farmers. As we noted previously, agrarian poverty resulted in a steady rise in tenancy. In 1917, 51.7 percent of the cultivated land was under tenancy with the tenants paying an average of 51 to 55 percent of the harvest as rent. Compared to a factory worker, a tenant's income was beggarly; for example, around 1917–1920 in Aichi Prefecture, a factory worker earned from 1 yen 80 sen to 2 yen 50 sen a day whereas tenant's income varied from 75 sen to 1 yen a day.

Disputes over rental rates began to increase after the recession of 1920, and the urban intellectuals and social workers moved into the countryside to organize the tenant farmers. In 1922, the All Japan Farmers Union (*Nihon Nōmin Kumiai*) was organized by Kagawa and other Christian leaders. Reflecting Kagawa's idealism, the union called for mutual aid, love and friendship, rejection of violence, and the uplifting of the peasants' lives. By 1926, there were more than 150,000 members in the union. Subsequently, other tenant unions were organized and, by 1927, more than 365,000 men were in unions, encompassing 7 percent of all farm families. The number of tenant disputes ran from fifteen hundred to two thousand per year from 1921 to 1925, and hit a high of over twenty-seven hundred in 1926. In many cases the altercations were settled by compromise, but in some instances the landlords got court orders to prevent the farmers from entering the fields held in tenancy. The landlords had the law on their side, thus creating a situation in which it was almost impossible for the tenant unions to make much headway. Nevertheless, they did succeed in getting rents reduced to some extent. After the Manchurian Incident of 1931 and the upsurge of right-wing nationalism, the tenant movement collapsed.

THE OUTCASTS AND THE *SUIHEISHA*

Despite the fact that legal discrimination against the eta had been abolished in 1871, social discrimination against these so-called outcasts continued. They still lived in separate communities, suffered discrimination in jobs, and were restricted to endogamous marriages.

Another aspect of the general reform movement that was emerging in the Taishō era was the effort launched by the eta leaders in 1922, to organize the *Suiheisha* (Levelers Society) for the purpose of pursuing their struggle for equality. The government extended financial aid to the eta communities after the rice riots in which a large number of eta were involved. The eta leaders, however, rejected this paternalistic approach and contended that true freedom could only be achieved through their own efforts. They urged their fellow eta to take pride in their heritage and fight for their dignity as well as economic and occupational freedom.

Initially, the Suiheisha leaders encouraged their members to denounce and extract public apologies from anyone who in any way insulted or expressed contempt for the eta. They hoped to eradicate social discrimination by taking aggressive actions against individual wrongdoers, but not surprisingly, this approach tended to harden and internalize the resentment and disdain that the other classes felt toward them. Consequently, the leaders decided that the social system itself had to be transformed, and they began to link their movement with the Marxist, proletarian class struggle.

MOVEMENT FOR FEMININE RIGHTS

Meiji Japan may have legally abolished the Tokugawa social class system, but it did nothing to change the status of women. They were still considered to be inferior beings subject to the control of the patriarchal head of the family. Legally, daughters could marry without the consent of the parents at the age of 25, but this seldom, if ever, happened. Marriages were almost invariably arranged by the parents. "Marriage for the Japanese girl meant losing individual freedom," wrote one feminist leader. "The relationship between man and wife in a Japanese home is not that of two supplementary personalities, but that of master and servant. It is the relation between the absolute possessor and the property." [7]

The wife was treated as a minor by law. She could not enter into any contract without her husband's consent; her property was placed at the

---

[7] Shidzue Ishimoto, *Facing Two Ways, the Story of My Life* (New York: Farrar & Rinehart, 1935), p. 349.

disposal of her husband; she could be divorced easily without her husband being required to provide for her livelihood; and in the event of divorce, the children were kept by the husband. Family property was inherited by the eldest son, with daughters seldom being given a share.

Except for factory work, few women were employed in the business or professional fields. The employment of married women in particular was very uncommon, and even those who worked in factories were released upon marriage. Politically, women were not only denied the franchise, but the Police Regulation Law prohibited them from joining political parties and even forbade them from sponsoring or attending public political discussions.

Female literary figures initiated the movement aimed at gaining recognition of rights for women. Among the leaders was Hiratsuka Raichō (1886–1971), who started a women's literary organization called the *Seitō* (Blue Stocking) Society in 1911. The main purpose of this group was to discover and develop the hidden talent, particularly literary capability, in women. It may not have sought the liberation of all women, but it did, nonetheless, constitute a pioneer effort in combating the ingrained customs that fettered Japanese women. The feminist leaders were willing to defy public opinion and challenge the conventional mores.

As might be expected, members of the Seitō Society were subjected to hostile criticisms, and their journal, advocating equal rights for women, was suppressed by the authorities. These actions, however, only served to inflame the members, who then went on to defy the established mores all the more vehemently. Hiratsuka rejected the existing marital system and practiced community living with a younger male artist. Another feminist, Itō Noe, refused to accept the marital arrangement made for her by her parents, and turned for intellectual inspiration to the anarchist Emma Goldman. Itō became increasingly conscious of the social injustices around her, and she grew steadily more radical. Eventually she became the companion of Ōsugi Sakae, the leading Taishō anarchist. She once wrote,

> When I was in girls' school all our teachers taught us
> that in order to attain happiness we must learn to be
> satisfied with our lot. They taught us to eliminate all the
> impulses that emanated from within our hearts. Why do
> they not teach us to destroy the environment and customs
> for the sake of the impulses that stir up from within? [8]

[8] *Itō Noe Zenshū* (*The Complete Works of Itō Noe*), 2 vols. (Tokyo: Gakugei Shorin, 1970), vol. 2, p. 19.

Hiratsuka began to work for equal political rights for women around 1919. She had the assistance of Ichikawa Fusae, who was active in the Yūaikai, and others in circulating a petition calling for the revision of the Police Regulation Law, which prohibited women from engaging in political activities. They also asked for measures that would prevent men afflicted with venereal diseases from getting married.

In 1920, the feminists organized the New Women's Association (*Shin Fujinkyōkai*) and asked not only for equal opportunities for women, but also for the protection of the rights of mothers and children. They sponsored numerous lecture series on a variety of subjects for the purpose of uplifting the political, social, and cultural awareness of women; published a journal; and agitated for universal suffrage. Their efforts did not produce much in the way of immediate results. In 1922, however, women were granted the right to sponsor and listen to political speeches, even though they were still prohibited from joining or organizing a political party.

In 1924, the League for the Attainment of Women's Political Rights (*Fujin Sanseiken Kakutoku Kiseidōmei*) was organized, mainly by middle-class women. At the same time, a socialist women's organization, the *Sekiran* (Red Waves) Society, was started by those who believed that discrimination against women was a by-product of the capitalistic system. This was a puzzling interpretation in light of the fact that it was so clearly a legacy of the feudalistic past.

Higher education for women was still limited even in the 1920s. The first women's college was established in 1911, and by 1928 there were only 37 college-level institutions for women as compared to 222 for men. There were 161,430 men in colleges or universities and only 14,127 women.

An increasingly large number of girls were beginning to be employed in white-collar jobs as typists, telephone operators, and clerks, but they were paid anywhere from one-half to two-thirds of the pay that men received for the same work. The society still looked upon these business women with considerable disdain.

The status of women was measurably enhanced by the emergence of a number of prominent females in the entertainment world. Miura Tamaki became a world renowned opera singer, gaining fame for her renditions in *Madame Butterfly*. Matsui Sumako became the first Japanese female stage star, appearing as Nora in Ibsen's *A Doll's House*. She uplifted the acting profession, which was held in low esteem, to the level of respectability. Her personal life outside the theater was publicly known and, like her career, it too clashed with existing conventions. For years, she carried on a love affair with her teacher, who was a married man with children. The movies and the female stars that emerged from them also became a vehicle for advancing the status of women. Such stars as Kurishima Sumiko frequently outclassed their male counterparts in popularity.

DEMOCRATIC AND SOCIALISTIC POLITICAL MOVEMENTS

The Taishō era was a period in which democratic concepts gained considerable support and influence. The chief spokesman for the theoretical underpinnings of this movement was Yoshino Sakuzō (1878–1933), a Christian humanist and a professor at the Imperial University of Tokyo. The political philosophy that he espoused did not advocate the establishment of a democracy in which sovereignty would reside with the people (minshu-shugi). Stated briefly, what he propounded was a democracy in which the government would be rooted in the people and have as its main goal their general well-being (mimpon-shugi). Public opinion would be the deciding force in politics, but it was not to be simply an assessment of what the masses thought about a particular subject. The ideas that constitute public opinion, according to Yoshino, would be originally formulated by a group of thinkers who would then have to win popular support for them. These ideas would have no moral value or political validity unless they received popular support. In the political system, public opinion would have to be represented by means of universal suffrage and party government. Yoshino's moderate political philosophy certainly did not appeal to the growing circle of socialists, but his ideas did find a receptive audience in liberal intellectuals, and his advocacy of universal (manhood) suffrage gave a strong boost to that movement.

Radical political thinking was represented by a wide range of socialist thinkers extending from democratic socialists, Bolsheviks, syndicalists, to anarchists. In December, 1920, a rather motley group set about organizing the Socialist League (Shakaishugi Dōmei). Among the more prominent leaders were Sakai Toshihiko, the veteran socialist agitator, Yamakawa Hitoshi (1880–1958), who had turned from Christianity to socialism, and Arahata Kanson (1887–   ), an anarchist and syndicalist. Probably the most interesting of the lot was Ōsugi Sakae (1885–1923), an anarchist agitator who was something of a charismatic leader. He was the son of a military officer, but his political awareness was initially aroused by an anti-military article written by Kōtoku. Ōsugi, like many other socialists, was also influenced by Christianity. He was baptized by a fiery evangelist, Ebina Danjō, who ironically enough was a right-wing nationalist.

Ōsugi was, to be sure, a dedicated anarchist and a defiant individualist, but perhaps above all he was a romantic. He said:

> I like that which is spiritual. But I dislike theorizing
> about it. . . . For this reason I really abhor scholars of
> law and government who talk about mimpon [see above]
> and humanity. . . . I have a strong aversion for socialism
> also. At times I even feel a distaste for anarchism. What
> I like above all is the blind actions of men, the natural
> explosion of the spirit. There must be freedom of thought,
> freedom of action, and freedom of impulses.[9]

The Socialist League was disbanded by the government just six months after its inception, but it nevertheless played a critical role in bringing together the labor leaders and the socialists. This was vitally important because until this point, the labor leaders never fully trusted these intellectuals and theorists who had never worked in factories. As a result of this cooperative venture, the influence of the anarchists and syndicalists came to be felt strongly in the labor movement. In fact, the cleavage they created between the radicals and the moderates rather effectively disrupted the Yūaikai.

The Socialist League itself was torn by internal dissension—there was constant feuding between the anarchists led by Ōsugi and the Marxists led by Sakai and Yamakawa. Ōsugi believed that the centralization of authority in Soviet Russia had destroyed the revolution; the Bolsheviks had been too eager to restore order. He maintained that if they had allowed anarchic conditions to prevail a bit longer, something approximating Kropotkin's ideal society would surely have come about. The socialists were divided further by the split between the revisionists, who took the name "Social Democrats," and the orthodox Marxists, who then used the term "Communists."

In July, 1922, Yamakawa, Sakai, Arahata, and Tokuda Kyūichi (who became the leader of the Communist party in the postwar period), secretly organized the Japanese Communist party (*Nihon Kyōsantō*), with Sakai as the chairman of the central committee. The party then received the official recognition of the fourth Congress of the Comintern.

Yamakawa and the other Communists held a negative attitude toward universal suffrage and were disinclined to support the bourgeois parliamentary system because it contributed to the fortification of capitalistic control. However, the Comintern under Bukharin directed the party leaders to support the bourgeois liberals in their fight against the semi-feudalistic forces that were still in control of Japan. The Bukharin Theses held that the Communists must begin work for the overthrow of

---

[9] Masumi Junnosuke, *Nihon Seitōshiron* (*Discourses on the History of Japanese Political Parties*), 4 vols. (Tokyo: Tōkyō Daigaku Shuppankai, 1965–1968), vol. 4, pp. 142–43.

the Emperor and the monarchic form of government by initiating a demo-cratic revolution. Hence, it was clear that they had to work for universal suffrage if they hoped to realize their goals.

In 1923, the government arrested the Communist leaders after obtaining the party membership list through an informer. In order to curb socialist and Communist activities, the government established the Higher Police Bureau in a number of prefectures. The task of this department was to combat advocates of "dangerous thought," an ever-growing category that began to encompass a larger and larger number of independent thinkers.

After their release, the Communist leaders voted to dissolve the party on the ground that the time was not yet ripe for the establishment of a Communist party in Japan. The authorities, however, did not cease harassing the Communists. In 1925, the government, headed by Katō Kōmei, drafted the Peace Preservation Law, which made it illegal to ad-vocate either change in the national polity or the abolition of private property.

Efforts were made to organize a broadly based socialist party, but the cleavage between the social democrats and the Communists kept the proletarian forces fragmented. By the end of 1926, there were several parties: the pro-Communist *Rōdō Nōmintō* (Labor-Farmer party) headed by Ōyama Ikuo; the socialist right-wing *Shakai Minshūtō* (Social Mass party) led by Abe Isoo and Yoshino Sakuzō; and the *Nihon Rōnōtō* (Japan Labor-Farmer party) led by Asō Hisashi, which stood midway be-tween the first two parties. The Labor-Farmer party was in effect an auxiliary of the Communist party, while the Social Mass party was closely affiliated with the *Nihon Rōdō Sōdōmei* (All Japan Federation of Labor). There was also the conservative and nationalistic *Nihon Nōmintō* (Japan Farmer party).

All of these various socialist parties were to continue to split and unite in a chaotic fashion, while seriously diminishing their influence and effectiveness. Some began to swing to the right and organize nationalistic, socialist parties; others aligned themselves with the militarists.

The Communists sought to revive their party under the leadership of younger men in late 1926, while some of the older leaders, such as Yama-kawa and Arahata, fell out of favor with the Comintern and were con-sequently isolated from the movement. The new organization was first led by Fukumoto Kazuo (1894–   ), who sought to purge the party of fellow travelers and social democrats because he believed that it should consist exclusively of pure Marxist thinkers. In 1927, the Comintern con-demned Fukumotism for its stress on the intelligentsia and ordered the party to get involved with the workers and peasants in order to achieve the socialist revolution.

The fragmentation in the socialistic political movement made it difficult for candidates from any of these parties to succeed in Diet elections. For example, in the 1928 election, the left-wing parties managed to win only eight seats (four of the victors were members of the Social Mass party).

The government under General Tanaka Giichi (1863–1929), who became Prime Minister in April, 1927, launched a vigorous campaign to ferret out and persecute the Communists. On March 15, 1928, midnight raids were staged throughout the country, and 1,600 persons were arrested. Torture was used freely during the interrogation of these men. The victims were beaten over their heads with bamboo poles, stabbed with thick needles, kicked, hung upside down with their heads bounced on the floor, or repeatedly choked until they became unconscious. The proletarian writer Kobayashi Takiji, who wrote a novel exposing such brutalities, was himself arrested, and after several hours of "questioning" he died. Mass arrests of Communists and those suspected of being Communists continued into the 1930s until the backbone of the movement was crushed. This relentless persecution of those who harbored "dangerous thought" resulted in many incarcerated Communists "converting" to the "imperial way" and renouncing their ideology. The conversion of two prominent leaders in June, 1933, was followed by 548 persons then under arrest or in jail disavowing communism. As a matter of fact, only a handful of leaders, including the postwar Communist leaders Tokuda Kyūichi and Shiga Yoshio, refused to recant.

Marxism had a considerable number of supporters in the academic community with many professors and students participating in Marxist study groups. The Red hunt, however, also hit the universities and a great many students were arrested while more than a few prominent scholars were dismissed from their positions.

In comparison to Marxism, Western liberalism, which entered Japan in early Meiji, constituted a much less serious threat to the traditional institutions, values, and way of life. To be sure, liberalism's stress on the worth and importance of the individual certainly challenged the traditional group-oriented values and life style, but it did not seek to bring about changes through violence or revolution. It was essentially an optimistic philosophy holding that self-interest would serve the good of the whole society. Its emphasis on reason and science was in tune with the desire of the ruling elite to modernize and industrialize the country. The Meiji liberals accepted the emperor system, supported nationalism, and stopped just short of introducing self-interest into the family. They upheld social classes insofar as they believed that the propertied class, the middle class, should play a dominant role in society.

Marxism, on the other hand, was primarily a revolutionary political movement. It rejected the emperor system and the propertied class, and advocated class struggles, thus challenging the traditional emphasis on social harmony. It was rigid and doctrinaire, offering only an either/or choice of becoming a Marxist or a slave of capitalism. Hence, it conflicted with the traditional proclivity for compromise. It forsook nationalism while looking to a foreign authority for guidance.

Initially, however, the Japanese socialists and Communists were not good Marxists; they were not at all well-versed in Marxian doctrines. In fact, the most potent influence on the early socialists was Christian humanism, although many of them drifted away from it later in their lives. For instance, the founders of the Social Democratic party, such as Katayama Sen and Abe Isoo, were Christians. Even Kōtoku, who denied that he was a Christian, was obsessed to the very end of his life with the problem of coping with Christianity.

The most influential of the Christian social reformers was Kagawa Toyohiko (1888–1960), who was born into a wealthy merchant family and devoted a major portion of his life to helping the industrial and agrarian poor. He was baptized at the age of sixteen and began working and preaching in the slums of Kobe at the age of twenty-one. He caught a variety of communicable diseases while living in the slums, including trachoma, which nearly blinded him. He nevertheless continued his evangelical work, pursued his own education, published a number of works based on his experiences in the slums, and participated in labor and agrarian reform movements. By 1920, he had become a prominent figure as both a Christian evangelist and a social reformer. His influence in the labor movement began to decline, however, as the anarchists, syndicalists, and Marxists extended their control, but he remained an active social reformer. Yamamuro Gumpei, the founder of the Salvation Army in Japan, compared Kagawa to St. Francis of Assisi, and he was often ranked with Albert Schweitzer by his American admirers.

CHAPTER 17

ERA OF
PARLIAMENTARY
ASCENDANCY (II)

CULTURE OF THE TAISHŌ ERA

The Taishō era was a period during which such concepts as individual rights, freedom, and democracy flourished in the intellectual and cultural realms. The Taishō intellectuals were not burdened with the task of "enriching and strengthening" the nation as were their predecessors in the Meiji era. These thinkers grew up in a relatively carefree atmosphere at a time when Japan had already joined the ranks of the world's major powers. The educational level of the people had been raised, and the intellectual and cultural sophistication of the better educated members of the society had been heightened. Consequently, this was also a period during which a "cultural elite," who cherished "cultural refinement," flourished. The number of well-educated urban dwellers had steadily increased as the economy expanded and the society was modernized. There was a growing number of professional men, executives, engineers, technicians, and office workers as well as government employees, educators, writers, and entertainers. These people made up the core of those who enjoyed and participated in Taishō culture.

Taishō Japan was also characterized by a thriving popular culture. Popular novels, magazines, newspapers, and the new media of radio and motion pictures disseminated "culture" into the countryside and the lower levels of the cultural and intellectual spectrum.

In order to meet the demand for better educated workers, the number of colleges, higher schools, and middle schools increased significantly.

423

By 1925, there were 34 universities, 29 higher schools, and 84 professional schools. There was a particularly impressive growth in the number of middle schools, those for boys increased from 218 in 1900, to 491 in 1924, and those for girls jumped from 52 to 576.[1]

A strong sense of individualism was manifested in the literary world through the White Birch (*Shirakaba*) School, whose journal was first published in 1910. Among the founding members were Mushanokōji Saneatsu, Shiga Naoya, and Arishima Takeo. The men who belonged to this school were usually young members of the upper class, most of whom attended the aristocratic Peers School. The philosophy of the White Birch School was explained by Mushanokōji (1885–   ), who said that the purpose of life was to be in harmony with the "will of mankind." This could be achieved by living in accordance with one's individual attributes or by letting one's individual personality have free play. The individual must place his trust in his own "spirit." "I do not believe that my spirit is only my own," wrote Mushanokōji. "It has something in common with the spirit of all mankind. . . . What I desire is what mankind desires." [2] Mushanokōji's philosophy was based upon the optimistic notion that "true happiness can be achieved by acting in accordance with the dictates of one's conscience. The value of man is found in the fact that the pursuit of one's authentic self-interest leads to the well-being of all of mankind." [3] This is not, however, to be confused with the prosaic concept of self-interest that was held by the nineteenth-century political economists. Mushanokōji's concept was that of an artist who believed in having "a heart that dances together with nature and mankind." [4]

In emphasizing the importance of individuality and the supremacy of subjectivity, Mushanokōji's circle made a deep impression on the Taishō youths. It induced some, who responded by limiting their attention to their own private lives, their immediate family members, friends, and nature, to become increasingly indifferent to the society in which they lived.

In turning inward to their private lives, the writers of the White Birch School produced a form of autobiographical fiction referred to as the "I" novel. The motivation for this kind of expression can be found in

---

[1] The elementary school, which was compulsory, consisted of six years; middle school for boys was five years; middle school for girls was four years; higher school was three years; and college was three years.

[2] Mushanokōji Saneatsu, *Atarashiki Mura no Seikatsu* (*Life in a New Village*) (Tokyo: Shinchōsha, 1969), p. 1.

[3] Imai Seiichi, *Taishō Demokurashii* (*Taishō Democracy*) (Tokyo: Chūō Kōronsha, 1966), p. 119.

[4] Mitsuo Nakamura, *Modern Japanese Fiction, 1868–1926* (Tokyo: Nihon Bunka Sinkokai, 1968), pt. 2, p. 36.

the remarks that Mushanokōji jotted down after being deeply impressed by the paintings of the French expressionists.

> A heart wants to embrace another heart. But man fears it
> for the sake of his own existence. He conceals where his
> heart is. He believes such an attitude is necessary to
> maintain his position in society. Thus every heart feels
> lonely. Recent art seems to be trying to satisfy this yearning.
> I feel that recent art is the exposing of one's heart boldly
> on paper, waiting for another heart to come to it to em-
> brace it.[5]

The object of the "I" novel, then, was to bring the heart of the reader into contact with the heart of the writer.

The most influential author of autobiographical fiction was Shiga Naoya (1883–1971), whose great success with confessional stories induced many young writers to follow his example. "I" novels came to dominate the literary scene to such a considerable extent that Shiga earned the acclaim of having influenced contemporary Japanese literature more than any other modern writer. Philosophically, he held with the doctrine of the supremacy of subjectivity as espoused by the White Birch School, and this led him to make his likes and dislikes the yardstick for good and evil. In his writings he dealt mostly with his feelings about his family and about nature.

The other prominent writer of this school was Arishima Takeo (1878–1923). He had studied in America, where he attended Haverford and Harvard, and was deeply influenced by both Christian humanism and socialism. His desire to become a part of the social reform movement was so enthusiastic and sincere that he gave his thousand-acre farm in Hokkaido to the tenants working the land. They were to operate the farm as a communal enterprise even though Arishima was convinced that communalism could not possibly succeed as long as the society remained capitalistic. However, as a member of the upper class he believed he had no right to meddle in the business of the proletariat. The working class, as far as Arishima was concerned, did not need the support of the intellectuals or scholars, not even of luminaries like Kropotkin or Marx. The struggle and eventual triumph of the working man will come out of his own proletarian experience. Arishima wanted desperately to participate in that struggle, but he could not do so because he was not a member of the working class. His growing sense of social impotence thrust him into a state of nihilistic despair, and seeking to find the ultimate meaning of life in love, he committed suicide with a female mag-

[5] *Ibid.*, pp. 32–33.

azine reporter in 1923. The philosophical rationale for this final act can perhaps be found in his theory that if there are three stages to human life—habitual, intellectual, and instinctive—true freedom is found in the instinctive or impulsive phase.

A group of young writers who were influenced by Natsume Sōseki started a literary journal called *Shin Shichō* (*New Thought*). Among them were Akutagawa Ryūnosuke, Kikuchi Kan, and Tanizaki Junichirō. Kikuchi (1888–1948) started his literary career by writing serious literature in which he sought to uncover the realities of life, but he soon abandoned the search for profound "truths" and shifted to writing for mass readership. His primary objective was no longer the creation of "pure" literature; he now sought to write entertaining stories by focusing upon a single aspect of human behavior, such as egoism, and treating it in a way that would appeal to the emotions of the reader. He may be accused of having succumbed to commercialism, but he did nevertheless contribute immensely to the popularization of literature.

The most brilliant member of the *Shin Shichō* circle was Akutagawa Ryūnosuke (1892–1927), whose work has been described as a manifestation of "pure intellect and refinement." Essentially, he had a pessimistic, almost cynical, attitude toward life, which he viewed as a wretched affair in which man is hopelessly entrapped in his egoism. Early in his work, Akutagawa was able to depict this with a sense of detachment, satirizing human foibles in a humorous vein. He also sought to find meaning in life through a philosophy that holds art to be transcendent above all else. "Life," he said, "is not worth one line of Baudelaire." Akutagawa could not, however, completely avoid ethical issues even though he believed that "morality was another name for convenience," and ultimately he lost confidence in the meaningfulness of art itself.

Akutagawa believed that unexpected events continuously prevent man from achieving happiness and the fulfillment of his desires. This view is reflected in the plot of "Jigokuhen" ("The Hell Screen"). In the story a court artist, who was commissioned by his lord to paint a screen depicting a scene in hell, asks that a woman be burned in a carriage so as to enable him to paint a realistic picture of a person burning in hell. The lord accedes to his request, but when the artist comes to paint the scene he finds that the victim, chained to the carriage, is his only daughter. He paints his masterpiece and then kills himself.

Akutagawa fell deeper and deeper into the abyss of pessimism and his thoughts were drawn increasingly toward death. In one of his later works he wrote, "If by chance we are made to feel the attraction of death, it is very difficult to escape from it. And as if we are going around a concentric circle we are drawn gradually toward death." Finally, in 1927, he committed suicide saying he felt "a vague sense of uneasiness about the future." To his children he left the words, "Do not forget that life is a battle that leads to death. If you are defeated in this battle of life commit suicide like your father." [6]

The writing career of Tanizaki Junichirō (1886–1965) extends from the Taishō to the postwar eras. He was influenced by such Western writers as Baudelaire, Poe, and Wilde, and in his early writings he revealed a strong interest in the sensuous as well as in sadomasochism. Tanizaki worshipped female pulchritude and considered men as being merely "manure" for the nurturing of feminine beauty, which often leads the men in his writings to commit abnormal acts of masochism and fetishism. Man's true happiness, in Tanizaki's opinion, consisted in being conquered by women.

Like many of his fellow writers who were opposed to naturalism, Tanizaki concentrated on evoking mood and atmosphere rather than defining things in concrete detail. His advice to aspiring writers was: "Do not try to be too clear, leave some gaps in the meaning. We Japanese scorn the bald fact, and we consider it good form to keep a thin sheet of paper between the fact and object, and the words that give expression to it." [7] He also believed that the Japanese prefer to see beauty left in the shadows rather than exposed to the harsh lights of critical scrutiny. "In the mansion called literature," he wrote, "I would have the eaves deep and the walls dark, I would push back into the shadows, the things that come forward too clearly." [8]

Another writer whose literary career spanned more than half a century was Nagai Kafū (1879–1959), who started out as a naturalist writer but soon turned for his subject matter to traditional Japan, manifesting particular nostalgia for the city of Edo. This shift in focus was fostered by his visit to France, where he was struck by the strong and enriching influence that traditional culture had on that country. He developed an intense dislike of what he considered the "false civilization" that had emerged in Japan as a consequence of the impact of an alien, that is, Western, civilization. He came to manifest a reverence toward the past. "Let us be respectful of the past," he wrote. "The past is the mystical spring from which the future must always flow. It is the torch lighting the uncertain way of the present." [9]

To find remnants of the past, Kafū turned to the brothels of Tokyo,

---

[6] Kadokawa Genyoshi et al., eds., Nihon Bungaku no Rekishi (A History of Japanese Literature), 12 vols. (Tokyo: Kadokawa Shoten, 1967–1968), vol. 11, pp. 199–215.

[7] Junichirō Tanizaki, Some Prefer Nettles, trans. Edward G. Seidensticker (New York: Knopf, 1955), p. xv.

[8] Junichirō Tanizaki, "In Praise of Shadow," in Perspective of Japan, an Atlantic Monthly supplement (New York, 1954), pp. 47–48.

[9] Edward G. Seidensticker, Kafū the Scribbler (Stanford, Calif.: Stanford University Press, 1965), p. 49.

where the old ways of Japan were still preserved. He extolled feminine beauty, but this was not his primary interest. The life of the geisha fascinated him for its manifestation of the manners and mores of traditional Japan. Later in his career he turned his attention to the modern counterparts of the geisha, that is, the café girls, the street walkers, and the dance hall girls.

Proletarian literature was given impetus during this period by the increasing activities of the socialists and the Communists. The proletarian writers, in some ways similar to the naturalists, were unconcerned about literary style and concentrated on an almost scientifically precisioned treatment of reality. Unlike the naturalists, they focused exclusively on the life of the working classes. A few novels dealing with the plight of the impoverished had been written before the Taishō era. The most prominent of these, *Earth* by Nagatsuka Takashi, was published in 1910; it depicted the very difficult and bleak life of the peasants. In 1921 a journal devoted to proletarian literature, *The Sowers of Seeds,* came into existence.

A considerable number of proletarian novels were published, but because Marxist writers believed that art and literature should serve political ends, much of the work followed the pat formula of socialist realism or were rather blatantly dogmatic propaganda tracts. Few revealed any serious literary quality. One writer, indignant at the proletarian disregard for the conventions of style and form, exclaimed, "Who is it that's destroying the flower garden?" Kobayashi Takiji wrote one of the best-known proletarian novels. In his *Cannery Boat,* published in 1929, Kobayashi described realistically the terrible conditions under which the crews of fishing and canning boats had to work.

A group of young writers referred to as the neo-perceptionists emerged as a reaction against the socialist realism of their proletarian counterparts. Their objective was to reaffirm the importance of literary values. Among them was Kawabata Yasunari (1899–   ), the winner of the Nobel Prize for Literature in 1968. The first of his works to be widely read was *The Izu Dancer,* published in 1926, and he is still writing today. He is not a prolific author, but each work that he has published has been praised for its lyrical qualities. E. G. Seidensticker, Kawabata's translator, compares his style to that of the haiku masters. "Haiku seeks to convey a sudden awareness of beauty by a mating of opposite or incongruous terms. Thus the classical haiku characteristically fuses motion and stillness. Similarly Kawabata relies very heavily on a mingling of the senses." Seidensticker goes on to point out that his novels, like those of many other Japanese writers, are not built around the form of a carefully structured beginning, development, and dénouement. Instead, Kawabata's novels "shift from one episode to another, each with rich lyricism, through a well-controlled flow of associations. . . . His expression is marked by extreme simplicity. He makes the most of all words and conveys to the reader meaning and atmosphere, not explicitly, but by a roundabout implicit style." After the Second World War, Kawabata said he would write only about "the grief and beauty of Japan. I will live with the mountains and rivers of Japan as my soul." [10]

Literacy became increasingly widespread with the consequence that newspaper circulations rose, popular magazines flourished, and novels designed to have mass appeal gained a large readership. There was frantic competition among the newspapers to capture the subscription market, and by the mid-twenties, those with nationwide distribution were claiming circulation figures of 1 to 1.5 million. In order to attract readers, entertainment features were emphasized. One of the most appealing of these was the serialization of novels by well-known popular writers, such as Kikuchi Kan.

Magazines dealing with political, social, and literary matters began to increase in number and circulation, but they were still primarily directed at the more sophisticated urban reader. Noma Seiji, a genius when it came to popular journalism, was particularly inventive and successful in his pursuit of mass readership. He began publishing monthly magazines that contained stories of samurai heroics, sentimental romance, melodramatic events, and didactic tales. He brought together many of the talented popular story writers, and put on a massive advertising campaign to draw attention to his publications. In 1925 he started publishing *Kingu* (*King*), which he vowed would become "the most entertaining, the most beneficial, the cheapest, and the best-selling magazine in Japan." The first issue appeared and 740,000 copies were immediately sold out. Noma also published an extremely popular women's magazine as well as magazines for the young. He attributed his success to the fact that he included articles that "were always a step behind the times." In 1930, the total circulation of his nine magazines came to six million copies. It is conceivable that Noma, as the indisputable leader of the popular magazine field, exerted more influence in molding popular culture from the 1920s to the end of the Second World War than any other person in Japan.

Many writers turned to the newly opened outlets, such as newspapers, magazines, and pocketbook editions, for the publication of their work. One of the more unusual writers to do this was Nakazato Kaizan (1885–1944). He wrote what is reputed to be the world's longest novel, *The Mountain Pass of the Great Bodhisattva*, which is three times the length of Tolstoy's *War and Peace*. Nakazato's novel depicts the life of a nihil-

[10] *Japan Report* (New York: Consulate General of Japan, 1968), vol. 14, nos. 20, 22.

istic warrior who is destined by his *karma* to wander about as a blind swordsman. Nakazato commenced writing it in 1912 and was still working on it when he died in 1944. He was influenced by Christianity, Tolstoy, and socialism when he was a young man, but he eventually turned to nihilism, perhaps in despair as he saw the real world crushing his idealistic dreams.

Another very significant writer who wrote historical novels and tales of valorous swordsmen was Yoshikawa Eiji (1892–1962). He had received only an elementary education but became the most widely read of the popular writers. "History," Yoshikawa said, "has to do with the affairs of the present," and he wrote stories that were appropriate to the mood of the age. Hence, the novels he wrote in the thirties manifested the militaristic temper of that era. The most renowned of his works is the historical novel *Miyamoto Musashi,* whose central character, Miyamoto, is a hero who uses the sword not only as a way to perfect himself, but also as a means "to regulate the people and govern the land." (See page 126 for a historical reference to this early seventeenth-century figure.)

The other forms of mass entertainment that began to capture a wide following were the phonograph, the radio (which was introduced in 1925), and the motion picture (which came to be mass-produced in the twenties).

Some scientists and philosophers made noteworthy contributions during the Meiji and Taishō eras. The field of science posed particularly difficult problems because work had to start virtually from scratch after the Meiji Restoration. Japan was dependent largely on foreign scholars for the first few decades, but by the latter half of Meiji some Japanese scientists began formulating new theories and making new discoveries. The first internationally renowned scientist to come out of Japan was Kitazato Shibasaburō (1852–1931), who discovered the bacillus of bubonic plague in 1894. He also isolated the bacilli of dysentery and tetanus and prepared an antitoxin for diphtheria. Fukuzawa supported him in establishing an institute for the study of contagious diseases, and then Kitazato went on to develop it into one of the world's finest bacteriological-research institutes.

Other notable Japanese scientists soon began to emerge. Nagaoka Hantarō (1865–1950) pioneered in the theoretical construction of atomic models, while also finding time to contribute to experimental research in atomic spectra. Kimura Hisashi (1870–1943) contributed to the verification of latitudinal changes. The renowned seismologist Ōmori Fusakichi (1868–1923) devised a formula for computing seismic tremors. Takamine Jōkichi (1854–1922), working in the field of pharmacology, discovered adrenaline and diastase. The internationally famous bacteriologist Noguchi Hideyo (1876–1928), who studied in the United States and did research for the Rockefeller Foundation, made discoveries concerning the cause and treatment of syphilis and yellow fever.

In the philosophical realm, the popularity during early Meiji of English utilitarianism and French positivism was followed by interest in Darwinism and the theory of evolution, which was fostered by E. S. Morse and Fenollosa. In the 1890s, however, German idealism began to dominate philosophical studies in the academic world, and Kantian and Hegelian concepts continued to influence the Japanese thinkers until the postwar era. The fact that German philosophy combined deep moral and religious characteristics with strictly logical approaches to thought, made it especially appealing to the Japanese.

As a result of this influence, attempts were made by Japanese thinkers to systematize their own thoughts by using the speculative and logical methods employed by the German philosophers. The first significant outcome of this approach came in 1911 with the publication of *A Study of Good* by Nishida Kitarō (1870–1945). Nishida continued to develop the basic concepts presented in this work for the next forty years and secured for himself the reputation of being the most important *original* thinker of modern Japan.

Nishida was influenced by many Western philosophers, such as Hegel, Bergson, Williams James, Husserl, and the Neo-Kantians. At the same time, he was also strongly influenced by Zen Buddhism; in fact it was Zen intuition that constituted the very foundation of his thinking. He attempted, however, to develop his method of thinking logically in accordance with the Western philosophical tradition. He sought to construct a philosophy that included religious and mystical elements as well as rational science.

In his *A Study of Good,* Nishida endeavored to define the nature of reality in terms of "pure" or "direct" experience, that is, a point before subject and object are separated. This pure experience is to be found in everyday life, but its most typical manifestations are "the dark consciousness of the infant, the creative process of artistic genius, and the consciousness of the religious man who has lost the distinction between himself and another." [11]

In his next work, *Intuition and Reflection in the Consciousness of the Self* (1917), Nishida extended the notion of pure experience into a concept of self-awareness in which "that which knows and that which is known are together identical as the self." He concluded from this that

---

[11] The quotations on Nishida's concepts are from Toratarō Shimomura, "Nishida Kitarō and Some Aspects of His Philosophical Thought," in Kitaro Nishida, *A Study of Good,* trans. V. H. Viglielmo (Tokyo: Japanese Government Printing Bureau, 1960), pp. 191 ff.

the ultimate character of self-awareness was "absolute free will." He sought to transcend the problem of the bifurcation of reality into subjective and objective realms by positing in their stead "the place of nothingness" wherein both subject and object exist and consciousness itself is established. In this domain of absolute nothingness "the form of the formless is seen and the sound of the soundless is heard."

POLITICAL DEVELOPMENTS: 1918–1932

The political parties had changed somewhat in character by the Taishō era. They were now led by new men who came from the bureaucracy, journalism, and the business world. Those fighters for freedom and popular rights during the Meiji era were, by and large, gone except for a very few old-time stalwarts like Ozaki Yukio and Inukai Tsuyoshi. The leaders were not the "rabble rousers" of the past; now they were "respectable" members of the community. The parties were more closely tied to the officialdom and big business than ever before.

The extent of the influence and involvement of big business in the political parties is indicated not only by the number of party members who came from the business field but, more importantly perhaps, by the amount of financial backing provided to the political parties, which were finding it increasingly expensive to run election campaigns. Much of the money went to purchasing votes. The total number of bribery cases that were reported increased steadily after the Russo-Japanese War. The ties between Mitsui and Jiyūtō-Seiyūkai as well as those between Mitsubishi and the parties that stemmed from the Kaishintō were well known. These allegiances, however, were not rigidly fixed and at times the companies would support the rival parties.

Party leaders solicited donations not only from the zaibatsu, but from wealthy individuals as well. Those leaders who were independently wealthy, like Katō Kōmei, were expected to contribute from their own funds. The government usually gave money to progovernment and neutral party members. The ability to raise and dispense political funds to party members gave party leaders a great deal of power, thus making party discipline much tighter than in the earlier years. Hara's control over the Seiyūkai, for example, was based partly on his ability to raise funds. Graft and corruption were the unfortunate by-products of the tremendous need for political funding.

The number of businessmen entering political parties had been increasing, and Hara actively recruited them for the Seiyūkai. Among those he persuaded to enter politics was the president of the Bank of Japan, Takahashi Korekiyo, who eventually succeeded Hara as the head of the Seiyūkai and Prime Minister. In addition to Hara himself, a number of prominent leaders emerged from the bureaucracy, including Katō Kōmei, Hamaguchi Yūkō, and Wakatsuki Reijirō.

Hara took charge of the government in September, 1918, and he was in a fairly strong position at the time. The Seiyūkai was the largest party in the Diet, although it did not have majority control. Yamagata had reconciled himself to a party government headed by Hara, a man he saw as being an essentially responsible leader. Hara had strengthened the Seiyūkai's ties with the business world and officialdom, and he was able to maintain relatively tight control over the party. He was a popular choice and was viewed as the man best suited to heal the wounds left by the rice riots.

The problems, however, that confronted Hara were enormous. Japan's relations with China were becoming increasingly strained; Japanese troops were off in Siberia; there were pressing economic and social prob- lems; the labor movement was growing stronger; and the demand for universal suffrage was gaining popular support. Hara was hardly the bold reformer that the times seemed to demand. He was basically a conserva- tive whose primary objective was the replacement of the Satsuma-Chōshū clique in the government with the Seiyūkai. His policies seemed to be based on the old objectives of Meiji Japan, that is, "enriching and strengthening" the nation. The four major goals proclaimed by him were: educational reforms, expansion of the means of transportation and communication, fortification of national defense, and industrial growth. These were certainly no different from the aims set by previous govern- ments. As a result, the Seiyūkai under Hara's leadership remained rela- tively unresponsive to the demands for reform that were being voiced by the spokesmen for the awakening masses. The Kenseikai, on the other hand, as the party in opposition, became the exponent of reform.

The left-wing critics called the Hara cabinet a rich man's govern- ment. The cabinet posts, with the exception of the war, naval, and foreign ministers, were filled by party men, many of whom were former businessmen having close ties with the zaibatsu. Hara's policies showed that he was not sympathetic to the working class movement or to the democratic forces advocating the adoption of universal suffrage. He was prepared to take a strong stand against strikers by using police and gen- darmes to disperse them and arrest their leaders. He also turned a deaf ear to the plea by the labor leaders that the Police Regulation Law, which restricted union activities, be revised. To counteract their work and possible effectiveness, Hara allowed his Minister of Home Affairs, Tokonami (also a former bureaucrat), to set up an organization of labor contractors, their workmen, and ruffians to serve as strikebreakers. The organization was named the *Dai Nippon Kokusuikai* (Japan National

Essence Society) and was supported by right-wing nationalists such as Tōyama Mitsuru. These "chivalrous patriots" insisted upon "the cooperation of capital and labor."

Hara pursued his repressive efforts by presenting an anti-subversive activities bill to the Diet, but it was opposed by the lower house. He was responsible for the suppression of the Socialist League, and he openly supported the dismissal of Morito Tatsuo, a professor at the University of Tokyo, for publishing an article on Kropotkin's anarchism.

The movement for universal manhood suffrage was gaining popular support, particularly among the moderate labor leaders who believed that the only way that reform could be achieved was through a Diet elected by universal suffrage. Hara was opposed to this but, recognizing the need to broaden the franchise to accommodate public opinion, he proposed that tax qualifications necessary for the privilege to vote be lowered from ten to three yen. The opposition parties (the Kenseikai and the Kokumintō) had favored a reduction to two yen, but Hara's proposal was approved by the Diet in 1919. The Diet also passed Hara's bill to reconstitute the electoral districts so as to replace the large electoral districts, from which anywhere from four to sixteen Diet members were chosen, with small, single-member election districts. Hara favored the small district because he believed that this would prevent men from the small splinter parties, especially socialists, from winning Diet seats.

The expanded franchise increased the number of voters from 2.6 percent of the population to approximately double that figure. That is, there was an increase from about 1.5 million voters to 3.3 million. This was still only a limited extension of the franchise and it did not, of course, satisfy the advocates of universal suffrage. They continued their agitation, eventually winning over Katō's Kenseikai and Inukai's Kokumintō to their cause.

In February, 1920, the Kenseikai and Kokumintō submitted a bill for universal suffrage to the Diet. Shimada Saburō of the Kenseikai criticized the existing class system that was based on wealth and demanded that qualification for the franchise be changed from "things" to "human beings." Seizing upon this as an excuse, Hara promptly dissolved the Diet.

Hara had strengthened the Seiyūkai's power at the local level by bringing men with community influence and prestige into the party. He had also used the technique of "pork barrel" legislation to enhance the Seiyūkai's authority. The party also had the strong support of big businessmen and landlords. The small election districts enabled the Seiyūkai to use these advantages effectively and it won an overwhelming victory at the polls. It captured 117 additional seats to occupy 279 seats in the new Diet, compared to 108 for the Kenseikai, and 29 for the Kokumintō.

This huge majority in the Diet made it possible for Hara to proceed with increases in the size of the navy, and expanded railroad, telephone, telegraph, and road construction. In the previous Diet, measures to increase the number of higher professional schools and colleges had been approved. Steps were taken to nationalize the industrial facilities, so the economy continued to grow following the brief recession at the end of World War I. As a result, Hara was able to achieve the four objectives he had set for his government.

The economic boom that started in the middle of 1919 collapsed in early 1920. In order to save the faltering banks and business firms, the government extended financial aid. Charges of graft and corruption involving government officials and members of the Seiyūkai buffeted the Hara government. In addition, there was the troublesome controversy that arose when it became known that the crown prince's fiancée, whose mother came from the Shimazu family, might pass on the defect of color blindness to the imperial family. Yamagata pressed for the cancellation of the proposed marriage agreement, while the Satsuma faction, with the support of right-wing nationalists such as Tōyama Mitsuru, resisted this move and managed to have the engagement upheld. In 1921, the crown prince took a trip abroad, and upon his return he became regent for the sick Emperor.

In spite of all these problems, Hara managed to fend off his critics because he possessed so strong a majority in the Diet. He appeared to be at the height of his political career when he was struck down by a young assassin in November, 1921. Thus he became the first, but not the last, of the incumbent prime ministers who were felled by fanatical assassins.

In order to preserve a continuity of policy in the Washington Conference to which Hara had just sent a delegation, the genrō asked Takahashi Korekiyo (1854–1936), Hara's Minister of Finance, to head the government. Takahashi was not the adroit politician that Hara was, and in fact, he had rather little interest in party politics. Consequently, he was able to preserve neither cabinet nor party unity when rival factions in the Seiyūkai began squabbling over cabinet posts, and he resigned after only seven months in office.

Yamagata had died in the spring of 1922, so the task of selecting a successor to Takahashi was now the responsibility of Saionji and Matsukata. Ironically enough, Saionji, who had been regarded as a liberal and a supporter of parliamentary government, spent the next few years trying to thwart the efforts of Katō Kōmei and the Kenseikai to gain power. He too resorted to the practice of establishing nonparty cabinets, thus in effect, following the practice that had been Yamagata's hallmark. The Kenseikai not only lacked a majority in the Diet, but Saionji had little confidence in Katō because of the manner in which he had managed the nation's dealings with foreign governments when he was Foreign Minister.

The Seiyūkai, on the other hand, was torn asunder by dissension and a lack of strong leadership. As a result, Saionji turned to Katō Tomosaburo (1861–1923), Minister of the Navy since 1915, to form the next cabinet. Katō hesitated because he lacked support in the Diet, and so the Seiyūkai leaders, who were more than a little anxious to keep the Kenseikai out of power, pledged him their support. As a result, Katō agreed to become Prime Minister and formed a cabinet consisting largely of members of the House of Peers.

Katō, in carrying out the agreements made at the Washington Conference, proceeded to withdraw Japanese troops from Siberia and reduce naval armaments. At the same time, a reduction of the army was also effected. Manpower in the two services was decreased by more than 100,000 and still further reductions were planned for the army. All this very clearly reflected a dramatic decline in the prestige of the military. No longer did bright young students aspire to join the army or navy; even officers began wearing civilian apparel when not on duty.

The Katō cabinet expired with the death of the Prime Minister in August, 1923. Again Saionji bypassed the political parties in his choice of Yamamoto Gonnohyōe to succeed Katō. Yamamoto was expected to form a nonpartisan cabinet with the three major parties.[12] Both the Seiyūkai and Kenseikai refused to enter the government because to do so would necessarily have entailed cooperating with rival parties. As a result, Yamamoto formed his cabinet with only Inukai's Kakushin Kurabu supporting him in the Diet.

Yamamoto had not completed forming his cabinet when Tokyo was struck by a major disaster, suffering damages second only to those caused by the massive air raids of the Second World War. On September 1, just before noon, the entire Kantō region was hit by one of the biggest earthquakes in Japanese history. The quake was followed by a major conflagration that turned the city of Tokyo into a virtual inferno, with thousands of people seeking to flee the rampaging flames that raged on until the morning of September 3. Landslides and tidal waves added to the death and destruction. More than 106,000 persons died or disappeared, 502,000 were injured, and 694,000 houses were destroyed. Property damages came to ten billion yen.

In addition to the havoc caused by the earthquake and fires, there were unfortunate by-products resulting from mass hysteria. In the chaotic situation created by the disaster all sorts of wild rumors began to spread,

---

[12] In October, 1922, the Kokumintō was dissolved, and some of its members, along with stray Diet members, organized the *Kakushin Kurabu* (Reformist Club).

the most pernicious of which was that the Koreans were responsible for the fires that broke out, and that they were still setting fires, looting, stealing, and raping. The police believed these rumors and caused the people to panic by announcing that the Koreans were grouping together to attack the people of Tokyo. The newspapers also helped to worsen the situation by reporting these rumors as facts. Stories also spread claming that the socialists were taking advantage of the chaotic conditions to start riots. As a result, vigilante groups were organized and many Koreans as well as a number of labor and socialist leaders were subjected to brutal abuses and atrocities.[13] In one area, the police arrested left-wing labor leaders and summarily executed them. Even the army, which was posted to guard the disaster areas, took part in the chaos by killing innocent Koreans. The number of Koreans who lost their lives in the Kantō region could not be determined precisely because of the confusion that prevailed, but the police estimated that 231 Koreans were killed; Yoshino Sakuzō, on the other hand, estimated that the victims numbered 2,613. The Chinese Embassy reported that between 160 and 170 Chinese were killed by hysterical people.

The police and army authorities denied committing atrocities against the Koreans. At the same time they justified whatever measures were in fact taken by blaming the socialists and Communists who, they claimed, had incited the Koreans to riot. Consequently, they continued to arrest socialists and Communists even after the initial panic had subsided. One prominent victim of this Red hunt was the anarchist Ōsugi Sakae who, on the evening of September 16, went out for a visit with his wife, Itō Noe, and his 6 year-old nephew. They were apprehended by Captain Amakasu, a military police officer, who then strangled the three and had their bodies thrown into a well. His object, Amakasu said, was to remove the poison that was destroying the state. The affair was hushed up until Ōsugi's friends, alarmed by his disappearance, began to press for an investigation. Amakasu was given a ten-year sentence, but after three years he was paroled and went to Manchuria, where he worked with the instigators of the Manchurian Incident.

The Yamamoto government was now faced with the tremendous job of reconstructing those areas that had been destroyed by the earthquake. The Minister of Home Affairs, Gotō Shimpei, had hoped to rebuild the city of Tokyo by using the latest ideas in city planning and asked for a budget of 3 billion yen,[14] but conservative, short-sighted politicians

[13] Earlier, in July, 1921, atrocities were committed against Korean workers employed in a construction project in the upper reaches of the Shinano River in central Japan. Efforts were made to unite the cause of the Koreans with that of the labor unions, but the movement failed to gain sufficient support.

[14] The government's budget for 1922 was slightly less than 1.5 billion yen.,

and businessmen opposed the plan because of the high cost and the fact that property owners would have to relinquish their lands for new thoroughfares. Consequently, Gotō acquiesced to the demand that the city be rebuilt in accordance with the former layout.

The second Yamamoto cabinet remained in power for only several months because of an unexpected incident involving an assassination attempt on the regent's life. The murder of Ōsugi had angered his fellow anarchists, who vowed to avenge his death by acts of terror. However, before they managed to take any action, one of their number acted independently and took a shot at the regent while he was on his way to the Diet on December 27, 1923.

The would-be assassin was Namba Taisuke, the son of a member of the Diet. He was aroused by the social injustices around him and deeply influenced by radical writings, particularly those of the French syndicalist Georges Sorel, and the Russian anarchists. The atrocities committed against the Koreans, socialists, and labor leaders during the Great Earthquake fortified his decision to turn to terrorism. Using a pistol, which had been given to his grandfather by Itō Hirobumi, he fired at the regent but missed, only managing to injure slightly one of the attendants. Namba was arrested, tried, and executed. The judges sought to make him repent but he refused to do so, claiming to the end: "I am not a criminal. I am a pioneer for social justice."

Yamamoto assumed the responsibility for allowing such an outrage as this assassination attempt to take place, and he resigned. Mortified, Namba's father relinquished his seat in the Diet and went into seclusion. Namba's former school teachers resigned their post for fostering such a heinous criminal, and his entire village went into mourning.

A movement was started to sharpen the vigilance against "dangerous thought" and "to guide people's thinking in the proper direction." Hiranuma Kiichirō (1867–1952), who was Yamamoto's Minister of Justice, brought together like-minded leaders from all fields and organized the *Kokuhonsha* (National Foundation Society) to rectify and uplift the national spirit. The government sharpened its surveillance over Communists and other left-wing reformers, and this in turn encouraged right-wing nationalists, such as Ōkawa Shūmei and Kita Ikki, to begin intensifying their activities.

The departure of the Yamamoto government left the genrō with the task of finding a successor to form a cabinet. Once again Saionji and Matsukata turned to a nonparty leader, Kiyoura Keigo (1850–1942), who was then president of the Privy Council. Kiyoura formed his cabinet in January, 1924, filling most of the posts with members of the House of Peers.

The two parties were left completely out of the government machinery and this finally led them to reconsider their policy of placing the rivalry between them ahead of the principle of party government. A new effort was made to bring the parties together in a movement aimed at defending constitutional government. The Kenseikai and the Kakushin Kurabu were willing to join the coalition against the Kiyoura government, but the Seiyūkai was irreparably split down the middle with Takahashi Korekiyo's supporters favoring the coalition and the more conservative elements headed by Tokonami opposing it. The Seiyūkai was splintered with 148 progovernment members leaving to form the *Seiyūhontō* (Main Seiyūkai party), while the remainder of the members joined the other two parties. The movement to defend constitutional government then called for the establishment of a party government, but it failed to arouse a great deal of popular interest. Finally, when Kiyoura dissolved the Diet, the three parties managed to gain a majority in the ensuing election. Faced with this new and very hostile Diet, Kiyoura resigned. Now Saionji had no choice but to turn to Katō Kōmei and the Kenseikai. In June, 1924, Katō at last came to power thus inaugurating a form of government that was to persist until 1932, when Prime Minister Inukai was assassinated; that is, the practice of having the president of one of the two major parties head the government. The principle of party government then finally became a reality, although it was to survive for only eight years.

Katō brought members of the Seiyūkai and Kakushin Kurabu into the cabinet along with such able nonparty men as Shidehara (Foreign Minister) and General Ugaki (Minister of War). He also selected men from his own party, such as Wakatsuki (Minister of Home Affairs) and Hamaguchi Yūkō (Minister of Finance), both of whom later became prime ministers. Takahashi (Minister of Agriculture and Commerce) and Inukai (Minister of Communications) also joined the cabinet. Katō succeeded in establishing a cabinet consisting of an aggregation of extremely capable men.

Katō possessed a patrician outlook even though he came from a lower-class samurai family, and he thus favored working with the upper classes rather than the masses. However, as the leader for so long of the party out of power, he was compelled to favor universal suffrage. This, together with financial retrenchment and the rooting out of corruption from the government, became his key objectives as Prime Minister.

Despite objections from those who would be affected adversely by budget cuts, Katō managed to effect some economies. The army accepted a reduction of four divisions, but only with the understanding that first, the savings would be used to mechanize the military by establishing tank and aircraft units, and second, military drills would be introduced in the schools at the middle-school level and above. Reductions in the bureaucracy were also made, but Katō had less success in decreasing "pork barrel" expenditures because of the considerable opposition of the Seiyūkai.

The major achievement of the Katō cabinet was the enactment of universal manhood suffrage. The bill that was finally passed in March, 1925, gave the right to vote to all male subjects over the age of 25 who had lived in their electoral districts for at least one year and were not indigent. This increased the number of voters from about 3.3 million to 12.5 million.

Ten days before the bill for universal manhood suffrage passed the Diet, the Peace Preservation Law was enacted. The purpose of this law, which had been contemplated since Hara was at the head of the government, was to curb "dangerous thought" that was being spread, it was argued, by anarchists and Communists. The law was designed to punish those who either advocated revolutionary changes in the national polity or rejected the system of private property. The law was prepared separately from the bill on universal suffrage, but its passage was clearly intended to mollify the conservatives, particularly those in the House of Peers. These men had insisted that safeguards be established to combat the spread of dangerous ideas that they were certain would follow in the wake of universal suffrage. The law was also intended to guard against the further diffusion of communistic ideas, which would result, it was feared, from the Japanese-Soviet Treaty that had just been concluded at the beginning of 1925.

The government also proposed a bill aimed at protecting the right of workers to organize unions and stage strikes, but this was effectively blocked by the powerful business interests. However, Article 17 of the Police Regulation Law, which had hindered labor union activities, was finally removed.

Members of the coalition parties also hoped to "reform" the House of Peers so that it would merely have the right to check or restrain the lower house, which would become the dominant legislative body. Katō, however, was unwilling to take such drastic actions; consequently, the only reform attempted was some slight change in the composition of the House of Peers, reducing somewhat the number of hereditary members.

Soon after the passage of the bill on universal suffrage, the coalition of the three parties began to disintegrate. Takahashi resigned as head of the Seiyūkai, and he was replaced by General Tanaka Giichi, a

Chōshū militarist. Tanaka assumed the presidency of the party, and almost immediately thereafter the Seiyūkai merged with the Kakushin Kurabu and another splinter party, and began challenging the Katō cabinet. Confronted with the collapse of the coalition, Katō resigned. The big surprise came when the Seiyūkai members, who had hoped to form the next cabinet in cooperation with the Seiyūhontō, found themselves in the lurch because Saionji asked Katō to take up the reins of government once again.

Six months after he formed his second cabinet Katō died and was succeeded by Wakatsuki Reijirō (1866–1949), his Minister of Home Affairs. Wakatsuki, a weak leader, resigned after slightly more than a year in office when the Privy Council opposed his financial policy designed to deal with the bank crisis besetting the nation. Saionji then turned to the head of the Seiyūkai, General Tanaka, who formed a new cabinet in April, 1927.

Tanaka came to power at a most critical moment when a financial crisis and a serious economic depression struck Japan. This was followed by severe agrarian hardship, urban unrest, an increase in ultra-right-wing activism, and expanded activities on the part of the military both at home, in the form of political assassinations, and abroad, in the form of aggression in China. Japan was about to enter the "valley of darkness," which was to involve her in wars on the continent and in the Pacific.

Tanaka saw two tasks before him: the solution of the economic crisis and the rectification of what he considered to be the soft policy that had been pursued by Shidehara during his tenure as Foreign Minister since June, 1924. The economy had been in a precarious state ever since the end of the First World War because overextended capital investment and production had not been retrenched. Instead, Hara had increased government expenditures in the hope of keeping the economy from collapsing. Foreign trade declined at a time when other industrial powers were actively rebuilding their economies. As a result, Japan's balance of payment deficit began to grow.

The Great Earthquake strained the economy further, not only because of the losses incurred by the business interests, but also because of the increase in government expenditures that were necessary to defray the tremendous cost of reconstruction. The yen weakened and inflation set in as new bonds were issued, and credit was extended to the banks and businesses that needed assistance. This, of course, further weakened Japan's foreign trade position. At the same time, unemployment and agrarian debt increased.

In March, 1927, the Minister of Finance inadvertently released the information that a certain bank was on the verge of bankruptcy. This produced a panic and the second-class banks of Tokyo were overwhelmed by terrified depositors trying to withdraw their money. As a result, these banks were forced to close their doors.

This panic was followed by the financial crisis of the Bank of Taiwan, which had over-extended credit to a company on the verge of bankruptcy. In an attempt to save the bank, the Wakatsuki government issued an emergency ordinance granting it funds, but this measure was quickly blocked by the Privy Council. Consequently, the Bank of Taiwan was forced to close its doors. This in turn caused another bank panic that led to the collapse of about twenty other banks. The run on the banks continued until the Tanaka government finally declared a three-week moratorium on bank payments and devised some measures aimed at saving the Bank of Taiwan. A temporary relief from the financial crisis was achieved, but the movement toward the elimination of middle- and small-sized banks was accelerated. The many depositors who felt safer with bigger banks certainly reinforced this trend, as did the government by its encouragement of mergers and consolidations. For example, at the end of 1926, there were 1,420 ordinary commercial banks, but by 1929, there were only 881.

The financial panic was followed by a recession. The producers of silk and cotton textiles found it necessary to curtail production in the face of declining demand. A similar situation beset the producers of paper, cement, coal, and ceramics. The trend toward concentration of the means of production and the reduction of medium-sized businesses was accelerated by the economic crisis. In 1928, companies with assets of more than 10 million yen constituted only 0.9 percent of the firms in existence, but they held about 55 percent of the capital assets; firms with assets of less than 50,000 yen constituted more than 55 percent of the companies, but they owned only about 1.5 percent of the capital assets.

In order to stimulate the economy, Tanaka increased military expenditures, exploited the colonies even more rigorously, accelerated the rebuilding projects of the Great Earthquake, and introduced agrarian aid programs. To finance these activities, the government issued bonds and was forced to dip into its reserve funds. These measures revived the inflationary trend and worsened the unfavorable balance of trade. They also led to a steady drop in the value of the yen in relation to the dollar (in March, 1927, the yen was worth .49 dollars, whereas by April, 1929, it had dropped to .44 dollars).

This unhealthy economic situation created social ills that intensified left and right-wing agitations. At the same time Tanaka, acting as both Prime Minister and Foreign Minister, adopted a bellicose posture toward China and stimulated nationalistic sentiments among the military and right-wing extremists. He also sought to turn the people against the soft policies that Shidehara, the former Foreign Minister, had pursued. Sentiments hostile to the "decadent" liberals, and "traitorous" Communists were also fostered by the government.

Tanaka was very aggressive in combating "dangerous thought," making full use of the Peace Preservation Law. In the election of February, 1928, he used the power of the government in trying to prevent the election of communistic candidates. In spite of his efforts, however, eight socialists were elected to the Diet. Tanaka responded to this threat by arresting all persons suspected of being anarchists or Communists. The campaign to root out "dangerous thought" was extended to the academic world and five professors, including Kawakami Hajime, a prominent Marxist economist, were dismissed from the imperial universities in 1928.

Tanaka also sought to add the death penalty to the Peace Preservation Law, and when this move was blocked by the Diet, he went ahead and issued an emergency ordinance putting this policy into effect. Hostility toward members of left-wing organizations was encouraged by the government, and this led to numerous incidents of violence. For example, in March, 1929, a former policeman murdered Yamamoto Senji, a socialist leader. This was followed by another massive arrest of socialists and Communists. In April, the government banned the Rōdō Nōmintō, the Communist led Labor Council, and Communist youth groups.

Tanaka adopted an aggressive stance toward China. About the time he assumed the premiership, Chiang Kai-shek was securing his control of the Nationalist party in China and taking decisive steps to unify the country under his authority. Shidehara's China policy was based upon the principle of nonintervention and cooperation, but this was rejected as being "weak and soft" by the military, the rightists, and the reactionary members of both the House of Peers and the Privy Council. Tanaka immediately dispatched additional troops into Shantung, ostensibly to protect the Japanese residents there, when Chiang began moving his troops toward Peking. In the summer of 1927, Tanaka held a conference with the top officials of the army and foreign office for the purpose of formulating a new China policy. During this conference the anti-interventionists in the foreign office managed to restrain the interventionists led by Mori Kaku, who was parliamentary Vice-Minister of Foreign Affairs, and the officers of the Kwantung Army (Japanese forces in Manchuria).

The participants in the conference agreed to respect the political integrity of China, but at the same time they also agreed to take decisive actions if and when there was a threat either to Japan's interests and rights or to the life and property of the Japanese residents. They also agreed that since Manchuria and Mongolia were important to Japan's security and well-being, it was essential that all necessary steps be taken to prevent those areas from becoming embroiled in the internal conflicts that were unfolding in China. Japan launched rather aggressive actions in China, and, consequently, much was made of the "Tanaka Memorandum," which was purported to be a blueprint for the conquest of China based on the formulations established at this conference. It was generally agreed after the end of the Second World War that this was a bogus document.

The conference developed a list of items that were to be negotiated in regard to Manchuria and Mongolia. The talks were to be conducted with Chang Tso-lin, warlord of Manchuria. Chang could not possibly accede to all of the Japanese demands because of the strong anti-Japanese sentiment that was so prevalent among the Chinese in Manchuria.

In April, 1928, as Chiang Kai-shek's army moved north, the Japanese commander in Shantung sent his troops into Tsinan to block the Nationalist forces. A clash resulted, and in order to overcome public opposition to dispatching reinforcements, the Japanese army claimed that more than three hundred Japanese residents had been massacred in Shantung. This was a gross exaggeration of an incident in which thirteen Japanese, who had been accused of smuggling opium into the region, had been killed. The *Minseitō* (Democratic party), which had been formed by the merger of the Kenseikai and the Seiyūhontō in June, 1927, opposed Tanaka's aggressive policies, but the newspapers stirred up public opinion in favor of intervention. Tanaka sent an additional division into Shantung and the Japanese forces launched an attack against Tsinan, killing and injuring thousands of Chinese residents.

Chang Tso-lin withdrew his troops into Manchuria as Chiang's forces advanced north. The possibility of the conflict spreading to Manchuria began to concern the Tanaka government, and so it notified the Chinese leaders that Japan would take "proper and effective measures to maintain peace and order" if the fighting spread to Manchuria. Chang was then persuaded by the Japanese authorities to return to Mukden without engaging the Nationalist forces in combat so as not to give Chiang the opportunity to extend the conflict into Manchuria.

The Kwantung Army officers hoped to disarm Chang's army and then move the Japanese troops beyond the areas they were entitled to remain in by treaty. Tanaka, however, refused to approve their plan. In order to create a situation that would provide the Kwantung Army with an excuse to control Manchuria, Colonel Kōmoto Daisaku, staff officer of the Kwantung Army, took it upon himself to insure Chang's assassination. In June, 1928, when Chang was returning from North China to

Manchuria, Kōmoto had the train in which he was traveling blown up.

Kōmoto expected local disturbances to break out after Chang's death, thus providing the Kwantung Army with an excuse to move its troops into key areas of Manchuria "to restore peace and order." The anticipated skirmishes, however, never did materialize, and Tanaka continued to oppose the army's proposal to move its troops beyond the areas in which they were legally entitled to be stationed. The role played by Kōmoto in the assassination of Chang was not revealed until the postwar years because the army and right-wing politicians opposed public disclosure of the facts.

In Manchuria, Chang Tso-lin's son, Chang Hsüeh-liang, took charge and, much to the chagrin of the Kwantung Army officers, pledged his allegiance to Chiang Kai-shek. The Nationalist government was so successful in extending its authority over China that Tanaka finally decided to withdraw the Japanese troops from Tsinan and recognize Chiang's government as the legitimate government of China.

Emperor Hirohito, who had succeeded Emperor Taishō upon his death on December 25, 1926, and Saionji both pressed Tanaka to punish the assassins of Chang Tso-lin. Tanaka was unable, however, to overcome the rigid opposition of the army leaders and he decided to resign his post. Contrary to Saionji's high expectations, Tanaka turned out to be a weak leader who failed to control the army. He had seriously damaged Japan's international standing and vastly increased the hostility of the Chinese people through his aggressive policies. He also left an ominous legacy when he failed to take vigorous action against Kwantung Army officers like Kōmoto who acted arbitrarily and independently, ignoring the wishes of the government officials.

In July, 1929, the president of the Minseitō, Hamaguchi Yūkō (1870–1931), succeeded Tanaka as Prime Minister. Hamaguchi adopted two basic policies: economic retrenchment and international cooperation. As his Minister of Finance he appointed Inoue Junnosuke, former head of the Bank of Japan, and as Foreign Minister he selected Shidehara, a man who was known to favor a peaceful policy toward China.

In order to solve the financial difficulties, the Hamaguchi government reduced the budget and also proposed a 10 percent reduction in pay for both civilian and military officials. Strong opposition by the officials, however, defeated implementation of the pay cuts. In the hope of buttressing the value of the yen and halting the trend toward inflation, Hamaguchi returned Japan to the gold standard and lifted the embargo on gold that had been in effect since 1917. A stable yen would, it was assumed, increase foreign trade, offsetting the outflow of gold. Unfortunately, this measure was adopted just at the time when the stock market crashed in the United States, and a prolonged worldwide depression followed. As a result, Japanese exports to the United States dropped sharply; raw silk in particular was seriously affected. The export of cotton textile goods and other sundry products that Japan normally sold to China and other Asian countries also decreased. Japanese exports dropped by 50 percent in the period from 1929 to 1931. At the same time, Japan's gold reserves diminished steadily after she returned to the gold standard. In 1929, it stood at 1.072 billion yen; by 1931 it had dropped to 470 million.

It was assumed that the government would be forced to go off the gold standard again. This, of course, would cause the value of the yen to drop. In anticipation of this, the rich, led by the Mitsui interests, began frantically to buy up American dollars, thus accelerating the outflow of gold. This kind of selfish indifference to the public good coupled with the many instances of graft and corruption involving high government officials and businessmen gave credence, in the minds of the people, to the charges being directed against big business and party politicians. The right-wing critics accused them of being selfish, unpatriotic traitors who had "sabotaged the nation to enrich themselves."

In December, 1931, the government, now headed by Inukai, finally took Japan off the gold standard and restored the embargo on gold. The damage, however, had already been done. The world depression, the drop in exports, and the outflow of gold all contributed to the onset of a severe economic depression in Japan. In 1931–1932, compared to 1926, the price index had dropped by 35 percent, and industrial and mineral production had decreased by 25 percent. The agrarian sector was hit especially hard. The price of raw silk dropped 67 percent from 1925 to 1931, while the price of cocoons dropped by more than two-thirds. Four years of abundant harvest, increased imports from Korea and Taiwan, and the decline in the demand for rice in the cities because of the industrial depression, caused a 55 percent drop in the price of rice. Rice and cocoons were the two major sources of income for the farmers, consequently, a simultaneous drop in prices of both these items proved disastrous for agrarian communities. The value of the net product of agriculture fell 58 percent during this same period, while the farmer's cost of living declined by only 28 percent.

As might be expected, the depression worked serious hardships on the masses, not only the workers and the farmers, but also the shopkeepers and the small and middle-sized businessmen. The only business that prospered was the pawnshop. Complete and fully accurate statistics are not available, but there is no question that unemployment rose considerably as many workers were released from their jobs because of declining business. Incomplete figures indicate that in 1932, 6.9 percent of the working population was unemployed. For the day laborers the figure was 11.6 percent. Only 1 out of 3 persons seeking jobs were able to find employment. It is estimated that as many as 3 million people were unemployed in 1930.

Actually, these figures can be somewhat misleading in the story they tell because many unemployed persons returned to the villages to share with their rural relatives what little work and food there was. A survey taken in 1931 showed that of the 660,000 factory workers who were released, 280,000 returned to the villages. The real problems, then, were hidden unemployment and the increased pressures on the rural communities, which were already suffering from the depression.

The factory workers who did not lose their jobs had to accept reductions in pay. The real wages of workers dropped from index 100 in 1926, to 69.5 in 1931. As might be expected, the number of labor disputes increased sharply—in 1929 there were 1,420 disputes, and in 1931 there were 2,456. In April, 1930, when the Kanebō Textile Company reduced wages by 40 percent, 35,000 workers went on strike. The salaried workers were also underpaid, and in some cases they were not paid at all. Of the 7,384 primary schools, 557 were unable to pay their teachers.

The social scene was characterized by a growing number of children begging in the streets, infanticides, suicides of entire families, deaths by the roadside, prostitution, and robberies. The crime rate doubled from 1926 (720,000 cases) to 1933 (1,550,000 cases).

Despite these deteriorating conditions and tremendous hardships, taxes in the rural areas remained high. A survey in 1933 showed that a fairly well-to-do independent farmer had an annual income of 723 yen and paid a direct tax of 96 yen, or 13 percent. Rural indebtedness continued to rise: the average debt per farm in 1932 was 837 yen as compared to 135 in 1914. Many independent farmers lost their lands and became tenant farmers because they were unable to pay their debts. The enormous pressures of poverty intensified, and many farm families were forced to sell their daughters to houses of prostitution in the big cities. In one village in northern Japan, for example, 110, or 23 percent, of the 467 girls between the ages of 15 and 24 were sold to the cities, primarily as prostitutes, some as factory workers. To make matters worse, the northern communities were afflicted by a disastrous crop failure in 1934, and the people were reduced to eating grass and tree roots.

These were the circumstances that led morally indignant young men and army officers, many of whom came from the rural communities, to turn to right-wing extremism. They were convinced that the politicians and the rich were wallowing in luxury, corruption, and decadence, while in the countryside their friends and relatives were starving to death. One of the army officers involved in the assassination of Inukai in 1932 said at his trial:

Some traditional agricultural methods are still employed in Japan: left, harvesting tea leaves; right, tilling a rice paddy field. Both courtesy of the Japan National Tourist Organization.

> The impoverishment of the farming villages is a cause of grave concern to all the thoughtful people. It is the same with the fishing villages and the small merchants and industrialists. . . . In utter disregard of the poverty-stricken farmers, the enormously rich zaibatsu pursue their private profit. Meanwhile the young children of the impoverished farmers of the northeastern provinces attend school without breakfast, and their families subsist on rotten potatoes.[15]

The depression tightened its grip on the economy and the people, while the Hamaguchi government made some ineffectual attempts to

[15] Masao Maruyama, *Thought and Behaviour in Modern Japanese Politics,* ed. Ivan Morris (London: Oxford University Press, 1963), p. 45.

alleviate the situation. Basically, the government failed to comprehend the enormity or the severity of the crisis and so it persisted in its policy of retrenchment. The policy-makers also had the notion that some degree of economic hardship would have to be endured in order to strengthen the economy. As a result, they concentrated on raising the efficiency of industrial production. This entailed increasing the productivity per worker, reducing the number of workers, and cutting wages. Thus, so far as the workers were concerned, greater efficiency meant aggravating the conditions created by the depression. This policy also resulted in a further concentration of financial power and the means of production into the hands of a few gigantic business combines, while at the same time more and more small and medium business enterprises disappeared.

Just as the Hamaguchi government's efforts to rectify the unhealthy economic situation resulted in a worsening of the crisis, in like manner, its efforts to establish harmonious relations with China and the other powers failed to produce positive results. Ever since Japan participated in the Washington Conference and adopted a policy of naval disarmament, each succeeding government adhered to the general policy of international cooperation. Even the Tanaka government participated in the Kellogg-Briand Pact of 1928, which outlawed war. Characteristically, the Privy Council objected to this peace pact because it contained the words "in the names of their respective peoples." The Minseitō joined the council in condemning this "insult" to imperial sovereignty.

In early 1930, the signatories of the Five Power Naval Treaty of Washington met in London to consider an extension of the earlier agreement and the reduction of other categories of warships besides battleships. The Japanese navy wanted to obtain a ratio of 10:10:7 in cruisers and other warships, while still maintaining a submarine tonnage of 78,000. Wakatsuki, the chief of the Japanese delegation, accepted a 10:10:6 ratio in heavy cruisers and succeeded in getting the United States and Great Britain to agree to a 10:10:7 ratio in destroyers. In submarines, Japan was allowed to maintain parity with the United States.

The leaders of the navy, directed by Admiral Katō Kanjū, chief of the naval general staff, were unwilling to accept an agreement that provided for less than what they wanted. The Seiyūkai supported the discontented naval officers and launched an attack against the Hamaguchi government. Inukai and Hatoyama Ichirō (a Prime Minister during the 1950s) took up the cudgels for the navy and accused the government of violating the independence of the supreme command. In this way, they gave support to the principle that the military was to use during the 1930s in order to undermine civilian control of the government. Hatoyama argued that the Hamaguchi government had no authority to overrule the naval general staff concerning matters of national defense.

Admiral Katō, exercising his right to have direct access to the throne, appealed to the Emperor, expressing his opposition to the government's action, and then resigned his post. Members of the Privy Council, led by Itō Miyoji and Hiranuma Kiichirō, sought to castigate the government, but Hamaguchi, with the encouragement of Saionji and a Minseitō majority in the Diet, refused to succumb to these pressures, and pushed through the ratification of the agreement.

The willingness of members of the oligarchy and the political parties to play upon the discontent of the militarists for political gains did not augur well for the future of parliamentary government. Those who had played a role in upholding the naval agreement were marked for elimination by army and navy extremists and right-wing civilian radicals. Among those picked as future victims were Admiral Okada Keisuke, who worked for the acceptance of the naval agreement, and Admiral Suzuki

Kantarō, who was then Grand Chamberlain. The first victim of the numerous assassination attempts that were made in the 1930s was Prime Minister Hamaguchi, who was shot and seriously injured by a right-wing extremist in November, 1930. The assassin was sentenced to death, but his sentence was commuted and he was released in 1940, at which time he again became an active participant in ultra-right-wing movements.

Shidehara was appointed to act as Prime Minister while Hamaguchi was incapacitated. Factional strife, however, seriously weakened the Minseitō, and the Seiyūkai continued to attack the government, labeling Shidehara as a traitor for defending the London agreement. In April, 1931, just a few months before his death, Hamaguchi resigned. He was succeeded by Wakatsuki, whose tenure was fraught with difficulties because of right-wing extremism as well as the arbitrary actions of army officers, particularly those of the Kwantung Army. Assassination plots were continuously hatched by right-wing nationalists and young officers in the army and navy. The Kwantung Army officers did not cease to contrive political intrigues in Manchuria, where they finally succeeded in starting an "incident" in September, 1931, which resulted in the establishment of a puppet state there. At home, civilian and military extremists managed to put an end to party government when they assassinated Prime Minister Inukai on May 15, 1932. These events marked the end of an era of parliamentary and democratic ascendancy and the beginning of a grim era of assassinations and wars.

CHAPTER 18

THE
ASCENDANCY
OF MILITARISM

RADICAL NATIONALISTS AND MILITARISTS

The Kwantung Army officers' conspiracy, which touched off the Manchurian Incident, and the assassination of Prime Minister Inukai heralded the end of party government in Japan and the advent of military domination of the political scene. These key events mark the beginning of Japan's long road to war, conquest, and destruction. Questions naturally arise as to how and why Japan got on this path of war and conquest. The conspirators who planned the Manchurian Incident were not acting at the behest of the government. There were no clearly defined domestic or foreign policies advocating such aggression. Nevertheless, these conspirators and assassins did put Japan on the road to war by virtue of the enthusiastic support they gathered to their causes from the general public and from the political circles.

Japan won one "glorious victory" after another on the continent after the Manchurian Incident and, in response, the public gave the military adventurers unrestrained support, while condemning Shidehara's "cowardly" policies. The press, in fact, greeted his efforts to settle the Manchurian affair peacefully with charges of treason. The public also sanctioned the many acts of violence committed by the so-called simple-hearted and patriotic young men who assassinated business and political leaders one after another. The trials following these treacherous assaults evoked wide public sympathy, not for the victims, but for the assassins.

This support was frequently manifested in the form of severed fingers sent to the courts to protest the trials of the "righteous patriots."

The ultimate responsibility for Japan's acts of aggression and her involvement in the China and Pacific wars cannot, of course, be ascribed to a handful of conspirators. It is true that army officers and ultranationalists schemed to effect the conquest of Manchuria and North China, but the really critical factor here was the considerable support these factions had from political leaders. They had the backing of members of the Privy Council led by Hiranuma and a significant number of political-party leaders. Their causes found champions even among the socialists; for example, the former left-wing activist Akamatsu Katsumaro committed the Shakai Minshūtō to a policy of expansionism on the continent. Those among the party politicians who were especially active in supporting the military expansionists were Adachi Kenzō (Wakatsuki's Minister of Home Affairs), and Suzuki Kisaburō and Mori Kaku of the Seiyūkai. For political purposes, the Seiyūkai as a whole supported the army and the navy, attacking the Wakatsuki government in general and Shidehara's foreign policy in particular.

The flames of nationalism, militarism, and imperialism were stoked by the economic and social frustrations felt by the masses as the depression brought them to the very brink of starvation. Their hardships were blamed on the selfish, decadent, and corrupt politicians and business leaders. The militarists and the ultranationalists spearheaded these attacks and offered the people the chance for a new order at home through a *Shōwa* (Enlightened Peace) Restoration[1] and economic relief through expansion abroad. The young officers were particularly disturbed about conditions in the agrarian villages because most of the army's recruits were from the rural communities. Many bright young boys from agrarian families who could not afford to go to college went to the military and naval academies. The sympathetic feelings expressed by the army officers toward the impoverished farmers were reciprocated by the farming communities displaying general admiration, respect, and support for the military.

The expansionist policies of the military were based on the belief that Japan's economic difficulties could be resolved by moving into Manchuria and other parts of China where supposedly unlimited reservoirs of wealth could be tapped. Kwantung Army officers Ishiwara Kanji and Itagaki Seishirō stressed the need to control Manchuria in order to improve the economic conditions of the Japanese people.

The economic depression that had beset Japan began to improve about

---

[1] Shōwa is the era name for the present Emperor's reign; Hirohito will be known posthumously as Emperor Shōwa.

the time she embarked on her path of conquest, but this recovery was not brought about by expansionism alone. Japan managed to pull herself out of the depression earlier than other major powers by abandoning the policy of retrenchment that had been pursued by Hamaguchi and Inoue, and by aggressively implementing a program to reflate the economy through greatly increased spending on arms and a substantial increase in exports. The appearance of the first signs that Japan was recovering from the depression coincided with the beginning of expansionistic activities on the continent, and thus the impression was created that imperialism was paying off.

The imperialists offered another excuse for expanding into the continent, and that was the need to acquire more space for Japan's surplus population. Colonel Hashimoto Kingorō, a leading jingoist, said after the Manchurian Incident, "We are like a great crowd of people packed into a small and narrow room." He argued that there were three ways to solve the problem: emigration, greater trade in the world market, and expansion of territory. The first two options, however, were blocked by other powers, so, according to Hashimoto, the only alternative left was expansion. He went on to point out that by developing the undeveloped resources, Japan would not simply be serving her own selfish ends but would be benefiting mankind.[2]

The army was growing increasingly concerned about the disarmament policies being pursued by the Minseitō government, which had participated in the London Naval Disarmament Conference. The Wakatsuki government was also determined to take part in the 1932 Geneva Conference on Armament Limitations. The military knew that the advent of an international crisis would put an immediate end to all talk of disarmament.

The desire to expand into the continent and the plan to introduce reforms at home were closely linked together. Both movements were led by middle-grade army officers and radical civilian nationalists. In the 1930s the army began more and more to interfere in political affairs. The factional rivalries in the army were intertwined with the desire to increase military influence in the government, and this served to complicate the political situation considerably. One issue that created a very serious cleavage in the army was the rivalry between the Chōshū and anti-Chōshū factions. Some of the more ambitious officers resented the long domination of the army by the Chōshū clique, even though the power of that controlling group had been declining since Yamagata's death, and

---

[2] Ryusaku Tsunoda, W. T. de Bary, and Donald Keene, eds., *Sources of Japanese Tradition* (New York: Columbia University Press, 1958), pp. 796–98.

began to establish an informal anti-Chōshū faction. They were led by two influential generals, Mazaki Jinsaburō and Araki Sadao.

The Chōshū faction had been led by Tanaka Giichi after Yamagata's death, but following Tanaka's demise it lacked a strong leader. General Ugaki Issei (1868–1956) was Tanaka's protege and although an influential general in the twenties, he failed to develop a power base in the army, not only because he incurred the resentment of the anti-Chōshū faction, but also because his military plans upset the traditionalists. Ugaki, who maintained that the army should be modernized with the greatest emphasis placed on tanks and airplanes, agreed to accept a reduction in the size of the army. Those who still believed in the primacy of the infantry criticized him for ignoring the "spiritual power" present in the Japanese soldiers.

Those army officers who agreed with Ugaki included Nagata Tetsuzan, Tōjō Hideki, and Yamashita Tomoyuki. This faction, led by Nagata, believed that future wars would require the total mobilization of the nation's resources, both natural and human. Consequently, they favored a comprehensive scheme coordinating military, political, and economic planning. The opposing faction, led by Araki, believed that future wars would still be won swiftly and decisively by superior Japanese troops imbued with the spirit of Yamato. The split in the army did not rigidly follow any particular lines, but by and large the Nagata faction tended to consist of officers serving in the Ministry of War, while the Araki faction drew most of its adherents from the general staff. The disagreement about whether to stress machines or the Yamato spirit contributed in part to the cleavage that divided the Control Faction (*Tōsei-ha*) and Imperial Way Faction (*Kōdō-ha*), a problem that will be discussed later.

As might be expected, the military officers were, in the main, opposed to the ascendancy of democracy and party government. Through the mechanism of the "independence of the supreme command," the army and navy maintained a degree of autonomy from the government. They had direct access to the Emperor, and the officers actually considered themselves to be the Emperor's immediate retainers.

The military officers did not see any conflict of interest between themselves and the government while Yamagata and the genrō were in control because it was their own patrons who were in power. The passing of the old patriarchs and the ascendancy of the political parties, however, radically altered the situation, with the consequence that the military officers became very wary of any government programs that affected either the army or the navy. They especially resented the disarmament policies fostered by the party government. The sentiments of the more radical of these military men were expressed in the statement of purpose drafted by an organization of politically-minded army officers, the Cherry Blossom Society (*Sakurakai*). It said:

> [The political leaders] have forgotten basic principles, lack the courage to carry out state policies, and completely neglect the spiritual values that are essential for the ascendancy of the Yamato people. They are wholly preoccupied with their selfish pursuit of political power and material wealth. Above, they veil the sacred light, and below, they deceive the people. The torrent of political corruption has reached its crest. . . . Now, the poisonous sword of the thoroughly degenerate party politicians is being pointed at the military. This was clearly demonstrated in the controversy over the London treaties. . . . It is obvious that the party politicians' sword, which was used against the navy, will soon be used to reduce the size of the army. Hence, we who constitute the mainstay of the army must . . . arouse ourselves and wash out the bowels of the completely decadent politicians.[3]

As we already observed, the army officers were critical of what they considered to be the gross indifference on the part of politicians and capitalists to agrarian impoverishment. In order to rectify these conditions, the concerned middle-grade officers favored introducing radical political reforms; that is, they proposed effecting another restoration, the Shōwa Restoration. The proponents of this change tended to be members of the anti-Chōshū faction because it was the Chōshū faction that had been a key component of the established order from the beginning of the Meiji era.

Military officers advocating reform began getting together to discuss political issues, and a number of societies were organized by them. One of these, the *Issekikai* (One Evening Society), was organized in 1929 and included among its members Kōmoto Daisaku (who had murdered Chang Tso-lin), Nagata Tetsuzan, Tōjō Hideki, Yamashita Tomoyuki, Doihara Kenji, Itagaki Taisuke, and Ishiwara Kanji. All of these officers were to play critical political roles in the next decade or two.

In 1930, another military society, the Sakurakai, was organized by Hashimoto Kingorō (1890–1957). The membership at first included about twenty-five officers, later growing to about one hundred. The Sakurakai favored the overthrow of the existing government and the establishment of a military regime in its stead. The group, with the support of Major

---

[3] Ōuchi Tsutomu, *Fasshizumu e no Michi* (*The Road to Fascism*) (Tokyo: Chūō Kōronsha, 1967), p. 297.

General Tatekawa, the officer in charge of military operations in the army general staff, planned to pursue the conquest of Manchuria once this military government was established.

Many of the military officers who favored internal changes and expansion abroad had established links with right-wing civilian nationalists. The latter also favored revolutionizing the existing political, social, and economic systems for the purpose of transforming Japan into a totalitarian state. Among such civilian radicals were Ōkawa Shūmei, Kita Ikki, and Inoue Nisshō.

Radical nationalist thinkers—civilian and military—may have disagreed about the best means to bring about the new order and about some minor details in analyzing the ills of Japan but, by and large, they all shared mystical notions about the superiority of the Japanese national character, the national polity, and the sacredness of the imperial institution, which was the source of all values. Another idea they held in common was the necessity of stressing spiritual rather than material values. Ōkawa Shūmei, for example, was opposed to capitalism and socialism primarily because they both pursued materialistic ends. The ultranationalists generally favored expansion into the Asian continent, development of a powerful military force, and the creation of a totalitarian state that inclined toward national socialism. Consequently, they opposed liberal, individualistic values as well as the democratic, parliamentary concepts that had entered the country in the mid-nineteenth century. In concert with these attitudes, they rejected the basically Western, urban culture in favor of the traditional, agrarian way of life and values. The family system, with its emphasis on the whole group rather than the individual, was envisioned as the appropriate basis for the structure of the state. The imperial household was to have the status of the main family, while all other families were to function as branch families.

In a sense, the conflict between the militarists and the radical nationalists on the one hand, and the bourgeoisie and the liberal intellectuals on the other, was a clash between the rural and the urban, the provincial and Tokyo, the traditional and the Western-oriented cultures of Japan. The triumph of the militarists and radical nationalists in the thirties was, at the same time, the triumph of traditionalism or "Japanism" over Western liberalism. This victory, then, was the denouement of the conflict between traditionalism and Westernism that had its inception in early Meiji.

The radical nationalists[4] believed that the use of force was necessary

---

[4] These men are often referred to as fascists, but because this term has become so fraught with associative significance, and in order to avoid the automatic equation of

for two primary purposes: first, to return Japan to her true character and values, which had been eroded by the artificial ideas imported from the West and by the evil advisers to the Emperor; and second, to extend the influence of the imperial way throughout the world. Aside from this kind of mystical notion about the special mission of Japan, there was a tendency to see the nation as the champion of Asia against the Western world. Ōkawa Shūmei (1886–1957), who became intimately involved with the young military conspirators, contended that in order to realize a new world order, one nation representing the East had to fight one nation representing the West. "It is my belief," he said, "that Heaven has chosen Japan as the champion of the East." [5]

The most important thinker among the radical nationalists was Kita Ikki (1883–1937). Kita started out as a socialist and struggled to remain one, if not through party affiliation, at least ideologically by attempting to reconcile socialism and the Japanese national polity (kokutai). He thus defined kokutai in a radically different way from the conventional interpretation by equating it with "socialism because sovereignty resides in the state, and [with] democracy because power rests with the people." [6] His view of the imperial institution resembled Minobe Tatsukichi's Organ Theory (see page 471). "The Emperor of Japan," Kita asserted, "is an organ who began and continues to exist for the purposes of the survival and evolution of the state." [7] His views on kokutai and the Emperor caused the authorities to look upon him with suspicion. On the other hand, he did not share the political opinions of the left-wing thinkers either. He disagreed with the socialists because they did not favor a strong state, while he complied with Luther's opinion that "the state is an ethical institution." He also favored imperialism because he considered it the natural precursor to internationalism.

Kita, however, was genuinely sympathetic to the fate of China, the victim of Western imperialism. Like many of his fellow Japanese, he favored extending a helping hand to China so as to enable her to break

---

the Japanese version of aggressive nationalism with European fascism, the use of this term has been avoided except in the instances of material quoted from other sources. One factor that distinguishes the political situation in Japan during the 1930s from European fascism during the same period is that a totalitarian system under the strict control of one party did not emerge. Even during the height of military ascendancy, a kind of collective leadership still prevailed with the imperial court, the imperial advisers, the aristocrats, the senior statesmen, the bureaucrats, and the big business leaders retaining considerable influence. On this question of "fascism" see Masao Maruyama, *Thought and Behaviour in Modern Japanese Politics,* ed. Ivan Morris (London: Oxford University Press, 1963), pp. 25 ff., and George M. Wilson, *Radical Nationalist in Japan: Kita Ikki, 1833–1937* (Cambridge, Mass.: Harvard University Press, 1969), pp. 90 ff.

[5] Tsunoda *et al., Sources of Japanese Tradition,* p. 796.

[6] Wilson, *op. cit.,* p. 27.

[7] *Ibid.,* p. 28.

her shackles and move along the path of progress. He spent some time working with the Chinese revolutionaries, but as Sino-Japanese interests began to clash, Kita concluded that the relationship between the two countries could only be adjusted after an internal reorganization of Japan was effected. Consequently, he turned his attention back to the Japanese situation and published *A Plan for the Reorganization of Japan* in 1923. This essay established his reputation as the spokesman for Japanese radical nationalists in the eyes of his admirers as well as his critics. His *Plan*, which had a tremendous impact upon civilian and military right-wing activists, is particularly worthy of examination because of the clear indication it yields of the kind of society that the reformers hoped to establish.

In his *Plan*, Kita called for a radical reorganization of the political, social, and economic institutions as well as a commitment to an expansionist foreign policy. Domestically, he proposed the removal of the privileged cliques so that a true union between the Emperor and the people could be achieved. The displacement of the ruling elite was to be brought about by a coup d'état. He advocated the abolition of the peerage and the House of Peers, the introduction of universal manhood suffrage, and the replacement of privy councilors, governors, and other officials. In the economic realm, Kita favored what was, in effect, national socialism—personal property and private landownership were to be limited and major enterprises nationalized. In the social sphere he envisioned the establishment of a welfare state in which the rights of the workers were protected with profit sharing and worker participation in management. Orphans, the aged, and the disabled were to be cared for by the state. In foreign affairs, Kita proposed that Australia and eastern Siberia be acquired by Japan as part of the proletarian nation's class struggle against wealthy capitalist nations.

CONSPIRACIES AND ASSASSINATIONS

The right-wing radicals among the civilians and the military began to hatch plots either to assassinate key officials as a prelude to the revolution or to stage a more elaborate coup. The first serious plot, devised by the members of the Sakurakai as well as other military officers, failed to materialize. This was the March Incident, which was planned by Hashimoto Kingorō and his cohorts, involving several generals as well as Ōkawa Shūmei. Among those who were consulted, or were at least aware of the plot, were generals Koiso Kuniaki, chief of the military affairs bureau, Tatekawa Yoshitsugu of the general staff, and Sugiyama Gen, Vice-Minister of War. The conspirators planned to stage a coup in March, 1931, and place General Ugaki, then the Minister of War, at the head of the new government. The plot fell through, however, when Ugaki, who had initially showed some interest, refused to co-operate. This action by Ugaki turned the militants against him, and they began to look to generals Araki and Mazaki for leadership.

Had vigorous action been taken at this time against the plotters, the possibility of future conspiracies breaking out might have been lessened, but wanting to avoid trouble with the army, the military and civilian leaders behaved cautiously. One historian has observed,

> This caution was the tragedy of all temperate and liberal opinion in Japan. Give us time, said army "moderates" to civilian ministers and Court officials, and we shall have extremists under control. Give us time, said Japanese diplomats to foreign governments, and the pendulum will swing back from militant nationalism to common sense and moderation. It was a recurring theme, from 1931 almost to the eve of Pearl Harbor.[8]

The young officers, with increasing audacity, continued to defy their superiors and civilian officials, thus posing a sharp contrast to the Meiji military men, who were strictly disciplined and accustomed to leaving political matters in the hands of their leaders. The Sakurakai conspirators, as noted below, were also intimately involved in the Manchurian Incident, which broke out in September, 1931. The efforts of Foreign Minister Shidehara to settle the episode peacefully through diplomatic negotiations angered the militant army officers and the radical civilian nationalists, who devised another plot to overthrow the government. The same men who planned the March Incident, Hashimoto and Ōkawa among others, were involved in this affair, labeled the October Incident. Their plan was to assassinate Prime Minister Wakatsuki and other high officials and place General Araki, then inspector general of military education, at the head of the revolutionary government.

General Araki Sadao (1877–1966) was a zealous advocate of "Japanism" and the Imperial Way (kōdō). He was critical of "frivolous foreign ideology," "egotistical foreign ideas," capitalism, Marxism, and materialism. Each Japanese, he said, must be clearly conscious of the thought, "I am a Japanese." He believed in the philosophy that mind has the capacity to conquer matter, and he contended that "if we have thirty million bamboo spears we can stand up to any major power." [9]

---

[8] Richard Storry, The Double Patriots: A Study of Japanese Nationalism (Boston: Houghton Mifflin, 1957), p. 68.
[9] Ōuchi, op. cit., p. 400.

In planning the October Incident, the young officers did not inform their senior officers of the plot this time, but nevertheless, word of the conspiracy leaked out, and the plan was squashed by Araki himself. Once again, however, the conspirators went unpunished, although the officers who were involved in the plot did get scattered to different posts.

The military plotters were blocked temporarily, but their conspiratorial offensive was soon taken up by a group of civilian extremists who were also concerned about the impoverishment of the peasantry and favored the establishment of a new order. They had organized a group called the Blood Brotherhood League (*Ketsumeidan*), whose goal was the destruction of the existing order by means of terror rather than through a military coup. Some of the league members were nevertheless still in touch with the Sakurakai as well as some naval officers. The Ketsumeidan also had the indirect support of older ultranationalists, such as Uchida Ryōhei of the Amur River Society, and Tōyama Mitsuru. The members pledged themselves in blood to eliminate those public figures who had enriched themselves at the expense of agrarian families and who had betrayed the country internationally. Their leader was a Buddhist monk, Inoue Nisshō (1886–1967).

The Ketsumeidan compiled a list of thirteen prominent men who were to be assassinated; among them were Inukai (who had become Prime Minister in December, 1931), Wakatsuki, Saionji, Inoue Junnosuke, and Dan Takuma (director of Mitsui). In early 1932, the terrorists had managed to assassinate only Inoue Junnosuke and Dan Takuma. Inoue Nisshō's connection with the killings was uncovered during the investigation, and he was sentenced to prison for fifteen years. This, however, failed to put an end to the activities of the Ketsumeidan. The remaining members conspired ever the more vigorously with navy officers who were in sympathy with their aims to assassinate Inukai.

Inukai, the champion of parliamentary government, had become Prime Minister after the fall of the Wakatsuki cabinet, which had been buffeted from all sides because of its efforts to resolve the Manchurian crisis peacefully. Ironically enough, it was Inukai himself who had in fact led the Seiyūkai in attacking Shidehara's so-called soft policies. Inukai was advised not to accept the premiership by his friend Tōyama Mitsuru, who knew that right-wing extremists were determined to put an end to party government. Unquestionably, as Prime Minister, Inukai would become the prime target of the assassins. He nevertheless accepted the assignment and, in accordance with the Emperor's wishes, set out to curb army actions in Manchuria.

As soon as Inukai's policy regarding Manchuria was revealed, the extremists, led chiefly by Koga Kiyoshi, a naval lieutenant, and Tachibana

Kōsaburō, a radical agrarian reformer who had worked with Inoue Nisshō, began plotting his assassination. Tachibana and his followers were influenced by a champion of agrarian radicalism, Gondō Seikyō, who was opposed to the highly centralized capitalistic state then in existence and favored a return to autonomous agrarian village communities united under the Emperor. Gondō was extremely critical of privileged groups, that is, the zaibatsu, bureaucrats, the military, and the political parties.

On May 15, 1932, the plotters—naval officers and army cadets led by Koga—put into effect their plot to assassinate both Inukai and Makino, the Lord Keeper of the Privy Seal. The plan also involved attacks on the Seiyūkai headquarters, the Mitsubishi Bank, the police headquarters, and various electrical power plants. They failed to accomplish all of their objectives save one: they succeeded in killing Inukai. The officers broke into the Prime Minister's home with drawn pistols, whereupon Inukai urged a discussion of their grievances. The assassins, however, recognized no need for talk and fired their pistols.

Inukai's assassination marks a milestone in the rise of the militarists and right-wing radicals. It effectively put an end to party government and presaged the domination of the political scene by the military. The removal of Inukai meant that the Kwantung Army could continue its arbitrary and aggressive actions without any serious restraints being placed upon it. In the future, few men would dare to oppose openly the wishes of the military.

Again the assassins were let off with light punishments. The heaviest penalty, life imprisonment, was meted out to the civilian participant Tachibana, who did not even take part directly in the murder of Inukai. The other plotters were sentenced to four to fifteen years in prison, but their sentences were soon commuted. For example, Ōkawa Shūmei, who had supported the conspiracy, was sentenced to fifteen years imprisonment, but he was released after serving only five years of his term.

THE MANCHURIAN INCIDENT

The desire on the part of the army to extend Japanese control over Manchuria and Inner Mongolia can, as we observed earlier, be traced back to the time of the Russo-Japanese War. However, the sense of urgency about accomplishing these aims was heightened in the twenties as the Nationalist party began to unify China and as the possibility that Manchuria might be brought under the control of a strong central government became increasingly evident. The concern was intensified as Chang Hsüeh-liang pledged his allegiance to the Nanking government.

The men who masterminded the Manchurian plot and thus set Japan on its road to conquest in 1931 were two Kwantung Army officers, Ishiwara Kanji (1886–1949) and Itagaki Seishirō (1885–1948). Their solution to the Manchurian-Mongolian question was to have the Kwantung Army take it upon itself to overthrow Chang Hsüeh-liang and then proceed to conquer Manchuria. The basic plan for these actions was worked out by Ishiwara.

Ishiwara and Itagaki wanted Manchuria under Japanese control not only for economic reasons, but also because they believed that the acquisition of that region of China was strategically essential in guarding against Soviet ambitions. They also rationalized this conquest with the argument that the Manchurian people would benefit from Japanese rule, which would see to the maintenance of public security and the development of the economy. To set their plan in motion, Ishiwara and Itagaki intended to contrive an incident that would provide the Kwantung Army with an excuse for extending control over all of Manchuria. Their desire to dominate this region was, of course, shared by other officers, such as Araki Sadao and Hata Shunroku of the army general staff. Support for the ambitions of the Kwantung Army was also found among officers of the war ministry, such as Nagata Tetsuzan, who believed in the concept of total war and who wanted to acquire the vast resources of Manchuria.

A number of minor incidents served to keep the Manchurian situation rather tense. In the late spring of 1931, a clash over water rights between Koreans and Chinese in Wanpaoshan, northwest of Changchun, resulted in the intervention of the Japanese police. In retaliation for the maltreatment of Koreans in Manchuria, Chinese inhabitants in Korea were attacked, and 109 persons were killed. Later, in June of that same year, two Japanese agents were caught in a restricted area in Manchuria, and they were summarily shot to death by the Chinese troops. This incident heightened anti-Chinese sentiments in Japan and intensified public criticism of Shidehara's policy of resolving Sino-Japanese problems peacefully.

Ishiwara and Itagaki decided that the time had arrived to put their plan into effect, and they went ahead and got the approval of key officers in the general staff and the war ministry. The tension continued to mount and rumors of impending action by the Kwantung Army began spreading until finally, the Emperor expressed his concern to the military leaders. As a result, Minister of War Minami dispatched General Tatekawa, who was actually a supporter of the plotters, to restrain the Kwantung Army officers, asking them to wait one more year. One historian has remarked that "To have sent Tatekawa to Mukden at the critical time was like telling a pyromaniac to forestall an attempt at arson." [10]

[10] Storry, *op. cit.*, p. 83.

Even before Tatekawa departed, the object of his mission was communicated to the Kwantung Army officers by Hashimoto, who advised them to act before Tatekawa's arrival.

On the night of September 18, 1931, a small group of Kwantung Army men were ordered to blow up a section of the South Manchurian Railroad in Mukden. The explosion was followed by a clash between the Japanese railroad guards and Chinese troops. Itagaki then sent reinforcements from the battalion headquarters in Mukden and turned the skirmish into a major offensive. By the next morning, the Kwantung Army had gained complete control of Mukden. It then issued a communiqué stating that the Chinese troops had blown up the South Manchurian Railroad and attacked the Japanese guards.

The Wakatsuki cabinet met as soon as the incident broke out and, at the insistence of Foreign Minister Shidehara and Minister of Finance Inoue, it decided to localize and settle the matter promptly. However, the army general staff contended that the cabinet decision was not binding upon the military forces because of the "independence of the supreme command" and the principle that the staff of field armies possessed complete freedom in the area of operational planning. The Kwantung Army rapidly moved ahead and occupied all of southern Manchuria without delay. Moreover, to extend the scope of the conflict, the Kwantung Army asked the commander of the Korean Army, General Hayashi Senjūrō, to send his troops into southern Manchuria. This Hayashi did, violating the principle that prohibited field commanders from sending their troops outside their command jurisdictions without first obtaining imperial sanction. Shidehara's insistence that Hayashi be censured was not approved, but the army promised to restrict further actions in Manchuria. The government in turn acceded to the army's demand that a new treaty be negotiated with the Chinese Nationalist government to guarantee Japanese rights and interests in Manchuria. The Kwantung Army nevertheless persisted with its aggressive operations by exercising the right of self-defense to carry out attacks against "bandits."

Chang Hsüeh-liang was unwilling to risk his army in a major confrontation with the Japanese forces, so the Nationalist government, which was not prepared to engage the Japanese because it was already deeply involved in conducting a civil war against the Communists, appealed to the League of Nations to stop the Japanese aggression. The Japanese government wanted to keep the League of Nations out of the affair and sought to negotiate directly with the Nationalist government. Following the lead of the British, council members of the League were initially inclined to accept the Japanese government's word that it intended to "prevent the aggravation of the situation." As a result, the council adjourned on September 30, without taking any action. The

Kwantung Army continued its activities, however, and so the council had to meet again in late October, at which time it passed a resolution calling for the withdrawal of Japanese troops by November 16.

In Japan, the army received the public's enthusiastic support for its bold actions, and criticism of Shidehara's efforts to achieve a peaceful settlement mounted even higher. Militaristic sentiments were buttressed throughout the country by the millions of members of the *Zaigō Gunjinkai* (Military Reservists Association). Not only did members of the Seiyūkai join Shidehara's critics, but even a member of Wakatsuki's own cabinet, Minister of Home Affairs Adachi, started to boycott cabinet meetings to protest the government policies advocating a peaceful settlement. Shidehara found himself in an impossible predicament because the Japanese army had absolutely no intention of withdrawing by November 16, and the Chinese government refused to participate in any negotiations before such a withdrawal. Shidehara now had virtually no support and even Saionji, who had backed him up until this point, concluded that he had to reconsider his position "from the point of view of living diplomacy when the entire national opinion called it mistaken and wrong." Shidehara finally gave up the struggle and on December 12, the Wakatsuki cabinet fell.

Wakatsuki was succeeded by the seventy-five-year-old Inukai of the Seiyūkai. Inukai served as his own Foreign Minister, but he appointed General Araki as the Minister of War and chose Mori Kaku, who favored establishing a dictatorship based on an alliance between the army and the Seiyūkai, as cabinet secretary. In spite of his attacks on Shidehara's policies, Inukai was deeply concerned about the army's arbitrary actions. Immediately upon his appointment, Inukai was informed of the Emperor's desire that the army be restrained from meddling in domestic and foreign affairs. He promised to abide by the Emperor's wishes and endeavor to curb the army.

Inukai hoped to devise a plan that would persuade the Kwantung Army to withdraw its troops to the South Manchurian Railroad zone in order to open the way for negotiations with the Chinese government. He even contemplated having the Emperor issue a rescript ordering the army to cease further operations in Manchuria. This step was never taken, however, possibly because it was feared that if the rescript were issued and the army defied the Emperor's command it would have a disastrous effect on the prestige of the throne. It was this very fear, in fact, that accounts for the civilian leaders' timidity in utilizing the imperial authority to curb the army throughout the 1930s.

Now that Shidehara was out of the way, the Kwantung Army proceeded to capture Chinchow and Harbin. It also moved north into Amur Province, overcoming the initial concern that this action might draw Soviet Russia into the conflict. In January, 1932, the Sino-Japanese conflict spread to Shanghai. In retaliation for the aggressive actions in Manchuria, the Chinese staged a boycott of Japanese goods, and some Japanese residents in Shanghai were molested by angry mobs.[11] For the protection of her own residents, the Japanese landed marines in Shanghai. This was followed, in the latter part of January, by a clash between the Japanese troops and the Chinese Nineteenth Route Army. Thereupon, the Japanese admiral in command ordered an aerial bombardment of a densely populated section of Shanghai. This outrageous action aroused world opinion against the Japanese and hardened Chinese determination to resist them. It is believed that it was this action rather than the Mukden Incident that turned American public opinion against Japan.

The Inukai cabinet, with great reluctance, acceded to Araki's proposal to send two army divisions into Shanghai and by early March, the Nineteenth Route Army was driven out of the city. The commanding general, Shirakawa, refused to listen to those who favored pursuing the fleeing Chinese forces and concluded an armistice in early May.

The Shanghai Incident further strengthened jingoistic sentiments in Japan. Consequently, Inukai found it increasingly difficult to continue his efforts to bring about a negotiated settlement with the Nanking government concerning Manchuria. Hostility toward the League of Nations mounted considerably after its adoption of Secretary of State Stimson's doctrine of nonrecognition.[12] The result of all this was that the proponents of a peaceful conclusion to the hostilities with China found themselves being overwhelmed by public indignation and chauvinism. This kind of atmosphere naturally yielded tremendous support to the Kwantung Army officers, who proceeded to establish the state of Manchukuo. They brought together former officials of the Ch'ing government who were willing to collaborate with them and organized the Northeastern Administrative Council. In February, the Council issued a declaration of independence and called a convention on the twenty-ninth of that month for the purpose of establishing a new state. The former Emperor of China, Hsüan-t'ung (Pu Yi), was made the head of the state as regent on March 9, 1932.

The Inukai government had no choice but to accept the machinations of the Kwantung Army, although it did not extend formal recognition to

[11] It was revealed after the war that, just as the Chinese had charged, the attacks on the Japanese were actually masterminded by Itagaki, who bribed some Chinese to incite the mob to touch off an incident.

[12] On January 7, 1931, Stimson declared that the United States "does not intend to recognize any situation, treaty, or agreement which may be brought about by means contrary to the covenants and obligations of the Peace of Paris of August 27, 1928."

the new state. Manchukuo was dubbed "a paradise where the way of the king prevails," but it was no more than a puppet state controlled by the Kwantung Army, Japanese officials, and the South Manchurian Railway. In September, 1932, the Saitō government recognized the puppet state; in March, 1934, it became a monarchy with Pu Yi on the throne. It did not succeed in gaining the recognition of other governments, with the exception of a few nations, such as Japan's Axis allies, Germany and Italy.

The Japanese government's failure to restrain the Kwantung Army compelled the council of the League of Nations to take a stronger position than its members initially desired. On December 10, 1931, the council appointed the Lytton Commission to look into the Manchurian situation. The five-member commission began its investigation in late February, and pursued its inquiry for six months. In September, 1932, a report was submitted to the League of Nations, which published it on October 2. The report held that the Japanese military actions of the night of September 18–19, 1931, could not be considered as legitimate measures of self-defense, and that the new state was not the product of a genuine and spontaneous independence movement. The report recommended the creation, under Chinese sovereignty, of an autonomous regime for the Manchurian provinces, and the withdrawal of all Chinese and Japanese forces. Japanese rights and interests were to be guaranteed by a Sino-Japanese treaty that would be designed to provide for the participation of Japan in the economic development of Manchuria.

The Lytton Commission's report was, as might be expected, wholly unacceptable to the Japanese army and the Saitō government. In February, 1933, the assembly of the League adopted a committee report based in large part on the Lytton report, at which point the Japanese delegation, led by Matsuoka Yōsuke, angrily responded by walking out. On March 27, Japan formally withdrew from the League, and embarked on a solitary path that, in the eyes of the world, made her an international outlaw.

The inability of the League of Nations to cope with Japanese aggression provided an unfortunate demonstration of the organization's fundamental impotence to future aggressors, Mussolini and Hitler. The post-World War I hopes for international cooperation and collective security were shattered, and it is in this sense that we can say that the road to the Second World War started in Mukden on September 18, 1931.

INTERNAL POLITICAL DEVELOPMENTS:
THE TRIUMPH OF THE MILITARISTS

Party governments, as we noted earlier, went out of existence in Japan with Inukai's assassination, and they were not to return until after the Second World War. Eleven men were to head the government from May, 1932, to August, 1945. Four of these men were admirals, four were generals, and only three were civilians. The admirals tended to be moderate, the generals were inclined to chauvinism, and the civilians were all very conservative members of the establishment who were acceptable to the military.

In selecting Inukai's successor, the Emperor told Saionji that the next Prime Minister had to be a man of integrity who was not sympathetic to the radical nationalists and who would uphold the constitution. Saionji believed that Admiral Saitō Makoto (1858–1936), the former governor-general of Korea, would fit the bill. Saitō was a moderate who was acceptable not only to the military, but also to the inner circle of court advisers. As a result, Saitō was given the task of forming a "united, national" government.

The Saitō cabinet included representatives from the two major parties as well as from the bureaucracy, the business world, and the armed forces. Takahashi Korekiyo once again became Minister of Finance and sought to curb the army, which was represented in the cabinet by Araki.

Saitō was not an aggressive individual, and he consequently failed to provide the strong leadership that was vitally needed if the many difficulties facing the nation were to be resolved. His cabinet, known as the "slow-motion cabinet," did restore a degree of calm to the turbulent political scene, but fundamentally, its policy of "letting sleeping dogs lie" merely provided a temporary respite while militaristic, authoritarian forces were sinking their roots in deeper and more securely. The political parties were split into factions, with a large segment joining the ranks of the militant nationalists in the hope of riding the tide of imperialism to power. At the same time, Saitō diminished the influence of the party men in the cabinet by establishing the Five Ministers Conference—an inner cabinet consisting of the Prime Minister and the ministers of war, navy, finance, and foreign affairs—as the key policy-making body. This practice, which was retained by subsequent cabinets, diminished the influence of the other cabinet ministers while giving the army and navy a much stronger voice in the setting of foreign and domestic policy.

The Saitō cabinet succumbed to the army's insistence that Japan withdraw from the League of Nations, although Minister of Finance Takahashi vehemently opposed such a move. On the continent, the Kwantung Army continued to pursue its own objectives as if it were an autonomous organ, and it compelled the government to go along with its actions. In February, 1933, it moved its troops against Jehol Province in Inner Mongolia and advanced south of the Great Wall in pursuit of the

Chinese forces. It also occupied Shanhaikwan Pass, but Minister of War Araki prevented them from going further into Chinese territory. In May, 1933, the Kwantung Army negotiated the Tangku Truce with the Chinese authorities, who at this time were more concerned about suppressing the Communist forces in the country than curbing Japanese aggression. Under this agreement Manchuria was extended into Jehol Province, the Kwantung Army gained control of the Shanhaikwan Pass, and a demilitarized zone was established north of Tientsin and Peking.

As a result of Japan's isolation from the international community and her successes in Manchuria, the tide of ultranationalism and militarism continued to sweep the country. One consequence of this was the campaign to rid the entire land of "dangerous thought." As we noted earlier, vigorous suppression of the Communists had been taking place since the time when Tanaka was Prime Minister. Now, as nationalistic sentiments began inundating the country, many of the incarcerated Communists recanted, pledged their loyalty to the Imperial Way, and embraced "Japanism." Many former left-wing socialists became staunch supporters of imperialism.

The initial effort to control thought may have been directed primarily at the Communists, but within a short period of time the scope of what constituted "dangerous thought" was gradually enlarged until eventually socialism, liberalism, pacifism, and internationalism were all deemed threatening ideologies, and consequently, their adherents became objects of persecution. The first victim of this renewed effort to purge the intellectual world of "dangerous thought" was Takigawa Yukitoki, a law professor at Kyoto University. Prior to this, professors had been expelled from the universities but the reason for their dismissal had been their espousal of communism. In Takigawa's case, his dismissal was ordered in 1933, by the Minister of Education, Hatoyama Ichirō, because the law books that he wrote were critical of the existing social and legal practices. This campaign to purge "Red professors" had the support of right-wing members of both houses in the Diet. Despite the protests of the president, faculty, and students of Kyoto University, Takigawa was dismissed and was prevented from publishing any of his works until the postwar period.

At the same time that this attack on "dangerous thought" was being launched, the military was able to win public sympathy for the "patriotic young men" who had assassinated Inukai. More than one million signatures were gathered on petitions asking for clemency. In July, 1933, another scheme to assassinate the Prime Minister and other leaders was uncovered. This plot, called the *Shimpeitai Jiken* (Divine Soldiers Affair), was led by a follower of Inoue Nisshō, and even Araki was among the projected targets.

The military became increasingly critical of the Saitō government as Minister of Finance Takahashi maintained tight control of the purse strings and as Hirota Kōki, who became Foreign Minister in September, 1933, pursued a policy of adjusting Japan's relations with China. In international affairs, tensions were reduced as Soviet Russia indicated its willingness to sell the Chinese Eastern Railroad in northern Manchuria to Japan. After prolonged negotiations the sale was finally consummated in March, 1935, and relations between the two nations improved considerably.

Right-wing nationalists grew impatient with Saitō's moderate policies and began to intensify their attacks against his government. For instance, the Minister of Commerce and Industry was forced to resign after it was exposed that ten years earlier he had written an article that was favorable to Ashikaga Takauji, the founder of the Ashikaga Bakufu. Saitō finally resigned in July, 1934, when it was charged that some government officials had taken bribes from a major rayon company.

In selecting Saitō's successor, Saionji introduced a new procedure. He called a conference of senior statesmen and conferred with all the former Prime Ministers as well as the Lord Keeper of the Privy Seal and the president of the Privy Council. Saitō recommended that Admiral Okada Keisuke (1868–1952) be appointed as his successor; Saionji and the others concurred with the choice. Once again the advisers of the Emperor had turned to a moderate admiral. The Okada cabinet was virtually an extension of the Saitō cabinet, but it lacked the cooperation of the Seiyūkai; in fact, the three Seiyūkai men who entered the cabinet were expelled from the party. This presaged trouble for the Okada government because it meant that the Seiyūkai would play the demagogic game of championing right-wing, ultranationalist causes by seeking to win the favor of the radical militarists.

The Okada cabinet may have enjoyed some success in adjusting Japanese relations with China, but by and large, it took a giant step backward in the realm of international cooperation when it acceded to the advocates of naval expansion, who were led by the chief of the naval general staff, Admiral Suetsugu, a long-time foe of disarmament. Going along with the wishes of the naval expansionists, the cabinet decided to abrogate the Washington and London naval agreements after the United States and Great Britain refused to agree to Japanese demands for parity. At the end of 1935, the departure of the Japanese delegation from the London conference catapulted the three powers into a naval arms race.

The Okada government was also influenced by Nagata Tetsuzan (1884–1935), who propounded the theory that in the future all nations had to be prepared to wage total war. To this end, Nagata argued, there had to be an autonomous national defense program in which all phases of the system, particularly military and economic planning, were coordinated. To lay the groundwork for such a scheme Okada established the Cabinet Research Bureau, whose task was the preparation of legislative proposals and position papers on important economic problems. Subsequently, this bureau became the agency responsible for formulating those laws that steadily diminished the rights and freedom of the people.

The Okada cabinet was confronted by an even stronger tide of right-wing nationalism than Saitō had faced. The attacks on the academic community were sustained by the ultranationalists, militarists, and political opportunists. A prominent authority on constitutional law, Minobe Tatsukichi (1873–1948) became a primary focus of their criticism. He supported the theory of the corporate state with a juristic personality and its corollary theory that the Emperor, because he is actually an organ of the state, is contained within the state rather than above or identical with it, as was argued by scholars who believed in a mystical notion of the national polity. Initially, arguments concerning Minobe's theory were confined largely to the scholarly world, and his interpretation was generally accepted by students of government and law. In the mid-thirties, however, as the forces of authoritarianism and ultranationalism gained strength, the theory that Minobe had first made public twenty-seven years earlier was turned into a major political issue by men who objected to all liberal and rational interpretations of the constitution.

The radical militarists objected to Minobe's Organ Theory because they favored an absolutist interpretation that would permit them to exercise power on behalf of the Emperor, whom they claimed to represent directly under the provision of the "independence of the supreme command." Minobe had angered the army on many occasions by consistently espousing a narrow interpretation of this concept and by criticizing the army for advocating total planning for war. The army, therefore, was more than a little anxious to join the scheme to discredit Minobe.

Ultranationalist scholars and politicians initiated the attack on Minobe. In February, 1935, a reactionary member of the House of Peers and a director of the Kokuhonsha, Kikuchi Takeo, publicly condemned the Organ Theory as being contrary to the national polity and then denounced Minobe as a "traitor, rebel, and academic bandit." Right-wing nationalists led by Tōyama Mitsuru formed an organization to destroy the Organ Theory. The scope of the attack was widened when the army called upon the Military Reservists Association to rally public opinion against Minobe.

Perceiving this as an issue that could readily be exploited to overthrow the Okada government, the followers of Hiranuma and the members of the Seiyūkai joined the attack on Minobe. They criticized officials who were sympathetic to Minobe and excoriated the government for defending the "defiler of the national polity." Both houses of the Diet passed resolutions condemning his theory, and a member of the lower house brought charges against the scholar for lese majesty. Minobe was finally forced to resign his seat in the House of Peers and his teaching post at the University of Tokyo, and his books were banned. The following year a fanatical ultranationalist attempted, unsuccessfully, to murder him.

The assault on the Organ Theory had far greater significance than being merely an attack on the life and ideas of one man. In effect it presaged the end of freedom of thought in Japan. During the succeeding years, a strict surveillance was imposed over all political theories. No idea that ran contrary to the mystical and irrational concept of national polity could be propounded even within the narrow confines of the academic world. The army and the ultranationalists, who made it their sacred mission to "clarify the national polity," set out to eradicate all vestiges of the Organ Theory.

In March, 1937, the Ministry of Education issued *Cardinal Principles of the National Entity of Japan (Kokutai no Hongi)*, a booklet describing the unique characteristics of Japan. It stated that

> Our country is established with the Emperor, who is a
> descendant of Amaterasu Ohmikami, as her center, and our
> ancestors as well as we ourselves constantly have beheld in
> the Emperor the fountainhead of her life and activities.
> For this reason, to serve the Emperor and to receive the
> Emperor's great august Will as one's own is the rationale of
> making our historical "life" live in the present; and on
> this is based the morality of the people.[13]

Here again the family system was made the linchpin of the whole society. "Our country is a great family nation," the treatise continued, "and the Imperial Household is the head family of the subjects and the nucleus of national life." The treatise went on to define and extol the virtues of loyalty, patriotism, filial piety, harmony, the martial spirit, and Bushidō. Western individualism was condemned as the root cause of democracy, socialism, communism, and anarchism, and it was blamed for "the ideological and social confusion and crisis" prevalent in Japan and in the West.[14] Thus, with the publication of this document, an

---

[13] Robert K. Hall, ed., *Kokutai no Hongi (Cardinal Principles of the National Entity of Japan)* (Cambridge, Mass.: Harvard University Press, 1949), p. 80.
[14] *Ibid.*, pp. 89–90, 54.

official doctrine of "Japanism" was promulgated, and conformity to this ideology became virtually mandatory.

The Organ Theory not only gave rise to an official formulation of national polity, but it was also responsible for creating conflicting factions within the army. In the midst of the controversy, the most vehement army critic of Minobe's theory, General Mazaki, was transferred from his post as inspector general of military education. His radical followers blamed Minister of War Hayashi and Nagata Tetsuzan, chief of the military affairs bureau, for this demotion. Hayashi had contended some time earlier that the Organ Theory had not had an inimical effect on military education and Mazaki, who favored military intervention in political affairs, openly contradicted this. The transferring of Mazaki was regarded as a plot on the part of the Tōsei-ha to diminish the influence in the army of the Kōdō-ha.

It has been customary to divide the army factions into these two groups, the Tōsei-ha and the Kōdō-ha, but the division was by no means rigidly fixed. There were no absolute and clearly defined disagreements about military and political matters between officers who supposedly belonged to these rival factions. Affiliation with one group or the other was informal, and the majority of the six thousand army officers actually took no part whatsoever in the factional rivalry. The Kōdō-ha, gathering around generals Araki and Mazaki, had among its adherents a group of young officers at the company-commander level. The more loosely grouped Tōsei-ha consisted of officers who objected to the tactics and the personnel policies of the Araki-Mazaki faction.

In order to bring about the Shōwa Restoration, the Kōdō-ha officers believed that senior statesmen, members of the zaibatsu, and corrupt politicians had to be eliminated by direct action. This approach was vigorously opposed by Nagata and other key officers of his faction, such as Tōjō Hideki and Mutō Akira, who believed that isolated acts of violence would only upset the order of things and consequently impede the plan to prepare the nation for total war. These army officers, who came to be called the Tōsei-ha, believed that the necessary changes could be brought about without violence by using legitimate means under the leadership of the army central headquarters. They insisted that the realization of this end depended on the entire army being united and disciplined under the tight control of army leaders at the center.

The conflict between the two factions[15] came to the surface after Araki

[15] It was assumed until recently that the two factions were also divided over key issues of foreign policy. That is, it was claimed that the Kōdō-ha believed in engaging the Soviet Union in a conflict, while the Tōsei-ha, on the other hand, favored moving against China. The demise of the Kōdō-ha following the unsuccessful insurrection of February 26, 1936, was seen as having paved the way for the invasion of China. This

became Minister of War late in 1931. He made personnel changes at the center by removing from key positions the followers of Ugaki, such as General Tatekawa, as well as some members of the Sakurakai. Among the latter was Hashimoto Kingorō, who had lost his enthusiasm for Araki when he disappointed the plotters of the October Incident. In their places Araki installed his friends and followers, including General Mazaki Jinsaburō (1876–1956), who was made the vice-chief of the general staff. This policy of filling sensitive posts with his own followers caused those who were ousted to form a faction called the *Seigun-ha* (Purification Faction) under the leadership of Tatekawa and Hashimoto. They called for the purification of the army through the elimination of cliquism. The Seigun-ha tended to align itself with the Tōsei-ha.

In January, 1934, Araki was replaced by General Hayashi Senjūrō (1876–1943) as Minister of War. The supreme war council, consisting of leading admirals and generals, had disapproved of Araki's personnel policies as well as of his repeated pronouncements that 1936 was going to be a year of crisis because a war with the Soviet Union was likely to break out at that time. Hayashi was thought to be sympathetic to the Araki faction, but upon assuming the post of Minister of War, he made Nagata the chief of the military affairs bureau. Nagata, as we noted earlier, was opposed to isolated acts of violence and believed in maintaining discipline in the army. In November, 1934, Kōdō-ha officers, Muranaka Kōji and Isobe Senichi, contrived an assassination plot, which also involved the cadets of the Military Academy. Their aim was to murder the senior statesmen and establish a military government, but before any action could be taken, the plot was uncovered by Nagata, who expelled the conspirators from the army. Nagata also removed Araki's men from the army's top positions, but he was unable to move immediately against Mazaki.

Now that Araki was out of office, the Kōdō-ha officers came to regard Mazaki as their main hope of regaining their influence. Their chances of ever succeeding in this regard were seriously threatened when, in the summer of 1935, Hayashi and Nagata finally made a move to place Mazaki on the inactive list. Mazaki was able to resist the plan to retire him, but he nevertheless lost his post as inspector general of military education. The Kōdō-ha officers were infuriated by his transfer, and they circulated statements in the army attacking the senior statesmen, members of the zaibatsu and their servants in the army who, they as-

---

interpretation has now been questioned. Factional strife in the army was not what determined the course of Japanese policies on the continent. The Araki faction was just as interested in extending Japanese influence into North China as was the Tōsei-ha. See James B. Crowley, *Japan's Quest for Autonomy: National Security and Foreign Policy, 1930–1938* (Princeton, N.J.: Princeton University Press, 1966), pp. 247 ff.

serted, had conspired against Mazaki and Araki. Nagata was singled out as the individual most responsible for the injustices committed against the two generals. Aizawa Saburō, a fanatical Kōdō-ha officer, decided to take matters into his own hands, and on August 12, 1935, he walked into Nagata's office and assassinated the man who was regarded as the most brilliant officer in the army. Hayashi, who all along was viewed as merely Nagata's puppet, shouldered the responsibility for this violent breach of army discipline and resigned. General Kawashima Yoshiyuki (1878–1945) was appointed as his replacement, but he turned out to be indecisive in dealing with radical army officers.

Aizawa's trial was held under the jurisdiction of the First Division, whose commanding general, Yanagawa Heisuke, was a follower of Araki. Consequently, the Kōdō-ha officers managed to turn the trial into a vehicle for denouncing the Tōsei-ha and for expounding their own political philosophy. The public, as a result, came to regard Aizawa as a sincere, selfless patriot, while Nagata was seen as an unprincipled schemer.

The Kōdō-ha officers decided that a propitious moment to stage a coup d'état had arrived since public opinion had been aroused to their advantage by a number of important events; namely, the Aizawa trial, the controversy over the Organ Theory, and the campaign to clarify the national polity. The conspirators were led by Muranaka and Isobe, now civilians, and officers of the First Division. Kita Ikki and his follower, Nishida Zei, another former army officer, were also informed of the projected coup d'état. The conspirators had the implicit support of generals Mazaki and Yanagawa, and they were given financial assistance from right-wing businessmen and politicians. It is also believed that General Yamashita Tomoyuki contributed to arousing the rebellious officers by talking of the need to cut down Prime Minister Okada. Minister of War Kawashima had a hand in supporting the conspiracy by hinting to the young officers that he would not intervene should they stage an incident. The insurgents decided that they would have to make their move in February, 1936, before they were fully prepared. They were compelled to act prematurely because of the announcement in December that the First Division, to which most of the conspirators were attached, was to be dispatched to Manchuria.

The rebels struck on the morning of February 26, by moving more than 1,400 men of the First Division into the streets of Tokyo to occupy key government buildings, and to murder a number of senior statesmen and high government officials. Among the intended victims were Prime Minister Okada, former Prime Minister Saitō, Minister of Finance Takahashi, General Watanabe, who had replaced Mazaki as inspector general of military education, the Grand Chamberlain, Suzuki Kantarō, and former Lord Keeper of the Privy Seal, Makino. Originally, Saionji was also on the list, but he was dropped when the rebels failed to agree on whether or not to liquidate him.

Three of the intended victims, Saitō, Takahashi, and Watanabe were killed. An official announcement was made that Okada had also been murdered, but the assassins mistakenly shot his brother-in-law, and Okada escaped. Suzuki Kantarō received several bullet wounds, but he managed to survive and later served as Prime Minister during the last months of World War II. Makino succeeded in eluding the assassins.

The rebels occupied the heart of Tokyo after staging the bloodbath, and then issued a manifesto justifying their actions. They accused the genrō, senior statesmen, military cliques, bureaucrats, and party politicians of undermining the national polity and of creating a critical situation abroad. They explained that these reasons motivated them to eliminate the men responsible for the national crisis. They called upon Minister of War Kawashima to take charge of the situation and implement the Shōwa Restoration. They also demanded that General Araki be placed at the head of the Kwantung Army, while generals Ugaki, Minami, Koiso, and Tatekawa be placed under arrest.

The rebels had no concrete plans beyond assassinating the top government officials and court advisers, so the success of their coup actually depended upon whether or not the army leaders would support them. The generals, however, were unable to agree on the course of action to be followed. The central figure, Minister of War Kawashima, was basically irresolute, but he did tend to sympathize with the insurgents. Mazaki and Araki naturally opposed any move to suppress the rebellion by force. Mazaki, in fact, urged Kawashima to persuade the Emperor to comply with the demands of the rebels. In sharp contrast, the officers of the general staff, Ishiwara Kanji in particular, insisted that the rebels be subdued, even by force if necessary. Ishiwara went so far as to advocate calling army divisions from the outlying districts into Tokyo.

The person most responsible for quashing the rebellion, however, was the Emperor, who was adamant in his insistence that the insurgents be subdued. The government, buttressed by the Emperor's strong stand, and headed by acting Prime Minister Gotō Fumio, proclaimed martial law in Tokyo on February 27. General Kashii, who was sympathetic to the rebels, was appointed the commanding general. The navy, also taking a strong position against the insurgents, brought its fleet into Tokyo Bay and moved the marines into the capital.

The rebels now pinned all their hopes on Mazaki and sought to have him appointed as Prime Minister. However, he began to waver after an imperial command was issued to the troops to return to their barracks.

Considerable pressure from Ishiwara and the vice-chief of staff, Sugi-yama, finally forced General Kashii to move his forces against the rebels, and he surrounded them on February 28. The next day, a last appeal was issued to the mutineers to surrender. The leaders of the insurgents finally yielded and the troops began moving back to the First Division com-pounds, and by evening the insurrection was over. Two rebel officers committed suicide, but the others decided to stand trial and use the court as a rostrum from which to present their case to the public. They were, however, tried very swiftly and in secret. Nineteen men, including Muranaka, Isobe, Kita, and Nishida, were condemned to death and executed.

Kita's connection with the uprising was tenuous. He had no part in planning or executing the rebellion, and although he had been informed of the plot, the planners of the coup had not definitely decided to put his political concepts into effect once they secured control. Nonetheless, Kita was held responsible for the influence his *A Plan for the Reorgan-ization of Japan* had on the rebel officers. Kita was a civilian but he was tried by a military court-martial and, a year after his sentence was handed down, he was executed. Mazaki's ties with the rebels were certainly stronger than Kita's, but he was absolved.

The attempted coup of February 26 was followed by a major purge in the army. The generals and officers who were linked to the Kōdō-ha as well as those officers who had caused strife in the army by participating in the activities of the Purification Faction were retired or removed from key posts. Araki and Mazaki were among those placed on the inactive list. In order to ensure that none of the generals who had been placed on the inactive list would return to power as Minister of War, the military regula-tions were revised again to make only active generals and admirals eligible to serve as war and naval ministers. This change, however, also gave the army a veto power over cabinets of which it disapproved.

The purge was conducted by officers who have been categorized as members of the Tōsei-ha, but actually they were men who disapproved of factionalism and mindless acts of violence. The men directly respon-sible for the purge were the new Minister of War, Terauchi Juichi (1879–1946), and his vice-minister, Umezu Yoshijirō (1882–1949), who in effect masterminded the entire affair. Mutō Akira, Ishiwara Kanji, and Umezu became the real wielders of power in the army.

The removal of the Kōdō-ha did not by any means put an end to the army's interference in political affairs. In fact, with internal strife eliminated, the army leaders became even more aggressive in meddling in politics. At the same time, civilians became very timid in dealing with the army, having had a taste of what a politically discontented military was capable of doing. The insurrection of February 26, therefore, greatly strengthened the army's hand and severely diminished the influence of the liberal senior statesmen and court advisers.

The army demonstrated the force of its newly won power immediately. Hirota Kōki (1878–1948), the new Prime Minister, set out to select his cabinet ministers, but Terauchi, who was chosen as Minister of War, insisted on exercising a veto over all the liberal candidates who were recommended for cabinet posts. Hirota meekly succumbed to the army's demand and as a result, Terauchi, with the assistance of Umezu and Ishiwara, rejected out of hand four of the men who were selected and shifted two others from the posts initially assigned to them. Yoshida Shigeru, who was serving as Hirota's chief adviser in selecting the cabinet members, was among those men rejected by the army. Yoshida was slated to become Foreign Minister but the army objected because, not only was he the son-in-law of Makino, who was a target of the insurrection of February 26, but he was also known to be openly critical of the militarists.

Saionji, before turning to Hirota, had asked Prince Konoe, president of the House of Peers, to serve as Prime Minister, but he refused, claiming to be in poor health. Saionji then selected Hirota because, although he was known to have ties with the right-wing nationalists, as Foreign Minister he had insisted that the foreign office, rather than the military, be the organ of government charged with formulating foreign policy. He had also advocated a policy of harmony and cooperation with China.

The chief tasks facing the Hirota government were the formulation of a clearly defined national policy and the resolution of the North China problem. In August, it adopted a policy statement entitled "The Fundamental Principles of National Policy," the basic points of which had been formulated by the officers of the army and navy. The primary objectives of Japan, according to this document, were held to be twofold: first, consolidate the position of the Japanese empire in East Asia, and second, advance into the region of the South Sea.

The navy had long been critical of the army's China policy, which it feared could lead to war with England and America at a time when Japan could not possibly match the combined fleets of those two countries. In order to gain access to the oil deposits in Southeast Asia, the navy wanted to adopt a policy of "defending in the north and advancing to the south." Consequently, a moderate policy in China had to be pursued, the navy argued, so as not to arouse British opposition there. This, in effect, was the very policy that was adopted by the Hirota government. At the same time, military defenses against Soviet Russia were to be strengthened. The move to the south was to be accomplished by peaceful means, but there was nevertheless to be a naval buildup so as to prepare for possible intervention by the United States.

Sweeping internal changes had to be made in order to achieve these goals. Not only was it deemed necessary to expand the military and naval forces, but it was also decided that administrative reforms and new economic and fiscal policies were essential. A reorganization of the Japanese way of life, including "the wholesome development of the people's mode of thinking," was considered vital. In other words, what was contemplated was a comprehensive plan that would make effective use of all elements of the national life in order to achieve these strategic objectives: peace and stability in eastern Asia through the establishment of hegemony over China; naval supremacy in the western Pacific; and superiority over the Soviet army in the Far East.[16]

The outbreak of the China War in 1937, coupled with Japan's inability to extricate herself from the quagmire effectively prevented the nation from realizing the strategic objectives that were outlined in "The Fundamental Principles of National Policy." Nevertheless, the goals embodied in that document were actively pursued by the government regardless of who headed it. Out of this policy, then, emerged the circumstances that ultimately led to the war in the Pacific. The International Military Tribunal, which tried and executed Hirota after the end of the Second World War, held "The Fundamental Principles of National Policy" to have been the blueprint for imperialism that actually led to the war in the Pacific.

The political parties had exercised very little influence ever since Inukai's assassination, but the army still regarded them as serious obstacles to its plan to place the nation on a wartime footing. It contemplated further restricting the role of the Diet in order to make the political parties wholly ineffective. Rumors of the army's plan aroused some of the party men, but a substantial number of them hoped to strengthen their positions by cooperating with the militarists.

In January, 1937, a member of the Seiyūkai, Hamada Kunimatsu, criticized the army for its political activities and charged that the military was permeated with sentiments favoring dictatorship. Minister of War Terauchi was infuriated at Hamada and accused him of insulting the army. Hamada responded by saying that if in reviewing the transcript he discovered that he had in fact insulted the army, then he would commit hara-kiri. If he did not, however, find this to be the case, then he

---

[16] These moves in the direction of total planning are what lead many historians to speak of the rise of fascism in Japan during the 1930s. One authority speaks of the developments under the Hirota government as an advance toward "a completed form of fascism." See Maruyama, *op. cit.*, p. 71.

believed Terauchi should do so. Incensed, Terauchi urged Hirota to dissolve the Diet. Hirota refused to comply and Terauchi resigned, bringing down the entire cabinet with him.

The masterminds in the army, such as Ishiwara, wanted Hayashi appointed as Hirota's successor but Saionji turned instead to Ugaki, believing that he would be able to keep the army radicals under control. Ugaki, however, was unacceptable to the army for at least three compelling reasons: first, he had been responsible for arms reduction while he was Minister of War under Katō Kōmei; second, he had equivocated in the March Incident of 1931; and third, he was regarded as being too intimate with party politicians. The army officers led by Ishiwara sought to dissuade him from accepting the premiership, but when he insisted on going ahead anyway, the army refused to provide him with a Minister of War. His numerous efforts to persuade at least several different generals to assume the post all failed. Reluctantly Ugaki abandoned his efforts to form a cabinet, and Saionji finally turned to the army's choice, General Hayashi.

Hayashi did not turn out to be the puppet that Ishiwara had expected him to be. For example, he refused to appoint Itagaki as Minister of War, and for his Minister of Finance he would not accept Ishiwara's recommendation of Ikeda Seihin, a Mitsui executive who was known to be sympathetic to the militarists. Yūki Toyotarō, who was appointed Minister of Finance did, however, favor cooperating with the military, and Ikeda was made the head of the Bank of Japan. Yūki reversed the Hirota government's policy of increasing government expenditures and reduced the budget by 10 percent, although he left the military budget untouched.

The Hayashi cabinet failed to include a single political party member, but the party men treated the new government gingerly and passed its budget and bills without offering much opposition. Nonetheless, Hayashi dissolved the Diet immediately after the session ended, claiming to be dissatisfied with the quality of the members. In what turned out to be the last prewar election contested by multiple parties, the Minseitō and Seiyūkai captured about the same number of seats. The especially notable result of this election was that 36 seats were captured by the Shakai Taishūtō, which doubled its membership in the Diet. This was the final, desperate resistance of the urban classes against the growing tide of militarism. Confronted by a hostile Diet, Hayashi resigned after staying in office for only four months.

The man who succeeded Hayashi was Konoe Fumimaro (1891–1945), who finally agreed to serve as Prime Minister. He belonged to the most distinguished family among the court aristocrats, and was regarded favorably by all segments of the society. Not only was he well-educated and cultured but, it was believed, he was politically sophisticated. The military approved of him and he also drew influential support from the political parties and from the business world. Saionji held him in high regard and in fact fully expected that eventually Konoe would take his place as the chief adviser to the Emperor. He was only forty-six, a rather young age for a premier. His political views were not clearly known so the newspapers spoke of "the attraction of the unknown quantity." Ironically enough the great hope of Shōwa Japan turned out to be a tragic failure—Konoe was hardly more than a tool of the military. During his tenure as Prime Minister the China War started and spread, and the circumstances that led to the war in the Pacific were allowed to get out of control.

The first Konoe cabinet, which came into existence in early June, 1937, consisted primarily of his followers, who hoped to form a new political party under his leadership. It also included Hirota Kōki as Foreign Minister, General Sugiyama as Minister of war, and Admiral Yonai as Minister of the Navy. Former Vice-Minister of Finance, Kaya Okinori, accepted the post of Minister of Finance only after Konoe agreed to implement a program of economic controls that would effectively prepare the nation for total war.

A little over a month after Konoe took charge of the government the China Incident broke out and Japan was plunged into a situation that was eventually to draw her into a much larger war. The wartime footing of this period enabled the advocates of total planning and total mobilization to implement their programs, and the vestiges of liberal, democratic tendencies that had survived since Inukai's assassination were all but eradicated by the triumph of militarism and ultranationalism.

ECONOMIC DEVELOPMENTS

The military and the zaibatsu began to cooperate with each other from about the time that the Hirota cabinet came into existence. Prior to this, as we noted, the army radicals were hostile to the big capitalists, who were in return opposed to the army's plan to regulate the economy for its own strategic purposes. This animosity on the part of the army was demonstrated when Manchuria was brought under military control. The Kwantung Army leaders, led by Ishiwara, sought to keep the zaibatsu out of the new state. They planned to develop the Manchurian economy by relying upon small and middle-sized business firms or by turning to state capitalism. The Manchurian economy, however, could not be developed without the injection of capital from Japan.

Initially, much of the investments were channeled into Manchuria through the South Manchurian Railway Company, but eventually other firms began to participate in its economic growth. Special emphasis was placed on the development of heavy industries such as steel, coal mining, light metal, and automobile production. Soy bean products had constituted 50 percent of Manchuria's industrial output before the Japanese takeover, but by 1940, 31 percent of the industrial output consisted of metals and machinery, and 15 percent was chemical products. The economy was dominated by Japanese interests, which held 84.1 percent of the capital investment. Some entrepreneurs managed to develop into "new zaibatsu" by using Manchuria as a base of operations and participating in defense production. All this was achieved by a ruthless exploitation of Chinese laborers in Manchuria, who were paid one-third the wages of Japanese workers.

The established zaibatsu also began to cooperate with the military in the building of defense industries as the military gained ascendancy and arms expenditures began to increase. In order to improve their image, the major zaibatsu families such as Mitsui and Mitsubishi, began contributing to social welfare programs. They also removed family members from the top administrative posts and replaced them by managerial executives in the hope of masking the fact that these gigantic combines were controlled by family groups. At the same time, a nominal amount of stocks were sold to the public in order to refute the charge that they were tightly-knit monopolistic combines.

The Japanese economy had recovered from the Great Depression sooner than the other industrial nations because of the tremendous increase in arms expenditures, which rose two-and-a-half times from 1931 to 1935. Recovery was also facilitated by the devaluation of the yen, which enabled Japan to compete more readily with other industrial powers. In 1931, 100 yen was worth 49.4 dollars, whereas in the following year it was worth only 20 dollars. The value of the yen rose somewhat after the United States went off the gold standard in 1933, but still 1 yen was worth only about 28 to 29 cents.

Japan's balance of trade steadily improved and in 1935, her exports exceeded imports for the first time since World War I. The price of her imports had increased by 202 percent since 1931, but at the same time the price of her exports had increased by only 40 percent. This favorable export price was made possible by extremely low wages coupled with greatly advanced efficiency in production. Cotton textiles replaced raw silk as Japan's major export commodity, and by 1936, she was the world's largest exporter of cotton piece goods. Textiles as a whole constituted 58 percent of her exports. The failure of raw silk to recover its status as a major export commodity affected the agrarian communities adversely since, as we noted previously, they relied heavily on the production of cocoons for supplementary income.

The influx of Japanese goods into foreign markets seriously disturbed her competitors and about 1932, they began to act to reverse the trend by raising tariffs and establishing quotas. These efforts to keep Japanese goods out of the Asian and African markets that were controlled by the Western powers aroused bitter sentiments in Japan and provided the militarists with additional excuses for seeking to establish a self-sufficient empire. It was essential for Japan to find markets for her manufactured goods because she had to import the bulk of her raw materials, and the imbalance in the export and import prices made it imperative that she sell more than she bought.

The emphasis placed on arms production resulted in the expansion of heavy industries. For instance, during the interval between the Manchurian Incident and the outbreak of the China Incident, the production of metals and machinery rose from 26 percent of the total industrial output to 34 percent. The textile industry, on the other hand, dropped from 37 percent to 26 percent. The established zaibatsu joined the new zaibatsu in developing strategic war industries. In shipbuilding, for example, Mitsubishi came to produce over 30 percent of the tonnage. It also moved into aircraft production and by 1940, the company was testing the Zero, a highly effective fighter plane. It also entered the automobile and electrical industries.

In contrast to the gains made by the zaibatsu, the small and middle-sized enterprises suffered a decline, particularly those who were engaged in the production of nonessential goods. Most of these businessmen were unable to obtain raw materials, capital, or workers. Consequently, many small and medium-sized entrepreneurs went bankrupt or were absorbed by the bigger companies. Only those factories and shops that managed to get subcontracts for the production of war goods were able to prosper.

The firms engaged in defense production increased their profits substantially, but money wages for the workers remained more or less stable while real wages showed substantial declines. Taking November, 1931, as index 100 we find that money wages stood at 93.5 in 1933, and 91.8 in June, 1937, while real wages dropped to 87.8 in 1933, and then down to 75.7 in June, 1937. Despite these serious declines, the president of a Japanese textile firm operating in China remarked that the capitalists in Japan were too timid in dealing with discontented workers. He went on to point out that in Shanghai they apprehended troublesome workers and summarily shot them. One Mitsui executive noted that the Manchurian workers were able to live on 10 sen a day while it cost the Japanese workers 50 sen a day. The Japanese workers, he concluded, should reduce their food costs by eating only rice and soybean cakes.

The period from 1931 to 1952, constitutes the second half of the second phase of modern economic growth according to the Ohkawa-Rosovsky schema. The development during this period is attributed not only to such stimuli as the export of cheap goods, but also to the "political solution," that is, military expansion.

The changeover to a wartime economy created hardship in the villages because the men were either drafted into the army or went to work in the factories, thus leaving only women, children, and the aged to do the farm work. The diversion of the nation's resources to war production resulted in shortages of chemical fertilizer and equipment needed on the farms. At the same time, the increased demand for rice in the cities and for the greatly expanded armed forces led the government to regulate prices and control sale and distribution. We shall now turn our attention to the political developments that caused these pressures on the economy to manifest themselves.

CHAPTER 19

THE
ROAD
TO WAR

CHINA POLICY TO 1937

Following the Manchurian Incident, the Japanese government under Saitō proclaimed the "Asiatic Monroe Doctrine," the primary objective of which was the preservation of peace in Asia through "cooperative and friendly relations among China, Japan, and Manchukuo under the leadership of the Japanese empire." Hirota became Foreign Minister in September, 1933, and echoed the intentions of this doctrine by announcing a policy of "harmony and cooperation" and by expressing his desire to improve Sino-Japanese relations. The Nationalist government refused to recognize the establishment of the state of Manchukuo, but in July, 1934, it did allow the passage of railroad traffic between China and Manchuria. This was soon followed by the establishment of customs offices, and the resumption of postal services. In May, 1935, Japan and China agreed to exchange ambassadors.

The Kwantung Army and the Japanese garrison in Tientsin, however, proceeded with plans to sever North China from the rest of the country. In late May, 1935, using the outburst of demonstrations against them as an excuse, the Japanese, represented by General Umezu, the commander of the Tientsin garrison, pressed the Peking Military Council to withdraw all Nationalist troops from Hopei Province. The Chinese acceded to the Japanese demands, whereupon General Umezu and the representative of the Chinese Nationalist government, General Ho Ying-ching concluded the so-called Ho-Umezu Agreement in June. Not satisfied with this political victory, the Japanese army then proceeded to conclude a similar agreement concerning Chahar Province. This was arranged by the head of military intelligence in Manchuria, General Doihara Kenji, who sealed an agreement with General Ching Teh-chin, the man in charge of Chahar. All Nationalist officials and troops were then expelled from that province.

In October, 1935, the Okada cabinet approved Hirota's Three Principles for presentation to China. They were: (1) the suppression of anti-Japanese activities and an end to the policy of dependence on Western powers; (2) the de facto recognition of Manchukuo and the resumption of economic and cultural relations between Manchuria and North China; (3) the establishment of facilities to combat the menace of communism, which threatened China, Japan, and Manchuria from Outer Mongolia. The army officers in Manchuria and North China were not fully satisfied with these principles and wanted a fourth one adopted stating that the unification of China by the Nationalist party was undesirable and unnecessary. This attitude reveals the basic reason for the eventual outbreak of the war with China.

The Japanese army officers on the continent, led by Doihara Kenji (1883–1948), proceeded to work for the establishment of autonomous regions in North China. In November, Doihara persuaded General Yin Ju-keng, the Chinese administrator of the demilitarized zone, which had been established by the Tangku Truce, to proclaim the creation of the East Hopei Anti-Communist Autonomous Council. Doihara then sought to persuade the local warlord, General Sung Che-yüan, to head an autonomous unit embracing Hopei and Chahar. These actions caused Chinese students and professors in Peking and Tientsin to demonstrate against the Japanese, who eagerly responded by gathering troops in Tientsin. In order to deprive the Japanese of an excuse to establish forcibly an autonomous state, the Nationalist government seized the initiative in December, 1935, and created the Hopei-Chahar Political Council under General Sung Che-yüan's direction. General Sung was considered to be pro-Japanese, but the council, rather than being an autonomous political entity, was actually an agency of the Nationalist government. Nonetheless, the authority and prestige of the Nationalist government had been seriously compromised in North China. Further efforts to improve Sino-Japanese relations failed because Japan insisted on using Hirota's Three Principles as a basis for discussion while the Nanking government was determined to bring North China under its authority.

As we noted earlier, when Hirota took the reins of government his cabinet formulated "The Fundamental Principles of National Policy," which called for a moderate policy toward China and a stronger defensive posture toward Soviet Russia. In line with this policy, the Hirota cabinet concluded an Anti-Comintern Pact with Germany, which on an official level simply called for an exchange of information for the purpose of guarding against the subversive activities of the Communist International. However, by secret provisions in the pact, the two nations agreed that in case either of the contracting parties were attacked by the Soviet Union or were under the danger of being attacked without provocation, the other party would not take any action that would be helpful to the Soviet Union. The agreement was intended to restrain the Soviet Union in the Far East while at the same time preventing Nationalist China from relying upon the Soviet Union for support against Japan. Contrary to expectations, the pact tended to harden Russia's position against Japan and also increase English and American distrust of Japan, who, as far as these Allies could surmise, seemed to be aligning herself with the European fascist powers. This impression was reinforced when Italy joined the Anti-Comintern Pact a year later.

The Hirota government sought to curb the activities of the field armies in North China and concentrate on economic penetration. It also endeavored to persuade the Nationalist government to join its camp by signing an anti-Communist military pact. On the other hand, it did nothing to restrain the Kwantung Army officers from plotting an invasion of Inner Mongolia. For example, in November, 1936, a Japanese collaborator, Prince Teh, led his army into Inner Mongolia in the hopes of establishing an independent state there. This attempted invasion failed and Teh's forces were defeated at Pailingmiao.

At this point, an important incident occurred that caused the Nationalist government to adopt a tougher position toward Japan. In December, 1936, Chiang Kai-shek flew to Sian to oversee the launching of a new offensive against the Communists in Shensi Province. He was kidnapped by Chang Hsüeh-liang, who hoped to persuade him to consent to a united front with the Communists in order to stop Japanese aggression. Evidently Chiang agreed to cooperate because, upon his release, he called an immediate halt to the campaign against the Communists.

When General Hayashi replaced Hirota as Prime Minister he pursued a policy of moderation toward China. He appointed as his Foreign Minister Satō Naotake, who favored maintaining friendly relations with England and America. However, Hayashi was not in power long enough to effect a significant improvement in Sino-Japanese relations.

A month after Konoe succeeded Hayashi as Prime Minister, war with China broke out. The conflict was touched off by a minor incident that occurred during the night of July 7, 1937, between Japanese forces out on maneuvers and the Chinese troops of General Sung Che-yüan at Marco Polo Bridge just outside of Peiping. Initially, the authorities on the spot seemed to have the situation under control and by July 11, a cease-fire had been concluded. It has never been verified as to which side was actually responsible for firing the first shot.

In Tokyo, the Konoe cabinet regarded the incident as a minor matter and adopted a policy of local settlement and "non-enlargement." The army was divided between those who wanted to seize this opportunity to strike a decisive blow against the Chinese forces and thus once and for all establish a separate state of North China, and those who opposed such drastic measures. The aggressive position was championed by Mutō Akira, a high-ranking general-staff officer, and Tanaka Shinichi, the chief of the military affairs department in the war ministry. Those who favored a policy of caution and restraint were led by Ishiwara, chief of the operations division of the general staff.

Ishiwara was convinced that Japan was neither militarily nor economically prepared to engage in a major war. Moreover, he felt that a full commitment to hostilities with China would surely result in a long drawn out war of attrition. This of course would then make Japan vulnerable to the Soviet threat from the north. Vice-chief of staff, Lieutenant General Tada Shun, and Colonel Shibayama Kaneshirō of the war ministry were also opposed to expanding the conflict. Of the officers in the field armies in China, it would be true to say that, by and large, the Kwantung Army officers favored an aggressive policy while the leaders of the army in North China favored a policy of localizing the conflict.

In the cabinet meeting that was held on July 9, Minister of War Sugiyama proposed sending three divisions from Japan and getting additional troops from Korea and Manchuria ready just in case a greater military involvement became necessary. The proposal was shelved by the cabinet, but as local negotiatiors began to encounter new difficulties, Sugiyama, in attendance at the Five Ministers Conference on July 11, again asked that five divisions be mobilized for service in North China. Minister of the Navy Yonai Mitsumasa (1880–1948) voiced the only opposition to the plan, which was approved with the understanding that it would be cancelled if subsequent events made these troops unnecessary. This decision was made only a few hours before a cease-fire agreement was concluded in Peiping.

On the same day, Konoe held a press conference in which he announced the mobilization plans and asked for public support. He also blamed the Chinese for the troubles in North China and demanded that they apologize, while at the same time he reiterated the government's intention of adhering to its policy of localizing the conflict. The Japanese officers in North China informed the government that it was now unnecessary to send reinforcements, but when word was received that the Nanking government was taking steps to strengthen its military position in North China, the war ministry decided to dispatch one division from Korea and two brigades from Manchuria.

As might be expected, public opinion in China grew increasingly hostile toward Japan, particularly after Konoe's announcement concerning the mobilization of five divisions for possible service in North China. Japanese public opinion, on the other hand, vigorously supported the government's tough posture.

The Japanese army officers in North China and foreign office officials remained confident that the affair could be settled amicably. However, on July 23, the Hopei-Chahar army ceased withdrawing toward the Paoting area as had been agreed by General Sung and the Japanese army in North China; instead it began reentering Peiping. It is believed that this reversal was ordered by Nanking. On July 25 and July 26, skirmishes broke out between Chinese and Japanese troops, whereupon General Katsuki, the newly appointed commander of the Japanese troops in North China secured the approval of army authorities in Tokyo and proceeded to launch an attack against General Sung's forces, driving them back toward Paoting.

The situation was further aggravated when, during the night of July 28, the militia in Tungchow, which was under the authority of the East Hopei Autonomous Council, attacked and killed 260 Japanese soldiers and civilians in retaliation for an accidental bombing of the Chinese barracks by a Kwantung Army plane. This incident was sensationalized to arouse anti-Chinese sentiments in Japan.

In order to prevent the situation from worsening still further, the Japanese government secretly dispatched an emissary to Nanking to try to settle the dispute. Even before serious discussions could be started, however, the conflict spread to Shanghai. The growing anti-Japanese sentiments had compelled the navy to land additional marines in Tsingtao and Shanghai so as to protect the Japanese residents there. On August 9, a Japanese marine officer and a seaman were killed by the Chinese security forces in Shanghai. Thereupon the navy, which had all along been insisting on moderation in North China, asked that three army divisions be sent to Shanghai because it considered central and southern China to be within its sphere of responsibility.

Minister of War Sugiyama was unenthusiastic about this proposal but the cabinet went ahead and approved it on August 13. As a result the army, which had long favored an aggressive policy in North China while opposing an extension of the conflict to the south, sent two divisions to Shanghai. This affair brought the Sino-Japanese strife to a point of no return, and the Emperor, who had insisted upon the localization of the hostilities in North China, resigned himself to the inevitable. The Minister of the Navy Yonai remarked that "the policy of non-enlargement is dead. The North China Incident is now a Sino-Japanese Incident."

On August 13, the Sino-Japanese forces in Shanghai began exchanging fire and by August 15, the Nanking government deemed it necessary to order a general mobilization. On the same day, the Konoe government announced its plan to discipline the Chinese army for its atrocities and force the Nanking government to reevaluate its position. The cabinet agreed on August 17 to abandon the policy of localizing the conflict and to turn its attention, instead, to preparing for a general war.

Thus the war in China commenced. Unlike the Manchurian Incident, it would appear that the episode that touched off this conflict, that is the Marco Polo Bridge confrontation, was not staged by Japanese officers aiming to provoke a clash. Once the incident occurred, however, the expansionists managed to take advantage of every opportunity to get the Japanese army and government more and more deeply involved until the point of no return was reached. On the other hand, the responsibility for the war cannot be placed on the chauvinists alone because, regardless of the rhetoric used to conceal Japanese ambitions, the men responsible for the formulation of Japanese policy in China more or less agreed on the desirability of bringing North China under their control. None of the high officials seemed to feel any compunction about violating the political and territorial integrity of China.

THE CHINA INCIDENT

In the north, the Japanese army moved against the Nationalist forces in Chahar, and then General Tōjō Hideki (1884–1948) led three brigades from there into Suiyuan Province in Inner Mongolia. Another contingent, led by General Itagaki, moved into Shansi Province. By October the Kwantung Army had established autonomous governments in Chahar, Suiyuan, and northern Shansi. To coordinate this campaign, the North China Area Army was organized under the command of General Terauchi. Those who had favored the establishment of a separate state of North China wanted to occupy the line delineated by Suiyuan-Taiyuan-Shihkiachwang-Tsinan-Tsingtao. General Terauchi also insisted that the Japanese forces must advance to the Yellow River. The general staff, under the leadership of the vice-chief, General Tada, and with the support of Ishiwara, sought to limit the military campaign but failed to do so. By the end of the year the North China Area Army had occupied Shihkiachwang, Taiyuan, and Tsinan, thus achieving the initial objective of their plan to occupy most of North China.

On the other front, in Shanghai, the Chinese forces put up a much stiffer resistance than the Japanese military had anticipated. The city finally fell in early November, but only after additional reinforcements were sent. Thereupon the army commanders sought permission to pursue the Chinese and occupy the capital, Nanking. General Tada was opposed to this plan but Foreign Minister Hirota and the commanding general in central China, General Matsui, insisted that it was necessary to capture the capital in order to inflict a serious blow against the Nationalist government. Konoe agreed with this opinion and General Tada finally approved the plan.

The offensive against Nanking began early in December and ended with the capture of the city on December 13. It was during this Nanking campaign that the Japanese troops committed some of the most heinous atrocities in the history of warfare. They went through the streets of Nanking indiscriminately killing Chinese men, women, and children without provocation. In the first two or three days after Nanking was captured at least 12,000 noncombatant Chinese were killed. During the first month about 20,000 cases of rape were reported and more than 20,000 Chinese males of military age were rounded up and shot. Similar atrocities were committed against residents living outside Nanking; 57,000 refugees were captured, some of whom were starved, some tortured, and some machine-gunned and bayoneted to death. Even Chinese soldiers who surrendered were indiscriminately killed. In the first six weeks after the fall of Nanking it is estimated that more than 200,000 civilians and prisoners of war were killed in and around Nanking.

One might speculate as to why the Japanese soldiers, who behaved in a relatively exemplary fashion during the Russo-Japanese War, abandoned all sense of humanity in perpetrating "an orgy of murder, rape, and pillage which is almost beyond power of belief." [1] The answer no doubt is to be found in the complicated intermeshing of individual and group psychological forces that were at work. The Japanese people, with their long tradition of living under a hierarchic social order, had developed a dual tendency of submitting docilely to power and authority from above while domineering over the weak and the powerless below. [2] The old samurai concept that the commoners can be cut down with impunity is an illustration of the application of this attitude. The Japanese masses, once they donned the uniform of the imperial army or navy, became warriors with imperial sanction behind their every action. A

[1] Robert J. C. Butow, *Tojo and the Coming of the War* (Stanford, Calif.: Stanford University Press, 1961), p. 100.

[2] Maruyama Masao, an authority on Japanese political thought and behavior, speaks of the "transfer of oppression" in which "people preserve the total spiritual balance by progressively transferring downwards the pressure that they incur in their daily life from those above them." (Masao Maruyama, *Thought and Behaviour in Modern Japanese Politics*, ed. Ivan Morris, London: Oxford University Press, 1963, p. 113.)

strong feeling of national pride coupled with a sense of superiority over other races had been instilled in the youths of the nation, particularly after the Russo-Japanese War when the officially prescribed textbooks emphasized the sacred nature of the Japanese nation.

The Japanese, who were essentially insular and parochial in their outlook, fell into an extreme state of hubris as a result of the indoctrination from early childhood about their insurpassable excellence and uniqueness. The attitude of superiority toward fellow Asians grew more intense as Japan joined the ranks of the world powers by successfully adopting Western science and technology. Her neighbor, China, seemed to Japan to be mired in reactionary immobility. This contempt for the Chinese grew stronger after the Sino-Japanese War.

Intermeshed with the merciless attitude of the warrior who has no compunction about cutting down the helpless and the weak, there was probably a venting of all the frustrations and hostilities that had long been developing. The life of the average soldier had been inflexibly regimented by narrowly confined social rules and hard economic necessities. Moreover, the exceedingly harsh treatment that the young recruits were subjected to in the Japanese armed forces no doubt brutalized their spirit and inclined them to behave in a bestial manner when restraining forces were absent.

In general, people do tend to lose a sense of individual responsibility when acting with a mob. This is an especially pertinent fact when speaking about the Japanese soldier, in whom a sense of individual responsibility had not been fostered. The individual could behave in a totally reckless fashion toward people outside the group to which he belonged, although a strong sense of responsibility toward his own group was retained. The dissolution of this sense of personal accountability in the psychological core of the mob enabled the Japanese soldiers to behave in an utterly undisciplined fashion.

The officers charged with the obligation of preserving discipline among the soldiers disclaimed all responsibility. At the Tokyo War Crimes Trial, the commanding general of the Central China Area Army, General Matsui, had the following to say in response to the prosecuting attorney: "As Commander-in-Chief of the Central China Area Army I was given the power to command operations of the two subordinate armies under

On the facing page: Formosa was ceded to Japan in 1895. Manchuria was occupied during 1931–1932 and Jehol during 1933. The occupation of northern and central China occurred primarily during 1937–1938 and of South China during 1944. Hainan Island was conquered in February, 1939, and Hongkong in December, 1941.

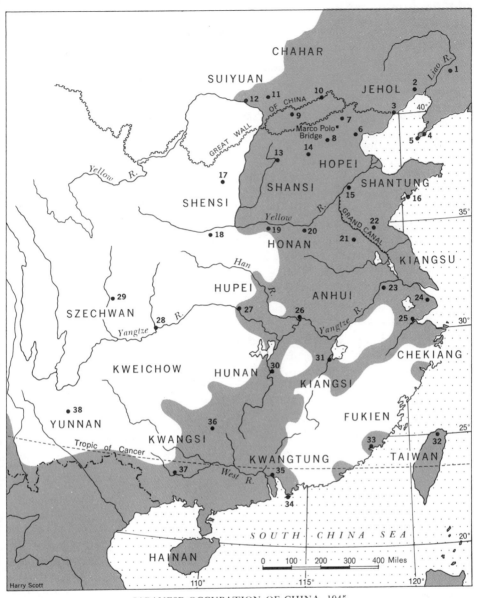

JAPANESE OCCUPATION OF CHINA, 1945.

Key to cities:	8 Paoting	16 Tsingtao	24 Shanghai	32 Taipei
1 Mukden	9 Tatung	17 Yenan	25 Hangchow	33 Amoy
2 Chinchow	10 Kalgan	18 Sian	26 Hankow	34 Hongkong
3 Shanhaikuan	11 Suiyuan	19 Loyang	27 Ichang	35 Canton
4 Dairen	12 Paotow	20 Kaifeng	28 Chungking	36 Kweilin
5 Port Arthur	13 Taiyuan	21 Hsuchow	29 Chengtu	37 Nanning
6 Tientsin	14 Shihkiachwang	22 Taierchuang	30 Changsha	38 Kunming
7 Peking	15 Tsinan	23 Nanking	31 Nanchang	

my command, but I did not have the authority directly to handle the discipline and morals within these respective armies." [3]

A commander of a brigade noted in his diary that angry soldiers, totally ignoring the officers' attempts to restrain them, massacred the Chinese troops who surrendered. However, the fact is that the officers actually condoned such behavior. This can be seen in his later remark that, in light of the death of many of their fellow soldiers and the hardships of the ten days' campaign, one is compelled to join the soldiers in saying, "Get them all."

The army authorities did little to prevent further atrocities from being committed; in fact as the officers and men began to boast of their exploits, the army central headquarters issued an order in February, 1939, prohibiting the release of information concerning atrocities that were committed, but no orders were issued forbidding the commission of atrocities themselves.

Perhaps the real explanation and cause for atrocities is war itself, which not only condones but glorifies killing and thus brutalizes the human spirit. The revelation that atrocities have been committed by nations that presumably did not have the psychological problems that prevailed in prewar Japan would tend to confirm this thesis.

The brutal behavior of the Japanese soldiers in Nanking did not break the Chinese will to resist the invaders. On the contrary, it reinforced the Chinese determination to resist and staunchly united the people around Chiang Kai-shek.

Despite the fact that Japan had committed an open act of aggression against her, China found that she could not rely on other powers to assist in her struggle to repel the invaders. The Chinese government appealed to the League of Nations for support as soon as Japan commenced her military operations, but it responded with only a lukewarm condemnation of Japan. The Soviet Union was the only nation that was willing to offer tangible support to China by signing a treaty of non-aggression in August, 1937, and by providing a certain amount of military equipment. A conference of the signatories of the Nine Power Treaty was called in Brussels but, because Japan boycotted the meeting, what little was produced had no significant effect. In the United States, President Roosevelt made a speech in October proclaiming the need to quarantine aggression, but no concrete measures were taken to restrain the Japanese. The more jingoistic Japanese army officers sought to start a conflict with the Anglo-American nations by attacking their gunboats, the U.S.S. "Panay" and the H.M.S. "Ladybird," in the Yangtze River in

[3] *Ibid.*, p. 117.

November. The matter, however, was resolved peacefully by prompt apologies and payment of reparations.

Germany was not enthusiastic about Japanese involvement in China because she felt this would prevent her from serving as an effective ally against the Soviet Union and the Western powers. This lack of ardor to have hostilities in China persist was shared by the Japanese general staff and cabinet, both of which still favored an early termination of the war. Consequently, when Germany offered to serve as mediator, the officials of the Japanese government accepted the offer and submitted their terms, which were then transmitted to the Nationalist government by the German ambassador in China. The terms were: creation of an autonomous Inner Mongolia; greatly expanded military zones in North China and Shanghai; an end to anti-Japanese activities; a pact against communism; and the reduction of tariffs on Japanese goods.

The Chinese officials believed that the terms were not particularly harsh, but they decided to wait before pursuing the matter further, at least until the results of the Brussels conference became known. That conference proved ineffective and Chiang immediately indicated his willingness to discuss the terms transmitted by the German ambassador, but by then Japan had captured Nanking and the militant expansionists insisted upon adding more stringent conditions, which they were careful not to spell out too concretely. The Nanking government asked for further clarification of the terms whereupon the Japanese leaders, including Konoe, Hirota, and Sugiyama, insisted that the Nanking government was not "sincere." They decided to terminate the negotiations, despite the protestations of General Tada of the general staff. On January 16, 1938, Konoe issued a statement to the effect that the Japanese government would no longer have anything to do with the Nationalist government. The Konoe government now concentrated its efforts on the establishment of puppet governments in northern and central China with an eye toward the eventual creation of a puppet government for all of China.

Japan was now involved in a full-scale war with China, but the government did not officially declare war in the hope that the other powers would not cut off strategic goods from Japan in the name of neutrality. It was also believed that an incident would be easier to settle than a war.

The next stage in the military campaign was directed toward linking the battlefronts of northern and central China. After suffering a setback at the battle of Taierchwang in April, the North China Area Army began its drive toward Hsuchow, a vital railroad center that linked Nanking and Tsinan as well as the Yellow Sea and Sian. In early May, the Central China Area Army drove from the south toward Hsuchow and captured it on May 19. In late August, an offensive was launched against the new capital, Hankow, and after encountering stubborn resistance, the Japanese forces were finally able to capture the city by the end of October. In the same month, a southern expeditionary force occupied the city of Canton.

The Japanese had expected the fall of Hankow to lead to the capitulation of the Nanking government but instead, the capital was shifted to Chungking and the battlefront was more or less stabilized, with Japan occupying the heavily populated and productive parts of China. The Japanese army now controlled the entire coast and the industrial centers. In the north it held the Peiping-Tientsin area and the outlet to the Yellow River. In central China it controlled both banks of the Yangtze from the mouth to Hankow. In the south it occupied Canton and controlled the West River.

Early in the war, the Japanese confidence that a quick victory would surely follow a series of knockout blows was crushed by the indefatigable determination of the Chinese to fight to the bitter end. Now, however, that the Japanese had control of the cities, railways, and rivers and could thus paralyze the Chinese economy, there was no question, the Japanese believed, that resistance would halt. Nevertheless, China did not capitulate, and the interminable war, which men like Ishiwara had feared, became a reality. Japan got trapped in a quagmire from which she could not extricate herself until seven years later when she, rather than China, surrendered arms.

Konoe, however, did not abandon all hope of effecting a political settlement and he continued to make additional diplomatic efforts. In May and June of 1938, he reshuffled his cabinet bringing Ugaki into the government as Foreign Minister, Araki as Minister of Education, and Itagaki as Minister of War. Konoe hoped that Ugaki's replacement of Hirota, who tended to follow the leadership of the army, would change the political situation regarding the China Incident. Konoe immediately informed his new Foreign Minister that the statement he had made earlier about not dealing with Chiang Kai-shek and the Nanking government was a mistake that he expected Ugaki to rectify.

Ugaki tried to conduct secret negotiations with H. H. Kung, the head of the executive branch of the Nanking government, but before the tentative feelers could be extended further, the expansionists, insisting on adhering to the policy of ignoring Chiang's government, proceeded with their own plans to create a puppet government. Konoe, contradicting what he had told Ugaki, sanctioned these efforts to establish a rival to Chiang's government in Chungking. A colonel in the war ministry was informed by his contacts with Chinese officials that Wang Ching-wei, the vice-president of the Nationalist party, was ready to break with Chiang. As a result, negotiations were conducted with Wang's friends to bring about his defection from Chungking.

The army also sought to restrict the role of the foreign office in the settlement of the China Incident and proposed the creation of a central organ that would be charged with the responsibility of managing Chinese affairs. This plan, which involved a substantial diminution of the functions of the foreign office, was approved by the Five Ministers Conference in September. Ugaki was displeased with this arrangement and resigned, having failed to make any contribution toward the settlement of the war. He was succeeded by Arita Hachirō, a career diplomat.

In order to retract the January statement about not dealing with the Nationalist government and to lay the groundwork for the establishment of a government to be headed by Wang Ching-wei, Konoe made a pronouncement on November 3, concerning his plan to establish a new order in East Asia, which was to be based upon the cooperation of Japan, Manchukuo, and China. The defection of Wang Ching-wei materialized in December when he fled Chungking for Hanoi calling upon his fellow countrymen to support his peace efforts. Wang had expected to establish a new government in the unoccupied regions of southwestern China, but failing to gain support from other Nationalist leaders, he was compelled to change his plans and become a puppet of the Japanese.

In another area of foreign relations, the Japanese suffered a serious setback at the hands of the Soviet Union. In July, 1938, a border dispute broke out at the Changkufeng-Lake Khasan area where the borders of Siberia, Manchuria, and Korea meet. A number of army officers who were more concerned about the Soviet threat than the China war decided to eliminate the Soviet menace by taking advantage of the border dispute and using it as an excuse to engage the Soviet Union in a limited war. They expected to inflict a crushing blow upon the Russian forces in the region of Changkufeng, and on July 29, the commanding general of the Japanese forces in the disputed area started military action on his own initiative. Contrary to the expectations of the Japanese military leaders, the Russians possessed superiority in airpower, heavy artillery, and tanks, and they were thus able to deal a decisive blow. The Japanese troops were forced to withdraw and the army was compelled to accept a negotiated settlement, although it remained adamant in its refusal to admit that it had suffered a defeat.

The self-delusion that the Japanese army so readily engaged in inhibited it from learning any lesson from the battle of Changkufeng and so in the middle of 1939, it once again engaged Soviet forces in another "border incident." The scene of this conflict was Nomonhan at the border of Manchuria and Outer Mongolia. The incident started in early May, when a segment of the Kwantung Army clashed with Mongolian border guards. During the first month fighting was limited to minor skirmishes, but as word was received that the Soviet Union was reinforcing its border forces, officials of the Kwantung Army began calling for a major offensive. This proposal was not well received by the army central headquarters because of their concern over the many Japanese forces that were bogged down in China. Minister of War Itagaki nevertheless gave his approval, and the Kwantung Army launched a large-scale attack against the Soviet forces on June 27. As a result, a minor border clash was transformed into a major conflict. In August, the Soviet troops commanded by General Zukhov launched a major counteroffensive using mechanized forces supported by air power. The Japanese soldiers, completely lacking in this kind of strength, were reduced to confronting the Soviet tanks with Molotov cocktails. In view of their considerable advantage in mechanical power, it was not difficult for the Soviet forces to win a decisive victory.

The Kwantung Army asked for reinforcements in the hope of possibly recouping their losses, but the army authorities in Tokyo remained adamant in refusing to allow a further enlargement of the conflict. On September 1, Hitler launched his offensive against Poland and the world political situation became extremely precarious. The Japanese government was not prepared at a time like this to get involved in a major war with Soviet Russia over minor border disputes. Consequently, in mid-September, a cease-fire was arranged with Soviet Russia, who was also anxious to avoid a war in the Far East while Europe was in a state of turmoil. The Kwantung Army had committed 56,000 men in the Nomonhan conflict and suffered losses of 8,400 dead and 8,766 wounded as compared to 9,000 dead and wounded for the Soviet and Mongolian forces. The Japanese losses were concealed from the public until the postwar era.

INTERNAL DEVELOPMENTS

The government moved to place the nation on an emergency footing immediately after the China Incident erupted. A Government Planning Board was established to regulate production, foreign trade, finances, consumption, and labor. All unnecessary imports were curtailed, and the use of such items as cotton and iron in nonessential production was restricted. All factories engaged in arms production were brought under government supervision, and military officers were assigned to act as overseers in these plants.

The need for a more comprehensive mechanism of control was felt as it became increasingly evident that the China Incident was turning into a rather protracted affair. In February, 1938, Konoe enacted a National

Mobilization Act, which provided for the full control and utilization of all the nation's manpower and resources for the purposes of national defense.

The government did not restrict its activities to subjecting the economy to increasingly stringent controls for military purposes. The threats posed by border incidents with the Soviet Union, hostilities with China, and international insecurity caused the government to intensify its efforts to suppress "dangerous thought" by restricting the freedoms of speech, press, and assembly. In July, 1936, and then again in the following February, there were mass arrests of Marxists as well as socialist professors, who were engaged in academic disputations about the nature of the Meiji Restoration and where Japan stood in its stage of historical development. In December, 1937, another mass arrest was conducted, this time involving more than 400 left-wing socialists.

The next victims were the liberals. The Ministry of Justice proclaimed that "democracy and liberalism are hotbeds that breed communism." In the fall of 1937, Yanaibara Tadao, who became the president of Tokyo University after World War II, was dismissed from his teaching post at that institution because he denounced the war in China. In the following fall, Kawai Eijirō, a liberal and a foe of Marxism, was fired from his post at the same university and his publications were placed on the prohibited list.

A watchful eye was kept on publications that might reveal the Japanese military in a bad light. Censorship became increasingly stringent and it was not at all uncommon to see the publication of articles and books in which one line after another was deleted. Newspapers and magazines that were in any way critical of the war effort were very effectively penalized by not being allotted their share of newsprint. Thus the authorities were able to weed out many undesirable papers and journals—by the end of 1939, more than five hundred publishers had gone out of business. As a result of this atmosphere of intimidation even the liberal newspapers headlined the news of the "glorious" victories of the "righteous" imperial army and condemned the "atrocious" Chinese "bandits." Military successes were exaggerated, defeats were never reported, and in this sense it can be said that the public was led blindly to the path of ultimate destruction and defeat while all along being firmly convinced that one magnificent victory after another was being won.

The government also began to place certain books, both Japanese and foreign works, on the "index of prohibited works," and the number of blacklisted titles increased year by year. In the early 1930s, any work containing anti-war sentiments was rooted out and banned. Studies in economics were hit the hardest; not only Marxist writings but the works of classical economists were also prohibited. Any work with the word "capitalism" in the title was immediately rejected. The only acceptable theories in this field, as one economist later remarked, were the kind to be found in the *Kojiki* or *The Analects of Confucius*. The proletarian novelists were, of course, banned; but even those works of other writers that had no political implications, such as Tanizaki's *Sasameyuki*, were ultimately proscribed because they were "useless literature of leisure." The censors did not restrict themselves to prohibiting contemporary literature or even the books of the Meiji period, they reached all the way back into the past to blacklist the works of prominent writers whose ideas they found objectionable.

The government did not rely only on negative means to rectify the people's thinking; it sought actively to instill the right attitudes and beliefs in the people. It revised the textbooks that were used in the primary schools in 1933, and again in 1941, in order to foster a more militaristic and nationalistic outlook among the children. Mythologies were presented as authentic history, and students were taught not to question, but simply to memorize what they were told they should learn. The teachers reinforced this approach by admonishing the children to develop into courageous soldiers and by punishing those who questioned the official truth. The indoctrination program in the schools proved highly successful for it produced innumerable soldiers who willingly gave their lives to the Emperor and the country. During the war in the Pacific many volunteered to become suicide pilots, no doubt sharing the conviction of one of these young fliers who said, "When I reflect upon the three-thousand-year history of our imperial nation, I realize the truth that matters concerning one puny individual or a single family are of no importance at all." [4]

In the realm of religion, periodic worship at Shinto shrines came to be almost a compulsory affair. At the same time, the persecution of Christians began to grow in intensity, and some Christian leaders were even forced to choose between the Christian God and the Sun Goddess (or the Emperor). By and large, however, the Christians cooperated with the war effort. The Buddhist community, naturally, said nothing critical about the war or about the growing trend toward totalitarianism.

The oppressive hand of the government was also extended to the labor unions. In December, 1937, the leftist Rōdō Hyōgikai was dissolved and in July, 1940, the moderate Sōdōmei was compelled to disband. Agrarian unions suffered the same fate, and in March, 1941, the Nihon Nōmin Kumiai ceased to exist.

The outbreak of the China Incident led the people onto the path of

---

[4] Ienaga Saburō, *Taiheiyō Sensō* (*The Pacific War*) (Tokyo: Iwanami Shoten, 1968), p. 134.

hardship, privation, sacrifice, and loss of freedom. Their life style became more sober and certainly more austere. These new times, when pervasive grimness characterized their lives, were in sharp contrast to the early thirties when, despite the depression, the Manchurian Incident, and the growing ascendancy of militarism, there was a good deal of carefree gaiety. Movies, musical revues, and light entertainment set the mood and the tone of the age. Fashionable young men and women, known as "mobo" and "moga" (modern boy and modern girl), went to dance halls, sang Western songs like "My Blue Heaven," strolled the neonlit streets of Ginza, and revelled in "ero-guro (erotic, grotesque) nonsense." The more traditional-minded danced in the streets in tune with the new folk songs such as the Sakura Chorus Song and the Tokyo Chorus Song chanting "yoi, yoi, yoi" ("It's good, good, good!"), and the young and old were entranced by the yo-yo.

Was all this carefree gaiety a form of escapism? In discussing possible answers to this question it becomes appropriate to note a rather lurid fad that came into vogue with the young and sentimental. In May, 1932, a young man and his girlfriend committed suicide on a hillside because their parents would not consent to their marriage. This incident was given extensive publicity, and twenty more couples committed suicide on the very same spot. The following year a couple of girls attempted to jump into the volcano of Mt. Mihara on the island of Ōshima off the coast of Izu Peninsula. This then became the favorite spot for suicides; in 1933, 804 men and 140 women jumped into the Mihara volcano, an average of three a day.

Another avenue of escape was through the "new religions," which were essentially cults and offshoots of established religions. They began to emerge in the unsettled days of the late Tokugawa era and they have continued to flourish to the present. The basic attraction of these new religions was that they were able to offer emotional solace to the downtrodden peasantry and townspeople who found little comfort in the established religions, which had become formalistic and stagnant. In the 1930s, one such new religion, the Ōmotokyō (Great Fundamentals), gained wide support, even among the well-educated, and claimed to have a following of eight million people. The leader, who was said to have direct access to the wishes of the Shinto gods, comported himself like an Emperor. In 1935, the leaders of the movement were accused of lese majesty and violation of the Peace Preservation Law, and the cult was banned. In the following years other religious cults were also suppressed by the government.

The seemingly carefree attitude that prevailed among the people in the first half of the thirties shifted, as was noted above, to a more austere, cheerless mood after the outbreak of the China Incident. The gloomy atmosphere was in part the product of the growing shortage of goods that resulted from the restrictions on imports and the diversion of raw materials to the production of war matériel instead of consumer goods. A variety of substitutes had to be used. Synthetic fibres were used instead of cotton; bamboo spoons took the place of metal ones; and charcoal-burning buses replaced gasoline-powered vehicles. Price control was introduced in 1939, and rationing of matches and sugar followed in 1940, and then during the next year, rice and charcoal were added to the list of rationed items.

The shift to a more somber, serious mood was caused also by the growing tide of nationalism and the attendant sense of national emergency. A rising current of anti-Westernism led to the condemnation of "frivolous, decadent" Western ways. These sentiments were so pervasive that even such things as permanent waves were frowned upon, not only because they wasted electricity, but also simply because they were Western. Women were admonished not to wear rings and jewelry or to dress in a stylish fashion. Western-style apparel, which was common in the cities, was soon replaced by khaki-colored "people's uniform" for men, and pantaloons for women. Western movies became increasingly rare, and it was not unusual to find serious-minded women on street corners admonishing people to stay away from all movie theaters and coffee shops. By 1940, dance halls were banned, and sentimental or gay love songs were supplanted by rousing war songs, and military and naval marches. Dancing in the streets was replaced either by ceremonies to send friends and relatives off to war or by solemn rituals to receive little white boxes containing the ashes and bones of men killed in action.

FURTHER FOREIGN ENTANGLEMENTS

Frustrated by his inability to resolve the China conflict, Konoe had frequently expressed his desire to resign. He was finally able to use Wang Ching-wei's defection from Chungking as an excuse to call for a fresh start in Japan, and he resigned his post at the beginning of 1939. The ultranationalist Hiranuma was, as successor, handed the task of heading the government. He retained five men from the Konoe cabinet, including the Minister of War, the Minister of the Navy, and the Foreign Minister. Konoe remained on as a minister without portfolio, and so the Hiranuma cabinet was virtually an extension of the Konoe cabinet.

One of the key tasks assumed by the new government was the plan to conclude a military alliance with the Axis powers. This project was championed by Lieutenant-General Ōshima, the Japanese ambassador to Germany. The negotiations floundered, however, because Germany, in anticipation of a possible conflict with England and France, wanted an alliance that would be directed against all potential enemies while the Japanese favored an agreement that would be restricted to deterring only the Soviet Union. The matter was debated back and forth and at great length between Minister of War Itagaki, who pushed for an alliance, even a comprehensive one, and the Minister of the Navy Yonai, who was against the alliance Germany was proposing for he feared it would draw Japan into a war with England as well as the United States, and he knew that the navy was not prepared to engage these two naval powers in battle simultaneously. Moreover, the naval leaders had always tended to be pro-British in their orientation. The army, on the other hand, was willing to broaden the scope of the projected alliance because it had become increasingly anti-British in its outlook. It was proving unable to resolve the war in China, and its leaders began to ascribe China's stubborn resistance to the fact that it was receiving British assistance. Rightwing organizations, with army backing, began to stage anti-British rallies with increasing frequency.

The disagreement between the army and navy prevented the government from arriving at a final decision on the alliance, and then Germany turned around and stunned the pro-German militarists by concluding a nonaggression pact with Soviet Russia in August. This compelled Hiranuma to resign his post, and as he did so he remarked that European developments had produced a "strange and complex" situation. His successor was a retired general, Abe Nobuyuki (1875–1953), a relatively uncontroversial figure. The Emperor took an unprecedented step when he made the appointment by insisting that either General Umezu or General Hata be chosen as Minister of War. He believed that either man would attempt to make the army behave more in accordance with his wishes. Hata Shunroku (1879–1962) was appointed as Minister of War and, as a matter of fact, during the four and a half months that the Abe cabinet was in office the army remained relatively subdued. This, of course, can be partially accounted for by the fact that the army was chastened somewhat by the reversal suffered by Hitler's rapprochement with Soviet Russia. Foreign Minister Nomura Kichisaburō (1877–1964), a retired admiral, sought to improve United States and Japanese relationships. One of the chief tasks confronting him was the need to negotiate a new commercial treaty with the United States, who had notified Japan of her intention to abrogate, as of January, 1940, the treaty that had been concluded in 1911.

The Abe government fell, however, before it was able to accomplish anything of significance because of public discontent over the growing shortages of food and goods and the rapidly rising prices. Particularly troublesome was the rice shortage caused by the drought of the previous summer. The political parties, which had been wholly ineffective during the past several years, sought to pass a resolution of no-confidence.

Lacking the support of even the army, Abe resigned in January, 1940.

The policy makers of the army failed to persuade Konoe to return to power, so their next move was to try and get the premiership passed on to Sugiyama or Hata. Contrary to their desires, Admiral Yonai, their arch rival, was chosen as the next Prime Minister thanks to the efforts of the Lord Keeper of the Privy Seal, Yuasa, who wanted to curb the arbitrary actions of the army. To prevent the army from blocking Yonai's appointment, the Emperor personally requested the cooperation of General Hata. Thus, one of the most forceful exponents of peace and moderation was given an opportunity to try to reverse the direction in which Japan was headed. The Yonai cabinet, however, turned out to be a tremendous disappointment to those who wanted to see the military restrained. The militarists and the ultranationalists were firmly entrenched in the political arena, and the spectacular successes that Nazi Germany was enjoying against the Western powers unquestionably redounded to their favor.

The expectation that Wang Ching-wei's defection would be followed by similar moves by other high-ranking Nationalist officials did not materialize; instead of setting a precedent for change, Wang was denounced as a traitor. Nonetheless, the Japanese government proceeded with the creation of a puppet regime headed by Wang even though it now realized that the conflict could not be settled unless direct contacts were established with Chiang Kai-shek. In March, 1940, a government was established in Nanking under Wang, who was bitterly disappointed because, contrary to what he had expected, he was given no real authority or power.

Hitler at this time was successfully overwhelming Europe with one victory after another, and this gave the pro-Axis elements in Japan an opportunity to begin to revive the plan to join Germany and Italy in a military alliance. This, the expansionists argued, would enable Japan to advance into Southeast Asia and bring all the European colonies under her control. The bellicose officers in the army insisted that Yonai, who favored cooperating with England and the United States rather than the Axis powers, be eliminated. In order to bring down the cabinet, Minister of War Hata resigned and then the army refused to recommend a replacement. Consequently, the Yonai cabinet fell in July.

Again the army's choice was Konoe; this time he was open to persuasion. Thus the stage was set for the implementation of the programs long sought by the militarists, the ultranationalists, and the thoroughgoing warmongers. Japan under Konoe joined the Axis powers, advanced to the south, and got ready for a decisive confrontation with England and the United States. Once again Konoe, to whom the moderates looked with great expectations, hoping he would restrain the expansionists, led the country directly down the path desired by the extremists.

The army chose Tōjō Hideki, a chauvinist who was reputed to possess a razor-sharp mind, to become its representative in the cabinet. To head the foreign office, Konoe chose the president of the South Manchurian Railway since 1935, Matsuoka Yōsuke (1880–1946), a flamboyant diplomat who was educated in the United States and who had led the Japanese delegation out of the League of Nations. He was considered to be "voluble and unconventional by nature," and guilty of the fault of "recklessly advancing in the wrong direction." He was an expansionist and thus favored concluding an alliance with the Axis powers.

On July 19, even before he filled all the cabinet posts, Konoe conferred with the men he had selected as war, navy, and foreign ministers and worked out the fundamental policies his government should follow. The basic ideas were embodied in a policy statement called "The Main Principles of Basic National Policy." On July 26, the cabinet approved the "Principles," which proclaimed Japan's intention to build a new order in East Asia, as the first step toward the achievement of world peace. It called for a military build-up; the settlement of the China Incident; internal administrative reforms; educational reforms aimed at emphasizing the basic principles of the national polity while eliminating "selfish thoughts"; and the creation of a strong new political structure. Economically, a planned economy was to be instituted at home with the goal of self-sufficiency being sought within the new order.

A conference was held on July 19, for the purpose of delineating the specific policies that were to be pursued in foreign affairs. The conferees agreed to strengthen Japan's ties with the Axis powers; conclude a non-aggression pact with Soviet Russia while at the same time strengthening defense measures against her; take active steps to bring the Asian colonies of the European powers into the new order in East Asia; and avoid unnecessary conflicts with the United States while at the same time preventing her from interfering with the construction of the new order in East Asia.

On July 27, a liaison conference of the cabinet and the supreme command was held to adopt officially the policies agreed to on July 19. The agenda was prepared by the middle-grade officers of the general staff and officers of the foreign service.[5] The policy makers in the liaison conference reaffirmed the basic points but spelled them out more concretely. A particularly significant decision was made regarding the use

[5] Regarding the usurpation of the decision-making power by the general staff officers, Robert Butow observes, "While lacking a basic understanding of political and diplomatic affairs, these virtually 'nameless ones' nevertheless possessed a confidence in their ability and in their program that was the more sublime because it was so misfounded. They proceeded, again and again, to draft policies to meet problems that were completely over their heads, and for which their narrow military approach was wholly inadequate." (Butow, *op. cit.*, p. 240.)

of force in advancing to the south. The participants agreed that whether or not the China Incident was settled, if domestic and foreign circumstances were favorable, Japan should move south at an opportune moment by resorting to arms. This, of course, would mean war with Great Britain and the United States, so military preparations were to be made with such a confrontation in mind. This decision to expand to the south even if this meant going to war constitutes a crucial turning point in Japan's road to the war in the Pacific.

The initial step taken to create what the Japanese hoped would be a strong new political structure was the voluntary liquidation of the existing political parties and the establishment of a single, all-embracing party. The idea for creating such an organization had been bandied about by Konoe's friends for several years. In June, just before he became premier again, Konoe made known his plan to resign from the presidency of the Privy Council in order to work for the establishment of a new political structure. The leaders of all segments of the society immediately expressed their approval of Konoe's plan and pledged their support. The military men, led by Mutō Akira, head of the military affairs bureau, favored the establishment of a promilitary, Nazi-type party that would facilitate their plan to establish a "national defense state," that is, a military state. It is believed that Konoe's supporters, many of whom were "reformist" bureaucrats and scholars, hoped to establish a mass party that would enable them to curb the military and at the same time set up a "modern, rational" social order. The party leaders sought to regain their lost political leverage by attaching themselves to the new movement. There were many right-wing, promilitary leaders in the parties who took the initiative in liquidating their organizations in order to be first in line to join the new party. The Minseitō leaders were the most reluctant to join the movement, but because there could be no doubt that they would be squeezed out of the political scene if they did not join the parade, they dissolved their party by mid-August. Thus did the successors of Itagaki and Ōkuma abandon the cause of parliamentary government.

In October, the Imperial Rule Assistance Association was established with Konoe as its head. This so-called party, however, turned out to be an ineffective agglomeration of diverse elements with irreconcilably different objectives. Some right-wing elements were critical of an organization whose leaders might eclipse the Emperor the way the Tokugawa shōgun had. The big business leaders were suspicious of the economic philosophies of the "reformist" elements in the association, and they tended to look upon the party as a Communist Trojan horse. The Emperor and the senior statesmen were also critical of the movement, and finally even Konoe lost his initial enthusiasm for the association.

A group of ultranationalists disapproved of the masses participating in politics, and what they wanted instead was for the association to function as an instrument to foster the "Japanese spirit" among the people. Konoe succumbed to their demands and turned the association into a nonpolitical organization that merely served as a vehicle that would transmit the government's wishes to the people and then rally them behind its policies.

The Imperial Rule Assistance Association stood at the top of the structure to guide the people, and "neighborhood associations," with each unit consisting of ten families, were organized at the local level. These were to serve as agencies that were specifically charged with the responsibility of dealing with the practical problems that arose as Japan was being transformed into a national defense state. Concerns such as rationing, air-raid practices, sending soldiers off to war, and public meetings, were managed by the neighborhood associations. They also very closely checked and supervised all aspects of the people's lives, making it difficult for anyone to violate the many new rules and regulations that were being issued by the government.

As for the implementation of the basic policies in foreign affairs, the Konoe government proceeded to conclude a military pact with the Axis powers, Germany and Italy. The army found a spokesman for the pact in Foreign Minister Matsuoka, who argued forcefully in favor of the alliance. The naval leaders feared that the alliance might draw the nation into a conflict with the United States, but they gave no voice to their misgivings. Officially they accepted Matsuoka's argument that the alliance would, on the contrary, serve as a restraining force on the United States while Japan moved south. Matsuoka had insisted that only by taking a strong stand could a war with the United States be averted. The Foreign Minister also contended that the alliance would improve Soviet-Japanese relations because of the nonaggression pact linking Germany and Soviet Russia. He assured the more cautious officials that even though the pact provided for Japan's entry into the war on the side of Germany, should the United States join the European war against Germany, Japan would under no circumstances automatically enter the conflict. Prior to getting involved she would make an independent decision, taking all factors into consideration.

A decision was finally made after careful deliberation to proceed with the alliance; the pact was signed in September, 1940. The agreement provided for Japan's recognition of the leadership of Germany and Italy in establishing a new order in Europe while those two nations in turn recognized Japan's leadership in establishing a new order in East Asia. Article III, the heart of the pact, held that if and when any of the signatories were attacked by any third power not then engaged in the European War or the China Incident, the other two would aid her with all political, economic, or military means. Article V stipulated that the alliance was not to affect the signatory nations' relations with Soviet Russia. It is rather clear, therefore, that the third power that the Axis nations had in mind was the United States. It was not at all difficult for the American officials to reach this conclusion also. Thus, rather than averting a conflict between the United States and Japan, the pact seemed to bring that eventuality one step closer. For the time being, however, the Japanese leaders felt that they could advance to the south with the assurance that they would not be standing alone.

The southern region that required Japan's immediate attention was French Indochina. The war with China continued endlessly to drag on and the Japanese became increasingly critical of the French for allowing supplies to be sent from Indochina to China. The European conflict broke out in the fall of 1939, and Japan immediately took advantage of the French preoccupation with the European crisis and began bombing the Yunan Railroad in South China, which had been built with French capital. It also launched a vigorous campaign in Kwangsi Province just north of the French colony. Just as soon as France fell before Hitler's armies, Japan began exerting greater pressure against her in Indochina. The Japanese government under Yonai asked Governor-General Catroux first, to grant Japan the right to station a group of military observers in Hanoi and second, to stop all shipment of war matériel into China. Being in no position to resist, Catroux acquiesced to the Japanese demands in June, 1940.

Immediately upon assuming his post as Foreign Minister, Matsuoka demanded that the French give Japan the right to send troops through Indochina, to construct and use air fields, and to station troops to guard military installations. Once again the French lacked the means to resist, and so when the ultimatum was presented they were forced to yield. By September 23, Japan completed the occupation of northern French Indochina. The United States and England felt compelled to adopt retaliatory measures in the face of Japan's actions in Indochina. The United States placed all types of iron and steel scraps under embargo, while the British informed Japan that it would reopen the Burma Road into China, a supply route that the British had agreed to close that summer.

France's difficulties presented Thailand with an opportunity to regain territories she had lost half a century earlier. The ensuing dispute between the countries provided Japan with still further opportunities to extend her influence into Southeast Asia. She purported to act as a mediator between the two nations, but in fact she applied pressure against

France on behalf of Thailand and thus laid the groundwork for an eventual alliance with Thailand. At the same time that the border dispute was settled, Japan obtained the assurances of both Thailand and French Indochina that neither would conclude with a third power any political or military agreements directed against Japan. This was designed primarily to prevent Thailand from aligning with England and the United States.

The region that Japan was most interested in because of its petroleum resources was the Dutch East Indies. The Japanese leaders hoped to gain access to the oil supplies without recourse to open hostilities since armed warfare would surely mean destruction of the oil wells and refineries. In September, 1940, a Japanese mission was sent to Batavia to negotiate an agreement by which the Dutch East Indies would supply Japan with additional oil and other essential materials. The negotiations foundered, however, and the talks were discontinued in June, 1941. Japan's failure to gain her economic objectives through diplomatic means only strengthened the argument of the militarists that she had to rely on military means in order to break through the ABCD encirclement, that is, the encirclement by America, Britain, China, and the Dutch.

During this time Matsuoka was pursuing the project that was to complement the Tripartite Pact, that is, the improvement of Japan's relations with the Soviet Union. He wanted to bring Soviet Russia into that agreement. In March, 1941, he left for Berlin and Moscow, but when he arrived in Europe he found that Soviet-German relations had deteriorated so considerably that he was forced to abandon altogether his plan to effect a broader military alliance. The Germans did not, however, inform Matsuoka of the impending attack on Russia. Instead, they sought to discourage him from trying to bring about a Soviet-Japanese rapprochement, and they tried to persuade him that Japan should enter the war against England by attacking Singapore. Matsuoka expressed his personal agreement with the suggestion but indicated that other Japanese officials would not readily consent to such action.

On his way back from Berlin, Matsuoka stopped over in Moscow and proposed that the Soviet Union sell northern Sakhalin to Japan and conclude a nonaggression pact with her. Molotov, however, countered instead with a proposal for a neutrality pact. Matsuoka agreed to this and, on April 13, 1941, he and Molotov signed a treaty that provided for the neutrality of the signatories in case one or more powers attacked either party. Japan also pledged to respect the territorial integrity of the Mongolian People's Republic while Soviet Russia pledged the same for Manchuria. Stalin, in a jovial mood, saw Matsuoka off at the station and clasping him in a bear-hug he said, "now Japan can move south." Matsuoka returned to Japan in a triumphant mood because he was convinced that he had achieved a diplomatic coup. However, it was scarcely two months later that Germany invaded Soviet Russia.

On June 25, following Germany's attack on Russia, a liaison conference of the cabinet and the supreme command was called to determine the policies to be pursued in light of the unexpected developments. Matsuoka, ignoring the nonaggression pact he had concluded with Soviet Russia and disregarding the strategic problems involved, sought to persuade his colleagues that Japan should abandon its plan to move south and instead immediately join the war on Germany's side and attack Soviet Russia.

The conference rejected Matsuoka's pleas and decided to proceed with the plan to advance southward. It agreed to seek air bases and access to harbors in French Indochina as well as the right to station troops in the southern portion of the French colony. If the Vichy government refused, the conferees agreed to use the force of arms to attain their objectives. The military planners argued that the occupation of southern Indochina would gain for Japan a foothold in the strategic defense line running from southern China, Thailand, Burma, and the Malay Peninsula.

On July 2, in a conference at which the Emperor was present, the cabinet and the supreme command adopted a policy statement that affirmed Japan's determination to construct a Greater East Asia Co-prosperity Sphere, end the China Incident, and advance to the south in order to establish the basis for self-existence and self-defense. They also agreed not "to decline a war with England and the United States" if such a conflict were necessary for the realization of Japan's objectives in the south.

NEGOTIATIONS WITH THE UNITED STATES

In March, 1941, the Japanese ambassador to the United States, Nomura Kichisaburō, opened discussions with Secretary of State Cordell Hull in an effort to resolve the difficulties between the two nations. The chief problems facing the negotiators were the expiration (as of January 26, 1940) of the commercial treaty; the China question; Japan's southward push; and Japan's alliance with Germany and Italy. In the lengthy discussions that took place between March and the end of November, the Chinese question turned out to be the thorniest problem in that both sides remained intransigent. The United States insisted on Japan's eventual withdrawal from that country while Japan intractably contended that complete withdrawal was not feasible.

Several private citizens from the two countries began exploring ways to resolve the difficulties confronting the powers at the same time that the official talks were being conducted. The initiative for these unofficial discussions was taken by two American Catholic priests, Bishop James E. Walsh and Father James M. Drought, in cooperation with a Japanese businessman and acquaintance of Konoe's, Ikawa Tadao. In early April, these men formulated a set of proposals that they thought could serve as a possible basis for official negotiation. The proposals called for the renunciation of force by Japan in the southwest Pacific, and her agreement to come to the support of Germany only if that nation were actually the victim of an attack by another power. In return, the United States was to restore normal trade with Japan, assist that country in obtaining the raw materials she needed in the southwest Pacific, and ask Chiang Kai-shek to make peace with Japan in accordance with specified terms. If Chiang refused, the United States was to cease supporting the Chungking government.

Secretary of State Hull wanted to discuss the following four basic principles: (1) respect for the territorial integrity and sovereignty of each and all nations; (2) support of the principle of noninterference in the internal affairs of other countries; (3) support of the principle of equality, including equality of commercial opportunity; (4) nondisturbance of the status quo in the Pacific, except as the status quo may be altered by peaceful means.

Matsuoka returned from his trip to Europe and he seemed petulant about Nomura's talks with Hull. He responded negatively to the Walsh-Drought proposals, claiming that they were based on 70 percent ill will and only 30 percent good will. He also advised Nomura to continue negotiations but only to achieve a neutrality pact. The United States, however, was not interested in such an agreement because it meant that she would have to remain neutral in the event that an Anglo-Japanese conflict broke out during the course of Japan's push to the south.

On June 21, Hull presented the position of his government on the outstanding issues to Nomura and, in effect, he asked Japan not to invoke the Tripartite Pact in case the United States entered the European war against Germany. He also called for the settlement of the China Incident on less favorable terms than Japan desired and without assuring her that normal commercial relations would be resumed after the settlement. These terms were wholly unacceptable to Japan and Matsuoka, bellicose as ever, proposed breaking off the negotiations, which were now practically at a standstill.

The United States' distrust of Japan was reinforced by the information she gained as a result of having broken the code by which the Japanese government sent diplomatic messages from Tokyo to its representatives abroad. Consequently, American officials were well aware of Japan's plan to move south and of her preparations for war.

Konoe was determined to continue his efforts to effect a rapprochement with the United States, but Matsuoka's pugnacious stand was making negotiations difficult. Consequently, Konoe decided to remove Matsuoka from the cabinet. To do this diplomatically, he asked for the resignation of the entire cabinet in mid-July. The senior statesmen immediately asked Konoe to form another cabinet, which he did by reshuffling his old cabinet, replacing Matsuoka with Admiral Toyoda Teijirō, who favored maintaining friendly relations with the United States.

THE OCCUPATION OF SOUTHERN FRENCH INDOCHINA

The new Konoe cabinet pursued the same policies as the old one. Just as soon as it was formed the supreme command of the army and navy asked it to adhere to the decision to occupy southern Indochina and to uphold the spirit of the Tripartite Pact. The Konoe government decided to put the occupation plan into effect, but they thoroughly misjudged the reaction that this would evoke in the Western nations, particularly in the United States. In deciding to occupy southern Indochina they completely disregarded Nomura's warning that the United States would consider such a move to be the first step in Japan's plan to invade Singapore and the Dutch East Indies.

Toward the end of July, Japan presented an ultimatum to the French Vichy government compelling it to permit troops to move into southern Indochina. In retaliation, the United States government froze the Japanese assets in the United States and followed through with a total embargo on exports to Japan, with the exception of cotton and food. As a result, Japan was cut off from her major source of oil. Great Britain and the Dutch East Indies followed suit by freezing the Japanese assets in their countries. Japan was thus confronted with the prospect of a total economic blockade.

Japan was heavily dependent on the United States for trade. For example, in 1939, 18.4 percent of her export trade and 38.7 percent of her import trade were carried on with the United States. In addition, 17.1 percent of her imports came from Asian lands under Anglo-American control, and 10.6 percent came from England and European nations aligned with her. In effect, 66.4 percent of Japan's imports came from the Anglo-American economic sphere. Of critical importance to Japan was the fact that most of the strategic materials that she desperately needed also came from these regions. Above all, she depended on the United States for oil, since domestically she produced less than 10 percent of the amount she needed; in 1939, 85 percent, and in 1940, 80 percent of her oil came from the United States. The most serious consequence of the trade restrictions was the severance of Japan from all major sources of oil. The navy's oil reserves were expected to last two years, or a year and a half if Japan became involved in a full-scale war.

This fact turned former moderates in the navy into advocates of immediate action. Their first objective was the oil fields of the Dutch East Indies. Aggression there would doubtless mean a general war in the south against England and the United States, since both Singapore and the Philippines would have to be occupied before the East Indies could be secured. Thus the navy officers who had previously wanted to avoid engaging both the United States and England in a war began talking of doing so even though they were not confident of winning. They were aware, however, that if the economic blockade continued and nothing were done, the navy would surely be immobilized without even firing a shot. The situation for Japan was like that of "a fish in a pond from which the water was gradually being drained away." [6]

The possibility of war, then, had become very real after August 1. Ambassador Grew concluded that "The vicious circle of reprisals and counter-reprisals is on. . . . Unless radical surprises occur in the world, it is difficult to see how the momentum of the down-grade movement can be arrested, or how far it will go. The obvious conclusion is eventual war." [7]

Konoe was aware of the desperate nature of the existing situation. A diplomatic breakthrough in the discussions with the United States had to be forthcoming or the military would unquestionably ask for positive action, that is, war. Time was running out on Japan as each day another twelve thousand tons of oil was being expended. Konoe decided to seek a conference with President Roosevelt in order to break the impasse. The navy supported the plan wholeheartedly, but the army insisted that Konoe be fully prepared to lead the nation to war if the conference failed as a result of America's refusal to change her position. The summit conference must, the army contended, bring about the end of American aid to China, acceptance by the United States of the Tripartite Pact, and the resumption of normal economic relations between the two countries. Hence, it is quite obvious that even if Konoe had succeeded in persuading Roosevelt to meet with him, the chances of reaching an accord would have been very slight indeed.

On August 8, Konoe's desire to meet with Roosevelt was communicated by Nomura to Hull, who responded negatively, indicating that no purpose could be served by such a meeting unless Japan changed its policies. At this time Roosevelt was busy holding a summit conference with Churchill on the Atlantic Ocean. In this meeting the two leaders

---

[6] *Ibid.*, p. 245.
[7] Herbert Feis, *The Road to Pearl Harbor* (Princeton, N.J.: Princeton University Press, 1950), p. 248.

agreed to issue a warning to Japan that "any further encroachment by Japan in the southwestern Pacific" might compel the United States government to take countermeasures even if these might lead to war. After returning from his conference with Churchill, Roosevelt procrastinated in deciding about Konoe's proposal, but both Hull and Secretary of War Stimson were skeptical of Japanese intentions. Stimson believed that it was "merely a blind to try to keep us from taking definite action."

On August 28, Konoe sent a personal message to Roosevelt reiterating his desire for a meeting. Nomura then met with Hull, who informed him that there had to be prior agreement on essential points before the meeting could be held. According to the Secretary of State, Japan had to first indicate her intention to withdraw from the Axis Pact and abandon her plan to retain troops in North China and Inner Mongolia. Nomura asked if perhaps other questions could be settled, leaving the China question alone for the time being, and Hull replied that, in fact, the China question was "one of the pivotal ones." As it developed, it was "*the* pivotal one" that made the resolution of United States-Japanese difficulties impossible.

Roosevelt finally agreed with Hull's opinion, and on September 3, he told the Japanese that the disputed points must first be settled before a summit meeting could take place. A confrontation between the two nations now seemed inevitable because each side believed it had to stand firm to avoid war. The United States remained resolute in its conviction that it could not compromise its moral principles against aggression: it could not abandon China, and it could not allow Japan to join Germany in destroying Britain or Russia. Japan, on the other hand, had been following an expansionistic policy ever since the Manchurian Incident, and with each step she became more deeply committed to the course of imperialism. It always seemed that just one additional step was necessary to consolidate the gains made with the previous step, until finally, after she had already stepped into southern Indochina, Japan was confronted with only two options: retreat or take the last fatal step forward.

THE DECISION FOR WAR

At the same time that Konoe was seeking a conference with Roosevelt, the supreme command of the armed forces began preparing for war in case diplomatic negotiations failed. If the differences between the United States and Japan were not settled at the conference table by early October, the decision as to whether or not to go to war was to be made at that time. Preparations for war were then to be completed by the end of October. The momentous decision was made, not as might be expected by the policy makers at the top, but by the staff officers, including the heads of the bureaus of military and naval affairs. The staff officers agreed upon the basic policies, and then the top officials of the government met to discuss these proposals in a liaison conference held on September 3. Some changes in the wording were made, but in the main the conference approved the basic policies formulated by the bureau chiefs of the army and navy. The representatives of the cabinet and the supreme command agreed to open hostilities against the United States, Great Britain, and the Netherlands if diplomatic negotiations failed to produce the desired results by the early part of October. The decision was presented to the imperial conference, that is, a meeting held in the presence of the Emperor, on September 6.

The day before the conference, Konoe and the chiefs of the general staff met with the Emperor, who had expressed concern over the fact that there seemed to be greater emphasis on war than on diplomacy. He pressed Konoe as well as the chiefs of staff, Sugiyama and Nagano, to affirm that efforts to achieve a diplomatic settlement would continue. The Emperor also castigated Sugiyama when the latter said that the military operations in the south would take only a few months. He reminded him that he had said in 1937 that the China Incident would be over in one month but here it was four years later and the conflict was still unsettled.

In the imperial conference on September 6, the Emperor reiterated his desire for peace and the need to give primacy to diplomatic negotiations. Even the military leaders, Tōjō, Sugiyama, and Mutō, were profoundly impressed by the Emperor's sentiments. Nevertheless, the conference did adopt the policy statement ("Outline for the Execution of National Policy") formulated by the army and navy, which avowed a determination "not to be deterred by the possibilty of being involved in a war with America (and England and Holland)." The statement also called for the continuance of diplomatic efforts to get Japan's demands accepted by America and England, and the commencement of war preparations if by the early part of October diplomatic negotiations failed to produce "reasonable hope" that these demands would be accepted.

The minimum Japanese demands were to be: (1) The United States and Britain were not to interfere in the settlement of the China Incident by Japan. They were to close the Burma Road and abstain from giving aid of any sort to the Chiang Kai-shek government. Meanwhile, Japan was to adhere rigidly to its plan of stationing troops in specified areas of China. (2) The United States and Britain were not to establish any military bases in Thailand, the Dutch East Indies, China, and far eastern Russia or increase their forces in the Far East. Japan was to retain her special relations with French Indochina as agreed upon with France. (3) The United States and Britain were to restore trade with Japan and, in particular, supply needed raw materials from their colonies in the southwestern Pacific area.

If these demands were met, Japan was to promise: not to use French Indochina as a base for operations against any neighboring country, except China; to withdraw her troops from Indochina as soon as a just peace was established in the Far East; to guarantee the neutrality of the Philippines; and to observe the neutrality pact with the Soviet Union. In case the United States should enter the war in Europe, the Tripartite Pact would not be automatically invoked by Japan, who would instead make an independent decision at that time concerning the applicability of the pact.

Japan's course was fixed by the policy statement adopted by the imperial conference, but Konoe seemed not to have attached any great significance to the statement. He believed that the one month or so still left for him to produce "reasonable hope" of having the Japanese demands accepted could be extended because of the ambiguity of the phrase "reasonable hope." During the month of September, Konoe continued to press for a meeting with Roosevelt. In fact, on the evening of September 6, after the imperial conference, he met secretly with Ambassador Grew to continue his plea for a conference with Roosevelt. However, Secretary of State Hull, now with Roosevelt's full concurrence, was intractable in his insistence that there be preliminary agreements on basic issues before such a meeting could take place. The American leaders felt that in light of his past record Konoe could not be fully relied upon to keep his promises. Moreover, the United States officials believed that Konoe did not have complete freedom and authority to negotiate and conclude binding agreements. All along it was believed that the military would have the final say.

Ambassador Grew urged his government to respond positively to Konoe's request instead of demanding clearly defined promises first. He insisted that to do otherwise would surely bring about the logical outcome, that is, the fall of the Konoe cabinet and the establishment of a military dictatorship. Evidently Konoe planned to have an imperial rescript issued that would prevent the extremists from opposing any settlement he might reach with Roosevelt, but even he himself was not confident that the diehard militarists could be held in check.

In the series of conferences that were held by the representatives of each of the governments, both sides persisted in their intransigence and consequently, the differences remained as great as ever. "The terms offered by the Japanese government would have permitted that country to emerge rewarded and strong from its ten-year venture in arms and stratagem." On the other hand, "the terms offered by the American government would have meant that Japan accept defeat; give up the gains of past effort, and the prospect of future expansion. They would have meant, also, a triumphant China." [8]

On September 7, Tōjō told Prince Higashikuni:

> The essence of the United States' demands is the severance
> of Japanese ties with the Axis nations of Germany and Italy.
> If Japan were to move in this direction England and
> America would demolish Germany and Italy, and then
> turn to the destruction of Japan. The United States asks
> for the withdrawal of Japanese troops from French
> Indochina and all of China, a full peace settlement with
> Chiang by the mediation of England and America, and
> the open door in China, but neither I, as war minister, nor
> the army can ever accept these conditions after having
> sacrificed so many precious lives on the continent. [9]

On October 2, Hull wrote a note to the Japanese reiterating his position that there could not be a meeting between Roosevelt and Konoe until there was an agreement concerning the four principles he had submitted in the spring. This, in effect, ended Konoe's hopes for a summit conference. The early part of October had come, and the diplomatic situation seemed even worse now than it had been in March, when the talks first started.

If the United States seemed more rigid in October than in March it was probably due to the fact that she was in a much stronger position. American defense production was increasing rapidly, the situation in the Atlantic was improving, the British still had the Suez Canal, and it appeared as if Hitler would not be able to capture Moscow as swiftly as he had expected.

Hull's note arrived and the army immediately asked Konoe to make the final decision to go to war with the United States. They cautioned that the longer Japan procrastinated the worse her economic and military situations would become. Tōjō told Konoe that a time comes in the life of every man when it becomes necessary to close his eyes and jump from the veranda of Kiyomizu Temple (in Kyoto) to the ravine below. On the other hand, the naval officers, led by Minister of the Navy Oikawa, still wished to avoid a war with the United States but were unwilling to state their position officially because they were afraid of bearing the stigma of having turned away from a showdown with the United States. They equivocated instead by saying they were willing to

---

[8] *Ibid.*, p. 273.

[9] Hayashi Shigeru, *Taiheiyō Sensō* (*The Pacific War*) (Tokyo: Chūō Kōronsha, 1967), pp. 240–41.

leave the decision to the Prime Minister. Only Admiral Nagano, the chief of the naval general staff, agreed with the army and favored engaging the United States in a war. The army leaders repeatedly urged their counterparts in the navy to make their position clear. They contended that if the navy would officially declare its opposition to war, the army leaders would then be able to keep their subordinates in line and even consent to further negotiations. The navy leaders, however, adhered to their contention that it was up to the Prime Minister to decide whether or not to go to war. They were placing their trust in a man who was less capable than they themselves were in making difficult decisions. Konoe favored continuing the talks with the United States, but he was unable to persuade the army to make concessions concerning China, which would make possible an agreement with the United States. In the face of this adamant position on the part of the army and the equivocal stand of the navy, he resigned his post on October 16.

Tōjō favored Prince Higashikuni, the Emperor's uncle, as Konoe's successor. This appointment, he believed, would make possible a general review of the situation and the restoration of harmony between the army and navy. Kido Kōichi, the Lord Keeper of the Privy Seal, opposed the idea of having a member of the royal family head the next cabinet because it would mean that responsibility would devolve directly upon the imperial family if war were to break out under the new government. He was convinced that in the event a decision were made to reverse the policy of September 6, the only person who could keep the chauvinistic army officers under control was Tōjō. Konoe concurred and, despite opposition by some senior statesmen, Tōjō was selected as the next premier. He was asked by the Emperor to reexamine the existing situation without being bound by the decision of the imperial conference of September 6; he was to start with a clean slate.

The impression created by the selection of Tōjō as Prime Minister was that Japan had decided upon war. Ambassador Grew, however, was somewhat encouraged when he learned that Tōjō planned to continue the negotiations, and he admitted that perhaps it was still a bit early to brand the Tōjō government a military dictatorship. The chauvinists in the army were of course delighted with the choice of Tōjō, and they insisted that the new government have a war cabinet.

In forming his cabinet, Tōjō retained his status as an active officer in the army and occupied the post of Minister of War; he also assumed the post of Minister of Home Affairs. Tōgō Shigenori (1882–1950), a career diplomat who was not at all enthusiastic about the alliance with Germany, was chosen as Foreign Minister. Admiral Shimada Shigetarō became Minister of the Navy, Kayo Okinori became Minister of Finance, and Kishi Nobusuke became Minister of Commerce and Industry.

Tōjō held a liaison conference with the supreme command after the cabinet was formed in order to reexamine the national policy. They deliberated from October 23 to October 30, trying to evaluate how they would fare in a war with the United States. Both the army and navy were confident of initial victories, but the navy expressed less confidence about the outcome of a lengthy war. The foreign ministry argued in favor of delaying the start of the war until March, but the general staffs of both branches of the military vigorously opposed the suggestion and insisted that it be set for November. Regarding negotiations with the United States, Foreign Minister Tōgō favored agreeing to the withdrawal of Japanese troops from China and Indochina, but the army general staff insisted on the need to station troops in China in order to guard against communism. Three options emerged after a week of discussions: (1) avoid war at all cost and "swallow the bitter pill"; (2) decide immediately upon war and direct all political and military planning to this end; (3) decide on war, and complete military preparations while at the same time continuing diplomatic negotiations with the hope of peacefully resolving the problems.

The conferees met on November 1 to make a final decision on the momentous question. The army general staff, as might be expected, chose the second alternative, calling for the commencement of hostilities by early December. The general-staff officers went so far as to ask the army chief of staff to disrupt the liaison conference if any of the other alternatives were chosen. The war ministry decided, however, to adopt the third alternative because it believed this would be the best way to lead the foreign ministry and the navy to the path of war. The navy favored the third alternative as did the Minister of Finance, and the head of the cabinet planning board, Hoshino.

Foreign Minister Tōgō was strongly opposed to the second alternative and, in the course of the discussion, he made it clear that if the third alternative were chosen the terms of negotiations would have to be made more flexible. In particular he wanted more time than the military leaders were willing to give him. The army general staff reluctantly agreed to continue negotiations but wanted the talks ended by November 13. It was, however, persuaded to accept December 1, as the deadline. If, however, diplomatic negotiations proved successful by that date plans for war were to be abandoned.

The conference next took up the question of the new proposals that were to be submitted to the United States. Two sets of proposals were presented by the foreign office. "Proposal A" included the following terms: Japan's willingness to uphold the principles of nondiscriminatory treatment in trade throughout the entire Pacific area and China if those principles were applied to the entire world; Japan's independent determination of the applicability of the Tripartite Act; Japan's withdrawal of her troops from China in two years with these exceptions: certain specified areas of North China and Inner Mongolia, and Hainan Island, where troops were to be stationed for twenty-five years after the conclusion of peace; and Japan's immediate withdrawal of troops from Indochina after the end of the China Incident.

A *modus vivendi* was to be arrived at if "Proposal A" was rejected by submitting "Proposal B," which called for the following: the United States and Japan were to refrain from advancing any troops into Southeast Asia (except French Indochina) and the South Pacific; the two countries were to cooperate in the acquisition of needed raw materials from the Dutch East Indies; the commercial relations that had prevailed before the freezing of the Japanese assets were to be resumed; the United States was to abstain from taking any actions that would be prejudicial to the restoration of peace between China and Japan; Japan was, in return, to withdraw her troops from southern Indochina to the north.

The army officers objected to "Proposal B," which would have provided only a temporary respite, but Tōjō persuaded them to go along with it because he considered the likelihood of the United States accepting it to be very slight. As expected, Secretary of State Hull condemned it as a proposal that would condone Japan's past aggressions, assent to her future conquests, give her dominant control of the entire western Pacific, and pose a most serious threat to American national security.[10]

On November 5, the imperial conference formally approved a decision to go to war in early December if diplomatic negotiations failed to produce a settlement by the first of that month. The army immediately began preparations for war in the south by appointing General Terauchi to command the Southern Area Army. The navy also prepared for war and by November 22, it managed to bring together at Etorofu Island in the Kuriles the very task force that was to attack Pearl Harbor.

The negotiations with the United States failed to produce any positive results. On November 7, Nomura submitted "Proposal A" to Hull. President Roosevelt deliberated and then responded on November 10, suggesting that Japan first prove her good intentions by starting to move her troops out of China and Indochina. Thus, "Proposal A," as was expected, failed to break the deadlock in the negotiations. At this point, Nomura was joined by Kurusu Saburō, a professional diplomat who was supposed to assist him in the talks. His arrival, however, did little to improve the situation, and in fact, his presence had a negative effect because Hull distrusted him and suspected that he was "deceitful."

---

[10] There is some indication that mistranslations of the intercepted messages by the United States' decoders tended to fortify Hull's distrust of the Japanese. Cf. John Toland, *The Rising Sun* (New York: Random House, 1970), pp. 133–35.

Nomura believed that the presentation of "Proposal B" would only make matters more difficult, but he was instructed to submit it. He did so on November 20, and once again Hull's reaction was negative. Hull did, however, entertain the thought of submitting America's own terms for a *modus vivendi* in order to delay the military confrontation. Interestingly enough, the United States and the Japanese military leaders were in agreement about the effects of a delayed confrontation. The Japanese general staff opposed putting off the commencement of the war beyond early December because it was believed that any further delays would enable the United States to strengthen its defenses while Japan's economic situation grew ever more precarious. On the other hand, the United States military leaders wanted to delay the start of the war so as to gain more time in which to prepare and strengthen their forces.

Secretary of State Hull considered the possibilty of devising a *modus vivendi* to keep Japan on a peaceful course for three months. The possible terms of the arrangement were scribbled out by President Roosevelt. They were: "(1) U.S. to resume economic relations—some oil and rice now—more later; (2) Japan to send no more troops to Indochina or Manchurian border or any place south; (3) Japan to agree not to invoke Tripartite Pact if U.S. gets in European war; (4) U.S. to introduce Japs to Chinese to talk things over. . . ." [11]

The suggestion to work out a *modus vivendi* was opposed by England and China, and consequently the idea was dropped. Instead, it was decided that the Japanese envoys would be handed a comprehensive basic proposal for a general peace settlement. This plan restated the basic principles Hull had been insisting upon from the outset of the talks; it called for a nonaggression pact among all nations who had interests in the Far East, and proposed the withdrawal of all Japanese forces from China and Indochina. In effect, the months of discussion had led absolutely nowhere—the negotiators were as far apart as they had ever been. The Hull note was handed to the Japanese envoys on November 26, and Hull told Stimson the following day, "I have washed my hands of it, and it [the situation] is now in the hands of you and Knox, the Army and Navy." [12]

The officers of the Japanese army general staff looked with great enthusiasm upon the Hull note for at last here was something that would enable them to end all talks of negotiation and start the war. The Tōjō government received the note as if it were an ultimatum and decided to go ahead with its war plans. In light of the previous decision to go to war if diplomatic talks failed to bring about a settlement by December 1, the Hull note left the opponents of the war without any ground to stand on.

The Japanese envoys, Nomura and Kurusu, appealed to their government not to decide on war. They asked Kido, the Lord Keeper of the Privy Seal, to have the Emperor send a personal message to Roosevelt, but Kido rejected the suggestion because, as he claimed, any effort to negotiate a settlement on the basis of the Hull note would indubitably touch off a civil war. President Roosevelt sent a message to the Emperor at the last minute on December 6, but it was not delivered to him until some time after the war had started.

The participants in the liaison conference that was held on November 27, agreed with Tōjō's interpretation of the Hull note as an ultimatum and had decided on war. On November 29, Tōjō set up a meeting with the senior statesmen, that is, the former Prime Ministers, in the presence of the Emperor. Wakatsuki, Okada, and Yonai expressed their concern about the decision in favor of war, but not one of those present was willing to take a strong stand against that decision. The plan to go to war was formally ratified by the imperial conference on December 1. The following day, the precise date of the attack was set at December 8 (December 7, in the United States). Admiral Yamamoto Isoroku, commander of the combined Japanese fleet, ordered the task force, which had left Etorofu Island for Hawaii on November 26, to attack Pearl Harbor on December 8.

Ironically enough, Admiral Yamamoto had all along been opposed to engaging the United States in a war. Immediately after the Tripartite Pact was signed, he told Konoe that the Japanese navy could dominate the seas for a period of only six months to a year. He maintained that Japan's chances of victory would dimisish tremendously if the war dragged on for two or three years. At the end of September he had informed Nagano, chief of the naval general staff, that all the fleet commanders agreed with him that a war with the United States would necessarily be a protracted one and that the Japanese fleet lacked the resouces to win such a war.

The supreme command wanted the Japanese attack to be a surprise, but they acceded to the foreign ministry's insistence that a declaration of war be delivered prior to the commencement of battle. The officers of the supreme command asked that the note be delivered to the United States government at 1 P.M. on Sunday, December 7, but they did not inform the Foreign Minister of the exact time that they planned to commence military operations. The message was intercepted and deciphered by the United States government even before the Japanese embassy in Washington managed to do so. The envoys had made an appointment to see Hull at 1 P.M., but because of technical difficulties there was a delay on their part in deciphering the message, and it was 2 P.M. by the time they arrived at the State Department. Finally at 2:20 P.M. they saw the Secretary of State—an hour after the first bombs had fallen on Pearl Harbor.

The war crimes trials placed the responsibility for the war on the shoulders of a handful of leaders. This assumes that the course of history is determined by a small group of men, and that the rest of the populace plays no role in molding the course of events. The Japanese public, however, with the exception of a small minority of thoughtful people, were completely behind the decision for war. By and large, the Diet members and the press were to all appearances more jingoistic than the government officials. In November, a veteran party politician in the Diet admonished the government "to stop grazing by the side of the road" and take action. A *New York Times* correspondent in Tokyo reported, "In so far as Diet members speak at all, they are so belligerent that the government appears moderate by comparison."

The ultranationalist extremists were naturally even more zealous in their desire to go to war with the United States. They constantly petitioned Tōjō to fight, and one ultranationalist openly accused him of "failing to heed the real voice of Japan." He called on Tōjō to listen to the voices in the streets and shops, which he said were clamoring for action. Any leading figure suspected of being an advocate of peace was in danger of being assassinated.[13] No doubt the danger of being murdered made the proponents of peace behave cautiously. It is nevertheless extremely unlikely that a small band advocating peace could have changed the course of events. Japanese public opinion had by this time been thoroughly conditioned to support the quest for a larger empire. That the Japanese people had come to support imperialism was not simply the result of the nationalistic, imperialistic propaganda that grew more intense after the Manchurian Incident.

Militaristic thinking originated in the ancient past and got stronger with the emergence of the samurai as the ruling class. The ethnocentrism of an island nation was transformed into a powerful force of nationalism in the nineteenth century as Japan encountered the West and felt compelled to revolutionize her institutions and way of life in order to survive in the international arena of power politics. The growth of Japan's strength soon transfigured the nationalistic sentiments into

[13] Admiral Yamamoto was assigned to sea duty after mid-1939, so as to lessen the chances of his being assassinated. An ultranationalist tried to kill Hiranuma because he had not severed his ties with the cabinet after Matsuoka had been dropped by Konoe. Another group of fanatics also had him on a list of victims they planned to liquidate. There was, in addition, a plot to assassinate Konoe on September 18, 1941, but this was uncovered and quashed by the police.

a hunger for more power and a desire to expand into the Asian continent.

Loyalty to the Emperor and defense of the nation were the ideals that were inculcated into the Japanese as soon as they entered elementary school. Textbooks began to take on an increasingly militaristic coloring with each successive revision of the officially compiled editions. For instance, the first-grade reader issued in 1933, starts off with the words: "Forward March, Forward March, Soldiers, Forward March." The outbreak of the Manchurian Incident caused the militaristic tone to grow increasingly pronounced in the schools, newspapers, journals, radio, and movies—in fact, in all media of communication and entertainment. The China Incident heightened the jingoistic, expansionistic sentiments of the people even more. Unquestionably, by the time Pearl Harbor was attacked, the Japanese as a whole, that is, both the civilian population and military personnel, were a war-minded people who believed in the justice of their cause. One historian writes, "The official brainwashing policy which had been directed at the Japanese people for more than a decade had by now taken full effect upon the leaders as well." [14] These leaders were no doubt right when they contended that the people would never have permitted them to accept a de facto defeat by agreeing to the terms that had been submitted by the United States. They had become the slaves of their own creation.[15]

The driving force (if there is in fact such a thing) in a nation's history would be the aggregate of the will and thought of the millions of people who constitute the "will" or the "mind" of that nation. The character and orientation of a nation cannot be changed except by a slow process of reeducation or by a truly soul-wrenching experience, such as the shocking defeat suffered by Japan in 1945. It is highly unlikely that any leader or group of leaders could have reversed the direction in which the "mind" of the people was moving during 1940–1941. Moreover, it would have taken leaders of much greater moral and intellectual calibre than those who led Japan along the road to war to even attempt to reverse the historical trend. Shōwa Japan lacked the leaders that Meiji Japan had; Konoe was certainly not Itō, Tōjō was not Yamagata, and Emperor Hirohito was not Emperor Meiji. Furthermore for change to have been even remotely possible, a dramatic shift in the thinking of the military itself was needed. This, of course,

---

[14] Butow, *op. cit.,* p. 327.

[15] "People in an undemocratic society are . . . liable to become the slaves of fanatic xenophobia, the frustrations of their daily lives being effectively sublimated into jingoism. The rulers of such countries are only too ready to encourage these tendencies in order to counter the backwash of dissatisfaction below; yet in time of crisis they are themselves mastered by this irresponsible type of 'public opinion' and end by losing their autonomy of decision." (Maruyama Masao, *op. cit.,* p. 114.)

was the last thing that one could expect to have occurred. The military leaders were governed by "a sort of a superpolitical auto-propulsion." [16]

The specific events that led to the war in the Pacific can be traced back to the outbreak of the China Incident or even to the start of the Manchurian Incident in 1931. Each succeeding event drew Japan closer and closer to the larger confrontation until 1941, when it was clearly too late for Japan to turn back. The military leaders were perhaps correct in saying they could not withdraw from China after having sacrificed thousands of lives on the continent since 1937. Too much blood had been spilled, too many promises had been made, too many emotions had been stirred, too much poison had been spread, and too much fanaticism had been fostered.

The strong feelings that had been aroused were not confined to Japan alone. The enmity and hostility that Japan had incurred abroad —in China, the United States, England, and Soviet Russia—might have resulted in what Tōjō believed would be the fate of Japan. That is, even if Japan had not initiated the war, once the war in Europe was settled, it is possible that an isolated and weaker Japan would have been the next target of the victorious powers. Given this possibility, it was not wholly irrational for a samurai like Tōjō to conclude that "rather than await extinction it was better to face death by breaking through the encircling ring to find a way for existence." [17] There was a degree of inevitability after 1937 in the events that led to war. Japan probably could not have averted war in 1941; perhaps with the right leadership this could have been accomplished in 1937.

The final rupture in relations between the United States and Japan must be viewed from a broader historical perspective than from that of the immediate circumstances that led to the war. A complex web of political, economic, and psychological factors transformed what was a warm relationship following the Meiji Restoration into outright animosity. Until the Russo-Japanese War the United States had sympathetically looked upon Japan's emergence as a "modern" nation, but the interests of the two nations began to come into conflict with growing frequency and intensity as Japan began to assert herself as a major power in the Far East. The United States, as an exponent of the open-door policy, was committed to the preservation of the territorial integrity and independence of China. As a result, Japan's expansion into China became the central issue of contention between the two nations.

Economically, Japan had to trade with other nations in order to grow as a modern industrial state. When the Great Depression occurred she was faced with economic barriers established by nations that had marked

[16] *Ibid.*, p. 115.
[17] Feis, *op. cit.*, p. 293.

out large sections of the world as their colonies and spheres of interest. Thus the pressure to stake out her own "co-prosperity sphere" grew in intensity.

Psychologically, a complicated ambivalence had developed in the Japanese attitude toward the United States. After the Meiji Restoration, the United States became the object of admiration and in many respects the model which the Japanese sought to emulate. Elementary school textbooks that were issued by the government and used until the eve of World War II contained numerous stories of such outstanding Americans as Washington, Lincoln, and Franklin, presenting them as models to follow. As Japan began to extend her power into the Asian continent, however, acrimonious feelings were aroused. This situation was aggravated by the difficulties over Japanese immigration into the United States. Whatever political, social, or economic reasons there were for the immigration policies adopted by the United States, the manner in which the opposition to Japanese immigration was expressed was unmistakably racist. This was a particularly galling pill to swallow for the Japanese, who thought of themselves as a unique race. The continuous talk of the Yellow Peril in the United States strengthened the position of the anti-American, radical nationalists in Japan. The central issue, however, was China, and by December, 1941, public opinion on both sides had become so fierce that the outbreak of the war was greeted by many people with almost a sigh of relief.

CHAPTER 20

WAR
AND DEFEAT

THE OFFENSIVE WAR

At 7:55 Sunday morning, December 7, 1941, Japanese torpedo planes attacked Pearl Harbor and the sanguinary struggle between the United States and Japan began.

The surprise attack on Pearl Harbor was conceived and planned by Admiral Yamamoto Isoroku (1884–1943), Commander in Chief of Japan's combined fleet, who believed that Japan could protect her expansion in Southeast Asia only by dealing a crippling blow to the American fleet in the Pacific at the outset of the war. The task force, commanded by Vice-Admiral Nagumo Chūichi, consisting of thirty-one ships, including six carriers, had left Tankan Bay on Etorofu Island in the Kuriles for Hawaii on November 26. The United States fleet at Pearl Harbor was caught completely off guard when the attack commenced. Every responsible official was aware that a war was imminent; but the American naval authorities were convinced that the Japanese navy could not mount more than one major naval or amphibious operation at a time, and all evidence pointed to a Japanese offensive to the south.[1]

---

[1] As to why the warnings from intercepted messages were not heeded, the following has been suggested: "It is much easier after the event to sort the relevant from the irrelevant signals. . . . We failed to anticipate Pearl Harbor not for want of the relevant materials, but because of a plethora of irrelevant ones." (Roberta Wholstetter, *Pearl Harbor: Warning and Decisions,* Stanford, Calif.: Stanford University Press, 1962, p. 387.)

Eighteen American ships had been sunk or seriously damaged by the time the Japanese planes ceased their attack at 10 A.M. In addition to these serious losses to the United States fleet, 188 planes were destroyed and 159 were damaged. Nearly 80 percent of the crew of the "Arizona" was lost; 47 officers and 1,056 men were killed or missing. The total casualties were 2,403 killed and 1,178 wounded. In contrast, the Japanese lost only twenty-nine planes, and five midget submarines, and suffered about a hundred casualties.

The raid was hailed as a great victory in Japan. A rather different evaluation of this event has been offered by the historian Samuel Eliot Morison:

> The surprise attack on Pearl Harbor . . . was a strategic imbecility. One can search military history in vain for an operation more fatal to the aggressor. On the tactical level, the Pearl Harbor attack was wrongly concentrated on ships rather than permanent installations and oil tanks. On the strategic level it was idiotic. On the high political level it was disastrous.[2]

The Japanese attackers did not even destroy the American naval repair ships, which were able to restore to service the less severely damaged vessels at an amazingly fast pace. Nor did they attack the power plant or the oil tanks, whose loss would have weakened the United States navy in the Pacific far more than did the damage to the fleet.

Strategically, it is believed that had the Japanese not attacked Pearl Harbor, the United States would not have ventured to the southern or southwestern Pacific to contest Japanese expansion. The Japanese could have acquired the Philippines and Malaya without touching Pearl Harbor, since the strategy of the United States called for defending the Marshall and the Caroline Islands in the South Pacific, which, it was estimated, would take six to nine months. Politically, of course, the attack on Pearl Harbor united the American people behind their president more than any other event could have.

Coincident with the attack on Pearl Harbor, military operations were directed against Guam, Wake Island, the Philippines, Hong Kong, and Malaya. The Japanese aim was to wrest the resource-rich regions in the south from their European protectors and to ring their prize with an impregnable defense perimeter of fortified bases.

On the same December morning that Pearl Harbor was attacked,

---

[2] Samuel Eliot Morison, *History of the United States Naval Operations in World War II*, 15 vols. (New York: Little, Brown, 1947–1962), vol. 3, p. 132.

Japanese planes took off from Formosa and bombed Clark Field and other American bases near Manila. They damaged or destroyed seventeen B–17s and thirty fighter planes, thus reducing American bomber strength by one-half and fighter strength by one-third. Within a week the Japanese controlled the skies over the Philippines and were thus able to launch amphibious operations on the key islands of Luzon and Mindanao. Lacking air or naval support, General Douglas MacArthur, commanding general of the United States forces in the Far East, ordered his troops to pull back to the Bataan Peninsula, declaring Manila an open city on December 26.

On January 2, 1942, Japanese forces occupied Manila, and as they moved on to Bataan the army commanded by General Homma Masaharu met determined resistance. It was not until April 9 that Homma could claim Bataan, and even then the island fortress of Corregidor, long an American stronghold, still held out.[3] General MacArthur, on personal order from President Roosevelt, had slipped away from Corregidor in March and escaped to Australia, vowing to return. General Jonathan Wainwright, who was left in command, defended the island until May, when he was compelled to surrender. The Philippine campaign was over, although guerrilla activities were continued by the Filipinos. The beleaguered commanders of the American Pacific bases at Guam and Wake Island were also forced to submit to overwhelming odds. Guam fell on December 10; Wake Island was able to resist only until December 23. On the China coast the British colony of Hong Kong was captured on December 25.

To the south, Singapore was the objective of the Malayan campaign. This great British port city had long dominated maritime trade in Southeast Asia. On December 8, Japan dispatched troops to southern Thailand, effecting an alliance with the Thai government on the 21st. At the same time, Japanese troops deployed from northern Malaya, proceeded south toward Singapore. The British fleet guarding that city was virtually wiped out on December 10, when the battleship "Prince of Wales" and the cruiser "Repulse" were destroyed by torpedo and bomber plane attacks. On the Malay Peninsula the Japanese soldiers moved rapidly through the jungle and arrived at Singapore on February 8. On the 15th, General Arthur E. Percival surrendered to General Yamashita Tomoyuki.

Elsewhere, the Japanese were equally successful. On January 23, 1942,

[3] In the course of moving the prisoners of war from southern Bataan 65 miles north to San Fernando, the infamous Bataan Death March took place, in which an estimated five thousand men died because of the brutalities of the Japanese captors. At the trials conducted after the war, General Homma was held responsible for this, and he was later executed as a war criminal.

the Australian airbase at Rabaul on New Britain Island in the Bismarck Archipelago was captured. The campaign in Burma resulted in the capture of Rangoon on March 8 and Mandalay on May 1. By the middle of May Burma was in Japanese hands.

The coveted prize of the entire southern campaign was the Dutch East Indies with their vast oil deposits and prodigious supplies of rubber, tin, rice, and bauxite. By the middle of December, Japanese soldiers were advancing on northern Borneo, southern Borneo, the Celebes, Amboina, Timor, and Bali. In mid-February, Japanese parachute troops landed on Sumatra. The invasion of Java was launched at the end of the same month. On March 9 the Dutch defenders of Java surrendered unconditionally.

Prior to the invasion of Java, the first surface-to-surface naval battle of the war in the Pacific was fought off Surabaya on February 27, 1942, between Japanese and British, Dutch, and American warships. The Japanese fleet won the Battle of the Java Sea, sinking four Allied ships without losing a single vessel. On the following day, Japanese warships engaged American ships in a naval battle at Sunda Strait and sank three more cruisers. On March 1, Japanese warships sank three British vessels off the coast of Java. In April, they attacked British warships in Ceylon, sinking several vessels including one carrier. Victory in these battles enabled the Japanese navy to gain control of the seas in the Southwest Pacific.

The initial campaigns by the Japanese armed forces had been far more successful than the military planners had anticipated. In less than six months the Japanese flag was flying from Burma to Wake Island. The Japanese had driven the Dutch, the British, and the Americans from Southeast Asia and the Southwest Pacific, and gained control of the vital resources of these areas. Japanese strategists had expected the conquest of the Philippines, Malaya, and the Dutch East Indies to take five months and they had further calculated that an additional six months would be needed to get the oil fields operating again. However, the Dutch policy of destroying the oil fields failed, and Japan was consequently able to gain access to these in half the estimated time.

A liaison conference was held in March, 1942, and it was decided that Japan must now consolidate her control over the newly won areas and strengthen her defense against an anticipated American counteroffensive. This was expected to begin sometime after 1943. By and large the leaders made an optimistic assessment of the overall situation even though a few saw protracted war as a distinct possibility. Actually, Foreign Minister Tōgō seemed to favor halting Japan's expansion, but, except for a few military and naval officers, no one shared his caution in the face of the spectacular successes of the war effort. The imperial advisers might have noted a portent of things to come when, on April 18, 1942, a squadron of B-25s led by Colonel James H. Doolittle flew 668 miles from the carrier "Hornet" to drop incendiary bombs on Tokyo. The actual damage inflicted was slight, and the raid seemed merely to demonstrate that Admiral Yamamoto was correct in placing the destruction of American cruisers at the top of his list of military objectives.

As a result of the initial successes, plans to extend the Japanese defense perimeter further into the Pacific were activated earlier than had been expected. A line of fortifications would be established at: (1) Tulagi on the Solomon Islands and Port Moresby in southeastern New Guinea; (2) Midway Atoll and western Aleutians; and (3) New Caledonia, Fiji, and Samoa (by which Australia would be cut off from the United States). The first objective resulted in the Battle of the Coral Sea, the second in the Battle of Midway, the third, however, was abandoned before any military engagement took place.

The Battle of the Coral Sea occurred on May 8, 1942—the first naval battle in history in which the fighting was done primarily by carrier-based planes. In this engagement the Japanese sank the American carrier "Lexington," a fleet oiler, and a destroyer, and damaged the carrier "Yorktown." The Japanese lost a light carrier, a destroyer, and three auxiliary vessels. Both sides claimed a victory. For Japan it was a tactical victory insofar as she exacted a heavier toll than did the United States, but it was a strategic defeat insofar as she was prevented from capturing Port Moresby.

The encounter that turned the tide in the Pacific, was the Battle of Midway. The assault on the American naval base at Midway Island was conceived by Admiral Yamamoto, who believed that by extending the defense perimeter to the Aleutians and Midway the United States fleet would be drawn into a vulnerable position, thus providing the Japanese navy with an opportunity to destroy it.

In early June, the campaign to invade Midway Island and to engage the United States fleet commenced with a diversionary attack against the Aleutian Islands that was designed to lure the American fleet north.

On the overleaf: Following the attack on Pearl Harbor, Japan launched military campaigns against the Philippines, Malaya, Burma, Borneo, the Netherland Indies, New Guinea, the South Pacific islands, and Attu and Kiska in the Aleutians. By May, 1942, these areas were under Japanese control. Earlier in 1941 Japan had occupied Indochina, and Thailand joined the war on Japan's side soon after the commencement of the Pacific War. The turning point of the war came with the Battle of Midway (June 4–7, 1942) and the Guadalcanal campaign (August, 1942–February, 1943).

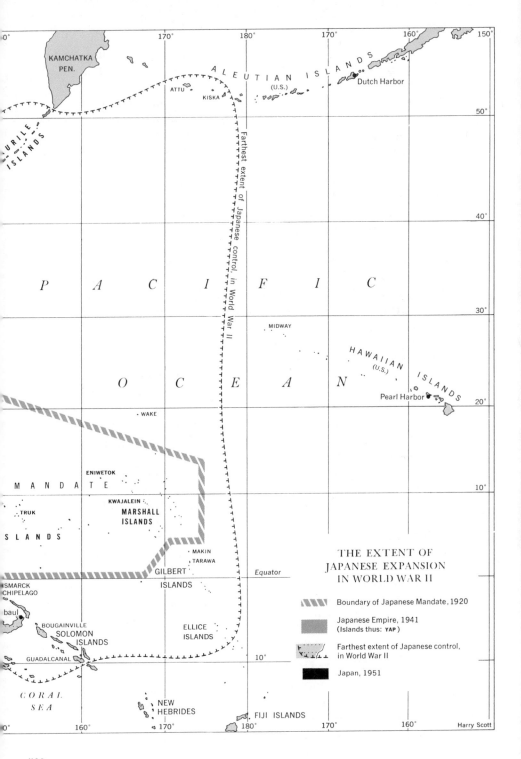

THE EXTENT OF
JAPANESE EXPANSION
IN WORLD WAR II

Boundary of Japanese Mandate, 1920

Japanese Empire, 1941
(Islands thus: YAP)

Farthest extent of Japanese control,
in World War II

Japan, 1951

Harry Scott

The carrier striking force with four carriers, led by Admiral Nagumo, and the Midway invasion force moved toward the island, while Admiral Yamamoto followed at a distance with the main force, waiting to ambush American warships as they sped to the defense of Midway. This time, however, Yamamoto was in for a surprise. Unknown to him, the Japanese military code had been deciphered by United States intelligence, and consequently the American navy knew of the Midway plan a month in advance and was prepared. Confident in the secrecy of their strategy, the Japanese admirals had not maintained strict aerial reconnaissance and their search planes failed to detect the American warships steaming forward to intercept the Japanese striking force. Included in the American fleet were three carriers, the "Yorktown," "Enterprise," and "Hornet."

On June 4, the fateful encounter began shortly after the initial Japanese air attack on Midway Island. Not anticipating a counterattack from the air, Nagumo's planes were armed with land bombs with which they intended to blast Midway Island a second time. Their plans were crushed when the American aircraft carrier "Yorktown," which the Japanese thought they had sunk in the Coral Sea, came into view. Frantic efforts were made by the Japanese plane crews to replace the land bombs with torpedoes, but even before their aircraft could take off American bombers were overhead. The Japanese carriers dodged torpedo bombs, but they were quite helpless beneath the onslaught of the American dive bombers. The carriers "Akagi," "Kaga," and "Sōryū" were destroyed almost simultaneously. A fourth carrier, "Hiryū," sent up planes against the "Yorktown" but was hit in turn by dive bombers from the "Enterprise." Crippled, the "Hiryū" sank the next morning.

Confronted with the destruction of his carriers, Yamamoto abandoned the invasion of Midway and pulled back his remaining ships. He had lost four great aircraft carriers, one heavy cruiser, and 332 planes; a half-dozen other vessels were damaged. The United States lost one carrier, one destroyer, and 147 planes. Three hundred and seven Americans died during this encounter in contrast to about thirty-five hundred Japanese. Among those were one hundred of the most experienced navy pilots. Thereafter the Japanese would be plagued with a shortage of able pilots. News of this disastrous defeat was kept from the Japanese public.

THE WAR AT HOME

Immediately after the outbreak of the war in the Pacific, the government, headed by Prime Minister Tōjō, enacted an emergency law to control speech, publication, assembly, and association. No war news could be released without the approval of the supreme command; hence, only favorable information concerning the battle was made available to the people. At the onset of the war, of course, the news was most favorable and so in the first weeks after the attack on Pearl Harbor, victory after victory was reported. The exuberant joy of the Japanese people knew no bounds. Even sophisticated intellectuals reveled in the heady emotional outburst of national pride. One writer commented on the news of Pearl Harbor: "I did not believe that I would experience in my lifetime such a happy, exhilarating, joyous day. The oppressive, gloomy cloud that has been hanging over us for the past few years has suddenly been lifted." [4]

The news of Pearl Harbor was followed in eighteen days by the announcement of the capture of Hong Kong, and in seven more days of the occupation of Manila. A Victory Day was celebrated just seventy days after Pearl Harbor to triumphantly herald the conquest of Singapore. A second Victory Day followed the seizure of Rangoon and the Dutch East Indies. The government proclaimed its intention of establishing the Greater East Asia Co-prosperity Sphere once the liberation of Asian nations from their European overlords was achieved. The imperial forces seemed invincible, and it was said that the American soldiers, in the face of the advancing Japanese, were "trembling in their shoes." Some of the more astute leaders, including Prime Minister Tōjō, might have been a bit less sanguine, but even they believed that the "Japanese spirit" would triumph over American material strength. To be sure, the government leaders counted on Japan's European partners in the Tripartite Pact to aid in crushing the enemy. At the end of 1942, Tōjō saw clearly that the real war was just beginning, but he was not able to formulate a policy appropriate to this knowledge.

Tōjō is frequently depicted as having been a dictator as absolute and sinister as Hitler, but in fact, his powers were nothing like Hitler's. President Franklin D. Roosevelt probably had greater authority as a wartime leader than did Tōjō, who was subject to constraints by "establishment" leaders who exercised considerable influence as senior statesmen and advisers to Emperor Hirohito. Collective leadership characterized the Japanese political scene even in wartime.

Tōjō, as the head of state during wartime, had but limited influence over the army general staff, which insisted on the "independence of the supreme command." It was the supreme command that held ultimate power, not Tōjō, and he was not allowed to forget it. The story is told that once when the army general staff was not allocated certain supplies that it had demanded, a staff officer confronted Tōjō and screamed at him, "You stupid fool!" Such an incident would have been unimagin-

[4] Hayashi Shigeru, *Taiheiyō Sensō (The Pacific War)* (Tokyo: Chūō Kōronsha, 1967), p. 320.

able had Tōjō been a dictator like Hitler. Dealing with the military leaders was not a simple matter, however. There existed many petty rivalries between the army and the navy, and the progress of the war was consistently hampered because they refused to coordinate their efforts. The war situation worsened throughout 1943, and it was not until February, 1944, that Tōjō at length received imperial sanction to assume the post of chief of the army general staff himself. He hoped this would put him in a better position to coordinate administrative and command policies. However, no amount of this kind of reform could roll back the tide of war, which by then was running strongly against Japan.

If Tōjō lacked sufficient power to shape events, the Diet lacked power even to question them. In the middle of the war, in April, 1942, a Diet election was held. At this time the Diet was almost completely ineffective, but the government nonetheless endorsed a roster of 466 candidates— the exact number of seats in the lower house—to make quite certain that the new Diet would be compliant. More than six hundred unendorsed candidates competed in the election, but not surprisingly, those who were officially favored won a huge majority. The Diet functioned as a rubber stamp until the end of the war.

In order to integrate the areas that had been brought under Japanese control into an overall framework, the government proceeded to establish what it called the Greater East Asia Co-prosperity Sphere. This plan, as a theoretical scheme, possessed considerable merit. In practice, however, the areas that were "liberated" actually remained under the jurisdiction of the military. Their harsh administrative policies alienated many potential allies, and the arrogant behavior of Japanese occupation soldiers, especially those in Singapore and Malaya where many atrocities were committed, aroused bitter hatred among the inhabitants of these areas toward the Japanese. To counteract this, in the middle of 1943, when the fortune of war was steadily growing more adverse, the Tōjō government decided to grant independence to the Philippines and Burma. In August, 1943, Burma, led by Ba Maw, was granted independence; in October, an independent state headed by José Laurel was established in the Philippines. Both these countries, however, remained under Japanese domination. Malaya, Sumatra, Java, Borneo, and the Celebes were annexed to the Japanese Empire though the policy was to allow the people limited participation in political affairs. Other areas were to continue under military control. The Japanese authorities supported the independence movement of the Indian nationalist, Chandra Bose, but as Japan's plan to invade India was never implemented, Chandra Bose's dream of freeing India from the British with Japanese help failed to materialize.

In November, 1943, a meeting of the Greater East Asian Nations—Japan, China, Manchuria, Thailand, the Philippines, and Burma—was held in Tokyo. The assembled leaders however, were, with almost no exception, Japanese puppets or collaborators, who were wholly dependent upon Japan for whatever power they had. Consequently the conference served little purpose, and when Japan's fortunes waned, anti-Japanese nationalist movements began to emerge throughout the Greater East Asian Co-prosperity Sphere.

THE DEFENSIVE WAR

The defeat suffered by the Japanese navy at the Battle of Midway was of such significant magnitude that its effects would entirely alter the course of the war. Thereafter the United States would slowly assume the initiative in the Pacific. American marines commenced the invasion of the Solomon Islands of Tulagi, Florida, and Guadalcanal in August, 1942. On Guadalcanal a grisly war of attrition was fought for six months. A ground battle continued to rage on that island while a series of air and naval battles were fought elsewhere in the Solomons. Before dawn on August 9, a Japanese naval force at Ironbottom Sound off Savo Island sank four American cruisers and thus inflicted upon the United States navy "one of its worst defeats in history." In the several encounters that ensued both sides lost twenty-four combat ships. The losses, however, proved more telling for the Japanese, and by the end of 1942, the United States had gained aerial and naval supremacy in the region of the Solomon Islands.

In February, 1943, Japanese troops, decimated by combat, in need of reinforcements and equipment, and unable to reestablish their supply lines by air or sea, were forced to withdraw from Guadalcanal. In that half-year period of fighting, Japan lost 893 planes and 2,362 airmen. In the following year she would lose 6,203 planes and 4,824 aviators. These figures combined represent three times the number of planes Japan had had in the Pacific at the beginning of her expansion and a grievous proportion of her experienced aviators. She would have to use hastily trained pilots as time went on, and lacking the productive capacity of the United States, she would find herself increasingly incapable of replacing her aircraft. The United States air and sea power, on the other hand, would expand during the conflict. By the end of the war the United States would have 40,893 first-line planes and sixty aircraft carriers. There can be no doubt that after the Battle of Guadalcanal the United States definitely moved on to the offensive in the Pacific while the Japanese were forced to the defensive.

The Japanese supreme command stepped up defense measures in the South Pacific following the Battle of Guadalcanal. Reinforcements were ordered to Lae in eastern New Guinea. A convoy of sixteen ships left the huge Japanese bastion on Rabaul in New Britain at the end of February, 1943. It was overtaken by American planes on March 3–March 4, in the Bismarck Sea and all eight transports plus four destroyers were sunk. The Allies, realizing that their drive across the South Pacific would be constantly challenged by the Japanese at Rabaul, now launched an offensive aimed ultimately at that seaport. It began with attacks on certain little islands in the upper and central Solomons group that stretched out between the American bases at Guadalcanal and Buna and the Japanese stronghold at Rabaul. Confronted with this very serious threat to their possessions in the Solomons the Japanese took prompt steps to protect their bases. In general there was a notorious lack of cooperation between the imperial army and the imperial navy in planning operations, but after the disaster in the Bismarck Sea the two services made some attempt to coordinate efforts in the campaign in the South Pacific. Admiral Yamamoto came to Rabaul to take charge of air strategy, and between April 7 and April 11, he dispatched a series of air raids against the new American airfields in the Solomons and against the warships protecting them. His planes returned with reports of splendid success. Believing that the operation had accomplished its purpose, Yamamoto terminated the raids. His aviators, however, had claimed more hits than they had in fact scored.

It was at about this time that American intelligence decoded details of a plan for Yamamoto to visit his troops in the Solomons to bolster morale. Knowing his exact flight schedule, American planes took off to intercept him in the air, and they shot him down over Bougainville Island. His death, according to one Japanese admiral, was "an almost unbearable blow to the morale of all the military forces."

Possession of the Solomon Islands was contested throughout 1943, with Bougainville the initial prize. Before long, however, the Allies adopted a policy of bypassing isolated enemy strongholds. Bougainville in the Solomons and Rabaul on New Britain were therefore left in Japanese hands to the end of the war. Cut off from reinforcements, they were in effect neutralized.

THE ALLIED STRATEGY

In May, 1943, the United States and Britain formulated a strategic plan for the defeat of Japan that encompassed three offensives. One offensive would recapture Japanese-held bases in the Aleutian Islands close by Alaska. A second offensive would drive through the South and Southwest Pacific. For this phase of the plan General MacArthur would lead the Allied armies up through New Guinea, the Celebes, the Sulu Seas, and Hong Kong. The third offensive would be largely naval and would strike through the Central Pacific islands. Admiral Chester Nimitz was to be commander in chief of the assaults on the Gilberts, Marshalls, and Truk in the Carolinas. His fleet would join MacArthur's forces at the Sulu Seas. In the fall of 1943, this plan was changed to allow Admiral Nimitz to move on to the Mariannas to establish airbases for the new B–29s on Saipan, Tinian, and Guam.

MacArthur vigorously opposed the third phase of the strategy, arguing that the essentially overland route through the islands of the Southwest Pacific was surer, and that the naval resources of the Pacific fleet could best be used in support of the invading army. However, the Pacific fleet, strengthened by the first of the fast new carriers, was newly capable of conducting assaults over long stretches of ocean at high speed. By March of 1944, the Central Pacific phase of the overall plan was confirmed, and submarine activity was to be intensified in all areas.

The first part of the comprehensive plan was put into effect on May 11, 1943, when Allied soldiers landed on the Aleutian island of Attu which, with the island of Kiska, had fallen to the Japanese during the previous summer. The small Japanese contingent on Attu, some twenty-five hundred men, fought ferociously. More American troops were brought in, and by the end of May, some eleven thousand Allied soldiers had disembarked on the island. Almost all the Japanese defenders had fought to the death, and nearly five hundred of the soldiers blew themselves up with grenades rather than face capture. Kiska was known to be more heavily fortified than Attu and preparations for the attack there were carefully laid. Prior to the American landing in mid-August, however, Japanese naval vessels secretly evacuated their fifty-six hundred men. Thirty-five thousand Allied soldiers came ashore and they were met with a strange silence. They searched in the fog for the Japanese for five days but found only two or three mongrel dogs.

The second phase of the comprehensive strategy was put in the hands of General MacArthur. He was to lead the South–Southwest Pacific offensive through New Guinea, Mindanao, Luzon, Formosa, and north. Later Mindanao and Formosa were eliminated, and Okinawa became the target after Luzon. In June, 1943, MacArthur's forces moved against Japanese bases in eastern New Guinea. The Japanese there had received neither reinforcements nor supplies since the destruction of their transports in the Battle of the Bismarck Sea. Those who survived the Allied advance would be left to struggle in the jungle for the rest of the war. This was also to be the fate of the Japanese troops in other sections of New Guinea. At the end of the war the Japanese forces in New Guinea surrendered, and only thirteen thousand of the original one hundred and forty thousand men were still alive.

In November, 1943, the third phase of the comprehensive strategy was activated when the Central Pacific naval forces, under the command of Admiral Nimitz, launched an attack on the atolls of Makin and Tarawa in the Gilbert Islands. The amphibious landing, followed by a four-day battle for Betio on Tarawa, began one of the bloodiest engagements of the war. American casualties came to one thousand dead and more than two thousand wounded, but the entire Japanese marine force of forty-eight hundred men died in the battle.

By the end of the year, the Central Pacific offensive was making significant headway in conquering the key islands and constructing airfields from which huge land-based bombers could attack the Japanese home islands. In the Marshall Islands, the western edge of the Japanese defense perimeter, Admiral Nimitz bypassed many fortified atolls to focus on capturing the critical islands of Kwajalein and Eniwetok. Supported by the crushing efficiency of carrier-based bombers and preceded by naval gunfire, the marines landed on Kwajalein on February 1, 1944, and in three days of fighting they captured the island, killing 7,870 Japanese. American losses during this battle were 372 dead or missing. At Eniwetok, which was also captured, the Japanese burial count came to 2,677, compared to the American toll of 195.

After the fall of the Marshall Islands, the Japanese withdrew their forces to a new defense line stretching from the Marianas and Palaus to New Guinea. Accordingly, the Allies decided to bypass occupation of the heavily fortified island of Truk in the Carolines. Nevertheless, Truk, a major airbase in the old Japanese defense perimeter, was bombarded by massive naval and air attacks that smashed Japanese aircraft and transport ships. The fifty thousand Japanese soldiers on Truk were cut off from aid and thus effectively neutralized.

Further to the south, MacArthur gained control of the Admiralty Islands in March, 1944, capturing Seeadler Harbor, which became one of the largest naval bases in the Pacific, with elaborate repair facilities for all types of vessels. Moving swiftly, MacArthur attacked Hollandia in Dutch New Guinea in April. There the Japanese fought fanatically; of eleven thousand men, fewer than one thousand were alive at the end of the engagement. Some three hundred Japanese aircraft and two destroyers were lost.

In Burma during the spring of 1944, the Japanese suffered another costly reversal. Determined to sever the British-American supply route from India by which Allied air bases in western China were maintained, the Japanese mounted an offensive in March against Imphal in Assam. Ignoring severe problems of logistics, extreme difficulties of terrain, and the sheer fact of British air supremacy, they relied on brute determination and fighting spirit. Hindered by stiff resistance, the attackers were still in the field when an unexpectedly early monsoon struck. Having had their supply lines cut, the Japanese ran out of munitions and food. Nonetheless their commanders fanatically insisted that the campaign continue. By July, when withdrawal was finally ordered, many of the retreating troops starved to death before they could reach safety. The Japanese casualties in the Imphal campaign came to thirty thousand dead and forty-two thousand sick and wounded.

During this same period, Allied forces under General Joseph Stilwell launched a counteroffensive in northern Burma and captured Myitkyina in the Mogaung Valley. Simultaneously, a Chinese army advanced from Yunan and captured Bhamo. Thus the Allies won firm control of the overland supply routes into China, linking the Ledo Road with the Burma Road. The Allied offensive continued into 1945, when in May, Rangoon was recaptured. From the autumn of 1944 to that time, the Japanese war dead mounted to two hundred thousand men.

By the spring of 1944, the Imperial High Command in Tokyo could anticipate the direction of MacArthur's stunning offensive in the South and Southwest Pacific, and it determined that the Allied forces must be engaged before they could move forward to the Philippines. Furthermore, MacArthur's advance threatened Japan's very lifeblood, for if her oil supplies were cut off, she could neither continue the war effort nor produce domestic necessities. Admiral Koga Mineichi, Yamamoto's successor, was charged with preventing the enemy from entering the Philippine Sea. Koga began to reorganize the fleet and draw up defense plans, but before he could act on these new strategies, he was killed in a plane crash in March, less than a year after Yamamoto's death. Admiral Toyoda Soemu now took command and placed his best combat vessels into an assault force, designated the First Mobile Fleet, with aircraft carriers at the center of its strength. Vice-Admiral Ozawa Jisaburō, a navy flier, was put in command. His unit included nine carriers, five battleships, four hundred and fifty carrier planes, and one thousand land-based planes that were stationed at various air bases in the islands. Toyoda believed that the Allies would advance unilaterally and he supposed that their protecting navy would come either from the northern coast of Australia toward the Philippines, or from the Caroline Islands toward Palau. The possibility existed that the advance might come past the Marianas, but those islands were fortified to the last degree and the nearest enemy approach base was Eniwetok Atoll, nearly 1,000 miles to the east. Toyoda was confident that the Allied offensive would come from the South or Southwest Pacific, and accordingly he held the main part of his fleet in readiness off the southwestern coast of the Philippines. He believed that one major naval encounter could decide the supremacy of the seas, and with this in mind, he formulated a battle plan called Operation A.

On May 27, American assault troops landed on the tiny island of Biak just north of western New Guinea. The landing strip on this island would provide critical air mastery and Operation A depended to a great extent on land-based air support. In view of its strategic importance, the Imperial High Command decreed that the island must be recaptured. Ozawa was dispatched with his First Mobile Fleet, and planes from Japanese bases in the Carolines and the Marianas were rushed into action. Large numbers of these sorely needed aircraft were shot down, carrying with them their irreplaceable pilots.

Early in June, 1944, the electrifying news was radioed that the U.S. Fifth Fleet was moving across the Pacific Ocean and shaping course for the Marianas. Admiral Toyoda immediately pulled his warships out of Biak and sent the combined fleet to the Marianas to put Operation A into effect.

The enormous Allied task force steaming toward the Mariana Islands consisted of 535 combat ships, auxiliaries, and transports carrying 127,571 men. Its destination was the Japanese strongholds of Saipan, Tinian, and Guam. As the task force neared the Marianas, planes from the carriers began a series of saturation bombings that lasted from the 11th to the 13th of June. Shortly before the first marines went ashore on June 15, naval bombardments pummelled the shores of Saipan in preparation for their landing. By June 17, a beachhead was secured.

The defending Japanese force had thirty-two thousand men, but not all of them were fully armed. The lethal efficacy of American submarines had made it impossible to receive supplies. Nonetheless, the Japanese in Saipan were determined to hold out until Admiral Ozawa's First Mobile Fleet could counterattack under the strategy prescribed by Operation A. Ozawa's force was outnumbered in carriers and aircraft by about two to one, yet his ships were armed with newly designed planes that had longer range than the comparable American equipment. He hoped therefore to attack the American carriers before they could get within range of his fleet. He also banked on the support of land-based planes from nearby island airfields.

On June 19, Ozawa launched four major air attacks on the Allied task force. Intercepted by U.S. fighter planes, they all failed to accomplish their mission. At the same time American bombers attacked the Japanese airfield on Guam, destroying many of the land-based planes. American submarines then moved out against Ozawa's fleet, sinking his flagship "Taihō" and the carrier "Shōkaku." The Japanese fleet finally withdrew northward, but the tracking Allied task force soon came within range and administered a crushing blow, sinking one carrier and damaging four more. In the two-day engagement Ozawa had lost three carriers, had seen four more crippled, and 395 carrier planes downed or destroyed on deck. He had but thirty-five carrier planes left as he escaped to Okinawa. In all, the Japanese lost 476 aircraft, and 445 badly needed aviators. The United States had lost 130 planes and 76 airmen. Operation A was a disastrous failure.

Meanwhile, fighting on Saipan was ferociously intense with the Japanese troops desperately holding until the "invincible fleet" could come to their rescue. The Americans consolidated their beachheads and moved inland while the Japanese retreated to the hills with the civilian residents, and fought fiercely to the end, conducting *banzai* (suicidal) charges. On July 9, when the Allies announced the subjugation of Saipan, only one thousand of the thirty-two thousand Japanese troops remained. Identified among the dead was Admiral Nagumo, commander of the fleet that attacked Pearl Harbor, who had committed hara-kiri. Ten thousand civilian residents had also perished, many committing suicide with the soldiers who exhorted them against surrendering. "Men, women and children cut each others' throats, deliberately drowned, embraced death by any means they could. Parents dashed babies' brains out on the cliffs and then jumped over themselves; children tossed hand grenades to each other." [5] American casualties were also high: 3,426 dead and 13,099 wounded.

The Allied assault forces moved on to Tinian, $3\frac{1}{2}$ miles away. It was during the encounter over this island that the United States first used napalm, dropping tanks containing gasoline and this highly incendiary substance from fighter planes onto the defenders, who were dug in below. The island fell on August 2. Japanese losses were thirteen to one compared to Allied casualties. The campaign for Guam had started on July 21, and organized resistance by the Japanese ended by August 10, 1944. The Marianas invasion was over.

The defense of these islands cost Japan the terrible human toll of fifty thousand men lost. In addition, she suffered a strategically devastating blow. Saipan had been "the naval and military heart and brain of Japanese defense strategy." On Saipan now, and on Tinian, the United States engineers would construct the airfields from which deadly B-29 superbombers would fly over Tokyo and other cities. The first of these raids took off from Saipan on November 24, 1944. In August, 1945, two B-29 bombers would leave Tinian for the fateful flights to Hiroshima and Nagasaki. On Guam the Allies would establish the naval base that serviced a third of the Pacific fleet, enabling it to penetrate deep into the Japanese defense perimeter and cut the vital supply lines to the south.

---

[5] Morison, *op. cit.*, vol. 8, p. 338. For a vivid account of the grisly story of Saipan, see John Toland, *The Rising Sun* (New York: Random House, 1970), pp. 504–19.

THE TRANSFERENCE OF LEADERSHIP
FROM TŌJŌ TO KOISO

The fall of Saipan touched off a political crisis in Tokyo that led eventually to the fall of the Tōjō government. Senior statesmen Okada, Konoe, Hiranuma, and Wakatsuki, as well as other political leaders, were deeply dismayed as early as March, 1944, by the course of the war. Quietly they explored the possibility of removing Tōjō to pave the way for a negotiated peace. Anti-Tōjō feeling ran high among naval officers, many of whom were angered by the government's allocation of precious war matériel. They felt that Admiral Shimada, Minister of the Navy and naval chief of staff was merely Tōjō's pawn and consequently functioned much to the detriment of the navy's interests. Okada proposed that Shimada be replaced by Admiral Yonai. Opponents of Tōjō readily endorsed this demand because they viewed Shimada's ouster as the opening move to tumbling the Tōjō government. Prince Konoe also favored overthrowing the Prime Minister, but at the same time he observed that if the war should end unfavorably for Japan, it would be useful to have Tōjō (who was as much detested by the world as Hitler) around as Prime Minister to assume full responsibility, thus eliminating the possibility that the Emperor might be held liable.

Tōjō was, of course, aware of the critical nature of the situation, and soon after he assumed the post of chief of the army general staff he told a member of the staff to investigate ways in which the war might be ended. Then when Saipan fell he expressed to Prince Higashikuni a desire to resign, but was told that since he had started the war it was his responsibility to remain at his post until he found a satisfactory way to conclude it. There was, of course, only one way that would be considered satisfactory, and that was through victory. No one dared even speak of defeat.

The senior statesmen continued to press for Shimada's resignation until Tōjō finally decided to accede to their demands. At the same time he proposed that former premiers Yonai and Abe be added to the cabinet as ministers without portfolio, and that Minister of Commerce and Industry Kishi resign so as to make room for them. Tōjō believed that the presence of Yonai and Abe in the cabinet would neutralize the efforts of the senior statesmen to overthrow his government. Yonai, however, declined to join the cabinet. The Lord Keeper of the Privy Seal Kido, whose influence was considerable, now began to lean in favor of the anti-Tōjō faction. At this point Kishi challenged Tōjō by refusing to resign and calling for a dissolution of the entire cabinet. Faced with opposition from his own cabinet members, Tōjō relinquished his authority and resigned on July 18, 1944.

As Tōjō's successor the senior statesmen selected Koiso Kuniaki (1880–1950), governor-general of Korea. In order to lend support to their choice the statesmen persuaded Yonai to serve as his deputy. Koiso failed to win the complete support of the army, and was prevented from combining the post of Prime Minister with that of Minister of War as Tōjō had done. General Sugiyama became Minister of War, and many of Tōjō's followers continued to hold key posts in the war ministry.

Koiso immediately set about the task of implementing certain practical reforms. To coordinate the policies of the cabinet and the supreme command more effectively, he replaced the liaison conference with the Supreme Council for the Direction of the War, consisting of the Prime Minister, the ministers of war, navy, and foreign affairs, and the chiefs of the army and naval general staffs. The Supreme Council, however, soon proved as vulnerable to schism and rivalry as the liaison conference.

One of Koiso's chief concerns was to try to establish closer ties with Soviet Russia in order to prevent her from joining the Allied powers in the war against Japan. To this end, he attempted to mediate between Germany and the Soviet Union, but the Russian government would not agree to having a special emissary sent to Moscow, and Germany indicated she would not negotiate with the Soviets. On November 7, 1944, Stalin denounced Japan as an aggressor. In February, 1945, at the Allied summit meeting in Yalta, Stalin formally promised to enter the war against Japan after Germany's defeat. This pledge was not made in public at that time, but when in April the Soviet government announced that it would not renew the neutrality pact with Japan, the apprehension of the Japanese leaders was intensified.

Meanwhile, Koiso was seeking to settle the war with China, and he conferred with Miao Pin, an official of the puppet government in Nanking. Miao Pin claimed to have contacts in Chungking and volunteered to serve as a go-between. His reliability was questioned by Foreign Minister Shigemitsu, who, together with the army leaders, argued against working with him. Kido persuaded the Emperor to express opposition to the Miao Pin venture, thus placing Koiso in an awkward position. This, and the deteriorating war situation, contributed to the fall of his government.

THE BEGINNING OF THE END

No longer could the government hide the fact that the war had turned against Japan. On November 24, 1944, the first massive raid of B–29 bombers left Saipan for Tokyo, where a major aircraft factory was all but destroyed. Raids against aircraft plants in other cities followed. Then in March, 1945, the dreaded planes sought out not factories but people, and concentrated on fire-bombings of congested, inflammable cities in order to coerce Japan into surrendering. On March 9, 334 bombers from the Marianas flew over Tokyo and dropped 2,000 tons of incendiary bombs. The raid left 83,793 dead, 40,918 injured, and a million homeless. It also destroyed a quarter of the city. It was the most destructive air attack in history up to that time. Similar fire-bombings hit Nagoya, Osaka, and Kobe. The attacks continued for the remainder of the war and accounted for a large part of the devastation that Japan was to suffer. Before the end of the war, ninety-eight Japanese cities would be bombed and fire-bombed from the air or shelled by warships. On the average, these cities were 40 percent destroyed. Approximately 2,300,000 houses had gone up in smoke by the time it was all over, that is, about 20 percent of the habitations in all of Japan.

Almost one million Japanese soldiers were garrisoned in China during the war in the Pacific. On the whole they constituted an occupying rather than a fighting force although on the northern provinces Chinese Communist guerrillas created continuous harassment. In the spring of 1944, the Imperial High Command perceived that the supply routes between the north and the south were threatened by the presence in western China of Allied air bases. Fearing that even the home islands might be subject to attacks from that quarter, they accordingly broadened the front in China. The campaign accomplished little since most air attacks against Japan originated from Pacific island bases. Furthermore, broadening the front in China made guerrilla activities all the more difficult to contain.

By the summer of 1944, Japan's last fortifications stood in jeopardy. General MacArthur's Southwest Pacific forces were preparing to link with Nimitz's Central Pacific force, now under the immediate command of Admiral William F. Halsey. A massive offensive against the Philippines was the next objective. Japan's installations on these islands represented her last-ditch defenses for the precious cargo ships and tankers bringing oil and raw materials from the East Indies. In September and October, 1944, the remains of her outer defense perimeter crumbled as the Allied air, naval, and amphibious forces attacked Peleliu and Angaur in the Palau Islands and converted the bases into landing fields for American bombers. Japanese airfields on Mindanao and in the East Indies were repeatedly struck by bombers. Close to home, air and shipping installations on Formosa and the China coast were blown up by bombers from carriers and from the Allied bases in western China. Hundreds of Japanese planes were destroyed on the ground. American submarines stalked the sea lanes in search of ships bringing goods to Japan.

During one attack on Formosa, the Japanese naval and air forces succeeded in downing seventy-eight planes and damaging two cruisers, a negligible victory compared to the mountainous evidence of imminent defeat. The jubilant Japanese pilots, however, were convinced they had scored far more spectacularly and sent home highly exaggerated accounts of victory. As a result, the Imperial High Command abandoned its plan to await the Allied invasion at Luzon and resolved to confront Mac-Arthur at Leyte instead. To defend the home islands and to secure the bases on the Philippines, Formosa, and the Ryukyus, the strategists devised a master plan, Operation *Shō* (Victory).

THE BATTLE FOR LEYTE GULF

In mid-October 1944, the combined Allied invasion forces, with some seven hundred vessels, had gathered for the momentous assault on the Philippines. Before dawn of October 20, the entire invasion force had converged on Leyte Gulf, and throughout the early hours of the day, the surrounding beaches were strafed, bombed, and shelled in an implacable barrage. At 10 A.M. the first ground forces were ferried to the shore and by sundown more than sixty thousand Allied soldiers were on the beaches with one hundred thousand tons of supplies.

Without land-based planes and unable, through lack of fuel, to maneuver at sea, Japanese forces were powerless to prevent the Allied invasion at Leyte. Nevertheless, they were determined to contain it and save Japan from blockade. On October 18, 1944, the First Striking Force, commanded by Admiral Kurita Takeo, left its base at Lingga Roads near Singapore and moved to Brunei Bay on Borneo to refuel. On the 22d, it set forth across the Sibuyan Sea and headed for the Leyte Gulf. Among the warships under Kurita's command were the gigantic battleships "Musashi" and "Yamato." At dawn of the 23d, two American submarines guarding approaches to the Philippines sighted the fleet and loosed their torpedoes with incredible accuracy. Two heavy cruisers went down, including the flagship, and a third was disabled. Kurita escaped to a destroyer and thence to the "Yamato." On the 24th, American carrier-based planes attacked and sank the reputedly unsinkable "Musashi."

At the same time that Kurita was heading toward Leyte, a decoy unit of Admiral Ozawa's Mobile Fleet moved out of Japan's Inland Sea luring Halsey's Third Fleet away from guard service at the north side of Leyte. Operation Shō called for Kurita's force to move to this side of the island and enter the Gulf through San Bernardino Strait, now left unprotected by Halsey's departure. Simultaneously, Vice-Admiral Nishimura Shōji, backed up by Admiral Shima Kiyohide, was to come up from the south across the Sulu Sea and enter Leyte Gulf through Surigao Strait. These naval forces were to meet in Leyte Gulf—one from the north, two from the south—and together, in a great pincer movement, they were to destroy the invasion support ships. The battle evolved quite differently from the plan, however, as Nishimura's advance unit of the southern force was virtually destroyed at Surigao Strait. The American Seventh Fleet, commanded by Admiral Thomas C. Kinkaid, had been apprised of the approaching Japanese force and lay in wait for the enemy to emerge from the narrow passage of Surigao Strait. Thereupon two battleships and three destroyers were blown out of the water and a heavy cruiser and a destroyer were severely damaged. Admiral Shima, following Nishimura by a few miles, observed the disaster from afar and retired his element of the force from the fray. American ships and planes pursued the remainder of Nishimura's fleet, sinking the crippled cruiser, and then went after Shima's retreating forces and sank another cruiser and a destroyer.

Meanwhile, Admiral Kurita with a reduced force proceeded to the north side of Leyte. Radio contact was erratic among elements of Operation Shō, and Kurita was not aware that Halsey, with the powerful Third Fleet, had been successfully decoyed to the north. He had, however, received word that Nishimura was under deadly attack in Surigao Strait. Therefore, he proceeded with extreme caution through San Bernardino Strait. Near Samar Island he sighted from afar the outlines of ships that he guessed to be part of the Third Fleet. Halsey at that moment was in fact some 300 miles away, and Kurita, with his powerful though depleted warships, was within range of Leyte Gulf. The ships he espied actually were a small task force on patrol, and they were scarcely prepared for combat with so formidable a force. Kurita, however, far from recognizing his great advantage and conscious that he could not count on help either from his southern units or from the gutted airfields within range, maneuvered badly. Consequently, the smaller American force was able to send three of his heavy cruisers to the bottom while crippling a fourth. Kurita managed to sink one carrier and four destroyers. Thereupon, he withdrew, leaving the vulnerable cargo vessels in Leyte Gulf unmolested.

Halsey, whom Kurita thought he had encountered, had pursued Ozawa's decoy unit northward and had sunk four carriers and a destroyer. He was about to close in on the main unit of Ozawa's force with every expectation of overwhelming it, when he was informed of Kurita's presence in Leyte Gulf. He immediately turned south to engage him, but by the time he arrived, Kurita had already departed. In the course of four days of combat, the Japanese lost three battleships, four carriers, six heavy cruisers, three light cruisers, eight destroyers, and six submarines. Thereafter the Japanese navy was virtually nonexistent as an effective fighting force.

THE END OF THE FIGHTING

It was at this juncture that the Japanese sent the first of their suicide planes into battle. The idea of establishing units trained for this kind of combat was conceived by Vice-Admiral Ōnishi Takijirō, commander of the First Air Fleet in Manila, and inspired by the fierce code of military honor. The pilots, known as *Kamikaze* (Divine Wind), were trained to crashdive into enemy ships with planes loaded with high explosives.

The same spirit of self-sacrifice that motivated the suicide pilots now seized all combat forces with new fervor. The Japanese defending their home islands were expected to fight to the death, and many thousands of them did. For example, on Leyte, Japanese soldiers yielded the island inch by inch, and about eighty thousand of them died in the battle.

In January, 1945, the troops of the American Sixth Army landed at Lingayen Gulf and fought their way to Manila. They claimed the island on March 4, and thus MacArthur fulfilled his vow to return. The contest for the Philippines did not cease with Manila, however. On Luzon some 170,000 Japanese troops were entrenched under the command of General Yamashita, who had just been recalled from semi-exile in Manchuria to lead the final defense of the Philippines. By the end of June, the American Sixth Army had moved into all key points on Luzon but Yamashita fought on. Many of his soldiers starved to death in their isolated strongholds. American casualties in the Philippines from January to June, 1945, came to 8,140 killed, 29,557 wounded, and 157 missing. The Japanese lost through battle, starvation, and disease 250,000 men and 7,297 prisoners of war.

At the same time that MacArthur's forces battled through the Philippines, a segment of the Central Pacific force laid siege to the rock citadel of Iwo Jima. Bases on the Volcano Islands and the Bonin Islands were of great strategic importance to Japan's defense chain since they lay midway between the American B–29 base on Saipan and the Japanese home islands. From these bases Japanese planes could both intercept bomber missions before they reached Japan and conduct harassing raids over the Marianas. If the Americans were to capture an island in this region they would then have a base from which medium-range bombers and fighter escorts could operate over Japan. It would further provide a refuge for damaged bombers returning from Japan to Saipan.

On February 19, 1945, after seventy-four consecutive days of preliminary bombing, American marines stepped ashore on the lava beaches of Iwo Jima. The Japanese defenders fanatically resisted, and bitter fighting lasted a month. On March 16, the United States finally declared Iwo Jima secured, though pockets of Japanese soldiers concealed in labyrinthine tunnels remained to be dealt with one by one. Virtually the entire Japanese garrison died in battle. The conquest of Iwo Jima's 8 square miles cost the United States 6,821 lives and more than 19,000 wounded. Japanese dead numbered 22,500. Just two weeks later American fighter planes were already lifting off the airstrip at Iwo Jima on the first of countless missions of escort, accompanying B–29s to Japan.

The last bastion of Japanese defense was Okinawa, largest of the Ryukyu Islands. Long before the liberation of the Philippines was complete and even before the fighting ended on Iwo Jima, final plans had already been completed for the capture of Okinawa. Amphibious, naval, and air elements of the Central Pacific force massed for the offensive. The beaches that were designated for invasion were readily accessible for attack from Kyushu, southernmost of the Japanese home islands and only 350 miles north of Okinawa. Therefore, preparation for the invasion required intensive bombardment of the airfields on Kyushu and of the remaining Japanese navy in the Inland Sea. Retaliating Japanese aircraft bombed four American carriers, damaging the "Yorktown," "Enterprise," and "Wasp," and wholly disabling the "Franklin." Antiaircraft emplacements downed 116 American planes; but 528 of Japan's last aircraft were also destroyed.

On April 1, 1945, a vast landing force stood off the shore of Okinawa and the first companies of marines were ferried to the beach. They met little challenge. Deep in the rugged interior, however, some one hundred thousand defenders, entrenched in pillboxes, blockhouses, tunnels, and caves, awaited their advance. No longer capable of meeting the invaders on the beach, the Japanese were instructed to conserve ammunition until the enemy came close. They were pledged to prolong the defense as long as possible.

American troops swarmed across the 15 miles of beachhead, while at the same time in Kyushu the last vestiges of the Japanese army and navy charted a final desperate counterattack. On the 6th of April, 341 bombers accompanying 355 suicide planes took to the skies to seek out and destroy invasion supply ships and the warships guarding them. About two hundred Kamikaze pilots reached Okinawa, where 135 of them were downed by fighter planes and antiaircraft guns. Those that reached targets sank six vessels, including two destroyers, and damaged eighteen others.

Simultaneous with the air attack, the battleship "Yamato" with a deep-load displacement of 73,000 tons, escorted by eight destroyers and a cruiser, sailed out of the Inland Sea fueled with just enough oil for a one-way passage to Okinawa. There she would fire her guns into the beachholds until her ammunition was spent. En route, however, she was spotted and set upon by carrier planes. She withstood bombardment for two hours, but at noon on April 7, the colossal warship went to the bottom, her admiral lashed to her bridge. The "Yamato" alone lost about 2,500 men and officers, and the other warships over 1,100. Only four destroyers of the entire task force survived to limp back to port. Japan no longer had any surface fleet.

The vicious land battle for Okinawa raged into June. By then some 190,000 American soldiers had been debarked to oppose 77,000 Japanese and 25,000 Okinawan militiamen. The Japanese would not be subdued, and day by day the bloody attrition assumed more horrifying proportions. At the end of two months of combat, American soldiers had killed 62,500 Japanese. On June 22, 1945, the commanding general of Okinawa, General Ushijima Mitsuru, committed hara-kiri and official resistance ended. In the gruesome slaughter 110,000 Japanese soldiers and Okinawan militiamen died. It is estimated that some 100,000 Okinawan civilians also perished in the conflict. American casualties included 5,000 navy men killed by Kamikaze attacks and an equal number wounded; the army counted 7,374 dead, 31,807 wounded, and 239 missing. Thirty naval vessels had been sunk and 368 ships were damaged.

THE ECONOMICS OF WARFARE

The key factor that ultimately halted the progress of the war was not the numbers of Japanese dead, staggering though those figures were. Even after the carnage of Okinawa there were still Japanese soldiers to fill up regiments. The major single element in Japan's military defeat was the collapse of her economy. At the onset of the war she had stockpiles sufficient for a limited military engagement, during which time she was to appropriate the resources of Southeast Asia, especially Borneo and the Dutch East Indies. In comparing the raw materials necessary for waging warfare, it is estimated that in 1941 the United States had seventy-eight times the available resources that Japan had. Furthermore, most of Japan's supply of raw materials had to be obtained elsewhere. The Japanese planners knew that to prosecute a war for longer than two years they had to control the economic resources of Southeast Asia. Equally necessary, they had to be able to transport the raw materials back to Japan. For this, it was essential to control the sea lanes and to maintain adequate shipping tonnage. Early in the war the head of the cabinet planning board, Lieutenant-General Suzuki Teiichi, estimated that 3,000,000 tons of non-military shipping would be needed to maintain adequate war production. It was calculated that if Japan lost 1,000,000 tons of shipping the first year and 800,000 tons in the years following, the 3,000,000 level could be maintained by constructing 600,000 tons annually. The actual toll, however, was much heavier. Japanese shipping losses for the first year were 1,250,000 tons, the second year 2,560,000, and the third year 3,484,000.

In 1944, non-military shipping had fallen to 2,560,000 tons, and by the end of the war it was down to 1,560,000 tons. The drop in tonnage, of course, represented a steady dwindling of vital raw materials. Japan's stockpile of scrap iron and steel dropped from 4,468,000 metric tons in 1941 to 449,000 in 1944. More critical than these declines was the lack of crude and refined oil as stores dropped from 48,893,000 tons in 1941 to 13,816,000 in 1944 and to 4,946,000 in the first half of 1945. This fuel oil shortage virtually immobilized the Japanese navy by the end of the war. In April, 1945, of the five battleships still afloat, only the "Yamato" could be fueled for the battle of Okinawa. Coal stocks similarly diminished from 63,448,000 metric tons in 1941 to 51,746,000 in 1944 and then down to 11,003,000 in the first half of 1945. Bauxite, essential for the production of aluminum, dropped from a December, 1941, supply of 254,740,000 metric tons to 176,241,000 in June, 1944, and then down to 2,651,000 in December of that year.

The Japanese economy was doomed once the raw materials essential for industrial production were depleted and replenishment made impossible by the ever-tightening Allied blockade. Obviously, the manufacture of the tools of warfare halted; but even before access to essential materials was cut off, the Japanese economy failed to expand rapidly enough to match the vastly expanded wartime production that was going on in the United States. From 1940 to the peak war year of 1944, total output in Japan increased by only one-fourth whereas in the United States it increased by two-thirds. In the early years of the war, when one might expect a great surge in output, the Japanese gross national product increased only slightly. In 1942 it had increased by only 2 percent over 1940. During the same period in the United States it had grown by 36 percent.

In aircraft production, Japan increased her output from an index of 100 in 1940, to a peak of 339 in September, 1944; by July, 1945, however, the production fell 59 percent from the peak period. In the construction of naval vessels a 133 percent increase over December, 1941, was reached in September, 1943, but by the end of the war it had dropped 53 percent from the peak month. In the construction of merchant ships a 347 percent increase over December, 1941, was attained in September, 1944, but it dropped 81 percent from the peak month by July, 1945.

A comparison of the aircraft production figures of Japan with those of other nations during the four-year period between 1941–1944 shows what Japan was faced with. In this period she produced a total of 58,822 aircraft: Germany, however, built 92,656; England, 96,400; and the United States, 261,826.

Just as raw materials diminished and production slowed, so also did industrial manpower decrease during the last year and a half of the war. At the onset of the war 2,400,000 men were in the Japanese armed forces. By February, 1944, there were 3,980,000 men in uniform. This represented about 10 percent of the male population and 17 percent of the male working population. The figure for military personnel increased to 5,360,000 men at the end of 1944, and when the war ended there were 7,190,000 men in the armed forces. There was no overall plan to exempt skilled workers from the draft, so the quality of the labor force was continuously lowered. Women, students, and Korean laborers were mobilized to work in the factories to replace the men who were drafted, and consequently, per capita production lagged. In 1941, the average output in the Japanese steel industry was 54 tons of ingot steel per worker; in 1944, this average fell to 21 tons. In the coal industry, output per employee per year dropped from 164 metric tons in 1941, to 119 in 1944. In contrast, in the United States in 1941, the figure was 1,021 metric tons of coal per worker, and by 1944, this figure rose to 1,430.

Farming communities also suffered from serious shortages of help as farm workers left the villages for the factories. Coupled with the conscription of the male farmers, this left the work of cultivating the land largely in the hands of women, children, and old men. Actually the rice yield did not diminish during 1941–1944, but rice imports from the colonies and Southeast Asia did fall as a consequence both of the shipping lanes being severed by the Allied sea and air forces, and of the severe crop failures in Korea.[6] As a result, total rice imports fell to 30 percent of normal in 1944, and 11 percent of normal in 1945. A disastrous drop in domestic rice production occurred in 1945, when bad weather resulted in a yield 27 percent below that of 1944.

Sugar became acutely scarce after shipping from the mandated islands and Formosa was slowed by American submarines and planes. Per capita consumption of sugar before the war averaged 30 pounds per year, but by 1945, it was down to 3 pounds. The supply of fish, an important item in the Japanese diet, reflected the attrition of both fishermen and fishing boats as well as of the areas where they could safely venture. By 1945, the total supply of fish dropped 65 percent from the 1939 norm. During the war, food consumption in general was reduced to 1,782 calories per capita per day and 58 grams of protein, compared to the minimum requirement of 2,165 calories and 76 grams.[7]

---

[6] Japan had to import about 20 percent of her rice supply from Korea, Formosa, and Southeast Asia.

[7] The figures in this section have been taken primarily from Jerome B. Cohen, *Japan's Economy in War and Reconstruction* (Minneapolis, Minn.: University of Minnesota Press, 1949).

Textile production was drastically curtailed because wherever possible textile plants were converted to war production. In consequence, clothing of all sorts was scarce. All daily necessities, such as rice, milk, meat, and charcoal were rationed as well as cigarettes, matches, soap, paper goods, and footwear. This critical economic situation was aggravated by the intensive bombings that began to devastate the major industrial cities at the end of 1944.

THE FINALE

Immediately after the American troops landed on Okinawa, Prime Minister Koiso resigned. The senior statesmen and Kido chose as his successor a retired admiral and head of the Privy Council, Suzuki Kantarō (1867–1948), who had narrowly escaped assassination during the uprising of February 26, 1936. In the Suzuki cabinet, General Anami Korechika became Minister of War, Yonai remained as Minister of the Navy, and Tōgō, who was Foreign Minister at the time of Pearl Harbor, reassumed that post. The Suzuki cabinet may have been seen as a "peace cabinet" by some observers, but outwardly there were no changes in policy. In fact, the critics of the war continued to be harassed by the gendarmes.

The Japanese nation lost all hope of support from other governments as defeat followed defeat. On April 5, Molotov informed the Japanese ambassador in Moscow that the Soviet-Japanese neutrality pact would not be renewed and would be allowed to expire in a year. On May 7, Germany surrendered; henceforth the Allied might would concentrate upon the defeat of Japan. In mid-May, the Supreme Council for the Direction of the War soberly considered how they might prevent the Soviet Union from entering the war, cultivate her friendship, and seek a negotiated peace through Soviet mediation. The Minister of War strenuously objected to the last item, but the Supreme Council agreed to pursue the first two possibilities.

Despite all evidence of their dire plight the army was still determined to fight a decisive battle on the Japanese homeland and, if necessary, to continue the struggle until the last Japanese fell. It claimed 2,250,000 soldiers in uniform who, with the navy's 1,300,000 men, stood ready to fight for the home islands. About ten thousand airplanes, mostly converted training planes, were prepared for use in suicide attacks. On June 8, the imperial conference adopted the army's policy of defending the homeland to the bitter end, and for this purpose a national militia was to be organized. The conference also agreed to negotiate with the Soviet Union to prevent her from entering the war against Japan.

Many senior statesmen and influential subjects realized that the war was in fact lost, and privately they even discussed the need to declare an end to the fighting, but no one attempted to start a peace movement. At last, however, Kido, who had previously worked hand-in-glove with the militarists, concluded that the time had come to terminate the war before the army's policy of defending the homeland to the last Japanese became a reality. He was concerned above all about the preservation of the imperial court and the protection of the national polity. He proposed a plan by which the Emperor would call for a solution of the "current difficulties" by requesting the Soviet Union to act as a mediator. On June 22, the Emperor summoned the members of the Supreme Council and asked for approval of Kido's plan. Confronted with the imperial command, the army reluctantly agreed.

Soon after the mid-May decisions of the Supreme Council, Hirota, who was assigned the task of negotiating with the Soviet Union, had expressed to the Russian ambassador, Malik, Japan's desire to improve Soviet-Japanese relations. Once again, after the Supreme Council meeting of June 22, Hirota met with Malik, and this time he offered concessions in return for a nonaggression pact. Malik agreed to transmit the proposals to Moscow and suggested that further discussion be postponed until he received a reply from his government. More than once thereafter Hirota sought to make an appointment, but Malik repeatedly claimed to be ill and refused to see him.

Foreign Minister Tōgō then decided to send a special envoy to Moscow and, with the approval of the Supreme Council, he asked Prince Konoe to undertake the assignment. Konoe, although convinced that it was too late to talk of "peace with honor" or "a negotiated peace," nevertheless agreed to go. He was prepared to end the war on any terms so long as the imperial household and the national polity were preserved.

The Japanese ambassador to Moscow, Satō Naotake, was instructed to inform Molotov of Japan's desire to send Konoe as a special envoy. Molotov was busy preparing for an impending visit to Berlin so Satō saw the vice-foreign commissar, Lozovsky, and transmitted his government's message on July 13. On the 18th, Lozovsky responded by saying that the message was too general, and the purpose of Konoe's visit was not sufficiently apparent. Tōgō then instructed Satō to make it clear that the object of Konoe's visit was to ask the Soviet Union to extend its good offices to end the war short of unconditional surrender.[8] Satō saw Lozovsky on the 25th, and he asked him to transmit Tōgō's message to Molotov in Berlin. Stalin, however, was not interested in acting as

---

[8] Following the Casablanca Conference of January, 1943, President Roosevelt announced that the Allied nations had agreed to continue the war against the Axis powers until they surrendered unconditionally. This policy was reiterated in the Cairo Declaration of December 1, 1943. (See below, footnote 10.)

a mediator to end the war. At Yalta in February, he had secretly agreed to enter the war against Japan after the surrender of Germany in return for certain concessions.[9] Now while the Japanese foreign office was desperately trying to persuade the Soviet Union to act as a mediator to end the war, Soviet officials were making arrangements at Potsdam to enter the war against Japan.

The United States had deciphered the Japanese code and so it was aware of the efforts to persuade the Soviet Union to proffer its good offices. Indeed, Stalin had informed Truman about this but held that the Japanese proposal was a maneuver to prolong the war.

On July 26, the United States, Great Britain, and China issued the Potsdam Declaration calling upon Japan to end the war or face "prompt and utter destruction." The terms set forth were: (1) the elimination of the authority and influence of those who led the Japanese people into the path of world conquest; (2) the occupation of Japan until her war making powers were destroyed, and a new order of peace, security, and justice was established; (3) the implementation of the terms of the Cairo Declaration,[10] and limitation of Japansee sovereignty to Honshu, Hokkaido, Kyushu, Shikoku, and such minor islands as decided upon by the three powers; (4) the complete disarming of the Japanese military forces; (5) the punishment of war criminals, the removal of all obstacles to the development of democratic tendencies among the Japanese people, and the establishment of freedom of speech, religion, and thought, as well as respect for fundamental human rights; and (6) the restriction of Japanese industries to those activities that would enable her to sustain her economy and still permit the extraction of just reparations in kind, but that would not allow her to rearm. The declaration also stated that the occupying forces would be withdrawn as soon as these objectives had been accomplished, and a peacefully inclined, responsible government had been established. It concluded by asking the Japanese government to proclaim the unconditional surrender of all Japanese armed forces.

On July 27, the Supreme Council for the Direction of the War and the cabinet were convened to discuss the Potsdam Declaration. Foreign

[9] These were: (1) the preservation of the status quo in Outer Mongolia (that is, it was to remain in the Soviet sphere); (2) the restoration of the southern part of Sakhalin Island to Russia; (3) the internationalization of Dairen and the leasing of Port Arthur by China to Russia; (4) Sino-Soviet control of the Chinese Eastern Railroad and the South Manchurian Railroad; and (5) the transference of the Kurile Islands to Russia.

[10] The Cairo Declaration proclaimed that "Japan shall be stripped of all the islands in the Pacific which she has seized or occupied since the beginning of the First World War in 1914, and that all the territories that Japan has stolen from the Chinese, such as Manchuria, Formosa, and the Pescadores, shall be restored to the Republic of China. Japan will also be expelled from all other territories which she has taken by violence and greed."

Minister Tōgō opposed an outright rejection of the declaration, but, on the other hand, he did not openly advocate its acceptance. The chiefs of the general staff and the Minister of War favored its unequivocal rejection, but Tōgō persuaded the Supreme Council and the cabinet to postpone a response to the Allied proclamation until the Soviet Union replied to Japan's request for mediation. They agreed to inform the public of the Potsdam Declaration without any official comments. When the press broke the news on July 28, however, it reported that the government considered the declaration to be of no significance and that it planned to ignore it. That afternoon Prime Minister Suzuki held a press conference at the insistence of the military leaders, who argued that an unequivocal denunciation of the declaration was needed to sustain the morale of the troops. At the press conference Suzuki stated: "I consider the joint proclamation of the three powers to be a rehash of the Cairo Declaration. The government does not regard it as a thing of any great value; the government will ignore it. We will press forward resolutely to carry the war to a successful conclusion." [11]

The Allied powers interpreted this as an outright rejection of the Potsdam Declaration. The *New York Times* headlined the story: "Japan Officially Turns Down Allied Surrender Ultimatum." At this moment the United States government came to the grave decision to use the atomic bomb, which had just been perfected. From the start scientists and military advisers concerned with its development were sharply divided about its use. Weighing the possibility of a protracted war mile-by-mile over the Japanese home islands, President Harry S. Truman, who had succeeded Roosevelt in April, agreed to permit the use of the atomic weapon. On the morning of August 6, at 8:15, the bomber *Enola Gay* flew over the city of Hiroshima. The single bomb it carried was dropped on the central section of the city and exploded with a force equivalent to 20,000 tons of TNT. A white flash of blinding intensity and a searing heat wave emanated from the point of explosion. The huge mushroom cloud spread overhead while the city below was turned into a living inferno. One eyewitness recollected: "It was a horrible sight. Hundreds of injured people who were trying to escape to the hills passed our house . . . Their faces and hands were burnt and swollen; and great sheets of skin had peeled away from their tissues to hang down like rags on a scarecrow." [12] Another witness observed: "The sight of soldiers . . . was more dreadful than the dead people floating down the river. I came onto I don't know how many, burned from the hips up; and

[11] Quoted in Robert J. C. Butow, *Japan's Decision to Surrender* (Stanford, Calif.: Stanford University Press, 1954), p. 148.

[12] Michihiko Hachiya, *Hiroshima Diary*, trans. and ed. Warner Wells (Chapel Hill, N.C.: University of North Carolina Press, 1955), pp. 14–15.

where the skin had peeled, their flesh was wet and mushy. . . . And they had no faces! Their eyes, noses and mouths had been burned away, and it looked like their ears had melted off." [13] One survivor trying to help the afflicted reached down and "took a woman by the hands but her skin slipped off in huge, glove-like pieces. . . . He remembered uneasily what the great burns he had seen during the day had been like: yellow at first, then red and swollen, with the skin sloughed off, and finally, in the evening, suppurated and smelly." [14] And yet the injured bore their suffering with stoic dignity. Father Kleinsorge, a Catholic priest in Hiroshima, observed, "The hurt ones were quiet; no one wept, much less screamed in pain; no one complained; none of the many who died did so noisily. . . ." And when he "gave water to some whose faces had been almost blotted out by flash burns, they took their share and then raised themselves a little and bowed to him, in thanks." [15]

The victims of Hiroshima were some two hundred thousand dead, missing, and injured. Radiation sickness afflicted a considerable number who had seemingly escaped without injury. "Many people," recalled a doctor who was injured in Hiroshima, "who appeared to be healthy . . . were beginning to die with symptoms of vaginal bleeding, nose bleed, bloody sputum, bloody vomitus, and hemorrhages beneath the skin and in the tissues." [16] The city of Hiroshima itself was turned into a wasteland; over 80 percent of the buildings were destroyed.

Even this horrendous disaster failed to shake the determination of the militarists to continue the war and fight the foe on Japanese soil. Civilian leaders such as Tōgō, however, realized that the war must be ended at once. Before the leaders could assess the true significance of the atomic raid on Hiroshima, however, Soviet Russia declared war on Japan on August 8, 1945, fulfilling Stalin's Yalta pledge and complying with Truman's request. On the 9th, Russian troops entered Manchuria, once the stronghold of the Kwantung Army but now weakened by the withdrawal of the bulk of the troops to the homeland.

On the morning of August 9, the Supreme Council met to discuss and reevaluate the Potsdam terms now that Russia had entered the war. Suzuki, Tōgō, and Yonai favored accepting the terms with only the one proviso that the national polity, that is, the imperial household, was to be preserved. Minister of War Anami, along with Umezu, the army chief of staff, and Toyoda Soemu, the naval chief of staff, insisted that in addition to the preservation of the national polity the following considerations be set forth: (1) Japan proper was not to be occupied; (2)

[13] *Ibid.*

[14] John Hersey, *Hiroshima* (New York: Knopf, 1946), p. 49.

[15] *Ibid.*, p. 60.

[16] Hachiya, *op. cit.*, p. 69.

the Japanese forces abroad were to be withdrawn and disarmed by the Japanese themselves; and (3) war criminals would be tried by the Japanese themselves. In the midst of this meeting the news arrived that the city of Nagasaki had suffered atomic attack and was even then ablaze with the same infernal fire that had swept Hiroshima. Later it would be ascertained that thirty-five thousand people had been killed, sixty thousand injured, and five thousand lost without trace. It was also announced at the meeting that on that same morning a Soviet army had invaded Manchuria. The military leaders refused, even in the face of all this overwhelming news, to modify their demands, and the meeting ended in a deadlock.

Later in the day the cabinet convened to discuss the terms of the Potsdam Declaration. Here, too, the army refused to retreat from its position. Suzuki decided to call upon the Emperor to make the final decision. An imperial conference was called around midnight, and after both sides presented their views, the Emperor expressed his agreement with the advocates of peace and called for the acceptance of the Allied terms and the termination of the war

The decision to accept the Potsdam Declaration with the proviso that "the said declaration does not comprise any demand that prejudices the prerogatives of His Majesty as a Sovereign Ruler" was sent to the Allied nations through the Swiss and Swedish governments. The Allied response, in effect the American response, to the Japanese statement regarding the prerogatives of the Emperor was: "From the moment of surrender the authority of the Emperor and the Japanese government to rule the state shall be subject to the Supreme Commander of the Allied powers. . . ." It also stated that "the ultimate form of government of Japan shall, in accordance with the Potsdam Declaration, be established by the freely expressed will of the Japanese people." [17]

The statement was drafted by Secretary of State James F. Byrnes, who believed that the United States, not Japan, should set the terms. At the same time, he also wanted to make it possible for the Japanese to accept them. Hence, the imperial institution was to be allowed to remain, but it was to be subject to the authority of the supreme commander.

The reply placed the Japanese peace advocates in a difficult position because it failed explicitly to uphold the prerogatives of the Emperor, and it was feared that this could provide the militarists with an excuse to reject the Potsdam Declaration. However, Matsumoto Shunichi, the vice-minister of foreign affairs, and Sakomizu Hisatsune, the chief cabinet secretary, convinced Suzuki and Tōgō that the American response,

[17] Raymond Dennett and Robert R. Turner, eds., *Documents on American Foreign Relations, 1945–1946* (Princeton, N.J.: Princeton University Press, 1948), vol. 8 pp. 107–108.

that is, the Byrnes rider, was satisfactory, and that it in no way conflicted with the national polity.

The military leaders objected vehemently. The two chiefs of the armed forces appealed directly to the Emperor to reject the Allied terms. Moreover, Minister of War Anami and Privy Council President Hiranuma nearly convinced Suzuki that the response of the United States violated the national polity. Tōgō managed to enlist the support of Lord Keeper of the Privy Seal Kido, who persuaded Suzuki to accept the foreign offices' interpretation of the Byrnes rider.

The Supreme Council met on August 13, and the old division remained, with the Minister of War and the two chiefs of the armed forces contending that the term "subject to" meant "subordinate to" not "restricted by," and the foreign office arguing that such subordination was not intended. The military leaders also maintained that allowing the freely expressed will of the people to determine the form of government would conflict with the national polity. Again an impasse ensued. The issue was once again passed on to the cabinet, which, as on the previous occasion, failed to resolve the disagreement. Suzuki now petitioned Emperor Hirohito to make the final decision. On August 14, an imperial conference was held, and the issues were argued again. After listening to the military leaders' arguments against accepting the Byrnes note, the Emperor finally spoke, saying that he could no longer allow his people to suffer death and destruction. He asked his officials to endure the unendurable, that is, to accept the Allied terms and end the war. He declared his intention to broadcast his decision to the people on the following day. Upon hearing his words, the opposition of the military leaders was immediately withdrawn. However, as word spread through the army, a hard core of fanatical middle-grade officers interpreted the decision as a betrayal and plotted a desperate coup d'état to rescue the Emperor from "evil advisers." The vice-chiefs of the two services were also irreconcilably opposed to surrender. The vice-chief of the naval general staff, Ōnishi, originator of the corps of Kamikaze pilots, argued that Japan should be ready to sacrifice twenty million lives in a Kamikaze attack to win the war. The coup d'état failed when key generals refused to lend their support. Minister of War Anami was sincerely opposed to the surrender, but he would not defy the Emperor. General Umezu, chief of staff of the army, also rejected the planned coup. The commanding general of the First Imperial Guard Division, Mori Takeshi, refused to fall in with the plotters, and they murdered him on the spot. At length, the commanding general of the Eastern District Army, Tanaka Seiichi, took steps to quell the rebellion. The plan by the rebels to prevent the imperial broadcast from being made was also foiled.

In the early hours of August 15, General Anami committed hara-kiri in true samurai fashion, leaving the words, "Believing firmly that our sacred land shall never perish, I—with my death—humbly apologize to the Emperor for the great crime." [18] Among other high-ranking officers who committed suicide were General Sugiyama, General Tanaka Seiichi, General Honjō, and Vice-Admiral Ōnishi. More than five hundred military and naval personnel committed suicide following the surrender.

On August 15, 1945, the people of Japan heard the voice of their Emperor for the first time as he broadcast his decision to terminate the war. On September 2, the instrument of surrender was signed on board the battleship "Missouri" in Tokyo Bay with General Umezu representing Japan and General MacArthur, the Allied powers. Thus ended the costliest venture Japan had ever embarked upon, a dire calamity for Japan as well as for the victims of her aggression. The suffering inflicted upon the victims of Japanese imperialism remains incalculable. According to the estimates of the Nationalist government of China, the number of Chinese soldiers killed and wounded since the start of the China Incident came to about 5,620,000. Chinese civilians that were killed and injured in the occupied areas was estimated at 350,000, and the victims of air raids at 760,000. Property damage suffered by the Chinese was calculated at 29.42 billion prewar Chinese yüan.[19]

There were some significant, though indirect, consequences of Japanese imperialism. For instance, the triumph of the Communists in China was made possible in part by the Japanese invasion, which weakened the Nationalist government and created political, economic, and social conditions that fostered the spread of Communism. It is equally true that the independence of the Southeast Asian nations from European colonial powers was facilitated by the defeat of these powers by the Japanese during the early phase of the war in the Pacific.

Japanese casualties from the outbreak of the war in the Pacific to 1945 included for the army: 350,000 dead (200,000 of whom died in banzai charges), 146,000 wounded, and 4,470,000 sick (of whom 40,000 died). The casualties for the navy included: 157,000 dead and 1,400 missing. The victims of air raids numbered 240,000 dead and 310,000 injured. Over 2 million houses were completely burned while 110,000 were damaged. The death and destruction, brutalities and atrocities, and hardships and agonies resulting from the war proved once again, as has been demonstrated throughout history, that the factor most responsible for the miseries of mankind is man himself.

At the end of the war all the major cities of Japan, except for Kyoto, which was spared by the United States because of its historical and cul-

---

[18] Quoted in Butow, *op. cit.*, pp. 219–20.
[19] At that time, one hundred yüan was worth approximately thirty dollars.

tural value, lay in waste. The economy was at a virtual standstill; there was an acute shortage of food, housing, and all basic necessities. In the midst of this the people awaited the arrival of the occupation forces with fear and trepidation.

CHAPTER 21

THE POSTWAR
YEARS: REFORM
AND RECONSTRUCTION

THE MACARTHUR ERA

The aftermath of war and defeat found Japan in an appalling condition. Most of her major cities lay in ruins. Tokyo had lost 57 percent of its dwellings and Osaka about 60 percent. Nationally about 20 percent of the houses had been destroyed by the air raids. The transportation system, telephones, power plants, and other utilities were on the verge of breaking down, having been used to the limit without replacements during the war. United States air attacks had destroyed 30 percent of Japan's industrial capacity, 80 percent of her shipping, and 30 percent of her thermal power. At the end of the war industrial production stood at scarcely 10 percent of the normal prewar level. In January, 1946, it was still severely depressed and had climbed to only 18.3 percent. For the entire year of 1946, it remained at 30.7 percent of 1934–1936.

Territorially Japan was now back to where she was when Commodore Perry first arrived. She was compelled to relinquish Formosa, the Pescadores, Korea, and southern Sakhalin. The Kuriles were now occupied by the Soviet Union and the Ryukyus were placed under American administration. Millions of soldiers and civilians from these areas and from the Asian mainland and Southeast Asia began to return to the already crowded Japanese islands.

The immediate problem and truly a matter of life and death for the urban dwellers was the food shortage. Bad weather had caused rice pro-

Two aerial views of Tokyo: left, the center of the city in August, 1945, at the end of World War II; right, downtown Tokyo today. Left, courtesy of the Ministry of Foreign Affairs, Japan; right, courtesy of the Consulate General of Japan, New York.

duction to drop 27 percent below that of 1944, and about 32 percent below the prewar average. Having lost her colonial possessions, Japan could no longer obtain additional food from Korea, Formosa, or Manchuria. The fishing industry, which she had relied upon as a major source of food, had also deteriorated and was about 40 percent below normal. Official food rations for each person per day came to 1,050 calories. The chief preoccupation of the urban dwellers was to scurry about in search of additional food. They scoured the black market or went out into the villages to acquire sweet potatoes from the farmers, a venture that frequently ended without success. If a person obeyed the law and abstained from getting food through the black market, he was apt to starve to death. One such man of principle, a judge in a Tokyo

court, died of malnutrition in November, 1947, but he left behind a diary in which he had written,

> The food control law is a bad law. But as long as it is the
> law of the land we must observe it strictly. Regardless of how
> much agony it causes me I will not buy food in the black
> market. I have decided to fight the black market and accept
> death by starvation. I live each day in the presence of
> death.[1]

Mass starvation of the Japanese people was avoided, however, by the American occupation authorities, who began transporting food to the country after the spring of 1946.

[1] Quoted in Tsurumi Shunsuke *et al.*, eds., *Nihon no Hyakunen* (*The Hundred Years of Japan*), 10 vols. (Tokyo: Chikuma Shobō, 1961–1964), vol. 2, pp. 301–302.

The shortage of basic necessities and the issuance of an excessive amount of currency caused the development of a serious inflation in the economy. In 1945, the amount of currency in circulation was fourteen times greater than that of 1937, and by 1949, it was six and a half times greater than it had been in 1945. The occupation authorities sought to impose price controls and curtail the flow of currency, but the cost of living continued to rise by about 10 percent each month for about two years. The wholesale price index in 1945 was three and a half times that of 1934–1936, and in December, 1949, it was 212.8 times; the consumer price index during the same period rose 240 times the prewar level. Eventually the yen, which was worth about 25 cents before the war, was fixed at 1/360 of a dollar.

In the throes of a virtually collapsed economy, and under a politically impotent government, a thoroughly bewildered and apprehensive Japanese people awaited the arrival of the occupying forces. To prepare for the unprecedented event, Prince Higashikuni (1887–   ) was appointed Prime Minister immediately after the termination of the war. On August 28, 1945, the first contingent of the occupying troops arrived at Atsugi airforce base outside of Tokyo. On the 30th, General MacArthur, who was appointed the Supreme Commander of the Allied Powers as well as the commander of the American military forces in the Far East, arrived at Atsugi. Corncob pipe in hand and dressed casually in his work clothes the new ruler of Japan stepped off his plane. Thus began the occupation of Japan, which was to last until April 28, 1952.

General MacArthur was supposedly acting on behalf of the Allied powers, the policies of which were theoretically formulated by the eleven-member Far Eastern Commission. In fact, however, the United States government held the truly decisive power. If, for example, the commission failed to agree on a matter of policy, the United States was empowered to issue "urgent unilateral interim directives." There was also an advisory council in Tokyo, the Allied Council for Japan, consisting of the representatives of the United States, the British Commonwealth, the Soviet Union, and China, but it had little real influence over General MacArthur. Essentially, it became primarily a forum in which the Soviet Union berated American occupation policies. The strong personality of General MacArthur tended to make the occupation of Japan a one-man show. His forceful leadership, self-assurance, dignified bearing, sense of mission, and sound political sense won him the respect of the Japanese and made his "reign" a highly successful one.

Contrary to the expectations of some Americans who had been impressed by the fanaticism of the soldiers of the imperial army, the Japanese people cooperated willingly with the occupation authorities, and, in fact, the initial period was characterized by a remarkable degree of harmony. The Emperor's acceptance of defeat and his submission to the Allied authorities of course made it easier for the people to do likewise. Moreover, the Japanese were conditioned to bow to authority and accept the established order of things. In times of extreme stress they might resort to desperate actions of fanaticism, but under normal circumstances the Japanese show themselves to be a highly practical people who are very rational and sensible, as well as friendly, cooperative, and courteous. The defeat and devastation of war swept away the self-confidence and psychological props that had for so long supported the people. Now that these were suddenly knocked out from under them, they lacked the will to resist the conquerors. The defiance came as time passed and the Japanese regained their self-assurance. Then the demonstrations against the United States military bases started.

Cooperation with the occupying authorities was facilitated by the fact that the conquerors themselves displayed very little rancor and hostility toward the Japanese people. The general friendliness and spontaneous warmth manifested by the occupying troops made the relationship between the two peoples a relatively harmonious one. The United States military did not display the kind of pomp and ceremony and the overbearing haughtiness that had so frequently characterized the tyrannical rule of the Japanese military over conquered peoples. The ends pursued by the occupation authorities were not vengeance or exploitation; instead, reforms were sought that would enable Japan to achieve a free and democratic society. Even if some of the measures and methods used to realize these ends lacked good sense from the Japanese point of view, no other conquered people in history was treated more humanely and benefited more at the hands of its conquerors.

The task facing the Supreme Commander of the Allied Powers (SCAP) was the implementation both of the terms of the Potsdam Declaration and of the policy for Japan that was formulated by the United States departments of state, war, and navy, and approved by President Truman on September 6, 1945. It was the American policy that provided the guidelines for SCAP in introducing reforms in Japan. In theory the occupation authorities were not to function as a military government. SCAP was to exercise supervisory authority, while the task of governing the country was to be left to the Japanese government. In fact, however, there was no question but that the real power in Japan resided with SCAP, from whence all important directives emanated.

The initial tasks that SCAP had to attend to were the demobilization of the Japanese forces at home and the repatriation of the troops and residents abroad. The stupendous task of returning to Japan the 3,300,-000 troops and 3,200,000 civilians was more or less completed by the beginning of 1948. Those who had not been repatriated by then were mainly prisoners of war under Soviet control. In May, 1949, a total of 900,000 people had been repatriated from Soviet controlled territories still leaving, according to Japanese estimates, 420,000. The Soviet Union claimed they had only 105,000 more prisoners and returned 95,000 by the end of 1949. It is estimated that 55,000 persons died while in Soviet detention camps. In contrast to the Soviet performance, repatriation from China, where the largest contingent of Japanese overseas troops was located, was facilitated by the goodwill and magnanimity of Chiang Kai-shek, who told his fellow countrymen to cease regarding the Japanese as enemies and treat them as friends.

The military installations and equipment were destroyed, and what remained of the navy vessels, with the exception of those ships needed by the occupation forces to carry out their assignments, were divided among the four principal Allied nations. The trial and punishment of war criminals was undertaken by the Allied powers as part of both the demilitarization process and the implementation of the Potsdam Declaration. Two generals had already been tried and executed by ad hoc military courts immediately after the end of the war. These were Yamashita Tomoyuki and Homma Masaharu, who were held responsible for the atrocities committed by the Japanese troops in the Philippines.

The International Military Tribunal for the Far East was created by the Allied powers for the purpose of trying the political leaders who were responsible for "crimes against peace." Twenty-eight major or Class A war criminals were charged with "the planning, preparation, initiation, or waging" of aggressive war. Most of these men were also charged with violations of the laws and customs of war as well as crimes against humanity. The trial, presided over by eleven judges, was started on May 3, 1946, and was not concluded until April, 1948. The sentences were finally handed down in November of that year. Seven persons, including Tōjō, were sentenced to death by hanging; sixteen were given life imprisonment; one was given twenty years; one was given seven years; two died during the trial; and one went insane. Those who were hanged with Tōjō were generals Itagaki, Doihara, Matsui, (commanding general of the forces that assaulted Nanking), Mutō Akira, Kimura Heitarō (the Vice-Minister of War in the Konoe and Tōjō cabinets and the commanding general of the Japanese forces in Burma), and Hirota (the only civilian). Among those who were sentenced to life imprisonment were: Kido, Hiranuma, Araki, Koiso, Umezu, and Hashimoto. Former foreign ministers Tōgō and Shigemitsu were sentenced to prison for twenty and seven years, respectively. In 1957, the sentences of war criminals of all classes who had been tried in Tokyo were commuted. Many had died during incarceration, but some managed to return to play active political roles after their release.

Matsuoka, Admiral Nagano, and Ōkawa Shūmei were also charged as Class A war criminals, but the first two died and Ōkawa lost his sanity during the trial. Konoe committed suicide when he discovered that he was to be arrested. Tōjō also sought to commit suicide before his arrest but failed.

The question of trying the Emperor as a war criminal was raised but the idea was quashed by American officials who felt that if this were done it would make their task in Japan very nearly impossible. General MacArthur wrote: "I believe that if the Emperor were indicted and perhaps hanged as a war criminal, military government would have to be instituted throughout all Japan, and guerrilla warfare would probably break out." [2]

About twenty high-ranking military officers were charged as Class B criminals, that is, they were accused of violating the laws and customs of war and were charged with command responsibility for the troops who had committed atrocities. They were all acquitted. Lesser officers and soldiers were charged as Class C criminals, that is, they were accused of crimes against humanity, such as mistreatment of prisoners of war and minor atrocities. They were tried by military commissions under the United States Eighth Army and by the Allied military authorities where the crimes were committed. Approximately 4,200 persons were categorized as Class C criminals and of these about 400 were acquitted, 700 were executed, and the remainder were sentenced to prison. These proceedings were more or less completed by the fall of 1949.

In addition to trying and punishing war criminals, the occupation authorities, in accordance with the directives of the United States government, sought to remove from positions of responsibility and leadership all those who had been exponents or agents of militarism, aggression,

[2] Douglas MacArthur, *Reminiscences* (New York: McGraw-Hill, 1964), p. 288.

In *Japan's Imperial Conspiracy* (New York: Morrow, 1971), David Bergamini contends that the Emperor was the mastermind behind Japanese aggression in Manchuria and China as well as the instigator of the war against the West. If we were to accept this thesis we would have to ignore the roles played by many other persons and groups, as well as the political, economic, and psychological circumstances that led to these conflicts. Nonetheless, if the political considerations mentioned by General MacArthur were not present, the Allied powers would no doubt have brought the Emperor to trial as a war criminal. It is true that the image of the Emperor as a peacemaker has been blown up and that the question of his complicity in the aggressive actions taken by the Japanese military and political leaders has been avoided, but to suggest, as Bergamini does, that there is a conspiracy of silence among the Japanese on this matter is untenable. The imperial system has come under harsh criticism by certain intellectual and political groups in postwar Japan, and they would be the first to denounce the Emperor if concrete evidence could be uncovered that he was in fact the chief culprit, as Bergamini asserts.

The legal and historical bases of the Tokyo trial are questioned by Richard Minear in *Victors' Justice: The Tokyo War Crimes Trial* (Princeton, N.J.: Princeton University Press, 1971), which was published almost concurrently with Bergamini's book.

and militant nationalism. This entailed the purging of all army and navy officers as well as most of the high government officials and leaders of business and industry. The SCAP directive ordering the Japanese government to implement these investigations of undesirable individuals was issued in January, 1946, and by May, 1948, some 220,000 persons, including 180,000 former military officers, had been purged. These men endured forced inactivity for six years or more.

Initially SCAP had adopted a policy of having Japan pay reparations in the form of industrial equipment to the nations that had been victimized by her imperialism. This course of action, however, was terminated in May, 1948, because it conflicted with the policy aimed at stabilizing the Japanese economy and helping it to become self-sufficient. Reparation arrangements were made by Japan with several Asian nations after she regained her independence. By April, 1964, she had paid $477 million as reparations to six Southeast Asian nations.

In addition to the punitive measures that were taken, the occupation authorities introduced radical changes in the economic, educational, and political fields in order to foster and strengthen democratic forces in Japan.

ECONOMIC REFORMS

To encourage the rise of democratic elements by effecting a wider distribution of income and the ownership of the means of production and trade, the United States policy statement of September 6, 1945, directed SCAP "to favor a program for the dissolution of the large industrial and banking combinations which had exercised control of a great part of Japan's trade and industry."

The first step in the plan toward "zaibatsu busting" was to require the key holding companies of the zaibatsu to dispose of their stocks to the general public. An antimonopoly law was also passed prohibiting such things as trusts, cartels, interlocking corporate controls, and agreements in restraint of trade. The third step of the plan was the most controversial. It involved the enactment of the Law for the Elimination of Excessive Concentration of Economic Power.

A commission under SCAP was given the authority to dissolve any company that it regarded as being too big or monopolistic. It was reported that the commission had in mind the dissolution of about twelve hundred companies but the program aroused considerable opposition among American business and political leaders who complained that the plan was socialistic and as such would retard the economic recovery of Japan. As a result a review board was created in May, 1948, to reexamine the program and eventually the number of companies destined for dissolution was reduced from twelve hundred to nine. Nonetheless, eighty-three zaibatsu holding companies were broken up and about five thousand other companies were forced to reorganize by means of the deconcentration and antimonopoly laws. The Mitsui and Mitsubishi organizations, for example, were fragmented into two hundred and forty separate firms. The effort to eliminate big business combines turned out to be the least enduring of the occupation reforms since most of the old zaibatsu firms reunited, albeit in a looser form, after SCAP departed. The mergers increased with the rapid economic growth of the late 1950s and 1960s.

The land reform program was another economic measure designed to bring about a more equitable distribution of wealth, and it turned out to be much more effective than zaibatsu busting. In fact, it was perhaps the most successful reform measure implemented by SCAP. At the end of the war, 70 percent of the farmers were tenants or had to rent some land to augment what they owned. About 46 percent of the cultivated land was tenanted, but there were, however, no gigantic landowners. Only about two thousand landlords owned as much as 100 acres; most individuals owned no more than 10 acres.

Under the direction of SCAP, the Diet passed the Farm Land Reform Law in October, 1946. This law prohibited absentee landlordism. A landlord who lived in the community where he owned his land could hold a maximum of 2½ acres. An active farmer could own a maximum of 7½ acres for his own use plus an additional two and a half acres that he did not cultivate. The government purchased the land from the landowners and sold it to former tenants, who were required to repay the government over a thirty-year period at an interest of 3.2 percent. The transfer of land was managed by thirteen thousand locally elected land commissions.

The rapid growth of inflation and the consequent decline in the value of money between the time when the amount of compensation was determined and the time when the transaction was actually completed resulted in a situation in which the landowners ended up receiving practically no compensation. In some instances the price per acre that was paid to the landowners was the same as the cost of a carton of cigarettes on the black market. This, of course, made it possible for any tenant, no matter how impoverished, to purchase his share of land. The transfer of land was completed by August, 1950, and about 2.8 million acres of rice land and 1.95 million acres of upland had been purchased from 2.34 million landowners and resold to 4.75 million tenants and farmers who possessed less land than the legal maximum. Only 12 percent of all arable land remained under tenancy, and low rents were fixed by law on this land. The percentage of full tenants dropped from 27.7 percent of the farmers in 1941 to about 5 percent in 1950. In addition, 600,000 acres of pasture land were acquired by the government for redistribution.

Another feature of the United States' policy of strengthing democratic forces and effecting a more equitable distribution of wealth was the attempt to foster an independent trade-union movement in Japan. A number of labor laws were enacted by the Japanese Diet at the instigation of SCAP. In particular, a trade-union law was passed in December, 1945, that guaranteed workers the right to organize, engage in collective bargaining, and strike. In 1946, legislation was enacted to set up grievance procedures for the settling of labor disputes, while at the same time denying public-safety and administrative employees the right to strike. In 1947, a labor law was enacted that set minimum standards for working hours, vacations, safety and sanitation safeguards, sick leaves, accident compensation, and restrictions on the hours and conditions under which women and children could work.

It was thus through the paternalistic policies of SCAP that the workers acquired the protection and rights that had been denied them under the old regime. The number of unions and union members mushroomed by virtue of these sanctions, and by 1949 more than six and a half million out of a total of fifteen million industrial workers were enrolled in the more than thirty-five thousand unions. A drop in membership occurred when the unions began engaging in controversial political activities, but it began to rise again in the 1950s. In 1969, there were close to fifty-nine thousand unions with a combined membership of more than eleven million workers.

EDUCATIONAL REFORMS

Educational reforms were initiated in order to remove militaristic and ultranationalistic influences from the schools and to inculcate democratic values in the students. In March, 1946, an educational mission headed by George D. Stoddard submitted a report to SCAP that called for the purging of militaristic, ultranationalistic teachers, a revision of textbooks, and numerous changes in the curriculum. It also recommended the extension of compulsory education to nine years; decentralization of control; establishment of more institutions of higher learning; and fundamental revision of the basic educational program, which stressed rote learning, to one that would encourage students to think by responding to new situations and by taking the initiative in exploring new ideas.

Changes in the educational system were introduced on the basis of the Stoddard report. The school system was reorganized in accordance with the American 6-3-3-4 (elementary, junior high, senior high, and college) system instead of the former 6-5-3-3 (elementary, middle, higher, and college) system. Control of the public elementary and secondary schools was turned over to locally elected boards of education. Prefectural boards, which were elected by the people, were established to coodinate the educational program within each prefecture, to certify teachers and administrators, and to approve all the textbooks. The control that the Ministry of Education formerly exercised was eliminated; it was to provide only technical aid and professional counsel to the boards.

To increase the facilities for higher education, sixty-eight national universities and ninety-nine other universities were newly established in 1949. The quality of many of these institutions, however, was poor because they formerly had been higher schools, normal schools, and technical institutions. Consequently, the prestige of the older institutions was enhanced even further, and this, of course, led to fierce competition among the young who wished to enter the esteemed institutions. Students underwent years of preparations and cramming to pass the entrance examinations of reputable schools like the University of Tokyo.

The radical changes introduced in the public school system created many problems because of the initial confusion that was caused by the changeover, the lack of funds to construct the necessary facilities, and the scarcity of qualified personnel and board members. Japanese educators also complained that the positive aspects of the former system had been hastily ignored in an effort to achieve a wholesale transplantation of an alien system. They also argued that the changes produced lower educational standards, and that the introduction of the one-track system (effected by eliminating the former technical schools) hindered those students who were apt to benefit more from a good technical education than from a general education program. These Japanese educators further contended that the incorporation of the philosophy of the progressive educationists in the school system reduced education merely to the science of life adjustment. Nevertheless, the educators did agree that in general the freer atmosphere in the schools and the emphasis on "independent thought and initiative and on developing a spirit of inquiry" was beneficial.

Part of the postwar changes was the emergence of a new force in the educational field. This was the Japan Teachers Union (*Nihon Kyōshokuin Kumiai*), a militant labor union strongly influenced by left-wing political sentiments. It has to the present kept a watchful eye over any trend that might presage a reversion to the former ways of imperial Japan. The militancy of the union leaders was heightened by the government's campaign in 1949 to remove all Communists from the school system. At the college level, another powerful political force emerged in the form of student organizations. The National Student Federation

(*Zengakuren*), which was organized in September, 1948, provided forceful leadership in staging political demonstrations to combat whatever it deemed as being antidemocratic.

POLITICAL REFORMS

The most significant efforts at democratization of the Japanese nation occurred in the political realm. In this area the United States set the following objectives: eliminate the power of the Emperor; make the executive power of the government responsible to the people or their representatives; establish a legislative body that would be directly responsible to all adult citizens; and develop democratically controlled political parties.

On an official level it was claimed that the new constitution was drafted by the Japanese government, but in actuality it was written by the officials of SCAP on the basis of a directive formulated early in 1946 by the United States departments of state, war, and navy. The Japanese had in fact been working on their own version but it was rejected by SCAP as being too reactionary. The power of the Emperor, for example, had not been reduced at all. The draft that was prepared by SCAP, although it disturbed many of the Diet members who wished to retain the Meiji constitution, was finally passed and proclaimed the law of the land on November 3, 1946. It went into effect in May, 1947.

The new constitution changed the identity and role of the Emperor from that of an absolute monarch to "the symbol of the State and unity of the people." Sovereignty was now vested in the people. The cabinet was made directly responsible to the Diet, which was made "the highest organ of state power." The members of the two houses were to be elected directly by the people. The upper house (House of Councillors) was given less power than the lower house (House of Representatives), which could override a negative vote in the House of Councillors by passing a bill a second time with a two-thirds majority.

An extensive listing of the rights of the people is included in the new constitution. In addition to the rights and liberties provided for in the American Bill of Rights, the Japanese constitution has provisions concerning social welfare. It states that "All people have the right to maintain the minimum standards of wholesome and cultured living. In all spheres of life, the State shall use its endeavors for the promotion and extension of social welfare and security, and of public health." It also guarantees the following: the people's right to an education; the right of labor to organize and engage in collective bargaining; and the equality of husband and wife. The constitution provides for full legal protection against arbitrary arrest and punishment. In other words, rule-of-law had finally become a reality in Japan.

In order to bolster the bill of rights, a law on habeas corpus was enacted in 1948. The judiciary was made independent of the Ministry of Justice and the Supreme Court was given the responsibility of supervising the lower courts. The concept of judicial review was also introduced, and the Supreme Court was made "the court of last resort with power to determine the constitutionality of any law, order, regulation or official act." The structure of the courts remained largely unchanged except for differences in appellation. The Court of Administrative Litigation was abolished, thus making it necessary to take disputes involving government agencies to the regular courts. The jury system, which was adopted in the early twenties as an option given to the defendant, was seldom used and consequently it was not incorporated into the new judicial system.

A unique feature of the new constitution is article nine, the "no-war clause:

> Aspiring sincerely to an international peace based on
> justice and order, the Japanese people forever renounce
> war as a sovereign right of the nation and the threat or use
> of force as means of settling international disputes.
>
> In order to accomplish the aim of the preceding paragraph,
> land, sea and air forces, as well as other war potential, will
> never be maintained. The right of belligerency of the State
> will not be recognized.

This article of the constitution later proved to be an embarrassment to the Japanese government and the United States, who, in the course of the growing tension between herself and the Communist powers, began to favor a rearming of Japan. Consequently, a tortuous reinterpretation of the clause condemning war was made to enable Japan to establish "self-defense" forces.

Changes were also introduced on a local level so as to strengthen the autonomy of local government and to foster democratic tendencies. The authority that the Ministry of Home Affairs formerly exercised over local governments was removed. The prefectural governors, who formerly were appointed by the central government, are now elected by the prefectural voters. The governors can no longer override the prefectural assemblies, to which they are now responsible. In the town and village governments fewer changes were necessary because they already had a greater degree of autonomy than the prefectural governments. The mayors are now elected directly by the voters rather than by the town or village assemblies as had been the rule before. In addition, the principles and procedures of referendum, initiative, and recall were introduced at the municipal and prefectural levels.

Significant reforms were also introduced in the police system. In 1947, a police reorganization law was enacted to decentralize the police, which formerly was under the authority of the Ministry of Home Affairs and its agents, the prefectural governors. Municipalities with a population of more than five thousand were required to maintain their own police force. A small national rural police force, under the control of a five-man National Public Safety Commission, was created for less populated rural areas. In a national emergency the Prime Minister has the right to assume operational control of both the rural and local police, subject to approval of the Diet within twenty days. Efforts were made to inculcate democratic values among the police to expunge the arrogant, overbearing attitude commonly manifested by the former police force.

Other changes on behalf of democracy included the introduction of universal suffrage in April, 1946. Women were given the right to vote, and the voting age was lowered from twenty-five to twenty. On New Year's Day of 1946, even before the constitution limited the role of the imperial throne, Emperor Hirohito, with the encouragement of SCAP, officially announced the fact that he was not divine. The Emperor also began more and more to come out of his closely guarded palace in an effort to mingle with the people.

The ties between the government and Shinto shrines were also severed. SCAP prohibited the teaching of Shinto doctrines in the schools and abolished state control and support of Shinto shrines. In addition, another pillar of imperial authority, the peerage, was eliminated. As a result, 913 families ranging from barons to princes lost their special status and privileges.

In the domain of social reforms, the most significant legal changes occurred in the family system, in particular in the status of women. The equal right of the wife with her husband was guaranteed; the wife was given the right to own property independently; and she gained the right to divorce her husband on the same grounds that he could appeal to in divorcing her. Primogeniture was abolished and daughters were given the right to inherit the same share of the family property as sons. The authority formerly held by the head of the stem family was removed. Family registries were compiled on the basis of the nuclear, conjugal family. A male at the age of eighteen and a female at the age of sixteen could now marry without the consent of the parents. Legal changes, of course, did not bring about an immediate end to the old ways. Women continued to play a subordinate role in the family and the society, although it should be noted that in the first election in which women were allowed to vote and run for office, thirty-nine women representatives were elected to the Diet. In recent years, emancipated women have been playing an increasingly prominent role in all areas of the society.

Among the social reforms initiated by the Japanese was the anti-prostitution law of 1956, which finally removed the many brothels that had occupied fixed quarters of the towns and cities for centuries. Another movement that gained popular support was birth control, which resulted in the legalization of abortion in June, 1949. The campaign to limit birth has enabled Japan to reduce her birth rate drastically (see p. 594).

POLITICAL DEVELOPMENTS

The form of the Japanese government was retained under the occupation, but the cabinets and the Diet were merely handmaidens of SCAP until the peace treaty went into effect in April, 1952. The Higashikuni cabinet, which was established at the end of the war, was replaced by the Shidehara cabinet in October, 1945. Shidehara (1872–1951), who had fought the expansionists at the time of the Manchurian Incident, was at the head of the government until May, 1946, when his party came in second in the first postwar election held under the new provisions of universal suffrage. By this time the political parties had reemerged and 363 of them, including numerous one-man parties, contended for Diet seats. The Liberal party emerged as the front runner, but just as its leader, Hatoyama Ichirō (1883–1959), was about to become Prime Minister, he was purged by SCAP for his prewar and wartime activities. As a result, Yoshida Shigeru (1878–1967), a wartime peace advocate and the Foreign Minister in the Shidehara government, was persuaded by Hatoyama to fill in for him while he went into temporary retirement.

The new constitution was to come into effect in May, 1947, so SCAP ordered new elections in April of that year. The result of these was that the Socialist party emerged as the largest party, and its leader, Katayama Tetsu (1887–   ), formed a cabinet by effecting a coalition with the Democratic party, headed by Ashida Hitoshi (1887–1959). The first and, thus far, the only socialist government in Japanese history turned out to be wholly ineffective, and consequently, it fell in March, 1948, as Katayama was unable to keep the contending factions in the party together. He was replaced by Ashida, who presided over the same coalition, but his cabinet proved even more ineffective. It was beset by charges of graft and bribery and fell in October, 1948. These cabinets did not have any real power, so their rise and fall did not significantly alter the course of political developments in the country.

In October, the second Yoshida cabinet came into existence and the Japanese government began to assert itself more forcefully in its relationship with SCAP. Yoshida managed to remain in office for over six years, a longer term than any of his predecessors enjoyed. Under his leadership Japan gained her independence and began showing signs of an economic recovery which, in the years to follow, was to result in the most spectacular economic growth in her history.

In the elections of January, 1949, Yoshida's Democratic-Liberal party won a decisive victory and became the first postwar party to hold an absolute majority in the 466-member Diet. It rather dramatically increased its seats from 152 to 264, while the Democratic party dropped from 90 to 68 seats, and the Socialist party fell from 111 to 49. The Communist party reached its highwater mark, rising from 4 to 35 seats.

Soon after SCAP took charge in Japan, all political prisoners were released. Among the three thousand men who were freed were Communist leaders Tokuda Kyūichi and Shiga Yoshio, who had been incarcerated since early 1928. They immediately set about organizing the Communist party, and they were soon joined by Nozaka Sanzō, who had fled abroad during the years of the Red hunt and worked with the Chinese Communists in conducting antimilitarist propaganda campaigns.

In the early years of the occupation the number of unions rapidly increased until two major rival federations of these labor organizations came into existence. One was dominated by Communist leaders who tended to use the labor movement for political purposes. As a result, political strikes became as prevalent as strikes for economic betterment. SCAP's earlier enthusiasm for an active labor movement cooled somewhat as the Communists came to dominate those unions involved in state-owned services, such as the railroad and telecommunication systems. In February, 1947, and then again in the following year, SCAP was forced to intervene to prevent a general railway strike. Consequently it persuaded the Japanese government to restrict the right of the employees of state-owned enterprises to strike, and in late 1948, legislation to this effect was enacted. In 1949, the trade union law was revised to ensure democratic control of the unions by the members in order to prevent the takeover of these organizations by the more aggressive Communists.

In order to win public acceptance the Communist leaders sought to create the image of a "lovable Communist party" and began pursuing a policy of moderation. As a result they managed to capture thirty-five seats and 10 percent of the votes in the elections of January, 1949. Its party membership rose to one hundred thousand. This policy of moderation, however, came under criticism of the Cominform, and the Communist party was compelled to assume a more militant posture. In 1949, the government adopted a policy of retrenchment in accordance with the advice of Joseph Dodge, a Detroit banker who was sent to study the Japanese financial situation. This resulted in the dismissal of 260,000 employees in state-run enterprises. Now the Communists had a popular issue with which to berate the government.

In June, 1950, the Communist leaders were forced to go underground again as SCAP ordered the purge of the Communist party's central committee members and the editors of the Communist organ, the *Red Flag*. The ostensible reason given by SCAP for the purge was the Communist advocacy of revolution by force; but no doubt it was the growing tensions in the Cold War that compelled it to adopt a tough policy toward them. It was not just SCAP that was becoming concerned about the ascendancy of the Communists. The members of the Japanese establishment were even more nervous, and they bitterly complained about the leniency of SCAP's policy toward the Communists.

Non-Communist leaders began to come to the fore in the unions, and in 1950 the General Council of Trade Unions of Japan (*Sōhyō*) was organized by them. More than half of all the union members soon joined this federation, which was the largest in the country. From around 1950, however, even the non-Communist union leaders began to adopt an increasingly hostile attitude toward SCAP and the United States. They objected to the tougher labor policies being instituted, and they resented the close alliance that was developing between the SCAP and the conservative political parties.

Tension in the international Cold War continued to mount, and the union leaders tended to grow increasingly sympathetic to the Communist nations, or else they favored maintaining a position of "positive neutrality." The leadership of Sōhyō also fell to men with leftist or Marxist leanings, and in 1953 the federation claimed that "monopoly capital at home and abroad supported by the United States is planning to throw the peoples of the entire world into the crucible of war." This remained more or less the position of Sōhyō and its political arm, the Socialist party, throughout the fifties. The union leaders who became disenchanted with the drift to the left broke away from Sōhyō and formed a separate federation that threw its support to the right-wing socialists. In 1962, three moderate, right-wing labor groups merged to organize the Japanese Confederation of Labor (*Dōmei Kaigi*), the second largest federation of labor unions.

Yoshida, an ardent anti-Communist, purged all Communists from government posts and government corporations following the outbreak of the Korean War. The Red purge was also extended to the press and private industry. Consequently, twenty-two thousand persons were discharged, including six hundred in the press and radio, and more than ten thousand in industry. In July, 1952, after the occupation ended, the Yoshida government enacted the Subversive Activities Prevention Law to keep the Communists under check. In 1955, the Hatoyama government was seeking to improve Japan's relations with Soviet Russia, and thus the Communist leaders began to reappear on the public scene.

The United States decided to terminate the occupation because they had achieved their major objectives, and the country, under the capable direction of Yoshida, had apparently assumed a significant degree of political, social, and economic stability. General MacArthur had always believed that a prolonged occupation would have adverse effects, and as early as the spring of 1947, he began advocating the conclusion of a peace treaty. Moreover, the international situation had changed radically since the occupation policies were first formulated. The primary concern of the United States involvement in Asia was no longer the prevention of Japan's reemergence as a major power. The issues that began dividing the Western powers and Soviet Russia immediately after the end of the Second World War soon turned into the Cold War and the foremost aim of the United States consequently became the containment of communism throughout the world. In the Far East the victory of the Chinese Communists in the fall of 1949 made fears about the revival of Japanese militarism seem to be merely a phobia of the past. MacArthur believed that the "consummation of a just peace for Japan is one way—possibly the most dramatic and dynamic way open at this time—of asserting our leadership and regaining our lost initiative in the course of Asian affairs." [3] Then, after the outbreak of the Korean War in the summer of 1950, the chief concern of the United States in Japan became the defense of the country from the potential threat of the Communist powers.

In the spring of 1950, John Foster Dulles was assigned the task of preparing the groundwork for the peace treaty with Japan. In September, 1951, it was completed and the powers concerned met in San Francisco to sign the document. Notably absent from the roster of signatories was the Soviet Union, who refused to sign the treaty, and China, who was not invited because the United States and Great Britain were unable to agree on which government, Taiwan or Peking, should be asked to come.[4] Forty-eight nations signed the peace treaty. On the same day the United States and Japan signed a security pact, which provided for the protection of Japan from external aggressors and internal rebellions supported by external powers. For this purpose American troops were to continue to be stationed in Japan. The terms of this arrangement were spelled out in an administrative agreement signed in February of the following year.

The left-wing socialists and the Communists opposed the ratification of the peace treaty and the security agreement with the United States,

---

[3] MacArthur, *op. cit.*, p. 323.
[4] Japan and Taiwan signed a separate peace treaty in April, 1952.

while the right-wing socialists accepted the former and opposed the latter. Consequently the Socialist party split into two separate political organizations. Yoshida's Liberal party had a majority in the Diet so the treaties were easily ratified in October, and they became effective on April 28, 1952. Thus ended the period of American rule during which revolutionary changes had been brought about. General MacArthur, the man most responsible for the transformation of Japan, was gone from the country, having been relieved of his post in April of the previous year because of his disagreement with President Truman regarding the Korean campaign. He was succeeded by General Ridgway.

Freed from the authority of SCAP, the Yoshida government moved to revise some of the reforms that had been introduced, thus giving rise to a trend that was labeled by the opposition as "reverse course." The confrontation between the government and its critics, led by the opposition parties, labor unions, students, and intellectuals, became increasingly acrimonious.

The antagonism of labor toward the Yoshida government, and the strident opposition of cultural and intellectual leaders to the projected law concerning the prevention of subversive activities touched off, on May Day of 1952, the first of a series of violent confrontations between demonstrators and police. The other issue that the opposition forces strenuously objected to was the government's agreement to permit American military bases to remain in Japan. Any move by forces of the United States to increase military facilities evoked massive demonstrations under the leadership of left-wing politicians, labor leaders, students, and intellectuals.

At the same time, a series of confrontations between Yoshida and the opposition parties rocked the Diet. The Prime Minister sought to enact legislation that would serve to modify some of the laws that had been passed during the occupation era. In addition to the anti-subversive activities bill, Yoshida sought to introduce restrictive legislation in the field of education. He claimed that he was concerned about

> the decline in public morals, the need for curbing excesses arising from a misunderstanding of the meaning of freedom, the neglect into which respect for the nation and its traditions had fallen due to mistaken ideas of progress, the biased political outlook prevalent among university students . . . the need for raising the standards of teachers.[5]

[5] Shigeru Yoshida, *The Yoshida Memoirs*, trans. Yoshida Kenichi (Boston: Houghton Mifflin, 1962), p. 172.

His primary object, however, was to curb the influence of communism in the public school system. For this purpose he introduced two bills: one prohibiting teachers of elementary and junior high schools from engaging in political activities, and the other proscribing the introduction into the schools of educational material on politics by the teachers' union. There was much opposition to the bills, but with some modifications they were passed by the Diet in May, 1954.

Another controversial measure that was sponsored by the Prime Minister was the centralization of the police. Yoshida contended that fragmentation of the police into local units caused inefficiency and prevented the force from being used effectively on a national scale. Opponents of this plan feared that Yoshida's move was in reality an effort to return to the prewar system in which the police suppressed political and ideological dissent. The bill was nevertheless introduced in the Diet, where it faced a vigorous battle with opposition parties, who ultimately resorted to physical force in attempts to prevent its passage. However, in June, 1954, the bill was passed with the opponents boycotting the session. The measure provided for the abolition of municipal police and their replacement by prefectural police forces, who were to be coordinated at the top by the National Public Safety Commission and the national police.

Another aspect of the so-called reverse course that disturbed the leftists, the liberals, and the opponents of militarism was the rebirth, under new appellations, of a military force. Shortly after the outbreak of the Korean War, SCAP issued a directive to the Japanese government calling for the creation on a national scale of a reserve police force consisting of seventy-five thousand men. The object was to have this force replace American troops being transferred to Korea. The National Police Reserve came into existence in August, 1950, and the government justified its creation, even in the face of the no-war clause of the constitution, by contending that it was designed to maintain order within Japanese territory. As soon as the peace treaty went into effect, the National Police Reserve was increased to 110,000 men. The maritime safety force, which was functioning as a coast guard, was also strengthened at this time by a loan from the United States of eighteen frigates and fifty landing craft. A security board, under the direction of the cabinet, was placed in charge of all the land and sea forces.

In order to be eligible for further military aid under the United States mutual security act (which provided for the extension of military aid to countries prepared to defend themselves), Yoshida, in 1954, submitted to the Diet two bills to transform the police force into a defense force. These were the Defense Agency Establishment Bill and the Self-Defense

Force Bill. The Socialist party vigorously opposed the bills, asserting that they constituted the first steps in the rearmament of Japan. The Progressive party, led by Shigemitsu, supported the bills and managed to get them passed, thus bringing the Defense Agency into existence. It was charged with the task of defending the peace and independence of Japan. The Ground Self-Defense Force, the Maritime Self-Defense Force, and the Air Self-Defense Force were established under the aegis of the Defense Agency. The apparent violation of article nine of the constitution, which expressly prohibited the maintenance of military forces, was dismissed by the creators of the defense forces, who contended that the constitution did not rule out self-defense. Yoshida, insisting that there was a difference between rearmament and the creation of the self-defense forces, remarked that "the idea of rearmament has always seemed to be one verging on idiocy." [6] The pressure to rearm was exerted with greater intensity by the United States as the Cold War became more critical.

Yoshida, after having guided Japan through the difficult occupation years and having set her on the path to recovery as a self-sufficient and independent nation, suddenly found himself out of power. He was a strong leader but had never been very popular. He was tactless, cocksure, and autocratic, and his critics charged him with conducting a "one-man" government. Yoshida's downfall was engineered by members of his own party who broke with him to support Hatoyama, who had been eyeing the premiership ever since he resumed his political life in 1951. This defection of his supporters cost Yoshida his majority in the Diet, and he was forced to resign in December, 1954.

Hatoyama became the next Prime Minister, but the Democratic party, which he had joined, lacked a majority in the Diet. Consequently, he was forced to dissolve the Diet and hold new elections in February, 1955. In this contest his party emerged with 185 seats, now the largest faction in the Diet. The Liberal party won 112 seats, giving the various parties representing conservative interests a majority of 297.

Two major objectives were set forth by Hatoyama: the pursuit of an independent foreign policy and the revision of the constitution. The first goal involved a readjustment of Soviet-Japanese relations, and the second goal meant an effort to have the no-war clause removed from the constitution. Hatoyama initiated talks with the Soviet Union, and when the two parties failed to agree on the disposition of the southern Kurile Islands under Soviet control, Hatoyama decided that in order to avert a breakdown in the discussions it would be wise not to press the issue. In October, 1956, Hatoyama journeyed to Moscow and personally con-

[6] *Ibid.*, p. 191.

cluded an agreement normalizing relations between the two countries. Agreements concerning commerce and fishing were made, and trade between the two countries began to increase slowly.[7]

Hatoyama failed to realize his second objective, the revision of the constitution. In December, 1956, he was forced to resign because of poor health. He was succeeded breifly by Ishibashi Tanzan, a man of liberal political inclinations, but Ishibashi became ill after only two months in office. The Conservative party thereupon turned to Kishi Nobusuke (1896–   ), who had been active in Manchuria in the thirties and Minister of Commerce and Industry in the Tōjō cabinet. He spent over three years in prison as a war crime suspect but was released at the end of 1948. He made a comeback in the political world as an active member of the Liberal party. He left that organization for Hatoyama's Democratic party, but when the two conservative parties merged to form the Liberal-Democratic party in November, 1955, he became its secretary-general.

Kishi remained in office from February, 1957, to September, 1960. He believed that the constitution needed revision so as to enlarge the Emperor's authority somewhat and curb the Diet's power. He also favored increasing the power of the police and restricting the influence of communism in the schools, but by and large he failed to achieve his objectives.

In the realm of foreign affairs, Kishi renegotiated the security treaty with the United States in order to give Japan a larger voice in determining the uses to which American troops stationed in Japan could be put. The United States agreed to consult the Japanese government before sending any of these troops on combat missions abroad and before bringing nuclear weapons into the country. The pact was to remain in effect for ten years and was to continue automatically thereafter unless either side gave a year's notice of abrogation.

Kishi and his supporters hailed the new security agreement as an improvement over the former treaty because it was a pact concluded between equals. However, the socialists, labor leaders, students, intellectuals, cultural leaders, and pacifists objected vehemently, contending that the agreement drew Japan into a military alliance against the Communist nations, particularly Communist China. A massive campaign was launched to prevent ratification of the treaty. Those who opposed the pact feared not only the revival of militarism and the possibility of being drawn into a war, but many also expressed distrust of American foreign policy which, they held, represented the forces of imperialism. In contradistinction to this attitude toward the United States, there was a tendency to view the Communist nations as the friends of peace.

---

[7] On the other hand, no official initiative was taken to normalize Japan's relations with mainland China, although private commercial arrangements were made following the end of the occupation.

From late 1959, street demonstrations against the security pact grew larger and more frenzied. Kishi, however, remained resolute in his determination to have the treaty ratified, and he whipped into line those conservative party members who were wavering. The left-wing socialists were bent on blocking ratification by physical obstruction if necessary. On May 19 and May 20, 1960, the Diet was turned into a virtual madhouse as the supporters and the opponents of the treaty ignored parliamentary protocol and used violence as a method to achieve their objectives. Diet members literally wrestled with one another while thousands of demonstrators snake-danced outside, voicing their angry opposition to the pact. The opponents even sought to block the treaty by preventing the speaker from occupying his chair. Finally, Kishi's faction summoned the police, who removed the obstructors and placed the speaker in his chair. Then, as the socialists boycotted the session, the Liberal-Democrats approved the treaty.

The manner in which Kishi pushed the treaty through the Diet aroused tremendous public indignation and a movement claiming an enormous following was started to unseat him. Political agitators as well as radical leaders of the National Student Federation were responsible for organizing the mass demonstrations against him, but this should not obscure the fact that there was also widespread public support for the movement "to defend democracy." Millions of petitions were signed calling for new elections; hundreds of thousands of people marched through the streets of Tokyo demanding both Kishi's resignation and rejection of the security treaty. The demonstrations were taking on an increasingly anti-American cast, and on June 10, President Eisenhower's press secretary, who was in Japan to prepare for the President's visit, was made the target of a student demonstration. A few days later, after violence erupted between demonstrators and the police, Eisenhower's visit was cancelled. The protest movement finally subsided as the treaty went into effect on June 19, 1960.

The demonstrators may have failed to prevent the ratification of the security treaty, but they did succeed in bringing about the downfall of Kishi, who resigned as soon as the ratifications were exchanged on June 23. His resignation was actually contrived by the leaders of the rival factions in his own party, who used the manifestations of public hostility against him and his tactics as an excuse to replace him. A political struggle ensued among Liberal-Democratic leaders to assume the premier's post. The contest was finally won by Ikeda Hayato (1899–1965), who had climbed up the ranks of the bureaucracy as an official in the Ministry of Finance. He assumed the post in July, and served until November, 1964.

Ikeda set forth economic expansion and the doubling of the national income in ten years as the primary objectives of his government. The economy had been expanding throughout the fifties and Ikeda hoped to sustain the growth. He formulated a ten-year expansion plan, liberalized government controls, and provided for greater government investments.

The general economic prosperity wrought by the conservative parties in the fifties and sixties made their grip on the reins of power secure. The socialists continued to wallow in their doctrinaire quagmire, and consequently they failed to make any inroads into the electoral base of the conservatives. Even after an acrimonious confrontation in the first half of the year, when Ikeda dissolved the Diet in the fall, the conservatives won a resounding victory, gaining 296 seats as compared to the Socialist party's 145 and the Democratic Socialists' 17.[8] The decline of the socialists continued and in the election of December, 1969, the Socialist party won only 90 seats; that is, 50 less than the number they had won in the election of January, 1967.

At the same time that the socialists were losing their strength, a new political party that began gradually to increase its representation in the Diet was emerging. This was the Kōmeitō (Clean Government party), which was sponsored by the militant Sōka Gakkai (Value Creation Society), a secular organization linked to the Buddhist Nichiren sect. In the election of December, 1969, it won 47 seats, a significant gain over the 25 it had captured in 1967. The Communist party had been unable to win more than 4 or 5 seats since its capture of 35 seats back in 1949, but in the 1969 election it made inroads into the socialist votes and emerged with 14 seats.

The nature of the postwar political parties has not changed very much from their prewar counterparts although the socialist parties have become a more significant force. In general, the parties have retained the traditional attribute of being faction-ridden, with half a dozen or more factions led by bosses contending for power. This is true even of the socialist parties. The mergers and fissures that have taken place have frequently occurred because of factional rivalry rather than as the result of disagreements about basic principles or policies. The man who emerges as a factional leader must have access to funds, like his prewar counterpart, to defray the political expenses of his followers.

The conservative Liberal-Democratic party is closely allied with big business in many-respects. More than half of the party's Diet members have some ties with industry. Furthermore, influential businessmen play a significant role in selecting the leaders of the party and even in the making and unmaking of cabinets. The merger of the Democratic and

---

[8] The left-wing and the right-wing socialists had effected a merger in October, 1955, but they split again over the issue of the tactics to be used in opposing the security treaty. As a result the right-wing socialists, led by Nishio Hiroo, organized the Democratic Socialist party in January, 1960.

Liberal parties in 1955 was, in fact, brought about partly because of pressures from business leaders who were displeased about the cleavage between the conservatives. Efforts have been made by the business community to minimize intra-party factional strife in the Liberal-Democratic party. The conservative government never makes major economic decisions without consulting the top business leaders and the Federation of Economic Organizations, who collectively represent the major trade organizations and large corporations. Political contributions, marital connections, school ties, personal friendships, and business links all participate in the preservation of the close ties between big business and the conservative Liberal-Democratic party.

The Liberal-Democratic party also claims among its leaders many former government officials, who are, in general, preferred by the interests of big business. The factions led by Kishi, Ikeda, and Satō have had a notably high percentage of these men. The elitist nature of the conservatives is further indicated by the fact that a large number of the party leaders are graduates of the prestigious schools, particularly the University of Tokyo, whose graduates occupy key positions in government, business, and education.

Members of the Liberal-Democratic party tend to be nondoctrinaire, pragmatic individuals. Their primary objectives are material progress and the reestablishment of Japan as a major power through economic growth. The electoral support of the Liberal-Democratic party is found among the rural communities, small businessmen, and large sections of the salaried class, who tend to be suspicious of the class slogans and disruptive tactics of the socialists. The conservatives have managed to retain consistently about two-thirds of the voters' support.

The socialists tend to be rigidly doctrinaire and adhere tenaciously to timeworn Marxian concepts, such as the need to carry on the class struggle against capitalist exploiters. They have had the vocal backing of the intellectuals, many of whom manifest a distinctly Marxist bias, but the main source of their support has come from the labor unions, in particular the General Council of Trade Unions. If the Liberal-Democratic party is the party of business, the Socialist party is the party of organized labor. Consequently, the political position of the Socialist party resembles that of Sōhyō. They both favor closer ties with the Communist nations, the renunciation of the security treaty with the United States, and such things as tighter government controls over big business, higher wages, and more generous social welfare programs.

The continued economic prosperity and expansion under conservative rule has resulted in a steady decline of the Socialist party. The members of this party have long seemed to be talking about an abstract society far removed from the realities of contemporary Japan. In 1962, some party leaders called for a more pragmatic, eclectic approach but they have failed to effect a breakthrough, and in the 1969 election they were reduced almost to a minor party.

In November, 1964, Ikeda was forced to resign because of poor health, and he was replaced by Kishi's brother, Satō Eisaku (1901–   ), whose different family name reflects the fact that he had been adopted as a child by the Satō family. Like Ikeda, Satō had risen as a career officer in the Ministry of Finance. Upon assuming office, Satō, with the support of a powerful block of business leaders, pledged to continue Ikeda's economic policies and to improve living conditions and welfare programs. The economy continued to grow during his tenure in office, making Japan the third most productive nation in the world by the end of the 1960s. In the realm of foreign relations Satō achieved a degree of success in 1969 when he obtained President Nixon's agreement to return Okinawa to Japan in 1972.

ECONOMIC DEVELOPMENTS

The most spectacular achievement of postwar Japan is to be seen in the phenomenal economic recovery that took place in the country. As noted earlier, industrial production was at a virtual standstill at the end of the war, and recovery was slow. In 1946 industrial production stood at 30.7 percent of what it had been during 1934–1936. In the few years following 1946 it rose slowly: to 37.4 percent in 1947, 54.6 percent in 1948, 71.0 percent in 1949, and 83.6 percent in 1950. Then the Korean War broke out and the figure jumped to 114.4 percent in 1951, although real consumption per capita still remained at 84.8 percent of the prewar level. In 1953, however, industrial production rose to 155.1 percent and real consumption surpassed the prewar average. The truly spectacular growth occurred after this period—between 1953 and 1960, the economy grew at an average rate of 9.3 percent each year. By 1965, manufacturing as well as the economy as a whole had risen to nearly four times the level reached before the war, while the population had only grown from sixty-nine to ninety-eight million. The average family in 1965 consumed 75 percent more goods and services than did its counterpart in the mid-thirties. The economic growth continued, and the gross national product, which stood at $10.9 billion in 1950, reached $202 billion in 1970. This was third largest in the world, after the United States, whose gross national product in the same year came to about $1,000 billion, and Soviet Russia, with $350 billion.

In specific areas we find that the production of crude steel was 5 million tons in 1950, and by 1969 it had risen to 82 million, thus making Japan the third largest steel producer in the world after the United States and Soviet Russia. Already in 1956 Japan had become the world's leading shipbuilder, and in 1969 she produced 48.2 percent of the world's merchant vessel tonnage. In 1950 Japan produced only 1,593 passenger cars whereas in 1969 she produced 2,611,499 and in doing so became the world's third largest manufacturer of passenger cars.

In the prewar years Japanese products were equated with shoddy workmanship and cheap materials, but in the postwar period the Japanese industrialists concentrated on the production of high quality goods such as cameras, watches, radios, televisions, precision instruments, electronic devices, electrical appliances, and heavy industrial goods. The phenomenal economic growth during the sixties of about 14 to 15 percent per year was expected to continue in the seventies, barring some unforeseen economic crisis, particularly in international trade.

The precarious footing of the Japanese economy was exposed when in August, 1971, President Nixon imposed a 10 percent surcharge on imports to the United States and exerted pressure on the Japanese government to revalue the yen upward. This touched off an acute economic crisis in Japan, which sends about 30 percent of its exports to the United States.

As a result of the rapid rate of industrialization, about 18 percent of Japan's labor force was employed in agriculture and forestry in 1969, in contrast to about 50 percent in the mid-thirties. Even though there were fewer workers on the farms, agricultural production, nonetheless, also increased. In the prewar period about 20 percent of the rice needed by the country had to be imported; today Japan herself produces a surplus. This, of course, is due in part to changes in dietary habit, but the primary cause is greater rice yield. In 1935, Japan's total rice production came to 8,619,000 tons and consumption amounted to 10,631,000 tons; in 1967, the figures were 14,453,000 and 12,386,000. Rice yield per hectare of land was increased from 2.71 tons in 1935, to 4.5 tons in 1969, the highest yield in the world. There also has been tremendous growth in the fishing industry with the annual haul, excluding whaling, increasing from 3,374,000 tons in 1950, to 7,851,000 tons in 1967. The catch in whaling has doubled compared to the prewar years.

Japan's economic growth and prosperity depend primarily on foreign trade. In 1950 she exported $820 million worth of goods and imported $974 million while in 1969 her exports came to $16.7 billion, showing an excess of $4 billion over imports. In that year 69.3 percent of her exports consisted of metal products, machinery, and chemicals, which before World War II averaged about 16 percent. In the prewar years textiles accounted for half of Japan's exports while in 1969 it came to only 14.2 percent. Her imports consist largely of raw materials, fuel, foodstuffs, and ore.

Throughout the prewar period Asian countries accounted for 64 percent of Japan's total exports and 53 pecent of her imports, but in 1969, the figures were considerably down to 33.8 percent and 30.4 percent, respectively. Immediately after the war, Japan's foreign trade was heavily dependent upon the United States: in 1946, 65 percent of her export trade and 86 percent of her import trade were conducted with the United States. In 1969, the figures were down to 31 and 27, but the United States was still unquestionably Japan's most important trading partner. Her trade with the Communist bloc was still relatively insignificant. In 1969 only 4.8 percent of her total exports went to mainland China and Soviet Russia and 5.6 percent of her imports came from these countries.

What were the factors that made the spectacular recovery and growth of the economy possible? Initially, the economy was given a boost by the United States as it turned away from the vindictive policy of having Japan pay for initiating the war and suffer the consequences of defeat. By 1951, the United States had poured more than $2 billion into the Japanese economy. The Japanese economy also received a strong impetus from the Korean War boom. By the mid-fifties the United States had spent about $4 billion in Japan for "special procurement," i.e., the purchase of supplies, equipment, services, and recreation for American troops. As a result the Japanese economy during this period began to grow by 9 percent or more each year. There was, of course, a complex of other factors that helped to sustain the initial upswing and thereby kept the economy growing.

In terms of world conditions, one of the very beneficial outcomes of the Cold War was that it resulted in the United States adopting liberal political and economic policies toward non-Communist nations, including Japan. Generous commercial arrangements were made with a minimum of effort to keep Japanese goods out of the American market. The United States also encouraged other non-Communist nations to keep their markets open. She sponsored Japan's entry into the General Agreement on Tariffs and Trade and made tariff concessions to other nations in order to secure favorable treatment for Japan. Moreover, the United States readily extended technical assistance and credit.

The fact that Japan renounced militarism meant that she would have to spend only a minimal amount, 1 or 2 percent of her gross national product, on defense. The government could, therefore, invest much of its public funds into programs for developing the nation's industries. The resources and the technological skills that were expended in the construction of tanks and huge warships in the prewar era were now devoted to the manufacturing of ships, machinery, and instruments for export.

The circumstances that had enabled Japan to develop into a substantial industrial power in the first half of the century were still present. She had an ample supply of well-educated, skillful, well-disciplined, hardworking laborers. Moreover, the level of education had been raised after the war, thus enabling the average worker to cope with the new technology of the postwar era. As a result of improved technology, labor productivity per hour increased at the rate of 7.2 percent annually during 1953–1962.

The leadership provided by the government and management has been vigorous, enterprising, and at times even ingenious. Management moved swiftly to modernize industrial facilities and production techniques by borrowing from the advanced technological knowledge of the West. Between 1949 and 1963, 2,563 contracts were concluded with Western firms to acquire patented processes and technical assistance. Nearly 70 percent of these were with American firms. The Japanese companies began to invest increasingly larger sums of money into their own research projects. They have also adopted modern methods of corporate management, giving more attention to marketing than before.

The government has made it a point to work closely with the business community, providing assistance wherever needed and regulating the economy, particularly foreign trade and fiscal affairs, so as to ensure healthy economic expansion. In 1949, and then again in 1953, it relaxed the antimonopoly laws in order to allow for the reemergence of large combines and thus enable Japanese business firms to compete more effectively with foreign companies. It has made state funds available to large private banks; cut taxes whenever possible to stimulate the economy; and invested in public works projects.

Another significant factor in the growth of the Japanese economy has been the high rate of savings, which has made available substantial capital for investment. In the early sixties, about 40 percent of the gross national expenditure was used each year for the replacement and expansion of capital stock. Some of the funds used for this purpose came from abroad, but about 96 percent of the corporate investment funds came from domestic sources. The government did make some public funds available, but most of it was derived from the private sector. The traditional emphasis on thrift and frugality has resulted in high personal savings: about 15 percent of disposable personal income went into savings. This was two times greater than what prevailed in the United States.

One consequence of the government's policy of economic expansion has been the rebirth of huge business combines. The old zaibatsu have reemerged under new leadership; the old families who controlled the former combines are gone; so are the old holding companies. Formerly, the four top zaibatsu firms controlled 24.5 percent of all paid-up capital in corporate industry and finance, but now there are eight or ten groups loosely organized around big banks. There are also huge independent firms such as Tōshiba Electric, Matsushita Electric, Toyota Motors, and Yawata-Fuji Steel. Each of these has its own circle of subsidiaries but none have the interlocking connections that the prewar zaibatsu had. Banks have replaced the old holding companies; thirteen city banks were in control of 60 percent of all bank assets in the early sixties, but there is keen competition among them and the dominant banks do not exercise tight control even over their operating affiliates.

Combines are also formed around huge companies that are involved in foreign trade, such as Mitsubishi Mercantile Company and Mitsui Products Company. The big firms in this area have managed to achieve the kind of predominance they had held in the prewar era. Cartels and cartel-like agreements have also come into existence, but efforts on the part of major firms to fix prices, limit outputs, and so on have often resulted in their being outdone by smaller competing firms. The government has of late been pursuing a policy of protecting Japanese firms against foreign competition and has as a result been sympathetic to the trend toward bigness by allowing mergers. For example, in 1970, two gigantic steel companies, Yawata and Fuji, were allowed to merge in order to curtail "excessive competition." Despite the trend toward bigness, however, there are still a large number of small and medium sized companies, where more than 50 percent of the nation's workers are employed.

Economic growth has not only resulted in huge profits for the more successful firms, but it has also brought higher wages for the workers. Rather severe privation was endured immediately after the war, but by 1952 the workers were earning wages equivalent to the prewar level. Wages have continued to rise with the growing demand for labor. Taking 1965 as index 100, wages for all industries stood at 61.1 in 1960 and 162.8 in 1969. From 1960 to 1969 wages increased by about 10 percent each year while consumer prices rose at an annual rate of 5.7 percent. In 1970 wages rose by 21.4 percent over the previous year. Workers in larger factories received better pay than those in small plants; factories employing less than one hundred workers paid only about 75 percent of the wages being paid in plants with more than five hundred employees. This disparity in wages had been greater in previous years, but in the sixties wages in the smaller factories rose more rapidly than they did in the larger ones. Women continued to receive less pay than men—in 1967, the average pay per month for women employees was about $76, less than half the amount earned by men.

LIVING CONDITIONS

The tremendous economic growth naturally resulted in a rise in the standard of living. The per capita income increased in a decade from

$284 in 1958, to about $1,122 in 1968.[9] In 1970 it reached $1,518 but it still placed Japan no higher than fifteenth in the world. Taking 1955 as index 100, the real per capita consumption was 89.2 in 1935, while in 1962 it had risen to 154.7; it has continued to rise. In 1945, Engel's coefficient (the ratio of expenditures on foodstuffs to the total expenditure) for urban households was 63 percent, and in 1950 it was still rather high at 57.4 percent, but by 1969 it was down to 32.8 percent. The monthly household income of the urban worker averaged about $81 in 1955, but rose to about $230 in 1967. The differences between income and expenditure per household, which stood at $6.7 in 1955, rose to $37.5 in 1967. The farm households have also fared almost as well. In 1950 the average monthly income of a farm household was $50, whereas in 1966 it had risen to about $200. The difference between income and expenditure per month rose from $8 in 1950 to $34.7 in 1966.

The caloric consumption of food, however, has not changed significantly from the prewar era. It was about 2,300 per capita per day in the twenties and thirties, and in 1969 it was just slightly higher at 2,450. It is believed, however, that when physical size and other factors are taken into consideration, this is an adequate amount for the Japanese. There has been a slight improvement in the quality of the food consumed. In the prewar years 78 percent of the food intake consisted of starch, but in 1965 this was down to 62 percent. Nonetheless, this hardly approaches the standards of the Western nations; for example, the percentage of starch consumption in the United States for the same year was 24.1 percent. In 1966, 56.4 percent of the food consumed in Japan consisted of cereals, and only 10 percent was of meat and meat by-products, as compared to 71.8 percent and 3 percent in 1934. In 1965, figures for the United States were cereals, 21.2 percent, and meat and meat by-products, 34 percent.

The extent of the material betterment in Japan can be seen in the widespread use of mechanical devices, which is quite comparable to that in the West. Television broadcasting was started in 1952, and by the end of 1969, there were over twenty-five million television sets in use, with 90 percent of the households owning a set. A private car was a rare luxury in 1950, with only 48,309 passenger cars in existence, but by 1969 there were 6.9 million cars in use. Washing machines, refrigerators, and other electrical appliances that were luxury items a decade ago, have become

[9] Since the purchasing power differs from country to country, comparative figures do not very accurately reflect the differences in living standards, but they are helpful as a general indicator. In 1969 the per capita income was $3,814 for the United States, $1,910 for West Germany, $2,106 for France, and $1,513 for the United Kingdom. It was much lower for Asian countries: $283 for the Philippines, $270 for Taiwan, and $126 for Thailand. For India in 1968 it was $73 and South Korea $163.

common household appliances. The vastly expanded use of mechanical devices has not necessarily improved the quality of life. The increased use of cars, for example, has caused horrendous traffic problems in the major cities. The noise index has risen, and pollution of the air and water has become a serious health hazard.

The one area in which a serious shortage prevails is housing, where construction has not kept up with the influx of people into the cities. About 70 percent of the population now dwells in urban areas. The congestion is particularly acute in Tokyo, where about ten million people are crowded together in cramped houses and apartments, which sell or rent for exorbitant prices. The sewage and sanitation systems have not been modernized, and there is very little modern plumbing; only about 9 percent of the homes have flush toilets. Most homes have no central heating or hot-water systems. Housing is not available in the center of the cities so people spill over into the outskirts, spending hours every day commuting in overcrowded buses, electric trains, subways, and cars.

In the area of health, great improvements were made in the postwar era. In 1969, life expectancy had reached 69.2 years for men and 74.7 for women, compared to 47 and 50 for 1933–1937. The infant mortality rate was lowered to 15 per one thousand live births in 1967, compared to 67 during 1947–1949, and 115.1 during 1933–1937. The American occupation authorities contributed greatly to the improvement of medicine and hygiene. Smallpox, diphtheria, typhoid, and tuberculosis were still prevalent when the occupation started. SCAP initiated a massive inoculation and vaccination program and within three years, cholera was eliminated, smallpox was curbed, diphtheria was reduced by 86 percent, tuberculosis by 79 percent, and typhoid was practically eliminated. It is estimated that two million lives were saved in the first two years of occupation by these health measures. Life expectancy during the occupation was raised to 60.8 for men and 64.8 for women by 1951.

As we noted earlier in this chapter, serious efforts to control the growth of the population have been made by means of contraceptives and legalized abortions. The birth rate was reduced from 30.8 per thousand in 1933–1937, to 18.4 in 1969. There has also been a drop in the death rate from 17.4 per thousand in 1933–1937, to 6.8 in 1969. The population in 1969 was 103.7 million, compared to 80 million in 1948, and 71 million in 1937. Japan is the fifth most densely populated country in the world, having 721 persons per square mile, compared to 56.6 in the United States. Only mainland China, India, the Soviet Union, the United States, and Indonesia have larger populations.

The social welfare program is still inadequate although benefits have been increasing. At present most of the population is covered by some type of health insurance. Pension insurance is also improving and annuities are rising. In 1963 Japan spent only 7 percent of her national income on social welfare programs, compared with 14.6 percent in the United Kingdom, 20.3 in France, 21.2 in West Germany, and 8 in the United States. In 1970, however, the Japanese government spent 2.2 times more money on social welfare programs than it did in 1965.

CULTURAL AND INTELLECTUAL DEVELOPMENTS

Japan had managed to raise its level of literacy to well above 90 percent in the prewar years. Today the literacy rate is about 98 percent, with enrollment in the nine years of compulsory education nearly 100 percent. About 75 percent of the school children in the nation go beyond the compulsory level, and by 1967 more than 1.3 million students were enrolled in colleges and universities, almost eight times the prewar figure. The enrollment of women in institutions of higher education has increased sixteen times the prewar level. By 1969 one out of every five persons of college-age was in a two or four-year college.

The Japanese are avid consumers of books. In 1969, 31,009 books were published, thus placing her fourth in the world behind the Soviet Union, the United States and West Germany. In the same year the daily newspaper circulation came to 503 copies per 1,000 persons, compared to 305 for the United States. In 1968, the papers with the first and second largest daily circulations in the world were Japanese, and they claimed figures of 8.9 million and 8.6 million. The newspaper with the largest daily circulation in the United States published 2.1 million copies in the same year.

Japan is a country where learning is held in high regard, and as a result, educated people have retained a strong influence in the society and "an overcredulous trustfulness in the pronouncements of 'men of culture' prevails." [10] In light of the fact that many intellectuals have had a noticeable Marxist bias, the general intellectual climate in Japan in the postwar years has had a strong slant in this direction. Magazines, books, and papers have all tended to reflect the dogmas and clichés of Marxism. Consequently a strong ambivalence toward the United States is displayed.

The impact of America on postwar Japan, as might be expected, has been enormous. It has rivaled, if not actually surpassed, the influence that the West had upon Meiji Japan. This is evident not only in the technological realm and in the profound institutional changes brought about by the occupation, but it also can be seen in such aspects of life and culture as rock music, pinball machines, Coca Cola, hot dogs, dating, public dis-

[10] Donald Keene, "Literary and Intellectual Currents in Postwar Japan and Their International Implications," in Hugh Borton et al., Japan Between East and West (New York: Harper & Row, 1957), p. 155.

play of affection between young couples, burlesque shows, beauty queen contests, professional wrestling, professional baseball, American television shows, movies, books, garish advertisements, Japanized English words, and fashionable apparel. Whatever becomes the vogue in the United States seems to appear instantly in Japan.

At no time in the history of Japan has there been so much direct contact with foreigners. A large number of American troops have remained in the country for more than two decades. Thousands of businessmen, students, scholars, missionaries, government officials, and professional men have resided in Japan. Now tourists in plentiful numbers are visiting the country. Moreover, thanks to the Fulbright program, innumerable Japanese students and scholars have been able to spend a few years studying in the United States.

Perhaps too much of the American presence has contributed to the extreme sensitivity displayed toward the United States by the molders of public opinion, the so-called men of culture. Numerous factors have contributed to the growing criticism of the United States: the shift in SCAP's emphasis from democratization to making Japan safe from communism; the fear of remilitarization under American auspices; disagreement with American policies in the Far East, particularly on Vietnam; and apprehensions about being dragged into a nuclear war.

The confidence of the Japanese in their intellectual achievement has been enhanced by the emergence of three Nobel Prize winners in the postwar era. In 1949, Yukawa Hideki received the prize for his work in physics and this event contributed greatly to bolstering the Japanese morale, which had been shattered by the defeat in the war. In 1965, Tomonaga Shinichirō won the prize for his work in physics and in 1968, Kawabata Yasunari was honored for his achievements in literature.

In the postwar era literature enjoyed a renaissance of a sort. During the war years, writers were compelled to produce novels that would inspire the people to work for the glory of the state and the Emperor. If they could not do this, they were forced to remain silent. Depiction of any "unhealthy," immoral, or unpatriotic ideas and behavior were proscribed by the censors. For the writers, the defeat of Japan in the war signified the restoration of their freedom of artistic expression. Whatever they wrote was read avariciously by the people, who immediately emptied the bookstores of literary magazines and books. Publications were limited, however, because of the paper shortage. In the immediate postwar years the authors with established reputations enjoyed a revival, and men who had been producing since the Taishō era, such as Nagai Kafū, Tanizaki, and Kawabata, continued to bring out new works. In a few years a host of talented younger writers, who commenced working in the thirties or in the postwar era, began to replace the older men as the literary masters.

Among those whose works have been translated into English are Dazai Osamu, Noma Hiroshi, Ōoka Shōhei, and Mishima Yukio.

Dazai Osamu (1909–1948) started his literary career in the thirties and was among the writers of the literature of despair that flourished in the postwar era. In his *The Setting Sun* and *No Longer Human,* the heroes, alienated from society and their fellowmen, seek consolation in dissipation, which leads ultimately to their destruction. Dazai relentlessly analyzed in the most minute detail the inner thoughts of his heroes, who invariably recognize the essential emptiness of life. The novelist was not interested solely in making the reader share his sense of futility and anguish; he also sought to make people laugh. Seeing himself in the role of a clown, Dazai injected some humor into his writings and thus saved his work from being irretrievably bleak. Not unlike the heroes of his imagination, Dazai finally succeeded in bringing about his own self-destruction.

As might be expected, writers from the left made a strong comeback in the postwar era. Among them was Noma Hiroshi (1915–   ), who was subjected to oppression by the army because of his political beliefs. He is a Communist writer, but he does not simply write novels of socialist realism; he probes the inner struggles of the intellectual who seeks self-realization within the masses. He is also concerned with his experiences in the army, which are brilliantly evoked in his masterpiece, *The Zone of Emptiness.*

Ōoka Shōhei (1909–   ) won renown with novels dealing with his experiences as a soldier in the Philippines. *Fires on the Plains* is a vivid depiction of the plight of a soldier who, reduced to insanity and on the verge of starvation, wanders about alone in Leyte struggling to survive. Ōoka forces the reader to stare directly at the horrors of war and even those of life itself as he describes rotting corpses and men reduced to cannibalism.

The most talented and versatile of the postwar writers was Mishima Yukio (1925–1970), who was well versed in both Western and traditional Japanese literature. He wrote novels, short stories, poems, and Kabuki as well as Nō plays. Mishima took for his themes the manners and mores of the postwar generation, the sense of despair and emptiness that faced the young, as well as the subject of homosexuality. In his *The Temple of the Golden Pavilion* he focuses upon the thematic contrasts of love and hate, reality and illusion, selflessness and self-assertion. The plot of the novel has to do with the story of the Buddhist acolyte who, in 1950, burned down the Golden Pavilion (*Kinkakuji*) built by Shōgun Ashikaga Yoshimitsu in 1397. The acolyte, who is a cripple, is obsessed with a sense of his own inadequacy and sees in the perfect beauty of the Golden Pavilion merely another reminder of his own ineptness. He awaits its destruction by American bombers, but the war ends without the anticipated air raid and the Golden Pavilion still stands. In a desperate act of defiance and self-liberation, the acolyte sets fire to the temple.

In the sixties Mishima began addressing himself to the problems of student unrest and the apparent lack of mooring in the younger generation. His solution to this absence of spiritual anchor has a remarkably traditionalist cast. In the early sixties he wrote: "To the Japanese whatever is new is desirable. Then, when we are so surrounded by new inventions that we are unable to move—every twenty years, that is—we Japanese suddenly begin to feel that old things are much better after all." [11] Hoping to revive the old samurai spirit, he organized a group of university students into a small private army to teach them patriotism, body building, and the fine art of combat. He became increasingly distressed over the disappearance of traditional values among the young. Mishima was deeply influenced by Wang Yang-ming's teaching that one must act on his beliefs, and in accordance with this dictum he decided to sacrifice himself "for the old, beautiful tradition of Japan, which is disappearing very quickly day by day." [12] In November, 1970, after failing to arouse the members of the National Defense Force to follow his philosophy, he committed hara-kiri in classical samurai fashion.

Significant creative works have also been produced in other realms of art. Probably the most notable achievements can be seen in the folk arts. For instance, in pottery Hamada Shōji (1894–   ), among others, has won international recognition. Wholly without vanity and pretension Hamada lives and works among village artisans. Considering himself merely a craftsman, not an artist, he does not even sign his work. Hamada has studied under the English potter, Bernard Leach, and has been greatly influenced by Korean pottery. He has, nevertheless, developed an individual style that is characterized by a rugged strength of shape in concert with somber colors. He creates spontaneous and striking designs with the freedom of movement displayed by a master calligrapher.

There has also been a revival of interest in woodblock printing. The most prominent artist in this field is Munakata Shikō (1903–   ). Working very rapidly, he has produced a prodigious number of prints. Munakata is a Zen Buddhist and much of his work has to do with religious subjects. Carving dynamic and rough-hewn figures, Munakata endows his prints with enormous strength of design, movement of line, and dramatic tension.

In the art of the cinema several Japanese directors have won international renown. An authority on Japanese films has written the following

---

[11] Yukio Mishima, "Party of One, Japan the Cherished Myths," in *Holiday*, October, 1961, p. 13.

[12] *The New Yorker*, December 12, 1970. p. 41.

"The Barking Dog" (1959), *a woodcut by Munakata. Courtesy of the Museum of Modern Art, New York, Blanchette Rockefeller Fund.*

very revealing statement regarding the significance of movies in understanding the culture of a nation:

> The Japanese movie continues to show . . . the most
> perfect reflection of a people in the history of world
> cinema. . . . If the American film is strongest in action,
> and if the European is strongest in character, then the
> Japanese film is richest in mood or atmosphere, in presenting

people in their own context, characters in their own surroundings. It reflects the oneness with nature which constitutes both the triumph and the escape of the Japanese people.[13]

The sudden international fame that was gained by Japanese films during the postwar period has made it appear as if the art of the cinema attained instant maturity after the war. This, of course, is not at all the case; the style and technique had been evolving since the twenties. A number of outstanding directors such as Mizoguchi, who produced *Ugetsu*, and Kurosawa, who made *Rashōmon* and *The Seven Samurai* among many other outstanding films, helped to bring about this triumph of cinema as an important art form. Kurosawa (1910–   ), perhaps the greatest of the Japanese directors, combines an interest in film aesthetics with a deep concern about social issues. Commenting on what he has been trying to do in his films, Kurosawa said, "I keep saying the same thing in different ways. If I look at the pictures I've made, I think they say, 'Why is it that human beings aren't happy?' " [14] He is continuously experimenting and devising new techniques and approaches, endeavoring to make the style fit the story, the form fit the content. He is a master at producing scenes of striking pictorial beauty. Regarding his *Rashōmon* he remarked, "I wanted to return to the simple pictorial values of the silent picture."

THE AGE OF UNCERTAINTY

It would appear that, like young people all over the world, the Japanese youths of today are making radical departures from traditional values and institutions. The defeat in the war and the changes introduced in the postwar years have wrought a revolution more rapidly developing and more far-reaching than has occurred in any other period in Japanese history. The old values and ways were still strongly embedded in the society that emerged immediately after the war because the young people of that era, having been raised and educated in the most authoritarian period of modern Japan, still retained the traditional values and attitudes.

The youths of today, on the other hand, are entirely the products of the postwar era and have grown up in a completely different intellectual and cultural climate. Today for the first time a generation embracing a wholly new attitude and perspective seems to be emerging. The young are no longer as respectful and deferential to their elders as the Japanese youths used to be. Another important barometer of change is the fact

---

[13] Donald Richie, *Japanese Movies* (Tokyo: Japan Travel Bureau, 1961), p. vii.
[14] Quoted in *ibid.*, p. 161.

that the style of speech in which the hierarchy of age, sex, and status has historically been reflected is beginning to show signs of erosion.

Students have turned from protesting the political actions of the government to challenging the traditional authority embedded in the citadels of learning, the universities, where formerly the professors were treated with esteem, if not veneration. Ironically enough, in many ways it has been the preachers of democracy, equality, freedom, and justice that have been the ones to retain the most "feudalistic" attitude in their interaction with students. The traditional master-follower relationship has always been strongly embedded in the academic world. Yet, until the present, students were unable to free themselves from their inhibitions and their traditional sense of deference and were thus unable to direct their attacks against the universities and the professors. In the spring of 1968, the cultural restraints were shattered and the "occupation" of the institutions of higher learning, and the confrontation between the students and the professors commenced. Students locked up professors and conducted group criticisms. Some of these sessions lasted for days while the students intimidated their teachers. True, only a small minority have actually been involved in the more radical actions, but when the lines are drawn many young people in the middle would rally to the support of the extremists.

Many of the radical students are Marxists or Maoists and consequently have a sense of direction and purpose. Among them are anarchists who see the destruction of the existing institutions as the first step toward the construction of an ideal society. The majority of the youths, however, seem not to have a sense of direction, or the defined sense of identity that the contemporary radicals have or that the prewar youths had.

Man has always had a sense of purpose founded upon a mythical or religious interpretation of the cosmos. He has also had a sense of identity. Earlier, tribal ties had given the individual a strong sense of community and security, but as the circle of man's association widened, these primitive ties weakened. In early Japan there were the clans (uji), the imperial household, the military chieftains, and the feudal lords, who provided the people with a sense of community and identity. Throughout the nation's history there were also family and village ties that endowed the individual with a sense of community. Even after the Meiji Restoration had occurred and Japan had entered the industrial age, the family bonds continued to remain strong. In addition the revived emperor system and the unfolding of extremely strong feelings of nationalism gave the people a resolute sense of purpose and identity. In postwar Japan, for the first time in its history, these institutions have virtually collapsed or, at least, have seriously eroded.

Legal changes that have been effected since the war have served to weaken the stem-family as the strong unit of foundation in the societal order. Liberation of the individual has also contributed to this by loosening family ties. In the prewar era the eldest son and his wife and children lived with his parents. Today, 65 percent of the young couples live apart from their families. There may be some sense of affection for the imperial family but no one would die for the Emperor any more. It is probably true that nationalistic sentiments are behind some of the outbursts against American policies, but these seem not to be representative of the kind of commitment in which the individual submerges himself wholly to a transcendent ideal.

In the postwar period of confusion and chaos, a large number of new religions came into existence, but none has won a large enough following to become a significant force in the society. The only truly vigorous religious movement to emerge has been the Sōka Gakkai. It was started in the 1920s by an obscure schoolteacher who maintained that within the uncertain flux of human existence the happiness of people could be furthered by the adoption of proper value judgments. It was essentially a cult of faith healing that linked itself to the Nichiren sect. In the postwar period it was invigorated by strong, dynamic leadership and became an aggressive, proselytizing religion. It tends to be moralistic and emphasizes the power of positive thinking. The religion has been tremendously appealing to the lower ranks of the working classes, who feel alienated from the rapidly developing bourgeois culture, and consequently the membership of the Sōka Gakkai has increased swiftly; it rose above fourteen million by the end of 1968. Nevertheless, it has had only limited appeal so far to the majority of the people; it has not been at all successful in converting the more sophisticated and prosperous middle class, and it has yet to capture the imagination of the youths of the nation.

It is likely that the spiritual drift will continue until a religious or intellectual force that can attract the young comes into existence. The form that this will take cannot be foreseen, but if it is true, as has often been said, that the Japanese do not like new things, despite the superficial affection they might display, then there is still a good chance that today's generation of young people will eventually achieve a sense of being whole again by reembracing some aspects of traditional Japan.

Robert J. Lifton, after studying the psychology of postwar Japanese youths in the early 1960s, remarked upon "the absence in contemporary Japanese youth of vital and nourishing ties to their own heritage—*a break in their sense of connection.*" [15] The Japanese youths that he

[15] Robert Jay Lifton, *History and Human Survival* (New York: Random House, 1970), p. 26.

talked with were affected by traditional, cultural elements but regarded them as irrelevant and inadequate to meet the demands of the modern world. Half a decade later Lifton interviewed the same young Japanese and found that "they were preoccupied with their cultural and racial heritage—with various aspects of their 'Japaneseness'—to such an extent that I wondered whether [in the essay written in 1961] I had overemphasized the psychological importance of postwar Western influence." [16]

The problems confronting Japan today are not unique. The decline of traditional values and institutions, and the search for meaning and purpose continue elsewhere in the industrialized, Westernized societies that have also left their tribal and familial stages far behind. Like other societies, Japan faces such problems as the dislocations and disorientations caused by the exceedingly rapid pace of change that has been brought about by science and technology; air and water pollution; the desecration of nature; the threat of nuclear destruction; the population explosion; the undermining of the sense of mystery and awe by rationalism and science; the abandonment of the sense of unity with nature and the universe that was at the root of Shinto; and the continued inability of man to stop abusing his fellowmen.

If the tasks facing man throughout history have been to relate meaningfully to the cosmic order through some sort of mythical view of life and the universe, to cope with the problems posed by nature, to order his relationship with his fellowmen, and to govern his own inner life, then it must be said that man has made very little progress. In fact today he may be even worse off than his primitive counterpart. Man has lost the sense of the mythical; he has conquered nature but in the process he has created greater problems by poisoning his environment and destroying the ecological balance of his world; he has yet to devise a just, humane, and meaningful system of human association; and he has still failed to gain some sort of inner peace.

Of course man will never achieve final solutions to these problems. The flow of history guarantees that there will be no ultimate solutions. If there were, history would cease to be. The ultimate meaning in life and history consists in the continuous struggle to cope with these problems. It is in the course of that struggle that man, in spite of all his frailties, has managed from time to time to create meaningful myths, tools, systems, works of art, and philosophies that have enabled him to cope with the challenges posed by the cosmic order, nature, his fellowmen, and himself.

[16] *Ibid.*, pp. 29–30.

APPENDIX A

Chronological Chart

PRE- AND PROTO-HISTORICAL ERAS

?–ca. 250 B.C.	Jōmon culture
ca. 250 B.C.– A.D. 250	Yayoi culture
660 B.C.	Mythical date of the accession of the first Emperor, Jimmu
ca. 100 B.C.	Rice cultivation in wet fields commences.
A.D. 57	The Japanese Kingdom of Nu sends an envoy to the Chinese court of the Later Han Dynasty.
139	The ruler of Yamatai, Himiko, sends an envoy to the Chinese Kingdom of Wei.

YAMATO PERIOD (CA. A.D. 300–710)

ca. 300	The imperial family establishes its hegemony over Japan.
ca. 400	Writing is introduced from Korea.
538 (or 562)	Buddhism is introduced from Paikche in Korea.
562	The Japanese colony of Mimana in Korea is conquered by Silla.
593–622	Prince Shōtoku is regent.
604	The "Constitution of Seventeen Articles" is issued.
607	The Hōryūji is constructed.
645	The Taika Reforms are initiated.
701	The Taihō Code is completed.

605

NARA PERIOD (710–784)

710	The capital is established in Nara (Heijōkyō).
712	The compilation of the *Kojiki* is completed.
720	The compilation of the *Nihongi* is completed.
743	Private ownership of reclaimed land is permitted.
752	The Great Buddha of Tōdaiji is dedicated.
ca. 780	The compilation of the *Manyōshū* is completed.
784	The capital is moved to Nagaoka.

HEIAN PERIOD (794–1185)

794	The capital is moved to Kyoto (Heiankyō).
794	Seiitaishōgun is appointed to subdue the Ezo.
858	Fujiwara Yoshifusa is appointed regent.
939–940	Taira-no-Masakado leads a rebellion.
ca. 1002–1019	*The Tale of Genji* is written.
1016	Fujiwara Michinaga is appointed regent.
1086	The cloister government is established.
1167	Taira-no-Kiyomori is appointed chancellor (dajō daijin).
1175	The Pure Land Sect is founded by Hōnen.
1180	Minamoto-no-Yoritomo challenges the Taira family.
1185	The Taira family falls.

KAMAKURA PERIOD (1185–1333)

1192	Yoritomo is appointed shōgun.
1205	Hōjō Yoshitoki becomes regent to the shōgun.
1224	The True Pure Land Sect is founded by Shinran.
1253	The Nichiren Sect is founded by Nichiren.
1274	The first Mongol invasion occurs.
1281	The second Mongol invasion occurs.
1333	The Kamakura Bakufu collapses.
1334	The Kemmu Restoration is established under Emperor Godaigo.
1335	Ashikaga Takauji rebels against the imperial government.
1336	Emperor Godaigo flees to Yoshino and establishes the Southern Court.

ASHIKAGA PERIOD (1338–1573)

1338	Takauji becomes shōgun.
1392	The Southern and Northern courts are united.
1401	The third shōgun, Yoshimitsu, establishes relations with Ming China.
1467–1477	The Ōnin War
1495	Hōjō Sōun captures Odawara.

1506	The painter Sesshū dies.
1543	A Portuguese ship arrives at Tanegashima.
1549	St. Francis Xavier arrives to propagate Christianity.
1568	Oda Nobunaga occupies Kyoto.
1573	The last Ashikaga shōgun is deposed by Nobunaga.
1582	Nobunaga is assassinated.
1586	Toyotomi Hideyoshi is appointed chancellor (dajō daijin).
1587	Christianity is banned by Hideyoshi.
1588–1598	A land survey is conducted under Hideyoshi.
1588	Hideyoshi confiscates arms from the peasants.
1592	Japan invades Korea.
1598	Hideyoshi dies.
1600	Tokugawa Ieyasu triumphs in the Battle of Sekigahara.

TOKUGAWA PERIOD (1600–1867)

1603	Ieyasu is appointed shōgun.
1635	The system of alternate attendance of daimyō in Edo is introduced.
1637–1638	The Shimabara Rebellion
1639	The nation is closed to the outside world.
1643	Buying and selling land is prohibited.
1716	Tokugawa Yoshimune becomes the eighth shōgun and initiates the Kyōho Reforms.
1720	The ban on Western books is relaxed.
1724	The playwright Chikamatsu dies.
1782–1787	The Temmei Famine
1787	Matsudaira Sadanobu becomes rōjū (senior councilor) and initiates the Kansei Reforms.
1792	A Russian vessel commanded by Laxman arrives in Hokkaido, asking for commercial relations.
1793	The novelist Ihara Saikaku dies.
1801	Motoori Norinaga dies.
1825	An edict to drive off foreign vessels is issued.
1833–1837	The Tempyō Famine
1837	Ōshio Heihachirō leads an insurrection.
1841	Rōjū Mizuno Tadakuni initiates the Tempō Reforms.
1849	The woodblock artist Hokusai dies.
1853	Commodore Perry arrives.
1854	The Treaty of Kanagawa is signed with the United States.
1858	Ii Naosuke is appointed great councilor (tairō); a commercial treaty with the United States is concluded; the woodblock artist Hiroshige dies.

1867   Shōgun Keiki restores political power to the imperial court.

MEIJI PERIOD (1868–1912)

1868   A new government is established;
            Tokyo (formerly Edo) becomes the capital.
1869   Four major daimyō relinquish control over their han to the imperial government.
1871   The han are replaced by prefectures;
            the postal system is introduced;
            Tokugawa class distinctions are eliminated;
            the Iwakura mission is dispatched to the West.
1872   The Tokyo-Yokohama railroad is opened;
            the freedom to buy and sell land is granted;
            compulsory elementary education is instituted.
1873   The Gregorian Calendar is adopted (Dec. 3, 1872 of the old lunar calendar is converted to Jan. 1, 1873);
            universal military conscription and a new land tax are instituted.
1874   A request for the establishment of a national assembly is submitted by Itagaki and others.
1876   The wearing of swords by former samurai is banned.
1877   Saigō Takamori rebels.
1879   The Ryukyu islands become Okinawa Prefecture.
1881   A national assembly is promised by the government.
1884   The peerage is created;
            The Chichibu uprising occurs.
1885   The cabinet system is adopted;
            Itō Hirobumi becomes the first Prime Minister.
1887   Electric lighting is introduced.
1888   The Privy Council is established.
1889   The Constitution is promulgated.
1890   The First Diet convenes;
            the Imperial Rescript on Education is issued;
            telephone service is introduced.
1894   A treaty revision is agreed upon between Japan and England.
1894–1895   The Sino-Japanese War
1898   The Ōkuma-Itagaki cabinet is formed.
1902   The Anglo-Japanese Alliance is concluded.
1904–1905   The Russo-Japanese War
1910   Korea is annexed;
            Kōtoku Shūsui and others are executed.
1912   Emperor Meiji dies.

TAISHŌ PERIOD (1912–1926)

1914	Japan enters the First World War.
1915	The Twenty-One Demands are presented to China.
1918	The Hara Cabinet is formed.
1921	The Washington Conference on naval arms limitations convenes.
1923	The Great Earthquake
1925	Universal manhood suffrage is enacted; radio broadcasting commences.
1926	Emperor Taishō dies.

SHŌWA PERIOD (1926–)

1931	The Manchurian Incident
1932	Prime Minister Inukai is assassinated; party government ends.
1933	Japan withdraws from the League of Nations.
1935	Minobe Tatsukichi's Organ Theory is condemned.
1936	Prominent leaders are assassinated by radical militarists; the Anti-Cominteran Pact with Germany is concluded.
1937	War with China breaks out.
1940	Japanese troops move into French Indochina; a tripartite alliance with Germany and Italy is concluded.
1941	Japan attacks Pearl Harbor and the Pacific War begins.
1942	The Battle of Midway (June);
1944	the tide of war shifts. Saipan falls; Prime Minister Tōjō resigns; U.S. bombers carry out massive air raids on Japanese cities.
1945	U.S. troops land in the Philippines and Okinawa; atomic bombs are dropped on Hiroshima and Nagasaki; Russia enters the war; Japan surrenders; Allied occupation under General MacArthur begins.
1946	A new constitution is promulgated.
1948	General Tōjō and others are executed.
1951	The peace treaty is signed in San Francisco.
1952	The Allied occupation ends.
1953	A United States-Japanese Mutual Security Agreement is signed; television broadcasting begins.
1956	Japan is admitted to the United Nations.

1960   A new United States-Japan Mutual Security Agreement
            is concluded.
1971   The United States agrees to relinquish control of Oki-
            nawa by 1972.

APPENDIX B

List of Prime Ministers

Itō Hirobumi (took office on December 22, 1885)
Kuroda Kiyotaka (April 30, 1888)
Yamagata Aritomo (December 24, 1889)
Matsukata Masayoshi (May 6, 1891)
Itō Hirobumi (August 8, 1892)
Matsukata Masayoshi (September 18, 1896)
Itō Hirobumi (January 12, 1898)
Ōkuma Shigenobu (June 30, 1898)
Yamagata Aritomo (November 8, 1898)
Itō Hirobumi (October 19, 1900)
Katsura Tarō (June 2, 1901)
Saionji Kimmochi (January 7, 1906)
Katsura Tarō (July 14, 1908)
Saionji Kimmochi (August 30, 1911)
Katsura Tarō (December 21, 1912)
Yamamoto Gonnohyōe (February 20, 1913)
Ōkuma Shigenobu (April 16, 1914)
Terauchi Masatake (October 9, 1916)
Hara Kei (September 29, 1918)
Takahashi Korekiyo (November 13, 1921)
Katō Tomosaburō (June 12, 1922)
Yamamoto Gonnohyōe (September 2, 1923)
Kiyoura Keigo (January 7, 1924)
Katō Kōmei (June 11, 1924)

Wakatsuki Reijirō (January 30, 1926)
Tanaka Giichi (April 20, 1927)
Hamaguchi Yūkō (July 2, 1929)
Wakatsuki Reijirō (April 14, 1931)
Inukai Tsuyoshi (December 13, 1931)
Saitō Makoto (May 26, 1932)
Okada Keisuke (July 8, 1934)
Hirota Kōki (March 9, 1936)
Hayashi Senjūrō (February 2, 1937)
Konoe Fumimaro (June 4, 1937)
Hiranuma Kiichirō (January 5, 1939)
Abe Nobuyuki (August 30, 1939)
Yonai Mitsumasa (January 16, 1940)
Konoe Fumimaro (July 22, 1940)
Tōjō Hideki (October 18, 1941)
Koiso Kuniaki (July 22, 1944)
Suzuki Kantarō (April 7, 1945)
Prince Higashikuni (August 17, 1945)
Shidehara Kijūrō (October 9, 1945)
Yoshida Shigeru (May 22, 1946)
Katayama Tetsu (May 24, 1947)
Ashida Hitoshi (March 10, 1948)
Yoshida Shigeru (October 15, 1948)
Hatoyama Ichirō (December 10, 1954)
Ishibashi Tanzan (December 23, 1956)
Kishi Shinsuke (February 25, 1957)
Ikeda Hayato (July 19, 1960)
Satō Eisaku (November 9, 1964)

APPENDIX C

Genealogical Chart of the Major Political Parties

I. **The *Jiyūtō* (*Liberal party*):**

founded, October, 1881

dissolved, October, 1884

revived, September, 1890, as *Rikken Jiyūtō* (Constitutional Liberal party)

renamed the *Jiyūtō*, 1891

merged with the *Shimpotō* (Progressive party) to form the *Kenseitō* (Constitutional party), June, 1898

split with the *Shimpotō* faction, October, 1898

joined Itō's *Rikken Seiyūkai* (Association of Friends of Constitutional Government), September, 1900

dissolved, July, 1940

revived as the *Nihon Jiyūtō* (Japanese Liberal party), November, 1945

merged with the *Minshutō*, November, 1955, and renamed the *Jiyū-Minshutō* (Liberal-Democratic party)—to the present.

II. **The *Kaishintō* (Reform party):**

founded, March, 1882

renamed the *Shimpotō* (Progressive party), March, 1893

merged with the *Jiyūtō* to form the *Kenseitō*, June, 1898

split with the *Kenseitō* to form the *Kensei hontō* (Main Constitutional party), November, 1898 became the *Rikken Kokumintō* (Constitutional Nationalist party), March, 1910

split into the *Kokumintō* (this faction eventually merged with the *Seiyūkai*, May, 1925) and the *Rikken Dōshikai* (Constitutional Association of Friends), December, 1913

became the *Kenseikai* (Constitutional Association), October, 1916

merged with a splinter group of the *Seiyūkai*, the *Seiyūhontō* (the Main Seiyūkai), to form the *Rikken Minseitō* (Constitutional Democratic party), June, 1927

dissolved, July, 1940

revived as the *Nihon Shimpotō* (Japanese Progressive party), November, 1945

renamed the *Minshutō* (Democratic party), March, 1947

renamed the *Kaishintō*, February, 1952

renamed the *Nihon Minshutō*, November, 1954

merged with the *Jiyūtō*, November, 1955 to form the *Jiyū-Minshutō* —to the present.

III. **The *Shakaitō* (Socialist party)**

founded as *Nihon Shakaitō* (Japanese Socialist party), November, 1945

split into left- and right-wing factions, October, 1951

factions merged October, 1955

right-wing faction split off to form the *Minshu-Shakaitō* (Democratic Socialist party), January, 1960—to the present.

SELECTED BIBLIOGRAPHY

This is of necessity a selected list of a growing body of Western books on Japan. The following bibliographies can be consulted for additional titles:

American Universities Field Staff. *A Select Bibliography: Asia, Africa, Eastern Europe, Latin America*. New York: American Universities Field Staff, Inc., 1960. Supplements were issued in 1961, 1963, 1965, 1967, and 1969.

Borton, Hugh, *et al. A Selected List of Books and Articles on Japan in English, French, and German*. Cambridge, Mass.: Harvard University Press, 1954.

Hall, John W. *Japanese History: New Dimensions of Approach and Understanding*. Washington, D.C.: Service Center for Teachers of History, 1961.

Silberman, Bernard S. *Japan and Korea: A Critical Bibliography*. Tucson, Ariz.: University of Arizona Press, 1962.

The Journal of Asian Studies issues an annual bibliographical number.

Works in English

HISTORICAL DICTIONARIES

Goedertier, Joseph M. A. *Dictionary of Japanese History*. New York and Tokyo: Walker/Weatherhill, 1968.

Papinot, Edmund. *Historical and Geographical Dictionary of Japan*, 2 vols. New York: Ungar, 1964. (Reprint of a 1910 edition.)

GEOGRAPHICAL WORKS

Cressey, George B. *Asia's Lands and Peoples*. New York: McGraw-Hill, 1963.

Dempster, Prue. *Japan Advances: A Geographical Study*. New York: Barnes & Noble, 1968.

Isida, Ryujiro. *Geography of Japan.* Tokyo: Kokusai Bunka Shinkokai, 1969.

Trewartha, Glenn T. *Japan: A Physical, Cultural and Regional Geography.* Madison, Wis.: University of Wisconsin Press, 1965.

GENERAL HISTORIES

Hall, John W. *Japan: From Prehistory to Modern Times.* New York: Delacorte, 1970.

Ienaga, Saburō. *History of Japan.* Tokyo: Japan Travel Bureau, 1956.

Inoue, Mitsusada. *Introduction to Japanese History, Before the Meiji Restoration.* Tokyo: Kokusai Bunka Shinkokai, 1968.

Murdoch, James. *A History of Japan,* 3 vols., each with 2 parts. New York: Ungar, 1964. (Reprint of a 1903–1926 edition.)

Reischauer, Edwin O. *Japan: The Story of a Nation.* New York: Knopf, 1970.

Reischauer, Edwin O., and John K. Fairbank. *A History of East Asian Civilization: East Asia the Great Tradition.* Boston: Houghton Mifflin, 1960.

Sansom, Sir George B. *Japan, A Short Cultural History.* New York: Appleton, 1943.

SPECIAL ASPECTS OF JAPANESE HISTORY AND CULTURE

Akiyama, Terukazu. *Treasures of Asia: Japanese Painting.* Cleveland: World, 1961.

Anesaki, Masaharu. *History of Japanese Religion.* Tokyo and Rutland, Vt.: Tuttle, 1963.

———. *Religious Life of the Japanese People.* Tokyo: Kukusai Bunka Shinkokai, 1961.

Aston, W. G. *A History of Japanese Literature.* New York: Appleton, 1899.

Barrett, William, ed. *Zen Buddhism: Selected Writings of D. T. Suzuki.* Garden City, N.Y.: Doubleday, 1956.

Beasley, W. G., and E. G. Pulleyblank, eds. *Historians of China and Japan.* London: Oxford University Press, 1961.

Benedict, Ruth. *The Chrysanthemum and the Sword: Patterns of Japanese Culture.* Boston: Houghton Mifflin, 1946.

Binyon, Lawrence. *Painting in the Far East.* New York: Dover, 1959.

Boger, H. Batterson. *The Traditional Arts of Japan.* Garden City, N.Y.: Doubleday, 1964.

Borton, Hugh, ed. *Japan.* Ithaca, N.Y.: Cornell University Press, 1951.

Bunce, William K. *Religions in Japan: Buddhism, Shinto, Christianity.* Rutland, Vt., Tuttle, 1955.

Chamberlain, Bail H. *Things Japanese.* London: Routledge & Kegan Paul, 1939.

Craig, Albert M., and Donald H. Shively. *Personality in Japanese History.* Berkeley, Calif.: University of California Press, 1971.

Dumoulin, Heinrich. *History of Zen Buddhism.* New York: Random House, 1963.

Eliot, Sir Charles Norton. *Japanese Buddhism.* London: Edward Arnold, 1935.

Hall, John Whitney. *Government and Local Power in Japan, 500 to 1700: A Study Based on Bizen Province.* Princeton, N.J.: Princeton University Press, 1966.

Hall, John W., and Richard K. Beardsley. *Twelve Doors to Japan.* New York: McGraw-Hill, 1965.

Hasegawa, Nyozekan. *The Japanese Character: A Cultural Profile.* Trans. John Bester. Tokyo and Palo Alto, Calif.: Kodansha International, 1965.

Hearn, Lafcadio. *Glimpses of Unfamiliar Japan,* 2 vols. Boston: Houghton Mifflin, 1894.

———. *Japan: An Attempt at Interpretation.* New York: Macmillan, 1913.

Herrigal, Eugen. *Zen.* New York: McGraw-Hill, 1964.

Holtom, Daniel C. *The National Faith of Japan: A Study in Modern Shinto.* New York: Dutton, 1938.

Honjo, Eijiro. *The Social and Economic History of Japan.* New York: Russell, 1965. (Reprint of a 1935 edition.)

Keene, Donald, ed. *Anthology of Japanese Literature from the Earliest Era to the Mid-nineteenth Century.* New York: Grove, 1955.

———, ed. *Japanese Literature: An Introduction for Western Readers,* New York: Grove, 1955.

———. *Living Japan.* Garden City, N.Y.: Doubleday, 1959.

Kitagawa, Joseph M. *Religion in Japanese History.* New York: Columbia University Press, 1966.

Lee, Sherman E. *A History of Far Eastern Art.* Englewood Cliffs, N.J.: Prentice-Hall, and New York: Abrams, 1964.

Munsterberg, Hugo. *The Arts of Japan: An Illustrated History.* Tokyo and Rutland, Vt.: Tuttle, 1957.

———. *The Folk Arts of Japan.* Tokyo and Rutland, Vt.: Tuttle, 1958.

———. *Zen and Oriental Art.* Tokyo and Rutland, Vt.: Tuttle, 1965.

Nakamura, Hajime. *Ways of Thinking of Eastern Peoples: India, China, Tibet, Japan.* Honolulu: East-West Center Press, 1964.

Nitobe, Inazo. *Bushidō, the Soul of Japan.* New York: Putnam, 1905.

Okakura, Kakuzo. *The Book of Tea.* Tokyo and Rutland, Vt.: Tuttle, 1956.

Paine, Robert T., and Alexander C. Soper. *The Art and Architecture of Japan.* Baltimore, Md.: Penguin, 1955.

Reischauer, Edwin O. *The United States and Japan.* New York: Viking, 1965.

Sagara, Tokuzo. *Japanese Fine Arts.* Tokyo: Japan Travel Bureau, 1955.

Saunders, Ernest Dale. *Buddhism in Japan; With an Outline of its Origins in India.* Philadelphia: University of Pennsylvania Press, 1964.

Seidensticker, Edward. *Japan.* New York: Time-Life, 1968.

Silberman, Bernard S., ed. *Japanese Character and Culture: A Book of Selected Readings.* Tucson, Ariz.: University of Arizona Press, 1962.

Smith, Robert J., and Richard K. Beardsley. *Japanese Culture, Its Development and Characteristics.* Chicago: Aldine, 1962.

Suzuki, Daisetsu T. *An Introduction to Zen Buddhism.* New York: Grove, 1964.

———. *Essays in Zen Buddhism.* New York: Harper & Row, 1949.

———. *Zen and Japanese Culture.* New York: Pantheon, 1959.

Swann, Peter C. *The Art of Japan, From the Jomon to the Tokugawa Period.* New York: Crown, 1966.

Takekoshi, Yosaburo. *Economic Aspects of the History of the Civilization of Japan.* 3 vols. New York: Paragon, 1967. (Reprint of a 1930 edition.)

Tokyo National Museum. *Pageant of Japanese Art,* 6 vols. Tokyo: Tōto Bunka, 1952–1954.

Transactions of the Asiatic Society of Japan. Tokyo: Asiatic Society of Japan, series 1, nos. 1–50, 1872–1922; series 2, nos. 1–19, 1924–1940; series 3, nos. 1–　, 1948–　. This collection has a wealth of material on all aspects of Japanese history and culture.

Tsunoda, Ryusaku, W. T. de Bary, and Donald Keene, eds. *Sources of Japanese Tradition.* New York: Columbia University Press, 1958.

Ueda, Makoto. *Literary and Art Theories in Japan.* Cleveland: Case Western Reserve, 1967.

Warner, Langdon. *The Enduring Art of Japan.* New York: Grove, 1952.

Watanabe, Shoko. *Japanese Buddhism, a Critical Appraisal.* Tokyo: Kokusai Bunka Shinkokai, 1968.

Yashiro, Yukio. *Art Treasures of Japan,* 2 vols. Tokyo: Kokusai Bunka Shinkokai, 1960.

EARLY HISTORY TO 1185
(CHAPTERS 1, 2, AND 3)

Aston, W. G., trans. *Nihongi (Chronicles of Japan from the Earliest Times to A.D. 697).* New York: Paragon, 1956. (Reprint of a 1924 edition.)

Brower, Robert Hopkins, and Earl R. Miner. *Japanese Court Poetry.* Stanford, Calif.: Stanford University Press, 1961.

Campbell, Joseph. *The Masks of God: Oriental Mythology.* New York: Viking, 1962.

Chamberlain, Basil H., trans. *Kojiki (Records of Ancient Matters).* London: Routledge & Kegan Paul, 1932.

Kidder, Edward J. *Japan Before Buddhism.* New York: Praeger, 1959.

Komatsu, Isao. *The Japanese People: Origins of the People and the Language.* Tokyo: Kokusai Bunka Shinkokai, 1962.

McCullough, Helen C., trans. *Tales of Ise: Lyrical Episodes from Tenth-Century Japan.* Stanford, Calif.: Stanford University Press, 1968.

Miner, Earl. *An Introduction to Japanese Court Poetry.* Stanford, Calif.: Stanford University Press, 1968.

Morris, Ivan I. *The World of the Shining Prince: Court Life in Ancient Japan.* New York: Knopf, 1964.

Murasaki Shikibu. *The Tale of Genji.* Trans. Arthur Waley. New York: Random House, 1960.

Nippon Gakujutsu Shinkokai (The Japan Society for the Promotion of Scientific Research). *Manyōshū: One Thousand Poems.* New York: Columbia University Press, 1965.

Philippi, Donald L., trans. *Kojiki.* Princeton, N.J.: Princeton University Press, 1968.

Sansom, Sir George B. *A History of Japan to 1334*. Stanford, Calif.: Stanford University Press, 1958.

Seidensticker, Edward G., trans. *The Gossamer Years: A Diary by a Noblewoman of Heian Japan*. Tokyo and Rutland, Vt.: Tuttle, 1964.

Sei Shōnagon. *The Pillow Book of Sei Shōnagon*, 2 vols. Trans. and ed. Ivan Morris. New York: Columbia University Press, 1967.

Tsunoda, Ryusaku, trans., and L. Carrington Goodrich, ed. *Japan in the Chinese Dynastic Histories: Later Han Through Ming Dynasties*. South Pasadena, Calif.: Perkins, 1951.

Wheeler, Post, ed. and trans. *The Sacred Scriptures of the Japanese*. New York: Abelard-Schuman, 1952.

Young, John. *The Location of Yamatai*. Baltimore, Md.: Johns Hopkins Press, 1957.

THE ASCENDANCY OF THE MILITARY HOUSES: FROM 1185 TO 1600 (CHAPTERS 4, 5, AND 6)

Asakawa, Kanichi, ed. *The Documents of Iriki, Illustrative of the Development of the Feudal Institution in Japan*. Tokyo: Japan Society for the Promotion of Science, 1955.

Boxer, Charles R. *The Christian Century in Japan, 1549–1650*. Berkeley, Calif.: University of California Press, 1951.

Cooper, Michael, S.J., ed. *They Came to Japan: An Anthology of European Reports on Japan, 1543–1640*. Berkeley, Calif.: University of California Press, 1965.

Dening, Walter. *The Life of Toyotomi Hideyoshi (1536–1598)*. Tokyo: Hokuseido Press, 1955.

Duus, Peter. *Feudalism in Japan*. New York: Knopf, 1969.

Hall, John W. "Feudalism in Japan—a Reassessment," in *Comparative Studies in Society and History*, 5, no. 1 (1962).

Keene, Donald, trans. *Essays in Idleness: The Tsurezuregusa of Kenkō*. New York: Columbia University Press, 1967.

———, ed. *Twenty Plays of the No Theatre*. New York: Columbia University Press, 1970.

Kirby, John B. *From Castle to Teahouse: Japanese Architecture of the Momoyama Period*. Tokyo and Rutland Vt.: Tuttle, 1962.

McCullough, Helen C., trans. *The Taiheiki: A Chronicle of Medieval Japan*. New York: Columbia University Press, 1959.

———, trans. *Yoshitsune: A Fifteenth-Century Japanese Chronicle*. Stanford, Calif.: Stanford University Press, 1966.

Nakamura, Yasuo. *Noh, the Classical Theater*. Trans. Don Kenny. New York and Tokyo: Walker/Weatherhill, 1971.

Reischauer, Edwin O. "Japanese Feudalism," in Rushton Coulborn, ed., *Feudalism in History*. Princeton, N.J.: Princeton University Press, 1956.

Sadler, A. L., trans. *Heike Monogatari (Tale of the Heike)*, in *Transactions of the Asiatic Society of Japan*, series 1, vol. 46, part 2 (1918), and vol. 49, part 1 (1921).

Sansom, Sir George B. *A History of Japan, 1334–1615*. Stanford, Calif.: Stanford University Press, 1960.

Shinoda, Minoru. *The Founding of the Kamakura Shogunate, 1180–1185*. New York: Columbia University Press, 1960.

Varley, H. Paul. *Imperial Restoration in Medieval Japan*. New York: Columbia University Press, 1971.

―――. *The Ōnin War: History of Its Origins and Background, with a Selective Translation of the Chronicles of Ōnin*. New York: Columbia University Press, 1967.

Waley, Arthur. *The Nō Plays of Japan*. London: Allen & Unwin, 1911.

THE TOKUGAWA PERIOD (CHAPTERS 7, 8, AND 9): POLITICAL, SOCIAL, AND ECONOMIC AFFAIRS

Borton, Hugh. "Peasant Uprisings in Japan of the Tokugawa Period," in *Transactions of the Asiatic Society of Japan*, series 2, vol. 16 (1938).

Hall, John W. *Tanuma Okitsugu, 1719–1788, Forerunner of Modern Japan*. Cambridge, Mass.: Harvard University Press, 1955.

Hall, John W., and Marius Jansen, eds. *Studies in the Institutional History of Early Modern Japan*. Princeton, N.J.: Princeton University Press, 1968.

Kaempfer, Engelbert. *History of Japan*, 3 vols. Trans. J. G. S. Schenchzer. Glasgow: MacLehose, 1906.

Sadler, A. L. *The Maker of Modern Japan: The Life of Tokugawa Ieyasu*. London: Allen and Unwin, 1937.

Sansom, Sir George B. *A History of Japan, 1615–1867*. Stanford, Calif:. Stanford University Press, 1963.

Sheldon, C. D. *The Rise of the Merchant Class in Tokugawa Japan*. Locust Valley, N.Y.: Augustin, 1958.

Smith, Neil Skene, ed. "Materials on Japanese Social and Economic History: Tokugawa Japan," in *Transactions of the Asiatic Society of Japan*, series 2, vol. 14 (1937).

Smith, Thomas C. *The Agrarian Origins of Modern Japan*. Stanford, Calif.: Stanford University Press, 1959.

Totman, Conrad D. *Politics in the Tokugawa Bakufu, 1600–1843*. Cambridge, Mass.: Harvard University Press, 1967.

Webb, Herschel. *The Japanese Imperial Institution in the Tokugawa Period*. New York: Columbia University Press, 1968.

Wigmore, John H. *Law and Justice in Tokugawa Japan*, 2 vols. Tokyo: University of Tokyo Press, 1969.

THE TOKUGAWA PEROD: INTELLECTUAL DEVELOPMENTS

Bellah, Robert N. *Tokugawa Religion: The Values of Pre-industrial Japan*. Glencoe, Ill.: Free Press, 1957.

Boxer, Charles R. *Jan Compaigne in Japan: An Essay on the Cultural, Artistic and Scientific Influence Exercised by the Hollanders in Japan from the Seventeenth to the Nineteenth Centuries*. The Hague: Nijhoff, 1950.

Dore, Ronald P. *Education in Tokugawa Japan*. Berkeley, Calif.: University of California Press, 1965.

Earl, David M. *Emperor and Nation in Japan: Political Thinkers of the Tokugawa Period*. Seattle, Wash.: University of Washington Press, 1964.

Kenne, Donald. *The Japanese Discovery of Europe, 1720–1830*. Stanford, Calif.: Stanford University Press, 1969.

Matsumoto, Shigeru, *Motoori Norinaga, 1730–1801*. Cambridge, Mass.: Harvard University Press, 1970.

Norman, E. H. "Andō Shōeki and the Anatomy of Japanese Feudalism," in *Transactions of the Asiatic Society of Japan*, series 3, vol. 2 (1949).

Ogyū, Sorai. *The Political Writings of Ogyū Sorai*. Trans. J. R. McEwan. London: Cambridge University Press, 1962.

Passin, Herbert. *Society and Education in Japan*. New York: Bureau of Publications, Teachers' College and East Asian Institute, Columbia University, 1965.

Sansom, Sir George B. *The Western World and Japan*. New York: Knopf, 1950.

THE TOKUGAWA PERIOD: CULTURAL DEVELOPMENTS

Ando, Tsuruo. *Performing Arts of Japan: Bunraku, the Puppet Theater*. New York and Tokyo: Walker/Weatherhill, 1970.

Blyth, Reginald H. *Haiku*, 4 vols. Tokyo: Hokuseido Press, 1950–1952.

Bowers, Faubion. *Japanese Theatre*. New York: Hill & Wang, 1959.

Chikamatsu, Monzaemon. *The Major Plays of Chikamatsu*. Trans. Donald Keene. New York: Columbia University Press, 1961.

Ernst, Earle. *The Kabuki Theatre*. New York: Oxford University Press, 1956.

Henderson, Harold G. *An Introduction to Haiku*. Garden City, N.Y.: Doubleday, 1958.

Hibbett, Howard. *The Floating World in Japanese Fiction*. New York: Grove, 1960.

Hillier, J. *Japanese Masters of the Colour Print*. London: Phaidon, 1954.

Ihara, Saikaku. *Five Women Who Loved Love*. Trans. William T. de Bary. Tokyo and Rutland, Vt.: Tuttle, 1956.

———. *The Life of an Amorous Woman and Other Writings*. Trans. Ivan Morris. Norfolk, Conn.: Laughlin, 1963.

Michener, James. *The Floating World*. New York: Random House, 1954.

Toita, Yasuji. *Performing Arts of Japan: Kabuki the Popular Theater*. Trans. Don Kenny. New York and Tokyo: Walker/Weatherhill, 1970.

THE LAST YEARS OF TOKUGAWA RULE (CHAPTER 10)

Alcock, Sir Rutherford. *The Capital of the Tycoon: A Narrative of Three Years' Residence in Japan*, 2 vols. New York: Harper, 1863.

Beasley, W. G., ed. and trans. *Select Documents on Japanese Foreign Policy, 1853–1868*. London: Oxford University Press, 1955.

Black, John R. *Young Japan: Yokohama and Yedo 1858–79*, 2 vols. London: Oxford University Press, 1969.

Craig, Albert M. *Chōshū in the Meiji Restoration*. Cambridge, Mass.: Harvard University Press, 1961.

Harootunian, H. D. *Toward Restoration: The Growth of Political Consciousness in Tokugawa Japan*. Berkeley, Calif.: University of California Press, 1970.

Jansen, Marius B. *Sakamoto Ryōma and the Meiji Restoration*. Princeton, N.J.: Princeton University Press, 1961.

Satow, Sir Ernest M. *A Diplomat in Japan*. London: Seeley Service, 1921.

Walworth, Arthur. *Black Ships Off Japan: The Story of Commodore Perry's Expedition*. New York: Knopf, 1946.

GENERAL HISTORIES OF MODERN JAPAN

Beasley, W. G. *The Modern History of Japan*. New York: Praeger, 1963.

Beckmann, George M. *The Modernization of China and Japan*. New York: Harper & Row, 1962.

Borton, Hugh. *Japan's Modern Century*. New York: Ronald, 1970.

Fairbank, John K., Edwin O. Reischauer, and Albert M. Craig. *A History of East Asian Civilization: East Asia, the Modern Transformation*. Boston: Houghton Mifflin, 1965.

Michael, Franz H., and George E. Taylor. *The Far East in the Modern World*. New York: Holt, Rinehart & Winston, 1964.

Storry, Richard. *A History of Modern Japan*. Baltimore, Md.: Penguin, 1965.

Yanaga, Chitoshi. *Japan Since Perry*. New York: McGraw-Hill, 1949.

SPECIAL ASPECTS OF MODERN JAPANESE HISTORY AND CULTURE

Allen, G. C. *A Short Economic History of Modern Japan, 1867–1937*. New York: Macmillan, 1946.

Anderson, Joseph L., and Donald Richie. *The Japanese Film: Art and Industry*. New York: Grove, 1960.

Brown, Delmar M. *Nationalism in Japan*. Berkeley, Calif.: University of California Press, 1955.

DeVos, George, and Hiroshi Wagatsuma. *Japan's Invisible Race: Caste in Culture and Personality*. Berkeley, Calif.: University of California Press, 1966.

Dore, Ronald P., ed. *Aspects of Social Change in Modern Japan*. Princeton, N.J.: Princeton University Press, 1967.

Henderson, Dan F. *Conciliation and Japanese Law*, 2 vols. Seattle, Wash. University of Washington Press, 1965.

Holtom, Daniel C. *National Faith of Japan: A Study in Modern Shintō*. New York: Paragon, 1965. (Reprint of a 1938 edition.)

Jansen, Marius B., ed. *Changing Japanese Attitudes Toward Modernization*. Princeton, N.J.: Princeton University Press, 1965.

Kaigo, Tokiomi. *Japanese Education, Its Past and Present*. Tokyo: Kokusai Bunka Shinkokai, 1968.

Keenleyside, Hugh L., and A. F. Thomas. *The History of Japanese Education and Present Educational System*. Tokyo: Hokuseido Press, 1937.

Lederer, Emil, and Emy Lederer-Seidler. *Japan in Transition*. New Haven, Conn.: Yale University Press, 1938.

Lockwood, William W., ed. *The Economic Development of Japan: Growth and Structural Change, 1863–1938*. Princeton, N.J.: Princeton University Press, 1954.

———, ed. *The State and Economic Enterprise in Japan*. Princeton, N.J.: Princeton University Press, 1965.

MacNair, H. F., and D. F. Lach. *Modern Far Eastern International Relations*. New York: Van Nostrand, 1950.

Nakamura, Mitsuo. *Contemporary Japanese Fiction, 1926–1968*. Tokyo: Kokusai Bunka Shinkokai, 1969.

———. *Modern Japanese Fiction, 1868–1926*. Kokusai Bunka Shinkokai, 1968.

Neumann, William L. *America Encounters Japan, From Perry to MacArthur*. Baltimore, Md.: Johns Hopkins Press, 1963.

Piovesana, Gino K. *Recent Japanese Philosophical Thought, 1862–1962*. Tokyo: Enderle, 1963.

Richie, Donald. *Japanese Movies*. Tokyo: Japan Travel Bureau, 1961.

Scalapino, Robert A. *Democracy and the Party Movement in Prewar Japan*. Berkeley, Calif.: University of California Press, 1953.

———. *The Japanese Communist Movement, 1920–1966*. Berkeley, Calif.: University of California Press, 1967.

Schwantes, Robert. *Japanese and Americans: A Century of Cultural Relations*. New York: Harper & Row, 1955.

Shively, Donald H., ed. *Tradition and Modernization in Japanese Culture*. Princeton, N.J.: Princeton University Press, 1971.

Skrzypczak, Edmund, ed. *Japan's Modern Century*. Tokyo and Rutland, Vt.: Tuttle, 1969.

Steiner, Kurt. *Local Government in Japan*. Stanford, Calif.: Stanford University Press, 1965.

Takahashi, Masao. *Modern Japanese Economy Since 1868*. Tokyo: Kokusai Bunka Shinkokai, 1967.

Takeuchi, Tatsuji. *War and Diplomacy in the Japanese Empire*. Garden City, N.Y.: Doubleday, 1935.

Ward, R. E., and D. A. Rustow, eds. *Political Modernization in Japan and Turkey*. Princeton, N.J.: Princeton University Press, 1964.

Ward, Robert E., ed. *Political Development in Modern Japan*. Princeton, N.J.: Princeton University Press, 1968.

THE MEIJI PERIOD (CHAPTERS 11 TO 15)

Akita, George. *Foundations of Constitutional Government in Modern Japan, 1868–1900*. Cambridge, Mass.: Harvard University Press, 1967.

Baelz, Erwin O. E. Von. *Awakening Japan: The Diary of a German Doctor*. Trans. Eden and Cedar Paul. New York: Viking, 1932.

Beckmann, George M. *The Making of the Meiji Constitution: The Oligarchs and the Constitutional Development of Japan, 1868–1891*. Lawrence, Kansas: University of Kansas, 1957.

Blacker, Carmen. *The Japanese Enlightenment: A Study of the Writings of Fukuzawa Yukichi*. New York: Cambridge University Press, 1964.

Chisolm, Lawrence W. *Fenollosa: The Far East and American Culture.* New Haven, Conn.: Yale University Press, 1963.

Conroy, Francis Hilary. *The Japanese Seizure of Korea, 1868–1910.* Philadelphia: University of Pennsylvania Press, 1960.

Fukuzawa, Yukichi. *Autobiography.* Trans. Eiichi Kiyooka. New York: Columbia University Press, 1966.

Hackett, Roger F. *Yamagata Aritomo in the Rise of Modern Japan, 1838–1922.* Cambridge, Mass.: Harvard University Press, 1971.

Havens, Thomas. *Nishi Amane and Modern Japanese Thought.* Princeton, N.J.: Princeton University Press, 1969.

Hirschmeier, Johannes. *Origins of Entrepreneurship in Meiji Japan.* Cambridge, Mass.: Harvard University Press, 1964.

Ike, Nobutaka. *The Beginnings of Political Democracy in Japan.* Baltimore, Md.: Johns Hopkins Press, 1950.

Iwata, Masakazu. *Ōkubo Toshimichi, the Bismarck of Japan.* Berkeley, Calif.: University of California Press, 1964.

Kaikoku Hyakunen Kinen Bunka Jigyō Kai (Centenary Culture Council), ed. *Japanese Culture in the Meiji Era,* 10 vols. (A translation of the *Meiji Bunkashi.*) Tokyo: Obunsha, 1955–1958.

Kublin, Hyman. *An Asian Revolutionary: The Life of Katayama Sen.* Princeton, N.J.: Princeton University Press, 1964.

McLaren, Walter W. *A Political History During the Meiji Era, 1867–1912.* New York: Russell, 1965. (Reprint of a 1916 edition.)

Nakamura, James I. *Agricultural Production and the Economic Development of Japan, 1873–1922.* Princeton, N.J.: Princeton University Press, 1966.

Nitobe, Inazo, *et al. Western Influences in Modern Japan.* Chicago: University of Chicago Press, 1931.

Norman, E. H. *Japan's Emergence as a Modern State.* New York: Institute of Pacific Relations, 1940.

Okakura, Kakuzo. *The Awakening of Japan.* New York: Century, 1905.

Okamoto, Shumpei. *The Japanese Oligarchy and the Russo-Japanese War.* New York: Columbia University Press, 1971.

Okuma, Shigenobu, comp. *Fifty Years of New Japan,* 2 vols. New York: Dutton, 1909.

Pittau, Joseph. *Political Thought in Early Meiji Japan, 1868–1889.* Cambridge, Mass.: Harvard University Press, 1967.

Pyle, Kenneth B. *The New Generation in Meiji Japan: Problems of Cultural Identity, 1885–1895.* Stanford, Calif.: Stanford University Press, 1969.

Siemes, Johannes. *Hermann Roesler and the Making of the Meiji State.* Tokyo and Rutland, Vt.: Sophia University and Tuttle, 1968.

Smith, Thomas C. *Political Change and Industrial Development in Japan: Government Enterprise, 1868–1880.* Stanford, Calif.: Stanford University Press, 1955.

Sugimoto, Etsu. *A Daughter of the Samurai.* Garden City, N.Y.: Doubleday, 1928.

White, John Albert. *The Diplomacy of the Russo-Japanese War.* Princeton, N.J.: Princeton University Press, 1964.

THE TAISHŌ PERIOD (CHAPTERS 16 AND 17)

Arima, Tatsuo. *The Failure of Freedom: A Portrait of Modern Japanese Intellectuals.* Cambridge, Mass.: Harvard University Press, 1969.

Duus, Peter. *Party Rivalry and Political Change in Taishō Japan.* Cambridge, Mass.: Harvard University Press, 1968.

Griswold, A. W. *The Far Eastern Policy of the United States.* New York: Harcourt, 1938.

Iriye, Akira. *After Imperialism: The Search for a New Order in the Far East, 1921–1931.* Cambridge, Mass.: Harvard University Press, 1965.

Ishimoto, Shidzue. *Facing Two Ways, the Story of My Life.* New York: Farrar & Rinehart, 1935.

Jansen, Marius B. *The Japanese and Sun Yat-sen.* Cambridge, Mass.: Harvard University Press, 1954.

Najita, Tetsuo. *Hara Kei in the Politics of Compromise, 1905–1915.* Cambridge, Mass.: Harvard University Press, 1967.

Nishida, Kitaro. *A Study of Good.* Trans. V. H. Viglielmo. Tokyo: Japanese Government Printing Bureau, 1960.

Seidensticker, Edward G. *Kafū the Scribbler.* Stanford, Calif.: Stanford University Press, 1965.

THE MILITARY ASCENDANCY AND THE PACIFIC WAR (CHAPTERS 18, 19, AND 20)

Beckmann, George, and Genji Okubo. *The Japanese Communist Party, 1922–1945.* Stanford, Calif.: Stanford University Press, 1969.

Bergamini, David. *Japan's Imperial Conspiracy: How Emperor Hirohito Led Japan into War Against the West.* New York: Morrow, 1971.

Buchanan, A. R. *The United States and World War II,* 2 vols. New York: Harper & Row, 1964.

Butow, Robert J. C. *Japan's Decision to Surrender.* Stanford, Calif.: Stanford University Press, 1954.

———. *Tojo and the Coming of the War.* Stanford, Calif.: Stanford University Press, 1961.

Byas, Hugh. *Government by Assassination.* New York: Knopf, 1942.

Coffey, Thomas. *Imperial Tragedy.* Cleveland, Ohio: World Publishing, 1970.

Craig, William. *The Fall of Japan.* New York: Dial, 1967.

Crowley, James B. *Japan's Quest for Autonomy: National Security and Foreign Policy, 1930–1938.* Princeton, N.J.: Princeton University Press, 1966.

Feis, Herbert. *The Road to Pearl Harbor.* Princeton, N.J.: Princeton University Press, 1950.

———. *Japan Subdued: The Atomic Bomb and the End of the War in the Pacific.* Princeton, N.J.: Princeton University Press, 1961.

Grew, Joseph C. L. *Ten Years in Japan.* New York: Simon & Schuster, 1944.

Hachiya, Michihiko. *Hiroshima Diary.* Trans. and ed. Warner Wells. Chapel Hill, N.C.: University of North Carolina Press, 1955.

Hall, Robert King. *Shushin: The Ethics of a Defeated Nation.* New York: Bureau of Publications, Teachers' College, Columbia University, 1949.

Hersey, John. *Hiroshima*. New York: Knopf, 1946.

Ike, Nobutaka, ed. *Japan's Decision for War: Records of the 1941 Policy Conferences*. Stanford, Calif.: Stanford University Press, 1967.

Ito, Masanori. *The End of the Imperial Japanese Navy*. Trans. Andrew Y. Kuroda and Roger Pineau. New York: Norton, 1962.

Japanese Ministry of Education. *Kokutai no Hongi (Cardinal Principles of the National Entity of Japan)*. Trans. John O. Gauntlett, ed. Robert K. Hall. Cambridge, Mass.: Harvard University Press, 1949.

Jones, Francis C. *Japan's New Order in East Asia: Its Rise and Fall, 1937–45*. London: Oxford University Press, 1954.

Lord, Walter. *Incredible Victory (The Battle of Midway)*. New York: Harper & Row, 1967.

Lu, David J. *From the Marco Polo Bridge to Pearl Harbor: Japan's Entry into World War II*. Washington, D.C.: Public Affairs, 1961.

Maruyama, Masao. *Thought and Behaviour in Modern Japanese Politics*. Ed. Ivan Morris. London: Oxford University Press, 1963.

Maxon, Yale C. *Control of Japanese Foreign Policy*. Berkeley, Calif.: University of California Press, 1957.

Mayer-Oakes, Thomas Francis, trans. *Fragile Victory: Prince Saionji and the 1930 London Treaty Issue From the Memoirs of Baron Harada Kumao* (the so-called "Saionji-Harada Memoirs"). Detroit: Wayne State University Press, 1968.

Miller, Frank O. *Minobe Tatsukichi, Interpreter of Constitutionalism in Japan*. Berkeley, Calif.: University of California Press, 1965.

Minear, Richard. *Victor's Justice: The Tokyo War Crimes Trial*. Princeton, N.J.: Princeton University Press, 1971.

Morison, Samuel Eliot. *History of the United States Naval Operations in World War II*, 15 vols. Boston: Little, Brown, 1947–1962.

Ogata, Sadako N. *Defiance in Manchuria: The Making of Japanese Foreign Policy, 1931–1932*. Berkeley, Calif.: University of California Press, 1964.

Pacific War Research Society, comp. *Japan's Longest Day*. Palo Alto, Calif.: Kodansha International/USA, 1968.

Storry, Richard. *The Double Patriots: A Study of Japanese Nationalism*. Boston: Houghton Mifflin, 1957.

Tōgō, Shigenori. *The Cause of Japan*. Trans. and ed. Fumihiko Togo and Ben B. Blakeney. New York: Simon & Schuster, 1956.

Toland, John. *The Rising Sun: The Decline and Fall of the Japanese Empire, 1936–1945*. New York: Random House, 1970.

Totten, George O. *The Social Democratic Movement in Prewar Japan*. New Haven, Conn.: Yale University Press, 1966.

Wilson, George M. *Radical Nationalist in Japan: Kita Ikki, 1883–1937*. Cambridge, Mass.: Harvard University Press, 1969.

Wohlstetter, Roberta. *Pearl Harbor: Warning and Decision*. Stanford, Calif.: Stanford University Press, 1962.

Yoshihashi, Takehiko. *Conspiracy in Manchuria: The Rise of the Japanese Military*. New Haven, Conn.: Yale University Press, 1963.

THE POSTWAR PERIOD (CHAPTER 21)

Allen, George C. *Japan's Economic Expansion.* London: Oxford University Press, 1965.

Beardsley, Richard K., John W. Hall, and Robert E. Ward. *Village Japan.* Chicago: University of Chicago Press, 1959.

Brines, Russell. *MacArthur's Japan.* Philadelphia: Lippincott, 1948.

Borton, Hugh, *et al. Japan Between East and West.* New York: Harper & Row, 1957.

Burks, Ardath Walter. *The Government of Japan.* New York: T. Y. Crowell, 1961.

Cary, James. *Japan Today: Reluctant Ally.* New York: Praeger, 1962.

Cohen, Jerome B. *Japan's Economy in War and Reconstruction.* Minneapolis, Minn.: University of Minnesota Press, 1949.

———. *Japan's Postwar Economy.* Bloomington, Ind.: University of Indiana Press, 1958.

Colbert, Evelyn S. *The Left Wing in Japanese Politics.* New York: Institute of Pacific Relations, 1952.

Dore, Ronald P. *City Life in Japan: A Study of a Tokyo Ward.* Berkeley, Calif.: University of California Press, 1958.

———. *Land Reform in Japan.* London: Oxford University Press, 1959.

Farley, Miriam S. *Aspects of Japan's Labor Problems.* New York: Day, 1950.

Fearey, Robert A. *The Occupation of Japan, Second Phase, 1948–50.* New York: Macmillan, 1950.

Feis, Herbert. *Contest Over Japan.* New York: Norton, 1967.

Halloran, Richard. *Japan: Images and Realities.* New York: Knopf, 1969.

Hellmann, Donald. *Japanese Foreign Policy and Domestic Politics.* Berkeley, Calif.: University of California Press, 1969.

Ike, Nobutaka. *Japanese Politics: An Introductory Survey.* New York: Knopf, 1957.

Kawai, Kazuo. *Japan's American Interlude.* Chicago: University of Chicago Press, 1960.

Lifton, Robert Jay. *Death in Life: Survivors of Hiroshima.* New York: Random House, 1967.

———. *History and Human Survival.* New York: Random House, 1970.

MacArthur, Douglas. *Reminiscences.* New York: McGraw-Hill, 1964.

Maki, John M. *Court and Constitution in Japan: Selected Supreme Court Decisions, 1948–60.* Seattle, Wash.: University of Washington Press, 1964.

Martin, Edwin M. *The Allied Occupation of Japan.* New York: Institute of Pacific Relations, 1948.

Passin, Herbert, ed. *The United States and Japan.* Englewood Cliffs, N.J.: Prentice-Hall, 1966.

Scalapino, Robert A., and Junnosuke Masumi. *Parties and Politics in Contemporary Japan.* Berkeley, Calif.: University of California Press, 1962.

Sebald, William. *With MacArthur in Japan.* New York: Norton, 1965.

Supreme Commander for the Allied Powers: Government Section. *Political*

Reorientation of Japan, Sept. 1945 to Sept. 1948: Report, 2 vols. Westport, Conn.: Greenwood, 1949.

Thayer, Nathaniel B. *How the Conservatives Rule Japan.* Princeton, N.J.: Princeton University Press, 1969.

Tsuneishi, Warren M. *Japanese Political Style: An Introduction to the Government and Politics of Modern Japan.* New York: Harper & Row, 1966.

Tsurumi, Kazuko. *Social Change and the Individual: Japan Before and After Defeat in World War II.* Princeton, N.J.: Princeton University Press, 1970.

Vogel, Ezra F. *Japan's New Middle Class: The Salary Man and His Family in a Tokyo Suburb.* Berkeley, Calif.: University of California Press, 1963.

White, James W. *The Sokagakkai and Mass Society.* Stanford, Calif.: Stanford University Press, 1970.

Yanaga, Chitoshi. *Big Business in Japanese Politics.* New Haven, Conn.: Yale University Press, 1968.

————. *Japanese People and Politics.* New York: Wiley, 1956.

Yoshida Shigeru. *The Yoshida Memoirs.* Trans. Kenichi Yoshida. Boston: Houghton Mifflin, 1962.

MODERN JAPANESE FICTION
TRANSLATED INTO ENGLISH

Abe, Kōbō. *Friends.* Trans. Donald Keene. New York: Grove, 1969.

————. *Women in the Dunes.* Trans. E. Dale Saunders. New York: Knopf, 1964.

Akutagawa, Ryunosuke. *Japanese Short Stories.* Trans. Takashi Kojima. New York: Liveright, 1961.

————. *Rashomon and Other Stories.* Trans. Takashi Kojima. New York: Liveright, 1952.

Dazai, Osamu. *No Longer Human.* Trans. Donald Keene. New York: New Directions, 1958.

————. *The Setting Sun.* Trans. Donald Keene. New York: New Directions, 1956.

Kawabata, Yasunari. *House of the Sleeping Beauties.* Trans. Edward G. Seidensticker. New York: Ballantine, 1970.

————. *Snow Country.* Trans. Edward G. Seidensticker. New York: Knopf, 1956.

————. *Thousand Cranes.* Trans. Edward G. Seidensticker. New York: Knopf, 1958.

Keene, Donald, ed. *Modern Japanese Literature from 1868 to Present Day.* New York: Grove, 1956.

————, ed. and trans. *The Old Woman, the Wife, and the Archer: Three Modern Japanese Short Novels.* New York: Viking, 1961.

Mishima, Yukio. *After the Banquet.* Trans. Donald Keene. New York: Knopf, 1963.

————. *Confessions of a Mask.* Trans. Meredith Weatherby. New York: New Directions, 1958.

————. *Five Modern Nō Plays.* Trans. Donald Keene. New York: Knopf, 1957.

———. *The Sound of Waves.* Trans. Meredith Weatherby. New York: Knopf, 1956.

———. *Sun and Steel.* Trans. John Bester. Tokyo and Palo Alto, Calif.: Kodansha, 1970.

———. *The Temple of the Golden Pavilion.* Trans. Ivan Morris. New York: Knopf, 1959.

Mori, Ōgai. *The Wild Geese.* Trans. Kingo Ochiai and Sanford Goldstein. Rutland, Vt.: Tuttle, 1959.

Morris, Ivan, ed. *Modern Japanese Stories: An Anthology.* Tokyo and Rutland, Vt.: Tuttle, 1962.

Natsume Sōseki. *Grass on the Wayside.* Trans. Edwin McClellan. Chicago: University of Chicago Press, 1969.

———. *Kokoro.* Trans. Edwin McClellan. Chicago: Regnery, 1967.

———. *Light and Darkness.* Trans. V. H. Viglielmo. Honolulu: University of Hawaii Press, 1970.

———. *Wayfarer.* Trans. Beong-cheon Yu. Detroit, Mich.: Wayne State University Press, 1967.

Noma, Hiroshi. *Zone of Emptiness.* Trans. Bernard Frechtman. Cleveland, Ohio: World, 1956.

Oe, Kenzaburo. *A Personal Matter.* Trans. John Nathan. New York: Grove, 1968.

Ooka, Shohei. *Fires on the Plain.* Trans. Ivan Morris. New York: Knopf, 1957.

Osaragi, Jiro. *Homecoming.* Trans. Brewster Horowitz. New York: Knopf, 1955.

Ryan, Marleigh G., trans. and ed. *Japan's First Modern Novel: Ukigumo of Futabatei Shimei.* New York: Columbia University Press, 1967.

Tanizaki, Junichiro. *The Makioka Sisters.* Trans. Edward G. Seidensticker. New York: Knopf, 1957.

———. *Some Prefer Nettles.* Trans. Edward G. Seidensticker. New York: Knopf, 1955.

A Selected List of Works in Japanese

There is, of course, an inordinate number of Japanese works on Japanese history and it would be both unnecessary and impossible to present here a complete list of even the standard works on the subject. Those who are interested may consult Volume 3 of the *Bibliography of Standard Reference Books for Japanese Studies with Descriptive Notes* compiled by the Kokusai Bunka Shinkokai (Tokyo: Tokyo University Press, 1965). The following works are cited because the author has found them to be of special value and has relied heavily upon many of them.

GENERAL AND TOPICAL HISTORIES
FROM PAST TO PRESENT

Chūbu Nihon Shimbunsha, ed. *Shin Nihonshi no Kagi (The Keys to a New Japanese History)*, 4 vols. Tokyo: Tōkyō Daigaku Shuppankai, 1957.

Hagino Yoshisuke. *Nihonshi Kōwa* (*Lectures on Japanese History*). Tokyo: Meiji Shoin, 1920.

Ienaga Saburō *et al.*, eds. *Iwanami Kōza Nihon Rekishi* (*Iwanami Series in Japanese History*), 23 vols. Tokyo: Iwanami, 1962–1963.

———. *Nihon Bunkashi* (*Japanese Cultural History*). Tokyo: Iwanami, 1959.

———. *Nihon Dōtokushisōshi* (*History of Japanese Moral Thought*). Tokyo: Iwanami, 1951.

Inoue Kiyoshi. *Nihon no Rekishi* (*A History of Japan*), 3 vols. Tokyo: Iwanami, 1966.

Inoue Mitsusada *et al. Nihon no Rekishi* (*A History of Japan*), 26 vols. Tokyo: Chūō Kōronsha, 1965–1967.

Ishii Ryōsuke. *Nihonshi Gaisetsu* (*An Outline History of Japan*). Tokyo: Sōbunsha, 1953.

Ishimoda Shō, Matsushima Eiichi, and Kitashima Masamoto. *Nihonshi Gaisetsu* (*An Outline History of Japan*), 3 vols. Tokyo: Iwanami, 1955 and 1968.

Kadokawa Genyoshi *et al.*, eds. *Nihon Bungaku no Rekishi* (*A History of Japanese Literature*), 12 vols. Tokyo: Kadokawa Shoten, 1967–1968.

Kokushi Kenkyūkai, ed. *Iwanami Kōza Nihon Rekishi* (*Iwanami Series in Japanese History*), 18 sets of booklets. Tokyo: Iwanami, 1933–1935.

Kuroita Katsumi. *Kokushi no Kenkyū* (*A Study of Japanese History*), 2 vols. Tokyo: Iwanami, 1932.

Nakamura Kichiji. *Nihon Keizaishi Gaisetsu* (*An Outline of Japanese Economic History*). Tokyo: Nihon Hyōronsha, 1941.

Okada Akio *et al. Nihon no Rekishi* (*A History of Japan*), 12 vols. Tokyo: Yomiuri Shimbunsha, 1959–1960.

Saitō Tadashi, *et al. Nihon Zenshi* (*A Comprehensive History of Japan*), 10 vols. Tokyo: Tōkyō Daigaku Shuppankai, 1958–1964.

Toyota Takeshi. *Gaisetsu Nihon Rekishi* (*An Outline of Japanese History*). Osaka: Ōsaka Kyōiku Tosho, 1961.

Tsuda Sōkichi. *Bungaku ni Arawaretaru Kokuminshisō no Kenkyū* (*A Study of Japanese Thought as Manifested in Literature*), 4 vols. Tokyo: Iwanami, 1951–1955.

Tsuji Zennosuke. *Nihon Bunkashi* (*Japanese Cultural History*), 7 vols. Tokyo: Shunjūsha, 1955.

Wakamori Tarō *et al.*, eds. *Shin Nihonshi Taikei* (*A New Outline History of Japan*), 7 vols. Tokyo: Asakura Shoten, 1952.

Watsuji Tetsurō. *Nihon Rinri Shisōshi.* (*A History of Japanese Ethical Thought*), 2 vols. Tokyo: Iwanami, 1952.

WORKS ON PRE-MEIJI JAPAN

Aoki Kōji. *Hyakushō Ikki no Nenjiteki Kenkyū* (*A Chronological Study of Peasant Uprisings*). Tokyo: Shinseisha, 1966.

Furushima Toshio. *Nihon Hōken Nōgyōshi* (*Japanese Feudal Agricultural History*). Tokyo: Shikai Shobō, 1931.

———. *Kinsei Nihon Nōgyō no Kōzō* (*The Structure of Early Modern Japanese Agriculture*). Tokyo: Tōkyō Daigaku Shuppankai, 1943.

Hani Gorō. *Nihon ni Okeru Kindai Shisō no Zentei (The Background to Modern Japanese Thought)*. Tokyo: Iwanami, 1949.

Hayashiya Tatsusaburō. *Koten Bunka no Sōzō (The Creation of Classical Culture)*. Tokyo: Tōkyō Daigaku Shuppankai, 1964.

Hōnjō Eijirō. *Kinsei Hōken Shakai no Kenkyū. (A Study of Early Modern Feudal Society)*. Tokyo: Kaizōsha, 1928.

Inoue Tetsujirō. *Nihon Kogakuha no Tetsugaku (The Philosophy of the Japanese School of Ancient Learning)*. Tokyo: Fuzanbō, 1902.

———. *Nihon Shushigakuha no Tetsugaku (The Philosophy of the Japanese Chu Hsi School)*. Tokyo: Fuzanbō, 1902.

———. *Nihon Yōmeigakuha no Tetsugaku (The Philosophy of the Japanese Wang Yang-ming School)*. Tokyo: Fuzanbō, 1900.

Ishimoda Tadashi. *Chūseiteki Sekai no Keisei (The Formation of the Medieval World)*. Tokyo: Itō Shoten, 1946.

Kokushō Iwao. *Hyakushō Ikki no Kenkyū (A Study of Peasant Uprisings)*. Tokyo: Iwanami, 1929.

———. *Zokuhen Hyakushō Ikki no Kenkyū (A Study of Peasant Uprisings: A Sequel)*. Tokyo: Mineruba, 1959.

Maruyama Masao. *Nihon Seijishisōshi Kenkyū (Studies in the History of Japanese Political Thought)*. Tokyo: Tōkyō Daigaku Shuppankai, 1954.

Muraoka Tsunetsugu. *Motoori Norinaga*. Tokyo: Keiseisha, 1911.

———. *Nihon Shisōshi Kenkyū (Studies in the History of Japanese Thought)*, 4 vols. Tokyo: Iwanami, 1930–1949).

Nagahara Keiji. *Nihon Hōkenshakairon (A Discourse on Japanese Feudal Society)*. Tokyo: Tōkyō Daigaku Shuppankai, 1955.

———. *Nihon no Chūseishakai (Medieval Japanese Society)*. Tokyo: Iwanami, 1968.

Nagata Hiroshi. *Nihon Hōken Ideorogii (Japanese Feudal Ideology)*. Tokyo: Hakuyōsha, 1936.

———. *Nihon Tetsugakushisōshi (A History of Japanese Philosophical Thought)*. Tokyo: Mikasa Shobō, 1938.

Nakamura Kichiji. *Buke no Rekishi (A History of the Military Houses)*. Tokyo: Iwanami, 1967.

Naramoto Tatsuya, ed. *Nihon no Shisōka (The Thinkers of Japan)*. Tokyo: Mainichi Shimbunsha, 1954.

Rekishi-Chiri Gakkai, ed. *Nihon Nōminshi (A History of Japanese Peasants)*. Tokyo: Rikishi Chiri Gakkai, 1924.

Watsuji Tetsurō. *Nihon Kodai Bunka (Ancient Japanese Culture)*. Tokyo: Iwanami, 1951.

WORKS ON MODERN JAPAN

Asahi Shimbunsha, ed. *Meiji Taishōshi (A History of the Meiji and Taishō Periods)*, 6 vols. Tokyo: Asahi Shimbunsha, 1930–1931.

Hani Gorō. *Meiji Ishin (Meiji Restoration)*. Tokyo: Iwanami, 1956.

———. *Meiji Ishin Shinkenkyū (A New Study of the Meiji Restoration)*. Tokyo: Iwanami, 1956.

Harada Kumao. *Saionjikō to Seikyoku* (*Prince Saionji and the Political Situation*), 9 vols. Tokyo: Iwanami, 1950–1956.

Haraguchi Kiyoshi. *Nihon Kindai Kokka no Keisei* (*The Formation of the Modern Japanese State*). Tokyo: Iwanami, 1968.

Hattori Shisō. *Meiji no Seijikatachi* (*The Meiji Politicians*), 2 vols. Tokyo: Iwanami, 1954.

———. *Meiji Ishinshi* (*A History of the Meiji Restoration*). Tokyo: Perikansha, 1967.

Hattori Takushirō. *Dai-Tōa Sensō Zenshi* (*Comprehensive History of the Great East Asian War*). Tokyo: Hara Shobō, 1965.

Hayashi Shigeru. *Kindai Nihon no Shisōkatachi* (*The Thinkers of Modern Japan*). Tokyo: Iwanami, 1958.

Ienaga Saburō. *Taiheiyō Sensō* (*The Pacific War*). Tokyo: Iwanami, 1968.

———. *Nihon Kindaishisōshi Kenkyū* (*Studies in the History of Modern Japanese Thought*). Tokyo: Tōkyō Daigaku Shuppankai, 1953.

Inoue Kiyoshi. *Nihon Gendaishi: Meiji Ishin* (*Contemporary Japanese History: The Meiji Restoration*). Tokyo: Tōkyō Daigaku Shuppankai, 1951.

Ishida Takeshi. *Meiji Seijishisōshi Kenkyū* (*Studies in the History of Meiji Thought*). Tokyo: Miraisha, 1954.

Ishii Takashi. *Meiji Ishin* (*Meiji Restoration*). Tokyo: Yoshikawa Kōbunkan, 1961.

Ishikawa Kammei. *Fukuzawa Yukichi*, 4 vols. Tokyo: Iwanami, 1932.

Itō Masanori. *Gumbatsu Kōbōshi* (*The Rise and Fall of the Military Cliques*). Tokyo: Bungei Shunjūsha, 1958.

Kada Tetsuji. *Meijishoki Shakai-keizaishisōshi* (*A History of Early Meiji Socio-Economic Thought*). Tokyo: Iwanami, 1937.

Kaikoku Hyakunen Kinen Bunka Jigyō Kai. *Meiji Bunkashi* (*A Cultural History of the Meiji Period*), 14 vols. Tokyo: Yōyōsha, 1953–1955. (This series has been translated into English; see above.)

Karasawa Tomitarō. *Meiji Hyakunen no Kyōiku* (*A Hundred Years of Meiji Education*). Tokyo: Nihon Keizai Shimbunsha, 1968.

Kimura Ki. *Bunmei Kaika* (*Civilization and Enlightenment*). Tokyo: Shibundō, 1955.

———. *Meiji Tennō* (*Emperor Meiji*). Tokyo: Shibundō, 1956.

Kōsaka Masaaki *et al. Kindai Nihon to Kirisutokyō* (*Modern Japan and Christianity*), 2 vols. Tokyo: Sōbunsha, 1956.

Maruyama Masao. *Nihon no Shisō* (*Japanese Thought*). Tokyo: Iwanami, 1961.

——— *et al. Gendai Nihon no Shisō* (*Contemporary Japanese Thought*). Tokyo: Iwanami, 1957.

Masumi Junnosuke. *Nihon Seitōshiron* (*Discourses on the History of Japanese Political Parties*), 4 vols. Tokyo: Tōkyō Daigaku Shuppankai, 1965–1968.

Nakamura Kikuo. *Shōwa Seijishi* (*Political History of the Shōwa Period*). Tokyo: Keiō Tsūshin, 1958.

Nihon Kindaishi Kenkyūkai, ed. *Kindai Nihon Jimbutsu Seijishi* (*A Political History of Modern Japanese Leaders*), 2 vols. Tokyo: Tōyō Keizai Shimpōsha, 1955.

Nihon Kokusai Seiji Gakkai. *Taiheiyō Sensō e no Michi* (*The Road to the Pacific War*),7 vols. Tokyo: Asahi Shimbunsha, 1962–1963.

Nihon no Sōri Daizin (*The Prime Ministers of Japan*). A special issue of the magazine *Chisei* published by the Kawade Shobō, Feb., 1957.

Odagiri Hideo. *Kindai Nihon no Sakkatachi* (*The Writers of Modern Japan*). Tokyo: Hōseidaigaku Shuppankai, 1962.

———, ed. *Kōza Nihon Kindai Bungakushi* (*A Series in the History of Modern Japanese Literature*), 5 vols. Tokyo: Daigetsu Shoten, 1956–1957.

Ōe Shinobu. *Nihon no Sangyō Kakumei* (*The Japanese Industrial Revolution*). Tokyo: Iwanami, 1968.

Oka Yoshitake. *Kindai Nihon no Keisei* (*The Formation of Modern Japan*). Tokyo: Kōbundō, 1947.

———. *Yamagata Aritomo.* Tokyo: Iwanami, 1958.

Osatake Takeki. *Ishin Zengo ni Okeru Rikkenshisō no Kenkyū* (*Studies in Constitutional Thought Before and After the Meiji Restoration*), 2 vols. Tokyo: Hōkōdō, 1929.

Ōtsu Junichirō. *Dai Nippon Kenseishi* (*Japanese Constitutional History*), 10 vols. Tokyo: Hōbunkan, 1927–1929.

Rekishigaku Kenkyūkai, ed. *Meiji Ishinshi Kenkyū Kōza* (*Studies in the Meiji Restoration*), 6 vols. Tokyo: Heibonsha, 1958–1959.

Saitō, Eizaburō. *Senryōka no Nihon* (*Japan Under Occupation*). Tokyo: Gannandō Shoten, 1966.

Sakata Yoshio. *Meiji Ishinshi* (*A History of the Meiji Restoration*). Tokyo: Miraisha, 1960.

———, ed. *Meiji Ishinshi no Mondaiten* (*Critical Problems in the History of the Meiji Restoration*). Tokyo: Miraisha, 1962.

Sakisaka Itsurō. *Kindai Nihon no Shisōka* (*Thinkers of Modern Japan*). Tokyo: Wakōsha, 1954.

Shinobu Seizaburō. *Taishō Demokurashiishi* (*A History of Taishō Democracy*), 3 vols. Tokyo: Nihon Hyōron Shinsha, 1954–1959.

———. *Taishō Seijishi* (*Taishō Political History*), 4 vols. Tokyo: Kawade Shobō, 1951–1952.

Tennō Hakusho (*A White Paper on the Emperor*). A special issue of the magazine *Bungei Shunjū*, published by the Bungei Shunjū Shinsha, Nov., 1956.

Tōyama Shigeki et al. *Shōwashi* (*A History of the Shōwa Period*). Tokyo: Iwanami, 1959.

Tsurumi Shunsuke et al., eds. *Nihon no Hyakunen* (*The Hundred Years of Japan*), 10 vols. Tokyo: Chikuma Shobō, 1961–1964.

Watanabe Ikujirō et al. *Gendai Nihon Bummeishi* (*Cultural History of Contemporary Japan*), 14 vols. Tokyo: Tōyō Kizai Shimpōsha, 1940–1944.

Yanaibara Tadao, ed. *Gendai Nihon Shōshi* (*A Short History of Contemporary Japan*), 2 vols. Tokyo: Misuzu Shobō, 1961.

Yoshino Sakuzō et al., eds. *Meiji Bunka Zenshū* (*A Collection on Meiji Culture*), 24 vols. Tokyo: Nihon Hyōronsha, 1927–1930.

INDEX